D1478723

The Takeover 1968

Student Protest, Campus Politics, and Black Student Activism at Northwestern University

Jenny Thompson

Evanston History Center Press

The Takeover 1968: Student Protest, Campus Politics, and Black Student Activism at Northwestern University

©Jenny Thompson, 2019

Evanston History Center Press, Evanston, IL 60201

All rights reserved. No part of this book, except for brief quotations in reviews, articles, and scholarly publications, may be used or reproduced in any manner without written permission from the author.
For more information, contact Jenny Thompson, jthompson@evanstonhistorycenter.org

Published 2019.
Cover design: Jenny Thompson.
ISBN: 978-0-9906574-2-2
Library of Congress Cataloguing-in-Publication Data
Names: Thompson, Jenny, author.
Title: The Takeover 1968: Student Protest, Campus Politics, and Black Student Activism at Northwestern University.
Includes illustrations, appendices, index.
Subjects: 1. Northwestern University—History—20th Century. 2. African American College Students—Illinois—Political activity. 3. Discrimination in higher education—Illinois. 4. African Americans—Civil rights. 5. College Students—Political activity—1960s. 6. Education, Higher—United States—History. I. Title.

Photograph of Margaret Walker Alexander, reprinted by permission of the George Cleveland Hall Branch Archives, Vivian G. Harsh Research Collection, Woodson Regional Library, Chicago Public Library.
Photograph of students on Low Library ledge, Columbia University, April 1968, reprinted by permission of University Archives, Columbia University.
Herblock, May 5, 1968, A 1968 Herblock Cartoon, ©The Herb Block Foundation, reprinted by permission of the Herblock Foundation.
Photograph of Professor John H. Bracey, Jr., 1972, reprinted by permission of the Department of Special Collections and University Archives, W.E.B. Du Bois Library, University of Massachusetts Amherst.
Materials from the *Daily Northwestern,* the *Purple Parrot,* and the Northwestern *Syllabus* Yearbook are reprinted by permission of Students Publishing Co., Northwestern University.
Materials from the Northwestern University Archives reprinted by permission of the Northwestern University Archives.
Interviews and material quoted and drawn from Jeffrey Sterling, MD, and Lauren Lowery, *Voices and Visions: The Evolution of the Black Experience at Northwestern University* (NP: Sterling Initiatives, 2018) are the sole property of that work and are used by permission from Jeffrey Sterling, MD, and Lauren Lowery.

See illustration credits for information on image sources.
Evanston History Center website: evanstonhistorycenter.org
Author website: jennythompson.org

We did what we had to do for our own survival at Northwestern and in anticipation of the needs of the Black students coming here after us.
We were trying to make this place a better place.

Kathryn Ogletree, undergraduate leader of the 1968 takeover[1]

CONTENTS

Introduction

More than fifty years have passed since the 1968 student takeover of the Bursar's Office at Northwestern University. The narrative of what happened is sometimes reduced to a simplified version of events: Black students made demands; they occupied a campus building for two days; and the university administration responded by fulfilling their demands. But I have found that the full story is more complex—and more interesting.

For me, researching the history of the takeover started simply enough: I was interested in exploring student activism at Northwestern University in the 1960s, and I began looking into what happened over those two days in 1968, initially planning to write an article. I contacted James Turner, one of the graduate student leaders of the takeover, who is now an emeritus professor at Cornell University. He agreed to an interview and it was in our conversation that I first learned about the takeover's wider context.

Although, at the time, many people were surprised by the takeover, it was the result of many months and even years of the problems, frustrations, and hostility that Black students had encountered on the Northwestern campus. It was a strategic action planned by the students in response to their experiences as the first students to integrate the university. Their action took place at a time of widespread Black student activism across the United States. The students were influenced by the civil rights movement, the Black Power movement, and the efforts of other student activists to alter the structure of universities and colleges across the United States. In the South, in particular, and also on other college campuses nationwide, similar organized actions, from sit-ins to boycotts, were taking place, and the Northwestern students were inspired by those actions.

Facing their own untenable situation at Northwestern, the students had asked administrators, time and again, to listen to their concerns and act upon them. But their concerns had largely fallen on deaf ears. And so they decided that the only way to bring about real reform was to force the administration to acknowledge what they had long been saying. To do so, they would undertake a risky action, an action that would disrupt "business as usual" at Northwestern.

In that first conversation with Turner, I was surprised to learn that Northwestern had been officially integrated in the 1960s. I was unaware that the university had ever undertaken such an effort, believing that Northwestern had never been a segregated institution. But in fact, for decades, Northwestern had operated as a predominantly white school, as did many Northern universities and colleges. Once integration efforts were underway in 1965, Black students arrived on campus looking forward to a great adventure, but they were instead met with a stark, and in many cases, disheartening reality. They had arrived at a well-respected institution of higher education that, for more than a century, had practiced segregation, and was, in many ways, still shaped by the decades of racism and discrimination that preceded their arrival on campus.

Once I learned about Northwestern's history in this respect, I began to see that the story of the takeover was about far more than one specific group of students in 1968; it was part of the larger history of racism within Northern universities. It was about school integration. And, as I soon recognized, it was also part of the civil rights movement, the Black Power movement, and the 1960s revolution within the American academy.

After talking with James Turner, I wanted to know more, and I began contacting others, including other takeover participants, John H. Bracey, Jr., Kathryn Ogletree, and Eva Jefferson Paterson. I also contacted Jack Hinz, former dean of students and vice president for student affairs at Northwestern, in order to learn about his role as a representative of the administration during the takeover. I also wanted to learn about his experience as the former director of admissions for Northwestern, hired in 1965 to initiate integration at the university. In order to learn more about the wider student activist movement on campus at the time, I contacted Roger Friedman and Ellis Pines, two former Northwestern students who both played prominent roles in progressive politics on campus in the late 1960s.

The more people I talked to and the more I dug into the history, the more the story expanded. Soon, I was reaching back into the early twentieth century, finding a clear line between events in 1968 and those in 1901. I was also looking forward, investigating the months after the takeover and what transpired in its aftermath.

This book then is not only about the takeover; it is also a story about what led to the takeover. It seeks not only to examine what campus life was like for Black students at Northwestern in the 1960s, but also to trace the connections between their experiences and the experiences of students who attended Northwestern long before the takeover occurred. To that end, this book explores not only how the process of integration unfolded at Northwestern, but also why such a process was enacted to begin with.

The book also attempts to examine the impact the Baby Boom generation had on the campus in the 1960s, how activism among both students and faculty was both manifest and received by the larger university community, and how the varying interests of student groups intersected at the time. In this story, one can see that different campus factions—within the administration and among other student groups on campus—had interests that often intersected in positive ways. Indeed, recent scholarship on the student movements of the 1960s points to an increasing concern with the intersections among various elements within protest movements, both within and outside of the academy.[1]

The book also seeks to explore the aftermath of the takeover. In the weeks and months that followed it, the takeover would be debated and scrutinized; the press, the student body, alumni, and many others would both champion and deride it. For some observers, the action had newly exposed them to the true nature of discrimination as it existed on campus; for others, the action's "illegality" left them enraged. Whatever the response, it was clear that the impact the takeover would have was far-reaching. And in the events that took place in its aftermath, it was also clear that the takeover would not entirely resolve the problems and issues the students had raised. And thus, it would launch a complex series of responses and even further actions that now involved a wider group of people and whose implications are still felt today.

Drawing primarily from interviews, primary sources, archival collections, and media coverage of events, this book is an attempt to convey the larger picture of the takeover, and to tell the story of its lengthy prelude and its complicated aftermath. In order to tell this story, I focused on examining the ways events unfolded, how the press covered events and issues, and the nature of the reactions from a variety of factions. It is an attempt to piece together some of the historical complexity and context surrounding the takeover, to tell a story whose origins are found well before the events of May 3-4, 1968 took place, and whose impact was felt long after those events had concluded.

The broadest version of this story involves a man from Kentucky named Lawyer Taylor; Robbie Shields Terry (Michelle Obama's great aunt); and 107 students who, one spring morning in May 1968 undertook an action that would change their lives forever. It would also prove to alter the institution of Northwestern University.

The more intimate version of this story is found in the experiences, insights, and memories of the many people who shared their stories with me. This is a story of Evanston, too, and of its residents; it a story from a time in the United States when change, challenge, and protest were everywhere; when the anti-establishment, Black power, anti-war, and student activist movements were making strides; when critics and conservatives were alarmed at what they saw, predicting an impending "revolution" led by members of a younger generation who sought to change American institutions and re-write the rules that governed their lives. It is a story of sit-ins, marches, protest, organizing, civil rights struggles, and integration. It is an American story that spans the nineteenth, twentieth, and twenty-first centuries.

Overall, I see this history as instructive. The story of the takeover, and its broader historical context, offers insight into how and why students enacted change within an institution. Looking back at the ways a relatively small group of students produced profound changes within a powerful institution provides a valuable lesson. Their story underscores how change is neither easily achieved nor is progress something that always moves in a forward direction, and at times it may seem to be stalled indefinitely. But there is no question that almost revolutionary change occurred because of the actions of 107 students, most of whom were just eighteen to twenty-years old. As students were speaking up and demanding reform, challenging power structures, and looking to create a new kind of world, Black students at Northwestern took it upon themselves not only to take action, but also to define the new shape of a new university for themselves and for those who came after them.

Acknowledgments

I am profoundly grateful to those who took time to share their experiences with me. I appreciate their willingness to spend so much time talking with me and answering my many questions. Their generosity and openness made a great impact on me. I am in awe of such an incredible group of people whose life stories serve as blueprints for living, as examples of how to act with integrity and bravery. And so, I offer many thanks to John H. Bracey, Jr., Roger Friedman, Jack Hinz, Kathryn Ogletree, Eva Jefferson Paterson, Ellis Pines, and James Turner for sharing their insights, reflections, and memories with me. I am also grateful to those who shared items with me from their personal files, including photographs, articles, documents, and, in the case of Jack Hinz, the "I Back Hinz" button, which is reproduced here. I am further indebted to John H. Bracey, Jr., Roger Friedman, Jack Hinz, Kathryn Ogletree, and Ellis Pines for reading drafts of the manuscript and providing helpful comments, insights, and critical corrections. Having all these remarkable, generous people share their experiences with me was such a gift. Their stories are inspiring. I hope that readers will agree.

I am grateful to Northwestern University for allowing me to reproduce the documents, images, and illustrations from the university's archival collections that appear here. Many thanks go to many people at Northwestern for their assistance in this project. In particular, I would like to thank Stacia G. Campbell, general manager of Students Publishing Co., for granting permission to use materials from the Northwestern yearbook, the *Syllabus*, the *Purple Parrot,* and the *Daily Northwestern.* I would also like to thank Kevin Leonard, university archivist, for his help with this project. And many thanks go to Charla Wilson, archivist for the Black Experience at Northwestern University. Charla wrote and curated the excellent 2018 exhibit, *They Demanded Courageously: The 1968 Northwestern Bursar's Office Takeover*, which was on display May 1-July 31, 2018 at Northwestern's Deering Library, and the online exhibit of the same name, both of which I relied upon heavily in writing this book. Charla generously helped me locate a variety of sources and confirm details, and she provided me with access to a host of significant resources. She also read through a draft of the book and helped clarify and correct many details of this history. Her help, her support, and her incredible breadth of knowledge were simply invaluable. I am so grateful to her and for the amazing work she does at Northwestern University.

I am grateful to Jeffrey Sterling, MD, and Lauren Lowery for permission to quote from their work, *Voices and Visions: The Evolution of the Black Experience at Northwestern University.*

I am also grateful to all of the *Daily Northwestern* reporters who worked so hard over the years to report on what was happening at their university; they wrote a valuable "first draft" of history as they documented the changes their institution was going through, day by day.

I would like to thank Blake Spitz, archivist for Special Collections and University Archives at the University of Massachusetts Amherst, and Jocelyn Wilk, university archivist at Columbia University, for their assistance. Thanks also to Sarah Alex, executive director of the Herb Block Foundation, for granting permission to publish the 1968 Herblock cartoon. I am grateful to Cynthia Fife-Townsel, librarian at the Harsh Research Collection of the Chicago Public Library, for her assistance. And many thanks to Sophie Mollins at the University of Massachusetts Amherst for her help.

Many thanks to my colleagues at the Evanston History Center, and especially to Eden Juron Pearlman, executive director, for her support of this project. I also wish to thank the board members of the Evanston History Center for their support, with a special thanks to Janet Neiman Reed. I am indebted to Ethan Michaeli for his generosity and for his own inspiring work that delves into American history. I am grateful to Lisa Montgomery for her help and encouragement. I am also grateful to Robert Axtell for his insight into the manuscript. Many thanks also to Cate Whitcomb for her support. Matthew Marchione has been such a wonderful editor on many past projects and I am deeply indebted to him for his work on this book. I am so grateful for the support of my friends, Rodger Birt, Diana Turk, and Kim Hiltwein. Their continued interest in and enthusiasm for this project have been encouraging and sustaining. A great big thank you goes to Diana Benjamin, whose support, feedback, and magical emails truly kept me going. I am so grateful to Diana for her friendship. I owe a great deal and many thanks to my family for their encouragement. Many thanks to my mother, Barbara, my father, Ted, my stepmother, Mary, and my sister, Victoria. I am grateful for their love and faith in me. I can never begin to thank Penny Souhrada enough for taking so much of her time to read and proof the manuscript. I am grateful to her. And more than thanks are owed to Don Souhrada. He never stopped cheering me on through this project. His unwavering support and continued encouragement helped me more than he will ever know.

The Takeover 1968

Student Protest, Campus Politics, and Black Student Activism at Northwestern University

Part I

What is new in your fight is the fact that it was initiated, fed, and sustained by students.

Martin Luther King, Jr., 1960[1]

In spite of the remarkable progress which the Negro[2] *has made, in spite of his two centuries of unswerving fidelity to the principles upon which the republic is founded, he is still a slave, a slave bound down by the pernicious race problem. Of this problem, I speak with first hand information. For I am the son of a man who spent thirteen years of his life in slavery. I have felt the cruel fangs of that terrible menace to the black man's progress. I see and feel the wounds inflicted on the Negro's soul by that monster; I know what it means to be segregated, for I am segregated.*

Northwestern student, George Dewey Lipscomb, "The Negro's Struggle for Freedom," oration delivered at Northwestern University, May 2, 1919[3]

We are in a state of crisis, of tremendous crisis in this country. And we are observing a crisis in every phase of the so-called American way of life and as such, black people feel it more keenly because we are the ones who suffer most under it.

Margaret Walker Alexander, Northwestern graduate, class of 1935, statement before the President's Commission on Campus Unrest, 1970[4]

The Setting, Spring 1968

The pivotal year 1968 got off to a rough start in January with the launching of the Tet Offensive, a surprise assault on U.S. forces and its allies throughout Vietnam. The assault would cause a majority of Americans to decide that the war was not winnable. The assassination of Martin Luther King, Jr. followed on April 4, with uprisings in 115 American cities taking place in its wake. On high school and college campuses, protests and activism heated up, as students staged walk-outs, takeovers, strikes, and sit-ins to take a stand on a number of issues, from the war in Vietnam to racism to university politics.* It was a season of violence. It was a season of change. For many who looked toward building a better future, it was also one of possibility.

Crowd outside the Bursar's Office, 619 Clark Street, Northwestern University, Evanston, IL, May 3, 1968
(Northwestern University Archives, photograph by James Sweet)

Chapter 1

The Takeover Begins

Power concedes nothing without a demand. It never did and it never will. Find out just what any people will quietly submit to and you have found out the exact measure of injustice and wrong which will be imposed upon them, and these will continue till they are resisted.

Frederick Douglass, 1857[1]

Early Friday morning, May 3, 1968, Northwestern University Vice President for Student Affairs and Dean of Students, Jack Hinz, was sitting down to breakfast at his home at 1010 Sheridan Road, in Evanston, Illinois, when his phone rang. The campus chief of security was on the line: "We've got trouble," he told Hinz. "You'd better come to campus right away."[2]

Earlier that morning, just after 6 a.m., eighteen-year-old Northwestern student, Kathryn Ogletree left her campus dorm room in Allison Hall after a sleepless night. It was just a short walk to a nearby alley off Clark Street, the agreed upon meeting site. As she hurried along, she was "particularly nervous," as she recalled in a 2018 interview, feeling that she would be "responsible . . . if it went awry."[3] Full of anxiety about how the next few hours might unfold, she arrived early and waited to see how many others would show up.[4]

At about the same time that morning, twenty-seven-year-old Northwestern graduate student, John H. Bracey, Jr., made the quick walk from his apartment at 1116 Foster Street and headed for the alley.[5] He had worked hard to help plan the strategy that would be executed in the coming hours. Once he got to the alley, he "counted heads" and saw that among the initial group of about thirty students who had already arrived, the vast majority were women. The women would be the "powerhouse" behind this action, Bracey recalls thinking.[6]

Later that morning, twenty-six-year-old Northwestern graduate student James Turner left his Evanston home at 920 Main Street and headed to campus. He had been a bit delayed in leaving that morning; he had to wait for the babysitter to arrive to take care of his young son. His wife, Janice, was attending a conference in Wisconsin. She was unaware of what was about to transpire. It would not be until later that evening, when one of her colleagues told her that there was a man on TV who looked just like her husband, that she would find out what Turner had planned for that day.[7]

Thirty-six-year-old Jack Hinz hurried to campus, embarking on what would be a thirty-eight-hour ordeal. The "trouble" had begun at about 7:30 that morning. A lone campus security guard had been on duty at the Bursar's Office at 619 Clark Street when a group of students, intent on occupying the building, amassed secretly and unseen in the alley across the street. Campus security guards were reportedly on high alert that morning. University officials had warned them that a student takeover of a campus building was "in the air."[8]

At about 7:30 that morning, the guard at the Bursar's Office was standing just inside the door of 619 Clark when one of the students, political science major, Victor Goode, approached the front door and asked the guard if he could enter the building to pick up a form. His intention was actually to assess the situation more closely: to determine if the guard was armed and if the doors of the building were locked.[9] Soon, two other students, sociology major, Michael Smith, and music major, Steve Colson, rushed into the building, carrying locks and chains. They hurried past the guard, assuring him that they were not going to hurt anyone. They entered the building, proceeded to the back door and secured it, before going through the rest of the building, chaining and padlocking all the windows.[10]

Once Smith and Colson were inside, the students outside created a decoy to lure the security guard away from the front door. A few students began shouting and running at top speed toward the neighboring Rebecca Crown Center, the university's administration building, prompting a handful of guards from that building to come outside to investigate, leaving their posts unattended. Meanwhile, the guard at the Bursar's Office moved away from the front door, concerned with what was going on outside.[11] Within minutes, Kathryn Ogletree, John Bracey, and the other students were inside. Two members of Northwestern's clerical staff, who were already inside the Bursar's Office, stood up from their desks as the students announced, "We're taking over the building. Will you please leave?"[12]

"They picked up their pocketbooks and looked around, and they had that kind of look, like, well, you know, like are you all going to wreck the place?" John Bracey recalled in a 2018 interview. "We said, 'We didn't come in here to destroy the building. We just want to hold it for a while.' "[13] When the staff members hesitated, looking at their desks with their displays of family photographs and small personal effects, the students assured them that they were not going to harm anything in the building, but if they wanted, they could put their personal items in their desk drawers for safekeeping. If any damage was done to their property, the students promised to replace it.[14]

Outside, Northwestern security guards approached the Bursar's Office to find that the revolving front door had been chained and barricaded. The back door had also been chained. They surrounded the building, awaiting further orders from the administration which had now been alerted that an action was underway. The occupation of the building took roughly ten minutes.[15]

And thus the students began the "takeover," to use the term they used at the time.[16] They were, to use a more modern term, occupying Northwestern's central financial building, a building that housed the university's accounting, finance, and payroll operations, along with its IBM computer system.[17] A spokesman for the students, who answered a reporter's phone call to the bursar's office, confirmed that an action had begun. The students promised that they would do no harm to the building or its contents and they pledged that they were prepared to continue their occupation until the end of the summer if their demands were not met.[18]

At about 8:00 a.m., Hinz arrived at the Bursar's Office, followed by his colleague, William Kerr, Northwestern's vice president and business manager, whose office was located in the occupied building. Both men quickly surveyed the situation and left shortly afterward.[19] Students from the takeover were now posted at the building's back and front doors. Employees arriving for work at the Bursar's Office were told they could not enter. After the initial occupation, more students joined the takeover, entering through a window on the east side of the building. Soon, the total number of students inside reached 107.[20] Just after 8:00 a.m. a truck pulled up to the side of the building. A group of men got out and supplies, including food and blankets, were unloaded through a window.[21] Their work was just finished when the police arrived. They moved in to catch them, but they "took off like bullets" and each one got away.[22] A sign was hung at the building's entrance that read: "Closed for business 'til racism at NU is ended."[23]

Numerous Black students at Northwestern planned this action and many took on leadership roles, particularly among the undergraduates. But two students would serve as the takeover's primary leaders: Kathryn Ogletree, president of the campus group, For Members Only (FMO), and graduate student, James Turner, chairman of Northwestern's Afro-American Student Union (AASU).[24] The students had organized their action carefully, from planting a false rumor that an action was going to take place that morning at the Rebecca Crown Center to contacting WCFL radio host, Jeff Kamen, the night before and arranging for him to come to Evanston early Friday morning to cover an undisclosed event. The students would use Kamen's microphone to announce, live on the air, that the takeover had begun, with one of the students reading their demands, word for word, over the airwaves during the morning rush hour.[25]

The students had chosen to occupy the Bursar's Office for several reasons. It was located off the campus proper on a fairly busy street. It was a two-story, relatively modest size, stand-alone building with first-floor access to the street. The large parking lot on the building's east side allowed students to enter and exit, communicate with those on the outside, and receive delivered supplies.[26] Given the building's prominent location near the heart of downtown Evanston, it was clearly visible to passersby and motorists, but most importantly, it housed critical materials.

Once they were inside the building, one of the students, Roger Ward, entered the bank vault in the basement where the university's massive computer system was stored, fans whirring to keep the machine cool. Ward was an applied mathematics major and a "computer genius," according to John Bracey. Soon, Ward was sitting in front of the mainframe computer, running his fingers across the keys. All of Northwestern's financial records were stored on this computer, from payroll to fundraising information. And all could be deleted. But, as Bracey stated, that was one thing they did not want to do. The students had planned the takeover as a nonviolent action. It wasn't about destruction. It was about building something up. And in fact, the students viewed the computer as something of immense value to them. They felt that they would be protected by their own proximity to it should police try to evict them by force. The students' presence in the building, near such a critical system, gave them "countervailing leverage," as James Turner explained in a 2012 interview.[27] It would, in effect, "guard against white men using an irrational approach," he said.[28] If the administration "had to consider only our well-being," Turner surmised, they would have "pounce[d] on us."[29]

Just after the students had taken over the building, a phone rang inside. On the line was an Evanston police officer. He ordered the students to evacuate immediately. Bracey recalled that the police officer was informed that they were not leaving. He was also told that one of the students was sitting in front of the university's computer at that very moment. Pause. The officer responded, "We'll get back to you."[30]

By the time Hinz left the building that morning, news of the takeover had reached members of the university administration. Soon, Northwestern's vice presidents, including Hinz, gathered to strategize in a nearby building at 1808 Chicago Avenue, the university's investment office. Northwestern President J. Roscoe Miller, who was attending a Sears board meeting, was reached by telephone. "The officers met," Hinz recalled in a 2012 interview, "and I guess I wasn't the only one anxious, but I think the president's view was we have to resolve this as quickly as possible. It's not good for us. It's damaging and so forth and so on."[31] In fact, President Miller reportedly wanted all the students ejected from the building immediately.[32] Administrators had already made progress toward that end: they had begun "marshaling Northwestern's security force."[33] They had also alerted the mayor of Evanston, John Emery, and the Evanston police department, which sent out a call to the Cook County Sheriff's Office.[34] Soon two police vans were standing-by in Evanston. In the neighboring towns of Niles and Skokie, seventeen additional officers were placed on standby.[35] The police would make no arrests unless requested to do so by university officials, however.[36] Evanston's Chief of Police, Bert Giddens, informed Northwestern officials that assembling a force sizeable enough to evacuate the building would take some time. But once they had enough officers, an eviction of the building's occupants could be carried out "in just a few minutes."[37]

Soon after the initial takeover, reporters and television crews began arriving outside the occupied building, along with a crowd of onlookers. Local media, including reporters from the *Chicago Defender* and the *Chicago Tribune*, and all three national networks, ABC, CBS, and NBC, would soon file reports, covering the takeover on nightly newscasts and in papers nationwide. The *New York Times* would carry a story in its Saturday paper, complete with photographs. According to one source, at least two FBI agents were deployed to the site (surreptitiously) that morning and four confidential sources on the campus were feeding information directly to the FBI as events unfolded.[38] "Rebellion at N.U.," the *Chicago Tribune* announced dramatically.[39]

From inside the building, the students soon spied James Turner standing outside, talking to reporters. After his delay in getting to the building that morning, he arrived to confront an already sizeable crowd outside. He made a brief statement to the press before joining the others inside.[40]

Wary of the media circus that was now encamped on Clark Street, university officials knew that this was a story of immense public interest. There was no chance that it could be handled without sharp scrutiny by the curious public, not to mention parents and alumni. While they wanted to end the incident quickly, they were concerned with the larger issue of safety on the campus. What might happen if they mishandled this event? What if anyone got hurt? What if an eviction of the students incited more protests and more takeovers or even violence? This was, after all, a tense time in the United States, with student protests, uprisings, and strikes taking place on a seemingly weekly basis throughout the United States.

At the time, student protests focused on a wide range of issues, from ending discrimination to stopping the war in Vietnam, and the Black student movement in particular was growing exponentially, with efforts underway nationwide to protest discrimination, alter campus conditions, and assert Black cultural identity. "Since last fall, the Black cultural revolution has raged with unprecedented fury on high school and college campuses," historian Lerone Bennett, Jr. had written just that month in *Ebony* magazine.[41]

Northwestern officials worried about making things worse through their actions. In fact, they later revealed that the university had received intelligence "indicating that certain organized off-campus, activist groups from throughout the Chicago area were prepared at the first opportunity to attach themselves to any developing incident, with a view to a swift and major magnification thereof, aimed at visiting disaster upon the university."[42]

One recent disastrous incident stood out sharply: Just days earlier, in the early morning hours of April 30, 1968, Columbia University President Grayson Kirk had mobilized a thousand police officers to quash a weeklong student takeover of several buildings on the New York City campus that had shut down the entire university. Using tear gas, police entered the occupied buildings and dragged many of the students out by the arms and legs. In the end, 132 students, four faculty members, and twelve police officers were injured and 712 people were arrested.[43]

Having witnessed the chaos at Columbia, not to mention the recent uprisings following the assassination of Martin Luther King, Jr. a month earlier, officials knew that the potential for violence was real. Polite and proper Northwestern, with its history of having a rather tepid counterculture and very little protest in years prior, was facing the eye of the storm of the sixties.

Students on Low Library Ledge, Columbia University, April 1968
Various student groups at Columbia, including Students for a Democratic Society (SDS), occupied (in their word, "liberated") several buildings on the New York City campus, including the university president's office. They presented a list of demands to the administration that included halting construction of a university gym in Harlem and protecting students' right to protest. For a time, a university dean was "restrained" in his occupied office by one of the student groups. All students were ejected from the occupied buildings by police force on April 30, 1968.[44] Two Northwestern students, who later participated in the Northwestern takeover, visited Columbia students right before the April 1968 protests. During their meetings, they learned of the students' strategies and planned actions. They took this information back to Northwestern to share with the other students who would soon stage their own takeover. (Photogrraph courtesy of University Archives, Columbia University, Office of Public Affairs, Protest & Activism Photograph Collection, Collection number: UA#109.)

Bursar's Office, 619 Clark Street, Northwestern University,
May 3, 1968
(Northwestern University Archives, photograph by James Sweet)

Frame of Mind

Our young people, in disturbing numbers, appear to reject all forms of authority, from whatever source derived, and they have taken refuge in a turbulent inchoate nihilism whose sole objective is destructive. I know of no other time in our history when the gap between generations has been wider or more potentially dangerous.

Columbia University President Grayson Kirk, April 12, 1968[45]

Black Students Occupy This Building Because the Administration Has Turned a Deaf Ear.

Sign held by a Northwestern student during the May 1968 takeover[46]

As Northwestern officials were poised on the brink of ordering "a physical removal of the trespassers,"[47] Lt. Col. Lucius P. Gregg, Jr., associate dean of science, and the only Black administrator at Northwestern at the time, was summoned to the administrators' meeting. Also called to the meeting that morning was sociology Professor Walter L. Wallace. Wallace, one of a handful of Black professors at Northwestern, joined with Gregg in calling for restraint. He told the others that the students had to be "desperate to have taken such measures."[48] Not only were the students placing themselves in jeopardy through their action, but they were also jeopardizing their futures. Gregg and Wallace said they understood the students' feelings of "alienation" from the university and they affirmed the fact that the students had confronted "extreme hostility" on the campus.[49]

Jack Hinz and Franklin Kreml, vice president of planning and development, concurred with Gregg and Wallace, and they urged that they proceed with caution. Refraining long enough to consider what these four men had to say, the group began to engage in an "intensive discussion of the problem" as they sought to understand the students' "frame of mind."[50] The legal issue of a building takeover, they later stated, was now superseded by a moral issue: that of the students' well-being.[51]

President Miller also had other considerations. Had the university chosen to forcibly remove the students, he later explained, Northwestern's small security force—it numbered only eighteen officers at the time—would have been unable to execute the action alone.[52] Evanston police would have been required, along with police from neighboring towns. Once arrests had been made, Miller foresaw that more conflict and protests would have "spread" not only among "the white student body, activists, semi-activists, and others," as Miller stated, "but among the faculty as well." Charges of police brutality were sure to follow. More campus buildings would likely be occupied. And even more police would be called in. In no time at all, he concluded, the "resultant situation would probably have paralleled that which occurred at Columbia."[53]

This scenario was clearly unacceptable to Miller and others in the administration who agreed that evicting the students "would have disastrous results on the campus."[54] Thus, during that early morning meeting, Gregg, Hinz, Kreml, and Wallace were able to influence the group's next steps as they all called for adopting a calm approach. And it would be their perspectives that would largely shape the way the university responded to the students. "I'm pretty nonviolent myself," Hinz later reflected. "I abhor what violence I hear and see about . . . . I think the president thought long and hard about, do we call in the police and do we bust these kids out of that building? I encouraged that we not do that. That we try and settle matters."[55]

For Hinz, who would serve as the principal go-between during the standoff that was to unfold over the next thirty-eight hours, the attempt to settle matters was central to resolving the situation nonviolently. And, as far as understanding the students' frame of mind, perhaps no one more than Hinz could help in this respect. Upon first learning about the takeover that morning, Hinz knew exactly who the students were and what they wanted. In fact, many of them were at Northwestern to begin with largely due to his efforts to recruit them there. He was more than familiar with what had prompted their action. In April, the students had presented university officials with a list of demands, aimed at changing what they defined as unacceptable conditions on campus. And, long before those demands had been made, Hinz had learned of the extent of the racism the students faced at Northwestern University.

Chapter 2

A Fight of Long Duration

Complaints from Negroes[1] about life on this campus are not just of recent vintage.

Vernon Ford, takeover participant, April 1968[2]

The status of the Negro at Northwestern makes ridiculous our claim to glory as a liberal institution. The fight for Negro rights is the fight of every person who believes in democracy and freedom.

Daily Northwestern, December 1936[3]

All of the 107 students in the Bursar's Office that spring morning in 1968 were Black or multiracial; about half were women.[4] John Bracey and others credit the large number of women who were involved to Kathryn Ogletree, her strong leadership and the trust she instilled in everyone, but particularly in the female students. Like Ogletree, the majority of takeover participants were undergraduates. Roughly half were members of the 1970 or 1971 class year, making the average age of participants eighteen to twenty years old. Among them were those majoring in art, mathematics, physics, music, English, biology, journalism, and sociology, and those who had yet to declare their majors; they were from Evanston, Chicago, Cleveland, New York, and other American cities.[5]

Not only did these students represent the majority of Black students on the Northwestern campus, *they were the majority* of Black students on campus. By the spring of 1968, a grand total of 124 Black students were enrolled at Northwestern, out of a total of 8,900 students.[6] While the number was small, it was, at the time, the largest number of Black students the university had ever enrolled, the result of an official undertaking to integrate the university. That effort had started in earnest in 1965, following the passage of the federal 1964 Civil Rights Act and led by a newly-hired admissions officer, Jack Hinz.

In 1965, following a six-year stint at Western Reserve University (now Case Western Reserve University), Hinz arrived in Evanston with his wife and two young daughters. He had been recruited to Northwestern by a faculty committee focused on diversifying the student body.[7] At that time, only twenty-six Northwestern students—out of a total of roughly 6,300 undergraduate students—were Black. Most of those twenty-six students were male and most were athletes.[8] "[R]igid quotas" were also practiced limiting the number of Jewish and Catholic students admitted, a number that accounted for roughly eleven percent of the student body.[9] (In earlier years, that percentage had been even lower.)[10] Prior to Hinz's arrival, applicants were required to state their religion and to include photographs of themselves with their applications for admission. Altering the make-up of the student body was Hinz's mandate. "[T]hat's why I was brought here," he remembered. Up until his arrival at Northwestern, as he pointed out, "the place was notorious as a white, Anglo community."[11]

By the time Hinz arrived in Evanston, Northwestern had been in operation for more than a century. And there was a long history that connected the May 1968 takeover with decades past. What may have appeared to come out of the blue on that morning in May was, in fact, a manifestation of a legacy of discrimination practiced not only on the campus, but also in the university's hometown, the city of Evanston.

HOUSEBOY—COLORED
For Evanston fraternity: room, board, $90 per month. Call Greenleaf 9385.

WILLARD HALL
Northwestern University, Evanston.
Will have an opening for
1 dishwasher immediately.
1 experienced cook, white, Sept.
1 salad girl, white, Sept.
Call Mrs. Cowan. University 7300.

Newspaper help wanted ads for a "colored" houseboy and a white cook and salad girl, *Chicago Tribune,* December 30, 1946 (top) and *Chicago Tribune,* August 15, 1943 (bottom)

Pre-Integration Northwestern

Located near the shores of Lake Michigan, about twelve miles north of downtown Chicago, Evanston was known as Ridgeville at the time a group of Chicago Methodists selected the area for the founding of a private university in 1851. From its beginning, Northwestern was a secular institution, but for decades it maintained strong ties to the Methodist Episcopal Church. (Until 1890, all the university's presidents were Methodist ministers.[12]) The university promoted itself as protecting students from the evils of modern American society, and part of that protection translated into strictly controlling certain behaviors deemed destructive, such as drinking. Thus, from the very founding of the university, alcohol was banned within a four-mile radius of the campus.[13]

Despite its Northern geography, Evanston had its own history of Jim Crow-style policies and segregation. After the first Black residents settled in the area in the 1840s, the Black population steadily increased as people came from the South during the long years of the Great Migration. Over the decades, the community expanded and planted deep roots. By 1940, the largest Black suburban community in Illinois was located in Evanston.[14] By 1960, Black residents composed roughly twelve percent of the city's population. By the mid-1920s, segregation had been firmly established in the city through real estate practices and other methods, and by 1930, the majority of Black residents lived in the fifth ward, located on the city's west side.[15]

"There were no signs such as 'whites only,'" recalled residents concerning life in Evanston decades ago, "but everyone knew where they were allowed and not allowed to be."[16] For decades, segregation was enforced in numerous places throughout the city, including restaurants, movie theaters, beaches, and the city hospital. "Practically every restaurant in Evanston refuses to serve Negroes who, when they go to even the less respectable ones, are simply ignored," the *Daily Northwestern,* the university's student newspaper, reported in 1936.[17] No Black residents served in government. No Black school teachers taught in the city's schools.[18] Grammar and middle schools were segregated, and the majority of Black students attended a single school, Foster School. Although Evanston Township High School was integrated, there were a variety of practices deployed to separate Black and white students, from enrolling Black students in basic, rather than advanced, courses to barring Black and white students from sitting together in the classroom.[19] Occasionally, a very public case of discrimination arose, such as in 1929, when the high school's junior prom, scheduled to be held at the all-white Evanston Country Club, was canceled after a group of Black students insisted on their right to attend the dance.[20] In relation to Northwestern, few Black Evanston residents attended the university and they had "long been de facto excluded from the university in terms of employment."[21] Those who did find jobs on the campus were largely relegated to positions of menial labor, including cleaning and garbage collecting.[22]

From its founding, Northwestern, like many other colleges and universities in the United States, did not admit many Black students. While some educational institutions stood behind official policies that excluded Black students from admission, Northwestern did not have an official policy announcing that Black students were barred from enrolling, nor did it profess any official limit on the number of students who were Black, Jewish, Catholic, or any other ethnicity or religion that was not widely represented among the student body.[23] In 1869, officials dropped the university's ban on female students, allowing women to enroll.[24] Over the decades, through specific choices and practices, unwritten and written rules, omissions, behavior, and overt discrimination, the university functioned—as the students who undertook the 1968 takeover later defined Northwestern—as a "white institution."[25] As such, Northwestern was just one of many colleges and universities in the North that were, de facto, segregated institutions.[26]

Members of the Menorah Society, Northwestern University, 1937
For decades, only a small number of Jewish and Catholic students were admitted to the university. In the early twentieth century, the *Daily Northwestern* occasionally published statistics on students' religions. In 1914, the paper reported that one percent of students in the College of Liberal Arts were Jewish; three percent were Catholic. At Northwestern, the paper observed, there was a "decided leaning toward the Methodist church with the Presbyterians running a bad second."[27] In the 1920s, Jewish and Catholic students began organizing their own campus groups. In 1922, students formed the Menorah Society, whose aim was to "advance Jewish culture and ideals." In 1934, a group of students started the Hillel Foundation, (later known as Fiedler Hillel), a campus group affiliated with the larger inter-collegiate Hillel organization, founded in 1923. In 1939, a group of Catholic students inaugurated the Shiel Club, named after the auxiliary bishop of Chicago, the Reverend Bernard J. Sheil.[28] (Northwestern *Syllabus* Yearbook, 1937)

A perusal through volumes of the university's yearbook, *The Syllabus,* paints a stark visual portrait of a white institution: four fraternity members appear in blackface in their fraternity chapter photograph (1900); a column listing student goings-on refers to a "Negro vaudeville" show on campus that included a "big coon" (1905); a student lists her participation in a "minstrel show" (1916). But perhaps what is most striking is the sea of faces: portraits of white student after white student after white student compose the decades upon decades of classes at Northwestern, punctuated only very rarely by the appearance of a portrait of a Black student. For decades, the vast majority (in most cases, all) of the university's presidents, trustees, officials, administrators, deans, counselors, student committee and club members, student government officers, athletes, staff on publications, faculty members, students, and nearly each and every fraternity and sorority member were white.[29]

In 1903, Lawyer Taylor, a thirty-eight-year-old student from Louisville, Kentucky, made history when he graduated with a BS degree in mathematics, becoming the first Black student to earn an undergraduate degree at Northwestern.[30] In 1905, Naomi Willie Pollard (Dobson), a student from Chicago, graduated with a BA degree.[31] (Pollard might well have been the first Black woman to graduate from Northwestern.) But Taylor and Pollard's accomplishments did not serve as a prelude to more Black students being admitted to the university and, for decades, the number of Black students remained minuscule.[32] Even as late as 1966 one observer noted a "virtual absence of black students in the student body."[33]

It should be noted that such an absence was replicated at the majority of postsecondary educational institutions in the United States. For decades, the majority of Black American college students attended Historically Black Colleges and Universities (HBCUs), which were predominantly located in the South.[34] As late as 1939, Black students enrolled at white colleges or universities outside of the South accounted for just five-tenths of one percent of all college students in the North.[35]

From Northwestern's founding in 1851 and through the first half of the twentieth century, university administrators did not publicly acknowledge having any formal policies of racial segregation. There were, to be sure, few

Naomi Willie Pollard Dobson commuted to Northwestern from her family's home in Rogers Park in Chicago. Like many of Northwestern's earliest Black students, her roots were in the South. Her great-grandparents had been enslaved in Virginia.[36] (Northwestern *Syllabus* Yearbook, 1905)

Black students enrolled at the university at any one time, but this was simply viewed by officials as a matter of course. Occasionally, however, a university official would opine publicly on some aspect of American race relations. In 1906, for example, Northwestern President A. W. Harris made his view on the desirability of school segregation known when he stated that he was "shocked" whenever he saw Black and white students enrolled at the same school, arguing that separate schools were far more "wholesome."[37]

For many years, the small number of Black students at Northwestern faced widespread discrimination. They were often demeaned and isolated, and they were barred from fully partaking in university life. They were not allowed to use the university bathing beach or swimming pool. Black female students were not allowed to take physical education classes, despite a university requirement that all students take gym in order to graduate.[38] For years, as a result of "an unwritten, tacit understanding," Black students were barred from joining the basketball and swimming teams (part of widespread discrimination against Black student athletes at predominantly white universities).[39] Visiting Black athletes from other universities were refused accommodations with their white team members, but were, as was the case in one documented instance, "allotted . . . to a public house . . . kept by a colored man."[40] And some amenities, such as the Goodrich Grill, a campus dining facility, reportedly refused service to Black students.[41] But perhaps the most critical problem Black students faced was housing discrimination.

"[L]iving quarters are a fundamental educational area in which there are extensive opportunities for all-round development of students," announced a 1946 Northwestern brochure.[42] Concern over the moral well-being of its students was a founding principle of the Methodist institution, and the administration, like others around the country, enacted the doctrine of *in loco parentis* in relation to both male and female students. In short, university authorities assumed the "rights, duties, and obligations" of a parent to a child.[43] And in this role, officials closely oversaw many aspects of student life on campus, including the housing of students.

In the university's first decades campus housing for all students was limited. Many members of the small student body lived at home while attending school, while the majority of male students who did not live at home found lodgings with private families. In fact, university founders were not fans of dormitories. They felt that students would benefit most from living in respectable, private homes where they could be cared for both morally and otherwise.[44]

As enrollment increased over the years, however, the need for housing became critical and some students complained of the difficulties of living off campus, including eating in greasy spoon restaurants and living in drafty rooms in rickety homes. By 1903, the university was operating one dormitory for men and some rooms were also available at Heck Hall, a dormitory of the nearby Garrett Biblical Institute (now part of the Garrett-Evangelical Theological Seminary). Campus housing for female students was more plentiful, with three dormitories available, Willard, Chapin, and Pearsons halls. But many women also found housing beyond the campus in their own family homes, boarding houses, and private homes, whose owners rented rooms to students. For years, women who wished to board outside of the dormitories had to apply for special permission, warned that wherever they lived, they were expected to "conform" to the university's general regulations for conduct.[45] A list of "desirable rooms," recommended boarding places, and approved off-campus residences was made available to students, a practice that would continue well into the twentieth century.[46]

In the 1910s and 1920s, as enrollment increased, the growing need for student housing prompted the widely accepted idea that universities were obligated to provide campus housing for students. Additional university dormitories were constructed and fraternity and sorority houses multiplied on campus, and soon, the majority of students were housed in campus facilities. There was one exception: if you were Black, you were largely on your own.

With one notable exception, which is explained below, from roughly 1903 to 1947, Northwestern did not allow Black students or Black visitors to reside in campus housing, forcing them to find lodgings elsewhere.[47] Some students lived in their own homes, with many forced to make long commutes. Others sought lodgings near campus in apartments or rooming houses. But many landlords refused to rent to Black students and finding housing in segregated Evanston was difficult.[48] Well into the 1960s, Black students faced housing discrimination in Evanston. Two students who would participate in the 1968 takeover, Victor Goode and John Higginson, recounted looking for an apartment in Evanston in 1967, and "every time we would show up to an apartment," as Goode recalled, "it had 'just been rented!' "[49]

Black male students often roomed at a YMCA branch at 1014 Emerson Street in Evanston. (The Emerson Y, as it was known, was the city's "Black Y" since Black people were not allowed to join the city's main YMCA branch.) The facility's nineteen rooms offered accommodations for twenty-five individuals. The Y always had a waiting list for its rooms, and the staff kept a running list of private boarding houses for those seeking accommodations.[50] Female students and visitors often roomed at boarding houses, but housing conditions for Black women were "especially bad," as the *Daily Northwestern* reported in 1939.[51]

In the early part of the twentieth century, stories of "race prejudice" at Northwestern circulated around the country, with many Southern newspapers noting the trials faced by students who ventured North.[52] Prior to 1903, in the rare instances when Black students lived in campus housing at

Northwestern, their stories caused a stir on campus and were dramatically recounted in the press.

In 1901, a music student from San Antonio, Texas, twenty-two-year-old Isabella Ellis, "set a precedent" (and made headlines nationwide) when she successfully secured a room in a woman's campus dormitory, Chapin Hall. Until she arrived at Northwestern, officials were unaware that she was Black. She had been engaged in correspondence with the dean of Northwestern's school of music, P. C. Lutkin, who had encouraged her to apply for admission to the university.[53] Upon her arrival, she was greeted at the dormitory with consternation. A "prolonged discussion" with administrators took place, followed by a consultation with university trustees. Her assigned white roommate "refused to occupy the same room with her" and no one else was willing to room with her.[54]

Despite protest from some faculty and students, Ellis was given her own room. "She is the only person occupying a room on the lower floor," a local newspaper reported, "and she comes in contact with the other students only at meal time."[55] Over the course of the school year, Ellis was subjected to unknown humiliations by her "enemies" who resorted to "various means to force" her to move out of the dormitory.[56] But Ellis remained.

COLORED STUDENT AT NORTHWESTERN

Sarah Ellis of Texas Admitted to Young Women's Dormitory.

SETS A PRECEDENT

Educational Aid Association Holds a Long Discussion.

Isabella Ellis' story was not told accurately or fully in the press accounts. As just one example, she was variously referred to as Sarah, Mabel, and Isabella.[57] (*The Inter-Ocean,* October 19, 1901)

After her first year at Northwestern, Ellis returned home for the summer. From San Antonio, she wrote to the matron of the dormitory, Elizabeth Simpson, asking to secure a room again for the next year. But the new fall term had already been underway for a full month when Ellis, still at home in Texas, finally received word that a room could not be reserved for her. Another Black female student, Ellis' friend, had also applied to live in the dormitory, and she asked if the two women could room together. But she, too, was "refused permission."[58]

The refusal to grant Ellis a room for the new school term was partly the result of the objections of a dozen white female dormitory residents who threatened not to return to school if "colored coeds were admitted again."[59] The Women's Educational Association, which supervised the dormitories, responded by ruling that beginning in 1902, "no colored girls will be admitted to the halls."[60] The decision to exclude Black women from the dormitories was met by protest from some administrators and faculty, including some members of the Women's Educational Association. And Northwestern's President, Edmund Janes James, publicly opposed the decision.[61] But it was allowed to stand. The ruling did not "mean the exclusion of colored girls from the university," university officials pointed out. "They have permission to take rooms with private families."[62] It was clear, as one newspaper put it, that the "color line" had been drawn at Northwestern in the women's dormitories. And Ellis, still in San Antonio, reportedly "despaired of ever attending school in Evanston."[63]

COLORED GIRLS BARRED FROM CO-EDS' DORMITORIES

Race Line at Northwestern Causes Strife—Rebellion by White Students.

Co-eds at Northwestern university have objected to living in the same dormitory with colored girl students, and the authorities have rejected the application of two young women who sought rooms in the university halls. Miss Mabel Ellis of San Antonio, Texas, is the girl whose colored blood started the racial feeling at the Evanston school.

"Colored Girls Barred from Co-Eds' Dormitories," *The Inter-Ocean,* September 15, 1902. After Ellis and the other unnamed student were refused housing at Northwestern, newspapers across the country published news of the university's new policy. "Dormitories Reserved for White Women Only," announced the *Leavenworth Times,* while the *Atlanta Constitution* reported: "A colored girl student has been ordered out of the dormitory of the Northwestern University, the great Methodist institution at Evanston, Ill. Explanation-race prejudice."[64]

A new policy of discrimination was now in effect, whose source was outrageously traced to Ellis herself. According to the local newspaper, *The Inter-Ocean,* Ellis was "the girl whose colored blood started the racial feeling at the Evanston school."[65] National attention to the case soon faded, although, on a closing note, it was observed by one newspaper that the "color question has never come up among the young men students at the university."[66] In fact, as one newspaper reported, "in the students' dormitory at Sheridan road and Cook street, a young colored man, also from Texas, has roomed for three years" and no one had raised any objections.[67] That student was Lawyer Taylor. He was living in the dormitory, Heck Hall, and by 1903, there were a few other Black male students also living there.

In September 1903, the housing situation made headlines again after two Black students, Naomi Willie Pollard and John Porcius Faulkner, passed their entrance examinations, registered at Northwestern, and "aroused the ire" of some white students.[68] University officials were in a quandary after white students threatened to move out of their dormitories if Pollard and Faulkner were allowed to move in.[69] The "feeling at the Evanston institution," one newspaper noted, "has always been strong against colored students."[70]

Despite the fact that Pollard and Faulkner reported that they "had no residence," the dormitories would not only remain closed to them, but the handful of Black students already living in campus housing would soon be evicted.[71] Just as Pollard and Faulkner enrolled in the fall of 1903, and one year after Ellis and her friend had been barred from the women's dormitory, Lawyer Taylor and several other Black students were "cast out" of their dormitory and "ordered to seek other quarters."[72] (At the time, a total of five Black male students were enrolled at Northwestern.[73]) Their eviction was reportedly ordered so that members of the university's football team could take their rooms.[74] Along with his classmates, Taylor "tramped the streets for lodgings," only to be met by a "chilly reception" by Evanston landlords and a refusal to rent rooms to them.[75]

The policy of barring all Black students from campus housing was now in effect, confronting students for decades to come with the experience of racism, exclusion, and discrimination. Katherine MacDonald (also known as Kay Davis), who later went on to fame as a vocalist with the Duke Ellington orchestra, was born and raised in Evanston. She was one of just six Black students enrolled in Northwestern's school of music from 1938-1942, and, along with her Black classmates, she too was barred from campus housing. "We used to drool over Willard Hall, which was right across from the music building," Davis recalled. "I had a good time at Northwestern, but there were those limitations."[76] Evanston's first (and only) Black mayor, Lorraine Morton (elected in 1993), graduated with a master's degree from Northwestern in 1942. As a student, she too was barred from the dormitories. She lived

Lawyer Taylor served as Sergeant-at-Arms for his class at Northwestern University. He was also a member of the Rogers Debating Club. In 1903, he was evicted from his campus dormitory room. Later that year, he made national headlines when he became the first Black person to graduate from Northwestern.[77] At the graduation ceremony, class historian, Eddy S. Brandt, addressed the audience: "There is one who has been with us four years, and in every way has proved himself a scholar and a gentleman; Friends, I now ask you to join with me in giving three times three cheers for Lawyer Taylor, the first man of his race to be graduated from this institution."[78]
(Northwestern *Syllabus* Yearbook, 1903)

in a privately-owned boarding house on Lake Street along with five other Black female students.[79]

Along with facing a variety of forms of discrimination, Black students also found that they were generally not welcome in school activities.[80] John Porcius Faulkner had been hailed as a skilled orator since winning third place in Northwestern's oratory competition in 1903. Still, the all-white members of the Hinman Debating Society, the oldest literary club at Northwestern, refused to grant him membership, with some members waging a "hard fight" against him. But after Faulkner won a place in the prestigious Northern Oratorical League Society in 1904, Northwestern's debating society members narrowly voted to grant him admission. Thereafter, it was reported, the society was "divided."[81]

Black students also found that they were excluded from campus social life. The majority of Northwestern students belonged to Greek letter organizations, which dominated the campus social scene. But only a handful of Black students were ever offered membership in these predominantly white fraternity and sorority chapters, and those members were pledged in the 1960s.[82] Indeed, many Greek letter organizations had restrictive membership clauses in their charters, the last of which (at Northwestern) was removed in the early 1960s.[83]

Members of Northwestern's Hinman Debating Society, 1905
(Northwestern *Syllabus* Yearbook, 1906)

John Porcius Faulkner (back row, first on the left) drew attention to his oratorical talents in his speech titled, "The New Bondage," in which he challenged the ideas of Booker T. Washington. "The black man has no chance to free himself from these chains once he is educated to endure them," Faulkner argued, charging Washington and others with teaching Black people to accept "subservience." Faulkner advocated for "an equality of the races through the medium of education."[84]

Poet, author, and professor Margaret Walker Alexander (1915-1998) was born in Birmingham, Alabama. She earned a BA from Northwestern in 1935. Her mother and father, a Methodist minister, also graduated from Northwestern. Alexander was seventeen when she arrived in Evanston to attend Northwestern in 1932. Along with her fifteen-year-old sister, Mercedes, she roomed at a boarding house at 812 Emerson Street, operated by Lydia and James Landers.[85] It was a short walk from the house to campus, but it was with "great trepidation" that she and her sister took in their new surroundings. On campus, Alexander recalled, "racism was rampant," with professors telling "darky jokes openly in the classroom." When white students laughed, she wrote, "you burned with shame but you could do nothing about it."[86] At the time Alexander attended Northwestern, there were only forty Black students enrolled. After graduating from Northwestern, Alexander earned an MA and PhD from the University of Iowa. She was a member of Chicago's South Side Writers Group (along with author Richard Wright) and she worked for the WPA's Writer's Project in Chicago. From 1949-1979, she taught at Jackson State University where, in 1968, she founded the Institute for the Study of History, Life, and Culture of Black People (now known as the Margaret Walker Center). In 1974, Alexander received an honorary Doctor of Literature from Northwestern. Her books include *For My People* (1942) and *Jubilee* (1966).[87]

(Photograph from the George Cleveland Hall Branch Archives, Box 9, Photo 50, Vivian G. Harsh Research Collection, Woodson Regional Library, Chicago Public Library)

As a result of being excluded from campus social life, over the decades, Black students founded and joined their own organizations. They came together to socialize, organize, lobby, and work to better conditions for themselves and others. Chapters of two historically Black fraternities, Kappa Alpha Psi (Theta chapter installed at Northwestern in 1919) and Alpha Phi Alpha (Alpha Mu chapter, installed at Northwestern in 1920), would provide male students with a vital means to come together for support, networking, and friendship. And by the 1930s, the historically Black sorority, Alpha Kappa Alpha, would have an unofficial presence on campus.

But perhaps the most representative and influential group on Northwestern's campus was the (coed) Quibblers Club. Founded in 1926, the club's first and "only purpose," as member Lillian Bell explained, "was to provide a meeting place for students forced to commute, and plan parties."[88] Over the years, a majority of Black students on campus would join the Quibblers Club. In October 1930, the club was officially granted recognition as a student organization by the university, and it would evolve to become not only more expressly political, but also entirely integrated.[89] The club sponsored a variety of events, lectures, panels, dances, and, in February 1945, during Negro History Week, (precursor to Black History Month), it sponsored an exhibit of the work of Black artists and writers in the foyer of Northwestern's Deering Library.[90]

Due to the lack of campus facilities open to Black students, however, most fraternity, sorority, and Quibblers Club meetings and events were held off-campus, with Evanston residents sometimes serving as hosts for a variety of programming in their private homes. Unlike the majority of members of the predominantly-white Greek letter groups on campus, who resided in their own (privately owned) spacious fraternity and sorority houses, Black fraternity and sorority members were scattered around the city, residing wherever they found rooms.

For a time, William C. Pyant, Quibblers Club member and Alpha Mu's longtime secretary, lived at the same boarding house at 812 Emerson Street where Margaret Walker Alexander and her sister lived. When Pyant first arrived in Evanston as a graduate student in sociology, he found lodgings at the Emerson Y, which served as a location for many social activities hosted by Black students, including annual fraternity dances and the Quibblers Club's weekly Wednesday luncheons.[91] For a time Pyant also worked at the Emerson Y. He later settled in Evanston where he worked to advance civil rights and reforms in Evanston's housing policies.[92]

Over the years, a strong connection between Black students and city residents was established; a large number of Evanston's Black residents may not have enrolled at the university, but they became a vital resource for students, as the city's professionals, church pastors, activists, organizers,

Members of Alpha Mu, Northwestern's chapter of Alpha Phi Alpha, 1930. (Northwestern *Syllabus* Yearbook, 1930)
Both graduate and undergraduate students were members of Alpha Mu, along with students enrolled in the law school and professional schools. From left to right, back row: Lucius Lee, Rodney Higgins, Lyons (first name unknown), James O. Smith, Clarence Mason. Front row: George Robinson, Joseph Grider, Lee Verne Newsome, Howard Daniels, William Pyant. Alpha Phi Alpha was the first Black fraternity in the United States, founded at Cornell University in 1906. In 1945, the fraternity became integrated. Among its most famous members are W.E.B. Du Bois, Martin Luther King, Jr., Duke Ellington, and Thurgood Marshall.[93]

and average citizens socialized with the students and worked in tandem on civil rights issues related to the campus, the city, and beyond. In return, the students contributed to the local community. They worked for and supported (including raising money for) local Black organizations, including the Emerson Y, and also the Evanston Township High School, where, in the 1960s, Northwestern students volunteered as advisors and mentors.[94]

Throughout the 1930s, Quibblers Club members became increasingly focused on issues beyond their social life. Now they were concentrating on addressing issues facing Black students on campus and improving conditions in Evanston.[95] Working with local residents, club members hosted various speakers "to discuss problems pertinent to all Americans" and explore possible solutions.[96] Many of America's most prominent Black artists and intellectuals would come to Evanston upon invitation from the Quibblers Club and other campus groups that were also dedicated to promoting civil rights. Speakers included professor and diplomat Ralph Bunche (1937), writer and poet Langston Hughes (1938), poet Arna Bontemps (1938), poet and professor Sterling Brown (1940), and writer and NAACP official William Pickens (1941).[97]

In 1931, scholar and NAACP co-founder, W.E.B. Du Bois, came to Evanston to support Edwin B. Jourdain, Jr. in his campaign for a seat on the Evanston City Council. Jourdain had invited Du Bois to appear at a "mass meeting" in Evanston that constituted, as Jourdain told Du Bois, "the first organized attempt of 10,000 colored people to get representation in the city council."[98]

Members of Alpha Mu chapter had long known "Brother Jourdain." He was a founding member of Harvard's Alpha Phi Alpha chapter, and, after moving to Evanston in 1924, he had become involved with Alpha Phi Alpha's chapter at Northwestern.[99] His fraternity brothers wholeheartedly supported and celebrated his campaign, and Quibblers Club members also pledged their unanimous support.[100]

In 1931, in a historic first, Jourdain was elected the city's first Black city council member, representing the fifth ward. But shortly afterward, he was dramatically unseated from office, charged with (unsubstantiated) election "irregularities."[101] His supporters, including Alpha Mu and Quibblers Club members, were outraged at the underhanded ousting of Jourdain from office. During one bitterly cold night, a group kept a twenty-four-hour vigil at the door of city hall, waiting to file Jourdain's name on the upcoming ballot once more. (They wanted to be first to file in order to ensure his name appeared at the top of the ballot.)

In April 1932, Jourdain was elected, again, and thereafter, he would serve as a leader in the fight to end discrimination at Northwestern and in Evanston.[102] He also continued his friendship with Du Bois, keeping him informed of the "obstacles" facing Evanston's Black residents. "This fight has found all of us with plenty of moments when we felt more blue than we've wanted to admit," he wrote to Du Bois in 1939.[103] (Jourdain also kept Du Bois informed about the number of Black students enrolled at Northwestern.[104])

Edwin Bush Jourdain, Jr. (1900-1986) (Evanston History Center Archives) Originally from New Bedford, Massachusetts, Jourdain graduated with a degree in history from Harvard University in 1921. At the time, Harvard was facing opposition owing to its own practices of discrimination against Black students.[105] Jourdain moved to Evanston in 1924, seeking, as his son Spencer Jourdain later said, "economic opportunities." Jourdain worked as a reporter for the *Chicago Defender* and as managing editor of the *Chicago Bee.* He also worked as manager of the Regel Theater. He married Emmaline Hardwick, a Fisk University graduate, whose family had moved to Evanston around 1915.[106] He attended classes at Northwestern and became close with members of Northwestern's chapter of his own fraternity, Alpha Phi Alpha. During his tenure on the Evanston City Council, in 1931 and from 1932-1947, he successfully fought against many of the city's discriminatory laws. Through his efforts, rules forbidding "mixed" baseball games on city-owned diamonds and segregating the city's beaches and seating in movie theaters were abolished. From 1942-1944, Jourdain worked for the NAACP, and later, he taught at Roosevelt University in Chicago, a university that was integrated since its founding in 1945.[107]

Quibblers Club Members, 1945. First row: Mae Gordon Davis, Jeanne Ackiss, Lillian Bell, Beverlee Stams, Helen Leatherwood. Willa Cummings; second row: June Wells, Florice Green, Ernestine Gillebeaux, Juanita Wells, Dorothy Fowler, Dorothy Bartholomew, Connie Johnson; third row: Dorothy Bradley, Irving McCullom, Jimmy Dixson and Bob Waters. "Quibblers Club does not quibble," wrote member Lillian Bell. Formed largely as a social organization, the club evolved over time. "Such a frivolous name fitted then," Bell observed of the time of the club's founding in 1926, "but now it does not. But for sentimental reasons, the name clings."[108] The Quibblers Club may not have represented the majority of the Northwestern student body, but over the years, its members often managed to raise the issue of racial discrimination and hold it in the public eye as they advocated for various reforms, from the integration of student housing to an increase in the number of Black students admitted to the university. (Photograph from *Purple Parrot,* April 1945, Northwestern University)

In the 1920s, various small "interracial" groups, comprised of both Black and white students, along with a few faculty members, were formed to address the issue of discrimination and to educate students on a variety of issues related to American race relations.[109] In 1928, for example, a "reconciliation tour" of centers of "Negro Culture and Life" in Chicago was organized and Northwestern students visited the offices of the *Chicago Defender* and the Urban League, among other places.[110]

But it wasn't until the 1930s that the issue of discrimination would be more widely discussed. In that decade, several investigations would prove that discrimination and segregation on the campus and in Evanston indeed existed. And, in the decades leading up to the takeover, several campaigns for reform were undertaken. The primary issue that drew together reform-minded students, administrators, faculty, and city residents was the critical issue of housing discrimination.

There had long been a call for the passage of anti-discrimination housing legislation in Evanston, and many residents continuously decried segregation, unfair financing, and the demolition of homes in the city's Black neighborhoods. Residents had presented fair housing petitions to the Evanston City Council numerous times, demanding that the city pass an open occupancy law in order to assure that the housing market operated free of any restrictions or discrimination.[111] Student groups circulated petitions to demand the university support open occupancy and integrate university housing.[112] Pressure had long been applied to the university to desegregate its own real estate holdings and ensure that no landlord on Northwestern's list of approved student housing discriminated against potential renters. And a "fight of long duration and much intensity," as the *Chicago Defender* put it, had been waged against the policy of banning Black students from campus housing.[113]

In 1935, the issue of discrimination in campus housing took center stage when two Black students (both Alpha Phi Alpha members) William Yancy Bell, Jr. and Bernard Jefferson, moved into a vacant room in a campus dormitory, Pearson Hall, located on Orrington Avenue.[114] They were the first Black residents in university housing in more than three decades. A university official had approved their placement in the house, which was occupied by forty white male students. But after they moved in, "a violent opposition arose against them."[115] The Dean of Men's office polled the dormitory's white residents to determine the extent of the opposition. The result: a majority (twenty-nine out of thirty-five) wanted Bell and Jefferson to move out.[116] The dormitory president urged the administration to evict them. "Up to the present occasion there has been no racial controversy on this campus," he wrote in a statement, "but unless something is done, I fear that a great deal of ill feeling is likely to arise, which would be bad for all parties concerned."[117]

Facing opposition from a majority of the other dormitory residents, Jefferson, a first-year student, decided to move out. But Bell decided to stay.[118]

The administration announced that "it will not be placed in the unfavorable position of breaking [Bell's] contract."[119] But by staying in the dorm, Bell had "broken the unwritten law that no Negro shall be allowed to stay at a university dormitory."[120] The incident was labeled the "Pearson Hall Fiasco" and Bell himself was labeled a "troublemaker."[121] He was, the *Daily Northwestern* wrote, "castigated by members of the student body, faculty, and administration as 'a Negro who doesn't know his place,' 'a publicity monger,' [and] 'a person who deserves every slap he gets.' "[122]

Football Team, Northwestern University, 1936
(Northwestern University Archives)

Bernard Jefferson (back row, number 31) was a key player. The team was on the brink of winning the 1936 Big Ten Conference title just as Jefferson and Bell were voted out of their dorm rooms. Jefferson's teammate was Clarence Hinton (second row, first player on the left), a star athlete at Northwestern. Thirty years later, Hinton's daughter, Audrey, enrolled at Northwestern and later took part in the takeover. After Clarence Hinton graduated in 1938, he earned his medical degree at Howard University and then served in the U.S. Army. He went on to enjoy a groundbreaking medical career. Jefferson later flew one hundred missions in Europe as a member of the famous Tuskegee Airman during World War II. Jefferson was a member of Alpha Phi Alpha. Hinton was a member of Kappa Alpha Psi.[123]

William Yancy Bell, Jr. (c. 1914 -1967) (back row, second from left) with other members of Northwestern's YMCA chapter. Bell came to Northwestern after graduating from Clark High School in Atlanta. In 1936, he graduated from Northwestern with honors, with a BA degree in classics. He was a member of Alpha Phi Alpha Fraternity and Eta Sigma Phi, a national honorary classical fraternity. In 1936, Northwestern Professor Thomas D. Eliot defended Bell against his critics, describing him as "one of the most poised and objective students I ever had in his attitude toward race relations." Bell would go on to a career as a civil rights activist and professor. He worked for the Urban League and was a professor of sociology at City College of San Francisco.[124]
(Photograph from Northwestern *Syllabus* Yearbook, 1935)

What some described as Bell's "troublemaking" didn't end with his dormitory stance. He would prove to be a formidable force for change both on the Northwestern campus and in the city of Evanston. The son of a distinguished father—who had the notable distinction of being the first Black man to earn a graduate degree at Northwestern—Bell would become the first Black student to use the university swimming pool.[125] He also "fought for and won the right to sit on the main floor of the Evanston theatres, hitherto prohibited to any member of the colored race."[126] And, in August 1936, Bell was represented by the Chicago branch of the NAACP in a suit against Northwestern for $5,000 in damages after he had purchased a token for admission to an Evanston bathing beach, operated by the university, and was refused entrance. According to *The Crisis* magazine, when Bell "presented himself for admission, he was told he could not enter because he was colored." Bell insisted upon his right to enter and was told by the beach guard, (a player on Northwestern's football team), that "he would be thrown out if he tried to enter."[127] The lawsuit charged the university with violating Bell's civil rights. University officials responded that the 1885 Civil

Rights Act of Illinois was not applicable in this case since Northwestern was a "charitable" institution and, as such, exempt from the law.[128]

Bell's suit initiated a chain of reactions. In December 1936, an editorial, titled "Discrimination Against Negro Students," appeared in the *Daily Northwestern.* It excoriated university officials and a variety of policies both on campus and in Evanston. Black people are "discriminated against in rooming houses, the dining room, the theatres, the athletic field and the classroom," the editorial read. "A good part of the blame rests, directly and indirectly, with the administration."[129]

Aside from identifying the "question of Negro discrimination on campus," the editorial also called for the university to remove from its list of accredited rooming houses any that "refuse to rent to Negroes." It also demanded that officials conduct a survey to determine to what degree white students found "reprehensible" the idea of Black students being allowed to live in campus dorms or eat at the Goodrich Grill, the campus dining facility that reportedly refused service to Black students.[130] Finally, the editorial called for "all liberal organizations on campus to take up the defense of Negro rights."[131]

"I am hoping that it will be found to be untrue that Northwestern is in any way discriminating against those of its students who are colored," declared Ernest Fremont Tittle, pastor of Evanston's First Methodist Church and member of Northwestern's board of trustees. "It is now certainly incumbent upon the universities of the world to place human values above nation, race or class."[132] But, just one day after the above editorial appeared, a fact check confirmed some details about the nature of discrimination as it existed at Northwestern. No Black players were on the basketball team. One Black athlete had been told not to even try out for the team "because of the Western Conference's 'unwritten law.' "[133] It was also revealed that a Black member of the university's track team was not allowed to stay in the same hotel with his white team members during out-of-town meets and was instead "forced to make provision for sleeping and dining privately."[134] And, as a result of "the Pearson Hall Affair of last year," as the *Daily Northwestern* reported, "no Negroes are rooming in university dormitories . . . although at least one negro made application for quarters there."[135]

In response, a campus forum was held, bringing together seven organizations, including Northwestern's International Relations Club, the Peace Action Committee, the campus chapters of the YMCA and YWCA, the Hillel organization, and B'nai B'rith. The forum, which also included an address by Evanston City Council member, Edwin Jourdain, Jr., was described as the "opening gun in a campaign on alleged discrimination against negro students on the campus and in Evanston."[136] Soon, Jourdain, along with the Evanston Ministerial Association, whose members included representatives from Evanston's First Baptist Church, First Congregational Church, and

Westminster Church, appointed a committee to investigate the charges of discrimination at Northwestern and in Evanston.[137] "Out of this tempest must come action," the *Daily Northwestern* asserted. "It is not enough to reveal how flagrant the situation is."[138]

Over the years, various investigations would be conducted, but little progress was made. In 1936, a student-run Interracial Committee was launched with the purpose of investigating and reforming university policies, improving housing conditions for Black students, and promoting "better relations among various racial groups represented on campus."[139] The group, which included both Black and white students, met at the home of Thornton W. Merriam, director of the University Board of Religion.[140] In one of its several reports, the committee stated that "conditions for some students, in particular negroes, were deplorable as compared to accommodations for white students."[141]

Another investigative body, the Interracial Commission, was formed within the Student Governing Board (Northwestern's student government). It also conducted investigations into conditions on campus and in Evanston, including conducting a survey of discrimination in the city's restaurants. Included in the commission's reports was confirmation of the fact that: "negro students are still . . . excluded from university dormitories as a matter of policy."[142]

The commission also sought to promote "better relationships between racial and religious groups" on campus and it soon began hosting various lectures and events.[143] In 1940, it sponsored "Negro in America Week," a campus-wide slate of events that included an art exhibit, reception, presentations, and a panel discussion, whose speakers included Evanston City Council member, Edwin Jourdain, Jr.[144]

Meanwhile, the housing situation intensified when difficulties arose at Evanston's Emerson Y, where Black male students had long resided. In the spring of 1938, two current Northwestern students and one alumnus had been evicted from their rooms, while another student had been arrested and charged with disorderly conduct by order of the facility's executive secretary, P. J. Hauser.[145] Reportedly, some residents in the Emerson Street building complained that the students were disruptive. They held late night discussions and hosted card-playing parties and fraternity meetings in their rooms. Despite being asked by the management to stop, they reportedly refused and thus followed the evictions and arrest. Acknowledging the historical relationship between the Emerson Y and Northwestern, P.J. Hauser (who was a member of Alpha Phi Alpha and active in Northwestern's Alpha Mu chapter) defended his actions. For twelve years, he "had taken the major responsibility in helping room Negro students who come to Northwestern," he explained, and "this is the first time that I have had any difficulty of this sort with the hundreds of whom I have helped."[146] Indeed, Hauser even noted that despite the YMCA's desire to keep "a reasonable balance" between students and others residents, that balance was almost never achieved; the demand for housing Northwestern's Black students was simply too great.

The eviction of the students caused an uproar. Members of the Quibblers Club wrote an open letter to Hauser, deploring him for his handling of the matter and for what they saw as his negative view of "Evanston Negro youths." One of the signatories was Bernard Jefferson, who had been pressured to move out of his room in a Northwestern dormitory two years earlier.[147]

Northwestern's student government conducted an investigation into the matter and urged the president of the Evanston YMCA, George Folds, to conduct a public hearing and thereby alleviate any "existing tension."[148] Folds responded that it was "unwise to further discuss this matter." He did not believe any investigation was necessary, a position he had already communicated to Northwestern's administration.[149] Soon, university officials announced that the matter was closed.[150]

"Much bad feeling has arisen," the *Daily Northwestern* observed of the case, "but the basic blame in the case rests neither with the boys nor the YMCA, but on the doorstep of the University."[151] The newspaper once again took a stand against the administration, asserting that it "has often smoothly evaded responsibility by pointing out that dormitory regulations exclude no student for race or color." But, the paper charged: "This is brutal hypocrisy. On one pretext or another, factual history shows that no negro student has remained long in a dormitory. Inevitably they are thrown on the community, to drift about from one lodging to another as best they can."[152]

The situation remained unresolved, but students continued to strategize and organize. In February 1939, a group of female students, including several members of the Interracial Committee, sought to make good on a university administrator's pledge to allow an "interracial house" on campus.[153] They were assisted in their effort by the university's new counselor to women, Ruth McCarn, who would become well known for her work to improve campus conditions for Black, Jewish, and female students.[154] The students submitted a petition to the administration, along with letters of support from faculty members, requesting an integrated dormitory for women.[155] In April, they received a response. While the university was "deeply appreciative" of the group's "willingness" to undertake such an experiment, officials could not "afford the risk of failure." "We do not feel that conditions are sufficiently favorable to ensure the success of the plan for the coming year," the women were told, "and for that reason prefer that the experiment should not be initiated at this time. May I express my regret?"[156]

Ruth O'Brien McCarn (1896-1981) Counselor to Women, Northwestern University. (Northwestern University Archives)

McCarn was a strong advocate for fair housing on campus. Not only did she support a student petition asking the university to establish an integrated dormitory women, but she also asked the university to draw up a list of approved housing for Black women—requests that were rejected.[157] In 1948, a firestorm erupted on campus after McCarn took a leave of absence from her position, suddenly and without any explanation. It soon came to light that she had reportedly been asked to resign by Northwestern President Franklyn Bliss Snyder because she was judged to be "too liberal about Jews and Negroes."[158] (A charge denied by Snyder.) For years, Snyder and McCarn had reportedly been at odds, and he had reprimanded her before, asking her to discontinue her focus on campus "race relations."[159] In 1941, Harry L. Wells had written to Snyder protesting McCarn's "advocacy of interracial relations," stating that among other problems, it jeopardized future fundraising.[160] McCarn would later be hired at the University of Chicago.[161]

The practice of discrimination at Northwestern was now entering yet another decade and still nothing had been done to change conditions. Chair of the Interracial Committee, Virginia Kennelly, one of the students who had been a signatory to the petition for the integrated dormitory, said the committee pledged to "carry on" and to plan for "greater social opportunity" for Black students, even in the face of the administration's refusal to support interracial housing.[162] But one committee member, electrical engineering major, Mynor P. Payne, was not so positive in his outlook. A member of both Kappa Alpha Psi and the Quibblers Club, Payne soon wrote a letter that appeared in the *Daily Northwestern.* "It is no longer satisfactory or even possible to pass over these present social conditions with a gentle 'shame,' or a polite 'tsk, tsk, it'll soon blow over!' " he wrote. "The problem of equal rights has reached a crisis, not only here, but throughout the world."[163]

Indeed, World War II would prove to accelerate the demands for ending segregation and discrimination. Fighting to defend the ideals of democracy and freedom was antithetical to living within the restrictions that divided Americans on the basis of race, many charged. By World War II, the Quibblers Club, now seeing itself as more intensely political, set forth its primary aims of fostering "democratic ideals on campus, and the integration of all students in campus activities."[164] Its members also attempted to tackle the housing problem by launching a campaign against racial segregation on campus.[165] "All Quibblers took an active part in the campaign," one club member recalled, "which although unsuccessful, at least succeeded in making the campus aware of the situation."[166] Some of the staff on the *Daily Northwestern* joined the campaign, often publishing editorials that drew attention to campus conditions for Black students and other people of color. "We want action!" the paper demanded and its editors announced "the beginning of a new era at Northwestern" with yet another concerted effort to lift campus housing restrictions.[167]

In 1941, members of Alpha Kappa Alpha, a predominantly Black sorority that had an unofficial presence on campus for a number of years, petitioned for admission into the university's Panhellenic Council, a group that represented all campus sororities. They were supported by Ruth McCarn in their request. There were just nine members in the local, unofficial chapter of Alpha Kappa Alpha at Northwestern, and they did not, explained chapter president Eunice Randall, have a house on campus. Thus, they wished to "obtain certain privileges of a recognized group," such as the use of campus building.[168] In a unanimous vote, the council approved the chapter's membership. Just three months later, Kappa Alpha Psi fraternity's chapter was granted admission into the university's Interfraternity Council, which represented campus fraternities. The council was required to rewrite its constitution in order to allow Black fraternity members.[169] The formal recognition of these two groups was, the *Daily Northwestern* observed, "perhaps the most outstanding step of the year."[170]

Nanette "Nannie" Turpin Thomas (Hopkins) (1914-1994)
(Northwestern *Syllabus* Yearbook, 1933)

Thomas hailed from St. Louis. She entered Northwestern at the age of sixteen. Her uncle, Charles Turpin, was the first elected Black city official in St. Louis. Another uncle, Tom Turpin, was a seminal composer and ragtime musician. Thomas was a member of the Quibblers Club and Alpha Kappa Alpha sorority. The sorority did not have a recognized chapter at Northwestern at the time Thomas listed her affiliation in the yearbook in 1933.[171] In 1967, several Northwestern students would request permission to bring Alpha Kappa Alpha (back) to campus.

Despite these victories, the small number of Black students admitted to the university, along with the restrictions on housing, resulted in the gradual demise of predominantly Black Greek letter organizations at Northwestern. Alpha Kappa Alpha soon disappeared from campus. By 1949, Alpha Phi Alpha counted only six members in its Alpha Mu chapter. Lacking housing and campus facilities, the group conducted its initiations that fall at Evanston's Ebenezer A.M.E. Church. But soon after, due to low membership numbers, the chapter became inactive. By 1954, Kappa Alpha Psi's Theta chapter was also gone; the chapter, which boasted many prominent educators and leaders, such as Rufus Clement, who earned his masters degree in history at Northwestern and was later appointed president of Atlanta University, also became inactive.[172]

In September 1942, another effort was made to establish an integrated dormitory when a group of fifteen Black and white students presented the administration with a plan and budget for "cooperative" housing. Their request was rejected. University officials explained why: "real estate agents and property owners would not approve of Negroes living in the vicinity of the campus," they argued.[173] And, more pointedly, they insisted, "interracial living is against the mores of the community."[174] A few years earlier, staff on the *Daily Northwestern*, who supported an integrated dorm, pointed out that the prejudice that existed on campus was not only confined to the administration; it was also widespread among students and parents. An integrated dorm seemed an impossibility, the paper stated, since "too many students, and too many parents, simply would not stand for permitting Negroes to live with them."[175]

In 1943, Northwestern's Business Manager, Harry L. Wells, seemed to affirm this fact when he offered one of the clearest statements on the university's policy on housing: "It is the policy and the unwritten law of Northwestern University to prohibit all Negroes from living in any dormitory or house on the university campus," he said.[176] Wells argued that integrated housing would "stir up trouble" since, he claimed, so many Northwestern students were white Southerners.[177] (Wells elaborated further: "Don't tell me that I don't like colored people. In fact, I went down south and bought a plantation, where I employ a number of Negros, and I know them as well as anybody."[178]) Wells made this statement after a visiting music student from Chicago, Robbie Shields (Terry), lodged a complaint against the university, charging that she had been barred from Willard Hall, a university dormitory, because she was Black. (Shields' niece was Marian Shields Robinson, Michelle Obama's mother.[179]) Shields said she had been "humiliated, chagrined and insulted" when she arrived at Northwestern to take part in a music institute and was turned away by the dormitory director. Soon, her lawyers charged that the university had branded Shields "inferior to other normal young American women."[180] In December 1943, Shields sued Northwestern for $50,000.[181]

In 1944, the Quibblers Club members polled students about their attitudes toward the housing situation, revealing that ":a large majority of the Northwestern student body feels that something should be done about negro housing."[182] In response, the Interracial Commission announced its support for an "international house," which would be open to students of "all races, creeds, and nationalities."[183] Such a house, however, was conceived largely as one to be open only to Black and foreign students. (The university broadly classified foreign students, including in that category, for example, students from the U.S. territory of Hawaii.[184]) Many Quibblers Club members made their position known: they wanted all dormitories on campus open to all students and thus they opposed any such "international house."[185] Such a dormitory, they argued, would "cause the Negro to be looked upon as a foreigner, not as a citizen." They also opposed opening a dormitory for Black students only, arguing that it would prove to be "a fatal step . . . almost 'Jim Crow' segregation."[186] Further, they continued to argue that housing was but one issue related to a far more critical problem: the small number of Black students admitted to the university.[187]

After World War II, pressure continued to build on campus and beyond. In the summer of 1946, at a meeting of the Institute on College Quotas, several serious charges of racial and religious discrimination in the admission of students were "laid at Northwestern's doorstep."[188] The *Daily Northwestern* sought to confirm them. "We do not have a quota based on race at Northwestern," William Selden, Northwestern's director of admissions, told the paper, echoing the statements of other administrators who also dismissed the charges.[189]

But the calls for the end of discrimination intensified. The *Daily Northwestern* continued to run editorials "calling for a solution to the 'deplorable conditions of Negro housing,' " while Northwestern anthropologist Melville J. Herskovits, founder of the university's preeminent African Studies program and library, made public his position decrying racism.[190]

"Negro students are forced to live wherever they can find a bed," the *Daily Northwestern* reported. "Many of them commute daily from Chicago's South Side for want of accommodations. One student, a World War II veteran, slept each night for awhile sitting in the lobby of the Emerson Y.M.C.A. because there was 'no room at the inn.' "[191] In urging the administration to change its policies, the paper often sought to compare Northwestern's status to the advances some universities were making in the area of ending discriminatory policies. "Other Big Ten universities—Wisconsin, Chicago and Michigan — have long since dropped any racial restrictions concerning residence," the paper reported. "At Indiana U last year a similar campaign to make 'open' dorms open to all was successful. It seems Northwestern, as usual, is far behind."[192]

The housing issue came into such sharp relief in the aftermath of World War II due to the severe housing shortage that plagued the city and campus (and the nation, for that matter). The "housing famine," as it was dubbed, was partially the result of a wartime suspension of all residential construction for the war's duration. It was exacerbated by a sharp increase in Evanston's population, due to an influx of veterans eager to enroll in college and take advantage of the Service Men's Readjustment Act of 1944 (the GI Bill). In the fall of 1945, Northwestern reported a thirteen percent gain in registrations, and many students had nowhere to live.[193] A classified ad in the local paper paints the picture: "Discharged Navy man needs 3 or 4 room apt for wife and 3 mos. child while he attends Northwestern. Desperate."[194] At the Emerson Y, extra cots were set up in the dining room, and residents were now required to double up, with as many as four residents, including many returning veterans, assigned to a single room.[195]

To meet the demand, the Evanston City Council authorized the construction of Quonset huts near campus and on private property and Northwestern planned to launch a half-million dollar construction project to build twenty Quonset huts, fifty prefabricated metal cottages, and twenty-five prefabricated dormitories for incoming students.[196]

Many people were outraged that the university's facilities would not be open to Black veterans. And so, in 1946, when Northwestern applied for a city permit to build a 280-unit housing facility for returning (white only) veterans, critics called loudly for the university to "drop its color bar."[197] City Council member Jourdain urged the council to "demand that the school drop its color bar as a condition upon which permission would be granted" for the new structure.[198] As chairman of the city's building committee, Jourdain wrote to the National Housing Agency (NHA) to determine the legality of the restriction. "At this writing, nine Negro war veterans, — some with battle stars from the European and the South Pacific theaters, some drawing disabled war vets' pensions," he wrote, "are finding that their share in World War II means little to a university which today raises against them the very Hitler racist barriers they fought to destroy."[199]

The NHA informed Northwestern of its policy to "administer its functions with racial equity." All educational institutions that sought federal aid or support for emergency construction were required "to reply that in the administration of its temporary housing program, it will provide housing for racial minority groups substantially in accordance with its proportionate needs."[200] But university President Franklyn Bliss Snyder announced that the NHA's policy would have no impact on the planned construction. "It is not in my power to commit the university on the question of housing Negro veterans," he said, "the university recommends that they stay with Negro families in Evanston and not on the campus."[201] This policy was, he explained, "determined by the board of trustees and the public sentiment . . . There is no indication that it will change." [202]

By a majority vote of the Evanston City Council, the construction was approved. The "color bar" remained in effect.

In 1947, a group of students and faculty presented a resolution in favor of unsegregated housing to Dean of Students F. George Suelberger. Although Suelberger consented to present it to the administration, he made it known that he did not support the resolution himself.[203] He "vigorously" reaffirmed what he called the university's "selective housing" policy which banned Black students from the dorms. "We should maintain our present system of selective housing, and continue to house negro students in private rooming houses and the Emerson Street YMCA," he stated. Not only would many white students object to living in the same dormitory as Black students, but no students at Northwestern, his insisted, come from homes "whether they be apartments or private dwellings, where people are housed on an interracial basis," he said. Therefore, since the university sought to maintain conditions in dormitories which were "as near to normal home life as possible," as he explained, the act of providing integrating housing would "violate" that principle.[204]

In January 1947, editors of the *Daily Northwestern* launched a campaign which, they stated, "we hope will finally result in a workable solution to the problem as it exists at this University."[205] "Our Aim," read the headline of the first of several pieces, "To Correct Negro Housing Evils."[206] Their work prompted the first real systematic exploration of white students' attitudes toward integrated housing. After two campus groups polled 900 students for their opinions, the results were disheartening: 72.8% of white students said they would refuse to live with a Black roommate. And 42% said they would refuse to live in the same house or share facilities with a Black person.[207] What most white students would "allow" (76.4% of them) was a separate, on-campus housing unit for Black students.[208] And a majority (76.4%) favored "a voluntary international house" for both Black and white students.[209]

For what seemed like the umpteenth time, many Quibblers Club members made it known that they did not want a separate dormitory for the forty-one Black students currently enrolled at Northwestern: they wanted fully integrated housing, a demand the university continuously argued was impossible to meet. "Negroes are not interested in segregated housing on or off campus," Bill Branch, a Quibblers Club member, said.[210] (In 1949, perhaps to underscore the seriousness of their desire for complete integration, Quibblers Club members changed their club's name to the Interracial Club.[211])

The student poll had concluded that "unrestricted housing is not feasible on this campus," and the Student Governing Board concurred. But now the idea of a dormitory open to Black and foreign students was back on the

"No Room for Them??" Illustration accompanying the campaign to "To Correct Negro Housing Evils." (*Daily Northwestern,* January 24, 1947)

table, which was, to many, a less-than-perfect solution. The Quibblers Club and others continued the campaign for "unrestricted housing," calling for the complete "elimination of the racial barriers in Northwestern's housing policy."[212] But still, the idea of an integrated dorm now seemed feasible. "If an international house IS established by next fall," the *Daily Northwestern* opined in February 1947, "Northwestern will have accomplished something in a few months it had failed to accomplish in nearly 100 years."[213]

With a growing and intense pressure to do something to address the situation, some university officials now seemed willing to embrace a "separate but equal" attitude toward campus housing. And finally, the administration, supported by a vote from the board of trustees, relented. In September 1947, the university opened its first integrated housing unit for female students, the International House (also known as an "inter-racial housing unit") at 1827 Orrington Avenue.[214] Called the "first experiment on the Evanston campus in non-segregated housing,"[215] the residence had room for seventeen students. Seven students, including five Black women, one white woman, and one Asian-American woman, applied to live there.[216] Some viewed this first step at integrated housing as a mere concession since the dormitory "was visibly segregated from the other housing units on campus."[217] "So far success has been slight," the *Daily Northwestern* asserted. "We have one house . . . . But prejudice is still on the loose."[218] But others were enthusiastic. The establishment of the International House "marks the beginning of an era of greatness for this University," wrote Barbara Stoner, a Quibblers Club member, "for no institution divided by racial intolerance can be more than an empty gesture toward democracy."[219]

"Our work is by no means ended," wrote Bill Branch after the International House had been approved. Branch, a Quibblers Club member, was treasurer of the Student Governing Board, a member of the *Daily Northwestern*'s editorial board, and a member of the NAACP. Along with scores of others, he had put in "tremendous effort" to bring about the university's first integrated dorm. And, like many others, Branch called for true equality on campus. The next step along that road, he argued, was "to translate NU's new policy of democracy into reality."[220] "Unrestricted" housing must be made a reality for all students, he said.

Branch also provided a warning: "The conciliatory attitude" among Black people was "diminishing," he said. "They want action."[221] There was now a

Residents of the International House, Northwestern University (Northwestern *Syllabus* Yearbook, 1948)

"rising resentment" in this country, particularly among Black veterans, and many were no longer "going to stand by to see Negroes lynched or committed to slow lynching by supposedly legal methods in the North," he warned.[222]

Just months earlier, at the Unitarian Church in Evanston, Branch had led a student "fireside discussion" titled "Racial Dynamite."[223] He was seen on campus carrying around a copy of *An American Dilemma: The Negro Problem and Modern Democracy,* the influential and bestselling 1944 study of American race relations by Swedish sociologist Gunnar Myrdal. Rather than calling it the "Negro problem," Branch advised, we should call it, "the American problem." For, it was "the duty of all Americans to confront racism and ameliorate it," he said.[224]

In 1949, the university launched the construction of a million-dollar men's commons to replace the temporary and prefabricated housing units and Quonset huts that housed the swelling postwar student population. The four-story building, slated for completion in 1950, would have rooms for 175 male students, along with a private dining room and "spacious lounging."[225] This was just one of the major construction projects overseen by the university's new president. J. Roscoe Miller (who would also be responsible for the 1962-1964 "lake fill" expansion which nearly doubled the size of the campus).

When asked if Black students would be allowed to live in the new men's commons, Dean of Students F. George Suelberger responded: "It is planned

James Roscoe Miller (1905-1977) was Northwestern's twelfth president, serving in that role from 1949 until 1969. From 1969 to 1974, he served as university chancellor. A graduate of the University of Utah, Miller earned his medical degree at Northwestern, later teaching in the medical school and serving as its dean. He was known by his nickname, Rocky.[226] (University Relations, Northwestern University Archives)

that we shall continue our policy of having International houses to house both men and women negro students."[227] And so it was that in October 1949—one year after the U.S. armed forces were desegregated—the university announced plans to open Asbury Hall, its second integrated housing unit.[228] After renovation, a university-owned property at 1830 Sherman Avenue would serve as a men's dormitory "open to all races and nationalities."[229] For the first time in nearly half a century, Black male students would be allowed to live in university housing.[230]

Asbury Hall opened in January 1950. The dean of students' office received applications from both Black and white students to live in the forty-room dormitory that soon became, as one historian called it, the "cradle of the civil rights movement at Northwestern."[231] Students living there, and elsewhere, continued to fight to end discrimination at the university. And they would continue to pressure officials, asking, for example, why there were so few Black and Jewish students enrolled at Northwestern.[232]

Residents of Asbury Hall, Northwestern's first integrated dormitory for men, 1953. (Northwestern *Syllabus* Yearbook, 1953)

When residents first moved in, they discovered an old carving of a hand hanging by the front door. Soon, they attached their own meaning to this mysterious artifact: There was only one "law" at the dorm: all must give a "helping hand" to each other "regardless of their religion, color, or nationality." One of Asbury's residents, who also took part in the campaign to end discrimination at Northwestern, was John L. McKnight, who would later go on to help draft the first federal affirmative action legislation.[233]

Three years after the integrated men's dorm opened, a new poll revealed a changing perspective among white students: now, a majority (53%) answered "yes" to the question: "would you be willing to live with a negro roommate, upon a first-come-first-serve basis, if he is the next assigned to your room?"[234]

In February 1953, after several proposals were approved by various student and administrative bodies, an official policy to make "housing assignments without reference to race" in men's campus housing was adopted.[235] The new policy was not entirely enlightened: Black and white students would not be assigned to live together unless they requested to do so.[236] For graduate students seeking off-campus housing, university officials still maintained three separate lists of available housing (one each for "Caucasian, Negro, and foreign students").[237] This practice, which continued until 1959, was a result of some area homeowners' unwillingness to rent to "certain students," officials explained. Although not ideal, the lists were seen as efficient, since they protected students from "uncomfortable exposure to prejudiced homeowners."[238]

By the fall of 1950, a new campaign was underway: an effort to ban discrimination in student organizations, namely, in fraternities and sororities, whose membership was nearly entirely white.[239] The campaign would not be successful, however, as both fraternity leadership and Northwestern officials argued that any legislation enforcing the "complete abolition" of "racial and religious barriers in membership requirements" would ultimately curtail student freedom.[240] "The process of education through individuals and groups will more readily achieve the desired goal than will any ultimatum," James McLeod, Northwestern's newly appointed dean of students, noted in defense of a lack of such legislation.[241] As to why there were so few Black and Jewish students at Northwestern? That seemed a harder question to answer. Some university officials simply suggested that few "qualified" candidates who were not white Protestants ever applied to the university.[242]

Rumblings

The struggle for human rights is a constant fight, and one which the students do not plan to relinquish until full equality is won.

The Student Voice, publication of the Student Nonviolent Coordinating Committee, Volume 1, June 1960

A new left must consist of younger people who matured in the postwar world, and partially be directed to the recruitment of younger people. The university is an obvious beginning point . . . A new left must start controversy across the land, if national policies and national apathy are to be reversed. The ideal university is a community of controversy, within itself and in its effects on communities beyond.

The Port Huron Statement, 1962[243]

In the post-World War II era, as members of the Baby Boom generation prepared to enter college in record numbers, the insularity of Northwestern's policies was increasingly threatened as events far beyond the university would press against the boundaries and borders of the Evanston campus.[244] Many of the university's practices and policies would be called into question on a national stage, soon making it difficult, if not impossible, for the administration to ignore issues of discrimination. By the late 1950s, Northwestern graduate, Warren F. Spencer, president of Evanston's NAACP chapter, praised the progress that had been made on the campus since he had first enrolled there as a student in 1939. "Northwestern, because of its influence in the community, has made possible many advances for Negroes in Evanston," he observed.[245] But he also publicly charged the university with practising "flagrant discrimination" in a variety of areas, including in admissions and hiring practices.[246] In 1953, Walter F. White, executive secretary of the NAACP, speaking on the campus during Constitutional Liberties Week, concurred, and he went on to list the many areas in which Northwestern needed critical reform.[247] One year later, with the unanimous Supreme Court ruling on *Brown v. Board of Education of Topeka,* it became clear that many of the changes that had long been desired, both in Evanston and on the Northwestern campus, would ultimately be mandated by the federal government.

Through the late 1950s and into the early 1960s, the whole world was aware of what was happening in the civil rights movement, especially in Southern states. For those in the North, televised images of school desegregation, voter registration drives, freedom rides, boycotts, sit-ins, and the often violent and repressive reactions to activists and protesters, conveyed the dramatic events unfolding in scores of battles to desegregate the South. "I think we need to confess that we in the North are as sick as they are and thank the Southern Negros for pricking our conscience," Northwestern professor Arthur S. Link stated at a 1960 meeting to discuss "what to do in regard to Southern negro sit in demonstrations." "The question of relative guilt, North vs. South," Link observed, "is not the case."[248]

A small but significant number of Northwestern students would be influenced by the civil rights movement. As early as January 1950, members of the Interracial Club (formerly the Quibblers Club) planned a "crusade," as it were, traveling to Washington, D.C. to join other groups, including the NAACP, the American Jewish Congress, and the American Civil Liberties Union in a civil rights campaign.[249] By 1963, a small, new campus group had formed: Students for Civil Rights. The group began hosting events and discussions and invited civil rights leaders to campus. Among them was Curtis Hayes, a field secretary for the Student Nonviolent Coordinating Committee (SNCC), a national student-led civil rights group founded in 1960.[250] Hayes discussed his involvement in various civil rights campaigns in his home state of Mississippi, one of which resulted in his arrest for participating in a sit-in at a Woolworth's drugstore.[251] In April 1965, the group sponsored a rally on campus (emceed by Studs Terkel) where two noted civil rights workers, James Bevel and James Orange, along with three Northwestern students who had campaigned in Selma, Alabama, spoke about their experiences.[252] At the time, Bevel was joining forces with others in the nascent Chicago Freedom Movement, led by Martin Luther King, Jr. That movement would challenge racial discrimination and segregation in Chicago and its surrounding suburbs.[253]

In 1962, twenty-two-year-old Tom Hayden, a student at the University of Michigan, penned the first draft of one of the most influential political manifestoes of the student movements of the 1960s: the Port Huron Statement. Expressing the attitudes of many progressive, Northern white college students, and largely inspired by what Hayden had witnessed in civil rights actions in the South, the statement was considered a founding document of the rapidly-growing student activist organization, Students for a Democratic Society (SDS), and it would prove to shape a new movement, known as the New Left.[254]

The influence of the civil rights movement on the New Left was clearly visible as student groups on college campuses nationwide launched numerous protests and actions using the same nonviolent tactics, such as marches and sit-ins, that students were deploying in Southern states. In 1962, students at the University of Chicago staged a sit-in to protest segregated campus housing and discrimination in the university's real estate holdings. (One of the protest leaders was a twenty-year-old student, Bernie Sanders).[255] In 1964, student leaders of the Free Speech movement on the University of California at Berkeley campus, including the famous Mario Savio, made headlines as their protests grew exponentially, while various student groups at San Francisco State College (now San Francisco State University) also began staging actions.

In the fall of 1965, a white female student, Melva Fager (Okun), announced her plan to form an SDS chapter at Northwestern, saying she wanted to "raise issues of national prominence—specifically Viet Nam—among students."[256] "I always thought it would be out of the question to start a chapter at NU," Fager, a sophomore history major, observed. But a recent development changed her mind: Northwestern's student government, now known as the Student Senate, had issued a proposal to back U.S. policy in the war in Vietnam, prompting Fager and two friends to look for "an outlet" for students with opposing views. Fager also wanted to organize off-campus demonstrations against racial bias in Evanston and work to advance the university's "role in the Evanston civil rights struggle," she said.[257]

One hundred students showed up for the first meeting of the SDS chapter at Northwestern, which was held at the Hillel Center on November 17, 1965.[258] Soon, SDS had absorbed the group, Students for Civil Rights, along with two smaller clubs, the Student Peace Association and the Student Association for Liberal Action (a group in which Fager had served as secretary).[259] In its first six months, SDS members organized four anti-war marches in Fountain Square in Evanston, marched in area civil rights demonstrations, hosted folk singer, Phil Ochs, for a campus concert, and invited noted civil rights leader, Fannie Lou Hamer, head of the Mississippi Freedom Democratic Party, to campus. "You're not free in Illinois . . . until we're free in Mississippi," Hamer announced to her Northwestern audience in May 1966.[260]

In 1965, Northwestern held a five-day symposium on the topic of rebellion.[261] Among the several panels was one on the subject of "Negro Revolt." It was led by civil rights leader, Robert Parris Moses, director of the Mississippi Freedom Project and well known for his work with SNCC.[262] (SDS founder, Tom Hayden called Moses "perhaps the single greatest influence on the early SDS.")[263] "The real change must come right across the board in our society," Moses told his audience. "We're all involved. And right now we need deeper changes than people are willing to talk about."[264]

At the time, Northwestern's student-activist movement was very small and fairly marginalized, largely judged as unrepresentative of the predominantly white and conservative student body and likely to have no real long-term impact on the Evanston campus. Certainly, there were ongoing campaigns for equality. And by now the fight to end discrimination at Northwestern was decades old. But after years and years of investigations, continued efforts at reform, and numerous campaigns, Northwestern entered the 1960s with its reputation as a small, wealthy, whites-only country club-like school quite intact. And the number of Black students remained tiny, despite the university's growth over the decades. Never mind the way the wind seemed to be blowing on campuses across the country, Northwestern officials asserted. Smaller, quiet campuses like Northwestern "did not have the problems which have hit the headlines at the so-called 'multi-versities,' such as the University of California at Berkeley," Dean of Students James McLeod told the press.[265] There was just no real "rebellious spirit" among the student body, he stated. In fact, at Northwestern, hadn't it even been safe enough to offer students a five-day symposium on the topic of rebellion? "I think our students have approached these issues with a good deal of sanity," McLeod observed mildly.[266]

But major changes were about to come to the campus, changes that would reveal that Northwestern students might just have a significantly more rebellious spirit than university officials initially gave them credit for.

Soon after Melva Fager founded an SDS chapter at Northwestern, students organized anti-war protests in downtown Evanston. (*Daily Northwestern*, April 19, 1966)

Pre-integration Northwestern, early 1960s
(Northwestern University Archives)

Chapter 3

Enter the New Guard

Northwestern students are less radical and less rebellious than any other bunch I've come across. [But] things are improving. A small, shy breeze of change—to call it a wind would be going too far—is beginning to blow around campus.

Judy Innes, correspondent for the *Daily Mail*, 1965[1]

We want students from a broad cross-section of contemporary America to consider Northwestern.

Jack Hinz, Director of Admissions, Northwestern University, 1965[2]

"To quote C. William Reiley, our director of admissions, there is no quota system at Northwestern, but then how do you explain that only three Negro girls have been admitted to Northwestern in the past 3 years?"[3] This was the question posed in the fall of 1963 by Northwestern student Karen Neilson, head of the Student Senate's Human Relations Committee. Pledging an investigation into university admissions practices and discrimination by Evanston merchants, Nielson was working in tandem with the city of Evanston's Commission on Human Relations.[4] University officials denied any discrimination in Northwestern's admissions policies.[5] But the charges were nothing new.

Years ago, in 1954, the question of discrimination in the university's admissions practices arose after an investigation was conducted by the Student Governing Board's Human Relations Committee. At that time, the committee requested that the administration cease to require applicants to state their religion or to provide photographs of themselves as part of their applications for admission.[6] When nothing was done to change those requirements, pressure from faculty and students began to build. By 1956, Dean of Students James McLeod announced that the question about religion would be made optional on the upcoming year's application form.[7]

As 1957 began, a number of students and faculty sponsored a lecture series on the topic of "discrimination and the climate it created at Northwestern University."[8] After McLeod spoke at the series, he found himself facing a hostile atmosphere as audience members publicly challenged him over the university's admissions policies, charging that the question about an applicant's religion was used for "discriminatory purposes."[9] That information, McLeod responded, was never used to discriminate, adding that he saw "nothing discriminatory about asking a person his religion."[10] McLeod said he would continue to support the question remaining on the application since "a person's religion is part of his personality."[11]

A "general outburst" followed, as many students, faculty members, members of the Student Governing Board, staff on the *Daily Northwestern*, and other groups objected, arguing that such a practice was not only blatantly discriminatory, but it also lacked "moral integrity."[12] There was no doubt, they asserted, that the information concerning an applicant's religion had long been used "to discriminate in university admissions."[13]

Soon, President J. Roscoe Miller announced that the question would be struck entirely from the application beginning in 1958.[14] There had been a misunderstanding concerning the question's purpose, Miller asserted. He explained that there was a difference between the kind of discrimination used in the exercise of "good judgment" and the kind used in the "prejudicial sense." At Northwestern, information regarding an applicant's religion had always been used in the former, "constructive manner," he explained.[15] Officials pledged that from now on they would only collect information on a student's "religious preference" after that student had been admitted to the university and only in order to distribute the information to campus religious counselors and organizations.[16]

But by 1964, it became clear that the university had continued to employ "procedures by which religions of applicants were determined by the admissions office."[17] And once again, the question of the university's admissions practices took center stage. For months, Director of Admissions C. William Reiley would be questioned and university policies scrutinized. In January 1964, Chuck Scott, co-chairman of the Student Senate's Human Relations Committee, charged that a quota system had indeed been in place at Northwestern, limiting the number of students admitted on the basis of race and religion.[18] Reiley denied the charge.[19] In February, Al From, an editor and reporter for the *Daily Northwestern*, requested access to the university's admissions records. In response, Reiley reportedly "verbally attack[ed] the newspaper and threaten[ed]" From, telling him that his scholarship would be investigated if he didn't cease his inquiries.[20] This prompted university officials and the Anti-Defamation League to launch what would become a three-month investigation into Northwestern's admissions policies.

In March 1964, the *Daily Northwestern* published information drawn from an interview with a former admissions office employee, Prudence J. Scarritt. She revealed that during the time she worked in the office, from 1959-1961, one of her duties "had been to designate the religion and race of applicants."[21] She explained the procedure: A numerical code was used on each application: Number 1 designated a Protestant applicant, 2, Catholic, 3, Jewish, and 4, "Negro."[22] "If the applicant were either of the last two numbers," Scarritt said, "they were circled."[23]

By April 1964, it was confirmed that the admissions office had, in fact, kept records of applicants according to religion and race, but officials maintained that the practice had been stopped "by direct order from Dr. Miller."[24] But in September, Albert J. Weiss, head of the Anti-Defamation League of Chicago's B'nai B'rith Foundation, revealed that he had "evidence that, as recently as the spring of 1964, the university was coding applicants as to whether they were Protestant, Catholic, Jewish, or Negro."[25] Franklin Kreml, vice president and director of planning and development, responded: "I assure you that this practice has not been used (in the recent past.)"[26] The coding system had been abandoned within the last four years, another administration spokesman said. But Weiss charged that it had been used to process the university's most recent applicants. The Anti-Defamation League charged Reiley with "discriminatory practices."[27] Reiley soon admitted that the office had, in fact, "coded applicants according to race, color, and creed," but he denied that the information had been used to "discriminate."[28] He was now willing, he assured his critics, to "comply with the announced university policy of admissions without regard to race, color, or creed."[29]

But there was no need for such a promise. The university promptly removed Reiley from his position as director of admissions and appointed him dean of administrative services, a newly created position.[30] It was announced that a faculty committee, headed by Joe Park, professor of education, would be established to investigate the university's admissions procedures.[31] As the search for a new director of admissions was underway, the *Daily Northwestern* urged officials to seize the opportunity to commit to recruiting more diverse students and faculty members. Noting that the board of trustees of the University of Illinois had recently approved their own plan to broaden their recruiting practices, the newspaper encouraged Northwestern to "move rapidly and in just that direction."[32]

Northwestern would indeed begin to move rapidly in that direction as it launched a new set of policies aimed at diversifying the student body and specifically focused on recruiting more Black students. The new policies were crafted in response to the investigations, public pressure, and a larger, national program to eradicate "formal racial barriers in higher education," spurred, in part, by the civil rights movement. But they were also legislated by the 1964 Civil Rights Act and, later, the 1965 Higher Education Act.[33] Indeed, federal laws that took aim at ending segregation in public schools, ensuring equal educational opportunity, and expanding financial assistance programs (and providing matching funds to universities in order to diversify student populations) would prove to be the main catalyst for change not only at Northwestern,[34] but also at institutions across the country.[35] As a result, between 1964 and 1970, Black student enrollment at colleges and universities in the United States would double. (Although, it must be noted, the proportion of Black students in college would not significantly increase, underscoring the fact that federally mandated integration was not the sole solution to expanding educational opportunities for Black students.[36])

In July 1965, it was announced that Jack Hinz had been appointed Northwestern's new dean of admissions, effective September 1, 1965.[37] Upon assuming his new role, Hinz observed that Northwestern's current student body was "wholesome, well-dressed, and well-scrubbed."[38] "They would make a good impression on any visitor," he noted. "And they produce a pretty good intellectual output."[39] But what was needed, he insisted, was "greater diversity."[40] "There aren't enough minority groups here," he said pointedly.[41]

As Hinz undertook running the admissions office, he began implementing new policies to diversify the student body and headed up widespread recruitment of non-white students.[42] At the time, as Hinz recalled, he had "very significant support from faculty, by and large, particularly younger faculty who had some perspective on what I was being asked to do."[43]

He made a particular effort to recruit from Chicago, but elsewhere

Roland "Jack" Hinz, Northwestern University
(University Relations, Northwestern University Archives)

as well. Hinz's intent was to diversify students not only in terms of race, but also in relation to religion, region, and class. "I kind of opened up the place," as he later put it.[44] In effect, Hinz was responsible for desegregating Northwestern University.

At the same time, university officials were taking a long-term view of the institution's future. In December 1966, under President Miller's leadership, the administration announced a five-year plan to raise $180 million dollars, known as the "Plan for the '70s."[45] The changes in the university's admission policies were, no doubt, somewhat influenced by this ambitious undertaking.[46] And for several years, the two efforts—the fundraising campaign and the effort to diversify the university —would proceed along parallel and sometimes intersecting paths.

Hinz would run the admissions office for eighteen months before being appointed to a new position. In October 1966, as the new admissions policies were being implemented, Dean of Students James McLeod resigned after serving in his post for fifteen years.[47] After an extensive search for a successor was conducted, Hinz was selected. He was promoted to take McLeod's place, effective May 15, 1967.[48] At the same time, Hinz was also appointed to serve as vice president for student affairs, a newly-created position.[49] Although the administration planned to hire a new dean of students, it would be years before that new appointment was made. Thus, Hinz was saddled with two positions for the duration of his tenure at Northwestern.[50] (On September 1, 1967, William Ihlanfeldt replaced Hinz as director of admissions, while still retaining his job as financial aid director.[51])

Hinz took on his new role as dean of students after what was described as the "stormy term" of his predecessor. To the students, James McLeod had been "everything they disliked: he was old. He was authoritarian. He was distant. He had the annoying habit of having a student's record file open on his desk whenever the student entered his office."[52] In his successor, everything was different. "Hinz was young. He smiled. He met with students. He talked liberally. The students loved him."[53]

But Hinz's dual roles were tricky since they placed him directly between meeting the needs of the students and those of the administration. This dichotomy would prove increasingly difficult for Hinz, whose job required close contact with all matters relating to student life on campus and also burdened him with the responsibility of implementing university policies at the highest level. "I felt trapped in some ways," he said. "I used to describe it by saying, 'I've got students over here and the administration over here. And they're both pulling on my arms, and they both want them to come out.' "[54]

To make matters more complicated, the thirty-five-year-old Hinz, who was closer in age to the students than to his colleagues, (all of whom were white men in their sixties), assumed his duties at the very moment the 1960s broke loose. Integrating Northwestern would be his first challenge; thereafter he would deal with the takeover, a student strike, a student-led action that closed and blockaded one of Evanston's primary thoroughfares, Sheridan Road, numerous protests, including those staged after Ohio National Guard troops killed four students at Kent State University in 1970, and a whole spectrum of behaviors committed by those who had been warned not to trust anyone over thirty. Hinz's dealings with the students took moving, dangerous, dramatic, and even comic turns. In 1970, when one hundred students, led by SDS members, "pelted a naval ROTC building on the Evanston campus with snowballs and rocks," a few students threw snowballs at Hinz too. "One snowball struck Hinz in the face," the *Chicago Tribune* reported. "He marched up to a student and said, 'I do not appreciate being hit in the face with a snowball.' "[55]

During his tenure, Hinz became one of the most admired and reviled university administrators, known for his leniency on certain matters—"We are not going to drag a student down to the Evanston police station if he has been caught smoking marijuana," Hinz proclaimed in April 1968.[56] Meanwhile, he was also chastised at times for his unwavering commitment to upholding university policy. "They have my deepest sympathies," Hinz said in response to student complaints at one point, "but that's the way it is."[57]

As an indication of just how intense conditions were at Northwestern during this period, Hinz became a kind of lightning rod—for some, he was a paragon of enlightened, progressive thinking. Indeed, he became rather famous, winning critical support among many students and faculty members. But to others, he was a pawn of the "rebel" and radicalized students, an administrator who allowed his charges to run rampant over tradition, rules, and most of all, authority. One observer noted that after Hinz had "liberalized admittance policies," he had been promoted to dean of students in order to handle "the monster he created."[58] Indeed, Hinz was later said to have drawn "heat" from some alumni owing to his efforts to "actively recruit" Black high school graduates; these critics charged that he was lowering enrollment standards at Northwestern.[59] His critics didn't always stop at harmless words. While at Northwestern, as Hinz recalled, he received "bomb threats on my home [and] threats on my kids' lives."[60] His tenure at Northwestern was, as he described it, a "challenging, demanding, exhausting, interesting time."[61]

High Expectations

Hinz "has become known as one of the most progressive and able men connected with the University," an editorial in the Daily Northwestern *observed. "Under his guidance, the admissions office has implemented the policies which today are creating a heterogeneous student body. Hinz has the interest of students at his foremost concern."*

"The Benefit of Hinz Sight," *Daily Northwestern,* May 16, 1967

In 1966, Northwestern fell in line with the leading educational institutions by admitting sixty black undergraduates. Nothing in its past . . . could have furnished the university with insight into this new situation.

Takeover participant, James Pitts[62]

Jack Hinz's challenges (and critics) first emerged as he spearheaded efforts to integrate Northwestern. Working with high school teachers and guidance counselors, he and his admissions staff recruited top-performing Black students from about twenty high schools in Chicago's West and South Side neighborhoods, as well as from other cities, including St. Louis, Milwaukee, and Gary, Indiana, and also from areas outside of the Midwest—all places where recruitment had been weak in the past, as Hinz noted.[63] "There is a need in these low advantaged areas for a first-rate higher education," Hinz said, explaining the reasoning behind the university's new recruiting efforts. He was, he told the *Daily Northwestern* "excited about the progress" being made at Northwestern, "although we still have many things to learn."[64]

Some of the incoming undergraduate students recruited by Hinz and his staff came from middle-class backgrounds.[65] But most were from working-class families and many were first-generation college students. Some students, such as seventeen-year-old Juaquita Harris, class valedictorian at Parker High School on Chicago's South Side, were awarded full-tuition scholarships at Northwestern.[66] But most of the newly admitted students would receive financial aid packages, which included scholarships and loans, along with assistance from federally subsidized work-study programs, which required students to work campus jobs.[67] William Ihlanfeldt, director of financial aid, explained that some incoming students would also receive financial assistance from the federal government's opportunity grant program under Title IV of the 1965 Higher Education Act.[68] In fact, as Hinz later explained, it was a substantial increase in available financial aid that made the broadening of recruitment possible.[69] And later, it would also subject Northwestern to closer scrutiny by the federal government concerning racial discrimination.[70]

As the process of what was called "lower economic recruitment" was underway, Hinz also oversaw the university's new pre-enrollment programs, including Project Upward Bound and the Northwestern University Chicago Action Program (NUCAP).[71] NUCAP was designed to introduce top-ranked Black high school students to college life by offering them summer courses and enrichment activities on the Evanston campus prior to enrolling in the fall.[72] "I was ambitious," Hinz said of his attitude at the time. "I wanted to do a good job."[73]

In the fall of 1966, one year after Hinz started his job as director of admissions, the class of 1970 entered Northwestern. "The class of 1970 will stand out like a sore thumb," wrote Joan Schuman in the *Daily Northwestern.* "But its uniqueness is the first step in a changed student body, and administrators want Northwestern to become heterogeneous."[74] The largest class ever admitted to date (1,777 incoming students), the class of 1970 was also the most geographically diverse, with two-thirds of new students coming from outside of Illinois. It also included the highest percentage of Jewish and Catholic students ever admitted. And the new class would also include the highest number of Black students ever admitted in a single quarter to date. A total of fifty-four Black students would enroll at Northwestern that fall, constituting a dramatic increase from the total of five Black students who had entered the year previously.[75]

As the new class entered, a letter of welcome was sent out to all incoming students. "We shall do our utmost to orient you to this new life," wrote Dean of Students James McLeod. "May I offer a word of counsel? . . . Take time to adjust calmly and thoughtfully . . . We want you to enjoy your four years at Northwestern to the full."[76]

When the new class of students arrived on campus, they were welcomed by officials, and nominally feted, as it were, since their presence marked the official shift away from earlier discriminatory admission practices. The young and idealistic Hinz was enthusiastic, proud to usher in a new era and a new class of students.

Stanley Hill was one of the students who entered Northwestern in the fall of 1966. Over the summer, he attended a NUCAP session with a variety of classmates, the vast majority of whom would later take part in the takeover.[77]

James Turner was also among the students arriving at Northwestern that fall, having just graduated from Central Michigan University, where his work earned him a place on the dean's list all three years he was there.[78] Originally from New York City, Turner arrived in Evanston with his wife, Janice, who would serve as director of Evanston's nascent Head Start program, and their young son. Turner had chosen Northwestern in part because of its unrivaled

African Studies program and library.[79] He was pursuing graduate study in sociology, a field he first ventured into as a young man in Manhattan when he got to know sociologists at Columbia University and served as "a liaison between the academic community and Harlem youth gangs."[80] He was encouraged by these academics and he was also inspired by the books on Black history and politics that he found at the Fredrick Douglass Book Center on West 125th Street in Harlem. He was particularly affected by a single man whom he often saw around the neighborhood: Malcolm X. "After having seen him many times on the streets of Harlem, and having listened to him speak," Turner told an interviewer in 1968, "I was virtually lifted up by him out of the self-destructive life that I had been living."[81]

Born in Chicago, John H. Bracey, Jr. also arrived at Northwestern that fall as a graduate student in history. He "came to Northwestern because it was quiet," he said, and "wasn't a hotbed of activism."[82] In 1964, Bracey graduated with his Bachelor's degree from Roosevelt University in Chicago, where for several years he had been active in student protests and the civil rights movement. He was a member of numerous organizations, including the National Afro-American Organization, Chicago Friends of SNCC, the Freedom Now Party, and the Amistad Society, a group founded by Chicago area scholars in response to the "Negro's virtual exclusion from official American history" and dedicated to fostering Black "history, research and action."[83] In recent years, Bracey had become well known for his activism and for playing a leading role in many protests, including a July 1963 protest in Chicago's Grant Park that made papers nationwide, with a photograph of Bracey appearing on the front page of the *Chicago Sun-Times*.[84] Now, Bracey said, he wanted to buckle down and work. Like Turner, he was attracted to Northwestern because of its stellar African Studies library, and so, the offer of a graduate fellowship was a dream come true. He was content to attend his seminars, read history, and study.

Bracey came from a long line of academics. He spent his first year of college at Howard University in Washington, D.C., where his mother, Helen H. Bracey, worked for many years as Director of Student Teaching. (Among her many students were Roberta Flack and Toni Morrison.) Bracey grew up in a family full of teachers and within a world of Black intellectuals; he was just fifteen years old when he went to hear W.E.B. Du Bois lecture, and he recalls seeing great figures, such as Thurgood Marshall and historian John Hope Franklin, on the Howard campus. He was "surrounded," he recalled, by "intelligent black people."[85] His education was the focal point of his life, and it included all aspects of human experience, with a particular focus on Black history, art, and literature. "At Howard you have to take Shakespeare *and* Langston Hughes," he noted.[86]

That same fall, Kathryn Ogletree, a straight-A student at Harrison High

School on Chicago's West Side, was considering applying to an HBCU or a state school before graduating in the spring of 1967. At the time, she recalled, "Northwestern was not even on my radar."[87] Ogletree, the eldest of five sisters, was born and raised in Chicago. She was an award-winning editor on her school newspaper, a top-ranked student, and, like the other Black students Northwestern would recruit, she earned college board scores in the top two percent of all Black students who took the SAT or ACT tests. It was not long before her stellar academic qualifications drew the attention of the college recruiters who had just launched a "massive outreach to inner-city schools trying to get the best Black students."[88] After she narrowed down her choices to Northwestern and Cornell, she chose Northwestern and accepted the financial aid package that would make attending feasible. Ogletree would be the first in her family to attend college. Her parents were bursting with pride at their eldest daughter's achievements.

In the summer of 1967, Ogletree took part in NUCAP, one of Northwestern's new enrichment programs. Along with thirty other students from Chicago, she came to campus that summer to take math and English classes and to attend plays and other cultural activities. Ogletree described it as a kind of "summer camp" and remembers it as "an exciting experience."[89] "I think it was helpful in the sense that we weren't totally taken off guard by everything, by us knowing each other a little bit and being helpful to each other," she said. And in fact, the group of students, who lived together in the dorms on campus that summer, quickly "bonded together."[90]

Ogletree was one of the few students in the group who had experience attending an integrated school. And yet, she explained, even though "we knew we were going to have interactions with the white students," we "didn't really know what exactly to expect."[91] They were particularly uncertain of what it would be like when the fall quarter began and they would be living full-time on campus among thousands of white students.[92] To be sure, they were aware that they were somehow integrating Northwestern, although none of the administrators acknowledged this fact directly to them, nor did they talk to the students about what that might mean. As far as being members of one of the earliest classes to integrate Northwestern, Ogletree said: "I didn't have any concrete notion as to what that meant."[93] And none of the students knew very much about Northwestern's history. "All I knew," Ogletree recalled, "was that historically a lot of Black people did not go to Northwestern."[94]

James Turner also remembered that although most of the Black students arrived on campus with "very little understanding about what we could expect," everyone was "eager and excited and very proud and satisfied that we had achieved the recognition of being admitted to Northwestern University."[95] Victor Goode recalled his attitude upon enrolling with his classmates in

1966: "As freshmen we had high expectations of Northwestern," he said. "[W]e were affected favorably by NU's reputation like everyone else, and we expected an enjoyable four years."[96] But he too didn't know what he was in for. When he arrived on campus, not having attended a summer program, he saw no other students of color. He recalled that as a high school senior looking at Northwestern's admission materials, he had seen nothing in the materials "to suggest there were so few Black students on Northwestern's campus."[97] Upon reflection, he realized that the materials had only included photographs of Black athletes. He had made the assumption that Black students were not only on the sports teams, but were "also in the stands, in the dormitories and, otherwise, on campus."[98] On his first walk across campus, when he finally encountered two Black students, he "rejoiced."[99]

Once the fall 1967 quarter began, Ogletree and others were met with a stark reality. She and her new friends had been aware that they would not be allowed to room together as they had over the summer, owing to a university policy that barred Black students from living with one another. But they soon found themselves isolated, separated from each other and living in various dorms across campus. At the time, Ogletree reflected, "we didn't really fully appreciate the implications" of being "scattered across campus" by administrators who wanted to "maximize our exposure" to white students.[100] "It was actually articulated at some point," she recalled, that administrators "wanted as many people to 'experience' us as possible."[101] Years later, Ogletree would clearly recognize: "We were treated like objects."[102]

Stories began to circulate about upsetting encounters. Many Black students were encountering hostility from their assigned white roommates. A white roommate would "come in, leave the room, and then a change [of room assignment] would occur," Ogletree recalled.[103] Some white students were pointedly refusing to room with their assigned Black roommates, a fact that was experienced personally by many of the new students as they arrived in their dorm rooms.[104] When Eva Jefferson (Paterson) arrived in her dorm room for the first time in the fall of 1967, one of her two white roommates took one look at her, left the room, and spent the night in a hotel. Later, she requested her own room. This was, Paterson later said, just one of the experiences that amounted to her "rude awakening" at Northwestern University.[105]

In 1966, the year before Paterson and Ogletree arrived, the first sizeable class of Black students at Northwestern had encountered hostility, racism, and difficulty on the campus, including also being rejected by their assigned white roommates. University housing officials downplayed any problems with roommates, stating that reports of "problems in dorm living by Northwestern's increased number of Negroes in the freshman class have been unfounded."[106] As evidence, they cited only five total cases of white students who had requested room changes after learning that their roommates were Black (which was, in actuality, a high percentage of cases).

The experiences of the 1966 entering class would be duplicated and even intensified by the 1967 entering class. Ogletree recalled the rejection by white roommates as particularly "dehumanizing experiences."[107] And she explained that even those Black students whose white roommates chose to remain in their assigned rooms often encountered other kinds of conflicts, primarily centering on different tastes in music. She recalled that "[m]any white students would complain that the Black students played their music too loud and would demand that they turn their music down or off."[108]

Not having anticipated such reactions to their presence on the white-dominated campus, the students were not "psychologically prepared" to face this rejection and humiliation, Ogletree said.[109] They were not even able to "suffer together," she explained, since they had no recourse to change their own room assignments. White students could opt out from rooming with Black students, but Black students were not allowed to change their own rooms.[110] "We felt we should have had that option just like any other student," Ogletree said.[111]

Ogletree herself was lucky to be assigned a "relatively nice roommate." The two women were open to rooming with each other and they developed a "good understanding, a healthy acceptance on things," she said.[112] But as other students began "sharing stories and experiences," Ogletree was made "very much aware" of what was happening around campus.[113]

This, then, was the first experience of integration for many Black students at Northwestern. The hostility of some white roommates was the first of many racist encounters that students would experience, and slowly, as members of Ogletree's class began talking with those who arrived the year earlier, the critical situation on campus was brought into view, fueling a sense of uneasiness, fear, and apprehension among many students. Turner, who lived off campus with his wife and son, immediately recognized that "there was tension" on campus.[114] Black students were experiencing "conflict, hostility, tension, and racial insult," he recalled.[115] And the problems encompassed far more than roommate assignments.

Many Black students said they felt unwelcome at Northwestern, viewed with suspicion or derision by many of their white classmates. They felt judged as not having a right to be there, and felt that they stood out uncomfortably, as if they were "intruders" in violation of the university's white upper class "social order."[116] Some students recalled working at their campus jobs, such as in a dining hall, and being treated as "the help" by some white students who called them disrespectfully by their first names.[117] They did not feel welcome to join in the university's social life and found themselves on their own in terms of social activity and interaction.

"We didn't have a place to congregate," Ogletree remembers. "We lived in the dorms and technically anyone could be in the lounge area but . . . if there were more than two or three of us together, [white students] would be angered or threatened by that and would make complaints that we were talking too loud or making too much noise."[118] It became clear to Ogletree and many others that many white students "were threatened by our presence."[119] "People were annoyed or frustrated and complaining about us," Ogletree recalled. They would "complain about us," she said, "for our very existence."[120] At issue, fundamentally, was that of legitimacy, the Black students' right to be there.[121]

Nearly all Black students agreed that being isolated physically from each other was a significant problem, making it difficult to establish or strengthen ties with each other. But as they tried to connect with each other, they found that their efforts to organize events and activities were not supported by the university financially or through resources made available to them. Turner remembered that when some of the students organized a two-day "cultural heritage program to celebrate Malcolm X's birthday," they had to "run around borrowing phones from other organizations."[122]

Another problem lay in the intellectual climate. It wasn't long before John Bracey and his graduate student friends, including Turner, recognized that among the numerous problems on campus, one of the most significant was the fact that the university was "stagnant" at an intellectual level.[123] With a scant number of Black faculty members, the majority of the curriculum represented a decidedly white point-of-view.[124] Bracey was "not impressed at all" with his history seminars; not only were they not dynamic—with no debate over ideas and with students seemingly only eager to please professors—but also there was nearly a complete absence of Black history and Black scholars within the curriculum. In the syllabus for a seminar on the history of the American South, taught by historian George M. Frederickson, for example, only one work by a Black writer was included.[125] (Frederickson was a newly-appointed professor, whose 1965 book, *The Inner Civil War: Northern Intellectuals and the Crisis of the Union,* had recently been published.) Some professors appeared entirely ignorant of any Black historians and authors and they were unaware of the existence of Black scholarship and literature to any degree.

" 'Don't you know Gwendolyn Brooks, the poet laureate from Illinois?' " Turner remembered asking his professors. " 'Or Margaret Walker who is a graduate of Northwestern University?' " "But no," he said, "they didn't know any of it. They didn't know St. Clair Drake from Chicago who wrote the *Black Metropolis* . . . They didn't know W.E.B. Du Bois or John Hope Franklin. At that point they didn't know Frederick Douglass or Harriet Tubman or Sojourner Truth. They simply repeated the limitations of their knowledge."[126]

Both Bracey and Turner recalled that some white professors would even question whether there was even *enough* Black history to constitute studying it for an entire quarter.[127] Bracey, along with fellow graduate student, the later famous historian, Sterling Stuckey, began mentoring his professors, particularly Frederickson and another young history professor, Christopher Lasch.[128] They began to suggest additions to their syllabi. They discussed Black history and debated the merits of various historians' arguments and theories. Bracey and Stuckey even got Frederickson and Lasch to alter their syllabi to include more Black writers and works of significance by Black historians.[129]

Other professors, however, were not open to dialogue with their students. In some of his sociology classes, as Turner remembered, professors would advance racist arguments, arguing, for example, that Black people had a "less sophisticated culture" than white people.[130] Others argued that Black people were "boisterous, free-spirited and loud in their religious practice;" that they were "superstitious," lacked "personal discipline," and "did not know how to practice deferred gratification," as Turner recalled. "We wondered, what world do you come from?" Turner remembers thinking at the time. "After all, in a segregated, confined inner city, you practice a great deal of deferred gratification!"[131]

Some professors would single out Black students to "carry the burden," as Turner put it, by asking them specific questions about Black identity and history so that they felt pressured to represent all Black people. Students also felt pressure to serve as a "model Black student." Ogletree recalled that some professors would "call on the one Black student to tell the class what it was like to be on welfare when he or she may never have been on welfare, or what it was like to live in the ghetto even if he or she grew up in the suburbs and never experienced the ghetto. In other words, whatever racial stereotype there was being discussed at any time, the lone or few Black students in the class would oftentimes be called upon to speak on that topic"—an experience that made students feel, as she recalled, "angry and/or embarrassed."[132]

"I was confident as a student," Ogletree recalls. But she recognized that "some of the teachers expected less" from Black students. "I remember getting a 'C' or something on an English paper and didn't understand why it was just a 'C,' " she remembered. Having never received anything less than an 'A,' she approached the instructor who told her "given where you came from, this is actually pretty good."[133] "[F]reshman English teachers didn't seem to feel we belonged in their classes," another student, Charles Shepard, recalled. "[O]ne told me I couldn't expect better than a 'C' in the course because I was from a 'deprived background.' I was assigned a midterm on what my life would be like if I were white," he said. "I got a 'C.' "[134]

For many students, the challenges in the classroom were exacerbated by the demands of working campus jobs. As stipulated in their financial aid packages, many students had to work and the required hours made it difficult to balance the demands of their coursework. Officially, the university discouraged students from working while in school, and it would be some years before working students would become more of a norm, especially as tuition costs rose. (In January 1967, tuition at Northwestern was $1,800 per year.)[135] Ogletree, who worked on campus as a part of her financial aid package, soon saw that many students were on the verge of failing classes or even flunking out of school entirely owing to the hours they were required to work. Others felt exploited by the large loans they had to take out in order to pay their tuition.[136] But they had no resources, such as a counselor or other administrators to help them. "We needed someone who understood our situation," she said, "to be able to talk to."[137] But with almost no Black faculty or staff, it was clear that Northwestern had not yet been fully integrated. Ogletree recalls that the students soon agreed: "We want more Black people to be part of the university."[138]

The problems Black students faced did not only concern roommates, classes, faculty, and finances. They were also harassed, threatened, and assaulted. In April 1967, when students showed up for a Student Senate meeting to discuss the issue of discrimination in fraternities, they were confronted by a handwritten sign that someone (unidentified) had posted on the wall. It read: "Negroes in Rear." It was, the *Daily Northwestern*, lamely explained, "a joke." But like many others, student Leslie Harris did not find it funny. "This time at least you're not being hypocritical about it," he remarked.[139]

Racist incidents took place continuously, often on Sheridan Road, where Black students would be yelled at or threatened as they walked. White students would call out to them in "racially offensive language," as Turner remembered;[140] they would throw full cans of beer and soda and balloons full of urine at them from the windows of dormitories and fraternity houses. Sometimes people driving on Sheridan Road threw cans at them as they drove past and the students had to dodge them as they walked.[141] It was "quite terrible," Turner recalled.[142]

All female students on Northwestern's campus faced some degree of aggression or hostility from some white male students. Particularly threatening were the ritual nighttime "panty raids." Periodically, on a given evening, crowds of male students would storm the south campus, where the women's dormitories were, yelling, lobbing firecrackers at dorm windows, and demanding that the women throw their underwear out the windows to them. (By April 1968, head of campus security Ted Arndt reported that the raids were getting out of hand and some female students had been attacked.)[143] Black female students faced even greater hostility and they were often subject to verbal attack, insults, and physical assaults as some white male students directly and specifically targeted them.[144] Walking from north campus, where the male students lived, to the south campus, could be a harrowing experience for Black women, Ogletree recalled. White male students would often touch them or shout at them in inappropriate language.[145] "It happened enough," Ogletree remembered, "that you would be on guard walking on the campus."[146]

A source of particular anxiety for all Black students were members of some campus fraternities, whose offensive acts included one fraternity's hosting a "plantation-themed dance," with fraternity members announcing that they wanted to recruit Black female students to "dress up in bandanas and aprons and serve guests."[147] But it would be one incident in particular that would stand out, exemplifying the extent of the racism that threatened students on campus.

On May 11, 1967, a group of members of the Phi Gamma Delta fraternity (popularly known as "Fiji") paraded down Sheridan Road "in minstrel blackface" in order "to promote their 'Island' party."[148] That same night, four of the fraternity's members allegedly stopped a first-year Black female student, "insulted [her] racially and sexually" and "touched portions of her body."[149] The woman, along with some of her friends, immediately notified university officials about the incident. Days passed. One week passed. Two weeks passed. And nothing was done about it.

Over the course of those two weeks, the University Discipline Committee (UDC) held three separate closed-door meetings to consider the incident and what punishment, if any, was advisable. The UDC was the campus unit, comprised of faculty members, administrators, and two students, which was granted judicial power to hear cases and exact punishment against students. James McLeod, who was still serving as dean of students at the time, pending the appointment of his replacement, served as chair of the UDC.

For years, the UDC—long the "subject of rumor and myth"—had been the target of reform-minded students, including Student Senate president Richard Gephardt (later elected to the U.S. Congress), who advocated a shift of greater judicial control to students.[150] Critics objected to the UDC's secrecy (it always met in private), its members (appointed by University President Miller), and its unclear policies and standards for discipline. (No precise statement of its jurisdiction or operating procedure was available for public scrutiny.)[151] When UDC members convened to discuss the Fiji case, they announced that it would be "improper" to divulge the nature of their proceedings since, they admitted, the case was "potentially 'explosive.' "[152] Therefore, they announced, they would keep their proceedings secret and would be reluctant to "make public" the UDC's "recommendations" in relation to the case.[153] But in response to a request made by the Fiji chapter president, the committee acquiesced and agreed not to reveal the names of those fraternity members allegedly involved in the May 11 incident.[154]

On May 16, rocks were thrown at the Fiji fraternity house and several windows were broken.[155] The Evanston police department was asked to increase patrols around the house.[156] Rumors began to circulate that the Blackstone Rangers, a Chicago gang, "might be planning a raid" on the fraternity house.[157] Now, there was a sense that "a race war between blacks and fraternities" was imminent.[158]

On May 25, the UDC announced that the case of the alleged assault against the student by Fiji members had been dismissed with a warning to the fraternity members that they "must act carefully in the future."[159] The Evanston police announced that no charges would be pursued. For its part, the fraternity stated that its members "had volunteered to give up wearing blackface."[160] The fraternity members who had allegedly assaulted the student "volunteered apologies," and, in a gesture that was surely adding more insult to the injury already inflicted, they sent her flowers.[161]

That spring, in acknowledgment of the existence of problems on campus, administrators held a "series of meetings with interested black students" in order to discuss "campus, summer program, and admissions problems."[162] But as campus tensions intensified, the administration's lack of response to this case and the UDC's secrecy and protective attitude toward the fraternity were met by many students with dismay and outright anger.

Distant observers might have believed that relationships between Black and white students were harmonious, a fact (apparently) evidenced by the election of Northwestern's first Black homecoming queen, Daphne Maxwell (Reid) in the fall of 1967,[163] and the pledging of the first two Black members, Audrey Hinton and Detra Smith, into a predominantly white sorority, Alpha Omicron Pi, and a historically Jewish sorority, Alpha Epsilon Phi, respectively.[164]

"To assume that NU has reached a stage of enlightenment or that it is on the road to progress is presumptuous," speech major Vernon Ford wrote about these milestones that were so celebrated by the national news media and also by a nation "starving for signs of progress."[165] But those events did not convey the reality of conditions on campus. At the ceremony to crown Reid, President Miller reportedly revealed his "extreme discomfort" at having "to crown a Black Queen," as Reid later put it.[166] He held the crown of yellow roses that he was to place on her head. "I have to hold this on your head while they take pictures," he whispered to her. Once the pictures were taken, he abruptly walked away without a word. "Maybe Northwestern wasn't happy" to have a Black homecoming queen, Reid later said, but given the widespread press coverage of the event, "the damn world was."[167] (Reid would appear on the cover of the November 30, 1967 issue of *Jet Magazine* that announced: "Teen beauty is the first of her race to reign as Homecoming Queen at Northwestern Univ.") These experiences and others would lead all three of the above-mentioned women, Reid, Hinton, and Smith, to take part in the takeover just months later.

But before that drastic action was undertaken, students began to formalize a network. By the fall of 1967, undergraduate students who entered the previous year had already started to build alliances with graduate students and others. Those students, as James Pitts noted, had "experienced their first year as a disaster." And, by the end of their first year, the majority of Black students had become "disillusioned with integration."[168]

That disillusionment would spur the founding of a new organization for Black students at Northwestern. In the summer of 1967, undergraduate business major Herman Cage saw a sign at the nearby Skokie Country Club that read "for members only," announcing its exclusivity.[169] That sign sparked an idea: Black students at Northwestern "needed an entity that was theirs and theirs only," he later said.[170] In August 1967, Cage, along with undergraduate students Wayne Watson and Vernon Ford, and graduate student, James Pitts, formed a new campus group, For Members Only (FMO).[171] Initially, its founders intended the group to provide Black students with "a social, cultural, and intellectual outlet."[172] A secondary aim was to build "communion" and "race consciousness" and support for a Black Power movement among students.[173] But overall, its primary goal was simple: to create something they did not find at the university, "a supportive environment."[174] The founders decided not to apply for official recognition of FMO as a student organization for "fear of potential repercussions."[175] FMO would serve as the basis for the modern Black student movement at Northwestern.

Daphne Maxwell Reid (center) on the Northwestern campus, c. 1967.
(University Relations, Northwestern University Archives,
photograph by Jim Biery)

After Reid was elected Homecoming Queen, the university "just ignored me," she said. Her honor was also slighted in the yearbook, which did not even mention her as Homecoming Queen, but only included one uncaptioned photograph of her, while the year before, the Queen had "gotten a three-page spread." When Reid complained to the yearbook editor, she was told that the election just "wasn't important this year." "The university was not important to me," Reid responded. The humiliation, as she wrote in a letter to the *Daily Northwestern* in 1970, was "something that I shall never forget." It would be years before she would receive (and accept) an apology from Northwestern.[176]

As FMO first got off the ground, it was largely focused on hosting social and cultural activities for Black students, along with offering tutoring services. In the fall of 1967, FMO held its own off-campus orientation for incoming students.[177] Members also held the group's first election, with Herman Cage elected president and first-year student Kathryn Ogletree elected vice president. Ogletree was particularly supportive of FMO's tutoring services. "We were addressing some of these concerns collectively as an organization," Ogletree said of the group, "in an effort to try to keep as many people from getting on academic probation."[178]

As they formed their own organization, Black students also attempted to reach out to others and open lines of communication concerning the problems they faced at Northwestern. "Only by a conscientious effort on the part of the administration and the students can the situation improve," observed Vernon Ford in one of the several *Daily Northwestern* articles he wrote in order to "help build communication between blacks and whites on campus."[179] Letters to the editor of the *Daily Northwestern* written by students, including sociology major Clovis Semmes, frequently appeared, with comments and observations concerning a variety of issues affecting Black students on campus.

Two women from the class of 1970 chose to take the path of student politics in an effort to help initiate desired changes on campus. In the spring of 1967, Daphne Maxwell Reid won a seat on the Student Senate, and later, Eva Jefferson Paterson also decided to get involved in student government. Over time, Paterson would work her way up the political ranks. In January 1968, she was elected class treasurer, and by April, she was elected to the Student Senate. Later, she'd make a bid for president Northwestern's student government.[180]

In December 1967, the first meeting of a Black history and culture club was organized by students Leslie Harris and Amassa Fauntleroy, with Professor George Frederickson serving as faculty advisor. Black students "do not feel part of the university," Harris told the *Daily Northwestern*. The club, which was open to all students, was launched in an attempt to "offer a possibility for cultural exchange" between Black and white students.[181] But after two meetings it reportedly flopped. Most of those who showed up for the meetings were liberal white students, and some Black students felt marginalized and exploited by them. They viewed the white students' enthusiastic desire to plan the club's activities and define its goals as domineering. And they resented the fact that some of them seemed set on defining the needs and interests of Black students themselves.[182] (Vernon Ford, Clovis Semmes, along Leslie Harris and Amassa Fauntleroy, would all later take part in the takeover.) Over time, some Black students shared a sense of being mistreated even by well-meaning white students and faculty. Victor Goode later expressed frustration with those white students who seemed to have a "strange curiosity" toward Black students, while Jocklyn Harris said white students always wanted to "talk to me about black things, as if I didn't have other concerns."[183]

As the fall 1967 quarter unfolded, many students began to feel disillusioned about their efforts. "Because the university had shown reluctance to act decisively" regarding racist incidents on campus, as James Pitts noted, students "rarely spoke to officials about their present difficulties."[184] But they did continue to organize among themselves. Many, like Ogletree, had attended summer programs and had already forged friendships with other students, and soon their circle grew. The younger students were getting to know the older students who "would share their experiences" from previous years, Ogletree recalled.[185] In fact, several upper class and graduate students had been counselors for NUCAP and other summer programs where they first met the incoming students in 1967.[186] Eva Jefferson Paterson remembered being heavily influenced by these older students, as they discussed issues related to Black life and culture. Soon, FMO members, including Kathryn Ogletree, began to branch out, drawing on the support and advice from graduate students, including Sterling Stuckey, James Turner, and others. At one point, several undergraduates approached John Bracey, knowing that he had been involved in protest movements in Chicago. They asked him to attend a meeting with the undergraduate students because "they're having problems," as Bracey remembers being told. Bracey had not personally experienced any overt racism on the campus directed at him; he had even successfully integrated a block of Evanston's Foster Street.[187] So he wondered, "what kind of problems could they possibly be having?"[188] But he agreed to come to the meeting.

Once he got there, he thought, "Aw, geez, Northwestern's got a hell of a problem on its hands."[189] More than one hundred Black students had shown up at the meeting and it was there that Bracey first learned of the "horrible things" that had been happening. It was clear to everyone, including Bracey, that the students were ready to take action.

Several graduate students, including Bracey and Turner, took on informal advisory roles and began coaching the undergraduate students on how to go about organizing and approaching administrators with their concerns.[190] "I gave them knowledge that I had from being in the movement," Bracey recalled. "I gave them the organizational knowledge that I had." At first, it was hard work to get everyone on the same page, organized and focused, since, as Bracey recalled, emotions were high. "They were mad. I said, 'Ok, but you've got to go through the steps, don't just jump up and start screaming.' "[191]

Overall, Bracey said, the graduate students offered their advice, but they let the undergraduates take control; they had to be the leaders of this growing movement. The graduate students were there to "keep them from getting hurt," as Bracey recalled. "The bulk of these kids were first-generation college kids," he said, and their families wanted them to be successful at Northwestern. "I didn't want anything to get in the way of that," Bracey said, "because you couldn't replace that."[192]

With the help of their mentors, the undergraduate students, with Ogletree soon taking the lead, began to formalize a growing list of their concerns.

Going in Circles

To bring in what is considered by many to be a foreign element, and expect assimilation and acculturation to be a one-sided affair is bad enough. But to expect this university to benefit from the black element without making certain necessary alterations is to expect out-and-out exploitation.

Northwestern student, Vernon Ford[193]

It . . . appears that all the integration that is to be done is of the Negro into the White society. We contend that the door to integration swings both ways.

Marianne Jackson, letter to the editor, *Daily Northwestern,* May 18, 1967

"We need a place that we can go where we can congregate without interfering with the activities of other people, so people can't just complain about us for our very existence."[194] This was one of the many requests that Ogletree and other students made in their meetings with Jack Hinz, William Ihlanfeldt, Northwestern's director of admissions and financial aid, and other administrators, to discuss campus conditions. They were, Ogletree recalled, pointedly "raising their concerns to the university."[195] "If you are going to diversify the students, you also need to diversify the other type of people around them," Ogletree told them. "We needed a black counselor, someone who can help us adjusting to the situations that we were experiencing," she said. "We needed more Black teachers and staff." What the students ultimately needed, she argued, were all the resources and necessities "that white people would just take for granted."[196]

In meetings with university officials, the students asked for what they needed. They also expressed their concerns about how "the work requirements may be negatively impacting students," Ogletree recalled. Students simply wanted to be "able to study enough to not flunk out. And so the financial aid packages needed to be reassessed."[197] But their concerns were met with inaction or dismissive responses. When some students complained about the amount of debt they had been forced to take on and the compulsory hours they were required to work, for example, one university official reportedly responded that "in the future more attention would be given to recruiting blacks who possessed more substantial middle-class resources" since they would "present fewer problems in adjusting to the campus."[198]

The students asked for a site on campus where they could gather, such as a Black student union. And, as they sought to find ways to build their own networks of support, they also asked for permission to bring Black Greek organizations to campus—a request that would prove to cause discord for many months.

The request had first been made in the spring of 1967. Education major, Saundra Malone met with the Dean of Women Patricia Thrash to ask for permission to organize a Black sorority on campus. "We have a serious problem meeting the social needs of Negro students on campus," Thrash admitted, but her answer to Malone was no. Permission would not be granted.[199] A month later, two first-year students, Millicent Brown and Juaquita Harris, met with Thrash to discuss the campus social situation in general and to request formal recognition for a chapter of Alpha Kappa Alpha.[200] Soon, a group of male students, including Vernon Ford, Roger Ward, and Stephen Broussard, requested that the fraternities, Alpha Phi Alpha and Kappa Alpha Psi, be given permission to reactivate their charters and return to campus.[201]

Jack Hinz's predecessor, Dean of Students James McLeod told the students that he thought Black fraternities would have "difficulties surviving" at Northwestern.[202] Many other administrators, students, and faculty members were vehemently opposed to authorizing them, arguing that no more fraternities or sororities were needed on campus. (Twenty-nine fraternities and nineteen sororities were on campus at the time.) Many also argued that predominately Black Greek organizations would only separate Black students from the rest of the students, and that, in essence, their presence would constitute a "tragic relapse into a segregated past."[203] (For this reason, Vice President and Dean of Faculties Payson Wild called the reactivation of Black fraternities "morally wrong."[204]) Such fraternities were not "in keeping with the school's integration policy,"[205] these critics argued, since "Negro" fraternities would "tend to encourage segregation and discourage integration in present fraternities."[206] At least one student proposed that they might even encourage a "ghetto mentality" among Black students, which he defined as "a 'culture of rejection' similar to those in Chicago's slums."[207]

The issue prompted some students to encourage (yet again) passage of an anti-bias bill for all campus fraternities and sororities, advancing the idea that if none of the existing fraternities and sororities discriminated, all groups would become "heterogeneous."[208]

Meanwhile, members of the Student Senate voted (ten to six) to reactivate the charters.[209] The Council on Undergraduate Life (CUL) took the requests under consideration and spent three months debating the issue before voting to support reactivating the charters. (The CUL was a body composed of administrators, faculty members, and undergraduate students. It held the authority to pass legislation, formulate rules and policies, and veto student government legislation and policies related to non-academic aspects of student life.)[210] But the final decision rested with the administration. An entire summer would pass before an answer came. In October 1967, university officials announced that a decision concerning the reactivation of the charters would be deferred until the spring of 1968.[211] "This is a serious question," Hinz wrote in a letter to all Northwestern students, that "must be studied very carefully before a decision can be reached."[212]

For the students, the opposition to the groups stemmed from a particular form of hypocrisy, since members of white fraternities and sororities had long been allowed to choose their own members and even to be largely segregated from the rest of the student body within their own housing. But somehow it was the Black students who were being accused of advocating segregation.

As they awaited a decision, many students pledged the fraternities anyway. Alpha Phi Alpha even hosted a campus event to "stimulate interest" among students, with 1936 Olympic gold medalist and Alpha Phi Alpha member, Jesse Owens appearing as a featured speaker. Meanwhile, Andrew Rodez, president of Kappa Alpha Psi's alumni chapter, acknowledged that the fraternity's informal campus pledge group, The Scrollers, might apply for recognition from the administration. But Alpha Phi Alpha was not willing, its members said, to lower the fraternity's status to a social club. "Even if we aren't officially organized," student Andre Bell explained, "there will be Alpha men here. Our ties to the fraternity are stronger than our ties to the university."[213]

Many of the new members and pledges of Alpha Phi Alpha and Kappa Alpha Psi would soon take part in the takeover. (In fact, they would constitute roughly twenty percent of all the students who took part in the action).[214] "It's a messed up situation," Roger Ward said when it was announced that the decision would be delayed. He explained why the students wanted and needed the groups on campus. "It all boils down to the fact that Negroes like to be with Negroes," he said. "A lot of white people are under the illusion that Negroes want to be with white people. This is not true. Around the nation there is a feeling more towards the Negroes being proud of the fact that they are Negroes."[215]

The students' disappointment over the nature of the debate and the delay in responding to their requests was intensified as they continued to take their concerns to administrators. They repeatedly reported the racist incidents they had experienced on campus. But to no avail.

Later, Northwestern sociology professor Rolf Schulze would reveal that within campus security files, he found "documented instances" of full beer cans being thrown at Black students from fraternity houses. But, according to Schulze, "the chief of the campus security force did not deem it necessary to report most of these incidents to the Dean of students, or other administrators."[216]

Nothing was done to change anything. And no one seemed to be held accountable. The racist behavior on the part of white students "was just kind of treated as a matter of fact," Ogletree recalled. "It's not good that they do these things, but it wasn't seen as criminal. We felt if we had done something like that it would have been treated as criminal."[217]

The silence and inaction of administrators seemed to affirm what many Black students suspected: they were really just pawns, there to facilitate integration and provide positive PR for Northwestern while little was done to create a healthy environment or provide resources for the very people who were doing the work of integrating the university. "We came here with trust and optimism," Victor Goode said, "but it took time to realize this is a racist school. We're being used as catalysts to change NU's conservative reputation."[218] Many now looked cynically at the whole process of integration and its underlying motives. According to James Pitts, students "began to believe that their enrollment in the university was based on the university's calculation of self-interest in private and government funding and public relations."[219]

And in fact, officials did champion the work the university was doing to diversify its student body, sometimes citing a *Newsweek* article lauding Northwestern for having accepted more Black students into the class of 1970 than any other private university in the country.[220] But on campus, those very students felt ignored, silenced, threatened. "It got to the point where the administration didn't believe that these things were happening," Turner recalled of officials' reaction to what the students told them. "They wanted to keep down the level of tension on campus, and they thought the best way to do it was to sweep it under the rug."[221]

For Hinz, the reported racist incidents were shocking and surprising. "I think we expected that the community would not be hostile toward them," Hinz said. "Frankly it didn't occur to me that this kind of overt racism and hostility would happen. And it's not easy to change. [I]t's kind of like turning a battleship to get the university to say, 'Ok we can do more to make the community a friendly one to incoming students, African American, in particular.' "[222] Of his own work to diversify the campus, which had begun just two years earlier, he admitted that he "didn't realize how complicated it was."[223]

"I found him responsive," Ogletree said of Hinz. "He was empathetic.

But he didn't have the power. A lot of the things that we wanted transcended different people's authority."[224] Indeed, the students became frustrated by the deferred decisions, the continued talking, the small promises for improvement that never materialized, and the pledges to investigate matters, with little or no advances made. It wasn't long before they could see that they "weren't getting anywhere," as Bracey said.[225] They felt they were being given the runaround. "We were getting tired of just talking back and forth, submitting the same things back and forth and people saying, 'That sounds good,' 'We'll work on it,' or 'This is not my jurisdiction.' The buck was being passed. We felt like we were going in circles and not being taken seriously," Ogletree said.[226]

For their part, university officials held to their overriding goal of working to "assimilate" Black students within the university. And for many administrators, the lack of official segregation on the Northwestern campus (all living facilities were now fully integrated) translated into a perceived *absence* of racism. But as Bracey, Ogletree, Turner, Hinz, and many others knew, the campus was not at all integrated in spirit. The racism perpetuated by some white students and faculty and the hostility directed at Black students were evidence that this historically white institution was not going to change its identity simply owing to the presence of Black students.

It was not long before Turner and others came to see the ways Northwestern operated as a "predominantly white school."[227] "You don't think of Northwestern University, Dartmouth, Yale, and even the University of Illinois as historically white institutions," Turner explained, "but it's important to see that."[228] Seeing that fact clearly revealed a stark truth: "It wasn't by happenstance that it was predominantly white," Turner noted, and its "history of active exclusion" didn't vanish with new recruiting efforts.[229]

An Uneasy Quiet

All integrated schools are desegregated, but not all desegregated schools are integrated.[230]

Northwestern actually considers its disinterest about Negro undergraduates a virtue—a sign of tolerance.

Editorial, *Daily Northwestern,* January 26, 1968

Following the U.S. Supreme Court's 1954 decision in *Brown v. Board of Education of Topeka,* Black students had come to Northwestern because of the "growing pressure to desegregate American institutions, most prominently educational institutions," as James Turner explained.[231] Although there was widespread support for desegregation in the United States, there was also a great deal of opposition to it. Since institutions play a key role in the stratification of the social system, as Turner observed, universities such as Northwestern confer "status upon the people who attend." Thus, when (relatively) large numbers of Black students began arriving on campus, "many white people felt that their status was being diminished by African-American students attending." In short, Turner said, some people believed that "Black students devalued the social prestige of the institution." Black people were the "most visible people who'd been historically excluded" from the university, Turner stated, but he also recognized the attempt to shut out others, such as Jewish, Catholic, ethnic Irish, Italian, and Polish students. But, as Turner put it, "the problem telescoped most visibly with the problem of race."[232]

Once the process of integration began, the attitude of some white people toward Black students was revealed to be paternalistic, a view evidenced early on as the first steps toward integration had been taken, even before Hinz came onboard. In the summer of 1965, a kind of prototype integration program was launched. University officials invited thirty-three Black students from Marshall High School in Chicago's Lawndale neighborhood to the campus for a visit.[233] "For this first trip from slum to suburb," a *Chicago Tribune* reporter wrote about the experimental program, "a noisy jostling masked the emotions of the restless teenagers, chosen from among 5,500 students at their high school for a taste of college life. In tree-shaded Evanston, as the 33 looked out over Northwestern's lakefront campus, the easy camaraderie gave way to an uneasy quiet."[234]

The "uneasiness," the reporter suggested, derived from the students themselves, who were not prepared for the "culture" they encountered at Northwestern. After all, she wrote, these students had not yet "mastered every nicety in life" and they had to "overcome their suspicions" in order to be able to accept what Northwestern had to offer them. Such an attitude, prevalent among some white reporters and university administrators, was an early indication that integrating Northwestern might require more than the *students'* adjustment to the transition "from slum to suburb." But at the time, some administrators had a less than enlightened view. Indeed, in a description of the NUCAP program, university officials described one of its aims as helping students "overcome their cultural deficiencies," revealing an attitude that many students found disdainful and dehumanizing.[235] "I've heard so many people say that they cannot understand this fuss about the Negro," Northwestern's Dean of Faculties William C. Bradford said in 1965, as he discussed the university's program for the Lawndale students. "We didn't make this much to-do about the immigrants," Bradford went on, "these persons seem to forget . . . that the immigrants had culture, drive, and hope, and the Negro has not even had much hope in this country, that is not until recently."[236] The purpose of this early program, Bradford concluded simply, was to show the students that "someone cares."[237]

Such a condescending attitude toward students, potential or otherwise, was not only directed toward Black students. In fact, many university officials had a decidedly paternalistic stance toward students in general. They were largely viewed as children who had to be treated firmly, with discipline, and with an eye to ensuring their well-being, they believed. Their young charges were in need of parental figures when it came to many matters, from housing to social life on campus. And it was precisely this attitude that would come under attack from students across the board as a growing movement toward student "self determination" and greater autonomy gained momentum at the same time Black students were taking their growing list of concerns to administrators.

While students universally found Hinz decent and sympathetic, many found other administrators dismissive and disdainful. "You should be glad to be here," Bracey recalled of one official's attitude toward the students. "You need to learn to get along in the broader world," they were instructed. At the time, Bracey recalls thinking, "This guy is nuts. Who does he think he's talking to?" The idea that their admission to Northwestern released them "out of the confines of the ghetto" and into the "broader world" was insulting. "The South Side [of Chicago] is broader than the Northwestern campus," Bracey (silently) retorted.[238]

One of the primary problems facing Northwestern administrators was that the effort to diversify the student body was a process that was neither widely understood nor entirely accepted by the majority of the university and Evanston communities at large. And there were numerous examples that exposed insensitive, patronizing, and outright racist attitudes among multiple factions. For example, just as integration efforts began in earnest—at the time, there were only twenty-six Black students at Northwestern—the main problem facing Black students, as two *Daily Northwestern* reporters wrote in 1966, was that they were "invisible." Black students did not face any "overt discrimination" on campus, they erroneously asserted, but were instead more likely to feel "ignored."[239] That same year, in its April Fool's Day edition, the *Daily Northwestern* poked fun at the efforts to integrate the university. "Recruitment Plan Exceeds Hope, Hinz Announces," read the headline of the satirical article that reported that "1,744 Negroes and 56 students of other races" would compose next year's freshman class. "When high schools heard we were recruiting more Negroes," the article continued, "no one else applied."[240] And, as the largest number of Black students to date prepared to enter Northwestern, attention was repeatedly called to the fact that many of these new students were coming to Evanston straight from the "slums."

Beyond the campus, in the first year of integration, one of the most visible clashes between white residents and Black students centered on housing. In

1966, when newly enrolled Black students searched for off-campus housing, they confronted "the most open and blatant form of racial discrimination." "There has been considerable reluctance in the community to rent rooms to non-whites in the immediate vicinity of the campus," Northwestern administrators admitted at the time.[241] But university officials, the students later observed, had done "nothing to prepare the Evanston Community for our arrival."[242] "Most of the university, particularly the student body," James Pitts aptly observed, "had not anticipated this recruitment, nor the challenge it posed for the campus."[243] There were others, however, who had seen the coming challenges posed by integration. Just as John Bracey recognized early on "that Northwestern was going to have a serious problem," others predicted the same thing.[244]

For years, Black students at Northwestern had been forced into "a double life split between on-campus academics and off-campus social activities."[245] By the 1950s, the small number of mostly male Black students on campus responded to being excluded from activities by converging at a single off-campus location: the Evanston home of Charles "Doc" Glass and his wife Helen, at 1839 Brown Street. Glass, a custodian employed by the city of Evanston, was a graduate of Evanston Township High School and had played semi-pro football for more than a decade. Over the years, he became an important (but unpaid) recruiter of Black athletes for Northwestern. And once these students arrived on campus, he opened his home to them, serving as their "friend, advisor and adopted father."[246] His main concern, he said, was not whether the students became "star[s] in their sport," but that they would take full advantage of "the opportunity to get an education at a fine school like Northwestern."[247] Glass was well aware, as he said in 1965, of "what an NU education could mean in their future."[248] And so he made sure that they had a place where they could relax, talk, and get advice. "He's a Negro looking out for the best interests of another Negro," as one student said of Glass. "There's a lot of things you can say to him that you could never say to a White man."[249] Students found a home-away-from-home with Glass, and at the time, his house was the "center for social life" for Black students at Northwestern.[250]

As Northwestern actively started to recruit more Black students, Glass predicted that it would "cause problems." "There's no student union, or any activity for the Negro on campus," Glass told the *Daily Northwestern* in March 1966. "Those new students will probably flock to me. And I just can't handle those numbers. I don't have space in the house, and I couldn't afford it."[251]

It was clear that the administration didn't understand the "full extent of what they were asking" of the students, Ogletree observed. And when problems arose, they were incapable of confronting, never mind solving them.[252] "They did not understand the full extent of what they were doing to us," she said. They were "asking us to make all the changes" and behaving as if "they didn't need to make any changes."[253] Even though we "signed up to integrate Northwestern University," Ogletree stated, "we didn't sign up for that."[254]

The students were well aware that the origins of the problems lay in both the racist institutional structure of the university, as well as the racism and ongoing problems within society as a whole. But the presence and effects of racism were, as Turner described, largely invisible to many white people.[255] And many of the problems associated with the efforts to diversify Northwestern would remain largely invisible to the majority of the administration. Even Hinz admitted to a certain amount of naiveté when it came to his attitude. "I thought I was a student service officer, and these were students who needed my service. I was probably over-simplified in my outlook toward that."[256]

The two tracks of what Turner called the "ongoing antagonisms" on campus and the "offensive behavior of white students,"[257] along with the "intellectual problem" of the curriculum, were the key factors in leading students to demand changing conditions on campus. The university was "helpful and supportive to a certain extent, but I don't think they always understood what kind of support we needed as a group," Ogletree reflected. "We were just so alone."[258]

After approaching university officials with their concerns numerous times, in various ways, and with "very little consequence,"[259] the students became discouraged and disappointed. The "disappointments," as Turner remembered, "broke our hearts."[260] "We didn't come to the university expecting to be treated this way," he said. "We thought the university would take care of problems and that they meant what they said. It was a protracted process of discussions, meeting with administrators and the dean of students, asking to meet with the president. We thought that once they knew what was going on, they'd improve. But there was one broken promise after another and that brought us to a turning point."[261] "Things kept getting worse," as Bracey recalled. "They weren't responding to these kids' demands. They were not making their lives easier." "In fact," Bracey added, "I would never have been an undergraduate at Northwestern . . . I wouldn't have put up with the crap that they were putting up with."[262]

"By the time we got from '66 to the spring of 1968, the number of incidents had built up," recalled Victor Goode. "The unresponsiveness from the University had grated on people, the idea that we were to remain on campus as a voiceless, invisible minority, somehow melding into the broader white university was something we knew would not happen and could not happen."[263] After hearing administrators' excuses, promises, and even finding sympathy and concern among some of them, nothing had been done. And "that's where the pushback came from," said Ogletree. Growing frustration and tension would soon find a tangible form of expression. Meanwhile, the students continued to organize, strategize, and plan.

It was clear that if things were going to change, it wasn't necessarily going to be because those in power had suddenly understood what the students had long been saying. Change would only come once they had made themselves heard. Many other students at Northwestern had the same idea. The concept of *student power* was in effect.

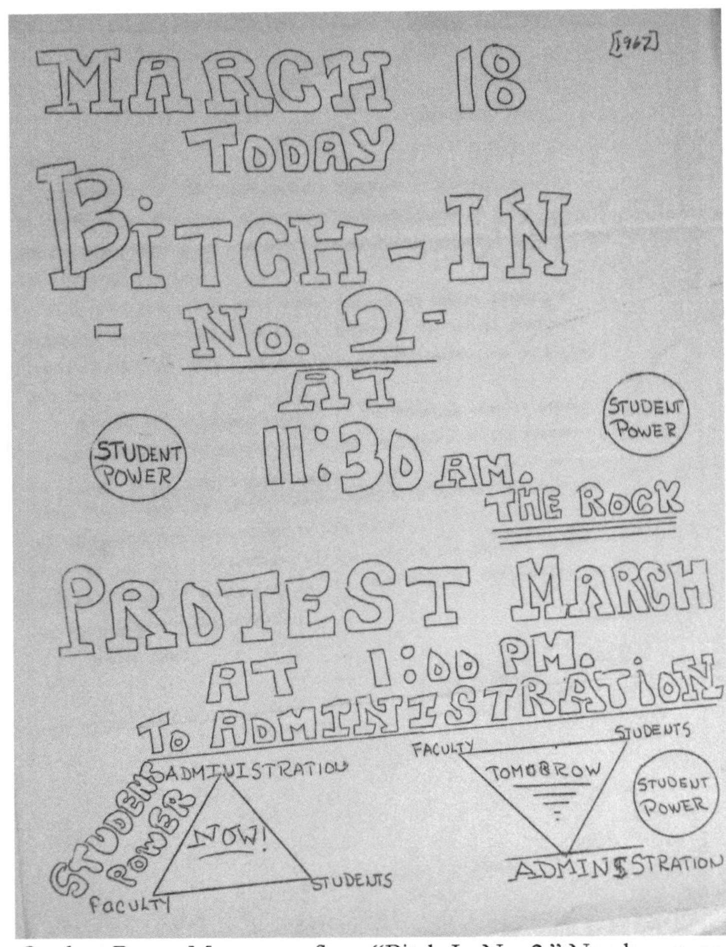

Student Power Movement flyer, "Bitch-In No. 2," Northwestern University, March 1967. (Student Activities Collection, Northwestern University Archives)

Many of the issues backed by the 1967 Student Power Movement at Northwestern were those that students had been advocating for years, and they were issues that other students would subsequently champion, including support for nondiscrimination in Greek letter organizations and open housing legislation in Evanston.

Chapter 4

Student Power

Demonstration fever has hit a group of Northwestern University students. It doesn't seem to be in the cards, however, for Evanston to be turned into another Berkeley despite some dire warning that this might happen.

"That Noise in Evanston," *Chicago Sun-Times,* May 10, 1967

Power is the ability to define your own terms.

Ellis Pines, Student Power Movement leader,
Northwestern University, 1967[1]

"There was a lot of distance between black and white students in general on campus," Roger Friedman recalled of conditions at Northwestern when he first enrolled in the fall of 1966, just as Hinz's new recruitment efforts were underway. "I was fully aware at the time that there were many more African-American and Jewish students in our class than ever before," he said. He also recognized that "many students, white and black, were becoming more radicalized by different forces." Overall, he said, "all of us were becoming more disgusted with things as usual at NU and more determined to be a part of a generation that was changing America. We felt that excitement and saw it in students all around the country and the world."[2]

A year earlier, when Melva Fager formed Northwestern's SDS chapter, she lamented the fact that the vast majority of Northwestern students "don't give a damn about anything."[3] When SDS first appeared on campus, it had been met with a large degree of apathy and a dose of diluted support. The *Daily Northwestern* announced its support for SDS's presence on campus, but it also labeled the group as marginal, its members representing "ultra-liberal thinking at Northwestern."[4] "It's indicative of the apathy at Northwestern," as one early SDS member observed of the unwillingness of most students to take any political stand.[5]

Aside from apathy, Northwestern's early SDS members had also faced open hostility from some students. In a letter to the editor of the *Daily Northwestern*, one student charged the newly-formed SDS chapter as serving as a "front" for subversive organizations, and he labeled its members as "sex deviants, marijuana smokers, and filthy little harlots."[6] "How could any decent Northwestern student associate his name with these sickening organizations," this irate student wondered.[7]

In April 1966, when Fager led one of several anti-war marches in downtown Evanston, the thirty-five protesters carried signs reading, "Loving our country and ignoring its faults are not the same thing" and "Bring the boys home!" "We just want people to think," Fager said of their intention. "We're against this 'my country right or wrong' attitude." As they undertook their silent march, they were met with curiosity. They were also confronted by a counter-protest of about thirty white male Northwestern students, chanting "we support the war." The group carried an American flag and held a sign that read, "McCarthy had the right idea."[8] At the end of the march, a water balloon was thrown at Fager's group from a department store window.[9] Fager and SDS persisted through that first year, organizing marches, protesting the draft, and handing out information to male students before they sat for a Selective Service Draft Deferment test on campus.[10] The organization continued to grow slowly, and by 1967, Steven Lubet, a first-year student, was elected chapter president.[11]

"Northwestern is not a bad place," wrote Christopher Lasch (1932-1994) upon accepting a position as professor of history at Northwestern in 1966, "but the students seem to be somewhat quiescent."[12] Lasch was one of many faculty members who not only supported various progressive student movements, but was also politically progressive himself. He and others would take part in the growing anti-war and progressive movements among the students. Among them were History Professor Robert Wiebe (1930-2000) and Raymond Mack (1927-2011), an influential sociology professor and later provost, who co-founded the university's Center for Urban Affairs in 1968. Lasch, Wiebe, and Mack were among the many faculty members who supported the takeover and the demands made by Black students.[13] (University Relations, Northwestern University Archives)

By the fall of 1966, things had started to change. Many of the members of the class of 1970 arrived at Northwestern ready to be politically engaged. One of the most notable was Roger Friedman, who would prove to be a remarkable force for change almost immediately upon first setting foot on campus. A speech major (communications, as it would later be known), Friedman was born in Houston and grew up in Austin, Texas. The son of "outspoken liberal Democrats," who were both originally from Chicago, he was a second generation Northwestern student.[14] His mother, Minnie Samet Friedman, graduated with a degree in education in 1940. She was one of the small number of Jewish students at Northwestern at the time.

Friedman had some experience with student activism in high school. He had served as student council president and engaged in what he called "some very mild anti-war education activity."[15] But once he arrived at Northwestern, the pace of his activism accelerated. At his dormitory, Bobb Hall, Friedman met other first-year students who were, he said, "pretty disgusted with the direction of the country at the time." And they wanted, as Friedman recalled, "to contribute to getting our voices heard at Northwestern."[16] In November 1966, just two months into his first year, Friedman ran for class president and won, becoming the first Jewish and non-Greek class president ever elected at Northwestern—signaling what he recognized as "a serious indication of culture change among students, white and black."[17] He pledged to avoid any of the conventional social activities that a class president would typically sponsor. Instead, his goal was "to educate and radicalize students."[18]

He didn't waste any time. Just weeks after assuming his office as class president, Friedman was expressing his concerns directly to university officials about a variety of issues, including the conditions faced by Black students on campus. The students were, he said, both "limited" and "ignored" by the administration, and he pledged to work toward bettering conditions.[19]

In March 1967, Friedman drafted a resolution, later passed by the Student Senate, aimed at confronting housing discrimination in Evanston. He argued that the resolution would "require the administration to take a stand on open housing or explain why it won't speak out."[20] (Franklin Kreml, representing the university's position, argued that Northwestern supported open housing and practiced it, but was against "applying corporate pressure to achieve open housing."[21])

Roger Friedman, 1966
Friedman used this photograph for his campaign for freshman class president at Northwestern. "I took as many courses as I could in social psychology . . . and American history," Friedman recalled of his studies. Two professors in particular had a major influence on him: Sociology professor Howard Becker and Christopher Lasch, who was, he said, "a mentor of mine at Northwestern and a lovely, brilliant man and professor."[22]
(Photograph courtesy of Roger Friedman)

In early April, Friedman launched an investigation into discrimination within fraternities and sororities. Those found to be practicing discrimination in pledging new members should have their charters revoked and they should be thrown off campus, he asserted.[23] By the end of a busy month, Friedman and another first-year student, Allen Foster, launched the NU Civil Liberties Union, designed to help students protect their civil rights.[24] Later, he took part in a panel discussion on the effects of discrimination and anti-Semitism at Northwestern,[25] and, upon the founding of FMO, he was one of many white students who pledged support for the new organization and its goals.[26]

Friedman was part of a small, but growing, progressive faction among white students whose early mobilizing would soon lay the groundwork for the emergence of the "Student Power Movement." As this group was in its nascent stages, many Black students increasingly recognized that they did have some allies among Northwestern's progressive white students. By the spring of 1967, that alliance would be represented most publicly in the surprising election of Ellis Pines, a sophomore from Dallas, Texas, as president of the Student Senate.

When Pines first arrived at Northwestern, he was unhappy. "Although I was not an outsider," Pines reflected years later, "I also experienced disaffection and, as dear [Northwestern] professor Remi Clignet would say 'anomie'. . . the buzz word for our problems."[27] Before coming to Evanston, Pines had made the dramatic transition from Barry Goldwater supporter to civil rights advocate, briefly involved with the Congress of Racial Equality (CORE) and later heavily influenced by civil rights activists, Melody Heaps, a Northwestern graduate and staff member for the Chicago Freedom Movement, and the Reverend William Cohea, founder of the Chicago Business Industrial Project.[28] Once at Northwestern, Pines became interested in the work SDS was doing on campus.[29]

In the spring of 1967, Pines launched his campaign for student government president on a "Student Power Movement" (SPM) platform. "It began as a lark," Pines said of his campaign, "but then, as people confided in me, I saw that there were very real problems . . . Most stemmed from the inability of the university to create anything close to an inclusive environment."[30]

Although the SPM platform reflected some of the ideas and spirit of the 1962 Port Huron Statement, it expressly avoided political issues, such as the war in Vietnam. To the distress of some more progressive and politically-oriented students, the platform focused almost exclusively on student life. As such, it advocated for better communication between the administration and students, curriculum reform, advancement of students' rights, and the abolishment of the University Discipline Committee. But the platform was, in fact, deeply political when it came to its stance against religious and racial discrimination.[31]

Pines was joined in his campaign by many supporters. But it was the "unexpected" support from Roger Friedman—whom the *Daily Northwestern* called the "most dynamic freshman leader in years"—that would prove critical to his campaign.[32] Both Friedman and Pines agreed on the fundamental issues facing students across the country and both were eager to bring changes to their own campus.[33]

Along with his supporters, Pines honed his campaign by organizing what became his signature event: the "bitch-in." The bitch-in proved popular as hundreds of students showed up at the Rock, a landmark boulder in the center of the campus, to discuss and debate a variety of issues. There, they also took turns expressing their various concerns and complaints. Pines compiled these grievances into a list which was then used to draft an SPM manifesto. Among the more than one hundred grievances collected were calls to end discrimination, reduce tuition costs, open channels of communication between students and the administration, and cultivate a more vibrant intellectual community.[34] The group that contributed to the SPM platform was not monolithic, but represented multiple campus factions: "sorority girls . . . fraternity guys, African-Americans, grunges and not grunges, regular students," as Pines recalled of the coalition.[35] Now, it looked like the students at the "Purple Island of the North Shore," as Pines referred to Northwestern, were mobilizing. "People don't like to come to meetings," he observed of the particular effectiveness of the bitch-in, "but are very happy to let the meetings come to them."[36]

At one bitch-in, a television news crew filmed Pines, dressed in a suit and tie and using a bullhorn to interact with the crowd of students and field questions. It was just days before the election, and a group, led by Pines, soon broke away and marched to the president's office with a copy of their Student Power Movement manifesto in hand. (Among other things, the manifesto called for a "student revolution" and a change in emphasis at Northwestern from a "concentration on publishing, research, 'parental' advice, and monetary profit" to a focus on "learning in an aura of controversy."[37])

At the president's office, they staged a brief sit-in. The next day they marched again, three hundred strong this time.[38] Vice President Payson Wild and Vice President Franklin Kreml came out of their offices to respond to their "gripes and questions."[39] As a result of this encounter, Pines secured a private meeting with President Miller and several other officials. Students Russell Barefield and Roger Friedman accompanied Pines to the meeting, and there they were afforded a chance to give the administration "an idea of what students are thinking" and address the problem of the "generation gap." Administrators are too far removed from the students, they told Miller. Many students feel alienated from the university, they said. Now, they want to be heard, to participate in decision-making, and to be represented by a new dean of students who would stand up for student rights. (A search for a new dean was underway at the time, and Jack Hinz would soon be appointed to that position.) Finally, they "specifically attacked the university for not taking a stand on alleged campus and Evanston discrimination."[40]

Pines mused that student apathy seemed to have vanished through the ritual of the bitch-in.[41] He and others were learning quickly that on-the-ground organizing, along with directly communicating with constituents, were the most effective means of advancing reform. Pines identified what he considered an essential tactic for a movement to be successful: "legitimize your power base." Securing meetings with administration officials was fine, he explained, but in order to be effective, such a meeting had to be backed by widespread support. "If I go in alone," he explained, "and say 'Now we need this,' the administration says, 'But whom do you represent?' [But] if you have 300 students outside the building, it demands an administrator's attention and you can meet him equally.'"[42]

Pines and the Student Power Movement enjoyed a "meteoric rise." By election eve, his two opponents were reportedly scared, worried that "previously apathetic voters would turn out in force" and vote for Pines. And so they did. Only four days after hosting his first bitch-in, Pines was "swept to victory," winning the election on April 19, 1967.[43] (Pines, who was in the midst of rehearsing for a production of Euripides' *Ion*, was dressed in a shepherd's costume when he learned the news that he had been elected president of Northwestern's student government.[44])

The SPM had plenty of critics, to be sure, and some students dismissed the movement as "immature."[45] But others were energized by what they viewed as the most dynamic student movement at Northwestern in a long time. On his first day in office, Pines directed all members of the Student Senate to attend a meeting on open occupancy in Evanston.[46] After collecting more than 1,600 signatures on a fair housing petition, he led a student march through Evanston to present it formally to the city council.[47] He also began presenting a series of demands and "ultimatums" to the administration, calling for the university, among other things, to protect students' rights, to expand student autonomy, to support an open occupancy law in Evanston, to reactivate the charters of predominantly Black fraternities, and to pass an anti-bias bill for fraternities and sororities.[48] (Newly-elected senator, Daphne Maxwell Reid would soon serve on Pines' committee investigating discriminatory practices in fraternities and sororities.)[49]

Pines also pressured a reluctant President Miller to appear at an open forum to answer questions from all interested students. Miller first reacted negatively to such a meeting, stating that he did not intend to negotiate with a "mob."[50] But on Friday, May 12, 1967, for the first time in his eighteen years as president, Miller appeared onstage before a crowd of one thousand students and answered questions on topics ranging from open housing to discrimination in fraternities.[51] The event was broadcast on the university's radio station, but no members of the press were allowed to attend.[52]

As the SPM took power, Pines was advised by a faculty member that he would garner broader support if he continued to refrain from commenting on the war in Vietnam. The war was becoming a hot topic and the small campus anti-war movement was gaining momentum. Those students who identified themselves as progressive or "radical" in their political outlook, especially in their stance against the war, may have supported Pines. But they were, as Roger Friedman recounted, "very discouraged by the avoidance of anti-war politics in the student power movement."[53] To them, the SPM agenda lacked "a political or historical context."[54]

Almost as soon as they arrived on campus in the fall of 1966, Friedman, Ed Steinhardt, and other student anti-war activists and SDS members continued the tradition established by Melva Fager the year before. At the Rock, they began to stage "silent vigils" against the war.[55] Later, they organized larger anti-war rallies and teach-ins. They also staged "creative protests," including orchestrating a succession of groups of students who approached military recruitment officers on campus and proceeded to press them to answer questions concerning the morality of the war in Vietnam.[56]

As Pines and the SPM had been on the verge of being swept into office, a group of Northwestern students traveled to New York City to take part in a massive anti-war rally and march to the United Nations to protest U.S. involvement in Vietnam, led by Martin Luther King, Jr. (Just days earlier, King had spoken out against the war in a now famous speech delivered at the Riverside Church in Manhattan.)[57] There, former Northwestern student and current research assistant, twenty-three-year-old Gary Rader and scores of others famously burned their draft cards. Rader was a U.S. Special Forces reservist (Green Beret) and during the protest, he wore his uniform. Days later, he was arrested by FBI agents at his home at 809 Simpson Street in Evanston.[58] His friends at Northwestern raised money to help post his bail. Weeks later, Rader appeared on campus to speak at an event sponsored by SDS,[59] and soon, he co-founded Chicago Area Draft Resisters (CADRE), a group that immediately had a presence on Northwestern's campus.[60]

Despite the fact that many SDS members did not approve of the SPM's silence on the war, they officially endorsed the movement.[61] In turn, SPM supported many of the actions staged by SDS, including an event dubbed, "Gentle Thursday." As described by its SDS organizers, the event was a celebration of "love and happiness" which would be held—coincidentally, organizers said—in close proximity to a scheduled Naval ROTC drill on Deering Meadow.[62] In reaction, officials saw fit to remind students of the university's policy regarding any student-led "disruptive tactics" and they issued a statement, authorized by President Miller: "the university cannot tolerate any attempt by any individual, group . . . or organization to disrupt the regularly scheduled activities of the university." Students found to be in violation of this policy would be met with disciplinary action.[63] The event went off without incident, however. It was "calm and serene," as the *Daily Northwestern* reported.[64]

In their anti-war activism, the students were supported by a small number faculty members, including math professor, Marvin Shinbrot, one of several professors who would become increasingly outspoken politically, especially concerning the war in Vietnam.[65] In May 1966, an open letter to President Lyndon Johnson, urging him to take a number of steps to "achieve peace" in Vietnam, was published in the *Daily Northwestern.*[66] The letter was signed by fifty-five faculty members, sixty graduate students, and 145 undergraduate students, including Melva Fager. On April 14, 1967, two thousand students attended a nine-hour campus teach-in on Vietnam sponsored by SDS, with several professors, including Shinbrot and Christopher Lasch, taking part.[67] The war, and specifically the draft, was becoming an unavoidable issue, and not surprisingly, it was "not only the beard-and-sandal crowd" who attended the teach-in, as the *Daily Northwestern* reported, "but also the curious, conservative students and Evanstonians."[68]

Still, there were plenty of critics who watched the rise of student and faculty activism, especially the SPM, with alarm. That fall, after a faculty committee circulated an anti-war petition signed by fifty professors, the action was reported to the administration by a faculty member who viewed it as inappropriate and dangerous.[69] Meanwhile, in a letter to President Miller, one critic labeled the SPM as a threatening, communist group and he warned that its members were seeking to seize control of the management of the university.[70] Others concurred, urging the administration to take immediate and decisive action to curtail protests and demonstrations among faculty and students. The administration acknowledged the growing alarm among some parents, alumni, and students. "Recent student demonstrations have distressed all of us in the administration," Franklin Kreml noted in May 1967. "It is important to observe that they have also distressed the great majority of students themselves."[71]

Some students were also distressed concerning what they saw as agitation among white progressive students in relation to the rights of Black students. One such student decided to put pen to paper. In May 1967, Dale J. Walther wrote an open letter, published in the *Daily Northwestern* and addressed to Roger Friedman and "his power puppets."[72] Walther lambasted Friedman for his activism and specifically challenged his efforts to confront discrimination on campus: "Just keep telling the Negro students how they are being discriminated against on this campus. I'm sure your vocal vociferation is really going to mellow the bitter prejudices you feign [*sic*] in every upper-middle class, white, Anglo-Saxon, protestant student on this campus. If you keep screaming loud enough you might even be able to sustain (or is it exploit) the persecution complex these colored kids have brought with them."[73]

It wasn't Friedman who responded to this attack, but another student, Marianne Jackson, who would later participate in the takeover. "This is an open letter to all Northwestern students, especially Dale J. Walther, from some of the colored kids at N.U. (Those with and without persecution complexes)," she wrote. "First of all if we didn't acquire persecution complexes living in 'White America' all our lives, we certainly wouldn't gain one after six months at Northwestern."[74]

"Secondly," Jackson continued, "we would like to say that contrary to public opinion, we are not running around with a bunch of empty heads, dying to gobble up everything the 'white man' lays down. In other words, we have the ability to think for ourselves, and nothing that Roger Friedman or anyone else lays down influences our way of thinking. We dance on the end of no one's strings."[75]

The criticism that some leveled at any kind of student activism was just one indication of the factions that existed within the student body. However, despite what Friedman recognized as a distance between Black and white students on campus at the time, he was also beginning to see "some close friendships forged across that barrier."[76] For his own part, Friedman was getting to know philosophy major, Eric Perkins, a member of the class of 1970, who would also prove to be a formidable student leader. The two shared a class and were soon having lunch together, ultimately building a friendship that would last for many years.[77]

For many, all the changes on campus seemed to point to a coming revolution. And an increasing number of critics lined up to make their fears known about these new trends. After President Miller responded to student requests for more freedom on campus by authorizing a trial run of parietal hours (allowing female and male students to visit each other in their dorm rooms), he set off a firestorm of protest: "What on earth are the schools coming to anyway!" one outraged alumnus wrote to Miller, "with boys pulling off panty raids-sit-downs... long shaggy hair-no shaves-sloppy clothes-dope use-LSD and other nonsensical stuff and/or stunts, when will this crazy end? Now they want to have their necking and sex parties right in their rooms!"[78] "Congratulations are in order," another critic wrote. "You will now have a free love campus. All you need is a large maternity hospital and a few doctors."[79] The outcry was so intense that administrators soon discontinued the experimental parietal hours and returned the issue to the Council on Undergraduate Life "for further evaluation and study."[80]

There was no shortage of opinion on how Northwestern should handle the push toward student power. In a May 1967 editorial, the *Chicago Tribune* recommended that the university dismiss protesters who did not uphold Northwestern's "rules of proper conduct and the standards of decency and patriotism" and it accused SPM leaders (and their bitch-ins) as "the sort of gross public indecency that has disfigured University campuses from Berkeley to Harvard."[81] Some Student Senate members agreed. Just after Pines assumed the office of the president, the Student Senate unanimously passed a resolution, voting to divorce itself from the SPM, explaining that the "Movement's methods are not representative of the student body."[82]

Pines, unfazed, responded that the resolution would have "no real effect" since the Senate could not be and never had been "connected officially" to the Movement.[83] But over one weekend in May, Pines and his steering com-

Ellis Pines, c. 1967. (Northwestern University Archives) Pines later described the SPM as "more lifestyle-oriented than political, whereas the African-American movement grew out of real inequality and prejudice with its roots in the civil rights movement. While I was running, I was told . . . that I had the faculty's support if I addressed campus issues and not international issues. Hence, I kept mum on Vietnam."[84]

mittee officially dissolved the SPM as an official organization. They wanted to ensure there would be no conflict of interest, real or perceived. Pines soon announced, however, that the Movement itself still existed and he remained "firmly committed to its ideas."[85] "We remain," he said, "representative of those who are interested."[86] But by September 1967, Pines was on his way out. Not only out of office, but also out of the university entirely.

Just five months after Pines had been elected, he resigned his office upon order of the administration, which (controversially) placed him on academic probation in the summer of 1967. Pines refuted the claim that his grades had not met mandatory requirements, but the administration forced him to resign his office nonetheless.[87] Soon after, Pines announced that he had been forced to withdraw from the university after his parents "cut off all financial support because they objected to his political activities." Pines said he'd rather withdraw from school than withdraw from politics. And so he told his parents, " 'I couldn't quit politics . . . political activity is human activity. I want to be a free person in a free society.' "[88]

Pines' SPM colleagues, including Roger Friedman, pledged to "continue to fight for student rights."[89] Friedman, Ed Steinhart, and Allen Foster issued an open letter to the university that outlined a plan to advance students rights, including a call to allow students to make their own rules concerning their social lives, to administer their own disciplinary measures, and to play a more active role in policy making.[90]

By the end of the spring 1967 quarter, Friedman had become "fed-up with student electoral politics," as he recalled. "It was too slow and all co-opted by the administration."[91] Soon, he dropped out of official student politics. He was now a member of SDS and ready to work to advance an agenda for reform from outside established student government. "It's time to get down and organize," he announced.[92]

"I knew at the end of freshman year in May 1967," Friedman said, "that the next fall was going to be exciting politically on campus."[93] In their first year at Northwestern, he and others, including newly-elected SDS president, Steven Lubet, had learned a lot about how to mobilize students.[94] "We were good organizers," Friedman said, explaining how they learned to build a coalition not only through the bitch-in, but also by going dorm to dorm, talking with students and listening to their concerns. Soon, he and others moved further to the left and began "experimenting with more active kinds of political mobilization."[95] For the next three years, Friedman would play a critical role, working with other students and faculty, organizing protests and rallies, and supporting a variety of reforms, including the adoption of a student bill of rights, an overhaul of the campus judicial system, and an expansion of student autonomy—something that "scared" the administration, as Pines believed.[96] In the fall of 1967, Friedman and other SDS members launched an underground campus newspaper, *The Real Press*, a one-page weekly.[97] "I was determined to use my energy to organize students against the war and radicalize them in general about the injustices in our corporate society," Friedman recalled.[98]

Such a pledge was being made on campuses across the country where a growing number of the country's seven million college students viewed the United States as a country fraught with inequality, racism, militarism, and injustice, and the university as an outmoded institution, authoritarian, woefully behind the times, and unable to educate students in a critical, meaningful way. "We felt connected with radical students all over the country," Friedman recalled, "and I'm almost embarrassed to say that we really did believe we could change the world."[99]

"Problems of Democracy," cartoon published in the *Daily Northwestern,* October 24, 1967.

Barb Caulfield became president of the Student Senate after Ellis Pines was forced to step down.[100] She was Northwestern's first female president of student government. Here, she is shown facing the challenges of representing Northwestern's various student groups. SDS is represented on the outskirts of the group, while FMO is not represented at all.

Alpha Omicron Pi sorority dance, Northwestern University, fall 1967 or winter 1968. (Northwestern University Archives, courtesy of Audrey Hinton) Seated left to right: Victor Goode, Diane Hinton (sister of Audrey Hinton, visiting from college), Michael Smith, Audrey Hinton. Standing: Lonnie Terry and Detra Smith. All five Northwestern students pictured here took part in the takeover just months after this photograph was taken.

A United Effort

Recently, many white liberals have expressed a concern and even fear over the rise of black organizations on Northwestern's campus. As a black student, feeling the neglect and even hatred of a racist society, I can recognize the need for a united effort of black students to fulfill their own needs.

Clovis E. Semmes, letter to the editor, *Daily Northwestern,* January 16, 1968

The goal of self-determination and black self-identity—Black Power—is full participation in the decision-making processes affecting the lives of black people and recognition of the virtues in themselves as black people.

Black Power: Politics of Liberation in America (1967)[101]

The rise of the SPM was only one indication that many Northwestern students were dissatisfied with the status quo. As Friedman, Pines, and others drew attention to a variety of issues related to student self-determination and equality, many Black students on campus were also in the process of creating their own network and drafting their own manifesto, as it were.

As much as university officials did not anticipate the problems that would come from integration, they also did not anticipate what the students recruited to enact integration would bring to the campus themselves. The university's self-perception as a benefactor, as graciously offering poor Black students opportunities that they otherwise would never have enjoyed, elided the very fact of who the students were themselves and all that they offered. They were bringing to campus not only their talents and ideas, but, in many cases, their experience in organizing and activism.

In its efforts to recruit high-performing Black students, Northwestern had "picked some of the most intelligent, radical, savvy young people who had already been part of a movement that had begun a decade before," as John Bracey explained.[102] And they came to Northwestern out of a "decade of struggle,"[103] with many already having been politically active and having engaged in civil rights protests, as Daphne Maxwell Reid had when living with her mother in public housing in New York.[104]

Before coming to Northwestern, Kathryn Ogletree did not define herself "as an activist or anything like that."[105] Like many students, it was only once she was on campus that "my eyes were opened," as she said, to the reality of many racial and social justice issues.[106] As editor of her high school newspaper, she had taken positions on current issues and knew about "black students marching and integrating lunch counters and things like."[107] But, as she later stated, "I had not had that type of exposure before coming to Northwestern."[108] And now she found herself in the presence of other students who *did* define themselves as activists, those who "had been involved in the actual civil rights movement," students including Eric Perkins, John Higginson, James Turner, John Bracey, and others.[109]

Bracey and Turner were particularly well versed in the civil rights movement and the particular demands of making changes within institutions that were not publicly or openly discriminatory, but practiced injustice through less visible methods. And both continued to serve in advisory roles to the undergraduate students who were in the process of organizing and expanding their activities. "They knew what they wanted," Bracey said of these students. And, later, he said, it was this group who "systematically took on this university."[110]

That process began once the students started meeting regularly and sharing their experiences, just as Black students on campuses across the country were doing. "There was a growing Black student movement in the country," Turner recalled. "This was not the classic fighting segregation in the deep South, but this was fighting a particular form in the Northern parts of the U.S."[111] Part of this fight involved the growth of Black student organizations. For the students at Northwestern, FMO soon took a leading role in their work to demand changes on campus.

Ogletree anticipated that she'd have "an ample amount of time" to learn the ins and outs of working in FMO while she served as vice president. But at the end of the fall 1967 quarter, Herman Cage unexpectedly resigned his position and Ogletree was elected president. "I willingly accepted that responsibility," she said, honored that her classmates had "entrusted me to lead."[112] She took her role seriously, immediately proving to be more than a capable leader. She effectively organized the group and held together its large and growing number of members. Indeed, many credit her with being *the* leader of the Black student movement at Northwestern. While she modestly argues that she was only one individual within the larger group, she has come to see more and more the significance of her role. "What was unusual was that I was an actual leader in the forefront," she acknowledged, at a time when "most women's leadership was always behind the scenes."[113]

Ogletree viewed the shaping of FMO as a "dynamic process" that involved all members, and she defined her role as "giving voice to FMO's evolving identity as expressed by the members."[114] Takeover participant and graduate student James Pitts saw it slightly differently, arguing that it was Ogletree who would bring the organization's identity and aims into greater focus. She "conceived of FMO of a social and political instrument," he observed. She incorporated within the organization the multiplicity of views of various students on race consciousness and racism, involved more students in numerous ways, and also helped shape FMO's identity as an "organization of blacks, by blacks, and for blacks."[115]

Ogletree's role was critical in another way: after she became president, the organization successfully achieved an equal ratio of female and male members. As the leader of FMO, she served as a role model, particularly for female students. While the feeling of being "on alert" while on campus became constant in the lives of many Black students, those feelings were intensified for Black women, since they were often subject to a broad spectrum of racist attacks and felt particularly threatened on campus.[116] And thus FMO became an essential resource for many female students.

FMO soon became, as Ogletree put it, "the mouthpiece of the black students to the university."[117] It continued to put the students' concerns in front of university officials. Meanwhile, the group held most of its activities off campus, including hosting lectures, social activities, and a fall orientation for incoming Black students. "We created," as Ogletree explained, "our own social environment."[118] By January 1968, the *Daily Northwestern* reported that seventy percent of Black students at Northwestern were FMO members.[119] But Ogletree puts that figure at one hundred percent, explaining that all Black students were drawn to the organization for various reasons, whether for its social and cultural activities, its advocacy and activism, or some combination of the two.[120]

Kathryn Ogletree
(Northwestern *Syllabus* Yearbook, 1970)

In February 1968, another student group, the Afro American Student Union (AASU), was formed by about ten students, with James Turner at the helm. Membership was by invitation only and the group also held its various events off campus. It was largely focused on fostering connections in Evanston and Chicago and strengthening alliances with other Black organizations and student groups across the county. It also worked to raise funds in support of various causes. For example, members launched a drive to raise money for funeral and hospital expenses after three Black students were killed and twenty-seven students were injured in Orangeburg, South Carolina.[121] The group also started "sending delegations to various Black student conferences around the country,"[122] engaging in a "broad exchange among Black student groups at other schools," as Turner explained.[123] Indeed, protests at other schools and throughout the South served as models for what might be accomplished at Northwestern, as Turner recalled. "We were sharing information and were aware of events at other schools, and the bitter history at other schools," he said.[124]

In March 1968, just two months before the takeover, students Eric Perkins and Victor Goode embarked on a visit to three eastern universities: Cornell, Columbia, and Harvard. They were, they later wrote, compelled by the "growing crisis situation that faced the black student . . . at Northwestern." They wanted to investigate conditions for students on other campuses and report their findings to Northwestern officials.[125] On their visits, Perkins and Goode met with students and administrators at each university, quickly learning that the problems they faced at Northwestern were similar to those confronting Black students across the country. They gleaned valuable information concerning how other students were handling their situations and they also learned specifics concerning their future plans. At Columbia, for instance, they met with Black student leaders and learned of the growing dispute between Harlem residents and the university over a planned construction of a gymnasium—a key element that would lead to the student strike and takeover on that campus a month later.[126] "When we returned from our trip," Perkins and Goode wrote, "we set about the process of organizing our information and applying what we had learned to the structure of F.M.O."[127]

Not all Black students joined the FMO and the AASU, and some students, including Ogletree, were members of both groups. "FMO was dealing with the basic needs day-by-day and the social needs of the students," Ogletree explained. It was far less politically focused than the AASU, whose members "did a lot," she said, "to help raise the consciousness of the Black students."[128]

As the students worked to cultivate their own organizations, administrators were not pleased. Theirs had been a call for assimilation, and, according to Turner, they were vehemently opposed to anything that smacked of segregation, even if self-imposed. University officials deplored the idea that the students who had been recruited to Northwestern to integrate the school were now retreating into their own organizations. In an article in the *Daily Northwestern*, reporter Tom Davies lamented that the Black student seemed "to be withdrawing into his own community and excluding the university from his social and cultural activities."[129] But others argued that they were only being practical; they were trying to meet their own needs, needs the administration seemed comfortable overlooking or ignoring. As Andre Bell put it, "We finally took matters into our own hands."[130]

In January 1968, *New York Times* film critic Bosley Crowther noted with barely concealed alarm what he took to be a growing "militancy" among Northwestern's Black students, apparent (to him) when he came to Northwestern to participate in a four-day symposium on violence in American life, where the topic of racism was addressed.[131] Crowther and other white observers were both outraged and dismayed by what they interpreted as the militancy of some of the symposium speakers themselves, whose messages they interpreted as advocating violence and revolution and encouraging a commitment from all Black people to do "whatever they can to switch the balance of power" away from white people.[132]

The negative and dismissive reactions of many white people to the symposium "upset me," wrote Carol Oliver, an undergraduate student who would soon take part in the takeover. "Before last week, I had naively, (and stupidly) maintained the attitude that white people, too, could hear and understand. Now, I am not sure about that at all."[133]

Indeed, for many Black students, the symposium had been a revelation. Among the speakers and seminar leaders were: James Lawson, civil rights activist and SNCC member; Ernest Chambers, activist and organizer; Charles Vernon Hamilton, political scientist, civil rights leader, and co-author, with Stokely Carmichael, of *Black Power: The Politics of Liberation in America* (1967); Staughton Lynd, historian and activist; and Eduardo Mondlane, who had earned his PhD from Northwestern in 1961 and was now leader of Mozambique's liberation movement, *Frente de Libertação de Moçambique* or FRELIMO.[134] The symposium speakers discussed a range of topics, from colonialism and police violence to racism in the U.S. and abroad. In several informal sessions held before and after the scheduled events, many students had a chance to meet with these influential leaders for "intimate" discussions.[135] There, as James Pitts recalled, they "not only learned new ideas," but they also saw that "black intellectuals, legitimized by the Establishment, if you will, spoke to them as racial brothers. This served as significant positive reinforcement to black students that they were part of a racial movement which was larger than themselves."[136]

The symposium sparked excitement among students, and it fed what was for many an increasing interest in Black political and social activist movements. At the time, as John Bracey observed, there was a larger "shift from civil rights to Black power" among students.[137] Hamilton and Carmichael's book, *Black Power*, was just one of many texts that spoke clearly and forcefully: "The concept of Black Power . . . is a call for black people in this country to unite, to recognize their heritage, to build a sense of community. It is a call for black people to begin to define their own goals, to lead their own organizations and to support those organizations. It is a call to reject the racist institutions and values of this society."[138]

The growing (re-)emergence of Black power and Black nationalism, points of view that represented a significant way of thinking for many of Northwestern's Black students, particularly among the members of AASU, but increasingly within FMO ranks as well, was being embraced by students across the country. As historian Joy Ann Williamson-Lott observed: "Black students actively participated in the Black Power movement and translated its goals and tactics into actions appropriate for a college campus. An umbrella organization coordinating protest on several individual campuses did not exist, and students at different campuses rarely chose appointed days for protest activities. But black students did talk to one another, learn from one another's struggles, and subscribe to a similar understanding of black power."[139]

For some students, it was their very experience at Northwestern that compelled them to shift their thinking, to become more interested in embracing the concepts of Black Power and Black nationalism and to become more expressly political in thought and action. The summer of 1967 (dubbed the "long, hot summer") also had a significant impact, as a series of uprisings took place across the United States, including a particularly devastating riot in Detroit. The uprisings left the county reeling as they underscored the volatile state of American race relations. It had been tense in Evanston that summer too, after a fire-bomb had been lobbed at a local lumber yard. Increased police patrols through the city were authorized and later, charges of police brutality were made after a young Black man had been reportedly beaten by two officers.[140] The city was on edge.

That summer, a group of students who were just completing the NUCAP program made their own politically-oriented ideas known to the rest of the campus. They left their painted statements on the Rock, which was always covered in graffiti, painted, and then repainted. "Detroit '67." "Black Power." "Rap." "Malcolm." "Stokely in '68."[141]

Moving away from calls for integration, some students now called for an assertion of Black rights and identity. They advocated advancing Black culture, history, and political and economic power. And they revealed the influence that radical political and social movements and organizations, such as the Black Panther Party (founded in 1966), were having on their thinking. "[B]lack students have taken it upon themselves to learn about their history, their literature, their culture in general and to develop a social life indicative of the mood and feeling of black people," Northwestern student Clovis Semmes explained in a letter published in the *Daily Northwestern* after the 1968 symposium concluded.[142] In *Ebony* magazine, James Turner would later explain that many Black people were no longer seeking acceptance by the dominant white culture. They were now simply refusing "to adjust themselves to the rules of success defined for them by white men."[143] Victor Goode remembered how being at Northwestern caused many students to shift their thinking. They had arrived on campus as "negroes," he said. But as they started earnestly to examine their own identity in light of their experiences on campus and within the context of the broader Black student movement across the country, they underwent a "transformation of consciousness."[144]

For Turner and others, the racism they experienced at Northwestern merely reflected the extent of inequality and racism within American society. "The university can be regarded as a microcosm, a miniature of the American social structure," Turner said in 1968. "And one thing Black people all over the country are asking is how they can survive in an overriding white context. Standards are set by the white group, standards of beauty, standards of evaluation, all of that. And that began to affect us here as Black students," he observed. And now, one of the overriding questions had become: "How do we hold ourselves together?"[145]

Black Power and Black nationalist viewpoints were embraced by many, but by no means by all of the Black students at Northwestern, as James Pitts observed in his insightful analysis of students' various beliefs, ideas, and philosophies at the time. They were certainly not monolithic in their thinking. Indeed, Bracey recalled many long, vigorous debates among students on a host of topics, related to the campus and beyond. And while there was some overlap in membership between FMO and the AASU, there was also a degree of discord concerning which group was viewed as being most effective in addressing their concerns, the (at first) less-politically oriented FMO or the almost exclusively politically focused AASU. Some students were far more dedicated to a Black nationalist ideology, embracing the idea that Black people should not seek entry into or acceptance by the dominant white culture, since that culture is inherently racist and oppressive. Others argued for integration within and access to the dominant white culture. Still, the various efforts and activities of the two different groups were aligned in many ways.

But soon, two critical events would "cause the entire Black student community to come together."[146]

The Closing of Ranks

Both internal and external changes must be made to change the plight of the black student. It is for this reason that I risk embarrassing what has proven to be an unresponsive institution into recognizing and implementing the necessary changes.[147]

Vernon Ford, *Daily Northwestern,* April 25, 1968

On Saturday night, December 2, 1967, members of the Sigma Chi Fraternity hosted a Roman toga party at their chapter house on the Northwestern campus. At a nearby recreation room in Sargent Hall, a birthday party was underway, hosted by a group of Black students, with a number of non-student guests from Chicago in attendance.

When a group of roughly six Black male students, some of whom were FMO members, along with a couple of their friends who were not Northwestern students, arrived at the Sigma Chi party, they were received "without hostility."[148] Indeed, many later reported that they had been invited to the party.[149] Soon, however, several other fraternity members arrived at the party and asked them to leave. They then "ushered [them] out of the house with some degree of force."[150] A fight broke out in a nearby parking lot, "apparently precipitated by a Sigma Chi member pushing a Black student against an automobile."[151] And, according to the *Daily Northwestern*, "the disturbance spread until about 100 youths were milling" near the intersection of Sheridan Road and Noyes Street.[152]

In the ensuing melee, at least two students were injured: one white student was stabbed and another white student would require stitches after being hit on the head. Campus security and local police were called. A large crowd of onlookers gathered and the police requested that everyone disperse. Two Black men, who were not Northwestern students, were reportedly maced and physically assaulted by the police.[153] They were arrested, charged with "mob action" and "resisting an officer."[154] Their bail was set at $5,000 each. [155]

The incident would not be widely publicized beyond the campus until months after it occurred.[156] It was one of "many encounters" between Black students and Sigma Chi members, and it scared many of the Black students on campus.[157] They were concerned with what they viewed as an escalating level of violence on campus, violence that was specifically directed at them. Many were also outraged by the degree of force used by the police during the incident, and they objected to the fact that the only people who had been arrested that night were Black. The charge of mob action and the high bail amount intensified their outrage.

At 10 a.m. on the morning after the incident, a group of more than one hundred Black students came together to "decide on a course of action."[158] They soon held a peaceful protest march to the home of Northwestern President Miller (who, it should be noted, was a member of Sigma Chi Fraternity at the University of Utah).[159] At the doorway of the president's home at 2870 Sheridan Place, they asked that he talk with them about what they saw as the "brewing racial tension" on campus.[160] Miller, who was reportedly "visibly annoyed," dismissed them, directing them to take their concerns to Jack Hinz whose responsibility it was "to look into" their "problem."[161] Ogletree later referred to Miller's response as a "slap in the face."[162]

On Monday, a large group of Black students showed up at the court for the scheduled hearing of the two men who had been arrested on Saturday night. There, they created a "stir in the building because of their impressive numbers."[163] Ultimately, the bail was reduced to $2,000 and the students worked together to raise the money.[164]

Soon, the students held a meeting to discuss their next steps. "We felt we were at odds with the university and also with the Evanston police department," Ogletree said, describing their feelings at the time. On Saturday night, there had been "equal fighting back and forth," she said. "But we were seen as the culprits as far as creating the situation."[165] During the meeting, held just one week before final exams, the students debated and strategized, not entirely in agreement over the best course of action to take. All were in agreement that they didn't feel safe on campus and that it was the university's responsibility "to protect the bodies of all its students."[166] Ultimately, they drew up a list of their concerns to present to the administration. Asking that the university investigate the incident and take disciplinary action against *all* of those who had been involved, including members of the Sigma Chi Fraternity, the students gave university officials two days to respond to their request "or else."[167]

The "or else" portion was not further defined, but it signified a critical method deployed by the students. Their action was viewed as "worthless without potential muscle" behind it, as James Pitts explained.[168] And while the students were not willing to make good on any threat or even define what the "or else" was, the strategy worked. Soon a meeting was called. After six hours of negotiation, the university agreed to their requests, placing Sigma Chi as well as FMO on "social suspension." The university also agreed to order the University Discipline Committee to conduct an investigation into the incident.[169] By January 12, 1968, the UDC convened to consider "further disciplinary pursuit" against all participants in the fight.[170]

The result of this organized action was clear: victory. After "being rebuffed by the president," Ogletree said, "we thought that we were up against the university as well as the Evanston legal court system."[171] Prior to this experience, university officials had seemed comfortable in ignoring the students as individuals with particular demands. But now the students recognized that "as a unified Black front, they had power."[172] "That experience did help pull us together," as Ogletree recounted.

The feeling of power, however, would soon be eclipsed by frustration. By February 1968, the UDC's investigation had yet to produce any outcome. Nearly two months would pass after the initial incident, with two subsequent UDC meetings called to "study the fight," and, according to Hinz, to discuss "broader-gauged implications for life on campus for Negro students."[173] Another six weeks passed without action from the UDC and meanwhile, hostility directed at Black students continued. On March 26, 1968, a full can of beer or soda was thrown from a window of the Sigma Chi house at a Black student who was walking by. The student looked up and saw no one. He continued on his way when he heard a man's voice coming from the house: "Next time it will be between your eyes."[174]

Northwestern's Dean of Men Seward Weber recounted this and other incidents allegedly involving Sigma Chi members. The alleged incidents, not all of which were directed at Black students, included vandalism, hazing, firing BB pellets, setting fires, turning a fire hose on a group of female students in a parking lot, and throwing firecrackers out of house windows. In a letter to Sigma Chi's chapter president, Weber wrote that the incidents "leave me with grave misgivings and cast doubt on the ability of your membership to conduct itself in a way commensurate with the academic goals of Northwestern University and the needs of the campus community."[175] If any more incidents occurred that could be confirmed, he warned, he would recommend to Jack Hinz that the chapter be expelled from campus. "This letter shall serve as a formal warning to the members of Sigma Chi that they must comport themselves in a manner more consistent with the academic and intellectual aims of this community," Weber wrote.[176]

Weber's action was taken as he and others tried to maintain some kind of order on what some judged to be an increasingly unruly campus. "I believe that anybody that has come into contact with officer Deese will agree that we cannot afford to lose him," wrote Ted Arndt, head of campus security, in an internal memo in April 1968. Venice Deese, Jr., Northwestern's only Black security guard, had been sitting in his car in a campus parking lot when someone had thrown a full can of Coke at his windshield. This was just one incident that Arndt saw as representative of a new trend which he partly blamed on the students' push for greater autonomy. "To put it in a nutshell," he wrote, "there is no discipline on this campus." In the past, students had been no problem, but after the rise of the Student Power Movement, "student security has become a bigger problem," he noted. As a result, Arndt explained, the campus relationship with the Evanston police department had become strained. University officials had instructed Evanston police that they should not be deployed on campus unless absolutely necessary, since their presence tended to incite students. The local police captain had thus advised his officers to keep off campus property unless directly requested by university officials. Now, when police "see something suspicious on campus as they pass, they call into their station and their station calls us by phone," Arndt reported. "All I am asking is for some help," he pleaded, as he requested additional support for his staff. "I am not sure what autonomy means," he concluded, "but from what I can gather from the students, it means that they can rule themselves or according to one student, we can do as we darn well please."[177]

Arndt's plea came as Northwestern's security force had recently been expanded (from eleven to eighteen officers) and several officers had been issued sidearms, a development that many students vehemently opposed. "Guns are dangerous," an editorial in the *Daily Northwestern* stated. "Their use must be stopped before they prove how dangerous guns can be."[178]

One day after the editorial appeared, on Thursday, April 4, 1968, Martin Luther King, Jr. was shot and killed in Memphis. For the students who were still awaiting some kind of justice in relation to the UDC's investigation into the December 1967 incident, King's murder was simply too much. "There was a feeling of defeat," Ogletree recalls, "because someone who epitomized nonviolence and peaceful protest had just been killed like that."[179] "My reaction," Turner told the *Daily Northwestern*, "was one of deep shock and hurt . . . A man who predicated everything on the belief in love is now dead."[180]

Disheartened and in disbelief, many students were also shocked by some of the responses to King's murder. At an evening Student Senate meeting, held just as the news of King's death was breaking, a debate was underway concerning a long-sought-after "self-rule" or "autonomy" bill which would expand student freedom in campus living units. Student Senate President Barb Caulfield interrupted the proceedings to announce that King had died. The news "stunned the audience for a few seconds" and then "the autonomy discussion resumed."[181] Some students were flabbergasted by the seemingly callous nature of this response. Howie Hill, an associate senator, watched in disbelief as the news was "pushed into the background." Finally, he took the floor. "I'm very deeply concerned about something that happened and the reaction I've just seen to it," he said.[182] In response, the Senate gave "hasty approval" to draft a letter to President Miller and Dean Hinz, "urging a strong NU corporate stand for stricter Evanston open occupancy laws."[183] The meeting closed with a moment of silence.[184]

On Friday, April 5, the day after King's death, flags on campus were flown at half-mast.[185] The university announced that the campus would close on April 9, the day scheduled for King's funeral. An official campus memorial service was being planned and an invitation was extended to a few

Black students to speak at the service. It was declined. On that day, many Black students held their own memorial service at Harris Hall and others attended one held in Evanston by city residents.[186]

As the weekend approached, it was clear that all over the country the reaction to King's murder would soon find physical expression in a form of grief and anger: rioting. King's assassination sparked uprisings across the United States. Chicago would be in chaos following the riots that broke out on April 5. After a weekend of violence, the city was placed under curfew with 16,000 federal troops, National Guard members, and police officers deployed to patrol the streets. The days and nights of looting and arson destroyed or damaged several hundred buildings and left hundreds of residents homeless. Twenty-eight blocks of the city lay in ruin. Hundreds of people had been injured.[187]

Many students came from the neighborhoods affected by the riots. And soon, they mobilized to provide assistance to those left homeless in the wake of the violence, eventually raising $1,570.[188] About two hundred student volunteers, including many FMO and AASU members, collected six truckloads of food and clothing to donate to city residents.[189] John Bracey and Wayne Watson drove one of the trucks downtown to distribute to residents in the heavily-patrolled neighborhoods.[190] On Saturday, April 6, at a Simon and Garfunkel concert held on campus, students collected an additional $700 in contributions "to aid Chicago riot victims."[191]

By Monday morning, some university employees were unable to get to campus from their homes in the areas affected by the riots and fires; two employees were now homeless as a result of the fires; and a graduate student had been injured while driving his car in Chicago's Near North Side on Friday afternoon.[192] But all was reportedly calm at Northwestern, which "had been quiet during the weekend of Chicago's troubles."[193] Ted Arndt credited the calm at Northwestern to Officer Deese. "If it had not been for his fine work," Arndt wrote one week after the riots, "we would have had trouble on the campus. We were advised that the white students on campus were going to cause trouble with the colored students. The colored and white situation on the north campus is not good and Officer Deese has been working with this matter. He put in many overtime hours on his own, which he has not been paid for."[194]

On Wednesday, Jack Hinz, "tanned and relaxed," returned to campus after a long postponed vacation in Florida.[195] Hinz had made the decision to get away for a while, thinking that after the Sigma Chi incident and others, "student disturbances at Northwestern might have quieted down a bit."[196] In his absence, though, "Northwestern experienced one of the most active periods of the year," and Dean of Men Seward Weber, who assumed Hinz's duties while he was gone, had an "embarrassing and difficult week." But, as

"King is Dead."
(Northwestern *Syllabus* Yearbook, 1969, photograph by Gary Price)

Weber said confidently, "I'm sure we'll get back on track now."[197]

The week had indeed been difficult. There was now a palpable mood of "tension, distrust, fear" on campus, as *Daily Northwestern* reporter, Bob Greene, observed.[198] Many people were on high alert, fearing that violence would break out in Evanston, a concern that even prompted some white students to leave campus temporarily.[199] At least one "riot-related" incident in Evanston occurred: a fire was set at local junior high. But a story was now circulating that a student had been reportedly attacked on campus by three unidentified Black men who fled after cutting him with a razor.[200] Along with other rumors, this story, which was reported in the *Daily Northwestern,* fed an irrational paranoia among many white students. Now, Black students "walking into a crowded room," reported James Pitts, "could bring it to almost complete silence."[201] Bob Greene saw the same thing. When two

Black students arrived at a dance over the weekend, the all-white crowd responded collectively: "The room quieted for an embarrassed moment, then conversation started again," he reported. "People were on edge. In a few minutes, the blacks left the party."[202] "Everywhere on campus," Greene noted, "rumors made their way from person to person. There was talk of a planned nighttime riot, talk of Northwestern blacks going downtown to take part in the disorders there. Nobody knew for sure; nobody bothered to ask."[203] And now, "there was little talk between groups of whites and blacks. Just whispered, scared, unknowing distrust." [204]

On Wednesday, April 10, a group of Black students assembled for a private meeting in Hardy Lounge in Scott Hall. They covered the window with newspaper so that no one could see inside. They talked quietly and reportedly would not let anyone else enter.[205] Aside from their grief and anger, they were insulted that "they were being watched as potential threats to white property and persons."[206] "What is it all about?" Ogletree recalls thinking at the time, "many of us had come from those various neighborhoods where

Students gather after the assassination of Martin Luther King, Jr., Northwestern University, April 1968. (Northwestern University Archives)

the rioting was occurring."[207] The fact that so many white students automatically viewed Black students as threats to their own safety was insulting and infuriating. "I think that did make us become more militant in our stance," Ogletree later reflected. Following the December 1967 incident with Sigma Chi, this was the second of two key experiences that would unite the students and ultimately transform what they previously defined as their *concerns* into their *demands*, as Ogletree explained.[208]

Indeed, the frustration and anger the students already felt would be intensified by King's murder. According to James Pitts, the killing of King and the reactions by some white students caused a "majority of Black students to come to the conclusion that liberal as well as conservative whites were committed to the repression of blacks."[209] King's assassination would prove to transform many other students across the country as well, compelling them to agree that they needed to act more directly and boldly. During the 1967-1968 school year, 150 campuses across the U.S. would experience some kind of protest led by Black students, and the majority of them occurred after King's death.[210] "At Northwestern, the closing of ranks among Black students was immediately evident," Pitts observed of the effect of King's assassination.[211] "That's how things kind of elevated," Ogletree reflected, "and then by the end of the month, we were in the situation of having the takeover."[212]

King's murder would also provoke others into action. On April 10, Hinz announced that the university had granted approval for Kappa Alpha Psi and Alpha Phi Alpha to return to campus. Also approved was the request of Alpha Kappa Alpha sorority to apply for official recognition.[213] It had been eighteen months since students first requested the reinstatement of the Greek letter groups and many reacted positively to the news. "It's about time we got action," said Stanley Hill, president of Northwestern's Alpha Phi Alpha chapter. But others remained frustrated. "It took them too long to make a decision," Dan Davis told the *Daily Northwestern*.[214]

In voting to authorize the groups, members of the Council on Undergraduate Life made it "clear that we do not feel that recognition of these predominately Negro groups would constitute an adequate response from the University for satisfying Negro students' present social needs." And they pledged that "[a]dditional efforts should be made in this direction."[215] Some white students predicted that the decision would only compel Black students to continue to "withdraw" from the greater university community. "The desire of many Northwestern black students for separate but equal social groups has been fulfilled with the rechartering of Kappa Alpha Psi and Alpha Phi Alpha fraternity," wrote Tom Davies in the *Daily Northwestern*.[216]

Just after the assassination, a group of students and faculty also sought to make good on the renewed pledge to demand that the university support the passage of an open housing law in Evanston. They drafted a set of demands and organized a march and a rally to be held on campus. At the rally, a crowd of more than three hundred formed to listen to speeches by Roger Friedman and Mathematics Professor Michael Marcus. There, they revealed several demands: the university must urge the city of Evanston to close all businesses on the day of King's funeral, as "a fitting tribute to the funeral of Dr. King;"[217] the university must make a substantial donation to the Southern Christian Leadership Conference for the Poor People's Commission as a memorial to King; there must be open occupancy law passed in Evanston; and Northwestern must desegregate all of its real estate holdings (which, it should be noted of this final demand, the university continuously stated had already been fulfilled.)[218]

But in all of this, some observed, there was an "obvious lack of black student support." "Why should we go?" senior Roger Ward answered when asked by the *Daily Northwestern* why no Black students attended the campus memorial service for King or the open housing march and rally. "[W]e decided to let you do it a while," Ward, who would soon take part in the takeover, explained. "You created the problems. You solve them. Everybody knows the blacks want it; we have to see if the whites want it."[219]

After months of being treated as objects and feeling the threats and injustices of racism, after weeks of holding ineffective meetings with officials, and after long hours communicating with other groups around the country and sharing strategies, Vernon Ford, Roger Ward, Kathryn Ogletree, James Turner, John Bracey, and more than one hundred other students were ready to take things into their own hands, set their own standards, and let administrators know that doing nothing—and remaining silent—was no longer an option.

Chapter 5

Petition

Student Reactions Mixed Over King's Death. Prayers, Plans and Riots are Outlets for Grief

Headline, *Chicago Defender*, April 8, 1968

We, the Black students at Northwestern University have found the academic, cultural, and social conditions for us on campus deplorably limited. In order to counteract the physical, emotional, and spiritual strains we have been subjugated to, in order to find some meaning and purpose in our being here, we demand that the following conditions be immediately met.

Preamble to the students' demands submitted to Northwestern administrators on April 22, 1968[1]

In the days after King's assassination, there was widespread talk that the nonviolent protest movement was now at an end. The uprisings, some speculated, seemed to signal that violence might be the preferred response to social injustice for the foreseeable future. But in Evanston, a group of Northwestern students had already begun work on *their* chosen response. They were moving forward, systematically, efficiently, and with a clear plan. "All these things are happening consecutively, simultaneously," Kathryn Ogletree remembers of the flurry of activity in the wake of King's death, a critical time when the students decided to proceed with formalizing their demands into a petition.[2] They would present the petition to administrators just nineteen days after King's murder.

By the time they were drafting their demands, members of AASU and FMO were working in tandem. FMO members had already contributed to "the development of the demands by continually bringing their concerns to campus administrators," while AASU members had helped raise the political awareness and race consciousness of the students, as Ogletree explained.[3] As a result of this partnership, AASU would eventually become fully absorbed within FMO.[4]

Ogletree took the lead in writing, rewriting, and fine-tuning the petition, which the students described as "an official list of grievances that would be submitted for redress."[5] Ogletree explained that the petition was really just a formalized version of the concerns they had already communicated to the administration many times before.[6] "They didn't become demands until after King's assassination," she noted.[7] Up until that time, they had never used the word "demand." But now, things were different. More critical. And certainly more urgent. Several graduate students, including James Turner and John Bracey, worked with Ogletree and the rest of the undergraduates as they all weighed in on the petition. As Ogletree saw it, "We all balanced each other out."[8]

"Northwestern was wrong to assume that in bringing us here, we would be able to dissociate ourselves from the injustices, sufferings, and mounting frustrations of our people," the petition read. "Like them, we, too, are tired of being talked about and we are weary of talking to people who cannot or refuse to do anything else but talk."[9]

The petition included a list of eight general demands. (See Appendix A for the full document.)

1. Northwestern must issue a policy statement "deploring the viciousness of 'white racism' " and pledging that any "conscious or unconscious racist policies, practices, and institutions existing now on campus will no longer be tolerated." Further, the university must state that it is willing "to go to any extent to enforce such a policy and also to protect the interests of the Black students on campus who have been negatively affected by such racist attitudes and practices."

2. Northwestern must pledge to increase the number of Black students admitted to the university. At least half of all incoming Black students must be recruited from inner cities. (This demand was partly crafted in an effort to ensure that the university would not begin to recruit only upper and middle class Black students, as one official had suggested earlier.)

3. There must be an increase in scholarships for Black students in order to cover the amount they currently must earn in working their "required jobs" on campus.

4. Black students must be furnished with their own living unit by the fall of 1968.

5. Courses in Black history, literature, and art must be added to the curriculum. The students must be given the "ultimate decision" on who is hired to teach these courses.

6. In order to help students "properly cope with the psychological, mental and academic tensions resulting from the dualism of our existence as 'black college students,' " the university must hire a counselor for Black students.

7. Students must be provided with a Black student union, as well as office space for FMO and all other Black organizations on campus.

8. The university must desegregate all of its real estate holdings. Evidence of the university's "subsequent progressive measures" related to its publicly stated commitment to open occupancy must be provided to the president of FMO each month.[10]

The students framed their petition within the overall idea that in fulfilling these demands, and particularly by offering Black students their own living unit, officials would "alleviate some of the tension of being 'a Black student at a white university.' "[11] But the prescribed way in which that tension would best be alleviated varied, depending on a student's given perspective. As James Pitts observed, the petition embraced two (conflicting) points of view that were represented among the students: a Black nationalist viewpoint that identified white power structures and their goal of oppressing Black people (reflected in the demands for a policy statement and a separate housing facility, for example) and what Pitts called an "integrationist" perspective that argued for equal treatment and opportunity *within* those power structures (reflected in the demands for increased admission of Black students and increased financial aid, for example).[12] The fact that these two perspectives were combined within the single document reflected the students' dedication to coming together to enact change.

Overall, the demands were crafted with a specificity and focus derived from the students' own experiences. In many ways, the petition can be viewed as a document that addressed the gaps and failures in the university's official integration program. And, while the students' demands were not the same as those made by earlier generations of students (who demanded integrated housing, for example), the petition can be seen as a culmination of a long history. In essence, it reflected the experiences of the many students who had come before them, those who had also faced challenges at Northwestern and who had tried to put an end to discrimination and segregation in decades past.

The students made it clear that they were submitting a set of specific, focused demands. "We are not about to solve America's race problems, if there is in fact a solution," they wrote. "We are concerned about the problem as it affects us on campus and in the city of Evanston."[13] Their call for Northwestern to desegregate all of its real estate holdings was of critical importance since they viewed the university as the "main promoter of segregation" in the city.[14] (For their part, university officials continued to assert that all of Northwestern's real estate holding were integrated and landlords wishing to advertise student housing were required to sign a non-discrimination statement.[15])

But now, there had been "too much idle talk about how to resolve some of the problems facing Black students here at Northwestern," the students asserted.[16] They were willing to "confer" with the administration," they wrote, but had "no intention of debating or conceding our stand. We have been to the administration before but with very little consequence. We want tangible results, not excuses or even promises. The University either responds to our demands or we have no other choice but to respond to its lack of response."[17]

There it was again: a variation on the "or else" clause that had been so effective in the prior negotiation over the Sigma Chi incident.

On Monday afternoon, April 22, 1968, the students submitted their petition to university administrators.[18] The document listed two students as contacts: Kathryn Ogletree and James Turner. The university had until 5 p.m. on Friday, April 26, to respond.

University officials were well aware of increased tension on campus—not only between administrators and Black students—but among all students. As recently as March 1968, President Miller informed the executive committee of the board of trustees that there "were indications of student unrest on the campus." Given "overall campus problems," he warned, there was a possibility that the unrest "might find expression in some form of student action."[19] The students' surprise visit to the president's home in December 1967 had indeed been an indication of the unrest that existed in the months prior to the formal submission of the petition. But officially, at least, university officials considered the April 1968 demands the first "formal notice of grievances" among Black students.[20]

On Wednesday, two days after receiving the petition, Jack Hinz and William Ihlanfeldt held a meeting with the students to discuss their demands. Roughly three-quarters of Northwestern's Black students were in attendance, including Victor Goode, Eric Perkins, Kathryn Ogletree, and James Turner.[21] At the two-hour meeting, the students were reportedly promised that certain demands would be met, others would be considered, and an official response from the university would be forthcoming. Afterward, Turner reported that "some of the issues were resolved (at the meeting) but some of the very important issues are still awaiting decision."[22]

In a seemingly unrelated matter, the next day Hinz appeared at an open meeting, held at the Cahn Auditorium on campus. It was a dramatic moment. Here, Hinz would announce the passage of a long-desired, "Student Self-Determination Bill."

The bill had arisen out of the movement for student autonomy which had "snowballed and crystallized" in recent weeks. In fact, the issue of student autonomy (often referred to as "self-determination") had reached fever pitch in recent months, following the Student Senate's unanimous passage of a student bill of rights in February 1968. That bill included a list of twenty-two student rights, including the right to freedom of association and the right to privacy. In a push for official recognition of the bill of rights, students were asking the administration to embrace the concept of student autonomy, hoping, ultimately, to force the university to abandon the concept of *in loco parentis*. In their campaign, they targeted their efforts on pressuring officials to lift various campus rules governing student living situations, arguing that students should "have the right to make their own rules on non-academic matters."[23] For well over a year, there would be "an almost endless hassle" over both the "format and content" of the student bill of rights.[24] But for now, after much debate and negotiation between members of the Student Senate and the Council on Undergraduate Life, students were being granted *some rights*: the freedom to follow their own rules (self-regulation) within campus living units, known as "self-rule."[25]

At first, university officials opposed any such measure, pledging "to meet the speeding autonomy drive with strict enforcement of existing rules."[26] But throughout the spring of 1968, they began to reconsider their stance in the face of mounting opposition. Newly-elected Student Senate President Fran Shanahan declared that students' rights to "social freedom" were not negotiable, while Roger Friedman and George Vickers proposed staging a sit-in or a student strike to force the administration to support students' rights.[27] Recently, in a show of force, thirty first-year female students staged a walkout from their dormitory, Allison Hall. In defiance of curfew, they left their housing unit at half-past midnight in an action that was orchestrated, they explained, to "show they weren't confused about their personal concepts of what autonomy is and how they were going to use it."[28]

The 1968 campaign for student autonomy had been foreshadowed by the Student Power Movement led by Ellis Pines. Just one year earlier, the Student Senate had denounced the SPM. At the time, SPM leaders had drafted an open letter to the university community which included "a four-part plan for the advancement of student rights."[29] "The rights campaign would continue," Pines and his colleagues had asserted then, "until significant change is achieved."[30] And now, many of the changes about to be enacted had been originally advocated by Pines, Friedman, and other SPM members.

Hinz entered the packed hall to announce that students had been freed (to some degree) from living under many of the university's restrictions governing their social life. "The university," Hinz told the audience of three hundred students, would now extend more "freedoms" to all Northwestern students, such as allowing those over the age of twenty-one to have alcohol in their dormitory rooms and extending the length of time male and female students could visit each other in the dormitories (parietal hours). Additionally, curfews for all students (except first-quarter first-year female students) would be eliminated. "This is not a license to do as one pleases," Hinz told students. "It puts responsibility on the students. We're betting on you."[31]

"I feel a little like Winston Churchill," Hinz said, in making his announcements, his "voice heavy with fatigue and emotion."[32] It had been a long hard battle to pass the bill. Hinz left the auditorium to a standing ovation. But before he did, he addressed one more issue. "[R]acism cannot be allowed to exist at Northwestern," he told the audience.[33] "Students must remember that the problem of racial tension is their most personal concern. I hope you'll not let that thought out of your mind for some time to come."[34]

Despite Hinz's statement, many Black students must have found the announcement of these new "freedoms" particularly hard to accept in light of their own situation. It appeared that officials were apparently capable of responding to the demands of some students while doing little to address the needs of others. After all, neither the student bill of rights nor the Student Self-Determination Bill addressed, in any real way, issues of racism or discrimination, and some felt that the white students' recent, and almost exclusive, focus on student autonomy had eclipsed any other campus issue.[35] Compared to the previous spring, which had seen the rise of the SPM, there now seemed, as James Pitts observed, "much less public passion displayed in crusading for the improved welfare of blacks on campus or in the Evanston community."[36]

Spring comes to Northwestern, Deering Meadow,
Northwestern University
(Northwestern *Syllabus* Yearbook, 1969)

Rite of Spring

N. U. Students Cavort Thru Spring Rites

Chicago Tribune, April 27, 1968

During the week that unfolded after the students submitted their demands and waited for the university's official response, much of the Northwestern campus was undergoing spring fever, with temperatures soaring into the sixties after a bitterly cold winter. The final weeks of the spring quarter were playing out, and it appeared as though all was serene, if a bit countercultural, at Northwestern.

That spring, the looming issue of the war in Vietnam had become more visible on campus. President Miller announced that those who had been admitted to Northwestern but were drafted before enrolling would be given the highest "readmission" priority, while Payson Wild announced that plans for a major expansion of faculty had been temporarily halted, largely as a result of university's expected revenue loss due to the war.[37] Now, a (still) small but increasing number of students were becoming more active in the movement against the war and they joined forces with other area protest organizations. On April 26, students would take part in a worldwide student strike to protest the war, racial oppression, and the draft. (Officials reported that the strike had no effect on campus operations.)[38]

But amidst all of this, little attention was being paid to the Black students' petition. In fact, no one beyond a small circle of administrators and the students themselves was even aware that it existed. While the students were meeting with Hinz and Ihlanfeldt on Wednesday, much of the attention of the greater student body was drawn elsewhere. About 900 students crowded into Tech Hall to see actor Dustin Hoffman, who had recently been nominated for an Academy Award for his role in the 1967 film, *The Graduate*. "The coeds wouldn't stop screaming to hear him speak," the *Daily Northwestern* reported. Once they did, it was clear that Hoffman was there on serious business: to take a stand against the Vietnam War and to endorse Senator Eugene McCarthy for the Democratic presidential nomination. "I won't lie to you," a grinning Hoffman told the standing-room-only crowd. "You make me very nervous."[39] He admitted that he had been instructed not to oppose the war publicly, that it would "hurt my box office," he said. But he did so anyway, urging those old enough to vote in the upcoming primary election to cast their ballots for the anti-war candidate, McCarthy.[40]

Two days after Hoffman's appearance was the deadline for the university's response. But on that day, Friday, April 26, much of the campus was again distracted: about 800 students gathered on the expansive green of Deering Meadow to dance, fly kites, blow bubbles, and "cavort" with two students dressed in gorilla costumes. This was a celebration, the students announced, of the "rite of spring."[41] "Bring a flower," a poster advertising the event read. "Do whatever you want to do," explained Michael Levine, the event's organizer, after a *Daily Northwestern* reporter asked what the purpose of the event was. "I just can't define this thing," he said, "because it would turn people off."[42] (Levine also admitted that he had not applied for permission to stage the event, even though he was required to. "If there's any charge for grass in this world," he countered, "then there's no sense in being in this world.")[43]

During the rite of spring event, there is no doubt that some students carried with them copies of that day's edition of the *Daily Northwestern*, now under the direction of a newly appointed student editor, John Walter.[44] On the front page were three photographs of Hinz, addressing students from the podium as he announced the "new freedoms" the day before. "NU Grants Self-Rule" announced the banner headline. Beneath the fold, so to speak, another headline appeared: "NU Black Students Make Demands of University." The article, which paraphrased the students' demands, ran after a "third party" leaked a copy of the petition to the newspaper the day before.[45] The unnamed source was reportedly neither part of the administration nor an FMO or AASU member. In fact, the paper reported, an unidentified Black student leader had "sought to withhold the text from publication because negotiations, he said, now are at a crucial stage."[46] Despite any effort on the part of the students to maintain silence while they awaited an official response, there was now a growing awareness of the tension that was brewing between Black students and the administration.

Jack Hinz announcing the passage of self-rule, Northwestern University, April 25, 1968.
("Nu Grants Self Rule," *Daily Northwestern*, April 26, 1968)

Later that same day, the administration issued its formal response to the petition.[47] (See Appendix B for the full document.)

"Racism of any character has no place at Northwestern," the seven page document, signed by Hinz, began.[48] The "university deplores incidents that have racial implications," it continued, "and asserts its determination to prevent any such events and to use its authority to employ disciplinary measures against those who violate the rights of others." The document went on to trace a basic history of the university's efforts to recruit Black students and the success of its first steps to diversify the campus. It also pledged that "increasing efforts will be made to improve the social and cultural welfare of all students," citing a recently drafted UDC report on issues facing Black students as an example of this effort.

In response to the students' specific demands, administrators pledged to continue to recruit Black students to the university and they welcomed "black students in University admissions activities."[49] Officials agreed to allow Black students to have a "separate meeting room." They would also reactivate the university's human relations committee in order "to hear grievances of minority students."[50] A counselor for Black students, Calvin Smith, had recently been hired and would begin work in September 1968. Smith, a graduate student in history at Northwestern, had accepted the position just a week after the assassination of Martin Luther King, Jr. He would work jointly in the admissions office and the office of the dean of students.[51] Administrators also supported the hiring of more Black faculty members and welcomed recommendations from the students. But the students were advised to take their specific demands concerning courses and curriculum directly to department chairs and committees.[52]

As far as financial aid went, the document stated that all loan and job offers were "optional" for students. It further explained that the amount of financial aid Northwestern was able to offer students with "demonstrated need" had made it possible to recruit more students. Without those jobs and loans, the number of "financial aid students" who had been "assisted in the past two entering classes at Northwestern would have been reduced by one-third."[53] The only suggestion to students "to help alleviate" their financial burden was that they should make use of the recently launched (1967) "summer job placement program." There, students might find available work study jobs "working with youth in innercity Chicago." "Because of the increasing needs for educated young men and women to work with innercity youth," the document advised, "the University encourages members of the black student community to seek such summer employment."[54]

Finally, the university rejected the demand for a separate living facility for Black students. "The housing policy of Northwestern University is not predicated upon any consideration of race, color, or creed of the applicant," the document stated, arguing that the university "strongly believes that organizing separate living for Black students is self-defeating and cannot contribute constructively to the academic purposes for which the University exists."[55] The document explained that not only was there presently a "severe shortage of on-campus housing," but there was also a philosophy behind the university's unwillingness to fulfill the demand for separate housing: The function of university housing, the document stated, "depends on a mixture of student types which cannot be achieved if certain groups are segregated from the rest of the living environment."[56] Without explicitly describing the problem of white roommates changing rooms once they learned they were to live with Black roommates, the document stated that as of January 1968, a sentence had been added to the housing information statement sent out to all incoming students: "All roommate assignments will be considered binding for all parties throughout the first academic quarter."[57]

The document nominally addressed all of the basic issues related to the students' demands: admission, scholarship, housing, curriculum, counseling, facilities, and open occupancy. But, as the students would soon assert, the administration's response had "rejected the basic principles on which our demands were based."[58] Professor Christopher Lasch would later tell the *Daily Northwestern* that the university's reply had been "lousy" and "weak." "It was just a rhetorical commitment to equality which bypasses the point about the needs of black students," he said.[59] Other faculty members chimed in, expressing their support, "in spirit and principle," for the students' demands.[60]

Some students recognized that Hinz was attempting to offer them *something.* "I think he probably had some things in the works," Ogletree reflected. But she also knew that Hinz alone lacked the authority to enact any real changes, and ultimately, that was the reason that "nothing crucial had happened" up to this point.[61] Moreover, the university's response ignored the students' fundamental concerns and their more politically focused demands, such as the role Northwestern played as a "white institution." Instead, it largely called for the students *themselves* to act. "While the crises which confront the nation and the university warrant the depth of this concern," the document stated, "it is essential that all members of the university act responsibly and with accountability in helping achieve the objectives of equal rights and dignity for all."[62]

After receiving the response on Friday, the students waited for three days believing that officials would offer another round of private negotiations to address their demands further. Three days later, on Monday, April 29, Hinz made public two documents: the university's formal response to the students' demands and a statement, dated April 15, 1968, from the University Discipline Committee concerning, among other things, the fight near the Sigma Chi Fraternity house in December 1967.[63] The UDC statement was later described by Hinz (who was chair of the UDC) as "an intensive study of the racial problems of black students on campus."[64] It reiterated some of the promises made in the university's response to the petition and offered a lengthy list of recommendations, including the hiring of Black staff members in student affairs; providing university facilities for Black students for meeting and social activities; pressing for "changes in all social groups and other organizations that will end de facto segregation;" and convening "a series of campus-wide meetings addressed to the problems facing a predominantly white academic community attempting to adjust to the new reality of a multiracial campus."[65] The statement concluded with the observation: "it is not integration or separatism which is at the center of current concern—it is rather for the entire university to modify institutions and attitudes of racism and recognize the Black student's existence, his right to be an individual, and the reasonableness of having his own values and goals respected."[66] The report also included the outcome of the UDC's investigation into the December 1967 fight: five students, three white students and two Black students, had been placed on disciplinary warning for their involvement in the incident.[67]

Although much of what was contained in the UDC report was in line with many of the students' demands, it was not a tool to effect any real reform. As many students saw it, it was purely rhetorical, and once more, full of promises. "We were working on things," Hinz said of the administration's efforts.[68] But he admitted that their handling of the whole situation had been inadequate. "[W]e were probably guilty of dragging our feet," he said, "partly because we didn't know what to do. And partly because we knew we couldn't do it all."[69] He also admitted to feeling some degree of frustration and disappointment. "I might very well have thought, well, you know, I tried very hard to diversify this community and bring these students here, and why aren't they more appreciative?"[70] Still, that attitude didn't last long. For, as Hinz said, "You can't spend a lot of time with that attitude and move things to a better place. I wanted to solve the problem."[71]

Hinz seemed to convey a deep understanding of the underlying issues related to the students' demands. The demands were not only about tangible things (curriculum, meeting rooms, dorms); they were also about attitudes, history, and culture. These were the issues that needed to be addressed before any real change could occur. Behavior could only be altered if the beliefs motivating that behavior could be transformed. Thus, Hinz asserted that the university must respond "more aggressively to the pressing social and cultural deficiencies in the campus community."[72] It was, he felt, "imperative" that Black students not be asked to "wait any longer to be accorded the respect and concern they deserve from this community."[73] But such demands, it appeared, were clearly difficult to meet, and for the most part, they seemed to be impossible to meet, given the fact that it seemed to be Hinz alone in the administration who was urging such a seismic shift in the university's collective attitude.

By the end of the day on Monday, April 29, the students had heard nothing directly from Hinz or any other administrator; no continued discussions were, apparently, in the works. In the eyes of administrators it seemed that the formal response, along with the UDC report, was sufficient to end the conversation.

"Black students have nothing at Northwestern University to call our own," the students had asserted in their petition. They were now ready to change that. They were ready to find another way to make themselves heard, to get the attention of administrators, and "make them confront the issues."[74] They would somehow make visible the so-called "invisible" to everyone.

Confrontation

There could be a physical manifestation of the next exchange between us and the university.

James Turner, Thursday, May 2, 1968[75]

Black students on campus see efforts to end racism on campus as a white responsibility. Racism was created by us (whites) and perpetuated by us and is therefore our obligation to end it.

Rolf Schulze, Northwestern sociology professor, May 1968[76]

Just twelve days would elapse between the submission of the students' demands and the beginning of the takeover. During this momentous period, tensions over a fair housing ordinance were heating up in Evanston, fueled by King's assassination. On April 11, 1968, the federal Fair Housing Act was signed into law by President Lyndon Johnson.[77] The act expanded existing laws and prohibited discrimination in the sale, rental, and financing of housing based on race, religion, and national origin. Many local governments had also passed their own fair housing laws, but still no such law existed in Evanston. In the days after King's death, Northwestern students and hundreds of Evanston residents took part in marches through the city in an effort to pressure the city council to pass an ordinance against housing discrimination.[78] The movement's leaders stated "emphatically and unequivocally" that if an ordinance was not passed on or before April 29, 1968, they would move "from non-violent protest . . . to nonviolent resistance," involving an "economic boycott of all Evanston businesses, transportation systems, and profit making operations within the city limit of Evanston."[79]

On April 29, the city council finally agreed to vote on an ordinance. That evening, two hundred people packed into the city hall chamber, while outside, a crowd of six hundred gathered to await the vote. Fifteen to one, city council members voted to pass the ordinance, forbidding discrimination in the sale or rental of housing and setting steep fines for brokers, realtors, and others who practiced discrimination.[80] The victory had come after years of organizing, strategizing, and keeping pressure on officials. For many Black students at Northwestern, who had also worked to bring fair housing to Evanston, this victory shored up their resolve that real change only comes when pressure is put upon those in power.

Meanwhile, the students were working on another version of their petition, what they would refer to as their "final demands." On Tuesday, April 30, James Turner held a press conference where he announced that the students had rejected the university's formal response to their petition, calling it a "public relations release."[81] "The whole idea of the legitimacy of our needs has been cast aside by their power," Turner asserted. "They have made a mockery of something we took very seriously."[82] At the April 24 meeting between students and officials, administrators had made specific promises, and now they were "reversing themselves" on those agreements.[83] The administration was acting in bad faith, Turner said. "It is an insult to our intelligence."[84]

Turner also denounced the outcome of the UDC's investigation into the December 1967 fight.[85] Arguing that the Black students had been the victims in that incident, he accused the university of trying to intimidate the two Black students who had been placed on disciplinary warning by the UDC.[86] The letters sent to the students, notifying them of their punishment, were a form of "intimidation," he said.[87] Justice had not been served in the case, and Turner called for it to be reopened.[88]

Turner announced that the students would hold another press conference on Thursday, May 2. There, they would release their final demands which would show, "point by point," why they rejected the university's response.[89] They would also outline a planned "confrontation" between Black students and the administration.[90] Turner invited Northwestern's white students, along with residents from Evanston, to take part in the undefined confrontation.

In response, SDS member and former SPM member, Roger Friedman, said he'd wait to find out just what the confrontation entailed before joining.[91] But Steven Lubet, SDS president, said he was interested in taking part. "Whenever a group of people has been exploited for 400 years like the blacks in this country have," he told the *Daily Northwestern*, "there are no demands that should be unreasonable, they should ask for everything they can get and take."[92]

On Tuesday night, Hinz was informed that the students had rejected the university's response to their petition. The response had been "as reasonable a response as we could make," Hinz told the *Daily Northwestern*.[93] The next day, Wednesday, May 1, Hinz "issued a plea for 'continued communication' between black students and the white university community."[94] In a meeting with members of the Council on Undergraduate Life, Hinz said, "I have no special wisdom to offer you at this time. I only pray we can discuss and try to resolve with students the things that must be done."[95]

Thursday, May 2, (the day before the takeover) was a beautiful sunny day. Students played Frisbee on Deering Meadow and relaxed and sunbathed on the grass. *Daily Northwestern* reporter Joann Lublin set out to interview white students about what was transpiring between the Black students and administrators. "[T]he sunshine was so warm," Lublin reported, "and the lake looked so enticing that not too many white students bothered to discuss the implications of the black demands."[96]

But, in an indication that some kind of action planning was now in full swing, one student said his Black friends had been missing from class that day. Most others admitted that they really knew very little about what had led to the students' demands, but they responded with sympathy, support, opposition, and outright fear concerning "what the consequences would be if their demands were not met."[97] "[W]hite kids are prejudiced," one student told Lublin, "but they won't admit it."[98] Another argued that the Black students "don't have any right to do what they're doing. They're not running the university."[99] And another observed: "white students are aware of it (the black crisis) but it hasn't affected them firsthand."[100]

Later that day, at 1:30 p.m., the students held their press conference in Scott Hall. There, they would reveal their final demands. Four students, James Turner, Kathryn Ogletree, Michael Smith, and Leslie Harris, took their places in front of the microphones. Turner made it clear that he wanted to speak only to members of the press and he requested that all Northwestern staff members leave the room. After objecting to this request, Sam Saran, Northwestern's director of public relations, departed. Assistant Dean of Men James F. Stull was told that he was not welcome as he tried to enter the room.

This was, the students announced, the last time that they would address their demands.[101] Turner described the long road that led to the drafting of their petition, including "a series of events on the campus over the last one-and-a-half years," the fight on December 2, 1967, and other racist incidents on campus.[102] He recounted how the students had taken their grievances to the administration time and again, but to no avail.[103]

"We have persisted," Turner said. "But we have reached the point where we find that the university is more concerned with eloquent statements than with solving the problems that affect us."[104] Turner reviewed the events of the last two weeks, including the university's response to their April 22 demands, a response which the students had rejected, describing it as unsatisfactory.[105]

Now, Turner announced, the students were submitting a revised and clarified final version of their demands, copies of which they provided to the press.[106] The document included a "point by point rejection" of the administration's response and significantly expanded the first version of the petition. It included the original eight demands and provided a breakdown of each demand into fourteen specific issues.[107] (See Appendix C for the full document).

"The university," the document read, "must show itself flexible enough to take in the 'peculiarities' of our culture and background. The only way, we feel, the university can display its understanding and flexibility is by the immediate approval and implementation of those demands submitted by the black student body."[108]

At the heart of the document was a call to "alter the racist structure" of the university.[109] The students demanded that the university realize and openly acknowledge "the extent of racism in American society," and they called for a policy statement to be issued by President Miller "asserting that the racism of American society which has penetrated all American institutions has also penetrated Northwestern University, and has thus affected the social and academic life here."[110]

This final version embraced more fully than the first a Black nationalist point of view. "No white institution can right our hundreds of years of history and experience by suddenly treating us the same as white people," it stated, "and call it justice and equality."[111] The students called for a declaration from the university that it would attempt to "provide a multi-racial and cultural society within the university walls and that any racist attacks and/or abuses shall be considered in direct opposition to the University's goals and a danger to the peaceful existence of such a society."[112] Those guilty of committing such acts, they asserted, must be "excluded from this institution."[113]

The document also made it clear that the students were demanding justice. To that end, they called for a reform of the university's "judiciary structures, attitudes, and practices."[114] The document cited specific encounters with Sigma Chi and Fiji as examples of the racism on campus that had not been dealt with effectively by the UDC. The students also denounced the UDC decision in the case related to the December 1967 incident, calling that decision "unacceptable in our eyes."[115] Making it clear that the UDC was "ineffective in dealing with racism on campus," they called for an overhaul of the entire judiciary system at Northwestern.[116] "Justice for Black people," the document advised, "at this time does not mean equal treatment before a law or rule which is insensitive to our oppressive position in this country."[117]

The document went on to elaborate earlier demands, citing admissions, scholarships, financial aid, housing, curriculum, counseling, facilities, open occupancy, and other areas for redress. It contextualized the issues faced by students by placing them squarely within a larger picture of an oppressive and unequal economic and political system within the United States. And it also addressed the process of integration itself: "We realize that the factors leading to our presently being students at Northwestern were basically politically motivated and had little or nothing to do with a social interest in the plight of Black people in America. Being brought here essentially for purposes of exploitation, Northwestern has subsequently shown little interest in our needs except for those which were compatible with theirs. Therefore, the main responsibility for reconciling the tension between us lies with the Administration and not with us."[118] "The legitimacy of these demands cannot be debated," the document concluded.[119]

"This is a call for *autonomy for black students*, for self determination on matters that concern us," Turner announced at the press conference, clearly echoing the recent movement for student autonomy at Northwestern.[120] "We're not asking for any control of this university outside the things that affect only us," he stated.[121] As far as any imminent confrontation went, Turner did not elaborate further. "We want to hold down an explosion on the campus," he noted. "If the response is positive, then we can see the way to affirmative talks."[122]

Would Northwestern become another Columbia? someone asked, referring to the recent protests and use of police force on that campus. "I should hope that Miller and Hinz are more enlightened men than they have there," Turner answered.[123] Ultimately, he instructed, the university had no choice but to approve and implement their demands.[124] This would be the last time the students would make any comments. The university had until "around dinner time" that day to respond.[125]

Meanwhile, the students were readying themselves for that imminent confrontation Turner had mentioned, although it had yet to be determined precisely what that would entail. Those details would be worked out in a closed and "completely secret" meeting held later that same day, on Thursday, May 2.[126] The meeting was "packed," as Bracey remembers. There, the students voted to pursue further action.[127] "And whatever was going to happen," Ogletree remembers, would "happen tomorrow."[128]

Planning the Takeover

All we can say is that if our demands are impossible, then peace between us is impossible too.[129]

Final Demands, 1968

After agreeing to move forward, the students now had to determine what action to take. Several ideas were considered, including having everyone show up at the registrar's office and ask for transfers to HBCUs; taking over the university president's office, as the students at Columbia had done; or occupying a university building.[130]

Bracey's recommendation was that the students collectively request to transfer out of Northwestern since only then, he argued, would the administration respond. "They need you here more than you need them," he said. Some students objected to the idea; what if the administration did nothing and they were all forced to leave? "But that's not going to happen," Bracey answered. "Because it would be too much of an embarrassment to Northwestern if you all walked away from it." He continued: "They have this image they're trying to project and you would be the direct repudiation of that image, that this is nonsense, that you don't want to participate in it, and that's the leverage you have . . . That would be on the front page of every paper in Chicago."[131] And, as Bracey explained, "Nobody likes chaos. Everybody likes things to be normal. [Administrators] realize that you have the potential for disrupting things. It's to their advantage to figure out how to work out something so you don't have to do that."[132]

But as the debate continued, a consensus emerged that taking over a university building would offer the best way to bring attention to the situation at Northwestern and compel administrators to implement their demands. And, in the true fashion of civil rights activism and nonviolent protest, such an action would also disrupt and impede "business as usual" from taking place at Northwestern. A collective transfer would ultimately impact the students themselves more than anything. Occupying the president's office was dismissed as an idea since it might not elicit an immediate and highly visible response from the administration. The students had learned through their study of student actions at other universities that an occupation of a critical building, one central to the university's financial and business operations, would be most effective.[133]

After the options were debated, the students took a vote. A majority voted to occupy a university building, staging a takeover until the university met their demands. Now, there was little time to muse over any concerns or hesitate; the plan had to be put in place rapidly. According to Ogletree, AASU members "directed the tactical aspects of the takeover,"[134] while FMO members took on a variety of related tasks. Various committees were tasked with collecting necessary supplies and renting a truck to bring those supplies to the building after it had been occupied. Others were given the job of purchasing locks and chains to secure the building's doors and windows. And still others focused on executing a public relations and media strategy.

Bracey reached out to his many connections in local civil rights groups and activist organizations in order to build a network of support. Without disclosing the precise nature of the forthcoming action, he also communicated with his contacts in the media, including a reporter at the *Chicago Sun-Times*. "We knew they were going to distort what we said," Bracey said of the press in general, and so he reached out to those he knew would be fair and even sympathetic in their reporting.[135]

A small group of students, including Steve Colson and Andre Bell, were tasked with selecting the building to be occupied. They soon chose the Bursar's Office, but only after a quick, but thorough assessment had been conducted. This included investigating campus security schedules, establishing planned entry points and exit routes to and from the building, and investigating rumors concerning the existence of an underground tunnel that connected the Rebecca Crown Center building with the Bursar's Office. Colson and Bell were reportedly assisted in their planning by a few students who had work-study jobs in the Bursar's Office.[136] After their investigation, they concluded that a takeover of that building was feasible. They would shut down the university's central financial building at 619 Clark Street until the university met their demands. Or else.

The vast majority of the students, including Kathryn Ogletree, would not know which building they were going to occupy until they were approaching it the next morning, Friday, May 3, 1968. They were only told to assemble at an alley off Clark Street at 6:30 a.m. the next morning. What would come next would remain unknown to most of the students until the moment arrived for the takeover.

Keeping the building's identity secret—known to just a handful of students—was key to their action. In part, they modeled the planning and execution of the takeover after lessons learned from the 1966 film, *The Battle of Algiers*, which documented Algeria's recent and victorious fight for independence from colonial France.[137] Thus, the students operated under a committee structure, with subsets of small "cells," composed of two or three students. "Everyone had different tasks," Ogletree recalled. "There was a division of labor."[138] The cell members worked together, only knowing the nature of their own task and not the entirety of the whole operation.

With the overall plan known only to very few, secrecy could be more easily maintained.[139] In fact, at the meeting the night before the takeover, Bracey encouraged the leadership to announce that they were going to take over Northwestern's administration building, the Rebecca Crown Center. "Why do that?" someone asked. Bracey responded: "Because there's a hundred people in this room and at least one of them is going to tell the administration. And it's not because they want to sell you out . . . But they're going to think they're helping you by doing that. Because what they're going to think is, 'Oh my God, if they're going to do this, they're going to get kicked out of school. I should go tell the dean so they can stop them before they do that.' . . . They don't want to get anybody hurt."[140]

The student leaders agreed, and, as Bracey anticipated, the intentionally false information was later leaked by someone who had been at the meeting, a fact revealed the next morning when police officers arrived at the Rebecca Crown Center, looking for an anticipated takeover, while the real occupation was already underway at 619 Clark Street.[141]

The takeover was not something the students took on lightly, and, ultimately, "people showed up for different reasons."[142] "There were very few Black students who did not support it," as Turner recalled.[143] But there was a small number of students who, for various reasons, decided not to participate. For the takeover leaders, this posed a problem. They were certain that the press would scour the campus and the city looking for any Black student who was not in the building the next morning and ask them why they weren't taking part. And that, as Bracey explained, "would be the headline."[144] So, as Bracey recalled, they told those students: "You don't have to be in it, but will you at least please be neutral?" They agreed, accepting five dollars each, and promising they'd go downtown the next morning, go to a movie, and "stay in the Loop all day."[145]

This was just one of the many steps involved in what was a highly organized action. The students assiduously worked to ensure that they did not appear divided or unorganized at any time. "You had to think through all of the steps," Bracey explained. Drawing from the experiences of Bracey and other students who had been involved in organized protests and the civil rights movement, the group worked to ensure that all the components of their action would be considered and any potential problems anticipated.

Even many of the students who agreed to take part in the takeover had reservations though, and it's probably fair to say that all were extremely apprehensive about what they were about to do. What had happened at Columbia was a recent and stark memory: students being dragged down stone steps, tear gassed, arrested. As they prepared, they were aware that Northwestern might very well have a similarly heavy-handed response, and considering that their experiences with the Evanston police had not been altogether positive, as evidenced by the arrests following the fight in December, they feared what might happen if police were called in to evict them. "We knew that," Bracey said of the potential for a violent police response, "and we prepared for that."[146]

Still, many feared that something irrevocable might happen as a result of their action; they could jeopardize their careers, lose their scholarships, disappoint their families, be expelled, arrested, or worse. Some of the graduate students were particularly concerned for the undergraduates. How would they ever justify themselves to proud parents after their daughters and sons had been arrested or expelled from college? As the takeover drew near, some students continued to advocate for continued negotiations, urging that they keep talking with administrators. Vernon Ford, as John Bracey recalled, "was one of those people who believed in mediation right up to the end. 'It's like, we don't want to do this. We don't have to do this, if you talk to us. If you're fair with us. We don't have to do any of this.' " And he held that position right "up until the minute he came into the building," Bracey said.[147]

FMO founder and business major Herman Cage, who always appeared neatly dressed in a suit and tie, volunteered to secure the necessary funds to purchase the supplies needed for the action.[148] Still, he was hesitant about the takeover. "He could have blown his whole career," as Bracey recalled. "He had a lot more to risk than a lot of us did." When some of the students assured Cage that it was ok if he decided not to take part, his response was: " 'No, No. I'm coming . . . I'm here to the end.' "[149] (Cage, dressed, as usual, in suit and tie, did show up on Friday morning and entered the building with everyone else.) Some students also argued that those students with more public profiles, such as many of the athletes, shouldn't feel bad if they chose not to participate since they faced an increased risk of having their scholarships revoked.[150]

"It was a heavy load on my mind as far as personally feeling that we did need to go to the next level," Ogletree recalled. She was tasked with organizing the large group of students and ensuring that as many as possible showed up the next day. "We all knew that anything could happen," she said, "that we could be thrown out of school. We could be arrested. We could be killed. There had been situations where people had died at demonstrations." Still, she said, "We felt justified in doing it."[151]

Even though the decision for the takeover was made quickly, it had, in many ways, been a long time coming. "We never went from A to Z," Wayne Watson later explained of the trajectory that led to their decision to undertake the action. "We always went to B and said, 'Let's talk about it,' " he said of their efforts to bring their concerns to university officials. "Then, when they didn't want to talk to us, we went to C. We only went to Z, meaning taking over the Bursar's Office, after we'd gone through the entire alphabet."[152]

Nothing was certain. And nothing seemed inevitable. As to whether they would be treated as the students at Columbia had been treated? "I wasn't so sure," Bracey said. But they knew that they had a broad range of support from a large number of people, particularly in Evanston and Chicago, "who would help us if they attacked us," as Bracey said. And the idea that the whole "South Side or West Side of Chicago" might arrive in Evanston in their defense might just cause officials to hesitate before using force, he said.

More than anything though, the students were assured by knowing that what they were doing was not only justified, but also necessary. They had witnessed examples of other similar actions all over the country. "We were influenced by the Black youth movements in the South, the civil disobedience," Turner said of their decision to undertake such a dramatic action. "In the South, sit-ins were commonly held in places such as movie theaters and Woolworth's lunch counters with the intention of forcing desegregation, confronting racism, and getting the world's attention."[153] In the North, as Turner explained, one emphasis of the civil rights movement lay on working to alter the "institutional climate" of higher education.[154] The tactics were the same as those used in the South: to point out the pattern of racial discrimination and ensure that there would be "no business as usual" until power conceded to demands. The planned takeover, Turner explained, was about "changing the culture of the institution from the inside out."[155]

As the plans were underway, little was known around the campus about what was unfolding, although there was just a hint of it in the air. Earlier that same day, both the students' final demands and the university's response appeared in the *Daily Northwestern* in the form of an "advertisement" "placed by a concerned individual who wanted to let both viewpoints be fully known."[156] Later that evening, the Student Senate issued two resolutions: one pledging "unqualified support for measures to end injustice on the Northwestern campus" and another calling for acceptance of a highly diluted version of the students' demands.[157] The first resolution had been introduced by three people, including Eva Jefferson Paterson, a newly-elected member of the Student Senate who was preparing to take part in the takeover the next day.[158]

Following the students' press conference on May 2, a copy of the students' final demands was provided to Hinz. For more than three hours that afternoon, Hinz met with President Miller and other university vice presidents, addressing the current situation. At 5 p.m., Kathryn Ogletree arrived at Hinz's office. She waited for a moment before he handed her the university's response to their final demands. It was a six-sentence typewritten paragraph, which "said, in effect, nothing," as Turner later described it.[159]

"Because of the seriousness of our concern for the issues involved in the discussion with the black student organizations," the statement read, "the president has asked me to call a meeting in which he and other officers will join at 4 p.m. on Friday, [May 3,] for all black members of the Northwestern University community."[160]

That meeting would not take place. The students already had other plans.

Sit-in at a Woolworth's Lunch Counter in Durham, NC, February 10, 1960. On February 1, 1960, in Greensboro, North Carolina, four students from the Agricultural and Technical College of North Carolina (NC A&T) walked into a Walgreen's drugstore and sat at a lunch counter marked "whites only." They waited to be served. They were not served. They returned the next day, accompanied by sixteen more students.[161] Soon sit-ins multiplied all over the South, including the one pictured above, held at a Woolworth's lunch counter in Durham, North Carolina, on February 10, 1960. The sit-in was a signature (and successful) act of nonviolent resistance, designed to point out injustice, demand change, and impede business as usual. When faced by the often violent response of some white people to these actions, protesters remained nonviolent, a key factor in the organizing philosophy of the civil rights movement. (Photograph from N&O Negative Collection, State Archives of North Carolina, Raleigh, NC)

Jack Hinz and James Turner in front of the Bursar's Office,
Northwestern University, May 1968
(Northwestern *Syllabus* Yearbook, 1969, photograph by Gary Price)

Chapter 6

The Takeover

Thirty-Eight Hours

May 3, 1968: "perhaps the most momentous in Northwestern's momentous years."[1]

Daily Northwestern

I was scared of my parents, of being expelled, and of going to jail. And so were most of us. But the unity of the other people kept us together.

Eva Jefferson Paterson[2]

Once the doors and windows of the Bursar's Office were padlocked and the takeover was underway, the standoff began. Over the next thirty-eight hours, the media reported. The crowd of spectators outside the building grew. And university administrators held their breath, so to speak. "They wanted things calmed down," Hinz said of his colleagues. "They wanted everything to be normal. They wanted no trouble."[3] As a result of their meeting earlier that Friday morning, university officials had agreed to work towards reaching an understanding with the students and, it was hoped, peacefully resolving the situation. An official press release from the university went out to all city news desks explaining that President Miller was now meeting with administrators and faculty leaders to go over "the latest demands point-by-point in order to prepare a formal response."[4] Meanwhile, "vice president for student affairs Roland J. Hinz has been talking to negro student leader James Turner and is maintaining a line of communication between the university and the Negro students."[5] An Evanston police officer was now posted in front of 619 Clark Street, but the rest of the police, at Hinz's request, had been ordered to stay away from the occupied building.[6]

Inside the Bursar's Office, the students sat tight. Participants Debra Avant Hill, Adrianne Hayward, and Sandra Hill said they knew little about what might transpire during the action. They had only been told by the takeover leaders where to show up that morning and to bring a change of clothes and Vaseline to protect against the possible use of mace against them. They were told to follow their "squad leaders" throughout the action.[7]

"It was dramatic," Kathryn Ogletree recalls of the actual takeover and of the feeling of being inside the building, its doors and windows chained and locked, the crowds of spectators and members of the press outside growing larger as the day wore on. But it was also rather studious. Throughout the takeover, most of the students were busy inside the building: They were doing their homework. "[We] were trying to stay on task because when we came out," Ogletree recalled, "you still had to go to class."[8] (Many participants in the 1960 lunch counter sit-ins at Woolworth's drugstores also brought their books with them to do their homework during their actions.[9]) Meanwhile, the takeover leaders held meetings to strategize and everyone was constantly "admonished," as Ogletree remembered, not to do any damage to anything within the building. The building's computer system was closely guarded since it alone gave them "leverage," as she said, "even though we weren't directly threatening to do anything with it."[10]

An Evanston police officer on duty at the Bursar's Office,
Northwestern University, May 3, 1968
(Northwestern *Syllabus* Yearbook, 1969)

But leverage also came from another significant fact. Earlier that morning, as Ogletree watched the other students show up in the alley, readying themselves to take over the university's main financial building, she had been relieved. By dawn, more than thirty students had already arrived in the alley, a number that John Bracey determined was great enough for the action to work. But soon that number grew to roughly ninety-four, and once inside the building, many of the students, primarily the female students, got on the telephone and called others, mostly the male students who had said they would take part in the takeover, but hadn't shown up in the alley. They urged them to get over to the Bursar's Office right away, directing them to enter the building through an east side window. (The leaders of the takeover told the students to keep track of their phone calls in order to reimburse the university for them).[11]

With the addition of the late arrivals, it was still morning when the number of students inside the Bursar's Office topped one hundred. "It was a good feeling to realize that over one hundred of us actually came out and went into that building," Ogletree said.[12] And, as a result, as Bracey observed, "the dynamic of it changed because in fact the numbers were so big. So that way we didn't have to deal with a whole bunch of people on the outside saying that we were crazy."[13] The turnout—as a reflection of student solidarity—was key to the action's success. "If it had only been a few, twenty people or so, there's no doubt in my mind that [university administrators] would have probably decided to act differently and to remove us or to dismiss us or to arrest us," Ogletree said. "But once they became aware that almost every Black student on campus was in there, then they took the time to consider what it was really all about."[14]

A majority of students would remain within the building throughout the takeover, while a handful would come and go temporarily. (James Turner even returned home on Friday night to check on his son, still in the care of a babysitter.)[15] Some were worried about what their parents would think when news of the takeover reached them. Because of the need for secrecy, most had said nothing to parents or family members about their plans beforehand. But as they anticipated the intense media coverage of the takeover, some students called home to tell their families they were ok.[16] A few were told by their parents to leave the building immediately. But they remained. "Some admitted that it was the first time they had disobeyed their parents," as Turner remembered.[17] Ogletree did not tell her parents, knowing, as most others did, that they "would have been against it. We knew that. So we didn't tell anyone. We just made our decision and then stood on principle and followed through with it."[18]

Newly-elected student senator, Eva Jefferson Paterson called her parents from the Bursar's Office during the takeover. "Guess where I am?" she asked. They were not happy. "If you don't get out of there," they told her, "we're cutting off your money." Paterson obeyed and reluctantly left the building. But she said she immediately felt "very alienated" and "left out." So she returned and re-joined the takeover for the duration. "And that's when I became independent," she said.[19]

Other parents had different reactions. When Daphne Maxwell Reid called her mother and told her where she was and what she was doing, her mother didn't miss a beat: "Ok, let me know if you need some bail money and I'll get you out."[20] At one point, another student, Saundra Malone, had a surprise visitor all the way from her hometown of Cincinnati: her father, who had flown in that morning out of concern for her. She leaned out of a window of the occupied building to have a conversation with him. "He told the newsmen that he feared for his daughter's safety," the *Chicago Defender* reported, "but after discussing the situation with her, he was in total sympathy."[21]

Students at an east side window of the Bursar's Office during the takeover, May 3, 1968. Stephen Broussard is pictured leaning out of the window.
(Northwestern University Archives, photograph by James Sweet)

Among the takeover participants were several Northwestern athletes: Vernon Ford and Dan Davis were members of the basketball team and Wayne Watson was on the wrestling team; all three were part of the takeover from the beginning. Two of Northwestern's star basketball players, Don Adams and Dale Kelley, joined the takeover after it began.[22] Adams told the press why they decided to take part: "off the field" he and other Black athletes "feel that they are not part of the NU community," he said. "I'm protesting," he continued, "not because I'm an athlete, but because I'm a member of the Black race." Kelley agreed, announcing that he and Adams were "both going to take our turn in [the Bursar's Office] with the others."[23] For many athletes, the choice to take part in the takeover was particularly difficult.

About a week prior to the takeover, Vernon Ford, who had come to Northwestern on a basketball scholarship, had outlined the "unique and inherent contradictions and paradoxes" facing a Black athlete at Northwestern: "He is the symbol of progress and the partial cause of stagnation," Ford wrote. "He is the pride of the alumni, but seldom their house guest. He is idolized by little white boys who may one day grow up to be his boss . . . . He is also expected to find an adequate social life within a racially unbalanced situation without causing controversy."[24] Because of their particular concerns associated with being such public figures at the university, some athletes chose not to risk taking part in the takeover. But many did come to the Bursar's Office on Friday morning, wearing their letterman jackets. They sat on the building's front steps and later remained outside in a show of solidarity with the students inside. Others had to make the choice to leave the Bursar's Office temporarily. Three of Northwestern's football players had no idea what might happen if they failed to show up at that afternoon's scheduled practice. At 3:45 p.m., they ran onto the field at Dyche Stadium just seconds before practice was to begin. "I knew they'd be here," coach Alex Agase said, relieved to see them. He told the *Daily Northwestern* that he no idea what he would have done if they hadn't shown up.[25]

The students also had support among Northwestern's staff. According to one account, when members of the Bursar's Office staff vacated the building earlier that morning or later showed up for work only to be turned away, a few employees smiled at the students and gave them the "thumbs up."[26] John Bracey argued that *all* of the staff who worked in the building supported the action, feeling that it was "about time" something like this occurred.[27] After they had been told by the students to leave the building that morning, the administrative assistants did not make any negative statements to reporters. "You can bet that the press asked them 'Were you scared?' 'Did you think the Negroes were going to tear the place up?' " Bracey recalled. "None of them said anything like that. You don't see anything in the newspapers about those secretaries saying they were afraid of us."[28]

In fact, Bracey revealed that the reason the students were even able to enter the building successfully was because of an act of solidarity on the part of a Northwestern employee: That morning, after Michael Smith and Steve Colson entered the building with chains and locks and the students deployed their decoy by running toward the Rebecca Crown Center, the lone security guard at the Bursar's office moved away from his post at the front door. But he remained close by, standing near the building's entrance. The guard was Venice Deese, Jr.[29] (Deese was the highly praised member of Northwestern's security staff who had recently been the object of an attack when a can had been thrown at his car.) As the students began streaming through the entryway of the Bursar's Office, Deese stood nearby with his back turned to the students as they filed into the building. Bracey watched him as he got on his walkie-talkie. "The building is being occupied. Please advise," he repeated calmly, as the students filed past him. He stood completely still and made no effort to stop them. As the last student entered the building, he said: "The building *has been* occupied. Please advise." Then he turned around, faced Bracey, and flashed a big smile.[30]

For many Evanston residents, the takeover represented a larger effort towards achieving justice in the city as a whole. "We were not alone," as Bracey said.[31] Although most of the students hailed from places outside of Evanston (Chicago, New York, St. Louis, etc.), many had ties to local community organizations, churches, and institutions, including Evanston's Ebenezer A.M.E. Church and Evanston Township High School, where several students, including Turner, Milton Gardner, and Wayne Watson, volunteered.[32] And numerous individuals and organizations in Evanston, as well as in Chicago, such as the Urban League, served as allies, pledging support in various ways. When the takeover began, community and religious leaders "spoke out in church and in press conferences; they came to campus and met administrators and cautioned against using police assault," as Turner recalled.[33] A group called the "Evanston Support Committee Coordinated," comprised of city residents, helped the students by delivering food and other supplies to the building.[34] And, on Friday morning, many Chicago activists and residents made the trip north from the city to show up outside the Bursar's Office in solidarity. Among them was twenty-one-year-old SNCC organizer, Bobby Rush, (later elected to the U.S. House of Representatives) who arrived at the Bursar's Office accompanied by Robert Brown, chairman of the Chicago branch of SNCC.[35]

At about 10:15 a.m. on Friday morning, several Black students arrived at the building and sat on the front steps; they were soon joined by two other students from inside the building. The two students, flanking the front entrance, held signs. "Black Autonomy Black Self-Determination," read one of the signs, in a clear statement contrasting Black students' demands with those of the largely white student campaign for autonomy and the administration's recent support for student self-determination. This small group of students served simultaneously as an announcement to the growing crowd and passersby that the takeover was underway and as a kind of symbolic barrier of protection for those inside. And soon, they would be joined by scores of others.

Northwestern students in front of the Bursar's Office, Friday morning, May 3, 1968. Those identified in the photograph are Laura Murray, seated on right, and journalism major, Stephen Broussard, standing, left. The students seated on the steps to the left of Murray, wearing letterman jackets, are Northwestern athletes.[36]
(Northwestern University Archives, photograph by James Sweet)

In a surprise development, at 10:30 a.m., just three hours after the takeover began, a group of about fifty Northwestern students, most of whom were white, showed up outside the Bursar's Office. They gathered in front the building, amassed on the front steps and the ground, in order to block the way to the door should police try to enter the building, while a large group assembled at the building's rear entrance to block entry there.[37] As they settled in on the steps, smoking, talking, eating, reading, and listening to transistor radios, it was clear that they were not moving.[38] They held a brief rally, with speeches and words of support for the students inside. And thereafter, a "communal mood of mutual interest prevailed" among them, and they "began to share everything from food, money, and blankets to thoughts and ideas," as Professor Rolf Schulze reported.[39]

These students had organized their action that morning with almost no planning. Roger Friedman, who was one of the students who showed up outside the Bursar's Office that morning, recalled that "progressive white student groups were surprised by the takeover, and we had to quickly figure out how to be supportive."[40] Among those who participated in the action were many SDS members, but there were plenty of others who also took part who were not affiliated with any activist organizations. In a document issued later, signed by the "whites who were there," the students involved in the action explained that "each one of us believed [the Black students'] cause to be just, and as such, a benefit to us all." They were, they explained, "each committed to doing whatever was necessary to help the Blacks achieve their ultimate victory."[41]

"[W]e hadn't calculated that," Turner said of the surprise action, "but once they came, we had some Black students who went outside of the building to speak at the rally the students were holding, to express appreciation and solidarity."[42] "I had no idea that we had white support that wasn't *left* support," Bracey said. But, as he later learned, "these were just regular kids."[43] For decades he had thought that all the students who created the line of defense around the Bursar's Office that morning were members of Northwestern's SDS chapter. He had been impressed, thinking, from the number of students out there, "Northwestern must have the biggest SDS chapter in the country!" Recently, he learned that they were not all SDS members, nor were they all necessarily "radical" students. Many of them were just "regular white kids," as he described them, who heard about what the Black students were doing and said, "We better go help them."[44]

"We were kind of pleased about that," Ogletree said of the action. Not only did it signify "general support among the white student body," as Bracey put it, but it also meant that the police "would have to come through the white students to get to us," as Ogletree explained.[45] "And they knew," as Turner saw it, "how would that play to the parents and the alumni to see the white students who had skin currency attacked by the police?"[46] This show of solidarity—and protection—played a significant role. All of a sudden, there was a "critical shift in the balance," Turner said, not fully of power, but of influence.[47] The students' presence now served as a protection for the students inside since the police would be unlikely to "bloody the white students," as Turner said.[48]

Northwestern students block the front entrance
to the occupied Bursar's Office, May 3, 1968
(Northwestern University Archives, photograph by James Sweet)

Around 11 a.m. on Friday, Hinz returned to the Bursar's Office after a lengthy meeting with administrators. He waited on the front steps for Turner and then the two men had a quick conversation. "No comment," Hinz said as he was leaving, reporters crowding around him, clamoring for a statement. Over the course of the day, Hinz, looking every inch the authority figure, wearing a suit and tie, and Turner, sporting a Northwestern sweatshirt underneath a light jacket, would meet on those steps many times, each appointed to represent his respective group. "James and I met at the front door [of the occupied building] repeatedly," Hinz recalled, "and we were back and forth." Hinz promised Turner that he would return to the building from his own "closed-door meetings" every two hours to consult with him.[49] And so, like clockwork, Hinz appeared on the steps at 1 p.m., 3 p.m., 5 p.m., and 7 p.m., and so on.

Jack Hinz leaves the Bursar's Office after a consultation with James Turner, May 3, 1968
(Northwestern University Archives, photograph by James Sweet)

Hinz was committed to the negotiating process, certain "that we would be able to work something out," as he remembered.[50] He had been given authority over the negotiating process, and he had begun by establishing a series of meetings at two-hour intervals throughout the day on Friday, meetings with administrators and faculty to address the students' demands and craft a more reasoned and substantial response, with the goal of reaching a settlement. Over the course of the day, fifteen hours of meetings would be held.[51] "I was the go-between," Hinz recalled of his role, ferrying back and forth each side's questions and concerns to the other. "I would take [the students'] concerns [to the administration]," he said. He was not, however, given the authority to bargain with the students without input from the administration. Only "occasionally I had been told I could make some decisions," Hinz remembered, "but by and large I wasn't. That's why we needed a collective negotiating activity."[52]

"We are going to give them a voice," Hinz said of the university's approach to the students.[53] Hinz made this statement on Friday afternoon during a meeting with Northwestern's faculty, which was closed to all students and members of the press.[54] Many of the nearly 450 faculty members in attendance applauded when Hinz asserted that the university "did not intend to use force" to evict the students from the building.[55] After the meeting, math professor Marvin Shinbrot appeared outside the Bursar's Office to report what university officials had said.[56] He was one of several professors who had already made known their support for the students, including history professor Christopher Lasch, math professor, Michael Marcus, and sociology professor, Rolf Schulze, among others. Schulze even took the opportunity to conduct sociological research while the takeover was in progress and in its aftermath.[57] English instructor Henry Lesnick canceled his classes that day in order to stand outside the occupied office in support, while another professor reportedly urged her students to go to the building in a show of solidarity.[58]

The fairly large percentage of faculty and administrators who supported the students was evident in the actions of two individuals who were privy to the closed-door meetings and secretly kept the students in the building informed about what was going on. "There were two people who were telling us what was happening at the meetings with the administration," Bracey recalled. "One was [history professor] George Fredrickson and the other was Lt. Col. Lucius P. Gregg, Jr., associate dean of science." Bracey explained that one of them would call the students in the Bursar's Office and let them know "this is what the administration is thinking about doing. This is what they're planning on doing." And then fifteen minutes later the other would call and "tell us the exact same thing," Bracey said. "And so that's how we knew we were getting accurate information. These were two different people; they didn't know each other. So in fact we had support on the administrative team."[59]

Lt. Col. Lucius Perry Gregg, Jr. (1933-) former Associate Dean of Sciences, Northwestern University.
(University Relations, Northwestern University Archives)

During the takeover, Gregg kept the students in the Bursar's Office informed about the administration's plans as they unfolded. Gregg attended high school in Chicago and later earned a bachelor's degree from the U.S. Naval Academy. He was the fourth Black man to graduate from the academy. He received an MS in aeronautics and astronautics from M.I.T. and served in the U.S. Air Force from 1955 to 1985. From 1965 to 1969, he was a research coordinator and associate dean at Northwestern. He later held positions with the Alfred P. Sloan Fund, Citibank/Citicorp, and Hughes Aircraft Company, among others.[60]

Historian George Marsh Frederickson (1934-2008)
(University Relations, Northwestern University Archives)

Frederickson was a renowned scholar on American race and author of numerous books, including *The Black Image in the White Mind* (1971) and *White Supremacy: A Comparative Study in American and South African History* (1981). He taught at Harvard and Northwestern and later at Stanford University. As a young professor at Northwestern, he was influenced by John Bracey and other students who broadened and expanded his understanding of the importance and significance of Black history and culture.[61] During the takeover, he and Dean Lucius Gregg, Jr., kept the students in the Bursar's Office informed about what administrators were discussing and planning in response to the action.

John Bracey leans out of a window in the Bursar's Office, May 3, 1968 (Northwestern University Archives, photograph by James Sweet)

As the students learned the content of the discussions underway by members of the administration, they were not surprised to hear that "Some people want to get you locked up," as Bracey recalled being told.[62] But they also learned an important detail: the administration had been informed by the Evanston police chief that "it would take eight hours to mobilize enough police" to evict them.[63] Before hearing this, the students had been worried about "how soon could they attack us," and knowing they had time gave them a degree of reassurance.[64] They were also reassured in hearing that there was a faction among the administrators who were insisting that they avoid any police involvement and that some, most notably Hinz, Gregg, and Wallace, were not only working towards a nonviolent resolution, but were also actively trying to "build support for the demands."[65]

Outside the Bursar's Office not all reactions were positive; they ranged from mild annoyance to outrage. Employees and students were unable to pick up or cash their checks at the Bursar's Office, as they usually did. "This is an awful inconvenience," one student told the *Daily Northwestern*.[66] Others were dismissive of the occupying students, arguing that their demands were "unreasonable;" "there is not enough housing on campus to give black students separate living units," one student said.[67] "I think they ought to kick everyone who's demonstrating out of school," said another.[68] Another referred to the occupying students as "disgusting human beings."[69] And many protested loudly. The outcry against the "militant" students had begun.

"Look at what they've done!" Turner recalled of the main charge from the opposition. "We've brought these inner city students to Northwestern University and they are bringing the inner city to the campus!"[70] Some critics characterized the students as "ungrateful" and chided them for disgracing the university. This was the era of flower power and hippies, after all, and many buttoned-up North Shore residents thought the generation gap had now widened to a canyon. These young people not only needed to be disciplined, they advised, but they should also be removed from university property by police force immediately, arrested, and expelled.

Throughout the takeover, fear of violence breaking out was present among both the students and administrators, as Turner remembers, and, as the standoff wore on, the "tension intensified."[71] At one point early Friday evening, nerves were set on edge when a group of twenty-five white men gathered outside to "taunt" the students from across the street.[72] And over the course of the day, various rumors circulated. A planned attack by "special squads of police" was imminent, Turner recalls hearing at one point.[73] And later, it was rumored that a network of secret underground tunnels leading to the Bursar's Office would be used to deploy police into the building. As far as the likelihood that officials might order police to drag the students out, Ogletree recalled: "We knew that was a possibility, a small possibility, that could happen. We knew that could be how Northwestern could decide to deal with it. We were hoping that because they were a different type of university, that they would choose to deal with it differently because this experience could make or break them too as far as how they chose to deal with minority students."[74]

Hinz remembered that the threat of violence was kept at bay through focusing on the task at hand: "the way you keep that from happening is to negotiate. Is to talk about it. That's very much what we did."[75] But privately, Hinz was also fearful. He was concerned about the possibility for violence, not from the students in the Bursar's Office, but from others who might be provoked by the situation. He kept this feeling to himself as he went about his job of mediating, representing both the students and the administration, walking the tightrope, as it were, that was woven by the different views of the two sides. (In fact, he was also up against counteracting some bold, "not-to-be moved" statements that seemed to undermine the attempt to reach a peaceful compromise when administrators, such as Vice President and Dean of Faculties Payson Wild, made statements to the press such as "we are not giving 'control' of the university away." The administration, Hinz added, was "trying very hard to be reasonable."[76])

Just before noon on Friday, another act of solidarity would occur: about thirty white students, including SDS members, Roger Friedman and George Vickers, showed up at Hinz's office in Scott Hall, just blocks from the occupied building. They announced to the administrative assistants, Jessie Robertson and Virginia Romans, that they "wanted to remain there."[77] "The black students expressed an interest in keeping the business functions of this university shut down until their demands are met," Vickers said. "We want to help them in that goal."[78] The staff summoned Assistant Dean of Men James F. Stull to the office and notified Hinz that a second takeover was underway. Hinz responded that "the students were not to be removed from the office or interfered with."[79] And so, with an office full of occupying students, the administrative assistants tried to get on with their work. But they weren't getting "much work done," Romans told a reporter. "We're really nervous, but the kids seem to be behaving themselves."[80] Stull stayed too, remaining in Hinz's office throughout most of the occupation, sometimes sitting on the floor and talking with the students. If any police arrived, Stull had indicated to Friedman, he wanted to be present in case there were "any arrests or brutality."[81] As the sit-in in Hinz's office continued, onlookers showed up outside, along with members of the media. Soon a crowd had gathered in front of that building too, obstructing traffic on busy Sheridan Road. Police were called in, but only to help break up the traffic jam.[82]

This second action, the students told the press, was undertaken in solidarity with the students in the Bursar's Office.[83] Roger Friedman announced that he was in contact with James Turner by phone and would "take his cues" from him.[84] Friedman explained to the *Daily Northwestern* that they had undertaken the action "because [the Black students'] demands are addressing the same root problems in the university community that we (*The Real Press,* Students for a Democratic Society and the Sandbox Committee) have been working for."[85]

The group made free use of Hinz's office, with students taking turns sitting at his desk and using his phone. (But they did not, it was reported, "disturb private property."[86]) They even dispatched a telegram to a student group at Columbia University who had engaged in the recent strike and famously occupied the office of University President Grayson Kirk. "This telegram is being sent from the office of the Dean of Students at Northwestern University," it read. "This office is being held by a group of white students in an act of support for the Afro-American Student Union who are currently occupying the financial building . . . We know that you support us in this action as fully as we support yours."[87]

Friedman traveled back and forth between Hinz's office and the steps of the Bursar's Office in order to talk with the other supporters of the takeover and try "to keep things calm."[88] As the actions around campus seemed to be multiplying, so did the onlookers outside the Clark Street building. One woman approached the students and asked, "Can I help? Do you need any food?"[89] "What's going on here?" a man in a green Volkswagen yelled at one point to Friedman and some of the students outside the occupied building. "We've taken over!" Friedman responded. "The hell you have!" the man yelled back.[90] And on it went.

James Turner, left, talks with members of the press outside the occupied Bursar's Office, May 3, 1968
(Northwestern University Archives, photograph by James Sweet)

Members of the press gather around James Turner (center), with Jack Hinz standing left, May 3, 1968. Also pictured is Professor Michael Marcus (between Hinz and Turner). Marcus was active in a number of progressive causes, particularly in the anti-war movement. He served as advisor to Northwestern's chapter of Chicago Area Draft Resisters (CADRE). Marcus was one of several faculty members identified in the FBI's reports documenting the takeover. Along with Professor Marvin Shinbrot, an FBI informant identified Marcus, and reported that both men were "seen helping to organize the white students on the steps on 619 West [*sic*] Clark Street, Evanston, where the Negro demonstrators were located."[91]

(Northwestern University Archives, photograph by James Sweet)

James Turner (right) outside of 619 Clark Street. Northwestern security officer, Venice Deese, Jr. (1936-2013) (left), stands by his side. Deese was an Evanston resident and a graduate of Evanston Township High School. The *Chicago Defender* described him as the "go between for students, police, and the school's administration."[92] Deese was the guard on duty at the front door of the Bursar's Office on the morning the students took over the building. Also pictured is Harold Daniels (behind Deese). Daniels played on Northwestern's football team from 1966-1970. On Saturday, May 4, 1968, Daniels would serve as one of the ten student representatives in the negotiations with university officials.[93]

(Northwestern University Archives, photograph by James Sweet)

James Turner being interviewed outside the Bursar's Office,
May 3, 1968
(Northwestern University Archives, photograph by James Sweet)

The press pool outside the building was growing too. Coverage in the *Daily Northwestern* was particularly extensive, with a special issue of the newspaper issued on Saturday, May 4. The *Daily Northwestern's* Bob Greene was just one of the many reporters in the crowd in front of the building, their microphones and cameras poised to capture the latest news. "Give us half a minute of privacy," Hinz asked as he pushed through the crowd on his way to one of his periodic conferences with Turner at the building's entrance. But the press would not be moved. To shield themselves from the cameras, the two men stepped behind one of the signs hanging from the door and conferred quietly.

As he was leaving, Hinz was "visibly irritated," the press noted.[94] But his irritation derived from the press itself. "I'm sorry," he said, as he pushed past the crowd of reporters. "You have to do your job and I have to do mine. I'd appreciate it if you'd let me go and do it."[95] Many outside the building applauded when Hinz made this statement, and later, they applauded again when Turner announced: "We're through with the press."[96]

The press coverage of the situation was causing both sides to bristle. For Hinz, claims that Northwestern officials were yielding to the demands of the "rebel students" were not only untrue, but they projected to the public the idea that the students had no legitimacy, and therefore the university was foolish to negotiate with them.[97] Further, the popular spin on the story was that the students were simply being allowed to "invade" and "seize" university property at will, while university officials feebly stood by and watched.

Turner had his own annoyances with the press, too. As the appointed spokesman for the students, he repeatedly ventured into the sea of reporters to make statements and answer questions. Some of the press had a penchant for describing the students as "militant," creating a false sense of them as being combative and potentially violent and not calculated and reasoned in their action. At one point, Turner called out some members of the press for "making a mockery of their demands" and resorting to racism in their reporting, as one UPI reporter did. A UPI story was now making the rounds, stating that one of the students' demands was that "chitlins and collard greens" be served in the Northwestern cafeteria.[98] (Thomas Picou, executive editor of the *Chicago Defender,* would later assert: "The unwarranted attack on Black students at Northwestern University by the white press after the students took over the school's administration building was malicious and racist."[99])

At one point, Vernon Ford, one of the takeover participants, leaned out of a window and summoned a Black photographer. A nearby white photographer called to him, "Hey, man, let me get a picture." Ford responded: "My name's not man. And I don't want you to take my picture."[100] The photographer that Ford called over was Joe Boyce of the *Chicago Tribune,* the newspaper's first Black reporter.[101] The students allowed Boyce to enter the building through a window. The only reporter with direct access to the students, Boyce would remain inside the Bursar's Office for the duration of the takeover.[102]

Allowing Boyce inside was a strategic move. Given the students' savvy understanding of the press, it was no surprise that they wanted to maintain authority over the event's narrative, beginning with their effort to contact members of the press beforehand, including radio host Jeff Kamen, who let them read their demands live on the radio that morning. John Bracey recalled that the students were prepared for the fact that some in the press would "distort"[103] what was happening and some newspapers would "print lies."[104] He and others wanted to get their story out unfiltered without distorting the meaning of their action.[105] While they were inside the building, members of the press and others also began to contact them by telephone, including leaders from the Nation of Islam, who soon dispatched a reporter from *Muhammad Speaks* to the campus.[106]

Despite Ogletree's critical leadership, the press and other observers would see little of her during the takeover. She did not make any statements to the press. "I was content with being behind the scenes at that point," she recalled.[107] She and the other leaders worked in a way that was, as she said, "complementary" to each other. By choice Bracey, too, would remain largely out of the eye of the press. He was focused on building "community" among the students and working his contacts behind the scenes. Turner thus served as the group's designated spokesperson. All agreed there could not have been a better one: he was brilliant, dynamic, and persuasive, the perfect "mouthpiece" for the takeover.

It was late Friday evening when university officials completed a draft of a new response to the students' final demands. At 10:40 p.m., Hinz was back at the Bursar's Office to give a copy of the document to the students.[108] After he left, Turner appeared at the window to announce that the students had been planning to meet with officials that evening for a negotiating session. "However," he stated, "we have heard from people we consider very credible that there might be an attempt at three this morning by the combined (police) forces of Evanston, Wilmette and Skokie to rush the building."[109]

When Hinz returned to the building a bit later, he anticipated that the students would be ready to negotiate. Instead, Turner asked him about the rumored planned raid to arrest the students. Hinz "categorically denied" such a police raid was being planned at "any level of the university."[110] Turner requested that the students be provided with a signed statement to that effect. He also requested that the university's response to their demands be signed by President Miller and all the administrators before the students would consider their own reply. Hinz had been the only signatory on the draft he had given them; and throughout the entire action, the students were careful to ask that everything be put in writing and signed by all those involved in the negotiations.

Hinz agreed and departed. At half past midnight, he was back again to give Turner the signed documents he had requested. The two men agreed that negotiations would begin at 9 a.m. the next day.

Just before 1 a.m., a brick was thrown by someone outside the Bursar's Office, shattering a skylight on the building's southwest side. The sound of the crash faded and a quick investigation was made, but the unidentified assailant had disappeared.[111] As dawn approached, some of the students in the occupied building tried to sleep, others talked together quietly; a few students remained at their posts, appointed to keep guard. Over at Scott Hall, the students occupying Hinz's office had settled in for the night, the corridors beyond the office plunged into darkness and quiet. Outside the Bursar's Office, many of the students who had assembled to protect those inside huddled under blankets, trying to get some sleep. At one point, a light rain fell.

Negotiation Table, 217 Scott Hall, Northwestern University, Saturday, May 4, 1968. Kathryn Ogletree sits just to the left of the head of the table. Turner and Bracey are on her right. Hinz sits on the right side of the table, along with other university officials.
(*Daily Northwestern*, May 6, 1968)

Point by Point

Negro student demonstrators at Northwestern University continued to hold the school's business office building today as a week marked by militant student activity at home and abroad came to a close.

The Associated Press, May 4, 1968

"[I]t was feared that if today's negotiations ended in disagreement, the sit-in could be a prolonged affair."[112] This was a statement given to the clamoring press as negotiations got underway Saturday morning, May 4, 1968. In a meeting room in Scott Hall on campus, ten students and ten faculty members and administrators sat around a large table and began to talk. Present at the meeting were Jack Hinz, along with Lucius Gregg, Jr., and Walter Wallace, all of whom had urged restraint in that first meeting among administrators, as well as John Bracey, Kathryn Ogletree, and James Turner, and others.[113] Neither President Miller nor William Kerr, Northwestern's vice president and business manager, were present. According to one source, Miller wanted Hinz to "handle the final negotiations."[114]

After Hinz had first requested that the negotiations be held, the students selected ten students who would represent all the students "very much as a team," as Turner said.[115] Each team member was assigned a specific demand and tasked with presenting that demand or a related issue to the administration. But as they prepared for the meeting, some students were reluctant to let the group leave the Bursar's Office. "I had to give assurances," Hinz remembered in organizing the negotiations, "because the students [in the Bursar's Office] were fearful that we would get the leadership there and then keep them away from the group still left in the Business Office. That hadn't occurred to me that we would consider doing that. That may have been in the minds of some of the other administrators, but I had to give James [Turner] and the others assurances that they would be able to return."[116]

As the negotiations got underway, the crowd in front of the Bursar's Office remained in place and the students in Hinz's office continued their occupation. At one point, an alumnus from the class of 1913 decided to walk over from his nearby home on Davis Street to investigate. "Nothing is in my blood like Northwestern and three generations of my name love it," he later wrote to Vice President Franklin Kreml. At first he stayed across the street because, as he said, he didn't want to be "roughed up." "What the hell!" he thought. "This is my school," and crossed over to the Bursar's Office. What he found was simply "a nice bunch of kids," he reported. "This may be Northwestern's finest hour," he concluded.[117]

That morning, more than one hundred students held a rally in support of the takeover, with SDS members leading the proceedings. Some members of campus fraternities were reportedly in the midst of planning their own counter-rally in opposition, but they were "dissuaded" by a university official from doing so.[118] Meanwhile, in Chicago, a demonstration—unrelated to the takeover—was underway at the Chicago Civic Center. It was rumored that some participants were planning to "depart for Evanston" afterward, but they, too, were dissuaded and "dispersed without incident."[119]

"The (negotiations) were difficult," recalled Robert Strotz, who was dean of the College of Arts and Sciences at the time (and later president of Northwestern). "Emotions were high, the air was tense. I felt that if the university failed on this one, it would be a rare thing for the university to see another Black student. They had the power to institute a 100 percent boycott of the university."[120]

For the students, the negotiations provided a long sought opportunity: the chance to sit down with those who had the power to initiate the changes they desired. "When we were at the table," Ogletree recalled, "they had everybody who needed to be there *there*, which made it impossible for anybody to just pass the buck."[121] "Who they send to the table tells you whether they were serious or not," as Bracey recalled. To him, it was no surprise that President Miller was not there. "You never send the president because the president can't contradict himself. But if there's an agreement made with somebody below him, then you can appeal to him. So that gives him a second shot," he explained. Bracey knew that the administration was serious about negotiating once Franklin Kreml walked into the meeting.

Franklin Kreml entered the room with all the full force of his long career

Franklin M. Kreml (1907-1998) served as vice president of planning and development at Northwestern from 1962 to 1971. A graduate of the University of Wisconsin-Madison and Northwestern University, he received a law degree from John Marshall Law School in 1932. During World War II, he served in the Office of the Chief of Transportation in the U.S. Army. He later served as a police officer in Evanston. An expert on traffic safety, he directed Northwestern's Traffic Institute for two decades. After retiring from Northwestern, he served as president of the Motor Vehicle Manufacturers Association.[122]
(University Relations, Northwestern University Archives)

behind him. "Kreml is one of the toughest people you're ever going to meet on the planet," Bracey observed. Kreml, a World War II veteran, former police officer, Chicago Police Board member, and Northwestern graduate, had just been appointed to serve on Chicago Mayor Richard J. Daley's commission investigating the riots that followed the assassination of Martin Luther King, Jr.[123] "He came in the door with an accountant," Bracey remembered. "With an accountant with an adding machine, sat right next to him. And he started off wanting to know why are we here. That's the first thing that started us off. He said, 'Why am I here? My job is not to talk to students. My job is to make money for the institution and to maintain the long-term security for the institution. Why am I even talking to you? Tell me that.' "[124]

When the students began to explain the reasons leading to their action, Kreml interrupted them. Why hadn't they taken their concerns to the dean, namely to the Director of Financial Aid and Admissions, William Ihlanfeldt? "We did," came the answer. "We talked to Dean Ihlanfeldt and we got no response."[125]

At this point, according to Bracey, Kreml turned to Ihlanfeldt, who was also seated at the table, and said: "Dean Ihlanfeldt, ask them does anybody want any refreshments." Ihlanfeldt stood and went around the table taking breakfast orders. ("I ordered a coffee with two and a half sugars and one cream," Bracey wryly recalled). Soon, Ihlanfeldt returned with the orders, distributed them, and sat down. But this time he didn't take a place at the table. He sat on a chair behind those at the table. Bracey recalled that Kreml then said to Ihlanfeldt, "I'll talk to you later."[126]

This mini-drama was a curious insight into the power structure of the Northwestern administration. Bracey and others recognized that Hinz had been working behind the scenes to take the steps that had resulted in this negotiation. And, as Bracey argued, the "only way this stuff got sold to Kreml" — meaning the willingness to negotiate seriously—was because of Hinz. The reason that the students had even been brought to the point of a takeover was because so many in the administration had either turned a deaf ear to their concerns or lacked the authority to institute any real reform. Up to this point, President Miller had "wasted Hinz's skills," Bracey argued. "He really did. He should have listened to Hinz. He only listened to Hinz after we had taken over the building." But now, with Kreml there, it was official. His presence announced, "I'm here. I'm representing Northwestern," as Bracey said.[127]

For his part, Hinz had continued to push for a fair resolution, one that sincerely took into account the students' point of view and responded thoroughly to their demands. Hinz remembers that he tried to explain to Miller how important dialogue with the students was, telling him, "you know, we need to talk about these things."[128] Hinz needed buy-in from the other administrators to reach an agreement with the students, although he would willingly have forged ahead alone had he been given the authority. "I'm not the one to make all of these decisions," he recalled saying at the time, reiterating the need for all the administrators to work with him, "unless you tell me to do that," he said. "And they knew better."[129]

It's likely that they "knew better" since Hinz was effective as dean of students, in part, because of the ways he connected with students. He had their respect and he wanted, above all, to make things better for them. Allowing him sole discretion to approve any changes or make an agreement with the students could result in an outcome that the administration would not support. And so Hinz had been left to work toward negotiations, building support for the students among faculty and staff, free but restrained. "I'm not sure they knew what to make of me," he said of his colleagues, "or how

I would behave and react to these things." But in seeking calm and peace, the administrators did know one thing for certain about Hinz: "I tended not to get excited very quickly," as Hinz himself observed.[130]

And so, for the next eight hours, the negotiations proceeded.[131] "We went point by point by point," Bracey recalled of the process. The group discussed each and every demand, sometimes arguing, sometimes talking through the nature of a specific issue. Perhaps not surprisingly, it was one specific demand—that Northwestern admit that it was a racist institution—that officials had the "most difficult time with," Ogletree recalled. "What they really argued about was could we do these things without admitting to being a racist institution," Bracey remembers. "They really got hung up about that one."[132] Turner concurred, remembering that a significant portion of the negotiations involved "an advanced discussion of institutionalized racism, not about blaming an individual. You didn't have to feel it was personal," he recalled telling them, "but institutional. We argued that you should not overlook the way the institution was developed, and that Northwestern University was racist in its history."[133] In a lengthy exchange, the students presented their views about "the shape, character and culture of this institution," and at one point, they had to explain the concept of "white privilege" to administrators.[134] "You don't understand how decisions are made," Ogletree remembered telling them.[135]

Ultimately, the administrators at the table apparently came to accept this idea and they would later acknowledge the history and presence of racism at the university. Still, they were "deeply offended," Turner said. " 'Are you out of your mind?' they said," he recalled of their initial response. " 'We agreed to bring you here! We gave you special funds to bring you here.' "[136]

Thus they proceeded, addressing each demand, focusing on the largest issue to the smallest detail. " 'What do you want?' Kreml, sitting next to the accountant, would ask," as Bracey recalled. " 'We want a newsletter.' 'How big? How many pages? How often?' He looked at the guy and said, 'How much do you think that would cost?' And the guy's cranking out numbers."[137]

When they discussed the demand for a separate building for Black student activities, Kreml said that it might violate federal law to have a segregated facility on campus. So he suggested adding the name of a largely white student group to the building's mailbox. When someone suggested SDS, Kreml agreed. "He was working with us," Bracey said. "He was moving to settle the thing." Still, they were well aware that he was "defending Northwestern's interest the whole time."[138]

Others at the table were aware that Kreml was working hard not only to peacefully resolve the takeover, but also to truly engage with the students and provide, as best he could, what they demanded. In a letter written after the negotiations concluded, Professor Walter Wallace, who was present at the table that day, wrote to Kreml. He thanked him for his "unexpected but unforgettable magnificence" at the talks. "You said you could not learn a new way after your 61 years," Wallace wrote, and yet he had proven himself capable and willing to be open to hear and understand the students' demands. "I respect and honor you, then and now, as a virtuous man," Wallace wrote.[139]

For Ogletree, being the only woman at the table was a unique experience. She knew that it was unusual for a woman to "be upfront with Turner and all the others at the negotiating table," she said. "The white men, powerful men, sitting there at the table that we were negotiating with, would not have been willing to negotiate with me," she reflected, "partially because of my style in terms of being kind of meek, but also they just didn't deal with women that way."[140] But in fact, the eighteen-year-old Ogletree had proven to be anything but meek. Sitting at the table, facing the ten administrators and faculty members, she continued in her leadership role, representing all of the other students and working to advance the discussion so that their demands could be both understood and met by the university. It was the kind of opportunity that the students had longed for and one that Ogletree was more than ready to take advantage of. They "would not have taken me seriously if I was just the president of FMO and trying to negotiate something with them," Ogletree recalled thinking. "It was just the nature of politics. It was not going to work."[141]

For Hinz, the meeting proved to be illuminating. "[T]hose from the Northwestern side," he recalled, "as opposed to the student side, learned a lot from the kids, from the students at the negotiating table, so there was a change of perspective that took place. But that's what negotiation is about and why it's important."[142]

In many ways, it was a change in perspective that would lead to an agreement. During that long day, when anxiety and resentment, fear and fatigue, must have been felt by all involved, the discussion focused on each issue raised in the students' demands, from admissions and curriculum to racism and the reality of a "white institution." Some of those representing the university would later state that they changed their attitudes as a result of the eight-hour session. Collectively, the university would concede that administrators had not understood the "true meaning" of the petition.[143] Most importantly, they would ultimately declare that the university "accepts the basic sentiments expressed in the Black students' petitions."[144] The "events of this week," they later wrote, "have given us new and broader insights [and] led us to a reappraisal of the attitudes with which we confront these problems."[145]

After hours of discussion, debate, and negotiation, an agreement was reached. (See Appendix D for the full document.) The thirteen-page document addressed all aspects of each demand. It began with a lengthy section titled,

Walter L. Wallace (1927-2015)
(University Relations, Northwestern University Archives).
Wallace received his PhD in sociology from the University of Chicago. Before coming to Northwestern, he taught at Spelman College and Atlanta University (his alma mater). He taught at Northwestern for nine years before joining the faculty at Princeton University in 1971, where he served as professor until 2001. He was the author of numerous books, including *The Future of Ethnicity, Race, and Nationality* (1997). At Princeton, Wallace served as an advisor to Michelle Robinson (Obama) on her senior thesis, which examined how the experience of attending a predominantly white university affected the perspectives of Black Princeton alumni.[146]

"Policy Statement." In it, the administration acceded to the charge that in its "overwhelming character," Northwestern had acted as a "white institution." As such, along with "virtually all institutions of higher learning in the United States," it shared the responsibility "for the continuance over many past years of . . . racist attitudes."[147]

It is true, the statement read, that the university had "in common with the white community in America, in greater or lesser degree, the racist attitudes that have prevailed historically in this society and which continue to constitute the most important social problem of our times."[148] The administration acknowledged its recent efforts to integrate Northwestern and to "improve race relations and to provide educational opportunities in greater measure than ever before for the black people in its community." But officials also recognized that those efforts needed to be reevaluated. Initially, the process of integration had been seen as one of "simply obliterating in our laws and in our personal relations the distinction between the races." "[I]f only man would ignore in his human relations the differences in skin colors," this attitude held, "racial problems would immediately disappear." But now, officials were altering this view. "We are now learning that this notion does not come fully to grips with the problems of the present turbulent period of transition . . . . Accordingly, we cannot be complacent with institutional arrangements that ignore the special problems of Black students. An important and difficult problem is that of an essentially white leadership coming to understand the special needs and feelings of the Black student, as well as the difficulty arising because the Black student does not regard the white university authorities as capable of appreciating all of the nuances of his decidedly separate culture."[149] Now, the university pledged, "special recognition and special concern must be given, for some unspecifiable time, to the black community that is emerging within our institution."[150]

What followed the policy statement was an outline of many of the changes that the students demanded. With some qualifications in meeting the specifics of some demands, the university pledged to: increase the recruitment of Black students, increase financial aid for Black students, hire more Black faculty members, add Black studies courses to the curriculum, ensure representation of Black students in university government, and make space available for Black students' social activities.

In the section on housing, officials acknowledged the university's policy of ensuring that "a mixture of student types should characterize living arrangements" on campus. But now, they were willing to "modify that position." The modification stemmed from both the "distinctiveness of existing racial concerns" and also the "admitted inconsistency" between the "ideal of nondiscrimination in housing and the recognized practice of discrimination that exists in certain living units of the University." (In their final demands, the had students argued that if Black students could not be provided with their own housing since that would constitute a form of segregation, then officials must "immediately get rid of the present fraternity and sorority housing arrangements" since those too allowed students to segregate themselves within their own housing.)[151] Officials were now willing to work toward providing "separate housing units for Black male and female students."[152]

There were some components to the demands that the university explicitly stated that it "could not in good faith offer."[153] These related to granting the students authority in decisions on hiring and admissions. They would not "share power in determining the admissibility of students," the agreement stated, nor would they be able to approve the appointment of a counselor for Black students.[154] But in fact, the students would exercise some authority to contribute in both these areas.[155] For, the agreement stipulated that a University Advisory Council would be formed, composed of ten Black student leaders, nominated by the larger group of Black students themselves and approved by the administration. The council would serve as "an instrument of University administration to function at all administrative levels as the administration deals with problems of the black community related to the University."[156] The university viewed the council as providing administrators "insight" and "advice" in order to ensure that the university will be "more responsive in reacting to the particular needs of its black students."[157] As a forward-looking document, the agreement also anticipated the future involvement of students in a variety of areas and it took a long-term view of the advisory role that the council would play in "future years."[158]

The agreement also addressed the issue of justice at the university. Affirming that any disciplinary action must be undertaken to "improve the standards of personal conduct rather than to punish per se," the university acknowledged that such procedures must take into account the "racial, cultural, and personal characteristics" of all students concerned.[159] In respect to the December 1967 fight, officials pledged that the UDC would be directed to undertake a review of that case.[160]

For the students, one of the most important outcomes of the negotiations was that the administration had finally acknowledged "the basic legitimacy of our concerns," as Turner said.[161] "One thing that was reassuring," Ogletree recalled, "was that there were a variety of people there who could speak for their particular areas, like only faculty could hire other faculty. So when we were talking about creating a department of African American studies or hiring someone to teach those kinds of classes, the administration could not just promise that. There were faculty agreeing to meet with us to try to work that out. So we kind of felt it was more of a commitment than just something to pacify us. And because the people who could have addressed the various concerns were there, we felt that it was on a different level than what people had done in the past, just giving us the runaround with the concerns that we were raising."[162]

With the agreement completed, which included the insertion of several addenda to the thirteen-page document, the meeting broke up. Bracey, Ogletree, Turner, and the other student leaders returned to the Bursar's Office. At 6:45 p.m., Hinz walked over to the Bursar's Office carrying a brown cardboard box which he handed to Turner. Inside were copies of the agreement signed by the ten administrators and faculty members. There would follow a tense waiting period while the students were given a chance to review the agreement and then inform the administration of their final decision to accept or reject it.

Back inside the still-occupied Bursar's Office, the students "had a collective meeting" and a "robust discussion," as Turner recalled.[163] Meanwhile, administrators waited on pins and needles. They had agreed that an official phone call would be placed by Turner to notify them of the students' response. And so, Hinz, along with Director of Public Relations Sam Saran, Dean Lucius Gregg, Jr., and others, went to Saran's office to wait. (Hinz's office was still being occupied.) Two *Daily Northwestern* reporters waited just outside Saran's office, while nearby, representatives from the "downtown press" also waited.[164] Occasionally the phone would ring and everyone would jump. But it was not Turner.[165]

Around 7:30 p.m. Hinz came out of the office and asked the reporters, "Have you been over to 619 [Clark]?" The crowd was "anxious but not unruly," one of them told Hinz. Soon after, one of the *Daily Northwestern* reporters decided to investigate for himself. He went over to the Bursar's Office and luckily ran into Joe Boyce of the *Chicago Tribune*. Boyce had been inside the building with the students since Friday. He had just filed his own story, reporting that the agreement had been accepted.[166] The reporter hurried back to Hinz." 'This may be old to you,' he said, 'but I've been informed that the agreement has been accepted.' 'Thank you,' Hinz said. 'That's not old to me.' "[167] But still, Hinz had to wait for the official word from Turner.[168]

Finally, just before 8 p.m., Hinz received word. The students had accepted the agreement. They had voted and reached consensus and were now ready to leave the building, "with promises," Turner recalled, "that the university would honor the agreement and there would be no prosecution or penalizing of the students."[169] A short time later, Hinz reemerged from the office to announce quietly: "They've accepted."[170]

Fifteen minutes after the students made their announcement, the students occupying Hinz's office departed. Now, it was time for administrators to prepare copies of the final agreement, with a security guard appointed to watch over them. It was also time to draft an official statement for the press. Hinz wanted to deliver the statement in front of the Bursar's Office, but his colleagues discouraged him. It would it be too loud and chaotic amidst the crowds there. So the neighboring Rebecca Crown Center was chosen.

"As distressing as the events of these past two days have been," Hinz said in his statement that night, "the entire Northwestern University community is heartened by the peaceful conclusion of the occupation at 619 Clark Street. The University administration took a serious view of the complaints and demands of the black student community, and the subsequent negotiations which resulted in the agreement early this evening were carried out in an atmosphere of earnestness and mutual concern. The black students comported themselves in a serious and responsive manner throughout this difficult period."[171]

Privately, Hinz was overheard telling a friend: "What we've done in the last three weeks at this university, I would have thought would have taken 10 years," he said. "And it's probably taken 10 years off my life," he added.[172]

The agreement had now been signed by the ten student representatives and ten university officials. Inside the Bursar's Office, the mood was a mixture of relief and happiness. "They gave us everything that we asked for," Bracey said.[173] "I was happy about it," Ogletree recalled, "but at the same time, kind of subdued."[174] For Ogletree, there was definitely "a sense of being victorious." After all, "everything that we were asking for, the university was willing to give us." But all the students knew "that we weren't really out of the woods yet," as she recalled. "This was the first time that we had any really serious commitment on this many of the concerns that we had raised."[175] Now, the students faced the long road to implement what would soon be known as the "May 4 agreement." In a statement Turner made later, he noted that the students pledged to "keep determined vigilance on administrators to see that these commitments are carried through."[176]

Before leaving the Bursar's Office, the students subjected the building to a thorough cleaning to ensure that it was vacated in pristine condition.[177] They still wanted to exercise control over the narrative, and by cleaning the building themselves, they made sure that staged images of "trashed" or damaged offices within the building would not emerge after they left.[178] (And sure enough, on Monday after the takeover, the *Daily Northwestern* published photographs of the interior of the recently occupied building.)

Shortly after 9:30 p.m., Hinz and other administrators arrived at the Bursar's Office and they pushed their way through the crowds of students, onlookers, and members of the press gathered outside. "Excuse me, please," Hinz said as he tried to make his way to the entrance.[179] But "no one paid very much attention," the *Daily Northwestern's* Kathy Waters reported, until they realized that "the man and those with him represented the university administration."[180] They were on their way to inspect the building. They found that it was in perfect order. "They left the place better than they took it," Hinz said later. "That was their whole approach to the situation, not to trash the place, but to make the university into a better place."[181]

The revolving front door of the Bursar's Office turned sixteen times as the flood of students came outside. A crowd of three hundred supporters was waiting, occasionally cheering and flashing the victory (peace) sign.[182] Under the bright lights of cameras and amidst a cheering crowd, Ogletree and Turner stood in front of the building's entrance.[183] "The situation at Northwestern University has been positively resolved," Turner announced. "The difference between this situation and the one at Columbia," he continued, "was due to the enlightened manner in which the administration conducted its response . . . They displayed themselves as men not only of responsibility but with a willingness to learn."[184] He thanked their supporters and soon, the group departed, singing "Lift Every Voice and Sing."[185]

Up to University Place, the students marched, for a brief rally. "We wanted this to be a model for change for the whole country," one student proclaimed.[186]

The takeover was over.

AN END – AND BEGINNING

Kathryn Ogletree (left) and James Turner (center) in front of the Bursar's Office after the agreement had been reached.
(*Daily Northwestern,* May 6, 1968)

Dear Northwestern University:

It's hard to believe that one of the great independent institutions of Higher Learning in the midwest had to give in to communistic agitators. Disgusted.

The response of the university on May 4th seems to me to be the most intelligent and courageous response yet made by any school to the demands of their black students. I am very proud that our university has stood up to be counted on the side of humanity.

Why don't you turn Northwestern into an all negro school?

Dear Jack [Hinz]: Now your friends have even more to admire you for! Congratulations! and continued best wishes.

The disgrace of the complete sell-out of the university to a militant minority has completely divorced me from Northwestern contributions henceforth. I am ashamed to have ever attended there.

I feel that the university has demonstrated the kind of leadership that is needed within "the white power structure" to bring about genuine quality in this country. The channels of communication, in which you played a great role in opening up, represent a great victory-a victory that will eventually defeat the kind of racist attitudes that were expressed in the Chicago Tribune *editorial today!*

Unbelievable-disgraceful. A complete sellout to black power! Disgusted.

I have never been prouder of our University.

Excerpts from letters received by Northwestern University after the takeover[1]

Chapter 7

This Was No Columbia

Northwestern university recognizes that throughout its history it has been a university of the white establishment. This is not to gainsay that many members of its administration, its faculty and its student body have engaged themselves in activities directed to the righting of racial wrongs. It is also true that for many years a few blacks have been members of its administration, faculty, and student body. But the fact remains that the university in its overwhelming character has been a white institution.

Northwestern policy statement, May 4 agreement, 1968[1]

"BLACK POWER WINS AT N.U." blazed the banner headline across the front page of the *Chicago Tribune* on Sunday, May 5, 1968, the day after the takeover ended.[2] The paper published a lengthy article documenting the takeover and negotiations and printed the thirteen-page agreement in full, charging that the university had "completely capitulated" by yielding to "rebel" demands.[3] Not only that, the article asserted, but "the administration publicly admitted guilt to white racism and begged forgiveness."[4]

The *Tribune* article was published without a byline. Joe Boyce, the reporter who had been inside the Bursar's Office with the students, had drafted an article about the takeover, drawing on his exclusive access. On Saturday night, right after the agreement had been reached, Boyce called in his story to the *Chicago Tribune* news desk. But soon, his story had been re-written by the paper's editor, Don Maxwell, who recast the piece in a decidedly negative light. Boyce was later told by the editor who initially took his story over the phone that he didn't think Boyce would want his name attached to such a scathing rendition of the event. And thus no credit was given to Boyce for his reporting.[5]

The next day, an editorial titled, "A Sad Day for Northwestern," appeared in the *Chicago Tribune* (soon reprinted in papers nationwide).[6] With a harsh, disdainful tone, it argued that any university with a "fit sense of values" would have "ended this insurrection within the first 15 minutes and driven out the interlopers." Afterward, it would have expelled each and every one of the students. Instead, as the editorial charged, Northwestern had "condoned the lawlessness with which they were challenged."[7] Equal vitriol was directed at both the students and the university administrators. And there were also a few harsh words directed at the "white sympathizers" who went "unmolested in their assertion of squatters' rights."[8] *Chicago Tribune* editor, Don Maxwell, who was also a member of Northwestern's board of trustees, later admitted that he wrote the editorial and the re-write of Boyce's piece "because I was incensed."[9]

There were plenty of others who were incensed. By Sunday morning, the university was facing "resounding criticism for treating its sit-inners with talk instead of immediate action."[10] Mail to the university "increased appreciably," as myriad critics wrote letters, sent telegrams, and drafted disdainful and insulting notes. A sizeable number of critics made overtly and deeply disturbing racist statements in their correspondence (some later labeled "obscene" in the Northwestern University Archives).[11]

Weaklings. Cowards. Pipsqueaks. Bunch of chumps. Communist agitators. Terrorists. Criminals. These were just some of the terms critics used to describe both university officials and the students. These critics were "disgusted." They were "outraged." And many were "ashamed" of Northwestern. Some alumni vowed to disassociate themselves entirely from the institution and others inserted their disparaging messages into otherwise empty Alumni Annual Fund return envelopes, deploring the fact that the university had surrendered its authority and had "rewarded" Black students "for their lawless act."[12] A few mailed in copies of Maxwell's *Chicago Tribune* editorial, torn out from the newspaper and accompanied by their own handwritten comments: "Shame is the word," one correspondent amended in red ink next to the headline, "A Sad Day for Northwestern."[13]

The hundreds of letters received from all over the country included a range of complaints, some more extreme than others. The fact that the students who participated in the takeover (and those who occupied Hinz's office) would not be disciplined was met with outrage.[14] The students did not seem to understand that attending Northwestern was a privilege and not a right, as many complained, and therefore they had no right to "demand" anything. Some argued that the May 4 agreement was only further evidence that radical students were part of a communist plot to take over America's universities. Others were furious that the administration had succumbed to a handful of radical, rebellious students. One alumna wrote to express her dismay in learning that the university had pledged to admit 2,000 Black students each year and lower the requirements for admission (which was, of course, untrue).[15] Hinz, in particular, was a target. "My guess is that you've got a radical on your staff as Vice-President and Dean of Students," one anonymous writer charged. Another addressed Hinz personally: "Following your statements and actions recently, we can only conclude that you are either an ass or that you have lost your reason. A child would do better, why not resign?"[16]

None of the critics acknowledged the larger context of racism or the long history of discrimination at Northwestern. Instead, they lambasted the *students*, deploring their "tactics of lawlessness and blackmail."[17] Even some members of Northwestern's Student Senate, which commended the administration for reacting to the takeover "with insight and educated clarity," decried the illegality of a building takeover, afterward issuing a statement that it could not "accede to its tactics."[18] At an Evanston City Council meeting held on Monday, just after the takeover, one council member went on the record saying he was "disappointed, disgusted and appalled at the way that Northwestern University had handled the case."[19] It had been a "lawless spectacle," another disgruntled observer wrote in the *Daily Northwestern.*[20] It was clear to many that the university had sided with a bunch of "militant" rebels, who were bent on defying authority and destroying Northwestern's reputation. The "selling out" of the university's authority had set a "dangerous precedent" amidst a country now undergoing widespread student revolt.[21]

Few if any statements appeared in the mainstream press acknowledging or reflecting on the legitimacy of the students' demands or the need for institutional change in light of the historic and long-standing effects of racism and discrimination. In fact, in a letter to the *Daily Northwestern*, one student called the takeover participants racists themselves, arguing that they were "demanding preferential, discriminatory treatment on the basis of skin color." No one, he wrote, "should give an iota of support to the ghetto-building racists."[22]

On Sunday, May 5, two white students staged their own protest in front of the Bursar's Office. Their homemade sign read: "NU Congradulations [*sic*] on your recent intimidation. We need Irish-Catholic Dormitories."[23] However tongue-in-cheek this demonstration may have been, it did get at the heart of one of the main points of contention many had with the May 4 agreement. Even some who supported the students viewed the university's pledge to provide a separate living unit for Black students as both "serious and harmful."[24] By May 8, 1968, syndicated cartoonist Reg Manning's "Soul Brothers" cartoon appeared in papers nationwide, accompanied by the caption, "Negro Students of Northwestern University." The cartoon depicted a Black student carrying a sign that read "We demand separate housing for blacks on campus," while nearby a KKK member, dressed in a robe and hood, raised his hand in solidarity.

In light of recently passed federal fair housing legislation and the open occupancy ordinance in Evanston, critics of a separate living facility charged that such an arrangement constituted segregation. The Evanston City Council vowed to study the legality of that portion of the agreement.[25] While the university was condemning itself for the "racist attitudes that have prevailed historically," read an editorial in the local newspaper, the *Evanston Review*, it was now "helping to prolong them."[26] Another critic wrote: "The ink is barely dry on the President's signature on the Civil Rights Act of 1968 providing open occupancy in housing. Let not Northwestern University violate the spirit of that law."[27] Many also questioned whether separate living quarters were even a legitimate right to demand: after all, as one writer for the *Chicago Defender* put it, it was "inconsistent with the basic assumption of the civil rights movement. For, open, unsegregated housing is the acid test of the democratic process."[28]

Immediately after the agreement was made public, calls were being made to nullify it. "The agreement made between the university and the extortionists who occupied the university's property and threatened to destroy its contents was obtained under compulsion," a Northwestern law professor told the *Chicago Tribune*.[29] Protest petitions in opposition to "the means used . . . to force the administration" to "yield" to the students' demands soon appeared on bulletin boards all over campus. Ultimately, more than four hundred Northwestern students signed them.[30] The co-chair of an upcoming Northwestern alumni reunion committee resigned his post in protest. He was "disappointed in Northwestern's naked capitulation," he wrote. "I am reminded of that sorry picture 30 years ago of Lord Chamberlain capitulating to Hitler."[31] Another alumnus flew halfway across the country in order to lead a protest march on campus.[32] His march was a "vigil of hope," he said, whose purpose was to void the May 4 agreement.[33] Hinz should be fired, he wrote in a letter to all Northwestern students, and the "militant group of fanatics"—the students who had taken part in the takeover—must be "dismissed, suspended, or placed on probation."[34]

As Jack Hinz returned to work on Monday, May 6, he repeated the same thing over and over again: The agreement was a *negotiated compromise*.[35] He was working furiously to ensure that the press, alumni, and everyone else understood the precise nature of what had occurred. At one point, he convened a closed door meeting with members of the Student Senate and staff on the *Daily Northwestern*. "I've been telling newspaper men all weekend," he told them, "if you could read, and if you would read, you'd see we have not come close to giving this school away." The agreement was made under a "very special set of circumstances," he stated.[36] "There were concessions made by both sides," he asserted. "There was humility on both sides of the table when that meeting ended Saturday."[37]

As Hinz publicly explained the nature of the agreement and the university's handling of the takeover, he continued to stress a key point: the resolution had been reached *peacefully*. "We had to weigh all alternative courses of action," he told the *Chicago Tribune*. "We felt the course of nonviolence was clearly the proper course of action."[38] Other university officials elaborated on the larger meaning behind the agreement. "The decision was a compassionate one made in recognition of the university's responsibilities to assist in providing education necessary if adequate Negro leadership is to emerge in this country," a university spokesman told the *Chicago Tribune.*[39] For his part, President Miller was unwavering in his support for the agreement and stood by the university's response to the takeover. He championed the agreement as signifying a great success. The "easiest and most popular action would have been to remove the students by force, since we clearly had the authority and the manpower to do so," he observed. "By use of understanding, restraint and compassion we feel we prevented what might have been a disaster at Northwestern University."[40]

Behind the scenes within the administration there was a bit of a scramble as mail continued to pour in and phones rang off the hook. Letters to President Miller were sorted into "pro" and "con" categories, with two appropriate uniform responses drafted:

> *Pro: I am grateful to you for taking time to make known to me your response to the University's action in the events of May 3-4. Your understanding and approval, together with the expressions of support we have received from others, give us encouragement and hope for the future.*

> *Con: Thank you for making known to me your views on the University's action in the student sit-in of May 3-4. I respect your opinion and regret that we do not see this incident in the same light.*[41]

But more than a form letter was needed. "An explanation should be offered to interested persons," one alumnus requested. "Critical reports by news media of what happened . . . are difficult to understand."[42] It was clear that the agreement had to be explained in depth. It had to be justified to the scores of critics who seemed to be lining up to share their opinions with Hinz, Kreml, Miller, and others in the administration.

On Monday, May 6, the *Daily Northwestern* published two photographs taken on Sunday afternoon inside the now quiet Bursar's Office, its rooms vacant. The images were a kind of visual cue to the rest of the campus: "It is now time," the paper stated, "to cool off."[43] And indeed, in the aftermath of the takeover, the mood on campus was strained. There was "tension in the air," as Turner recalled. Reports (later unsubstantiated) began to circulate that police patrols had been increased. Students reported sighting plainclothes officers roaming the campus and dormitory halls, apparently conducting "special patrols" in reaction to the takeover and the potential for further conflict or unrest.[44]

But the only known act of hostility that occurred was directed at Black students. At 3 a.m. on Sunday, just hours after the students left the Bursar's

Interior of the Bursar's Office. These photographs were taken right after the takeover ended and published in the *Daily Northwestern.* "The long hall leading to the bursar's office, 619 Clark St., was quiet Sunday afternoon, as were the offices there," the paper reported.
(*Daily Northwestern,* May 6, 1968)

Office, a water balloon had allegedly been thrown from the Zeta Psi fraternity house at seven Black students.[45]

"There was quite a bit of animosity among the white students," Turner said of the takeover's aftermath. While many white students were supportive, there were plenty who "were very vocal in their opposition" and thought that the university should have "beaten up" the students and "tied us up in sacks and thrown us in the lake," he said.[46]

Although the administration pledged that no participant would be punished for their involvement, there were reports of unofficial punishments. Steve Colson recalled returning to class after the takeover and being met by the professor who said, "I don't want to see you here again. Get out. Don't come back."[47]

Now, Black students were fast becoming "increasingly concerned with the hysteria sweeping the campus as a result of last weekend."[48] Hinz called for a return to equilibrium. This was a "critical time," he reminded everyone, and he forcefully declared that racist incidents have "got to stop."[49]

In an effort to calm the campus down, university officials were now busy preparing their written explanation of both the takeover and the agreement. It would soon be mailed to all alumni, faculty, students, and staff.[50] Prior to the official statement going out, the majority of mail the university received was classified as negative.

That proportion would not change. (By September 1968, a total of roughly 900 letters concerning the takeover had been received. A total of 615 letters opposed the administration's handling of the takeover and 222 letters expressed support.[51]) But once the official explanation had been received, many people seemed to have been appeased. The lack of information had only fueled the ire of the critics. Members of the board of trustees were also unclear on precisely what had transpired. And it was not until May 9 that they received an official report from President Miller himself. Prior to that, they had not been "informed of the negotiations and the ultimate solution," and so, for many, Maxwell's piece in the *Chicago Tribune* had been the only substantial account they received.[52]

Despite the vocal critics, there was, in fact, significant support for the agreement. By noon on Monday, a total of 390 fulltime Northwestern faculty members (out of a total of 722) had signed a statement endorsing the agreement and "both the rational conduct of the crisis and the moral solution of the problems it raised."[53] Petitions of support were also received from members of Northwestern's law school faculty, including alumna Dawn Netsch, a former *Daily Northwestern* editor who had been part of the campaign to end campus housing discrimination in the 1940s. University staff, representing a range of employees, from cashiers to administrative assistants, also submitted a petition of their own, stating "we wish it to be known that we, too, endorse the agreement reached by President Miller and all University representatives for the future conduct of the University with its black students."[54]

Many people specifically commended Jack Hinz for his role, lauding him for the way he handled the takeover, interacted with the students, and compelled everyone to the negotiation table. Soon, students and faculty around campus were spotted wearing "I Back Hinz" buttons.[55] The buttons were made by a group of students, led by Will Ris, who wanted to show their support for Hinz.[56]

In order to address the takeover and its implications in depth, events were organized to offer an opportunity for public discussion. Hinz took part in several town halls and panel discussions where he was the subject of both praise and derision. At a parents' town hall held at Cahn auditorium, many of the three hundred parents in the audience expressed support for the university's handling of the takeover and some articulated their support for the changes that were to be enacted. But others were furious. "The university," one angry parent fumed, "is never going to admit to all the resentment and opposition to this." Another said, "It's wrong to submit to the militant minority. If they want to complain, that's alright, but not violently. You've got to take a stand somewhere—now they will be off to the next conquest."[57] Hinz patiently explained that it was true, the university had several courses of action from which to choose to deal with the takeover. But, he told the parents, "we chose to address ourselves to the grievances in their petition."[58] For Hinz, the takeover's conclusion had been entirely positive and it bode well for a more

"I Back Hinz" button, 1968
(Courtesy of Jack Hinz)

open relationship between students and administrators. "A whole new stage of communication has been set up with our students," he insisted. "They realize now that we want to talk to them."[59]

Privately, Hinz soon became aware that the university's actions would affect him personally. At least one close friend unceremoniously "dropped" him afterward, and he continued to hear from plenty of critics who "thought my position was cowardly," as he said, and believed "that we should have put a heavy hand on the students."[60]

Kathryn Ogletree and James Turner also appeared at events to discuss the takeover. And they continued their effort to maintain control over the narrative. They were, as Turner said, "beginning to start defining what we feel is the significance of the weekend's events not only for ourselves, but for the entire University community."[61] On Monday, May 6, Eva Jefferson Paterson and two others formed a Student Senate committee and began drafting a letter to all campus living units in order to counter some of the "anticipated objections" to the agreement.[62] Days later, the Student Senate sponsored a panel of faculty and students, including Ogletree. Overall, the panelists praised the administration for the way that takeover had been resolved and Ogletree explained just why the action had been necessary in the first place, stating that "the University's bureaucratic structure prevented action on demands that some administrators favored."[63] At a "Black/White talk-in" held on campus, takeover participant Vernon Ford was joined by Thomas Picou, *Chicago Defender* editor, along with representatives from the Southern Christian Leadership Conference and the Evanston Urban League, to discuss the agreement.[64] Turner himself led a campus teach-in: "Black Students: After the Crisis." There, he spoke at length about the takeover, the issues confronting Black students, the Black Power movement, and the reasons behind the post-takeover "hysteria."[65] To him, the hysteria was generated by "conscious malice on the part of many people and perhaps some innocent ignorance on the part of others."[66] Ultimately, Turner explained, the hostility that the takeover elicited was derived from a "feeling that somehow Black students shouldn't have gotten what they got," that "they shouldn't have been somehow able to do what they did this past weekend."[67] "But what has it cost you?" Turner asked rhetorically and with the eloquence and force that made him such an effective spokesperson. "What does it cost anyone else in the university in terms of what Black students did?"[68]

Turner, unlike Ogletree, was cast further onto the public stage. The media could not get enough of him. He was profiled in a variety of newspapers and magazines, and just days after the takeover, he appeared as a guest, along with William F. Buckley and Abbie Hoffman, on "At Random," a local CBS news show, moderated by John Madigan.[69] He also appeared on David Susskind's nationally-syndicated television show and was a guest on the premiere of a television show, "For Blacks Only."[70] Locally, in Evanston, he was famous. "I'd go into a restaurant or a bank," he recalled, "and people would come up and say . . . 'We're glad you did what you did' and 'We admire your courage and principle.' "[71]

Of course, Turner also had more than his fair share of blowback. His critics were numerous, labeling him an "anarchist" and just one of many dangerous "college radicals" who were making so much trouble across the country. "The press and television stations ought to quit glorifying them as if they had something important to say," one critic said, disparaging Turner along with all other young "radicals."[72] Meanwhile, others saw something deeply nefarious going on within the student protest movement as a whole: "Both white and Black revolutionary groups are supported, influenced, and sometimes used by the Communists, as instruments of subversion," a *Chicago Tribune* reporter warned.[73]

For many critics, the takeover spelled a kind of social breakdown and their fears seemed to be affirmed every time they looked at a newspaper. Around the world, throughout the country, and right in Chicago, student protests were becoming so numerous now that some newspapers devoted a special column to them, giving a rundown on the current student-led protests, takeovers, sit-ins, be-ins, and other actions, sometimes using the word *spreading* to describe how they seemed to be multiplying exponentially. "[M]ilitant youths continue to disrupt academic life in the United States and abroad," one such article noted.[74]

But for defenders of the May 4 agreement, the disruptions on other campuses, including a weeklong protest launched just days after the takeover at Roosevelt University in Chicago, provided a wider context to frame the events at Northwestern. And soon, many were comparing the outcome of Northwestern's dramatic events with other protests around the country.

"This was no Berkeley or Columbia," Howard R. Rosenheim, president of Northwestern's alumni association, announced.[75] "When the dust is settled," he wrote in a press release, dated May 7, 1968, and "we look to the deeper meaning of the actions at Northwestern, I believe we will find a source of pride and hope for the future."[76] Still, he acknowledged the divisions left in the takeover's wake. "[N]ever before in the history of this great University," he observed, "have so large a group of our alumni been drawn apart from their Alma Mater as they have by the events of May 3-4."[77] But, as Turner, Hinz, and many others had already observed, the fact that a peaceful resolution had been obtained at Northwestern was crucial, a point that Rosenheim reiterated to other alumni.

It was hard not to compare the peaceful resolution obtained at Northwestern with the upheaval still being experienced at Columbia University following the forced ejection of student protesters and the injuries police inflicted on students and faculty. As Northwestern tried to resume a normal routine on Monday, May 6, Columbia officials announced that all classes on their campus would be suspended for a week; and all classes and final exams would be canceled for the year at one of the university's colleges. A campus-wide student strike was soon underway and the university was now in chaos, nearly paralyzed following the recent violence.[78] Columbia President Grayson Kirk was facing calls to resign.

During the weekend of the takeover, Kirk had appeared on the TV show, "Face the Nation," where he defended his decision to order the police to clear the occupied buildings. There seemed to be no alternative, he said, "except that of complete capitulation to the demands of those who had illegally occupied four of our buildings."[79] "I'm not going to resign under fire," Kirk pledged, "because that would be a victory for those who are trying to wreck the university."[80] But just three months later, under intense pressure from a growing body of critics who charged that he had catastrophically mishandled the event, Kirk would, in fact, resign from his position as president.[81]

The final authority on whether the May 4 agreement would go into effect now rested in the hands of Northwestern's board of trustees. On May 9, the board appointed a subcommittee to review the agreement before the entire board would vote to approve, reject, or qualify it. University officials, including Miller, Kreml, and Hinz, met with thirty-one of the fifty-four board members for three hours to discuss the agreement.[82] Prior to the vote, the heads of several academic departments implored the trustees to approve the agreement outright. "[I]f the agreement is qualified, in spirit or content, or if the trustees fail to backup president Miller and the administration," they predicted, it was likely that many faculty members would leave the university and there would be a "general loss of confidence in administrative decisions, from those made by the president down to those made by us."[83] Perhaps most importantly, they advised, approving the agreement also provided a unique opportunity. "We hope that the board will respond to these events by recognizing the remarkable opportunity provided the university for distinction as a private institution, which is pioneering in the achievement of viable solutions to the racial problems which beset this nation."[84]

Support for the agreement was certainly not universal among the trustees. Some stated privately that they held firm to their belief that police force should have been used to eject the students from the Bursar's Office.[85] Franklin Kreml, who had played such a significant role during the negotiations with the students, now played another major role as he sought to mollify trustees and build support for their approval of the May 4 agreement.[86] And so they did. On May 14, the board accepted the subcommittee's report and voted unanimously to approve the agreement.[87] "The board concurs in the administration's sincere efforts to understand the problems of the black student group and to seek a satisfactory program for resolving them," announced Tilden Cummings, the board's vice president. "The board therefore authorizes the administration to proceed with the terms of the agreement." Cummings also confirmed that the students (including those who took over Hinz's office) would not be punished or disciplined in any way.[88] Further, while the board acknowledged there had been "considerable adverse comment" about establishing separate housing for Black students, it nonetheless approved the administration's pledge to fulfill that demand. The students, the board noted, were "sincere in their belief that separate housing, on the basis of individual choice, was desirable in view of the special problems confronting them."[89]

The board did not qualify any part of the agreement, but it did raise some objections. It judged the agreement's policy statement (admitting that Northwestern was part of the "white establishment") "wholly unacceptable" "insofar as it is interpreted to impute to the University hostile and antagonist 'racism.' "[90] It also condemned as "unlawful" the students' occupation of the Bursar's Office.[91] "In order that there be no misunderstanding, negotiations will not again be conducted by the University while unlawful or disruptive activity is in progress," the board noted, pledging that in the future, Northwestern would "take whatever action is necessary to terminate unlawful activities."[92]

To this end, the board formally adopted a new resolution: The university would no longer "tolerate any attempt by any individual, group or organization to disrupt the regularly scheduled activities of the University. Any such effort to impede the holding of classes, the carrying forward of the University's business or the arrangements for properly authorized and scheduled events, would constitute an invasion of the rights of faculty and students and cannot be permitted. If any such attempt is made . . . the leaders and participants engaged in disruptive tactics will be held responsible and will be subject to appropriate legal and disciplinary action, including expulsion."[93] As a member of the board of trustees, Don Maxwell, author of the recent *Chicago Tribune* pieces, was present at the board meeting. He reportedly spoke only once: to vote "yes" on passing this resolution.[94]

The board also underscored the limit on the power to be exercised by the students in the wake of the agreement. The university had done well to refuse to "surrender administrative authority or faculty prerogative" to the students, the board stated clearly. "Under the terms of the agreement, students will be consulted in an advisory capacity only."[95]

President Miller responded to the board's unanimous vote to approve the agreement. "I am deeply grateful to the members of the board of trustees of this University for upholding the decisions made by the administration in the events of May 3-4," he stated. "Their approval enables Northwestern to go forward with programs of the utmost concern to the future of our country." The takeover had been "a single confrontation of a special type," he reiterated. "We will not again negotiate with any groups under such circumstances," he pledged.[96]

Inside the Bursar's Office, May 1968. Left to right: Michael Smith, Steve Colson, Dan Davis (wearing a Kappa Alpha Psi t-shirt), and Eric Perkins. (Northwestern University Archives, photograph courtesy of Steve Colson)

Residual Effects

Some are calling the peaceful settlement of the grievances a shameful capitulation. Is it ever shameful to redress wrongs?

Chicago Defender, May 13, 1968[97]

Hail to my brothers and sisters of Northwestern University for their significant victory over injustice.

Roger Williams, Jr.[98]

Once the students left the Bursar's Office, many of them faced the task of calling home "to let our parents know that we were okay," as Ogletree remembered.[99] They knew that their families had heard about the takeover through the media, and for the past two days they had agonized about them, imagining how worried they must have been, thinking "that we were going to be put out of school or arrested or hurt or killed," Ogletree recalled.[100]

"Their aspirations were for us to go to college and graduate," she noted, explaining that many parents had been concerned that their children, by their own actions, might have put those dreams at risk.

Before she enrolled in college, Ogletree's father "had been on his job bragging that his daughter had been accepted Northwestern University and he was very proud about that," she said.[101] After the takeover, she called home. Her father, she learned, had indeed found out about the takeover through TV and newspaper reports. At work on Friday, one of his colleagues confronted him, newspaper in hand, and asked, " 'Is this your daughter? In this takeover?' And he had to reluctantly agree that yes, that was his daughter."[102]

But it was her mother's reaction that concerned Ogletree more. Later, she joked that when she had been in the Bursar's Office, "my greatest fear was not of the police, but that my mother would appear outside that window and demand that I come out! Because if she had said I had to come out, I would have had to come out!"[103]

Relieved to learn that her parents stood by her, she recalled that even though her father hadn't "known any of the details" about the takeover, "the only thing that he knew was that I wasn't a rabble rouser or someone who would participate in riots. [So] if I had felt inclined to engage in such an activity there must be a reason for it, even though he may not have agreed or approved of it if I asked him in advance."[104] Ogletree's parents were also relieved, grateful that their daughter had not been harmed in any way.

It was only after the takeover that many parents would first learn about what their children had been experiencing at Northwestern. "Many of us from inner-city Chicago were first-generation college students," Ogletree recalled, and most parents hadn't known "what to expect from college anyway." "We didn't complain at home every day about all the things that we were experiencing, so they did not really know the subtleties of everything that we were enduring." It was only "afterwards when we had talked about things" that many parents not only understood what their children had been going through, but they also "became proud" of what they had done, feeling that, as Ogletree put it, "everything was going to be for the better."[105]

Overall, the students had a feeling that they had accomplished something quite momentous, and there was an overriding sense of relief and even awe at what they had done. "You didn't know what was going to happen; this was open-ended," Bracey said, describing their anxiety before the takeover. And now, they were rather amazed at the outcome. "When you look at it in retrospect, a whole bunch of stuff fell into place," Bracey said. "If one thing had not fallen into place . . . You would have read about Northwestern students being thrown in jail for disorderly conduct, resisting arrest, and illegal trespassing," he said. "That could have been the story."[106]

But now the students were looking at a copy of the May 7, 1968 issue of the *Chicago Defender.* A two-page spread was devoted to a series of photographs that documented the takeover. One of them, which Ogletree later described as a favorite, pictured a group of the students, including Bracey, Ogletree, and Turner, holding one of the chains that had been used to secure the Bursar's Office. The chain, the caption read, "signifies unity among black students at NU."

Some students were dismayed by the negative reactions to the takeover, but they weren't surprised. For them, their highly-organized and peaceful protest was the only rational way to initiate change. "It took taking over a building to get people to listen," as Bracey said. And really, their demands had not been so extreme. "They didn't demand that Northwestern become Tuskegee," as Bracey pointed out with his dry sense of humor.

As the students returned to classes and evaluated for themselves what had happened, there were plenty of people who not only lauded their action, but also celebrated it. They praised the brave students and commended the university's peaceful response. The *Chicago Daily News* applauded the university's "ability to cope with radical change,"[107] while the *Chicago Defender* stated that the university "deserves to be congratulated."[108]

Of the nine hundred letters the university ultimately received related to the takeover, many were written "in support of the university's action."[109] "It is the overwhelming consensus of the faculty and students with whom I have talked that you and your administration have performed a distinguished service to Northwestern University," wrote a Northwestern English professor to President Miller. "You have shown magnanimity and great moral courage. You have advanced us a giant stride into that greatness we all coveted for this university."[110] (He also noted that his daughter, a student at Barnard, was among a group of students at Columbia who, in the recent takeover there, had been "needlessly, recklessly, and brutally attacked by the police.")[111]

Support also poured in from generations of alumni. "I got a vicarious thrill out of the victory of this generation's black Northwestern students," Doris E. Saunders, a former Quibblers Club member, wrote in the *Chicago Defender.*[112] Saunders attended Northwestern from 1938 to 1940 when just twenty-seven Black students were enrolled. She recalled their own failed efforts in asking for "simple things" from the administration, such as being allowed to live in campus housing.

"I am particularly moved by the breadth of vision and compassion shown by graduates of classes as far back as 1911," President Miller later wrote.[113] Alumni wrote in to recall their own experiences on campus, from fighting for civil rights to personally experiencing racial and religious discrimination. All praised the university's enlightened response, acknowledging the widespread need for the entire country to come together to confront racial prejudice in just such a manner.

"I recall all too clearly my own active involvement while at Northwestern 1948-50 in various interracial activities which attempted, among other things, to obtain the university's approval of the 'radical' stuff of integrating student housing," wrote alumnus Thomas H. Floyd, Jr. "The somewhat Country Club atmosphere of the University at that time was also objectionable and I have welcomed president Miller's willingness to bring the university into modern times . . . We are still moving entirely too slowly to treat all humans alike and bring Negroes into full participation in both American and our University life. . . . I commend any efforts you can take in this direction."[114]

A current graduate student recounted the reason she, as a Jewish student, had left Northwestern as an undergraduate in 1955. "An orientation week of Christian prayers made me feel distinctly uncomfortable, unwanted," she wrote, "and I completed my education at the University of Chicago. In those years, this school did not even admit to having a quota system. Over the years I have watched Northwestern liberalize and finally open its admission policy, as though realizing that the right to educate was also a responsibility whose parameters reach beyond the white world."[115]

A recent graduate observed that "Mr. Hinz handled the situation with good sense. Black students were locked out of university life the way they had been locked out of American life in the past . . . it is beyond argument that black people in general are not citizens in the sense white people are—and we all recognize the symbolic aspects of these confrontations."[116]

Support also came from administrators and faculty at other institutions, government officials, and local residents. They wrote to express "gratitude to Northwestern University for setting an excellent example of how to handle student protests in a creative way."[117] "I hope you will not be deterred by bigoted statements," Chicago alderman Leon M. Despres wrote in offering "congratulations on the mature settlement of the dispute with black students." Despres lauded the university's willingness to negotiate with the students and thus provide a "powerful example for peaceful settlement of differences."[118]

Many current Northwestern students also viewed the takeover's resolution positively and with hope for the future. "Two years ago this couldn't have happened," a nineteen-year-old sophomore told the *Chicago Tribune*. "I think we can thank Dean Hinz for the change in attitude."[119] "The administration is fabulous," another student said, "because they kept their 'cool.' . . . I don't go along with sitting in buildings, but the administration's reaction was far better than the reaction at Columbia."[120]

It soon became clear that the university's handling of the takeover was having a positive impact on Northwestern's broader reputation. In a letter to a Northwestern trustee, an alumnus reported that he been at a seminar on the day the agreement was reached. He overheard a Harvard professor say that he was encouraged by the takeover and related actions since he had thought that all Northwestern students were interested in was "necking." Although this was clearly a joke, it revealed the negative view some held of Northwestern. But now, this alumnus was heartened to recognize that Northwestern would become more widely recognized as having a politically conscious student body and an administration that was seen as a leader in higher education, blazing a trail for others to follow.[121]

Although some feared that the university would see a decline in financial support after the takeover, Hinz publicly dismissed such a claim. He was confident that "the net result will be more gain than loss" in the coming years, he said.[122] And in fact, following the takeover, several major corporations, including Jewel Food Company and United Airlines, made donation pledges to Northwestern, while the Robert R. McCormick Charitable Trust made a $300,000 gift for the building of a new auditorium.[123] By June 1968, the amount of donations to the university exceeded that of the previous year.[124]

In the weeks and months after the takeover, its positive effects reverberated. The May 4 agreement was judged as "perhaps more comprehensive, and more understanding of the peculiar situations Black students face on predominantly white campuses than any other made so far,"[125] as one observer noted, and it was held up as a model for other student groups. And it wasn't long before others began to try to duplicate the takeover's results. Among the numerous protests launched in Chicago in the week following the takeover, at least two were organized by Black student groups: On May 15, at the University of Chicago, sixty Black students seized the administration building for more than three hours.[126] That same day, at De Paul University, members of the Black Student Union, representing the school's 129 Black students (out of 9,000 students) presented nine demands to University President John Courtelyou.[127] After peaceful negotiations concluded, the university agreed to take "positive measures" to meet their demands.[128]

There was no doubt that the issue of racial disparity and discrimination had also been made more visible in Evanston as a result of the takeover. One Evanston City Council member "congratulated the administrators of Northwestern University and others for the very difficult and fine handling of a tough situation."[129] It had been a "year of unprecedented turmoil in the community," as one Evanston resident observed.[130] But in the May 4 agreement and the passage of the city's fair housing legislation, many saw the possibility for further reform. By July 1968, the city established a Human Relations Commission, which adopted as one of its aims to help "institutional structures cease obstructing the legitimate aspirations of minority groups—particularly black people."[131]

Perhaps partly sparked by the events at Northwestern, a number of panels and talks addressing racism and discrimination would take place in Evanston in the months following the takeover. In July, at St. Mary's

Church, George H. Clements, a Chicago-based Catholic priest, active in the civil rights movement, addressed an audience of four hundred to share his "view of white racism."[132] In September, the National Council of Jewish Women invited four area women to speak about their own local experiences with "racial prejudice."[133] By 1969, the *Evanston Review* began running a series focused on the city's "racial problems." The fact that "the city's black community is subjected to vocational, economic, and educational discrimination" was "not new," the paper noted. But it was clear that the need to address discrimination was now being "accented by a tone of urgency."[134]

Many takeover participants would continue organizing, branching out, and networking both locally and nationally. In the days following the takeover, the students dispatched a telegram of support to students conducting a sit-in at Stanford University. The telegram was "received with cheers."[135] Many also joined with over two hundred Chicago-area students, including students from Loyola, Roosevelt, and the University of Chicago, who were inspired to strengthen their alliance. They founded Black Students Organized for Political Liberation, a group which aimed to "liberate the politics within the black community" and "organize more black students to help in the campaign."[136]

Meanwhile, many students continued to work in the local community. Along with other Northwestern students, James Turner and Wayne Watson helped set up a Black cooperative bookstore across the street from the Evanston Township High School, and they also continued to take part in a mentorship program for students.[137] Some Evanston high school students had been outside the Bursar's Office during the takeover in a show of support, and soon, they too would form their own organization and present their own list of demands to the school board, helped along the way by Turner, Watson, and others.[138] By August 1968, the school board announced plans to implement broad changes at Evanston's high school, including hiring more Black teachers and administrators and offering classes with an "emphasis on Negro culture and achievements."[139]

In the wake of the takeover, it was clear that Northwestern had undergone a dramatic change. And both behavior and attitudes would begin to change as a result. In a series of essays published in the *Chicago Tribune*, John Walter, editor of the *Daily Northwestern,* offered his insights from a student's point of view. He drew a sharp contrast between the parents, alumni, and trustees who were the "most vocal in criticizing the N.U. administration" and the "general support within the university community for the action Northwestern administrators took." Some students, he noted, had now become "aware of how 'institutional racism' can work—even if it is an unconscious racism on the part of whites."[140] As evidence of this new awareness, in a noticeable change, the *Daily Northwestern* soon largely ceased using the word "Negro" and replaced it with the more contemporary and preferred term, "black."[141]

For Ogletree, one of the most significant effects of the takeover was the emergence of a widespread "consciousness . . . concerning black people's problems."[142] Indeed, many people made it known that prior to the takeover, they had not "fully appreciated" what Black students had been going through.[143] In a letter to the *Daily Northwestern*, one student even admitted to seeing "for the first time the heretofore invisible Black student."[144] Making the existence of racism on campus apparent to so many people was a victory. This new enlightenment, however, had to be sustained. It "shouldn't be allowed to die or be put on the shelf in the next 2 or 3 weeks," Ogletree warned at the time. "Whether you know racism is a reality or not," she argued to those who still refused to recognize the reality of conditions at Northwestern, "we do, and we feel it every day."[145]

For Turner, the peaceful resolution was something to be admired, celebrated, and replicated. "I would like to think that this university has set a path that other people can emulate," he said.[146] Indeed, as he later reflected, the May 4 agreement was "the most sophisticated and productive to come out of confrontations between university administrations and students in this country."[147] And there was no doubt that the takeover and the agreement constituted what Turner called "a proud moment" not only for the students and the university as a whole, but also for Evanston's Black residents.[148] It was a turning point, a moment when Black students "stood up and told Northwestern University about itself," he said.[149] Prior to this, as he asserted, "you just didn't take on Northwestern University and not pay dearly for it."[150]

Among many Black Evanston residents were those who worked for the university as groundskeepers and mechanics; they worked in the dining halls and in building maintenance; they were among the university's clerical staff; and one Evanston resident, Venice Deese, Jr., worked as a member of the university's campus security staff. They were economically vulnerable, as Turner said, unable to fully express any concerns they might have to their employer.[151] And so, as Turner recalls, many residents viewed the success of the students' peaceful occupation of the building to advance changes on campus as a shared victory. They "talked about that event as if it were theirs," Turner reflected, like it was "their event."[152] It was, he said, "a big moment" for Black Evanstonians. And, one of the takeover's "unintended consequences" that Turner was most "proud and pleased about" was that many Evanston families now thought about Northwestern as a possibility for their own children. Before that, few Black city residents attended the university. Turner himself knew of at least three residents "who were positively influenced" by the takeover and, as a result, decided to apply for admission to Northwestern. "These residual effects," he noted, "multiplied in the Black community."[153]

As for those who viewed the students as militants, rebels, or anarchists,

Turner responded: it was not the students who were lawless agitators or troublemakers. They were the objects of injustice, not the perpetrators. "In this case the law, the rules, oppressed us," he said. "The students had decided that the white administration wasn't going to give them anything of their own will. When we occupied the building, [administrators] said they could finally begin to realize and understand what we had been saying. We thought, as with most men of power, they had understood all the time, and now they were forced to see it and deal with it."[154]

But was Northwestern, as an institution, really ready to change fundamentally? Was the "battleship" that Hinz once talked about, truly making a slow turn in another direction? Ogletree remembers "feeling reassured that [university officials] were making a commitment that was different than before." Still, she "knew it was going to be a lot of work" not only to implement the agreement, but also to ensure that true and lasting change would occur.[155]

Many students had their doubts that the May 4 agreement would cause an immediate revolution in attitudes and practices when it came to issues of racism and injustice. But they were still hopeful. Later, Eva Jefferson Paterson would observe that the quick resolution to the takeover "gave us all a false sense of how quickly change can come about."[156] And, as far as the climate on campus for Black students went, Ogletree recalled that after the takeover, "it was still probably about the same."[157] Overall, she said, "things did not immediately change."[158] Hinz concurred. After things quieted down a few weeks after the takeover, he had believed that things were better than they really were.[159] Victor Goode assessed the situation this way: after the takeover, "campus life was never really normal."[160]

In June 1968, at the close of a momentous year, Northwestern held its graduation ceremony. Elvis J. Stahr, president of Indiana University and former secretary of the U.S. Army, delivered the commencement address. "In complete disregard for the rights of others and careless of the institution's fate," Stahr asserted, "some seek to hammer and burn their individual views upon the face of the university."[161] No mention was made of the takeover directly. But it appeared, from Stahr's ominous condemnation of protest and student activism, that there might be some stormy seas ahead.

Part II

The Five Broad Causes of Campus Unrest:

The pressing problems of American society, particularly the war in Southeast Asia and the conditions of minority groups;

The changing status and attitudes of youth in America;

The distinctive character of the American university during the postwar period;

An escalating spiral of reaction to student protest from public opinion and an escalating spiral of violence;

Broad evolutionary changes occurring in the culture and structure of modern Western society.

Report of the President's Commission on Campus Unrest, 1970, 55-56.

Question:

This has been kind of a frantic year for Northwestern. When you became president, this was a very conservative university. Today, it has to be considered one of the most liberal in the country. Do you agree with all this change?

Answer:

It's a sign of the times.

Interview with President J. Roscoe Miller, *Daily Northwestern,* May 28, 1968

Herblock, May 5, 1968. This nationally-syndicated cartoon appeared in the May 8, 1968 edition of the *Chicago Sun-Times,* just days after the takeover concluded.
(A 1968 Herblock Cartoon, ©The Herb Block Foundation)

Chapter 8

Climate of Restlessness

It is no wonder that a new generation of students, trained by the mass media to detect events in the world affairs and conscious of the visible flaws in their society and its educational system, has risen to challenge the aimlessness and the intellectual lethargy of the big university in America.

"NU Sees the Light," *Chicago Defender*, May 8, 1968

The Present Culture

The summer following the takeover was anything but peaceful in the United States. On June 5, 1968, Senator Robert F. Kennedy was assassinated in Los Angeles on the night of his victory in the California Democratic primary. Several weeks later, in August, during the Democratic National Convention held in Chicago, police moved in on ten thousand protesters, beating, tear gassing, and arresting hundreds of people, including some members of the media. "The whole world is watching" went the refrain protesters chanted.

Over the course of a difficult summer, the national media continued reporting furiously on the scores of youth-led protests, which seemed to multiply each week, trying to make sense of it all. "Can you trust anyone *under* 30?" quipped *Time* magazine in its June 1968 cover story. "The spirit of '68 is at times uncomfortable and uncouth," the writer observed. "It may also turn out to be the most creative ferment ever to disturb the college campuses."[1]

With a hope that the ferment on its own campus was a thing of the past, Northwestern officials ushered in the fall 1968 quarter with a sense of guarded optimism. Seventy Black students were newly enrolled. And there were now roughly 180 Black students at Northwestern (out of 6,500 undergraduates).[2] Jack Hinz told reporters he was "cautiously optimistic" about the year ahead. He was "quite happy with the way things went last year," he said. "We accomplished a great deal."[3] On October 8, camera crews from ABC and other news organizations were present as Hinz joined Kathryn Ogletree, James Turner, and Eric Perkins at a press conference to report on the progress made in "carrying out promises made last May." They were off to a good start, they announced.[4]

Work to implement the May 4 agreement had been underway since the days following the end of the takeover. Over the summer, a subcommittee to monitor and investigate discrimination in housing had been appointed, along with a nine-member Human Relations Committee that would "hear grievances from anyone—student, faculty, or staff—who believes he is subject to unfair treatment."[5] The committee would also "elicit" and "recognize" the views and recommendations of Black students, as Hinz explained.[6] Two takeover participants, Saundra Malone and Amassa Fauntleroy, were appointed as student members of the committee.[7] The university had also integrated its three-year-old summer enrichment program, Northwestern University Chicago Action Program (NUCAP), which had previously been offered only to incoming Black students.

Not all went smoothly, however. The first integrated program had reportedly been "turbulent," with students engaged in emotional discussions often into the wee hours of the morning. Some students reported that they experienced "racial tension" within what was soon described as a "psychologically demanding" program. Despite the reported problems with the new program, however, administrators pledged their continued faith in its capacity to bring students together.[8]

Robert Strotz, dean of the College of Arts and Sciences, and one of the university representatives at the negotiating table on May 4, had been appointed to oversee an ad hoc committee to introduce Afro-American studies courses at Northwestern. By early 1969, the committee received support from the faculty to formulate a degree-granting program in Afro-American studies, and three distinguished visiting professors were hired to teach courses: Lerone Bennett, Jr., historian and influential editor of *Ebony* magazine; Margaret Walker Alexander, the prominent poet, writer, and Northwestern graduate, who would teach courses in African-American literature; and historian C.L.R. James, who would teach courses in sociology.[9] South African historian, Jeremiah Congress Mbata, who had recently been hired at Northwestern, would also teach a two-quarter course on the "History of Apartheid, Segregation and Partnership."[10] These first course offerings would serve as the basis for the university's Afro-American Studies program, and would eventually lead to the 1972 founding of Northwestern's African-American Studies department, with Lerone Bennett, Jr. serving as its first chair.[11]

"The university also hired its first Black financial officer, a recent graduate who had worked as an intern," as Turner recalled, "and they hired someone to recruit Black students to increase enrollment."[12] A new financial aid fund for Black students had been established over the summer with a private donation of $200,000.[13] Also in the works was the establishment of what would later be known as the Black House, a campus center for Black students. Initially located at 619 Emerson Street (and later moved to 1914 Sheridan Road), the Black House would offer students a "lounge, library study, small offices, conference room, and social area." A large portion of the building would be assigned to FMO, with office space also reserved for Northwestern's new counselor for Black students, Paul Black, who would join Hinz's staff.[14]

Want ads in the *Daily Northwestern* also reflected changes from the past year. In the section listing available rental housing, a new statement now appeared: "It is the policy of Northwestern University Student publications to accept housing advertising only from those whose housing is available without discrimination with respect to race, creed, or national origin."[15] The on-campus housing situation for Black students, however, was unresolved. In the May 4 agreement, the university had promised to "move toward providing separate housing units" for Black students, with a spring 1969 deadline set to fulfill this demand. In the interim, the university would reserve separate sections within existing housing units for those Black students who wished to room together. In response, two-thirds of Northwestern's Black students requested housing with other Black students for the fall 1968 quarter.[16]

But living arrangements in the crowded dorms were difficult: some Black female students were given a corridor on the second floor of the Northwestern apartments, half the rooms in Hobart House, and rooms at the North Shore Hotel in Evanston. Black male students had been given a corridor on the sixth floor of the North Shore Hotel, as well as rooms in other residence units around campus.[17] "Efforts will be made in the future to provide the opportunity for those students who wish to live in proximity to have that choice," Hinz pledged.[18]

Overall, the university put a positive spin on the progress that had been made thus far. "It is my hope that the new relationship which resulted from our discussions of May 3 and 4 will continue to improve and prosper in the future," Hinz said.[19] "There were times when we didn't listen carefully enough," Hinz said of the way the administration had handled interactions with students in the past. "There must be an effort to effect understanding on both sides. Without this, our growth will be stifled."[20] For his part, Turner believed that Hinz was working hard "to see that the university would put forward its best practice to live up to the agreement."[21] But Turner also acknowledged that the perceptions of students and administrators were not always "identical or harmonious."[22] "The black students will say to the university what else they want and where else they want to go from here," Turner noted of the ongoing process to implement the demands.[23]

With no separate housing facility yet provided for Black students, the housing situation was just one of the concerns weighing on Kathryn Ogletree's mind as she returned to school for the fall 1968 quarter. Not only did she have a full load of classes, but she was also involved in several committees formed just days after the takeover. Ogletree underscored the need for the students to continue to keep focused. "If we slacken up now," she told the *Daily Northwestern*, "the university will slacken up."[24] As the new fall quarter began, she knew there was much work to do. After all, the agreement would be useless if the students themselves did not work assiduously to ensure that progress would be made toward meeting all of their demands. "We realized that if we wouldn't show up to the committees and take everything seriously, they wouldn't either," she said. "Why should they?"[25] But the workload proved to be tremendous, with the students volunteering to work on the committees alongside faculty and staff who were being paid for their labor.

Ogletree also confronted changes underway in FMO, the organization she had so successfully led the previous school year. Now, in the fall of 1968, FMO members began to formalize many aspects of the organization, including drafting and ratifying a constitution and establishing permanent committees on issues such as admissions and financial aid. The group soon became known officially as "For Members Only: A Black Student Alliance." It received official designation as a campus organization and thus became eligible to receive student activity funds.[26] But just as the new year got underway, Ogletree had a rather unpleasant surprise. As president of FMO, she had steered more than one hundred students through the nationally famous and peacefully resolved takeover. But now, she learned, she would no longer hold office. This was the result of a majority of FMO members voting to impose a new committee structure on the organization. Now, "coordinators" would run the group, rather than a single leader. The new positions included a minister of campus affairs, a minister of communications, a minister of external relations, and a correlator of communications. Each new position was staffed by a takeover participant.[27]

To this day, there is still some debate concerning the reasons behind these changes and what was, essentially, Ogletree's ouster from office. To her, the change was sexist, and she felt strongly that "the guys were eager to . . . get me out of office."[28] Along with some other FMO members, she was "disturbed by the fact that all of the coordinators that were elected at the time were all male and that there were no women coordinators."[29]

Still, she viewed the changes within the larger social and political context of the time. Many organizations, including civil rights and students activist groups, held the belief that "the man should be in the lead and the women should be behind," as Ogletree observed. At the time, most groups were dominated and led by men, with female members often pushed into the background. From an "ego standpoint," Ogletree recalls, "I did want to be more prominent." But, she conceded, "I didn't argue it or anything," feeling at the time that "it was an anomaly that I was the female president."[30] But she also believed that she had done an excellent job, particularly during such a taxing period. "I executed my duties and responsibilities well," she said. "I thought I did and they thought I did too. But then they wanted to go back to the regular way that people thought things should be."[31] So, she said, "I just kind of sucked it up and dealt with it . . . I still had respect. And some people would come and consult with me about various things. So I still had the respect as a leader. But we never really openly talked about it."[32]

John Bracey recognized the fundamental unfairness of the leadership change. And he was not hesitant to call out the sexist impulse behind it. "It was only the obsession with the notion that militant, Afro and dashiki wearing males had to be the leaders that caused Kathy [Ogletree] and so many other young women like her to be overlooked and their contributions minimized or attributed to others," he said.[33] But Ogletree's experience was not unusual; at the time, many women were relegated to the sidelines within student activist organizations.

Although there were female students involved in Northwestern's progressive student movements, it was rare to see a woman mentioned in the *Daily Northwestern's* coverage of various student activist groups.[34] Over the years, the name Melva Fager, founder of SDS at Northwestern, seems to have disappeared from the official historical record, along with the names of her female classmates also active in SDS, including Niki Gekas, who organized a local boycott in support of a United Farm Workers strike in 1967.[35] Such omissions of women's contributions were not unique to Northwestern.

Barnard student Nancy Biberman documented the unequal treatment female students faced during the April 1968 protests at Columbia: "Despite the rhetoric of making decisions that affect our lives, we have often found ourselves behind desks answering phones and typing endless statements handed officiously to us by our bosses," she reported. "What we have to fight against as women and as political people is the idea that being feminine implies accepting powerlessness both within the College, and within those very political movements which are trying to change the power relationships."[36] (The sidelining of women activists would continue, with many even later "written out of the history" of the 1960s protest movements themselves.[37])

It was not only female students who found themselves on the outskirts of organized power structures. Women were also not represented in Northwestern's administration or faculty in any real number. At the time, Northwestern's schools of technology, journalism, and business each had *only one female faculty member*.[38] "We simply have a smaller reservoir to draw upon," the dean of the journalism school asserted, explaining the near absence of women faculty members. Another dean admitted that there may be some unconscious discrimination at work. Given equally qualified male and female candidates for a position, "the man would probably be hired over the woman simply because it is more 'natural' to see a man instead of a woman on the faculty," he said of the prevailing attitude.[39]

As Ogletree tried to accept her role "behind the scenes," the students received their first indication that the new year would not bring about a key change they had anticipated.[40] Ogletree's second unwelcome surprise came as she learned that the demand for separate housing for Black students would not be fulfilled.

The problem surfaced just two weeks after the board of trustees voted to approve the May 4 agreement. Almost immediately, Northwestern came under fire by the office for Civil Rights within the federal agency, Health, Education and Welfare (HEW). The university's pledge to provide separate housing for Black students was at issue. According to the board of trustees, this had been the agreement's most controversial section, but no real investigation had been made regarding its legality.[41] At the time, Evanston's City Manager, Wayne F. Anderson, stated that he did not think the university would be in violation of the city's fair housing ordinance—at least not until "a non-Negro student asks to get into the corridor and is refused."[42] Illinois Congressman Donald Rumsfeld, although supportive of the university's handling of the takeover, was one of the first to question the legality of the separate housing agreement.[43] (Later, Rumsfeld would also join his colleagues in approving a "halt to federal financial support to those students taking part in activities that disrupt a college's operations."[44])

On May 29, 1968, the university was notified that it could potentially violate Title VI of the 1964 Civil Rights Act which orders: "No person in the United States shall, on the ground of race, color, or national origin, be excluded from participation in, be denied the benefits of, or be subjected to discrimination under any program or activity receiving Federal financial assistance."[45] In particular, the act prevented recipients of federal assistance from allocating housing "on purely a racial basis."[46] A special delivery letter was sent to President Miller from HEW, stating that the section in the May 4 agreement pertaining to the intent to provide separate housing for Black students had to be modified in order to be in compliance with the law.[47] This was, reportedly, the first case in which the 1964 Civil Rights Act "applied to the discrimination of whites."[48] Northwestern officials, including Hinz, responded to the notification, stating that they were "continuing discussions" with the students "with the understanding that the agreement would not violate the civil rights act."[49]

Arguing that HEW did not "understand the spirit of the agreement," Turner and other students met with an attorney to draft a letter clarifying the agreement.[50] Turner also spoke to the press in defense of the housing section of the agreement, stating that it was not "restrictive," but offered students "the choice to live in close proximity with each other. If this violates the civil rights act," he added, "certainly fraternities are in violation also."[51]

In Hinz's words, Northwestern was "called on the carpet" by the federal government. Accompanied by legal counsel, he traveled to Washington, D.C., to meet with a HEW representative and discuss the situation.[52] Ultimately, the university revised the housing plan, finding a legal solution by allowing Black students to live together, while not banning white students from those same spaces. As a result of the potential violation, Northwestern would now undergo closer scrutiny by the federal government. In the fall of 1968, federal regulators would subject the university to a student survey, collecting data on students' race, ethnicity, residence, and amount of financial aid received, among other areas.[53] They would also conduct a routine on-campus investigation to ensure that the university was in compliance with Title VI of the 1964 Civil Rights Act.[54] When questioned about the upcoming investigation, Franklin Kreml "denied that the U.S. government was giving Northwestern any trouble over the [housing] situation."[55]

By the end of October 1968, five federal officials arrived in Evanston to conduct their two-day investigation.[56] Hinz hosted them as they interviewed students, staff, and faculty. At one point, Hinz arranged a meeting between the investigators and a group of Black students. The intent, investigators explained, was "to see if non-discriminatory policies are felt on their level."[57] Reportedly, the investigators did not "specifically refer to the May 4 agreement, but instead sought answers to general questions about how the university recruits, admits, treats and places its students."[58]

Ultimately, the investigators did not identify any violations of Title VI of the 1964 Civil Rights Act at Northwestern, but they did have some concerns and recommendations which they outlined in a final report.[59] They recommended that the university increase financial aid and recruitment of students from "ghetto areas" and underrepresented regions and that a study of the university's job placement center be conducted to ensure that "it does not refer students to prospective employers on a discriminatory basis." (A recommendation made, perhaps, in reaction to the university having previously steered Black students to take jobs working with "innercity" youth in Chicago.[60]) They also recommended "setting up a formalized procedure for students who feel they have been subject to discrimination."[61] The university responded that the Human Relations Committee had been organized in the summer 1968 "for that purpose."[62] Finally, HEW notified Northwestern officials that they must "rule . . . out the possibility of a separate black living unit."[63] By January 1969, HEW reported that Northwestern's response to their recommendations for compliance was "completely satisfactory."[64]

Case closed. (?) Not for the Black students who had been promised their own "autonomous living unit."[65] As the students continued to hold meetings with administrators and the Human Relations Committee, exploring "areas of satisfaction and dissatisfaction in the implementation of the (May 4) agreement," they would continue to press this, and other, issues. But it was now clear that their "advisory" role, as stipulated by the May 4 agreement, was, in many ways, limited.

By January 1969, FMO leaders were voicing objections on several counts, including delays in furnishing the Black House, enrolling more Black students, and providing more financial aid for Black students, along with the unresolved housing situation. University officials reiterated their commitment to upholding the agreement, but FMO leaders asserted that the "pace is not fast enough."[66]

Of course, Ogletree, Bracey, Turner, Hinz, and many others knew that the May 4 agreement was not the final step in solving all the problems on the Northwestern campus. "We made progress," as Hinz observed, "but we can still do more."[67] But even as discussions and negotiations continued, many students faced the reality that there were "still the same problems" facing Black students at Northwestern.[68] After the takeover, continued racist incidents on campus, as Hinz suspected, may well have gone unreported.[69] And in some cases, the problems worsened. As Turner observed, racist attitudes among some people "intensified" after the takeover.[70] Eva Jefferson Paterson concurred, stating that "it wasn't as blatant, but there was some horrible stuff going on."[71] Racism, one FMO member observed at the time, was still running "rampant on NU's campus."[72]

In October 1968, two Black students were pelted with eggs thrown from a campus fraternity house; in response, Northwestern's Inter-Fraternity Council considered a motion to fine and subject to disciplinary probation any student found guilty of "throwing an object from a fraternity."(Objects were defined to include eggs, rocks, and water balloons.) But the motion was tabled. "They don't realize the consequences of not handling it," said Leroy Richards, one of the students who had been the target of the attack, after the penalty motion failed to pass.[73]

In reaction to the continued campus tension, Black students "just kept to themselves," as Paterson recalled.[74] In November, FMO hosted its own homecoming dance at Patten Gym. The dance, which was open to all students, was organized under the theme, "I'm Black and I'm Proud (Say it Loud)." By popular vote, Kathryn Ogletree and Clovis Semmes were elected homecoming queen and king.[75]

Noting this continued trend in "separatism" among Black students, Elliot Brown, the *Daily Northwestern's* campus editor, went to talk with Paul Black, Northwestern's newly-hired counselor for Black students. Black had only been on the job for several weeks and said he didn't feel he'd been on campus long enough "to firm up his views." But he did have an opinion to share: it seemed to him that "black students feel they have made improvement and there has been some change but . . . it is a *beginning* of the kind of change they ultimately envision." That change, he noted, would come "in the form of taking care of basic student needs." When asked about Black students' apparent move toward "separatism," Black simply observed that it might be considered a "reflection of the present culture."[76]

Student rally, Northwestern University, 1969
(Northwestern Syllabus Yearbook, 1969)

Disruption

The tide of unrest that has swept American campuses has not left Northwestern untouched.

Chicago Tribune, February 2, 1969[77]

If you're going to be a revolutionary, it's time to start acting like it.

Eric Perkins, takeover participant, November 1968[78]

The present culture indeed. While some might have hoped that the student unrest of the spring 1968 quarter was well in the past, this was not the Northwestern of years past. "It was hoped," the *Chicago Tribune* observed, that the "concessions" made to Black students, along with the other "privileges" granted to all undergraduates in regard to student autonomy, "would bring things back to normal."[79] But no such luck. Students returning to school in the fall of 1968 now "faced a campus swept by changes during the last year."[80]

As observers watched this new Northwestern, some charged the administration with failing to maintain authority, and the one person most commonly criticized was Jack Hinz. Along with serving as the primary (and most public) mediator representing the university during the takeover,

Hinz had also been at the helm of many other "dramatic innovations" for Northwestern students, including self-rule, which now allowed for "complete self regulation of student affairs by students" and the proposed judging of student drug use cases by student courts.[81] His mounting critics disparaged Hinz, holding him accountable for "engineering most of these changes."[82] But many of the fundamental changes on the campus had nothing to do with Hinz.

A larger shift was occurring among a sizeable portion of this generation of students. If another kind of investigation could have seen conducted, it might well have revealed that there was a significant degree of discord lying just beneath the surface of the student body. All of the recent "upheavals," as Hinz observed, had "create[d] a kind of climate of restlessness."[83] As many Black students worked toward holding the administration accountable to the May 4 agreement, a significant faction of progressive white students was becoming increasingly vocal about a number of issues. And they were intent on shifting the university's focus toward providing young people with a more critical and even revolutionary education. Roger Friedman, who had begun advocating for reform two years earlier, recalls fighting "a good deal" with his parents at the time. "They were upset about my public anti-war and disruptive activity at Northwestern," he recalled, and their arguments arose "as I challenged them to be more radical in their politics and not settle with conventional liberalism."[84]

Along with Friedman, many other students were becoming more radicalized, and they were intent on posing a more direct challenge to the university itself as they sought to "wrest power" from the administration. "The days of absolute administration control are at an end," Fran Shanahan, president of the Student Senate announced.[85] As much as officials wanted to see only calm seas ahead, Northwestern would find itself confronting widening student protests. The university was, as one reporter described it, now "in the throes of an upheaval."[86]

"For years, Northwestern University enjoyed the reputation of being the conservative Country Club on Chicago's North Shore," wrote *Daily Northwestern* reporter Wally Judd at the close of the 1968 school year. But now, Judd observed, "it just ain't so anymore baby . . . This year, the students knew what they wanted and went after it. Most importantly, they were successful."[87]

Advocating for reform and fighting injustice had become more prevalent among many students nationwide, and now, the May 1968 takeover seemed to have emboldened progressive white students, such as those who had taken over Hinz's office during the takeover. "[S]ay anything bad about the administration," the *Daily Northwestern* observed of these students, and "they will show up." "Their very presence tends to turn whatever is being argued into another anti-administration cry."[88]

Welcome to the generation gap.

The successful takeover and the May 4 agreement, along with the passage of the Student Self-Determination Bill and other advances, seemed to offer clear evidence that students indeed had decisive power. The movement toward student power had been launched earlier, but after the takeover, its ideals would be reinvigorated, its aims expanded. As other students around the country successfully launched campaigns for reform, Northwestern students were doubly encouraged. Soon, a small number of Northwestern's female students would begin to push issues related to women's equality into the public forum. "Women are joining the ranks of America's minority groups rebelling against discrimination," as student Roberta Kirsten observed. By 1969, an overflow crowd was present for a talk by University of Chicago sociology professor, Marlene Dixon, who addressed the issue of discrimination within the academy. "Talking about women's liberation gets me into trouble," she told the students. "But it's very liberating." By the spring of 1969, the university would host a panel discussion on the topic, "Feminism-1969," and a campus organization, "Women's Liberation," would be launched.[89]

Changes were afoot among faculty too. In October 1968, Northwestern's faculty planning committee issued a 140-page report, urging the adoption of "new approaches to undergraduate education at Northwestern" and proposing major changes in the "academic and social environment" of the campus, including abandoning the concept *in loco parentis*, the traditionally held view that the university acts as a surrogate parent for students.[90]

FMO would not be alone in restructuring its organization; changes were also underway in other student organizations. In December 1968, members of Northwestern's SDS chapter announced a reorganized structure with many coordinated actions and protests to come.[91] Like others, they were now actively focused on challenging "the establishment" and taking a more aggressive stand against authority. This heightened intensity was largely fueled by opposition to the escalating war in Vietnam, which was now at its height, along with concurrent issues, including opposing the draft and protecting free speech and the right to protest itself. The issue of racial justice was also front and center within SDS, and soon, many progressive white and Black students would formalize the solidarity that had been most publicly manifest when the group of mostly white students blocked the entrances to the Bursar's Office on May 3, 1968.

Soon after the new school year began, a series of so-called "disorders" began to take place, beginning in September 1968, when SDS members and others hosted a weeklong "Dis-Orientation Week" for incoming students. From an all-day "be-in" held in Deering Meadow to a talk titled, "The Failure of Education at NU," the activities offered new students "a chance to find out about a lot of the things the university is afraid to tell you," as Professor Marvin Shinbrot, SDS advisor, explained.[92]

"Vote in the streets during election 68!!" This was the call from SDS members in their "Don't Vote" campaign to protest the 1968 presidential election.[93] "[O]ur 'democratic' process is a fraud," they asserted. "Just as the corporations of the midwest control Northwestern University through the Board of Trustees, so too, the Money Interests of America make the important decisions that affect all of our lives. We must organize ourselves, and together we can challenge their illegitimate power."[94] Joining forces with FMO and the AASU, SDS members organized a march and rally in downtown Evanston on the day before the election. There, they burned absentee ballots and voter registration cards.[95] Among the speakers were FMO's Eric Perkins and John Higginson, along with Clark Kissinger, former SDS national secretary, and Richard Flacks, one the founders of SDS.[96]

After Richard Nixon was elected president in November 1968, administrators were shocked when a group of students organized a "nude in" at the plaza in front of the Rebecca Crown Center, calling on other students to "shed your clothes for freedom."[97] (Three hundred students showed up, but, it turned out, no one took off their clothes.[98]) And university officials were appalled when students interrupted an address by Joseph A. Mendenhall, a former U.S. State Department official, by throwing a paper plate piled high with shaving cream in his face.[99] Later, at a university Founders Day event, several hundred "chanting pickets" interrupted the proceedings, embarrassing officials.[100] And, at a meeting of the Northwestern Club of Chicago, a group of students, including the president of the Student Senate, demanded, before an audience of outraged alumni, an end to "university racism" and the abolishment of the university's board of trustees.[101]

In January 1969, a weeklong campus symposium, appropriately titled, "Confronting Change," was disrupted when students "shouted down and ridiculed" nearly all of the eleven speakers, objecting not only to the symposium's authoritarian structure, but also to many of the speakers themselves.[102] " 'Negro? What is a Negro?' " a Black student shouted from the audience after Thomas Ayers, president of Commonwealth Edison and a Northwestern trustee, suggested that white businesses can help "Negro businessmen" start their own companies. " 'Black!' " another student yelled.[103]

Only those speakers judged sufficiently progressive or radical were allowed to speak uninterrupted; these included Claude Brown, author of *Manchild in the Promised Land*, who delivered a "passionate oratory" in which he demanded the death sentence for the white Southerners accused in the killing of Medgar Evers and the bombing of a Birmingham church that killed four young girls; Tom Hayden, SDS co-founder, co-author of the Port Huron Statement, and one of the "prime movers" in the 1968 Columbia protests;[104] civil rights activist Dick Gregory; and Jerry Rubin, leader of the Youth International Party or the "Yippies." (During his time onstage, Rubin wore a National Liberation Front or "Viet Cong" flag as a cape and shouted in "unprintable terms" at the audience.[105]) At one point, some panelists even engaged in a heated argument with each other. "You just can't bring people of divergent opinion to campus after 1968," concluded symposium co-chair Will Ris. "It just won't work."[106]

"I felt safer in Viet Nam," said Joseph A. Mendenhall after his reception by some Northwestern students.[107] At the time, Mendenhall was deputy assistant administrator for the U.S. Agency for International Development in South Vietnam. During his talk at Harris Hall, someone pulled all the fuses, casting the auditorium in darkness. Moments later, someone threw a plate of shaving cream in his face.
(*Daily Northwestern,* November 25, 1968, cartoon by Bill Reed.)

With a strong anti-establishment sensibility now prevalent among a sizeable percentage (but certainly not a majority) of students, more anti-war and anti-corporate protests were being planned, and all of these actions were viewed as having been buoyed, at least in part, by the May 1968 takeover.

At the time, the takeover seemed to have caught many white students by surprise. In the days after it concluded, some white students admitted that the action seemed to have occurred "all of a sudden," as if, incredibly, it had come out of nowhere.[108] But it did alert them to what many had not previously seen or fully acknowledged: the extent of racism not only on campus, but also throughout the country. It was soon clear that the takeover would have significant reverberations.[109]

Afterward, many white students seemed more acutely aware of racial and social injustices. And more progressive and radical white students would become involved in protests and politics, inspired both by national movements and events on their own campus. After the takeover, as Turner observed, more white students and faculty also began to recognize their own "complicity" in ignoring the university's "racist culture," and they started to engage in a major discussion of the "moral role" they should play in order to critique and dismantle that culture. Later, some white student activists would explain that their own subsequent protests were "implemented with the black stratagems as a model."[110]

But it was not only Black students who influenced the actions of white students. It also worked the other way: Eva Jefferson Paterson, who came from a conservative family and whose father served in the war in Vietnam, recalls that it was a political protest at Northwestern, largely organized by progressive white students, that "heightened my consciousness," as she said, leading her to reexamine some of her beliefs, especially her attitude toward the war.[111]

In January 1969, FMO members distributed a letter at registration, calling for the strengthening of the alliance between Black and white students.[112] As a result, an open committee of students was formed, headed by undergraduate student Richard Cohen.[113] The February 1969 issue of the *Daily Northwestern*'s "Emphasis," a weekly magazine focused on a single topic, was prepared by FMO members as a part of Afro-American history week. FMO's Milton Gardner, a journalism major and takeover participant, edited the issue, stressing its common theme: "We must deal with the institutions and persons who have used physical differences and racism to keep us fighting one another. We must realize who the enemy is. We must deal with reality and reality at Northwestern is that all of us are 'students' who are powerless."[114] Contributions by several progressive students, including Roger Friedman, were included in the issue.[115] "The university," wrote student Stephen Plotnick, reflecting the tone of many of the articles, "exists for the purpose of producing people for the racist, industrial and militaristic society outside."[116]

For his part, Hinz continued to welcome dialogue and change, arguing that both must be present for growth to occur.[117] But not everyone was so sanguine. "People are afraid a revolution is starting in this country and it's starting on the college and university campuses," one college chancellor observed.[118] "This can't go on anymore," a Northwestern alumnus complained to the *Chicago Tribune*. "We have to take some action. We have to return control of the university to adults."[119]

But methods of control were already in the works. "It is not likely that Northwestern will ever again tolerate a group of students taking control of a university building," the *Daily Northwestern* predicted just one day after the takeover ended.[120] And that prediction was correct. At the New Student Convocation in September 1968, President J. Roscoe Miller delivered an address to the university's 1,800 incoming undergraduates. "I suggest that you do your own thinking before endorsing the platform of any special group," he instructed. "Your right to responsible dissent carries with it the obligation of responsible thought." Miller closed his fifteen-minute address with a warning: the university will "not permit the development of actions or programs which are disruptive of the orderly process of education."[121]

By October 1968, university administrators, including Hinz, had drafted a confidential policy paper titled, "Procedure for University Administration in the Event of Campus Disorders." The new step-by-step procedures differed in several ways from the way the takeover had been handled. Now, students participating in any kind of campus disorder would be notified that they must desist immediately or be suspended from the university. An effort would be made to identify those involved, and they would immediately be served with a summons to appear at a university disciplinary hearing. The police would be called to the scene thirty minutes after any action began. Students would be notified a second time that they must desist. If they did not comply, the university would have "no alternative but to use force." Police would "enter the scene, preferably without weapons, arrest the participants and remove them."[122]

The new policy was a direct response to the 1968 takeover. It was also informed by the board of trustees' May 1968 resolution that future disturbances would be dealt with by "legal and disciplinary action."[123] No more negotiations would be undertaken with students engaged in any disruptive or illegal activity. Now, university officials looked upon any student protest or action that impeded "business as usual," not as an act of civil disobedience, but as an "invasion" of the rights of others.[124] And such actions would no longer be "permitted" at Northwestern.[125]

Northwestern was not alone in cracking down on student protests. In September 1968, on the campus of the University of Illinois, Urbana-

Champaign, nearly 250 Black students were arrested and charged with "mob action" after refusing to end their occupation of the campus student union.[126] "The universities are asking for it," raged the *Chicago Tribune* after the incident. "[I]f university administrators delay a moment in breaking up illegal occupations or stall around trying to mollify dissidents who refuse to honor public law or university regulations, the result is anarchy."[127]

"It was a rare occurrence that a protest did not lead to some promise of reform," as historian Ibram X. Kendi observed of the Black student protest movement of the 1960s. "Nevertheless, campuses that experienced protests also became virtual police states. Thus, reform and repression followed protests, diminishing their likelihood of recurrence and forever altering the racial *and* policing mechanism of the institutions."[128]

Four months after it was written, the university's new policy for responding to campus disorders would be tested.

Five Minutes To Clear The Street

This University recognizes that freedom requires order, discipline, and responsibility.

Resolution, Northwestern Board of Trustees, May 14, 1968[129]

This University . . . cannot tolerate any attempt by any individual, group or organization to disrupt the regularly scheduled activities of the University.

"Procedure for University Administration in the Event of Campus Disorders," October 1968[130]

Concentrated efforts to bring the university bad publicity can eventually "bring the administration to its knees."

Ellis Pines, quoted in the *Daily Northwestern*, January 1968[131]

Job recruiters from the Dow Chemical Company had come to Northwestern before. In fact, they routinely arrived on campuses across the country to recruit students into corporate jobs. But by 1966, Dow, a manufacturer of napalm, an incendiary chemical weapon used by the U.S. military in the war in Vietnam, was increasingly met with opposition.[132] Following the first anti-Dow protest in October 1966, more than one hundred protests against the company would be staged on campuses nationwide.[133] On October 18, 1967, a Dow protest at the University of Wisconsin-Madison turned violent, with police dispersing tear gas and dragging and beating student protestors.[134] That same fall, after students staged an anti-Dow sit-in at the University of Illinois, forty-seven students had been disciplined. Seven students had been expelled.[135]

In 1968, members of Northwestern's ad hoc Committee Against War Recruiting, composed of faculty and students, including Roger Friedman and other SDS members, prepared for their own protest against Dow. The action was planned to take place on the day Dow corporate recruiters would be interviewing students on campus. Among other things, the protest organizers charged the university with acting as an accomplice in the war in Vietnam due to its financial investment in Dow. For some, this charge was confirmed when the *Daily Northwestern* reported that the university owned $811,899 worth of Dow stock. In response, Northwestern's Vice President and Business Manager William Kerr asked, "What company does not participate in a war, popular or unpopular? I imagine most companies in our portfolio . . . have some connection with the war."[136]

In February 1968, the campus was in a heightened state of alert as both the scheduled Dow interviews and the protest approached, with students and faculty debating everything from the potential use of police force to the very right of students to protest. Planning events were held, with protest organizers announcing they intended to stage an entirely peaceful demonstration. They were dedicated to avoiding any outbreak of violence, they said.[137] Members of Northwestern's chapter of Young Conservatives pledged to protect the civil rights of the interviewees and they provided them with instructions on filing assault and battery charges "in case they were physically harmed by members of anti-war groups."[138] Letters to the editor appeared in the *Daily Northwestern*, both for and against the protest. "We feel these protesters represent a minority," wrote several students in opposition.[139] Meanwhile, the anti-draft group, Chicago Area Draft Resisters, requested permission to recruit its own employees on campus. The request was denied.[140]

On February 14, 1968, the Dow interviews took place while roughly five hundred people, mostly students and faculty members, held a peaceful demonstration.[141] Both the march and rally went off without incident. Ellis Pines, former Student Senate president and SPM leader, was there, having recently returned to Northwestern after a few months' absence.[142] Pines, whose always long hair was now much longer, as the *Daily Northwestern* noted, had returned to campus after working for the *Washington Free Press* in Washington, D.C. He was now "a self-labeled 'radical.' "[143] He was still involved in student organizing and had recently begun writing for Northwestern's alternative newspaper, *The Real Press,* where he implored others to critique the "system" and the ways Northwestern was "determined to turn out people to fit within the present system and not to think about changing it."[144] During the Dow protest, Pines addressed the crowd through a bullhorn, urging demonstrators to "redirect the uses of this university."[145]

"We want Miller! We want Miller!" the crowd chanted at one point during the rally. But instead, as the *Daily Northwestern's* Bob Greene reported, "they got Hinz." Hinz had come out of his office to join the crowd. And once he did, the television news crews turned their cameras on him right away.[146] Someone shoved a bullhorn in his hand. "No," Hinz responded. "I just came out here to listen."[147] "What did he think of the protest?" he was asked afterward. "It was a cracking good demonstration," he answered— a response that left many people stunned.[148] "This was an NU administrator talking?" Greene asked in disbelief.

But it was no surprise that Hinz should have made such a statement. During what amounted to the two months of tension concerning the potential for violence to break out at the Dow protest, Hinz had stood by the students' right to protest. Just two weeks earlier, the Student Senate passed a resolution,

"Policy on Free Speech at a University," which sought to protect protesters' rights and advocated for "the active presence of civil authorities *only* during the presence of violence on campus."[149] Hinz said agreed in "broad principle" with the resolution, but he did note that there could be some circumstances when police might be called in, even if no violence occurred. (If, for example, demonstrators blocked a person in a room for an extended period.) But he did not anticipate having to call the civil authorities to campus, he said.[150] Soon, a photograph of Hinz, published in the *Daily Northwestern*, announced this fact: "Roland J. Hinz. Hesitant About Calling Police."

Bob Greene asks: "Their man Hinz or is it our man Hinz?"[151]
(*Daily Northwestern,* January 30, 1968)

For many students, Hinz had become a hero. He had "done more to liberalize and improve the climate of this university than anyone connected with Northwestern in memory," Bob Greene asserted.[152] But to many conservatives and even some moderates, he was a symbol of what they saw as a growing trend on college campuses: revolution. "I'm not a revolutionary," Hinz stated firmly. "People are going to find out that I don't like revolution."[153] But there was no doubt that he had now come to symbolize a "changing Northwestern—liberal to the point of radicalism."[154] And for this reason, he was increasingly viewed as a threat to the establishment itself. (This view was affirmed by the fact that the FBI had already begun to compile a file on his activities, as Hinz would later learn.[155]) Now, as people witnessed the endless series of disorders at Northwestern, "they thought of Hinz."[156] President Miller's photograph had begun to "disappear from the front pages of the downtown papers. And in its place came the standard public relations shot of Hinz, his left eye half shut, smiling up at alumni over their breakfast coffee."[157]

The peaceful and well-organized Dow protest was judged as having set a good example for others to follow.[158] The only flaw in the event, noted the *Daily Northwestern*, was the *Chicago Tribune's* account which included "outright fabrications and slanted descriptions," such as describing the demonstrators as "bearded and scruffy." The *Daily Northwestern* also objected to the *Tribune's* characterization of fraternity members (who blared the "The Ballad of the Green Berets" during the protest) as patriots.[159] As the debate over the protest continued long after it ended, two students objected to the *Daily Northwestern's* apparent support for the protesters, writing: "You constantly stress the right of the lunatic fringes on the campus to parade and make noise . . . . the only 'credit' to be derived from Wednesday's events is that the vast majority of Northwestern's students laughed at those 'peaceniks' who would carry signs such as 'Make Death Pay. It's the American Way.' "[160]

One year later, in February 1969, after the takeover and followed by a tumultuous fall marked by numerous campus disorders and disruptions, Dow planned to return for another round of student interviews. Planning for a second Dow protest was underway.[161] The Committee Against War Recruiting, whose members included George Vickers, Roger Friedman, and Steven Lubet, announced that protests would be staged on campus and that Northwestern students would be joined in the action by students from Loyola University and the University of Chicago, along with members of the national office of SDS.[162]

But this time—one year after the peaceful protest against Dow and in the wake of the takeover—there was a great deal more apprehension concerning just how this demonstration might unfold. A rumor began to circulate that a building takeover was being planned for the day of the protest.[163]

Evanston police were alerted. Additional campus security were placed on duty. Hinz announced that the university was obligated to "keep disruption from happening."[164] Anyone engaged in "disruptive tactics will be subject to appropriate legal and disciplinary action, including expulsion," he warned.[165]

On the morning of February 25, 1969, the planned Dow protest got underway. It was small at first, then grew slowly as the crowd of protesters amassed near busy Sheridan Road. At one point, a group of demonstrators walked into the street, stopped traffic, and began handing out leaflets to drivers. When a single police officer arrived and demanded that they clear the street, they refused. More police arrived to divert traffic and the number of demonstrators grew. Now, a crowd of counter-demonstrators had gathered, booing and cat-calling. Several counter-protesters began to throw eggs at the protesters.[166] Both sides made use of megaphones and the noise level rose as onlookers and motorists stopped to watch the growing and increasingly audible crowd.[167]

By noon, the crowd had swelled to one thousand, equally divided between counter-demonstrators and protesters. Some passers-by shouted encouragement to the protesters, while others reportedly directed drivers at the protesters, shouting, "Run them down" and "Run 'em over."[168] Traffic was now at a standstill as protesters opted to sit down in the middle of Sheridan Road. At noon, twenty Evanston police officers arrived, "equipped for riot duty" (wearing helmets with face shields and carrying Billy clubs).[169] And, according to one account, it was their arrival that ignited events and "touched off a campus disturbance."[170]

As police attempted to disperse the crowd and divert traffic from the area, it was clear that there would be no negotiation this time. Police gave demonstrators "five minutes to clear the street."[171] A "scuffle" took place, as Hinz recalled.[172] And, after Steven Lubet, the former president of Northwestern's SDS chapter, was arrested, a crowd gathered around a police car and began shaking it.[173] More arrests soon followed. The police, who had previously been ordered to stay off campus unless their presence was requested by university officials, then "stepped onto the campus" after it was reported that someone was trying to lower the American flag at Lunt Hall.[174] Ultimately, six white students, all SDS members, were arrested and charged with disorderly conduct.[175]

After the arrests, the protesters dispersed. But they were not finished.

"Arrested!!!" read a quickly drafted flyer distributed by the student protesters right after the demonstration. Announcing the arrests of the undergraduates who were taken away in patrol cars during a "peaceful demonstration," the flyer warned that "25 armed Evanston police are presently on campus, and policemen with clubs, helmets, mace, and guns are on Sheridan Road." A meeting was called to "decide further action."[176]

Roughly two hundred students gathered at Scott Hall. There, they drew up a list of demands to present to university officials: the university must not discipline the six students who had been arrested or any other participant in the demonstration; the university must do all it could to prevent Evanston police from filing charges against the students; the university must provide legal and financial support to the arrested students; and the Dow Chemical Company must cease its campus recruiting activities.[177]

After a brief rally, the students announced that they were going to stage an all-night sit-in at Scott Hall. Around 2 p.m., as they prepared to occupy the building, another group of students showed up at Hinz's office intent on staging an occupation there.[178] Hinz's administrative assistant, Jessie Robertson, saw them coming. Robertson had been in the office the previous spring when students had occupied it for nearly two days. This time, she locked the office door as they approached. But they broke the lock with a screwdriver and entered. Robertson then packed up her belongings and locked her desk. "This is where I work," she told the students in exasperation and walked out.[179] The students remained, occupying Hinz's office and replacing Robertson's nameplate with a sign that read, "Dig freedom! Dig revolution!"[180]

At about 4:30 p.m., Hinz, who had been going back and forth between the sit-in at Scott Hall and his occupied office, along with visiting various points on campus, told the *Daily Northwestern*, "I'm not upset yet about people being in my office . . . but I might be."[181] But after he announced that he would keep Scott Hall open all night to allow the sit-in to continue, the students occupying his office "cleared out."[182]

And so, two hundred students stayed all night at Scott Hall discussing various needed reforms, including more student involvement in the running of the university and the appointment of a student to the university's board of trustees. The sit-in went on well into the wee hours of the morning, with Hinz's "blessing," as the *Chicago Tribune* noted disdainfully.[183]

The demonstration, the arrests, the office sit-in, and the all-night occupation made headlines across the country, with the *New York Times* reporting "Calm at Northwestern" the day after the demonstration, as if suggesting that a lack of upheaval on the Northwestern campus was, in fact, newsworthy.[184]

"Out of Place: What's a nice looking, neatly dressed young man on the right doing in a place like this." So read the caption of a UPI photograph that appeared in newspapers the next day. The photograph pictured an unsmiling Hinz, wearing his standard suit and tie, sitting on a chair in his office, legs crossed, hands resting on his knee, while a group of students milled around him. "Well, he's the only one who belongs here," the caption continued. "He's Roland Hinz, dean of students at Northwestern University, and the unkempt ones surrounding him are protesting students . . . who took over his office."[185]

In the document outlining the new procedures to handle campus disorders, it had been noted that the "university must be mindful of the complexities of public relations and public information which surround any demonstrative activities."[186]

Just one week later, Northwestern would make national headlines again.

Evanston police officers arrest a student protester, while counter-protesters applaud in the background, Dow protest (and counter-protest), Northwestern University, February 1969.
(Northwestern *Syllabus* Yearbook, 1969)

Chapter 9

Triangle

As described by witnesses, the students acted in unison. When their purpose was accomplished, they fled.[1]

On Monday afternoon, March 3, 1969, at Northwestern's Willard Hall campus dining facility, a white male busboy allegedly assaulted a Black female student. The busboy, a Northwestern student and member of the Triangle fraternity, would later deny the allegations against him.

Later that afternoon, the woman told Victor Goode what had happened to her at the dining hall. Goode was now working as a resident assistant at the North Shore Hotel, where many Black male students had been assigned university housing. Goode went to the director of Willard Hall and urged that the student's statement be taken and the incident be reported immediately since, after hearing about yet another alleged volatile encounter between a Black student and a white fraternity member, "emotions were running high among the Black students."[2] That night, telephone calls were made reporting the incident to Patricia Thrash, dean of women.[3] But an incident report, which did not include the student's full complaint, reportedly did not reach Jack Hinz until Wednesday.[4]

At some point on Monday evening, a group of about twenty Black male students went to Willard Hall to investigate. According to one witness, they were persuaded to leave without incident by counselor Paul Black.[5] The next day, the students went to the Triangle fraternity house at 1936 Sheridan Road. They demanded to meet with fraternity members. They particularly wanted to talk to the fraternity member who had been accused in the incident. (He was reportedly being hidden in the house's attic by fraternity members.[6]) They were turned away. They came back again later the same day, and again they were refused.[7]

At 8:30 p.m. that evening, the students were back at the fraternity house. This time they didn't wait to be refused entry. They stormed their way inside and proceeded to smash dishes and lamps, damage furniture, and break thirteen windows. "Their destructive action was instantaneous," according to a later court document, and their actions were concerted. "All the destruction, according to the witnesses, was done in about two minutes. From this evidence it appears that the students were engaged in the common design of committing criminal damage to property in the fraternity house;

that all in the group had knowledge of the common purpose and that each acted in furtherance of the venture."[8] In the end, four fraternity members suffered minor injuries.[9] The Triangle members soon evacuated their house, citing fear of another attack.[10]

"I got a call when that was just starting to boil," Jack Hinz remembered of the Triangle incident, "and raced to the campus."[11] In fact, he was so harried and hurried that he drove too quickly, hit a curb, and blew out the back tires of his car. Local police had been called and they arrived at the fraternity house shortly after the incident.[12] Fraternity members identified two students who had allegedly taken part in the destruction. Police issued warrants for their arrest.[13] Each faced two felony charges: burglary and criminal damage of property.[14] The attack was "unprecedented," Hinz announced publicly, and he pledged that the University Discipline Committee (UDC) would investigate.[15]

On the night of the Triangle house incident, Evanston police arrived at the men's residences at the North Shore Hotel. But, as one newspaper reported, "persons there refused to surrender the two sought."[16] The next day, ten busboys at the Willard Hall dining facility staged a walk-out, citing solidarity with the accused busboy and also protesting the fact that they felt they were in physical danger.[17] Now, a call went out for a mass meeting of all Black students at the North Shore Hotel.[18] The next day, FMO announced that as an organization it backed "the actions of blacks who took part in the Tuesday night disturbance."[19] Hinz reportedly urged all students not to take any action until he had a chance to talk with everyone involved.[20]

According to FMO, the Triangle house invasion may have been conducted by a small group of students, but *all Black students at Northwestern were involved* in the case.[21] Only ten months had passed since the peaceful resolution of the takeover. Throughout that time, as FMO leaders soon announced, Black students had continued to be threatened and harassed on campus. The Triangle house incident was, therefore, "the result of recurring racial incidents during the last year."[22] FMO leaders explained that there had been other racially-charged encounters at the Willard Hall dining facility, other encounters with Sigma Chi and Fiji fraternity members, and "smaller incidents" that had either not been reported to university officials or had failed to be investigated by the administration.[23] Thus, the news of an alleged "molesting" of a Black female student by a white busboy "brought about a spontaneous reaction by the entire Black community and the community at large," as FMO asserted. "We can no longer tolerate physical harassment and provocation," FMO spokesmen, Michael Smith, Milton Gardner, and Eric Perkins, stated.[24] As Kathryn Ogletree recalled, it was the male students, in particular, who felt compelled to act, not only because of past racist incidents, but also because "they felt that they needed to stand up for the integrity of a black woman."[25]

"There were still problems," Hinz later said about campus conditions long after the takeover. He recognized that the damage done at the Triangle fraternity house was "extract[ing] retribution of some kind."[26] While Hinz certainly did not advocate violence in any form, he was aware of the motivations behind the incident, since, as he knew, there were still "notable demonstrations" of hostility toward Black students, especially by some campus fraternity members. Hinz had been waging a battle of sorts, calling upon fraternities to "adjust" in the wake of the May 4 agreement. "Thus far," he had observed during an alumni meeting in mid-June 1968, fraternities had "not changed to meet the challenge of higher education."[27] One fraternity in particular stood out as allegedly causing a significant amount of trouble on campus, Sigma Chi.

The previous spring, a fight between two white Sigma Chi Fraternity members at the chapter house resulted in one member suffering a head wound. The university turned the matter over to the UDC. Hinz, who was chairman of the UDC, noted that there had been some "pretty darn deplorable" incidents involving Sigma Chi.[28] Charging fraternity members with repeated fights and various disturbances, on July 12, 1968, the UDC placed Sigma Chi on a three-month probation, banned social functions and parietal hours at the house for a quarter, barred the chapter for participating in rush for one year (thereby preventing any new members from joining the fraternity), and closed the house for the remainder of the summer.[29] The two students who had been involved in the fight were placed on probation. The fraternity had been "warned about disturbances in the past," officials noted.[30] Indeed, in April 1968, Dean of Men, Seward Weber, had written to the president of Northwestern's chapter of Sigma Chi, warning him that the fraternity must cease its alleged troublemaking. But Weber reportedly never received any response. Now, as Hinz instructed, the UDC's ruling offered the fraternity a chance "to take stock of its values and attitudes."[31]

Some students were incensed by the UDC's ruling against Sigma Chi, arguing that it was a renunciation of recent strides made in the movement toward student autonomy. Others charged that it symbolically constituted a return to the reign of the former dean of students, James McLeod, an excessively strict disciplinarian. In response to the punishment, Sigma Chi charged the UDC with "procedural irregularities" and both local and national fraternity officials wrote to Hinz and President Miller asking that the UDC's ruling be reconsidered.[32] They appealed to officials to overrule what they saw as an unnecessary, undeserved, and far too severe punishment, arguing that an injustice had been done that would cause future damage to the fraternity. Fraternity officials also asked to meet with Hinz and other UDC members.[33] Hinz responded that he held firm to the UDC decision. But he said he would agree to hold a new hearing as an "expansion and amplification" of the case.

By August 1968, Sigma Chi's punishment was being "reconsidered."[34]

On Saturday, October 5, 1968, UDC members, administrators, and fraternity representatives met for two and a half hours. On Monday, it was announced that Sigma Chi's social probation remained in effect, but the UDC had lifted the one-year ban on rushing, effective at the end of the fall 1968 quarter. Despite having won a new hearing and a reduced punishment, the fraternity's chapter president responded that he was still "very disappointed."[35]

Still, the rehearing of the UDC case and the reduction of punishments would prove to further strain campus relations. And now, in the wake of the Willard Hall and Triangle incidents, the UDC faced another difficult case, one whose outcome would be closely watched and debated.

As the public and the press took note of Northwestern's current troubles, many wondered if law and order would ever reign on the campus again. But the alleged assault at the Willard dining hall was quickly overshadowed by the Triangle incident. In the hands of the press, the incident was sensationalized and even caricatured. Stories appeared in papers nationwide with the caption "Pantry Raid" appearing below a photograph depicting the damage done to the kitchen in the fraternity house. That damage had been inflicted by a "band of negroes," as one newspaper put it.[36] The "militant" Black students, some asserted, were at it again. But this time, it appeared, they had escalated their tactics, opting for violence and orchestrating an organized "rampage" on campus.

For some, the peaceful resolution to the takeover had now been eclipsed by what had happened at the Triangle house. University officials would be wrong, critics argued, to negotiate with those who could perpetuate such violence. Others watched unfolding events to see how the university would handle yet another major disruption, this one calling into question whether conditions for Black students at Northwestern had really changed following the takeover. For many, recent events only proved that Black students continued to be threatened and harassed, and it was no surprise that some students had reached a breaking point, they surmised. Was the long-criticized UDC up to the task of meting out justice? The continuous press coverage emphasizing campus disorder and destruction exerted tremendous pressure on the administration. The university's next steps would be careful, calculated, and closely observed.

On Wednesday, March 5, one day after the Triangle house incident, Hinz began conducting interviews with witnesses and convened a closed-door meeting with UDC members and representatives of the Triangle fraternity. The meeting, he said, was an opportunity to engage in a preliminary discussion, prior to the beginning of formal hearings.[37] Hinz also invited several among FMO's leadership to attend. But FMO leaders responded that they believed that all Black students should be invited to attend.[38]

The meeting went ahead as planned, but at one point, a group of one hundred and fifty Black students arrived, reportedly interrupted the proceedings, and asked to meet immediately with UDC members. Hinz tried to dissuade them, asking them to return later, but soon, he and the committee members complied. They met with the students in a two-hour private session that later sparked controversy.[39]

The next day, under the banner headline, "Hinz Takes UDC to Black Meeting," the *Daily Northwestern* reported that Hinz had walked out of the first meeting after "the blacks demanded" that he and the other UDC members meet with them privately.[40] Campus Security Chief Ted Arndt had been stationed at the door of the room where Hinz, the other UDC members, and the students privately convened. Arndt informed anyone who inquired (including members of the press) that the meeting was closed and they were barred from entering.[41] Those nearby reported hearing speeches and applause from inside.[42] Afterward, UDC members accompanied Hinz to his office and met in closed session for an hour.[43]

This, at least, was the story that the *Daily Northwestern* and other sources reported, a story that was later challenged by FMO members. According to FMO leader Milton Gardner, the "Black students have adopted a policy that all Black students were involved in the Triangle incident," and therefore, they *all* wanted to attend the UDC meeting. But in order to do so, they needed to be accommodated in a larger meeting room. That was their only so-called "demand."[44] Gardner explained that they wanted everyone, including members of the Triangle fraternity, to attend that larger meeting.[45]

The next day, the *Chicago Tribune* published an editorial, arguing that Hinz's handling of the meeting was evidence that "candor, truth, and order have been casualties in the administration's attempt to sweep racial violence under the rug."[46] In its own editorial, the *Daily Northwestern* lambasted Hinz for having shown "favoritism" toward Black students by suspending the March 5 meeting to meet privately with them.[47] It charged him with "foolish and irresponsible behavior."[48] Hinz had failed, the editorial continued, to inform all students about the UDC's decision-making process and thus contributed to the fear that many white students were now reportedly feeling on campus. (The editorial writer claimed that some white students were now hiding "baseball bats in their closets, uncertain if, when and why they might find blacks storming their house.") The editorial concluded with its own demand as it issued an "ultimatum:" Hinz must either convene a public UDC hearing and "make the facts of this case clear to whites and blacks alike" or resign.[49]

A few days later, 4,000 of the *Daily Northwestern's* 6,000 copies were removed from the newsstands. An anonymous caller said they were taken because of the editorial's "racist attitude." "If things don't change in the next quarter," the caller reportedly warned, "we will escalate our action."[50]

An escalation did not occur, but things were about to change in a major way.

Shake Up

Students have the right to judicial due process, including a speedy trial, confrontation of plaintiff and his witnesses, counsel, presumption of innocence, protection against cruel or unusual punishment, and appeal.

Northwestern Student Bill of Rights, February 1968

One day after the incident at the Triangle fraternity house, the press began to circulate a rumor that President J. Roscoe Miller had submitted a revision of Northwestern's administrative structure to the board of trustees. Among other changes, the new plan reportedly called for the appointment of a new university president, with Miller stepping aside to undertake a new position, one focused primarily on "external relations" (fundraising, essentially).[51] When questioned, university officials offered no comment.

But just a few days later, following all the recent furor of the Dow protest and student arrests, the all-night sit-in at Scott Hall, the alleged assault of the student in the dining hall, the raid on the Triangle house, the issuing of arrest warrants for two Northwestern students accused in the Triangle incident, the accusations against Hinz, the reports of white students fearing impending attacks, and the continued allegations of racism on campus, it was announced officially that the board of trustees had approved a new administrative structure. After serving for two decades as president of Northwestern, President Miller was leaving his post. He would be appointed university chancellor, effective immediately.[52] This change, it was announced, would now pave the way for the selection of a new university president, someone "capable of best communicating with and understanding students and faculty."[53] Despite speculation concerning the reasoning behind this dramatic shift, a university spokesman said that it "was not related to the recent racial and anti-war turmoil that has beset the university."[54]

"Top-level shake-up!" the *Daily Northwestern* announced. The paper was quick to identify what could only be the reason for such a major reorganization, arguing that Miller had "been criticized for having spent too much time in pursuing large fund-raising campaigns and too little time with students."[55] Miller's resignation would "open the way for a younger administrative staff to deal with students," the paper happily noted. Although, it conceded, all university staff would still be responsible to Miller in his new post as chancellor.[56]

In the wake of the Willard Hall and Triangle incidents, it was clear that someone must find a way to ease the "rising tensions" on campus."[57] And it was no surprise that it was Jack Hinz, the youngest member of Miller's administrative staff, who was working furiously to calm things down and get to the heart of the matter related to both cases.

On Friday, March 7, Hinz issued an official statement (published in the *Daily Northwestern*) in which he sought to correct the "considerable misunderstanding" among students concerning events surrounding the Willard Hall and Triangle house incidents. Hinz recounted the events of the past few days, explaining that the "so-called 'closed hearings' " that he'd been accused of conducting with Black students had, in reality, been a "preliminary inquiry." The reasons such a large number of students had attended that meeting, he explained, was because they all claimed to be "involved" in the Triangle incident. The following day, he had held a similar inquiry with Triangle fraternity members.[58] Hinz explained the upcoming UCD proceedings and he outlined the potential charges students faced. Although UDC hearings were not open to the public, Hinz announced that there would be more access to these proceedings. "In recognition of the widespread student and public interest," he stated, "daily reports will be issued and print media, including the *Daily Northwestern*, will be entitled to send one representative to each proceeding."[59] He closed by imploring everyone to understand that he and the entire administration had "great and continuing concern for the welfare and protection of its entire student body."[60]

That morning, the UDC brought formal charges against five Northwestern students. In relation to the Willard Hall incident, one student, the accused busboy, was charged. And in relation to the Triangle house incident, four Black students were charged: the two students whose arrest warrants had been issued earlier, Michael Smith, FMO's governor of campus affairs, and one other student. All four had been participants in the takeover. Each student was charged with violating section 2-B of the student self-determination bill. Each faced charges including wrongful entry, property damage, and personal injury. All faced the possibility of probation, suspension, or dismissal for the university.[61]

Later that day, FMO members and Triangle fraternity representatives agreed to meet with Hinz. Afterward, they held a joint press conference to announce that they had signed letters of agreement "to bring proper justice" in the Willard Hall and Triangle cases. And all pledged "to keep the disagreement within the academic community."[62] To that end, both groups agreed that the university would handle the disciplinary proceedings. Although the fraternity "strongly condemned the actions of certain militant blacks on March 4, 1969," it announced that it would drop all criminal charges against the students whose arrest warrants had been issued.[63] For its part, FMO announced that it would "accept the authority of university officials."[64] There was just one stipulation: the all-white UDC must appoint at least one Black student or faculty member in order, as FMO's Milton Gardner said, to "properly adjudicate" the case.[65]

That same day, the two students who had been identified as taking part in the fraternity house incident surrendered to the police.[66] They were released on bond and notified that the charges against them could not be dropped until they appeared later in court.[67]

In an odd twist of fate, on Friday, March 7, the day before the hearings were set to begin, the *Daily Northwestern* announced that it would be suspending publication until March 31. Staff were preparing, as was everyone else, for final exams, followed by spring break.[68] However, a special issue would be published on Monday, March 10, in order to report on the UDC hearing. But for three weeks afterward, the campus would have no news from its daily newspaper of the dramatic events that were about to unfold.

On Saturday, March 8, the UDC proceedings (known officially as an "administrative hearing") got underway. John Ritchie, dean of Northwestern's law school, and Alban Weber, university counsel, conducted the hearings, which began with a consideration of the Willard Hall incident, followed by an examination of the Triangle house incident.

Eight witnesses went before the committee that first day. As the "story of a brief incident that grew until its ramifications reached startling proportions was told for the record for the first time," the *Daily Northwestern* reported, it soon became clear that not everyone had the same account of what happened in the dining hall.[69] Dean of Women Patricia Thrash testified, observing that the incident "was considered a problem of bad manners on Monday, but was considered a Student Affairs problem by Tuesday."[70] The accused busboy testified that he had neither insulted nor assaulted the student, and a variety of witnesses offered their own accounts, some affirming his story. According to his testimony, the student asked him to clear a table so that she and her friends could sit there and he only partly complied, clearing away some glasses. Victor Goode, the only Black student to testify, related his encounter with the woman just hours after the alleged incident occurred. She was "emotionally upset," Goode said, "she had never been grabbed like that by a white man before."[71] (Her mother would later claim that the busboy shook her daughter so hard that "she could have choked to death."[72])

The incident would not be recounted in front of the UDC by the woman herself, however. For undisclosed reasons, she, and the three students who had been with her in the dining hall, did not testify. Acting as her counsel in the proceedings, Michael Smith may have surprised everyone when announced that "she and Northwestern's black students wished to drop the allegations" against the busboy. "As far as black students are concerned," Smith said, "we are no longer interested in that case . . . it is irrelevant at this particular time."[73]

What they were interested in, Smith told the UDC, was the larger issue of justice at Northwestern. Smith asserted that it was university officials who were ultimately responsible for both the Willard Hall and Triangle incidents. They had failed to deal with racism on campus. They had failed to take swift or thorough action after the incident in Willard Hall. And, further, he argued, they had failed to ensure that Black students were treated fairly by the university's judicial system. Why was it, he queried, that there still was no Black member on the UDC?[74]

It had been less than a year since Smith had rushed into the Bursar's Office alongside Steve Colson, carrying the locks and chains that they would use to secure the building. And now, he stood before the UDC, quoting from the document that had been the outcome of that action. He concluded his statement by charging university officials with failing to fulfill parts of the May 4 agreement. "For the university to try to find scapegoats in the white community or black community for *their* negligence," Smith concluded, "is trying to shift the blame to those involved from those responsible for the flare-up on this campus."[75]

After the complaint against the busboy was withdrawn, the charges against him were dismissed.[76] The UDC next addressed the Triangle incident. Each of the four students facing charges in that case, including Michael Smith, pleaded not guilty.[77] The students' lawyer requested a continuance of the hearings in order to prepare a defense. The UDC granted the continuance, ordering the four students to appear before the UDC the following Friday, March 14.[78]

Afterward, FMO members continued to raise what they saw as a significant issue related to the case: the promise to appoint a Black member to the UDC had not been fulfilled. "I have to object to the fact that there are no black people on the UDC," Milton Gardner stated. "I don't think a completely white body can try a black person and have the black person get a fair hearing."[79] For many students, this was yet another example of an unfulfilled demand that had been promised by the university in the May 4 agreement. In their initial demands, the students had addressed the long-standing issue of justice at the university, particularly concerning the UDC. Any all-white judiciary which "intends to deal with racism" had to be reformed, they asserted, and "a new basis for administering justice must be developed and put into effect."[80] And now, Michael Smith and others advanced the idea that Black students might not accept any UDC ruling because the committee was not, in their estimation, a "proper authority."[81]

On Wednesday, it was announced that the charges against Michael Smith had been dropped. The UDC explained that Smith had been mistakenly identified as a participant in the Triangle raid.[82] Now, three students faced punishment by the UDC, including possible expulsion.[83]

On Friday, March 14, the hearing to consider the students' punishment got underway. At the outset, the students' lawyer, Leo E. Holt, presented a fifteen-page motion. He moved that the UDC was incapable of holding a fair and impartial hearing. He stated that the UDC must disqualify itself and cease proceeding any further.[84]

After a long recess to consider Holt's argument, the committee members announced that his motion had been dismissed. Holt then asked the UDC to consider a continuance of the case. The fraternity had not yet dropped the criminal charges against the two students who were scheduled to appear in court on April 14.[85] Their attorney had advised them not to testify before the UDC, since in providing such testimony they might incriminate themselves. After a lengthy recess to consider this motion, UDC members took a secret vote, ruling that a continuance would be granted. The UDC would reconvene on April 15, one day after the scheduled court date.[86]

After the hearing adjourned, Triangle fraternity members were incensed. They objected to the granting of the continuance and they criticized the UDC's handling of the entire case. One day later, fraternity leaders announced that they would not drop the charges against the two students who had surrendered to police. "The university is incapable of investigating and getting to the heart of the problem," J. Douglas Quick, president of the Northwestern's Triangle chapter, said.[87] There were "rabble rousers" among the Black students, Quick charged, and he was committed to showing them "that they cannot get away with things like this."[88]

In response, FMO accused Quick and others of "copping out" from their original agreement. As proof, in the *Daily Northwestern,* they would later publish the letters signed by Triangle members, including Quick, and several Black student leaders, in which they had agreed, among other things, that the fraternity would drop all criminal charges.[89]

Meanwhile, FMO leaders continued speaking out, hosting "fireside" chats to discuss racist incidents on campus and other issues.[90] At these gatherings, students addressed recent events and attempted to counter claims that the Triangle incident had been propelled by the racism of Black students toward white students. It was not a racist incident, they asserted. It had occurred solely because the university had failed to take action in previous racist incidents directed at Black students.[91]

Milton Gardner, who continued to pressure the press to provide fair coverage and accurately portray the Black students' position, explained: "Our quarrel is with the university—the way it handles problems of both black and white students."[92] At an FMO meeting, members voted unanimously that "the university should uphold and implement the May 4 agreement as stated."[93] The university had failed in a number of ways, they asserted. Officials had not called a campus-wide meeting to discuss the racial situation at Northwestern, as promised. They had not appointed a Black member to the UDC. And they still had not made good on the promise to provide a separate living unit for Black students. "We want," Gardner reiterated, "an autonomous living unit—a house, not a corridor. If enough blacks want to live there to make it 100% black, then that's what it would be. If there was a space open and a white wanted to live there, he could."[94] Hinz, meanwhile, insisted that university officials were indeed trying to fulfill the May 4 agreement within the law. But after HEW ruled out the possibility of a separate living unit for Black students, the university could not agree to fulfill that demand.[95]

The students were concerned with more than the May 4 agreement, however. They also expressed alarm at an increasing seriousness to the racist incidents they faced. Full cans of beer and soda were still being thrown at them from fraternity houses; they were still being nearly run down by cars; and female students were still being verbally and physically harassed. And now, they faced a frightening new form of harassment: fire. Early Monday morning, March 30, 1969, a beer bottle full of gasoline was ignited and left near a door of the Black House, causing some fire damage inside. Smoke from the fire had alerted those in the house and they had been able to extinguish it. Authorities later deemed the fire an act of arson.[96]

"There was no mass reaction from whites when something happened to the Black house," Victor Goode stated, referring to the fire, "but when the Triangle incident happened, there was nation-wide publicity."[97] The students made it clear that they believed that the university was incapable of dealing with the "causes of racial strife" on campus. And they called for support from the wider university community in order to overcome the "racist, reactionary policies of Northwestern's administration."[98] "Black students are dissatisfied with the way the university has handled the whole affair," James Turner told the press. "We feel the Triangle decision [to press charges against the students] is another example of the racism that infects the entire Northwestern University campus."[99] As a result, Turner said, all Black students might well choose to withdraw from the university in protest.[100]

On March 20, the UDC announced that along with the three students previously charged, seven other students, including Milton Gardner and Wayne Watson, were now also being charged "in connection" with the Triangle incident.[101] University attorney Alban Weber explained that some of the seven students had been identified as taking part in "fraternity fights" and others "were involved in related events."[102] Gardner and the others were ordered to appear before the hearing on April 15.[103] All faced the maximum penalty of expulsion from the university.[104]

Gardner was incredulous. He had not been involved in the Triangle incident, he said, and he could prove it. He also pointed out that the charges—showing "disrespect for the rights and property within the university community"—were entirely too vague, constituting yet another example of the lack of justice in the UDC proceedings.[105] Further, the names, ages, and addresses of all the students facing charges had been made public. That information was soon published in the press, including in the *Chicago Tribune.* The hypocrisy of releasing this personal information did not escape notice, especially since the members of Fiji fraternity, accused of assaulting a Black female student, had their identities concealed by the UDC just two years previously.

Of the ten students now facing expulsion, three were first-year students and were not enrolled at Northwestern when the takeover had taken place the previous spring. But the others were sophomores, juniors, and seniors, and *each one of them* had taken part in the takeover, including one student who had been a signatory to the May 4 agreement.[106]

Many viewed the charges, the judiciary proceedings, and their precipitating events as a continuation of a larger, troubled narrative concerning racism on campus. And many white students stepped up to express their solidarity with FMO. On April 11, the newly-formed student group, the "Concerned Whites Committee," headed by undergraduate student Richard Cohen, organized a rally at Deering Meadow to support Black students and "their struggle within the university."[107] The group circulated a petition, eventually signed by 1,000 students and faculty members. It demanded that the criminal charges now pending against the students be dropped and that the April 15 hearing be delayed until the UDC could be restructured "and/or an open hearing" called.[108]

More than 450 people turned out for the rally, which included numerous speeches. James Turner addressed the crowd, declaring that the past year had been full of "promises and no action" from university officials.[109] Several faculty members also spoke, including Raymond Mack, who had been a long-time ally of the students, particularly during the takeover. Other supporters also came forward: When Michael Smith asked Dean of Men Seward Weber to sign the petition, he did so, to the applause of the crowd. A peaceful march followed the rally whose theme was, noted Victor Goode, "order and rationality." As he explained, the "brothers' lives are in the balance. If you become disorderly, you ruin it for them."[110]

Meanwhile, Hinz reached out to Black students, pledging that "appropriate disciplinary action will be instituted" concerning any physical harassment or violence inflicted against them. He urged them to work with the university and to supply evidence or leads in any such cases.[111] In response, Gardner said that such a pledge "ignores the essential problem" at the heart of the matter: up to this point, the university had not dealt with incidents when Black students had been the victims of attacks. The students had indeed "furnished leads" to officials before, he said. But "no action has ever been taken."[112]

Now, the students knew that they needed to express themselves in a new and dramatic way. If "violence and disruption are antithetical to the very concept of the University community," Gardner announced, referring to Hinz's own statement to this effect, then "the university should see that there is no need for black students to use violence to protect themselves."[113]

Such a statement made it clear that the group of students involved in the Triangle incident had indeed adopted a violent approach as a means of self-protection. But now, the tactic of nonviolence seemed the most fitting next step, especially with so many lives in the balance. After all, the students were "all involved," as Gardner had said, and acting again in unison appeared to be the only possible way to save their friends from expulsion.

Twenty-One

We want total justice. We will not be satisfied until justice is done.

Milton Gardner, April 1969[114]

Without any prior announcement, a quickly called and unscheduled UDC hearing came to order on Sunday, April 13. It was just two days before the scheduled hearing of the ten students charged in the Triangle case. Hinz was out of town on university business and thus would not be in attendance for this hastily convened meeting.[115] The hearing had been requested by twenty-one Black students, including Michael Smith, who notified the UDC on Friday, April 11, that they "wished to appear before the committee and admit to various degrees of participation in the wrongful entry into Triangle fraternity house."[116] Represented by their attorney, Leo E. Holt, the students said they wanted to undertake negotiations with the UDC.[117]

At the Sunday hearing, the students requested that the charges against the ten students facing possible expulsion be withdrawn. In their place, new charges would be filed against all of them, the twenty-one students now coming before the UDC.

After hearing their plea, UDC members agreed to work out an agreement. They would drop the original charges and charge the twenty-one students instead. The students would agree to plead guilty and would guarantee financial restitution to the Triangle fraternity for the damage done to the house (an offer the students had already made).[118] University officials announced that representatives from Northwestern would appear in court in defense of the students facing criminal charges, formally requesting they not be punished further.[119] (Ultimately, the university failed to make good on this promise. In addition to the two students charged criminally, another student would also be charged in the summer of 1969. All three were among the group of twenty-one.[120])

The twenty-one students who came forward to work out this new agreement were acting "as a community," as Wayne Watson later explained.[121] They believed that some of the students who were facing potentially serious punishments, including probation, suspension, or expulsion, had too much to lose in respect to their current situations academically and professionally. (They were in the midst of applying to law school, for example). There were others, however, who could "afford to go through a disciplinary process," Watson said.[122] And so, together, they crafted a plan where one student who was facing charges "would be allowed to step back" and another "would step up, even though he may not have actually participated."[123] Among the twenty-one students who came before the UDC in an effort to save others from expulsion, fifteen had taken part in the May 1968 takeover.

The UDC unanimously agreed to the students' request. No students would be expelled. The twenty-one students who had come forward were now charged with violating section 2-B of the student self-determination bill (showing "disrespect for the rights and property within the university community.")[124] The students entered their guilty pleas. Dean John Ritchie then asked their attorney if the students "understood that such pleas entitled the Committee to impose such penalties as it deemed appropriate without hearing additional testimony."[125] Holt affirmed that his clients understood. There was some discussion concerning what "appropriate terms of discipline" might be. The UDC members then recessed to "consider the terms of discipline."[126] When they reconvened, they announced the following punishments:

Two students, including Michael Smith, had been charged with "very serious violations" of section 2-B. They were (immediately) suspended for the remainder of the school term, to be followed by one year's probation. Thirteen students, including the two students facing criminal charges, had been charged with "serious violations" of section 2-B. They were (immediately) suspended for thirty days, to be followed by one year's probation. Six had been charged with a violation of section 2-B and were placed on probation for two years.[127]

On Monday, April 14, news of the Sunday hearing was shared around the campus. "Blackmail!" "Whitewash!" These were the reactions from FMO and the Triangle fraternity, respectively, following the announcement of the punishments. The actions of the UDC now faced "criticism on both sides."[128]

Many were stunned by the severity of the punishments. Black students were being "penalized more harshly" than others, as Ogletree recalled of the main feeling after the UDC's decision was announced.[129] For nearly two years now, students had been "requesting a committee to evaluate the judicial process," she said.[130] And now with these punishments, it was clear that nothing had changed. And in fact, the punishments were serious. Suspension meant that students would fall behind in their course work, potentially delaying graduation and putting scholarships, internships, and jobs at risk. It also might hinder or delay applications to graduate school. Failure to satisfy the terms of probation also put students at risk of dismissal from the university.

"This is," announced Victor Goode, "no type of justice."[131] Gardner, one of the students who had been facing expulsion, said that the twenty-one students had been "blackmailed" by the UDC. He explained that after the UDC had agreed to charge the twenty-one students, the students had been threatened with expulsion if they did not accept the deal they were offered.[132] According to a document later issued by the UDC, at that Sunday hearing, the university's attorney Alban Weber "suggested appropriate terms of discipline to which the students agreed."[133] "The black students were fully aware of the penalties before they entered into the agreement," Weber said.[134] But the students disagreed. The UDC wanted "21 blacks not to be tried, but to be guilty," Michael Smith insisted.[135]

J. Douglas Quick, chapter president of Triangle, called the whole case a "travesty of justice," arguing that it was entirely improper for the UDC to even entertain making a deal with the students since the fraternity had not been consulted.[136] Attorney Weber confirmed that Triangle members had not been included in these most recent negotiations, although, he said, they had participated "in an earlier, unsuccessful series of negotiations."[137]

Quick accused the university of "whitewashing" the entire case. The UDC had entered into what he called a "sneak agreement." And he had a full list of accusations to make: university officials suppressed evidence in the Willard Hall case; they failed to provide adequate security for fraternity members; and they hindered the criminal proceedings against the students accused in the Triangle house raid. Overall, he charged, the administration's actions revealed the university's favoritism toward Black students. (Quick even charged that Hinz and others had "picked up furniture" in the raided fraternity house prior to the press arriving).[138]

Quick went on to argue against charging all of the twenty-one students who came before the UDC to begin with. Several fraternity members had identified other students who had been involved, he said, but those students had not been charged. He puzzled over the fact that some of those punished had definitely not been involved. All those who had participated in the raid should be expelled, Quick asserted. And now some students who were truly guilty would go free. They could "do it again tomorrow without fear of reprisal," added another Triangle spokesman.[139] "Because they're black," Quick said, "the university has given them every possible break to avoid the question of racism."[140]

FMO members formally denounced the punishments. (Gardner later stated that the agreement with the UDC had not been made with FMO per se, and therefore FMO members had every right to oppose it.)[141] Many other students also denounced the punishments. And now, "cameras and confusion" were back on Northwestern's campus as protests of the UDC ruling got underway and reporters showed up to cover the story.[142] Two hundred and fifty students, both Black and white, marched to the registrar's office to ask for withdrawal slips from the university.[143] That afternoon, a group of students convened a "People's Court" to pass judgment on the UDC and issue their own ruling: the UDC had enacted "totally arbitrary" procedures, they concluded. The students also distributed leaflets accusing the UDC of being "racist," "biased in make-up, intent and purpose," and not representative of the student body.[144]

By Monday, April 14, Hinz was back on campus. When he appeared in front of Scott Hall to answer questions from a crowd of students, he admitted that he was discouraged by the reactions to the UDC decision. Someone in the crowd demanded: Would the suspended students now face the likelihood of being drafted?[145]

Meanwhile, at the Black House, FMO members held a press conference where Gardner and Goode presented a formal response to the UDC decision.[146] The punishment handed down "was far too harsh," Gardner said. "We say this because white students who engaged in similar incidents involving property damage and personal injury have been given relatively light punishment i.e., at the most, disciplinary probation. As a result of arbitrating justice in the name of law and order, black students have been dealt a vindictive and racist blow."[147]

Gardner also publicly confirmed that the twenty-one students had indeed attempted to reach a negotiated agreement with the UDC in a pointed effort to save their friends from expulsion. They were "motivated by a strong moral conviction to assure the dignity and safety of black students on this campus," he said.[148] At the time, they saw their acceptance of the UDC deal as simply "politically expedient."[149] The students stepping forward to save their classmates was, as Ogletree recalled, "a very powerful statement in and of itself. And what a lot of people don't really know or understand." ("The Triangle incident," she added, "is probably one of the least understood."[150])

Now, the students hoped to overturn the UDC's punishments against the twenty-one students. After all, hadn't members of Sigma Chi fraternity successfully won reconsideration of their own case before the UDC and a reduction of penalties just six months previously?

FMO announced that its members would soon hold a meeting with concerned faculty and a series of protests was to come.[151] The first and most significant: twenty-one Black students would engage in a hunger strike in support of the twenty-one students punished by the UDC. The strike would continue until the punishments were rescinded and "justice has been met."[152] Milton Gardner, Victor Goode, John Higginson, Wayne Watson, and Eric Perkins would serve as strike leaders.[153] If they failed to persuade the administration to reduce the punishments, Black students might be "forced to leave the university 'en masse.' "[154]

Once the strike was announced, some SDS members objected to the tactic of a hunger strike. It was far too tame. As they saw it, the "complete adherence to nonviolent tactics" would have no effect to bring about any real change.[155] Some SDS members were now advocating for more aggressive, or, at the very least, more disruptive actions, a trend that was on the upswing among some student protest leaders around the country. (One idea floated at one point, unrelated to the Triangle incident: assign students to act as "bodyguards" for high-ranking university officials. The students would follow officials around campus in an effort to "protect" them from the student body.[156]) But others found SDS's proposed tactics disturbing and antithetical to the tenets of nonviolent activism. In fact, Ellis Pines would soon abandon SDS entirely after finding himself disillusioned by this and other aspects of the organization.[157] At this time, he said, he believed the group was on the "precipice of violence."[158]

But the hunger strike, as many saw it, was an effective form of nonviolent protest. Every day it seemed, hunger strikes were making the news, as students, prisoners, and political opposition parties all over the world were choosing to undertake hunger strikes as a means to call public attention to a variety of unjust conditions. In fact, on the same day the Northwestern students began their strike, another student hunger strike was underway at nearby University of Chicago in protest of punishments meted out to students who had recently been involved in a campus sit-in.[159]

At a press conference, Hinz announced that the university would allow the strike to go ahead, provided it was not disruptive.[160] He also responded to the allegations made by both the Triangle fraternity members and FMO. The fraternity's charges of "a sneak agreement" were unfounded, he said. He affirmed that the university had made no threats to the students in order to get them to plead guilty. The sole objective of the UDC proceedings had been to identify those responsible and deliver appropriate penalties. All of this was done with the overall intention to preserve "the developing cooperative character of interracial relations on campus," he said.[161] And to this end, Hinz said that he was committed to working toward revamping university discipline procedures.[162]

"Twenty-one" read the protesters' signs as students picketed in the plaza of the Rebecca Crown Center on Wednesday, April 16, 1969, the strike's first day. Other signs read: "Justice is good for the soul," "Northwestern is starving us," and "Hunger hurts; so does injustice."[163] A temporary shelter was erected in the plaza, and there, twenty-one Black students would undertake a hunger strike in opposition to the university's punishment of the twenty-one students in the Triangle incident.[164]

Members of the press immediately converged on the plaza, with reporters from a variety of news outlets, including from the *New York Times,* covering the strike. Television news crews were there en masse to interview participants.[165] The twenty-one students undertaking the strike were easy to identify: each wore a sign reading: "Feed Us Justice." The signs were numbered from one to twenty-one and each bore the name of one of the twenty-one students punished by the UDC.[166] A notable number of female students took part in the strike, among them were Adrian Williams, Melinda Jennings, Eva Jefferson Paterson, and the first-year student who initially brought the complaint against the busboy.[167] Kathryn Ogletree was also there in support of the strikers.[168]

"We 21 black students, in support of the 21 black men vindictively punished by UDC, which issued such harsh action contrary to all judicial precedent, commit ourselves to starvation until those men are allowed to return to campus."[169] This was the official statement read as the strike began. It was followed by a rally with students, faculty members, and Evanston residents turning out to show support. "Sympathy Picket to Back FMO" read the signs many white students carried to announce their parallel action in support of the students. Members of the Concerned Whites Committee were there, as were SDS members, who came out to decry "oppressive university policies" and call for the restoration of the twenty-one Black students to "full status."[170] Picketers handed out leaflets to passers-by and flyers posted around the plaza announced: "All Power to the People," a slogan of the Black Panther Party.

"We didn't even ask anyone to show up," one strike organizer said as the action got underway, but "groups of whites straggled through the square all afternoon. Today there will be hundreds in the square, with demands that the administrators come down from their fortress in [Rebecca] Crown [Center] and talk."[171]

For nearly a week, the strikers camped in the plaza. They slept in sleeping bags in a sheltered, but open-air, section under the building's eaves, often bearing freezing temperatures, rain, and high winds. They ate nothing, but by a doctor's order, drank fruit juice.[172] They had a small portable television to watch and one striker brought his guitar to serenade the others. At one point, the film, *Bridge on the River Kwai,* was projected on an outside wall for entertainment.[173] (Director David Lean's 1957 masterpiece set in a prison camp during World War II, which examined themes of injustice, brutal authority, and sabotage, seemed a particularly interesting choice.) Roger Friedman, who

Hunger strike rally, Rebecca Crown Center Plaza, Northwestern University, April 1969
(Northwestern University Archives)

supported the strike, visited with his friend Eric Perkins, one of the strikers, during the action. Friedman recalled "how thin and 'starved' he looked."[174]

Throughout the strike, supporters held marches, rallies, and nightly vigils. On the strike's first day, civil rights leader Julian Bond made an appearance, speaking briefly to the crowd before taking part in a candlelight vigil.[175] On Thursday, April 17, in solidarity with the hunger strikers, twenty-one SDS members, organized by Ed Steinhart, began their own "sympathy" hunger strike.[176] That night, Fred Hampton, chairman of the Black Panther Party of Illinois, appeared on campus to "talk revolution" at an event jointly sponsored by FMO, SDS, and the Concerned Whites Committee.[177] Hundreds of people turned out to hear Hampton speak, and afterwards, they took part in a demonstration in support of the strike.[178] Evanston residents also made their concerns and support known, with some offering to serve as mediators between strikers and university officials.[179] Their proposal was rejected.

In fact, there was an eerie silence from administrators.

Hunger strike participant, Rebecca Crown Center Plaza, Northwestern University, April 1969 (Northwestern University Archives)

Hunger strike participants, Rebecca Crown Center Plaza,
Northwestern University, April 1969
(Northwestern *Syllabus* Yearbook, 1970)

As the strike was underway, the results were announced of the newly-elected members of Northwestern's Associated Student Government. A moderate election turnout produced the winners: Mike Place was elected president and Eva Jefferson Paterson was elected vice president. The slate, which had been supported by both FMO and the Concerned Whites Committee, won by two hundred votes.[180] When the results were announced, Place ran over to the Rebecca Crown Center to tell Paterson they'd won.[181]

That night, at the installation banquet held at the Orrington Hotel in Evanston, Place called the hunger strike an "emergency situation." His first priority, he announced, was to "take action toward changing the judicial process by which 21 blacks were punished."[182] He made no speech after being sworn in, but instead left hurriedly to attend a meeting with faculty members who were working together to find a resolution.[183] (Paterson, camped out with the others at the Rebecca Crown Center, would be installed in her office after the strike ended).

At the meeting that evening, twenty-two faculty members and the newly-elected members of Northwestern's student government adopted a statement in "the interest of racial harmony and justice."[184] They asked for an immediate reduction of the UDC punishments and that "conciliatory action be taken by administration, faculty and students" under the leadership of the university's Human Relations Committee.[185]

Mike Place was now working in tandem with Gardner and other FMO leaders, along with Richard Cohen and members of SDS. Together, they continued to stage large rallies, notable, according to the press, since they included both Black and white participants and both Black and white speakers took the stage at the events.[186]

Still, as the strike wore on, some amount of disharmony emerged among some of the students who had been brought into closer alliance by recent events. A hearing for the six white students who had been arrested and charged with disorderly conduct during the February demonstration against the Dow Chemical Company was set for Friday, April 18. SDS members requested that FMO members attend the hearing to show support for these "political prisoners," as they referred to the students.[187] But no FMO members appeared at the court on Friday morning. In reaction, roughly half of the white hunger strikers withdrew from their own strike in protest.[188]

On Sunday, April 20, the strike's fifth day, another rally was held. Northwestern's Dean of Men Seward Weber and Dean of Women Patricia Thrash, along with members of their staff, were there.[189] Also present were three "equally unhappy" mothers of Northwestern students, dressed in their "Sunday coats and hats."[190] One of the women was the mother of the student who had been allegedly assaulted by the busboy.[191] Another, who was booed and jeered at, was Millicent Quick, whose son was chapter president

Reporter interviewing a hunger strike participant,
Rebecca Crown Center Plaza, Northwestern University, April 1969
(Northwestern University Archives)

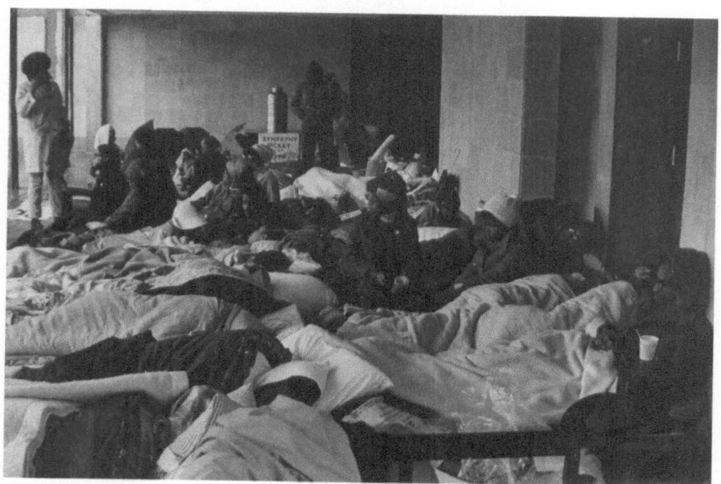

Hunger strike participants, Rebecca Crown Center Plaza, Northwestern University, April 1969. The strikers arranged their sleeping bags near the entryway to the Rebecca Crown Center, which housed the offices of university administrators. (Northwestern University Archives)

Hunger strike rally, Rebecca Crown Center Plaza, Northwestern University, April 1969 (Northwestern University Archives)

Crowds and sympathy picket members at the hunger strike, Rebecca Crown Center Plaza, Northwestern University, April 1969 (Northwestern University Archives)

of Triangle.[192] The third mother was there in support of one of the hunger strikers, her daughter, Marianne Jackson, a junior sociology major who had also been a participant in the takeover. As "a mother my heart goes out," she said, after embracing her daughter, tears running down her face, "because I feel what they are doing could have been done a long time ago. They are not asking for much—just equality." [193]

The strike would take its toll: over the weekend of April 19-20, four students were taken away in ambulances and hospitalized for complications related to fasting for up to one hundred hours.[194] As first-year student Winston Cenac was carried out of the plaza on a stretcher, he raised his fist in the Black Power salute. "How many of us must roll over with cramps before the administration hears?" Cenac had asked in a speech earlier.[195]

Many of the strikers were not only dismayed by the administration's complete silence during the strike, but they were also troubled by their treatment by Evanston police. On April 19, FMO member Ameen Ramzey called for an ambulance to aid one of the strikers, Bill Henderson, who was suffering from stomach cramps. "They kept asking me to repeat myself," Ramzey reported of his phone call to the police. Then one officer asked: "Why don't you feed him a hamburger?" (A complaint was later filed against the police department.) "They had no sense of urgency," Ramzey said of their reaction.[196]

The *Daily Northwestern's* Bob Greene was alarmed by the administration's failure to respond to the strike. "You can throw your ideology and your legalistic jargon out now," he wrote, "because what you have is people who believe in something so much that they are being carried away sick for it. And right and wrong are just words after you have seen a freshman coed shaking and crying as they put her in the ambulance."[197]

As the hunger strike continued, events surrounding the action moved quickly. Sociology professor Richard Schwartz was working with other faculty members to draft a proposal to demand a reduction of the UDC punishments.[198] More than one hundred faculty members had also organized a network of tutors for the suspended students in order to protect them "from harsh academic penalties," they said.[199] And a student government subcommittee was busy investigating possibilities for judicial reform and working on a set of recommendations to overhaul the UDC.[200]

The administration, Payson S. Wild announced, would accept plans for a revamped judiciary, but no official was even entertaining a rehearing of the Triangle case or considering any reduction of the punishments.[201] Aside from this statement, the administration remained silent as the strike wore on. Chancellor Miller, it was rumored, was in town somewhere. But, as Bob Greene reported, "no one had seen him in weeks."[202] In fact, Greene asserted, there had been no effort from any official to attempt any understanding of the Black students' position.[203] Franklin Kreml made only one statement as he affirmed that "no top-level administrators met with black students about the strike, and there were no plans for such a meeting."[204]

"It would not be necessary for them to offer to change the administrative position on the UDC decision," the *Daily Northwestern* stated, concerning the administration's silence, "but to ignore the strikers out of hand is arrogant, appalling and inhumane. We strongly feel nonviolent protest is the only form of protest acceptable for provoking and implementing change. At Northwestern, we are having one now, and it is being ignored."[205]

The week of the hunger strike had been marked by news of more major student protests around the country, including a sit-in at Stanford University, the continuation of a six-day strike at Harvard, and yet another building occupation at Columbia University. But two actions stood out starkly as evidence of an alarming escalation in tactics now being used by some students: at Atlanta University (now Clark Atlanta University) student protesters had locked twenty-two university trustees in a building for twenty-nine hours.[206] And at Cornell, a group of Black students seized a campus building after presenting demands similar to those made by Northwestern students the previous spring. But there was a notable difference in this incident. After reportedly being taunted by white fraternity members, who threatened to forcibly remove them from the building, the students armed themselves. Once negotiations with administrators concluded, granting many of the students' demands and offering amnesty to those involved, the students left the building and marched across campus, brandishing their weapons.[207] A Pulitzer-prize winning image of the armed students, taken by photographer Steve Starr, would be seen around the world, prompting an outcry against the students.[208] Despite the university's pledge to refrain from punishing the students who had taken part in the thirty-six-hour occupation, just a few weeks later, the students were under indictment.[209]

"In the wake of increased nationwide violent campus disturbances," observed undergraduate student Paul B. Hewitt in a letter to the *Daily Northwestern*, "the hunger strike currently being conducted by Northwestern black students represents a significant reversal of style."[210] Certainly nonviolence as a method of protest had long been used, but, as Hewitt observed, "on its effectiveness in 1969 may well hinge the form of protest for years to come." Should Northwestern administrators "choose to relax and ignore the protest because it is non-violent," Hewitt stated, "they will open the gate for militancy which will be very difficult indeed to close."[211]

After the hospitalization of the four hunger strikers, the students faced a dire situation. The strike leaders reluctantly decided that it was not in their best interest to continue. After 121 hours, on Monday, April 21, at 4:15 p.m., the six-day hunger strike came to an end. There had been no response from administrators. No effort to negotiate. And no real acknowledgment of their concerns. The seventeen remaining students, along with the sympathy strikers and other supporters, broke up their camps, packed up their belongings, and left.

The empty plaza, whose walls were still papered with flyers proclaiming, "All Power to the People," was quiet. "Our grievances have not been resolved," Gardner stated.[212] He promised that the students would confront the university in some other way.[213]

Chapter 10

A New Normalcy

Participants in a successful campaign for equality must "redefine themselves and create their own institutions."

Robert Parris Moses, address at Northwestern University, 1965[1]

But another confrontation did not occur. Instead, in the immediate wake of the hunger strike, the students suffered a sense of defeat. "Most us felt that that was a failure," Kathryn Ogletree recalled.[2] It "didn't work," Victor Goode said simply. And now, "from the elation and success of the building takeover in '68, we experienced a sense of loss and despair in '69," he said.[3]

By May 1969, four of the students suspended by the UDC in the Triangle case submitted applications to withdraw from the university; several others said they also planned to leave Northwestern. One student, who had not been punished by the UDC, said he also pledged to withdraw because he wanted to "accept the same punishment as the others." "It was a symbolic thing," as another student explained.[4]

Many students felt slighted by the administration's silence during the strike. They were left to ponder the reasons their action had not opened a dialogue with officials concerning the problems they continued to confront on campus. But others seemed only too grateful that the hunger strike ended without the administration making any concessions to the students. At this point, plenty of people were entirely fed up with student protests. All student activists, and Black student activists in particular, were fast becoming the subject of a widening backlash. "Angry, impatient, [and] distrustful," read a story in the *Chicago Tribune* describing Black students at Northwestern and at other universities across the country.[5] "A fast-spreading drive by American Negroes and their supporters," an Associated Press story asserted, "for special treatment in the schools has brought campuses in many parts of the country to a boiling point."[6]

Even though the administration had been unwilling to negotiate with the hunger strike participants, some white students began to complain about what they believed to be the university's overly attentive treatment of Black students. "If the university wants to let students have a voice in decisions," offered one undergraduate student, "all students should be listened to—not just the blacks."[7] Like others, she thought Black students had already been given disproportionate attention. "It seems clear that since May 4th, 1968," she wrote, "and perhaps since the hunger strike, the blacks . . . are the only ones who have anything to say in this university."[8]

Such resentment was just one indication of the numerous divisions within the student body. "Greeks are intolerant of any discussion of their system by others," John Walter wrote in an editorial in the *Daily Northwestern*. "Blacks are intolerant of any white point of view, and vice versa. The so-called 'radicals,' who should be a vital, probing part of the University campus, are intolerant of any suspected of being less enthusiastically left. Take an issue, define your side and try to figure out how willing you were to listen to anybody else even talk about the subject."[9]

It was nearly the end of the school year and many felt bedraggled and distressed. "[W]e put away our tired typewriters with a sense of depression and the feeling that we and you need a summer vacation," wrote the staff of the *Daily Northwestern*.[10] But before that vacation arrived, there would be a few final disruptions. And once again, Northwestern would make headlines.

On May 15, as part of a series of actions opposing the campus Naval Reserve Officer Training Corps unit (NROTC), a group of fifty students, led by SDS and including Roger Friedman, staged an "anti-drill" protest on Deering Meadow near the NROTC training site. A week later they were back, but this time 600 protesters took part in the action.[11] A third protest a week later turned ugly. On May 29, at the thirty-ninth annual President's review of the NROTC, two hundred protesters turned out. Several protestors accosted guests, preventing them from entering the event. They sprayed fake blood on several people, including Jack Hinz. A fistfight broke out among a group of several protesters, guests, and security. The police, in riot gear, were called in. One arrest was made.

This was the first time, the *Chicago Tribune* noted, that "the university had issued no invitations to the press to attend the affair."[12] Buttoning up from outside scrutiny in the wake of a disruptive, dramatic, and game-changing year, the university seemed to try to limit its public profile, for a while at least.

Roger Friedman was one of four students who were ordered to appear before the UDC for taking part in the protests.[13] Friedman recalled that he and the others were notified that the hearing would provide them with a chance to explain why they "shouldn't be put on academic probation or suspended."[14] But Friedman, who was about to leave town for the summer, said he felt that the university was escalating its efforts to curtail student protests against the war, and so he chose not to show up for the UDC hearing.[15]

One student, Dale Brandt, was suspended for eighteen months, and three others, Roger Friedman, Eva Blinder, and Sam Ho, were placed on academic probation until June 15, 1970.[16] These punishments also caused a sizeable uproar, especially after Brandt was reclassified "1-A" by his draft board and ordered to appear for a physical exam.[17]

That summer, Friedman received notice that he had been placed on academic probation. Friedman said he felt that this was "the cost" of participating in anti-war activity on campus. For a time, he considered whether he really wanted to return to Northwestern in the fall. He knew that students who dropped out of school were particularly vulnerable to being drafted. So he decided to make the best of his senior year. He decided that he would work toward completing his degree by June 1970, and then move on to undertake more radical political activity in Chicago.[18]

The final protests of the 1968-1969 school year only foreshadowed what was to come at Northwestern as students would continue to escalate their actions, take on the administration, and, in the hands of some radical students, raise the stakes. "We can predict a year of unrest, here and all over the world," the *Daily Northwestern* announced at the beginning of the fall quarter in 1969.[19] And that prediction would come true. During the 1969-1970 school year, a total of 7,200 students in the United States would be arrested (up from the total of 4,000 students arrested in the 1968-1969 academic year).[20] There was no question that the university, as well as the country as a whole, would continue to undergo unrest for the foreseeable future, and by the spring of 1969, many were already fatigued.

In the wake of the Dow protest, the Willard Hall incident, the Triangle incident, the hunger strike, and the scores of other major and minor disturbances of the past year, the campus was beset by resentment, anguish, and animosity. "This university is at a crossroads," John Walter observed in his end-of-the-year editorial. "The year has so awakened, so discouraged, and so exhausted some people here that I'm not sure we can see our way clear anymore. If we are to see clear at all, we are all going to have to change."[21]

Roger Friedman addressing an open housing rally in Evanston, April 8, 1968. (*Daily Northwestern,* April 9, 1968)

Owing to his early collaboration with Ellis Pines and the Student Power Movement, Friedman was identified as a "student power leader" throughout his time at Northwestern. For three out of his four years at Northwestern, he played a leading role as a student activist—an unusually long stint which was matched by several other student leaders, including Victor Goode and Eric Perkins. By his senior year, Friedman began to step back, figuring, as he said, that "I needed to make room for a younger group of students to assume leadership." That year, as he feared being drafted, he failed to pass the physical exam for military service and he received a medical deferment. He moved to Rogers Park in Chicago, where he became involved in community organizing activities. In 1970, he graduated from Northwestern with a BS from the School of Speech. He later earned an MSW and then a PhD in developmental psychology. Today, he is a psychologist and social worker. He works as a reformer in the child welfare system in Maryland and around the country, and teaches at the University of Maryland's School of Social Work. He also maintains a clinical practice as a psychologist. In 2016, he co-authored, *Tower Sniper: The Terror of America's First Active Shooter On Campus.*[22]

Change

It was no surprise that it was Jack Hinz who ultimately broke the administration's silence that lasted throughout the hunger strike.[23] One day after the strike ended, Hinz announced that he and three other university vice presidents wanted to meet with the students.[24] He had not interfered with the strike, he later said, because it had not been disruptive and he fully supported the students' right to protest. Now, he said, he didn't want to "rehash" the Triangle case, but instead welcomed a discussion with Black students concerning "all elements of their lives on campus," including the conditions that led to the "Triangle difficulty."[25]

One day later, after reportedly meeting with university officials and some members of the board of trustees, Chancellor Miller's own silence was broken.[26] It came in the form of a printed statement published in the *Daily Northwestern*, under the ironic title: "advertisement."

"[S]ince returning over the weekend from the East where I was attending the meeting of the American Association of Universities," Miller wrote, "I have been looking into the problem presented by the hunger strike of 21 black students of the university."[27] His conclusion: he supported the UDC's handling of the case and thus, the penalties imposed on the twenty-one students would not be reduced. Although he asserted that "the University cannot tailor its governing bodies to suit the parties in a specific case, nor restructure its procedures under duress," he "recognized the desirability" of undertaking a study of the structure of the UDC. Further, he noted that Jack Hinz had been tasked with undertaking "a review of basic problems with both Black and white student leadership."[28] "It is my expectation and hope that we proceed now to improve the character of interracial relations on the campus," Miller concluded.[29] (Milton Gardner would later state that he and others were not at all satisfied with Miller's statement.[30])

Miller's response (and preceding silence) was really no surprise. What had been identified during the strike as a "growing alienation" between Black students and university officials was, in part, the result of some administrators' desire to take a strong authoritarian stand in the wake of the 1968 takeover.[31] Never again would the administration be put in such a precarious position as to negotiate with lawbreakers and protesters, this point of view held. This was the position most clearly articulated by Miller.

At the same time, there was also a move to draw the administration closer in alliance with all students, both Black and white, and to find ways to negotiate, compromise, and reach agreement. This was the position most clearly represented by Hinz. As the strike had been underway, Hinz had been busy. He held a meeting with a few Black student leaders to discuss the housing situation, and he had already begun looking into reforming disciplinary procedures. And he was still interested in working to advance and broaden "the role of the student in developing school policy," he told the press.[32] But, always performing a kind of balancing act, Hinz also had to temper these statements, adding that the university's "support for greater autonomy of students should not be interpreted to mean that the university will accede to any and all pleasures."[33]

As Hinz performed his dual roles as representative of both students and the administration, he unintentionally reflected the nature of a Northwestern in the process of a large-scale shift, one that was witnessing many transitions within the institution—a transition from old to new guard, from segregated to integrated, from *in loco parentis* to student autonomy. And all the while the students themselves were shifting alliances, building networks, retreating, disrupting, debating, or trying to maintain the status quo.

By the end of the spring quarter, the *Daily Northwestern* saw fit to point out the ultimate absurdity of Hinz's position, "the position that makes a man a university vice president, a 'one of them,' and the position that makes the same man the dean of students, 'one of us.' "[34] But it was precisely owing to Hinz's skill in balancing his dual roles that made him effective.

Increasingly, Miller had turned to Hinz to handle any number of student-related issues, from the takeover to the housing situation. During all the turmoil of the 1968-1969 school year, as Hinz later explained, Miller's decision to step down as president was a reaction to many considerations. But the number one reason was *all the upheaval among the student body* (precisely as it had been rumored).[35] In the midst of the chaos, Miller simply "didn't know how to deal with it," Hinz recalled.[36] "Rocky [Miller's nickname] didn't understand the students very well," he said of the president, "and he had very, very limited interaction with them."[37]

"All of those men," Hinz said of the other university vice presidents "—all men—were past sixty. So that kind of gives you some information where they're from." According to Hinz, they "lived in a pretty passive world and they were accustomed to when there was a bit of upheaval or distress that it would be dealt with."[38] He remembered approaching Miller many times, informing him about a particular issue that students were talking about, something that might boil over at any moment. To be prepared, Hinz wanted to discuss it with Miller, craft a response, and be ready to have an informed discussion with the students. But the president's answer was simply: "Don't let them talk about that."[39] The upheavals and distresses—the takeovers, sit-ins, and the hunger strike—were annoyances and distractions to Miller, who feared that such disturbances "might turn away donors, might create a climate in which folks who might have given money to the university wouldn't give it."[40]

While Miller sought to adjust to the new reality of a more open, integrated, and responsive university, he also revealed his connection to the Northwestern of years past. It was 1949 when he had become president, long before so many "radical" changes had come to the campus. Indeed, Miller came from an era that predated integrated campus housing, much less the campaign for student power, SDS, and the Black Power movement.

In a letter to the board of trustees outlining the details of the takeover, Miller had revealed a kind of duality to his own view of the issues raised by the Black students and, in particular, of the way the takeover had been resolved. On one hand, he argued that the university's "mea culpa statement," (the May 4 agreement's policy statement that Northwestern had acted as a racist institution in the past), was acceptable. "[W]e felt that the University was great enough in size, spirit and power to permit such compassion and humility," he wrote.[41] But he also revealed a fundamental misinterpretation of the experiences of Black students. Their action to take over a building, he argued, stemmed from *their own* difficulty integrating within the university. "It was realized that the transfer from the ghetto to daily contact, without refuge, with upper middle class white students was for many a traumatic experience," he asserted.[42] Citing the university's mission to provide "educated leadership," Miller opined: "There is no segment of the society which is in greater need of such leadership than the Negro community."[43] (It should be noted that this view was held by those outside of Miller's generation, too. A May 1968 editorial in the *Daily Northwestern* asserted that many of the problems faced by Black students at Northwestern stemmed from their difficult "transition from ghetto to college."[44])

Miller echoed the negative and erroneous perception of some other observers of the "Black revolution" on campuses across the country. The revolution was about Black students' failure to assimilate, not the racism of white institutions, they argued. When students demanded rights and redress, many viewed them as disturbing or damaging the traditional structure of the university itself. They were asking for "privileges" they were not owed. They were disrupting "normal" life on campus. With an attitude that harkened back to the criticism heaped on an earlier reformer, William Yancy Bell, Jr., they looked upon the students as troublemakers.

For some college administrators, the increase in college enrollment of Black students simply could not be separated from the concurrent rise of student activism on campuses in general. To them, the demanding, "militant," and disruptive actions of the students were unacceptable. And Miller was certainly not alone in his reaction to student protests. By the late 1960s and into the early 1970s, university officials across the country began to focus efforts on limiting student speech and taking a hardline approach as they prepared for a "season of guerrilla violence," fearing that the "tactics of recent years will be abandoned in favor of guerilla and hit-and-run assaults."[45]

By 1970, thirty states would enact roughly eighty punitive laws to deal with campus unrest, with many calling for the expulsion of students who violated campus rules.[46] Many judged such laws as offering welcome relief from the "anarchy" on campuses around the country and, ultimately, it was hoped they would quell the protest movements led by both Black and white students.

There are "encouraging signs that the voice of responsibility may be restored on the campuses of the nation," as the *Chicago Tribune* asserted in 1969. "For a long time the revolutionists of the student left and the black militants have been having things their way, but countervailing forces are beginning to arise and make themselves heard."[47] By 1970, President Nixon would convene a special commission to investigate campus unrest, whose report included the observation that the U.S. was on the brink of "a chasm in society so dangerous that it threatened the survival of the nation."[48] Meanwhile, in a secret (and later proved illegal) program, FBI director J. Edgar Hoover expanded the controversial counter-intelligence program (COINTELPRO) which was designed to disrupt and discredit progressive organizations and individuals, including student activists. Among those identified in FBI reports concerning activism at Northwestern were James Turner, Kathryn Ogletree, John Bracey, and Jack Hinz, along with other Northwestern students, faculty, and administrators.[49]

But of course, the students on campus at the time were unaware of any of this. And so they did the only thing they really could do after the hunger strike: move forward. Despite any sense of failure, they still rode the wave of their earlier success a year before. Still compelling them forward were those aspects that led them to the takeover in the first place: an awakening of consciousness, a commitment to take action, and the building and organizing of a network, a network that had widened considerably by the time of the hunger strike. The hunger strike proved to be only one step in a long process that seemingly began after the students had left the Bursar's Office that night in May 1968. But in fact, that process had begun several decades earlier.

As so, in the spring of 1969, Black students would continue to "press for justice," as Eric Perkins announced after the hunger strike ended. Perkins stated that they planned to hold fast to the adoption of nonviolent means to initiate reform. Their future tactics, he explained, would include legal "possibilities" as well as nonviolent physical confrontations.[50] In short, they were not giving up. After all, to the students, engaging in an act of protest was not the problem; it was the means to force a solution to a problem. As some officials railed against student disruptions and disorders, they often failed to see the conditions that had given rise to the protest to begin with. They saw only the protest itself. And so it was that the students pledged to continue to take their concerns before the administration, to continue to try to make them see, to compel them to listen.

Just one week after the hunger strike ended, FMO leaders were back in talks with Hinz. "The issues that prompted last year's takeover live on," the *Daily Northwestern* aptly observed on the takeover's first anniversary.[51] That same month, Hinz was making good on some of his promises. No, there would be no separate housing for Black students, he confirmed yet again, but he was busy trying to make more space available for students in residential halls. Currently, he was overseeing the integration of Goodrich Hall, a campus dormitory. Twenty-four Black male students would be moved in, while some white male residents would be moved into other facilities, in order to achieve a fifty-fifty ratio.[52] Some disgruntled white students who lived in the dorm staged a brief sit-in in opposition to the plan. But after consulting an attorney, they found they had no legal recourse.[53]

Hinz and others also made good on the pledge to address issues related to the UDC. By September 1969, the UDC had been disbanded. In its place came a revised judicial system, made up of three levels of adjudication, with three procedural levels to hear cases, and providing for an expanded role for students in proceedings.[54] The new system, the Northwestern University Systems of Hearings and Appeals, was authorized by the board of trustees over the summer. The University Hearings and Appeals Board (UHAB), the highest board of appeals, was composed of six faculty members and three students. UHAB would now handle cases involving "major disruption" on campus, while the student board would conduct hearings on all routine cases. Over the course of the next year, eighty-six cases were heard. A total of nineteen students were found not guilty and twenty-three students received disciplinary probation or warnings. But no students were suspended or expelled.[55] The new system would also lead to changes in the types of cases undertaken for adjudication, partly as a result of the Triangle case.[56] When Milton Gardner was appointed as one of the eleven student judges on the newly-formed judiciary board, it did indeed appear that progress was slowly being made.[57] And, parallel to the dissolution of the UDC, other changes were underway.

After months of pressure by students, the Council on Undergraduate Life, which for years had formulated non-academic campus policy, would soon be abolished, too. It was replaced by the Northwestern Community Council, a body which would also have increased student representation.[58] And, in the midst of the hunger strike itself, in April 1969, Northwestern's student government underwent a major reorganization: The Student Senate had been replaced by the Associated Student Government, a change that would also allow for increased student participation.[59]

Changes to the university also came as the federal government continued to enforce the Civil Rights Act. In June 1969, Northwestern officials submitted the first of several Equal Opportunity Employment plans designed to oversee fair employment practices and initiate procedures to hire more women and people of color at the university. (By 1971, the plan would be approved, establishing the university's first central affirmative action office. In the fall of 1970, Richard C. Adams, Northwestern first equal opportunities officer, was hired. He told the *Daily Northwestern* that he was "working to end discrimination . . . at all levels of university employment."[60])

As the 1969 spring quarter wound down, FMO held a special election. In June 1969, Milton Gardner, Michael Smith, and Eric Perkins were replaced by Clovis Semmes, Charles Shepard, and Clinton Bristow.[61] These three new leaders were all takeover participants, and two of them had been part of the group of twenty-one who came before the UDC to save their friends from expulsion. They were elected to steer FMO through what one member called "another arduous year at Northwestern."[62] Negotiations with the university, they announced, would continue in the areas of financial aid, housing, admissions, and curriculum.[63] By October 1969, FMO presented administrators with a new list of demands for increased financial aid and admission of Black students. "I thought we had made progress," William Ihlanfeldt told the *Daily Northwestern* after receiving it. "It sounds now like we're just starting all over again."[64] But of course, they were not starting from the beginning, but continuing a fight that had begun decades before.

In the fall of 1969, 115 Black students would enter Northwestern. By that time, Black students were playing a "unique activist role" on campus, as FMO's Governor of Campus Affairs Clinton Bristow announced. A new admissions committee, comprised of seven Black students, was now accompanying admissions officers as they traveled to high schools to recruit students. The students spoke to audiences of predominantly Black high school students, giving "their interpretations of NU life and emphasizing the black role on campus." Black students, explained one committee member, "want to know how black students here live, and a white admissions officer can't tell them. The story has to come straight from the horse's mouth."[65]

"A scrappy little newspaper." The staff of the *Daily Northwestern.* (Northwestern *Syllabus* Yearbook, 1969)

While the paper, which had been founded in 1881, could annoy and outrage nearly everyone with its various editorial points of view, it served a critical function as staff documented campus life, opinions, events, and controversies. By the late sixties, the predominantly white staff would slowly become more diversified. In 1969, Milton Gardner was assigned to write a weekly column, and more women were appointed as reporters and editors. Among the paper's staff during the momentous years 1966-1969, were several female editors and reporters, including Joan Schuman (editor from 1966-1967), Marla Strassberger, Kathy Polhemus, Kathy Waters, Donna Rosene (editor from 1969-1970), and Joann Lublin, who later went on to become an editor at the *Wall Street Journal.*[66] All of these women covered student political movements and, in particular, the events surrounding the takeover, including the Triangle incident.

All of these advances spelled progress. And thus, despite the administration's silence throughout the hunger strike, the students had, in fact, already proved to have "confronted" the university in significant ways. The hunger strike had built on many of the advances made with the takeover. It prompted new alliances to form among students; it sparked debate and dialogue, however contentious at times; it drew the attention of the national media and national figures in the civil rights and Black power movements; and it also elicited the support of a large number of faculty members, local residents, and student government officials, all working together to try to address the issues confronting the university. In these important ways, the strike, like the takeover, had been effective.

It was owing to the alliances built in the previous few years—those among Black students and white students, along with a sizeable number of faculty members, administrators, and staff—that so many changes had come to Northwestern. Black student activism had both influenced and been accompanied by other significant movements to reform the institution, to change the ways the university operated, and to shift the ways officials perceived of and reacted to the student body. The drive for student autonomy and self-rule, the Student Power Movement, the anti-war movement, the New Left, AASU, FMO, SDS, and the Concerned Whites Committee, had all proven to present a critical, unavoidable force on campus. And, while all members of these various movements may not have worked perfectly in sync at all times, they collectively proved that *all were involved* in efforts to make Northwestern a "better place," as Kathryn Ogletree put it.[67] When Milton Gardner expressed his hope that out of their combined efforts "maybe black and white students can move together," he expressed the nature of a new more cohesive student body within a more enlightened institution.[68]

Ultimately, the hunger strike also prompted wider recognition of what was at stake at Northwestern. If Black students followed through on their threat to withdraw in protest, "this university will have lost everything it stands for," wrote the *Daily Northwestern's* Tom Davies. "The effects of such an action would be shattering. A black studies program down the drain. A university suddenly unable ever to recruit black students again. A barrier to recruiting even serious white students who want a liberal education, hence a Northwestern returned to its lily-white North Shore country club days."[69]

Dean of Women Patricia Thrash concurred. "The incidents at Triangle, Willard and [the hunger strike at] Crown were sad and unfortunate," she observed at the close of the spring 1969 quarter. But she also recognized that Black students had prompted "a hopeful breakthrough" on campus. By continuously expressing their concerns, engaging in a hunger strike, and also undertaking the takeover the year previously, they had "unveiled" many problems on campus, problems that needed to be addressed in order for Northwestern to evolve. Thus, Thrash concluded, Black students had ultimately helped the university "take the plunge into the genuine concerns of the real world."[70]

As the Northwestern administration feared ever more violence breaking out on college campuses (despite the fact that it was usually the police who initiated violence against students), the students had adopted entirely nonviolent tactics in both the takeover and the hunger strike. They had rejected calls to employ more aggressive and even violent tactics as advocated by a small but influential number of SDS members nationwide—a faction that would eventually cause the splintering of the organization in the summer of 1969.[71]

Theirs was a different kind of strategy: using a nonviolent approach to force "institutional change," the central concept that James Turner identified as governing the students' activism, particularly in the takeover. While their strategy might have seemed like a failure in the case of the hunger strike, it would prove to be a success in many ways: it caused yet another shift in the institution—at the time perhaps barely perceptible. Turner explained that following the perceived victory of the takeover, there had indeed been "some retrenchment in some areas and some disappointments."[72] But he also recognized that while the takeover was a significant event, it was only one action in a long, ongoing process which was focused on "changing the culture of the institution from the inside out."[73]

Both the takeover and the hunger strike were part of that process. And both, in a sense, can be seen as a part of the real work of integration. Both actions were intended to force the institution to change. Both were a means to challenge the university's underlying historical and social values and attitudes—"ways of doing things." And both, in a sense, caused a rupture in the university's routine, its "business as usual," and exposed the nature of the deeply embedded racism within the institution. Each action was a part of a larger process that did not conclude at the end of a single protest or an academic year. And, they were both part of a process, one can argue, that is still underway.

"[T]hings did not immediately change," as Ogletree said, describing the aftermath of the takeover. Nor did the process of change always move in a forward direction. "You take a step forward and two steps backwards," she said. Still, she reflected, "all in all, I think there was a sense of optimism over a period of time."[74] According to Turner, there would be a gradual reduction of overtly racist incidents in the years following the takeover. Despite some missteps and outright failures to fully embrace the reality of Black students' experiences and needs, the administration, represented especially by Hinz and Kreml, would increasingly attempt to mediate and resolve situations, to work from the inside out as they and other officials consented to alter some components of the very structure of the institution itself (curriculum, student regulations, housing, and the judicial system, for example).

In the case of the Triangle incident and the punishments handed down by the UDC, one could argue that there was a vindictive nature in punishing (and possibly expelling) so many Black students, especially when the majority had taken part in the takeover, and particularly because white fraternity members had not been subject to similar punishments—or even investigation—for allegedly violent actions in the past. But by the spring of 1969, it was clear that the university was more often working to seek official and public resolution to racist encounters on campus, rather than implicitly affirming them through silence or inaction. Indeed, however one judges what occurred at the Triangle fraternity house, the action can be understood—not condoned—in context: it was a response to the lack of justice Black students faced for many years, and the dilatory response of an administration that, by delaying, saying nothing, or turning a blind eye, seemed to offer tacit approval for the racism the students experienced at Northwestern.

The events that occurred after the takeover underscored the need for students to continue to pressure the university to make good on the May 4 agreement. That process, too, was ongoing, lasting not weeks or months, but years. As the administration continued to work with students on implementing the agreement, "we were feeling more optimistic because we thought things were going to be improving," as Ogletree recalled. "We felt that as more and more black students came to Northwestern it would lessen the likelihood that people would just take advantage and do things like dropping beer cans and stuff. [T]hey would have to deal with a larger number of people. Sometimes if you only have two or three people you think you can get away with things like that," she said. Ogletree also recognized that as the number of Black students increased, they would find more support from the established alliance of students who now held power to "advocate within the administration." And it was that position that would allow them to ensure that any further incidents would not go "unnoticed."[75]

Historian Joy Ann Williamson-Lott argues that top-down changes in official policies, as well as federal legislation, such as the 1964 Civil Rights Act and 1965 Higher Education Act, cannot be overlooked in their impact on integrating and reforming American institutions of higher education. But, she asserts, it was the students themselves who were at the "center of reform."[76] "Black campus activists did not succeed in revolutionizing higher education," historian Ibram X. Kendi concedes. But he too argues that their success was immeasurable. For, as he argues, "they did succeed in shoving to the center a series of historically marginalized academic ideas, questions, frames, methods, perspectives, subjects, and pursuits. They were able to succeed in pushing into higher education a profusion of racial reforms—in the form of people, programs, and literature. Most decisively, but least chronicled, Black campus activists succeeded in exchanging the academy's century-old racist ideals."[77]

Many view Black student activism at Northwestern, manifest namely in the takeover and its success in producing the May 4 agreement, as a critical component that first truly pushed the university to evolve, to become more open, modern, and connected, rather than remaining a regional institution whose borders, both physical and metaphorical, were staunchly defended. Ogletree argues that the administration's response to the takeover was connected to something more than meeting the needs of Black students. It was also about "how they were trying to position themselves as being an open and progressive Midwestern university," she said. And officials wanted to show that they were now willing to abandon "the isolation that they had been in prior to that."[78] Lucius Gregg, Jr. would later observe that the events of May 1968 "helped catapult Northwestern onto the national stage and increase its competitiveness."[79] And historian Martha Biondi perfectly describes the impact that both Northwestern students and students across the country had: they "forced a permanent change in American life, transforming overwhelmingly white campuses into multiracial learning environments."[80]

For many Black students, the experiences of 1968-1969 proved transformative. Not only did the students successfully organize and build their own network and means for demanding change, but they also experienced a new sense of power and even identity. "A theme for my life became nonviolence and peaceful protest," takeover participant Dorothy Harrell said of the deep impact the takeover had on her.[81] "One of the things that I think was significant," Victor Goode reflected, "was that we were trying to understand the political trends and events occurring in the nation as a whole and make them a part of our own experience. I can't emphasize enough how dramatic it was in our lives to come onto campus as eighteen-year-old Negroes and leave as African American men or women."[82]

As time passed, Turner explained, a "new normalcy" would slowly emerge at Northwestern.[83] As students presented their demands, undertook nonviolent protests and actions, marched and held rallies, and took a stand in order to save their classmates from expulsion, the administration was, in effect, put on notice; its actions were being watched and evaluated. As these events unfolded, Turner argued, many white students would increasingly become "apprehensive about acting out their animosity" toward Black students because there was no longer "tacit support or tolerance" from the university.[84] Achieving the "goal of undermining the institutionalization of racist attitudes is something not only hard to do, but also involves changing behavior," as Turner reflected.[85] In 2012, Turner conceded that the number of Black students at Northwestern was still disproportionately low.[86] But he also recognized that significant progress had been made, despite plenty of setbacks. And that progress can be traced to the takeover of 1968. "It was a very significant moment," as Turner said. "It made a great deal of difference in Northwestern's history. Afterward, there was no going back to what had been before."[87]

Cover, *Syllabus* yearbook, Northwestern University, 1969
(Northwestern *Syllabus* Yearbook, 1969)

A New History

November remember still
august and april and june
an NU view
SDSing, protesting, and
with an eagle-eye or young rep spy and young dem try and SOC
it to them-jam, damn the machine-the april-august scene
the new "obscene"
violence
blind reliance and compliance dies

The Syllabus, Northwestern University Yearbook, 1969

The 1968-1969 school year was finally coming to a close. After two particularly dramatic years of change, challenge, and disruption, the events of the recent past would soon become history. And, in the hands of the students themselves, a new narrative of Northwestern's history would be constructed.

At the end of the spring quarter in 1969, the Northwestern yearbook, *The Syllabus,* was released. Although the takeover had taken place the year earlier, it would not be included in the yearbook until 1969.[88]

The 1969 *Syllabus* yearbook begins with a lengthy account of the previous year or so. Scores of photographs and illustrations, accompanied by unconventional prose, guide readers through the year's events. The style appears intensely contemporary to the era, constituting a dramatic break with the formal, and now seemingly old fashioned, style of yearbooks past, when the image of a predominantly white, conservative, and fraternity and sorority dominated campus, with little "rebellious spirit," had been presented, an image that would appear wholly antiquated by 1969.

Five photographs from the takeover appear, including a full-page image of Hinz and Turner standing in front of the Bursar's Office on May 3, 1968, along with a brief text, recounting the event. "What happened at Northwestern is a small episode in a worldwide phenomenon," the copy describing the takeover reads, "a local manifestation of unrest brought on not only by general political and social dislocations but also by unprecedented changes in the American University."[89]

The pages surrounding the coverage of the takeover recount other events from 1968-1969, peppered with quotations from activists who had visited the campus, including Julian Bond and Benjamin Spock, and accompanied by photographs of protests, war, and student activism. The entire spread is crafted in a counter-cultural style that embraces the full force of world politics and the zeitgeist of the student movements of the 1960s. "[W]e're not depression children though we are depressed," the copy reads on one page, "because we know about the world and we don't like what we know."[90]

The yearbook's account of the takeover reveals how, by 1969, the once considered surprising and even anomalous event had been somewhat comfortably contextualized within the history of the university itself. The story now existed not as a rebellious act of a handful of "militant" students. Now, it was memorialized as a story of great significance and historical importance, and it took its place within a larger, interconnected narrative that told the tales of the late 1960s. It existed within a local, national, and global context, comprised of the assassinations of Martin Luther King, Jr. and Robert F. Kennedy, the war in Vietnam, the passage of the fair housing ordinance in Evanston, the protests against Dow, the riots in Chicago, the "rite of spring," and the hundreds of other student actions, disruptions, and protests at Northwestern and across the country—a host of generation-gap cavortings and serious political movements that belonged to an era of change, a climate of restlessness.

politickin—talking "68"
revealing, reveling, rebelling the Convention
the conventions
the conventional bally-ho . . . hopes bulletcrushed, maced, defaced but not gone. . .
(photographs from Northwestern *Syllabus* Yearbook, 1969)

If students care enough, and keep caring, we can at least keep from slipping two steps backward for every step we take forward.

"Retrospective: What Difference 10 Years Make,"
Daily Northwestern, December 10, 1969

The Bursar's Office, Northwestern University, April 2019
(Photograph by the author)

Epilogue

The Person You Needed

The temptation to moralize is strong; it is emotionally satisfying to have enemies rather than problems, to seek out culprits rather than the flaws in the system.

William Sloane Coffin, Jr.[1]

I learned that you can change an organization from the inside. From the outside, you don't have any power.

Dorothy Harrell, takeover participant[2]

The Northwestern and Chicago world of radical student politics at that time was a powerful crucible to grow up in, and it influenced my values and interests in large and small ways for the rest of my life.

Roger Friedman[3]

During those times during the takeover—every two hours like clockwork—when James Turner and Jack Hinz stood at the entrance of the Bursar's Office, they held "whispered doorstep conferences," as one reporter described their unrecorded conversations.[4] What did they say to each other? Certainly, they reported on the status of their respective sides. But there was likely something more unfolding in these encounters; something more human, more connected, perhaps. "Is James here?" Hinz asked at one point when he mounted the steps of 619 Clark. Using Turner's first name was just one indication that a relationship was developing between the two men. Respectful, even friendly. "I think there has been a symbolic turn," Turner told the press after one of these meetings. Hinz, Turner noted, "seems sincere."[5]

Turner later said that Hinz was a man of "honor and integrity." He "stood out as a man who was doing a great deal to try and provide insight. He was definitely the most creative and responsible member of the administration, the one who showed the greatest ingenuity, insight, and competence," he said.[6] Turner also noted that after the takeover, Hinz had been committed to seeing "that the university would put forward its best practice to live up to the agreement."[7] For his part, Hinz saw in Turner a man to admire and respect. Both shared an experience that was "meaningful on both sides," Hinz later reflected.[8]

There is no doubt that Hinz and Turner were the most visible leaders during the takeover, but Kathryn Ogletree's leadership had also been critical, a fact that the press never reported, and one that she has long downplayed herself. "I could not talk the way Turner did," she said. "I didn't mind being in the background in that regard because I was also, to a certain extent, traumatized by the whole experience. I did what I needed to do, but it was a lot of responsibility for an eighteen-year-old, I can tell you that. And so I was kind of overwhelmed with the experience and the responsibility of it all."[9]

In fact, fifty years after the takeover, Ogletree still vividly recalled her anxiety at "what it would have meant if everything had gone awry. I would have felt very, very bad, not just for myself, but for all the other people who were following behind me at that time, as the president of FMO, even though I couldn't make anybody do anything they didn't want to do. But it was still a lot of responsibility."[10]

Along with Ogletree, the responsibility for ensuring that all did not go awry was shouldered by several people, including Hinz. As those days unfolded, more than anything, Hinz wanted to reach an understanding between the students and the administration. "I didn't think it was unreasonable," Hinz later said of his attitude toward the students' petition.[11] And so he knew he would have to step up to represent their interests, a process that was not easy. Decades later, Hinz admitted that he had indeed been "advocating" for the students during the takeover and in the negotiations, even though he was officially representing the administration. He was "sticking his neck out," he said of his actions during that time. "You know," he reflected, "there were things that we could do that would make life better for Black kids on campus. So why not do those?"[12]

By June 1969, Ogletree was on her way to entering her junior year and declaring a major in psychology. She was still involved with FMO and "still kind of held in esteem," as she said. But she was now acting more as a consultant, or, as she described it, a "private citizen."[13] At this same time, James Turner announced that he had accepted an appointment as director of Cornell University's first Black Studies department. The Cornell faculty and administrators sought Turner partially in response to their own recent and dramatic campus protest, involving a building takeover by armed students. The fallout from that incident would be long-lasting (including the forced resignation of Cornell's president, James A. Perkins). But there was an effort to make good on some of the demands made by the students, including the demand to create a Black Studies department at Cornell. Administrators turned to Turner to head up the new department, describing him, with no apparent irony, as "militant but responsible."[14] As founding director of the new department, Turner would go on to develop the much respected Africana Studies and Research Center at Cornell University, where today he is professor emeritus of African and African American Politics and Social Policy.[15]

One month after Turner's announcement in 1969, Hinz made an announcement of his own. He was resigning from his position as dean of students, but would maintain his position as vice president for student affairs. He had "wanted to resign the job for more than a year," Hinz told the press. After all, he'd only been meant to serve as interim dean until a replacement could be appointed, and the demands of the dual positions were simply too much. "It's been quite apparent for two years that I am not able to be as many people or in as many places as I am needed to do my job," he said at the time. He also explained what many had long suspected: there was an inherent conflict in "representing the university as a vice president and the students as dean."[16]

Despite his resignation, Hinz would remain dean of students for more than a year. It was not until August 1970 that a new dean of students would be appointed: James F. Stull, the former assistant dean of men who had watched over Hinz's office during its May 1968 occupation.[17] Prior to Stull's appointment, over the course of the 1969-1970 school year, Hinz thus continued to be front and center in the most student-centered activities on campus and his work would continue along a dramatic path.

During the increasingly larger protests that took place in the year following the hunger strike, Hinz would find handling student disruption and unrest a bit easier, owing to a student working alongside him: Eva Jefferson Paterson. Nearly two years after the takeover, a milestone was reached at Northwestern. On April 14, 1970, in the largest election turnout in the university's history, Paterson was elected the first Black president of Northwestern's Associated Student Government.[18] The former takeover and hunger strike participant soon became nationally famous as she helped guide the campus—peacefully—through its largest and most potentially provocative anti-war protests to become a "leading voice in the youth movement because of her brilliant, frontal attacks on the 'system.' "[19] (She also famously debated Vice President Spiro Agnew on David Frost's nationally syndicated TV show.)[20]

Paterson worked with both Hinz and Franklin Kreml to maintain peace and protect the students' right to protest throughout a tumultuous time on campus when several massive campus-wide protests were staged. The most notable action was part of a national student strike staged in May 1970 after the killing of four students and the wounding of nine students by Ohio National Guard troops at Kent State University. Thousands of Northwestern students rallied, protesting not only the killings, but also the U.S. incursion into Cambodia. Students barricaded Sheridan Road. National Guard troops were placed on standby. Paterson, along with Hinz, urged the administration not to call them in. "We cannot have a clash of the students and the National Guard," Paterson told Northwestern officials upon learning that troops were awaiting an order from the administration to move in upon the striking students.[21] (The troops were not called in.) At another point, a group of students was planning to torch Lunt Hall, the campus building that housed the offices of the NROTC. Paterson's response was clear: "Stop." To her amazement, she later said, the students complied, and no campus building was burned. That was a "crossroads," Paterson said. At issue was whether or not Northwestern students would continue to engage in peaceful protests, and it was Paterson who played a central role in ensuring that violence would not be adopted as a protest tactic. She wanted, she said, to maintain peace and to build and support a "community" among all students, whatever their views.[22]

During the 1970 strike and the many other protests and events surrounding it, Hinz continued advocating for the students. (He even wore a black armband in sympathy for the students who had been killed at Kent State). Years later, he reflected on the way student activism at Northwestern

Eva Jefferson Paterson attempts to maintain peace on Northwestern's campus. Paterson was lauded for being "the focus of unity on campus—between the administration and the students, the whites and the Blacks, the young and the old."[23]
(Northwestern University Archives, photograph by James S. Roberts)

affected him: "In some ways, the strange behavior of people responding to student protests, I think radicalized me some," he said. "I think I became more and more of an anti-war person as it went on."[24]

In fact, Hinz was not alone. In the fall of 1969, Hinz and all of Northwestern's other vice presidents, including Franklin Kreml, publicly proclaimed their opposition to the war in Vietnam. "The Vietnam War not only disturbs the minds of the most vociferous students, but also those of the Northwestern administrative hierarchy," as the *Daily Northwestern* reported.[25] The war had proven to be a mistake, the vice presidents declared, and not one of them was in favor of continuing it. "Starting as a supposedly advisory group," said William S. Kerr, vice president and business manager of Northwestern, "we are now in an undeclared war of appalling magnitude."[26]

In Hinz's final year at Northwestern, "a lot of things happened," as he said of the escalating chaos on campus. "I remember [being] in the stairwell at Willard, grabbing a student by the belt as he tried to jump out a window because he was high on peyote. Now, you know, that gets lost in the relics of life at the university, but I mean there were all kinds of things going on!"[27]

Hinz's office would be occupied many times by protesting students that year. "The one time I remember the most," he said, "was that I had a subpoena to appear in court for jury duty and I didn't show up because I was barricaded in my office in Scott Hall. And the next day the [*Chicago*] *Tribune* had a photograph of the kids barricading me in my office and I got a summons from a bailiff saying you're in contempt because you didn't show up. And I sent him a copy of the picture and I never heard from him again."[28]

"[It] was a hectic time," Hinz reflected. "No question about that." His work, he said, was "exhausting." "[T]here was one month," he recalled, "either late '69 or early '70, when I was on campus something like 330 hours in a month and you know it just wears you out."[29] He began to think that "there had to be some other activity that I could do that gave me a different life, including some more time with my family because there were periods of time when I saw very, very little of the kids. I was lucky to see them at breakfast. I was often home after they turned in for the night."[30]

Hinz came home one night and told his wife, "I'm worn out. It's no fun anymore. It's not satisfying. I'm going to resign."[31] His job was "not easy to give . . . up," he admitted, but his decision to resign was a good "indication of how worn out I was."[32] On July 9, 1970, after five years at Northwestern University, including "three stormy years" serving as both dean of students and vice president for student affairs, Hinz submitted his resignation.[33] The administration, he recalled, made no effort to get him to stay. "I represented a lot of turmoil," Hinz said. "It wasn't particularly good PR."[34]

Upon Hinz's resignation, the *Chicago Tribune*, never his advocate, described how his tenure at Northwestern had seen an "increasing, sometimes violent, student rebellion against university regulations and procedures, and angry reaction by trustees and alumni against what they believed were student excesses."[35] "We hope Northwestern's next vice president for student affairs will last longer than Hinz did," the *Tribune* wrote. "But we place no bets. Unless he has the guts—and the backing—to say no to users of strong-arm tactics, he won't."[36]

Hinz is the first to admit that there was indeed "some pretty severe upheaval" during his time at Northwestern.[37] But, as he sees it, in the progress that was made and the changes that were initiated—from the university's first efforts at integration to the granting of more authority to students—it was ultimately a success. And keeping the peace was among the best of his achievements. Reflecting on the takeover, he said, "our having completed the settlement peacefully was very important to me and ultimately to the university, to the history of the university."[38] And he recognized how differently things had worked out at Northwestern compared with many other universities. "I've never gone back and looked at things at Columbia, things at Chicago, and things here. They were all within weeks of each other, practically speaking," he said. "But we didn't have severe property damage. We didn't have any injuries or loss of life . . . But, no, I think we did well. And I recall with some pride that the place never blew up," he concluded with a laugh.[39]

After Hinz left Northwestern, he interviewed for other university positions in student affairs, including one at the University of Utah. After a successful interview, the university president told him to expect a letter of appointment soon. But, as Hinz recounted, "I never got the letter. Nothing ever came. That was the last I ever heard."[40] Hinz was left to wonder how his tenure at Northwestern had affected his later job prospects. He wondered, laughing, "are the ghosts of the past haunting me? And they might be," he said. "And they very well might be."[41]

In November 1970, Hinz accepted an eleven-month appointment as a consultant and lecturer at Northern Illinois University.[42] Later, he accepted a position at the College Board, and remained in Evanston. For a long time he felt alienated from the university. "I'm not sure I needed to, as I look back on it now," he said. "But I just needed to be away. I just needed to be disconnected from [it]."[43]

In the spring of 1971, Ogletree graduated from Northwestern with a BS in psychology. She knew that she wanted to become a psychologist. After she took a job as a mental health specialist at Garfield Park Community Mental Health Center, a community mental health center on Chicago's West Side, she realized that a PhD was necessary in her field. She began working on an MA in counseling and guidance at Chicago State College and she soon applied to Northwestern's PhD program in Counseling Psychology and was accepted. Throughout her graduate studies, she said, James Pitts, her friend and fellow takeover participant, served as an important mentor to her. Once back at Northwestern, she was busy with her job and only came to campus to attend classes.

After earning her PhD, Ogletree joined the faculty at the University of Wisconsin, Milwaukee. She was recruited there by another takeover participant, her friend Michael Smith, to work in the newly-created Community Education program. (A program that awarded people academic credit for their life experiences.) Later, Ogletree and her husband, also a Northwestern graduate, who transferred to Northwestern from the U.S. Military Academy after the takeover, moved to Miami, where she taught at Florida Memorial College, an Historically Black College. In 1992, she was recruited to Ohio Wesleyan University by James Pitts, who was then serving as a dean at the university. Ogletree was appointed Director of Minority Student Affairs, a position she would hold for many years.

"I actually can trace it," she said of the impact the takeover has had on her life. "Almost everything that I've done has its roots in my experience at Northwestern as an activist student."[44] Along her career path, Ogletree has worked to be "more of an advocate psychologist," as she explained, focused on "helping people deal with their problems and issues" and adapt to their situations. But, she continued, "I also believe that institutions have to be confronted as to how they need to change, to facilitate change, for a greater number of people."[45] Her professional focus is almost an exact reflection of her stance as a student, when she advocated for change within the institution that was Northwestern University. Ogletree explained that in her work to encourage and support students on a diverse campus, she focused on helping an "institution understand it has a responsibility, too, to make changes, and that you can't just have the status quo and talk about diversifying, but not make changes that contribute to an appreciation of the diverse groups that you're bringing in."[46]

Almost all of the several professional positions she has held in her career, she notes, have had "something to do with playing a role as a person that I needed" as a student at Northwestern. My "whole career path, in retrospect," she said, has been "involved in activities related to that." Through her work, she has continuously focused on offering students the "things that we were looking for and needing when I was a student at Northwestern."[47] She became, in many ways, the very person she had been looking for, the person she needed as a seventeen-year-old student arriving on campus in 1967.

Despite having been FMO president and one of the ten student negotiators at the table on May 4, Ogletree has long "been reluctant to accept the role as leader."[48] She acknowledged that "people actually give me more credit than what I actually give myself."[49] But as she now looks back on the events of 1968, she has begun to see things differently. "I kind of think I was actually kind of frozen in time a little bit," she reflected. "I've kind of been pushing it off when people would say that you have to talk to Kathryn Ogletree. She was the leader at the time. And I would always say I wasn't the leader. And I don't really like the term leader. I do feel I was the representative, but we had different roles that everybody played and I played a critical role, but people do attribute me to being more the leader than I have accepted up to this time."[50]

But now, especially after attending the commemorations of the takeover's fiftieth anniversary in 2018, she is, she said, "beginning to develop a better appreciation of what I had done."[51] And she has only recently started to embrace her role as leader. In 2018, when she was invited to speak at Northwestern during Women's History Month, she was told by event organizers that they were interested in her perception as the most prominent female student activist leader at Northwestern at that time. That comment was eye-opening. "I had never been asked that," she said, "and I never really tried to look at my role as distinct—as being the only woman and what that meant. And it's been an interesting process of me looking at it more critically than I had up to that point."[52] Now, she says, she is starting to formulate a better "understanding of what was happening in terms of the gender roles that we were locked into during that time."[53]

Just as Ogletree's reflection on the events of 1968 has brought forth a new understanding, so too has John Bracey's viewpoint expanded over time. As he now looks back on the takeover and reflects on it, he's been "kind of surprised," as he said. "Seeing it all together. How things fell in line. Little things could have gone off and messed up the whole thing, but those little things fell in line. It was really kind of a unique circumstance."[54] In fact, Bracey calls the takeover the "most effective demonstration I've ever been part of."[55]

Jack Hinz's viewpoint has also evolved over time. After being away from Northwestern for many years, he would finally learn the extent to which so many people appreciated his efforts. In October 2011, a year after his eightieth birthday, Eva Jefferson Paterson organized a reunion party for the class of 1971 with Hinz as the honored guest. About fifty people were invited, including a few former faculty members and about forty former students. Paterson remembered that Hinz was initially apprehensive, but she reassured him. "We all are so appreciative of you," she told him.[56] The party was a big success. "[I]t was pretty amazing," Hinz said. "Many kids had an opportunity to say, 'Hinz you mattered to us' and that was really nice."[57] He was also able to revisit the history of the takeover and reconnect with many of its participants, including many of the students he had recruited to Northwestern so many years ago. "Dean Hinz" was the "exception," as John Bracey later said of Northwestern's administrators. "He was one of the few people that listened."[58]

Long after the takeover, Hinz would enjoy a moving encounter when he reconnected with James Turner for the first time in decades when Turner returned for a visit to the Northwestern campus.[59] For Turner, too, the past would never prove to be very far away. Turner has enjoyed a long career at Cornell University as a well-respected professor and director of the Africana Studies and Research Center.[60] But it was not always an easy road. In 1969, when the Turners first arrived in Ithaca, where they would raise their three children, "there were no black teachers in the Ithaca City School District, only a handful of black tenured professors and no courses in African-American history, life, culture or literature."[61] In April 1970, a year after they arrived, the building that housed the new Africana Studies Center was set on fire in an act of arson.[62] Turner's and other faculty members' belongings—including manuscripts, dissertations, and books—were destroyed.[63]

Amidst these new challenges, along with many achievements, Turner was often reminded of the events of May 1968. And he recognized how they shaped what came afterward for him in his life. The takeover was a "life-changing experience," he said, a "defining moment in my life experience."[64] It not only "shaped the course of my life," he said, it also "helped define me."[65] "It impacted me immensely," Ogletree agrees.[66] She also recognizes the impact her college experience has had on her family. Her sisters, she said, "all kind of looked up to me, as their older sister and as someone who had gone to college."[67] Ogletree is proud that "most of their children really credit me with their going on to college because I had gone to college and they were following my example."[68] As for her role in the takeover, her sisters knew she had been involved and they were proud of her, but it wasn't until the takeover's fiftieth anniversary that they would learn the true extent of the role she played. They were "excited," Ogletree said, "to learn all those details."[69]

Hinz too was personally shaped by the events of 1968-1969. "I'm sorry I never really had enough time to be as active in the civil rights movement of that time that I might have if I weren't working twelve and fifteen hours a day," he said, reflecting on his time at Northwestern.[70] When asked about his impact on changing the course of history at Northwestern, he reflected a moment, then stated simply: "You don't know you're doing that at the time. You live the best way you know how, and you hope that it doesn't hurt anybody, and if you're lucky, as I was, maybe it was helpful to some people." But, he said, "You didn't see that until much later."[71]

"It actually guaranteed that I had a career," John Bracey said of his participation in the events of May 1968. As a history major, he had always planned on a teaching career, but what he wanted to teach was Black history. When he was a student at Northwestern, though, he thought that there was really "no discernible career" in teaching Black history.[72] But he soon found that he was able to leave Northwestern and enter a field that he himself helped to create and define. Numerous job offers came his way as Black Studies departments all over the country began to form in the late 1960s, offering a whole new set of opportunities and allowing him the freedom to design and teach all of his own classes, a rare and welcome opportunity in academia.

After Bracey left Northwestern, he held a two-year appointment at Northern Illinois University. He then took a position at the University of Rochester, recruited there by his former professor at Northwestern, Christopher Lasch. In 1972, Bracey was recruited to the University of Massachusetts Amherst where he helped develop the W.E.B. Du Bois Department of Afro-American Studies. Today, he continues to serve as a professor, department chair, and co-director of the department's graduate certificate in African Diaspora Studies.

As he sees it, the generations who came before him made his work and career possible. "I'm armed with the wisdom and support of the people who were there before me," he said.[73] And it was in listening to and learning

Professor John H. Bracey, Jr. of the W.E.B. Du Bois Department of Afro-American Studies, University of Massachusetts Amherst, c. 1972. (Courtesy of the Department of Special Collections and University Archives, W.E.B. Du Bois Library, University of Massachusetts Amherst.)

from "older Black people who were there before me," as he said, that he has learned the most. And this is something that has been at the forefront of his own career. "My obligation was to do that for the people who were coming after me."[74]

This commitment to ensuring something better for the generations coming up behind them is woven throughout many of the takeover participants' lives. Wayne Watson turned to the community of Evanston for the topic of his doctoral dissertation. He recorded oral histories with city residents, many of whom had memories of an earlier era when few Black students attended Northwestern. Later, Watson would be appointed as a member of Northwestern University's board of trustees.[75] Other takeover participants would go on to serve in positions that allowed them to continue to expand opportunities for other Northwestern students. One notable example is Andre Bell, who served as Northwestern's Director of Admissions and Financial Aid from 1972-1987. Later, another takeover participant, Clovis Semmes would become Assistant Director of Admissions and Coordinator of Admissions and Financial Aid for Minority Students at Northwestern. Semmes replaced yet another Northwestern alumnus and takeover participant, as well as signatory to the May 4 agreement, Harold Daniels, who served as Northwestern's Assistant Director of Admissions, in charge of minority recruitment, from 1980 to 1986.[76]

Many takeover participants went on to earn advanced degrees, and many returned to Northwestern to earn master's degrees and Phds. They would go on to distinguished careers as artists and educators; college presidents and administrators; lawyers, judges, and civil rights workers. Isola Jones enjoyed a long career as a mezzo-soprano at the Metropolitan Opera in New York, while both Steve Colson and Chico (Earl) Freeman became internationally renowned composers and musicians. After earning a law degree, Eva Jefferson Paterson went on to co-found the Equal Justice Society, a legal organization focused on fighting discrimination in a variety of areas. Roger Ward went on to earn his PhD in biomedical engineering. Marianne Jackson, who took part in both the takeover and the hunger strike, went on to become a Circuit Court Judge in Cook County, Illinois. Daphne Maxwell Reid would enjoy a successful career as a model and actor. In October 1969, she became the first Black woman to appear on the cover of *Glamour Magazine*. She later appeared on the television show, *The Fresh Prince of Bel Air*.[77]

Milton Gardner (c. 1948-1985) went on to earn a law degree from Columbia University.[78] Stephen Broussard served as a Cook County assistant state's attorney before launching his own civil and criminal law practice.[79] Victor Goode graduated with a degree in political science and went on to earn a JD from Rutgers University. He later served as executive director of the National Conference of Black Lawyers and founder of the Affirmative

Action Coordinating Center. He is currently an associate professor of law at the City University of New York.[80]

Eric Perkins (1948-2011) graduated with honors with a degree in Philosophy. After earning a PhD in history, he served as a Faculty Fellow at the W.E.B. Du Bois College House at the University of Pennsylvania and later taught at Hunter College, City University of New York. In 1996, he edited the ground-breaking anthology, *Droppin' Science: Critical Essays on Rap Music and Hip Hop Culture*, hailed as a seminal study of hip-hop.[81] Others published volumes on Black history, taught courses in Black culture and literature, chaired and founded Black Studies departments, worked in university administration, and worked to advance civil rights, among many other undertakings. In short, they became the people they needed.

Remembering the criticism that was heaped upon the students at the time, Ogletree is clear: We were not "people out to do devilment or to bring harm or embarrassment or anything to the university."[82] Instead, she says, "We did what we had to do for our own survival at Northwestern and in anticipation of the needs of the Black students coming here after us. We were trying to make this place a better place."[83]

In retrospect, the students who integrated Northwestern, and who undertook such a bold and risky action to compel the university to recognize what integration actually meant and really involved, sacrificed a great deal. Along with the anger, fear, and frustration they felt, they also lost something intangible. Victor Goode later reflected on what was lost in 1968: "our youth," he said. We were not "able to be carefree college kids," but instead had "to shoulder the burden" of "breaking down doors."[84] Ogletree agrees. "When people talk about their feelings about their alma mater, I didn't leave with that kind of fuzzy feeling about Northwestern," she said, "because it was a struggle at the beginning." Even after the successful takeover, she said, college felt like "a tiring load over a period of years. And so it cut into the feeling of love, when you realize what other students had in terms of a fun time at college. I don't recall myself having a fun time like that."[85]

The second location of the Black House, 1914 Sheridan Road, Evanston. (Northwestern University Archives)

In the spring of 1972, students submitted another set of demands to the administration. Among their thirteen demands were: an increase in the number of Black graduate students admitted to the university, the appointment of Black counselors for each school, and that a university-owned property at 1810 Hinman Avenue be converted for use as a new (and larger) Black House. The administration offered use of another property, 1914 Sheridan. The students refused to move into that building after the administration failed to renovate the property which had, according to an FMO spokesperson, "bare wires, rickety railings, and peeling paint." Finally, the building was renovated and the students moved into the property in early 1973. The former Black House at 619 Emerson became home to Women at Northwestern and the Committee for the Program on Women, Northwestern's new interdisciplinary program in Women's Studies, founded in 1971.[86]

In 1973, Turner returned to Northwestern for a visit. "The mood of black students," he noted then, "had changed."[87] During a talk before an audience of students, Turner said that he noticed "less unity and zeal on the campus" than there had been when he was a student. He provided some encouragement: "We have learned," he told his audience, "that centuries of oppression don't slide away so quickly."[88] "[O]ur struggle is more like a long distance run than a sprint," he continued. "A sprint produces a sudden powerful burst. It is not lasting . . . The long-distance run, however, is constant, steady, and gains strength as the finish is in sight."[89]

A long-distance run began at Northwestern long before the 1968 takeover. And it has continued in the fifty years since. Over the decades, the history of the takeover continues to be remembered. It is recounted at FMO's annual orientation (known as *The Ritual*). Most recently, it has a new campus presence on a plaque near the front entrance of the Bursar's Office at 619 Clark Street. The plaque, which was installed during the commemoration of the takeover's fiftieth anniversary in May 2018, reads: "In honor of the more than 100 Black students who occupied the Bursar's Office for 38 hours on May 3 and 4, 1968. The University's first-ever sit-in led to an agreement that resulted in a better existence for Blacks on campus and a better Northwestern."[90]

In the fifty years that have unfolded since the takeover, however, many students and alumni have viewed with alarm what they see as an erosion of some of the advances made in May 1968. In 1978, Kathryn Ogletree collaborated with James Pitts, who was then serving as an associate professor of sociology at Northwestern, to conduct a survey of Black and white alumni who had graduated between 1970-1973. They published their findings in a paper titled, "Northwestern University's Recent Alumni: In Black and White."[91] They also co-hosted two campus forums to discuss their findings. As far as campus conditions went, they reported that there was still "a considerable amount of tension" and "almost no social interaction" between Black and white students at Northwestern.[92]

Northwestern students, Kevin Blackistone, Carolyn D. Davis, and Michael Wilbon, confirmed those findings. "It may be concluded that in May of 1968 Black Power did win a major battle," they observed, "but unless Black students continue to demand the right to quality education the hard work, determination and dedication" of those who undertook the takeover "will be a lost and meaningless memory."[93] Others noted the existence of "silent segregation" at Northwestern. "Racial tension" may not have been as overt as it had been in the past, reported Nancy Rawles in a 1978 story for the *Daily Northwestern,* "but it's still there." "Years after all discriminatory clauses have been erased from the books," Rawles wrote, "many Northwestern students say their school is 'racially segregated.' "[94]

As the fiftieth anniversary of the takeover approached, some observers asserted that there has been a nearly complete dissolution of "the gains of the May 4 agreement."[95] Every five years, remarked Jeffery Sterling, former president of the Northwestern University Black Alumni Association (NUBAA), Black students and alumni are forced to re-defend the Black House, for example, and must have an "additional conversation" with administrators to again "prove we need a safe space on campus."[96]

In 2015, a group called "Concerned Students of Northwestern University" submitted a list of demands to administrators. The demands were written by a number of student groups and reflected the needs not only of Black students on campus, but also Native American students, Asian American students, LGBTQIA students, and others. The 2015 document did, however, have many "common requests" with those made by the students in 1968, including calls for increased enrollment of Black students, increased hiring of Black faculty, and more resources, social spaces, and financial aid for Black students.[97] In response, the university formed a "Black Student Experience Task Force" to study issues facing Black students on campus. In 2015, university officials also hired Jabbar R. Bennett as Northwestern's first Chief Diversity Officer and Associate Provost.[98]

In its 2016 report, the task force revealed that many Black students at Northwestern felt "dissatisfied, exhausted and alienated on campus."[99] From feeling unwelcome in social activities (particularly in fraternities and sororities) to feeling isolated and alone on campus to experiencing a lack of "cultural competency" among professors and staff, many students reported exactly the same problems that plagued the campus in decades past. The report also revealed that "an alarming number of African American/Black students . . . have been threatened or insulted because of their race/ethnicity" or "have witnessed or experienced harassment or discriminatory behavior at Northwestern."[100]

It should be noted that universities and colleges across the United States have experienced a rise in reported hate crimes on campus. In 2016, the FBI recorded a twenty-five percent increase in reported campus hate crimes over the prior year. Since then, the number has increased each year, with the largest year-to-year increases in reported hate crimes occurring in crimes targeting Black, multiracial, and Jewish students and individuals.[101]

Administrators have pledged to continue to work to improve campus conditions at Northwestern. After the 2016 report was released, officials drafted a set of recommendations for improvements to be made in a variety of areas on campus, pledging, among other things, that the university "remains committed to creating a positive Black Student experience on our campus."[102] The university continues to report on the progress being made in these areas.[103]

In the meantime, the "takeover continues."[104] This sentiment was clearly expressed by a group of Northwestern students, representing the campus groups, Latinx Asian American Collective, Students Organizing for Labor Rights, and Black Lives Matter NU. On May 3, 2018, the students submitted forty-seven "Bursar Commemoration" demands to university officials.[105] Black Lives Matter NU submitted thirty-six of the demands, which, the group's members wrote, "reiterate the concerns raised in 2015 by Black Northwestern students addressing this institution's continuous failure to listen to Black students, internalize what they have to say, and act on their recommendations."[106] Al Cubbage, a university spokesman, responded: "We agree on the critical importance of these topics, and we also agree they merit further examination and additional solutions, wherever possible . . . This discourse is fundamental to the dynamic nature of Northwestern." Cubbage added that "administrators will continue to meet with students and alumni to further understand their points of view and work together."[107]

The same day the students submitted their demands, a group of students arrived at a campus auditorium. Northwestern University and the Northwestern University Black Alumni Association were in the midst of hosting a series of fiftieth anniversary commemorations marking the takeover, and a panel discussion, "Living the Legacy-From Protest to Progress," was about to get underway. The students held a large banner that read: "#The Takeover Today. You Never Completed Our Demands."[108] They stood in the aisle of the auditorium, holding their banner silently, while onstage John Bracey, Kathryn Ogletree, Northwestern President Morton Schapiro, and others prepared to begin a discussion about the takeover. It was Bracey who acknowledged the students: "Before we begin," he said, "can we look to the left and acknowledge the young brothers and sisters with the sign?"[109] The audience, which consisted of many takeover participants, including Eva Jefferson Paterson, alumni from various generations, former and current staff members, professors, and university officials, including Jack Hinz, applauded.

At the end of the panel discussion that day, the participants had covered a lot of ground, moving from discussing the attitudes, issues, and events of 1968 to those of 2018. And throughout, they revealed a clear trajectory between the two eras—a fact that was undeniable in the presence of the students who stood silently, holding their banner, during the entire panel discussion.

For Bracey, Hinz, Ogletree, Turner, and others, the momentous and difficult events of 1968 embody lessons for those engaged in contemporary struggles for justice. Ogletree watches the current generation of eighteen-year-old students taking a stand, for example, after the 2018 shootings at the Parkland, Florida, high school, and is in awe of their bravery: "It's been very impressive to me to see how articulate you can be at that young age," she said. Still, she recognizes that taking a stand comes with "a lot of responsibility." But like others, she agrees that for those who confront injustice, who are

"#TheTakeoverToday. You Never Completed Our Demands,"
Northwestern University, May 3, 2018. (Photograph by the author)

Student protest at Northwestern during an event marking the takeover's fiftieth anniversary, May 3, 2018. "The legacy of the Bursar's Takeover is not just the Black House and the African American Studies department," the students wrote, explaining their 2018 demands, "it is the Black students who continually fight to be not only heard, but also answered fully. Black students walking this campus today are living the reality that the demands from the Bursar's Office Takeover remain unfulfilled."[110] Some of the students' demands related specifically to the May 4 agreement and its aftermath, including a demand that the university publish "to its homepage the original preamble of the May 4th agreement" and that the university "redress its original stance in opposition to the Bursar Takeover by reversing its 1968 decree that it 'will not again negotiate whilst disruptive activity is in progress'. "[111] The students also objected to the way the university commemorated the takeover's fiftieth anniversary. "Throughout the commemoration process," they wrote, "Northwestern has taken credit for the work of radical Black students whose demands it never fulfilled, essentially co-opting student activism."[112] The issue of "ownership" of the takeover, so to speak, continues to be addressed, with some objecting to the way Northwestern now defines the event. At a symposium at Cornell University to honor James Turner in April 2019, John Bracey noted a distinction between the ways Northwestern and Cornell commemorate campus activism, and he observed that Northwestern now characterizes the takeover as "a Northwestern event," when it was, in fact, an "anti-Northwestern event."[113]

made to feel afraid, who are belittled and demoralized, and threatened for "their very existence," it is critical to speak up, to push back, and to try to make things better. James Turner concurred, underscoring the fact that it is essential for people to continue to "point out imbalances."[114] Only then can change occur, he said, and a "new normalcy" take the place of unacceptable conditions.

Isabella Ellis, Lawyer Taylor, Naomi Willie Pollard Dobson, John Porcius Faulkner, William Yancy Bell, Jr., Robbie Shields Terry, Edwin B. Jourdain, Jr., Bill Branch, Ruth McCarn, the members of the Quibblers Club, Charles "Doc" Glass, Melva Fager, Ellis Pines, Kathryn Ogletree, Roger Friedman, Venice Deese, Jr., John Bracey, James Turner, Jack Hinz, Lucius Perry Gregg, Jr., Eva Jefferson Paterson, and so many others. Over the decades, many have tried to bring positive change to Northwestern, to point out imbalances, and to fight for justice. Each individual's action may have cleared only a small portion along a narrow path, but each made just enough room for the next person behind them to continue forward. "Then it will expand to take on other issues," as Turner noted of the ways change occurs. Ultimately, he said, it is simply necessary for people to speak out. "We have a much healthier society when people don't feel repressed about expressing their concerns," he observed, "but can enter the public square to express them."[115]

Fifty years ago, 107 students gathered in such a public square, as it were, trying to make visible what had been unseen by so many for so long. They took great risks. They faced hostility and humiliation. Along the way, they encountered others who acted in solidarity, whether sitting nearby to protect them, speaking out in their defense, or working to help them achieve their goals, arriving on the steps every two hours like clockwork. The students "persisted," as Turner put it. When they left the Bursar's Office that night in May, it was an end, but it was also a beginning. They knew that their next steps along that path, forged over the decades, were yet to be taken. And today, it is clear that there are still more to come.

Appendix A

List of Demands, April 22, 1968 (Northwestern University Archives)

Copies of all of the following documents are available on the website of Northwestern University Libraries: https://sites.northwestern.edu/bursars1968/about/

N. U. ARCHIVES

BLACK STUDENT STATEMENT AND PETITION TO NORTHWESTERN UNIVERSITY ADMINISTRATORS, RECEIVED MONDAY, APRIL 22, 1968.

We, the Black students at Northwestern University have found the academic, cultural, and social conditions for us on the campus deplorably limited. In order to counteract the physical, emotional, and spiritual strains we have been subjugated to, in order to find some meaning and purpose in our being here, we demand that the following conditions be immediately met

I POLICY STATEMENT:

We demand, firstly, that a policy statement be issued from the administration deploring the viciousness of "white racism" and insuring that all conscious or unconscious racist policies, practices, and institutions existing now on campus will no longer be tolerated. This statement should make it clear that Northwestern is willing to go to any extent to enforce such a policy and also to protect the interests of the Black students on campus who have been negatively affected by such racist attitudes and practices. Furthermore, this statement should express Northwestern's readiness to exert its influences (both political and financial, in uprooting racism in the city of Evanston).

II ADMISSION:

Considering that Black people account for 12% of the total American population, we demand that Northwestern initiate a project which guarantees the gradual increase of the number of Black students to a more "realistic" figure which we shall decide. We demand also that we have some say in the development and initiation of such a project with Black students of our own choosing on the steering committee. We further demand that at least half (1/2) of each year's incoming Black students be from the inner school systems.

As for now, we demand a complete list containing the names of all Black students enrolled at Northwestern as of Fall Quarter 1967.

III SCHOLARSHIPS:

We demand that our scholarships be increased to cover what is now included in our "required jobs" and to include funds for those who want or need to attend summer school. We have found that students who work because they want to, and not because they have to, perform much better academically and with less mental tension and frustration. Furthermore, we have found it a contradiction that in view of the fact that we inadequately prepared for the type of competition we encountered here at Northwestern, we were still expected to keep up and hold down a job simultaneously. We strongly feel, as well, that those Black students who want to continue their intellectual pursuits through the summer should have the same opportunity to do so as any other Northwestern student. The University should not deny them that opportunity by requiring that they work instead, in order to substantiate their scholarships for the other three quarters.

IV HOUSING:

We demand that the University provide a living unit(s) for those Black students who want to live together. We demand that immediate action be taken to provide such a unit(s) by Fall Quarter 1968.

Inasmuch as that Black freshman women do not usually room with each other, we demand that they receive the same treatment as their white roommates. In the past, upon receiving room assignments, a white girl or her parents have been allowed to object to having a Negro for a roommate and upon either of their requests a shift in room assignments took place. We contend that if the girl or her parents wanted to be assured that she would not be rooming with a Negro, she should have stated on her housing form her preference of a Caucasian roommate to a Negro one. Black students did not even have the option to request another Black student for a roommate. We were told from the start that it was the University's intention to split us up and that we would not be allowed to room with each other.

Due to contradictory (racist) housing policies and practices, to the definite differences in social and cultural differences between us and our white roommates, and to the general tenseness of the racial situation, we demand that this Black living unit be made available to us by Fall quarter to help alleviate some of the tension of being "a Black student at a white university."

V. CURRICULUM:

We demand that a Black Studies Course be added to the curriculum including studies in Black history, literature, and art. In view of the fact that Black accomplishments have been underplayed and Black history misconstrued, we demand to have the ultimate decision in the choice of professors to be hired to teach these courses. There is no doubt, that since they inevitably must be "Black" professors, no one on the administration is capable of adequately judging their qualifications.

VI. COUNSELLING:

We demand that a Black Counselor be provided by the University in order to help us properly cope with the psychological, mental, and academic tensions resulting from the dualism of our existence as "black college students." There is a definite need for Black students seeking to overcome the contradictions of the demands placed on us by this white community, which offers little for us to identify with, and the demands of our own people and our native communities which look to us for some kind of inspiration, guidance, and instruction in the struggle to overcome white oppression, to have someone who can relate to us and understand us out of a common experience. The "Great White Father" image the university has been projecting must be destroyed if any real communication is to develop.

VII. FACILITIES:

We demand a Black Student Union, a place to be used for social and recreational activities, as well as, a place to office F.M.O. and all other Black organizations on campus. Black students have nothing at Northwestern to call our own. We need a place where we will feel free to come and to go as we please, a place which will substitute for the lack of fraternity and sorority houses and provide us with the necessary facilities to function as independently as the Student Senate office.

VIII. OPEN OCCUPANCY:

We are aware that Northwestern University has taken a stand in favor of Open Occupancy. However, what good, we ask, is such a stand when Northwestern is in effect the main promoter of segregation in the City of Evanston? We demand that the University immediately cease with this hypocrisy and take the necessary steps to desegregate all of its real estate holdings. We further demand that evidence be presented to us, verifying that Northwestern is doing more than taking "a stand on Open Occupancy," and that monthly reports be turned over to the president of F.M.O. indicating N.U.'s subsequent progressive measures.

There has been too much idle talk about how to solve some of the problems facing Black students here at Northwestern. Indeed, there has been too much talk and too little action in regard to the general racial situation. We are not about to solve America's race problems, if there is in fact a solution; however, we are concerned about the problem as it affects us on campus and in the city of Evanston.

Northwestern was wrong to assume that in bringing us here, we would be able to disassociate ourselves from the injustices, sufferings, and mounting frustration of our people. Like them, we, too, are tired of being talked about and we are weary of talking to people who cannot or refuse to do anything else but talk.

It would be useless to engage in further discussion--there are some things which will never be understood, and even if they were understood, it would make little difference anyway. These are our demands of the University. We are willing to confer with the administration, but we have no intention of debating or conceding our stand. We have been to the administration before but with very little consequence. We want tangible results, not excuses or even promises. The University either responds to our demands or we have no other alternative but to respond to its lack of response. The University has until 5:00 p.m., Friday, April 26, 1968, to notify us of its decision.

CONTACT: Kathryn Ogletree (F.M.O.), James Turner (A.A.S.U.).

Appendix B
University Response to the Students' Demands, April 1968
(Northwestern University Archives)

Confidential

Northwestern University responses to the

Black Student Petition received Monday, April 22, 1968.

I. Racism of any character has no place at Northwestern which as a University is an institution where tolerance and mutual respect are essential to the educational process and for the dissemination of knowledge. The University repeats that in the admission of students, the appointment of faculty and staff, and in the operation of all its facilities such as housing, dining halls, libraries, placement offices and the like, no discrimination on the basis of race, religion or color can be countenanced. The University deplores incidents which have racial implications, and asserts its determination to prevent any such events and to use its authority to employ disciplinary measures against those who violate the rights of others.

Increasing efforts will be made to improve the social and cultural welfare of all students in ways which will better prepare them for the roles of professional leadership which are in keeping with the educational objectives of a university.

To this end and pending receipt of reports from existing University Committees now considering these problems, a special University Committee on Human Relations will be established to consider the grievances wherein the human rights and dignity of students have been violated, to continually review all facets of the university life, and recommend new policies and procedures which will bring our student environment in line with Northwestern's national and international responsibility. While the membership of this Committee has not yet been determined, appointments will be made after consultation with all elements of the university community.

The University Discipline Committee (UDC) has recently completed an intensive study of the racial problems of black students on campus, and their aspirations and search for identity within the university and the community. This report has just been released for publication. The Committee on Human Relations will be asked to develop programs and recommendations which will implement the objectives of the UDC report.

While the crises which confront the nation and the university warrant the depth of this concern, it is essential that all members of the university act responsibly and with accountability in helping achieve the objectives of equal rights and dignity for all.

II. ADMISSION

Since the summer of 1965, the University has made a substantial effort to change the composition of the undergraduate student body.
The change has been from a homogeneous student body to a student body which is representative of the many different subcultures of our society.
The forces necessary to bring about this change were (1) increased recruitment efforts in a variety of high schools serving populations which traditionally had not been interested in the University in the past and, (2) a substantial increase in the University's financial aid program.

One result of this effort was the matriculation of 54 black students in the entering class of 1966, in contrast to 5 black students in the entering class of 1965. At least 35 of these students were from innercity high schools. In the fall of 1966, recruitment efforts were intensified in predominantly black areas. The results were more applications from these areas, more admitted students from these areas, but a nominal matriculation increase over the previous year. For example, 50 students from innercity Chicago schools were accepted for the fall of 1967, but only 31 matriculated. In 1966, 36 students were accepted from these same high schools and 35 students entered. Greater competition from other colleges and universities has affected the percentage of students who have entered the University. In the fall of 1967, the admission recruitment efforts were further intensified to include the innercity high schools of Chicago, St. Louis, Milwaukee and Gary, Indiana. In addition, the University has coordinated its efforts with the Cooperative Program for Educational Opportunity, the National Scholarship Service Fund for Negro Students and the National Achievement Scholarship Program.

These efforts resulted in more applications than in the year 1967 and the acceptance of approximately 100 black students to the entering class of 1968. The matriculated number will not be available until the end of summer. According to a recent article in NEWSWEEK, Northwestern has accepted more black students to the entering class of 1968 than any other major private university. The University will continue to increase its efforts in the innercity school systems and will continue to admit to the University those students who have a high probability of success at Northwestern. In terms of actual percentages, at least 50 percent of those admitted black candidates for admission have attended high schools serving the innercity. There is no reason to believe that this percentage should change with the University's intense interest and efforts in this area. The University will welcome the support of its black students in University admission activities.

In the spring of 1967, the University held a series of meetings with interested black students to discuss campus, summer program and admission problems. The Admission Office now seeks to formalize such meetings in order to acquire better counsel from the University's black community regarding the recruitment of black students. It is requested that a committee be appointed by the black student community to assist in University admission activities. One of the most immediate needs is to develop procedures to assure that a greater percentage of those black students accepted enter the University. Students selected to serve on such a committee should be undergraduate students. This is consistent with the University position in asking undergraduate students to participate more fully in the decisions governing those elements affecting student life.

The University further will provide the black community of Northwestern with the names of all black students who are known to the administration. In addition, the University will provide a list of names of all entering black students to the black community when all names of all entering students become available to campus organizations.

III. SCHOLARSHIPS

The financial aid budget of the University has been expanded for the last three years. This expansion has permitted Northwestern to offer more financial aid to a substantially greater number of its admitted candidates. However, the increased offers of financial aid would not have been possible without the packaging (job, loans and grants) of all financial aid resources. Acceptance of job and loan offers are optional. The packaging of financial aid is an agreed procedure by more than 600 universities which are members of the College Scholarship Service. The purpose is to assist as many students as possible who have demonstrated a financial need. If a maximum utilization of resources had not taken place, the number of financial aid students assisted in the past two entering classes at Northwestern would have been reduced by one-third.

Each application for financial aid is carefully evaluated relevant to the family background of the applicant. Special consideration is given to students from unusually limited economic circumstances. The University's Committee on Financial Aid to Students realizes that some students will not concur with the decisions governing their applications. In such instances, the University's Office of Financial Aid requests the opportunity to fully explain the relevant decision. Students receiving financial aid are made fully aware of their financial responsibilities before entering the University. This information is available in the University literature sent to the admitted candidate. The offer and acceptance of financial aid is a binding contract between the University and the student.

In the past, the University has established a temporary loan program in the Office of Financial Aid to assist black students. In addition, payment deadlines have frequently been waived and a mutually agreeable payment date has been determined. In several situations, awards have been increased after individual conferences with students. Realizing the pressures encountered by financial aid students, the University in 1966 eliminated the grade requirement for the retention of financial aid. Prior to that time students were required to maintain a minimum grade average of 2.5 if financial aid were to be continued.

To help alleviate any remaining financial burden of the student, a summer job placement program was established in 1967. The Office of Financial Aid assists students in securing summer employment. Earnings are as much as $800 to $1,000 for the summer through the Work-Study Program of the federal government. Summer jobs of this nature are available working with youth in innercity Chicago. Because of the increasing needs for educated young men and women to work with innercity youth, the University encourages members of the student black community to seek such summer employment.

The Office of Financial Aid also is willing to assist any student in acquiring additional University or federally guaranteed loans. A private university is unable to completely finance the education of any of its students without some financial demands put upon the students. However, better than eighty percent of the black student community is receiving outright grant assistance in excess of two thousand dollars a year.

To continue this kind of a financial commitment, the University is constantly seeking additional funds for the financial aid program. Recently, the University received a grant of twenty-five thousand dollars a year for the next four years for scholarships for black students from the Chicago innercity.

The Office of Financial Aid will attempt to assist those students who need to attend one summer school session in order to graduate with their class. This opportunity will be made available to such students between their junior and senior year. Students who are unable to graduate even with one summer school session will not be provided this opportunity. However, they will be considered for a fifth year of financial aid in order that they may graduate. This statement, of course, is predicated on the assumption that the student is progressing normally toward a degree. A student whose grade average consistently falls below a "C" is not progressing normally toward a degree. In addition, students will receive consideration for financial aid for summer school if a special course or program necessitates such consideration.

In summary, the University will not be able to categorically increase the scholarships of all black students. However, the Office of Financial Aid is willing to evaluate each student's request independently and discuss the decision with that student. This position is consistent with the guidelines established by the Committee on Financial Aid to Students which governs financial aid applicable to all of its undergraduate students.

IV. HOUSING

"The housing policy of Northwestern University is not predicated upon any consideration of race, color, or creed of the applicant. All roommate assignments will be considered binding for all parties throughout the first academic quarter." The foregoing is a direct quotation from the Housing Information statement which is sent to all new students. The University Housing Committee added the second sentence at its meeting in January of this year. Freshmen roommate assignments will not be changed during fall quarter. Thereafter, changes will be made by the Housing Office when possible and only upon the consent of all parties.

In addition, all landlords wishing to list a rental property with the University have been asked to sign a statement which specifies that they "agree to offer without regard for race, color, or creed the facility listed." In addition, they are sent a copy of the Housing Policy Statement.

While we can understand and appreciate the frustrations that lead to the demand for black living units, the University cannot accede to this request. For one thing, the University is living with a severe shortage of on-campus housing which in itself limits the policy options which are open to us. Given the need to house freshmen on campus, there are not enough spaces left over to permit the University to give any one group of students special exemption from the normal room assignment procedures.

The most important reason, however, for denying this request lies in the function the residence hall serves in the educational program of the University. The residence hall is far more than just shelter and a place to escape from the daily academic routine. Rather it is a place where students learn from each other and thereby further the educational process in which this institution is engaged. This function of University housing depends on a mixture of student types which cannot be achieved if certain groups are segrated from the rest of the living environment.

While the University believes there is much that must be done to accord the black student the rights and respect on this campus that he deserves, it strongly believes that organizing separate living for black students is self-defeating and cannot contribute constructively to the academic purposes for which the University exists.

The University will take every step it can to provide housing for black students wishing to live on campus. Black students wanting to live off-campus are urged to use University off-campus housing directory services and to report to those services all cases of suspected discriminatory renting practices so investigation and follow-up action can be taken by the committee on housing discrimination.

CURRICULUM

V. Perhaps the most appropriate way in which a University can contribute to the increase in understanding which is needed between the black and white segments of our society is through its academic program. The faculty has the sole authority and responsiblity for matters of curriculum with regard to course content as well as new courses. Any request for new credit bearing courses should be directed to the Curriculum Committees and Department Chairmen. Consideration should also be given to the development of special non-credit programs within such activities as the Evening Divisions, the Experimental College and Symposium.

While the recommendations for the appointment of new faculty emanate from the faculty, your assistance in identifying prospective faculty members would be useful. The University welcomes the addition of more qualified black faculty members to its ranks.

VI. COUNSELING

To improve relations between students and between students and the administration, the University is committed to increasing the counseling facilities available to all students. The University is pleased to announce that Mr. Calvin Smith accepted a joint appointment in the Office of Admission and in the Office of the Dean of Students on April 15, 1968, to be effective September 1, 1968. Mr. Smith is a graduate of Carver High School in Chicago, received his Bachelor of Science degree from Winston-Salem College in North Carolina, his Master's degree from DePaul University, and presently is a doctoral candidate at Northwestern. Mr. Smith also has been a high school teacher and administrator. The University encourages those students who are interested in meeting Mr. Smith to contact Mr. Ihlanfeldt so that a convenient time might be arranged.

VII. FACILITIES

The University realizes the special needs for activity space for black students. By September 1968 we will provide a room on campus in an attempt to meet some of these needs. The space should provide for general lounge activity and also be usable for meeting activity as well. It is clear that all of the space needs of black students cannot be met through the provision of such a room and every effort will be made to schedule other multiple-use-space to assist in meeting these special needs.

We ask that a committee of black students be selected by you to work with us in our efforts to meet these needs.

Some cultural activities and many social activities presently available on campus are irrelevant for the black students; new activities must be developed to meet these needs. In addition to space, financial support is also needed and while it is not possible at this time to specify what support will be available, every effort will be made to provide reasonable assistance.

VIII.OPEN OCCUPANCY

The University has taken a strong stand on open occupancy in Evanston, as evidenced by Mr. Kerr's recent statement to the Evanston City Council. In the housing under its ownership -- that is -- the N.U. Apartments, Dryden Hall, and faculty homes -- there is no segregation whatsoever. A list of occupants in this housing is available. Furthermore, when the Committee appointed to deal with discrimination in housing makes its report within the next two weeks, the University will be prepared to implement the measures recommended. The University is committed to working for just living space and conditions for all black people.

Roland J. Hinz

Appendix C
Revised and Final Demands, May 1968
(Northwestern University Archives)

Having rejected the basic principles on which our demands were based, the administration has forced us to speak for the last time on those matters discussed at the meeting of Wed., April 24, 1968. We demand that such action be taken to meet this, our final list of demands. The University must show itself flexible enough to take in the "peculiarities" of our culture and background. The only way, we feel, the University can display its understanding and flexibility is by the immediate approval and implementation of those demands submitted by the Black student body on April 22, 1968.

I. <u>POLICY STATEMENT</u>

Northwestern cannot begin to deal effectively with racism on this campus until it first realizes and openly acknowledges the extent of racism in American society. For this reason we reject the statement given to us in response and demand that a "new" policy statement be issued and made public from President Roscoe Miller asserting that the racism of American society which has penetrated all American institutions has also penetrated Northwestern University, and has thus affected the social and academic life here.

This statement is to include a declaration that the University is attempting to provide a multi-racial and cultural society within the university walls and that any racist attacks and/or abuses shall be considered in direct opposition to the University's goals and a danger to the peaceful existence of such a society. The extent of this danger is such that the perpetrator shall be immediately excluded from this institution.

In order to alter the racist structure of this University, a change has to take place in the judiciary structures, attitudes, and practices. As of now, the University Disciplinary Committee is ineffective in dealing with racism on campus (examples include the Fiji incidents and the many encounters with Sigma Chi). We demand that this judiciary be changed and implemented to bring about swifter and fairer decisions, or that a special judiciary be created to deal with these special cases.

On acknowledging the racist structure of this country and this institution, Northwestern is committed to understand the negative effects of racism on Black people and other oppressed people. The entire concept of justice has to be re-evaluated for this reason. Justice for Black people at this time does not mean equal treatment before a law or rule which is insensitive to our oppressive position in this country. We contend that justice for Black people means that extra consideration and efforts are to be made in order to balance the effects of racism. This means in effect that the U.D.C. decision to place 3 white students and 2 Black students on disciplinary warning is not justice and is thus unacceptable in our eyes.

Our experience in America has not been characterized by justice in any way. No white institution can right our hundreds of years of history and experience by suddenly treating us the same as white people (only at those times when it is strategic to do so) and call it justice and equality. No matter how one looks at it, idealistically or realistically, Black people know that we are still getting the short end of the deal. A new basis for administering justice must be developed and put into effect and it is with this that U.D.C., or any new judiciary which intends to deal with racism, has to concern itself.

The only concrete response from the administration was the establishment of a special University Committee on Human Relations. However, we are not satisfied with that response and demand the right of the Black student community to approve all appointments to this committee and to determine at least 50% of these appointments.

II. ADMISSIONS

We understand that Northwestern has suddenly made a "substantial effort to change the composition of the undergraduate student body." However this statement or any of the others which followed says nothing about a guaranteed increase of the number of Black students at Northwestern. We demand that each forthcoming freshman class be 10-12% Black and that it will be financially feasible for all those Black students accepted to come.

We demanded that 50% of each year's incoming Black students be from the inner city school systems. The administration emphasized that in the past the Black enrollment contained at least 50% from the inner city and ended with the statement "There is no reason to believe that this percentage should change." In lieu of this statement there is no reason why we should not be given a guarantee that this percentage will remain the same.

We agreed that a committee will be appointed by the Black student community to assist the Admissions Office, expecially in the area of recruitment. We demand that there be no restrictions placed on our selections, that this committee be in a salaried position, and that it have shared power with the Office of Admissions and Financial Aid in making all decisions relevant to Black students, including decisions on which Black students are to be admitted.

The University has agreed to provide us with the names of all Black students who are known to the Administration as well as a list of all entering Black students. We demand a list of all Black students accepted as well as those entering with information relevant to our purposes such as residence (city and state). We further demand that such lists be compiled and turned over to F.M.O. for each subsequent freshman class.

In addition, the University agreed to arrange a meeting between us and the incoming Black freshman.

III. SCHOLARSHIPS

As all Black people in America categorically suffer from the oppressiveness of this white society, we conclude that all Black students at Northwestern in turn categorically suffer from economic and social oppression and on that basis should categorically be given special consideration for increased financial aid which is not covered in the data of the financial aid form. The process of evaluating financial need and administering financial aid must be restructured to meet our vital needs. This re-organization can be done in conjunction with our established Admissions and Financial Aid Committee.

The acceptance of job and loan offers may be optional for white students attending Northwestern, but due to our plight in this country, they are not optional for us. Black students are forced to take jobs and loans to lessen the financial burden of our families who suffer categorically under the American political, economic, and social structure. Therefore the problems and pressures encountered by a Black student receiving financial aid are not the same ones encountered by a white financial aid student.

The University has already acknowledged the deficiency in our High School preparation. By virtue of this fact, we contend that this deficiency can best be removed by allowing all Black students to attend the Summer Session as they so desire. Also, we strongly feel that Black students should have the same opportunity to continue their education through the summer as any other Northwestern student. Whether or not we work or attend classes should be our option and therefore the University should not restrict us by requiring that we work in order to substantiate our scholarships for the other three quarters.

As it stands now, Northwestern has neither a fair admissions policy nor a fair financial aid arrangement. Equal opportunity and rights for us imply much more than whites care to admit. Our demands still stand that our scholarships be increased to cover what is now included in our "required jobs" and to include funds for those who want or need to attend Summer session.

IV. HOUSING

As taken from the University's reply to our demands of April 22nd: "While we (the administration) can understand and appreciate the frustrations that lead to the demands..." We, the Black students of Northwestern, cannot appreciate the frustrations that led to making these demands. How the University can claim to understand our problems and/or frustrations and not concede to our demands is beyond our comprehension!

The University might be living with a severe shortage of on-campus housing. However, this does not affect us in that a Black living unit would not necessarily call for additional space, only the relocation of students.

Furthermore, the Administration contends that the most important reason for denying this demand lies in the function the residence hall serves in the educational program of the University. "(The residence hall) is a place where students learn from each other and thereby further the education process in which this institution is engaged. This function of University housing depends on a mixture of student types which cannot be achieved if certain groups are segregated from the rest of the living environment." Why, we ask, are the fraternities and sororities exempt from this educational program?

The University evidently helps to support living units (fraternities and sororities) on this campus which are in direct opposition to the above quoted University policy. Therefore, the University should have no objection to supporting another living unit (Black) without this educational program.

Furthermore, according to the minutes of the March 5, 1968 CUL Subcommittee meeting, "Mr. Ihlanfeldt stated that as Director of Admissions, he feels his charge from the faculty is to recruit quality and dissimilarity within the student body. He sees the Greek groups as selecting others like themselves and opposes the extension of the system on that basis. He stated that he would accept the fraternity idea but not in the same way that it has been in the past where there is discrimination based on the same type of criterion. He would only accept an extension of the idea, such as converting Hobart and Rogers to models of the future that may tend to represent the philosophical idea of a master house plan. This could be all or predominantly Negro, but it would not be copying the fraternity system as it is." Evidently the idea of a Black living unit was at one time feasible. Why is it that this is no longer the case?

If the University genuinely believes that a Black living unit would be in direct conflict with their program and/or basic university policy, then we demand that the University should make a policy statement condemning the existing living units of this sort (i. e. fraternities and sororities) with a commitment to get rid of them immediately. Otherwise, on the basis of this argument, we restate our demand that the University provide us with a Black living unit.

V. CURRICULUM

Dean Strotz received a copy of our demands on April 21, 1968 as did the rest of the administration. It is our understanding that Dean Strotz heads the Committee for Curriculum Revisions. We have received no reply either from him or through the administration on the creation of a Black Studies Course. Therefore, we assume that he has either denied our request or he is thoroughly disinterested in the condition of the Black student at Northwestern.

Through University funds, the Administration has the influence to promote the hiring of Black faculty members. We demand that this influence be immediately put into effect and used to its fullest extent.

One concrete step in meeting our demand would be the creation of a visiting chair in Black Studies. However, we demand that the Black community have the ultimate decision as to which professor would occupy this chair from year to year.

VI. COUNSELING

We want it understood that any hiring of personnel in the position of counseling to the Black community of Northwestern University must be approved by the Black community. Without such approval, we will totally absolve ourselves from recognizing or interacting with such persons. Further understand our position on the hiring of Mr. Calvin Smith. We will review his "qualifications"; however, if he does not meet our approval, steps must be taken to find an acceptable Black counselor.

VII. FACILITIES

We acknowledge the Administration's reply to our demand for facilities.

VIII. OPEN OCCUPANCY

We acknowledge the University's efforts toward the passage of the Evanston Open Occupancy Law. However, we demand access to the committee which has been studying open occupancy and discrimination, as well as review rights to the matters which they are discussing so that we may determine both their relevance and effectiveness.

The legitimacy of these demands cannot be debated. What is important to Black people is not necessarily important to the Administration or this University as a whole. The Administration has demonstrated that they are less concerned about our reasons and motivations for presenting these demands than about their own intentions to maintain ultimate control over our lives. Likewise, we are not interested in the reasons why these demands cannot be met.

In lieu of this, tension between us is inevitable and it is this tension which has to be reconciled. We realize that the factors leading to our presently being students at Northwestern were basically politically motivated and had little or nothing to do with a social interest in the plight of Black people in America. Being brought here essentially for purposes of exploitation, Northwestern has subsequently shown little interest in our needs except for those which were compatible with theirs. Therefore, the main responsibility for reconciling the tension between us lies with the Administration and not with us. All we can say is that if our demands are impossible, then peace between us is impossible too.

In summary, we demand positive responses from the Administration to the following:

POLICY STATEMENT:

1. That the Administration will accept and issue a policy statement as outlined in this paper.

2. That the Administration restructure the UDC or create a new judiciary to adequately and justly cope with racial problems and incidents.

3. That the Administration effect a new judiciary standard (as outlined) and apply this standard retroactively to the UDC decision of April 15.

4. That the Administration allow the Black community to (a) approve all appointments to the Human Relations Committee and (b) determine at least 50% of those appointments.

ADMISSION:

5. That each forthcoming Freshman class consist of 10%-12% Black students half of which are from the inner city school systems.

6. That the Administration will institute a committee selected by the Black community to aid the Admissions Office, especially in recruitment, and which will have shared power with the Office of Admissions and Financial Aid in making decisions relevant to us.

7. That the members constituting this committee be in a salaried position.

8. That F.M.O. will be supplied with (a) a list of all Black students presently enrolled at Northwestern (b) a list including names, addresses, etc. of all accepted and incoming Black freshmen, (c) a similar list of each forthcoming Freshman class.

FINANCIAL AID:

9. That the process of evaluating financial need and administering financial aid be restructured in conjunction with our Admissions and Financial Aid Committee.

10. That our scholarships be increased to cover what is now included in our "required jobs and that funds be allocated for those who want or need to attend Summer Session.

HOUSING:

11. That the University provide us with a Black living unit or commit themselves to immediately getting rid of the present fraternity and sorority housing arrangements.

COUNSELING:

12. That any hiring of personnel in the position of counseling the Black community of NU be approved by that Black community.

FACILITIES:

13. That a committee of Black students selected by us work with the Administration in meeting our needs for a Black Student Union.

OPEN OCCUPANCY:

14. That we have access to the committee studying open occupancy and discrimination with review rights to the matters which they are discussing.

Appendix D
Draft of the May 4 Agreement, 1968
(Northwestern University Archives)

Draft Agreement Between

Afro-American Student Union and FMO
and a committee representing the
Northwestern University Administration

May 4, 1968

I. POLICY STATEMENT

Northwestern University recognizes that throughout its history it has been a university of the white establishment. This is not to gainsay that many members of its administration, its faculty, and its student body have engaged themselves in activities directed to the righting of racial wrongs. It is also true that for many years a few blacks have been members of its administration, faculty, and student body. But the fact remains that the University in its overwhelming character has been a white institution. This it has had in common with virtually all institutions of higher learning in the United States. Its members have also had in common with the white community in America, in greater or lesser degree, the racist attitudes that have prevailed historically in this society and which continue to constitute the most important social problem of our times. This University with other institutions must share responsibility for the continuance over many past years of these racist attitudes.

A few years ago, the Northwestern Administration became increasingly concerned with the problem of doing something to improve race reations and to provide educational opportunities in greater measure than ever before for the black people in its community. Within a relatively short period the number of black students, though still small, has grown to the point at which it can now be said that there is a definite, significant, and important black community within the larger community of the university. Despite the difficulties of understanding that have attended this process, we mean to and shall approach our problems constructively in this area. We wish to face these new challenges and to enhance, both quantitatively and qualitatively, the role of black men and women in the activities of the University at all levels.

The events of this week, which have given us new and broader insights, have led us to a reappraisal of the attitudes with which we confront these problems. For many of us, the solution has always seemed to be one of simply obliterating in our laws and in our personal relations the distinction between the races: that is, if only many would ignore in his human relations the differences in skin colors, racial problems would immediately disappear. We are now learning that this notion does not come fully to grips with the problems of the present turbulent period of transition. In short, this means that special recognition and special concern must be given, for some unspecifiable time, to the black community that is emerging within our institution.

Accordingly, we cannot be complacent with institutional arrangements that ignore the special problems of black students. An important and difficult problem is that of an essentially white leadership coming to understand the special needs and feelings of the black student, as well as the difficulty arising because the black student does not regard the white university authorities as capable of appreciating all of the nuances of his decidedly separate culture.

The University therefore accepts the basic sentiments expressed in the black students' petitions, and urges the following in addition: that there be established a special Northwestern University Advisory Council as an instrument of University Administration to function at all administrative levels as the administration deals with problems of the black community related to the University. We believe that membership on this council should consist only of black leaders who have distinguished themselves within the black community in educational and professional affairs. This council, to consist of ten (10) members, should be chosen by the University Administration from a list of twenty (20) nominees to be made by the black members of the University community. We believe that the insight and the advice of this council will be valuable in assuring that the University will be more responsive in reacting to the particular needs of its black students.

An urgent function for such a council would be to recommend to the university what changes in its procedures are needed to handle better the problems of black students. We believe that such a council could play in future years an important role in recommending the selection of members for the newly appointed University Committee on Human Relations. But until the council if formally constituted, the President will appoint a University Committee on Human Relations and will make appointments in a way that elicits and recognizes the views and recommendations of the black students.

The university also recognizes in the matter of student discipline that the intent of disciplinary action is to improve the standards of personal conduct rather than to punish perse, and it recognizes that in this purpose it is necessary to take account of the racial, cultural, and personal characteristics of all students concerned. In keeping with this principle, the Administration will instruct the University Discipline Committee to review the case growing out of the December 2 incident. It also agrees with the complaint that the judiciary function must proceed as rapidly as is consistent with the justice of decisions. All ways of expediting the judiciary process will be pursued.

ADMISSIONS

We acknowledge and respect the black students' desire for a guarantee of an immediate proportionate representation in Northwestern freshman classes. We cannot in good faith offer such explicit guarantees and wish to explain why. Hitherto, we have confronted three major problems in this regard: recruitment, competition from other colleges and universities, and support for a program of financial aid to black students.

The University welcomes assistance in resolving these problems from black students at Northwestern and from any other interested quarter, but especially we welcome assistance on recruitment and related issues, including admissions criteria.

It is hoped that in the future, through the combined efforts of the black students and the Office of Admission, a greater number of applications will be received from black high school students. If such efforts are successful, it is realistic to assume that the black community in the nation at large will soon be proportionately represented in the Northwestern student body. It should be noted that the University has received the following number of applications from black students in the past three years: in 1965-66, seventy; in 1966-67, ninety; and 1967-68, one hundred-twenty. The Office of Admission will provide an annual progress report of the number of black students who have applied and who have been accepted by the University.

The Office of Admission of the University is committed to increase the number of black students at Northwestern as rapidly as possible, and to seek at least fifty percent of these students from the inner-city school systems. The University is further committed to intensify present recruitment efforts in order to assure such an increase. Although the University is committed to accelerate the increase, it is unable to cite a specific number because of ever-increasing competition from other colleges and universities.

In pursuing this goal of a guaranteed increase in black students the Office of Admission will welcome a committee of black students selected by the black community to advise, assist and counsel the Committee on Admission. Salaried positions in the Office of Admission will be created for such students who assist in student recruitment.

The University, however, cannot permit students to make individual admission decisions. The evaluation of a candidate's folder is confidential and is a privileged communication between the candidate and the Office of Admission. The University is legally and morally bound to honor such privileged communication.

The Student Affairs Office of the University routinely provides lists of students to campus organizations. A list of all black students, as far as they are known to the Student Affairs Office, will be provided to F.M.O. Such a list will include names and addresses of presently enrolled black students and those accepted in each entering freshman class.

FINANCIAL AID

In principle, the University agrees that the amount of grant aid for black students should be increased. The Development Office of the University is constantly seeking additional funds for financial aid purposes. An example of this effort is the recent gift which has been committed and restricted to black students from inner-city Chicago.

The University agrees to a committee selected by the black student community to advise the University's Committee on Financial Aid to Students on policy matters regarding financial aid to black students. A special sub-committee will be established comprised of equal representation of black students and faculty members of the Committee on Financial Aid to Students. The purpose of this committee will be to review and advise on individual black students' complaints regarding financial assistance. It is anticipated that such requests will include the elimination of job requirements, the increase in a student's assistance, and the granting of special funds to students to attend the Summer Session.

The University wishes to reply to the statement made by the black student community, "The University has already acknowledged the deficiency in our high school preparation." That acknowledgement by the University only is relevant to individual cases and cannot be categorically applied to all black students at Northwestern.

HOUSING

While reaffirming our previously stated belief that a mixture of student types should characterize living arrangements within the University, we have modified that position in response to two impinging influences: one is the distinctiveness of existing racial concerns; the other is the admitted inconsistency between the ideal of nondiscrimination in housing and the recognized practice of discrimination that exists in certain living units of the University.

Accordingly, starting with the Fall of 1968, the University will reserve separate sections of existing living units of the University in which black students, upon their individual requests, will be housed.

CURRICULUM

The Administration shares your concern as to the importance of expanding studies of black history and black culture in the University. The introduction of such material through visiting lectureships, courses, and research is a matter which the Dean of the College of Arts and Sciences will urge upon his departmental chairmen for consideration. The procedure for the introduction of new courses is their recommendation by the department or departments concerned, approval by the Divisional Council which is elected by the faculty, and their approval finally by the faculty of the College. The Curriculum Committee of the College recommends degree requirements, but does not officially recommend new course offerings. We encourage you to present curricular suggestions to the individual members of departmental faculties, the department chairmen, or the Dean of the College.

Further, we welcome suggestions from the black community as to qualified potential faculty members. Nevertheless, it should be pointed out that faculty appointments are initiated by the departmental faculties and they are the groups to whom suggestions should be addressed.

We must, in all candor, state that the Administration cannot provide more specific replies to the demands under this heading since the initiative in all these matters is a prerogative of the faculty.

Signatories

For A.A.S.U. and F.M.O.	For Northwestern Administration and Faculty
James Turner	Payson S. Wild
Kathryn Ogletree	Franklin M. Kreml
Amassa Fauntleroy	Robert H. Strotz
John Bracey	William Ihlanfeldt
Victor M. Goode	Joe Park
Vernon Ford	Lucius P. Gregg
Roger Ward	Gail M. Inlow
Michael Smith	Robert H. Baker
Harold Daniels	Walter L. Wallace
Arnold Wright	Roland J. Hinz

Addendum to POLICY STATEMENT, page 3, last sentence, first full paragraph as follows:

....recommendations of the black students. The University will inform the black student community of the date by which recommendations for membership on the committee must be submitted.

Addendum to ADMISSIONS, substitute the following in place of paragraph 2:

The University welcomes assistance in resolving these problems from black students at Northwestern and from any other interested quarter, but especially we welcome assistance on recruitment and related issues, including admissions criteria for black students.

Insert the following as sentence 2, paragraph 5:

The faculty Committee on Admission prescribes policy governing the philosophical concerns of admission, for example, it determines criteria for admission. In the daily operations of the admission office black students will be asked to provide direction as to which high schools, other institutions or persons the Office of Admission should contact. In addition, black students will be asked to advise with respect to the admission and financial aid candidacies of individual black applicants and on other operational concerns as they arise. Salaried positions.....

Final paragraph:

We agree that an orientation program will be arranged for entering black students. For students entering in the summer program, block-time will be allocated for scheduled meetings and programs which will be organized and conducted by an orientation group selected by the black student community. Similarly, two days will be arranged at the beginning of the fall quarter for the orientation of entering black students. A minimum amount of $500 will be made available for these purposes.

Addendum to HOUSING, final paragraph:

Moreover, the University will move toward providing separate housing units for black male and female students, and will inform the black students of progress in this direction during the Spring Quarter of 1969.

Addendum to CURRICULUM, final paragraph:

Dean Strotz will also arrange for a meeting of the black students with Prof. Jean Hagstrum, Chairman of the Faculty Planning Committee, so that their views and ideas regarding curriculum may be expressed to him.

New section on FACILITIES:

The University realizes the special needs for activity space for black students. By September 1968 the University will provide a room on campus in an attempt to meet some of these needs. The space should provide for general lounge activity and also be usable for meeting activity as well. It is clear that because all of the space needs of black students cannot be met through the provision of such a room, every effort will be made to schedule other multiple-use space to assist in meeting these special needs.

Some cultural activities and many social activities presently available on campus are irrelevant for the black students; new activities must be developed to meet these needs.

The University asks that the black students select a committee to work with it in all these efforts.

Specific consideration should be given to the following details:

1. Adequate library and artistic display space.
2. Flexibility of house to meet the special social needs of black students.
3. The provision of maximum privacy of the area.
4. Sufficient financial resources to carry on a reasonable program.

Addendum to OPEN OCCUPANCY, to be inserted as first paragraph:

The University has taken a strong stand on open occupancy in Evanston, as evidenced by Mr. Kerr's recent statement to the Evanston City Council. In the housing under its ownership--that is-- the N. U. Apartments, Dryden Hall, and faculty homes--there is no segregation whatsoever. A list of occupants in this housing is available. Furthermore, when the committee appointed to deal with discrimination in housing makes its report within the next two weeks, the University will be prepared to implement the measures recommended. The University is committed to working for just living space and conditions for all black people.

This document has been drafted by and is concurred in by the President, the several Vice Presidents, certain other officers of administration and several senior faculty members.

Transmitted by

(signed) Roland J. Hinz

Roland J. Hinz
Vice President for Student Affairs
and Dean of Students

5/4/68

Appendix E: List of Takeover Participants

(From the exhibit, "They Demanded Courageously: The 1968 Northwestern Bursar's Office Takeover," Northwestern University Libraries, Northwestern University) Not included on this list is Harold Daniels, who was a signatory to the May 4 Agreement. He and others, especially some Northwestern athletes, may not have participated in the takeover per se, but can be considered to be part of and integral to the action. (See chapters 5 and 6.)

Barbara Atkinson (Perkins/Melendez)
Lee Banks
Andre Bell
Ermetra Black
John Bracey
Elaine Brazil
Clinton Bristow
Josephine Bronaugh
Stephen Broussard
Floyd Brown
Millicent Brown
Janice Bumphus
Nona Burney
Barbara Burton
Widmon Butler
Herman Cage
Dorothy Carter (Higginson)
Paula Christopher (Kelley)
Leon Coleman
Steve Colson
Floyd Crider
Dan Davis
Lawrence Dillard
Amassa Fauntleroy
Vernon Ford
Chico (Earl) Freeman
Milton Gardner
Renee Gay
Victor Goode
Gregory Harper
Dorothy Harrell
Juaquita Harris
Jocklyn Harris
Leslie Harris
Freddie Heard
John Higginson
Debra Avant Hill
James Hill
Sandra Small Hill
Stanley Hill
Audrey Hinton
Valeria Howell
Michael Hudson
Gail Hush
Gail Irving
Marianne Jackson
Eva Jefferson
Nelson Johnson
Isola Jones
Lillian Jordan
Loester Lewis
Saundra Malone
Daphne Maxwell (Reid)
Charles McBride
Mario McHarris
Herbert Melton
Robert Miller
Maxine Mitchell
Janice Morris
Laura Murray
Harvette Nelson
Kathryn Ogletree
Carol Oliver
Dorothy Parson
Eric Perkins
Roland Person
Mark Phillippe
James Pitts
Sharon Pitts
Anthony Porter (Soji Adebayo)
Thomas Preston
Christine Price
Travis Pumphrey
Lonnie Radcliffe
Robert Ray
Lea (LeEasther) Redmond
Cora Regalus
Sue Rhoden
Regina Rice
Ronald Riley
Robert Scott
Clovis Semmes
Thomas Sharpton
Charles Shepard
Janice Sims
Detra Smith
Jinx Smith
LeRoy Smith
Michael Smith
Eleanor Steele
Dianne Strickland
Ibrahim Sundiata
Lonnie Terry
Adrianne (Hayward) Thomas
John Trimble
James Turner
Mae Tyler
Tom Vance
Joyce Wade
Roger Ward
Wayne Watson
Bill West
Joanne Williams
Judy Willoughby
Dolores Wilson
Arnold Wright
Cherilyn Wright

Archival Collections

Department of Special Collections and University Archives, W. E. B. Du Bois Papers, University of Massachusetts Amherst.

Evanston History Center Archives, Evanston History Center, Evanston, IL.

Franklin M. Kreml Papers, Northwestern University Archives, Northwestern University, Evanston, IL. Cited as Kreml papers, NUA..

Records of the Bursar's Office Takeover, May 1968. Northwestern University Archives, Northwestern University, Evanston, IL. Cited as Bursar's Office Takeover, NUA.

Student Activities Collection, Northwestern University Archives, Northwestern University, Evanston, IL. Cited as Student Activities Collection, NUA.

Student Protests and Strikes at Northwestern University, Northwestern University Archives, Northwestern University, Evanston, IL. Student Protests, NUA.

University Presidents, J. Roscoe Miller Papers, Northwestern University Archives. Northwestern University, Evanston, IL. Cited as Miller Papers, NUA.

Notes to Introduction

1 See for example, Blake Slonecker, "The Columbia Coalition: African Americans, New Leftists, and Counterculture at the Columbia University Protest of 1968," *Journal of Social History* 41, no. 4 (2008).

Note to frontispiece quotation: Kathryn Ogletree, interview with the author, May 25, 2018.

* Student activism certainly did not begin in 1968. For many years, protests had been staged on campuses across the country, and anti-war protests had taken place at Northwestern earlier than 1968. In November and December 1967, two protests at UCLA and San Francisco State College (now San Francisco State University) made headlines, and protests would continue. As 1968 began, the momentum was building for more actions, from walk-outs to sleep-ins, occupations to strikes. These actions were not limited to the United States, but were a global phenomenon.

Notes to Introductory Quotes

1 On February 16, 1960, at the White Rock Baptist Church in Durham, North Carolina, Martin Luther King, Jr. "acknowledged the emerging importance of young people" within the movement for civil rights. Quoted in Charlie Cobb, "The Story of SNCC," ND, SNCC Digital Gateway, https://snccdigital.org/inside-sncc/the-story-of-sncc/.

2 Throughout this book, I quote materials that use the term "negro" and other antiquated and racist terms. I do so in original context only. The term "negro" was still in use during the time period documented here, although by the mid 1960s, it was rapidly being replaced by the word Black.

3 *Orations of the Northern Oratorical League* (Ann Arbor: Ann Arbor Press, 1920), 5. "The Future of the American Negro." This was the title of George Dewey Lipscomb's award-winning 1916 oration in a state-wide oratorical contest in Illinois. Lipscomb was a student at Freeport High School in Freeport, Illinois, when he was awarded a scholarship to Northwestern. In 1919, he represented Northwestern in the Northern Oratorical League competition and later was awarded the Sargent Prize for excellence in declamation. He graduated from Northwestern in 1921. He later became an author and professor at Wiley College and at Howard University. Northwestern University, *Sixty-Third Annual Commencement,* June 15, 1921, 15; "Social Progress," *The Crisis,* May 1919, 35; "Prizes and Honors," Northwestern University, *The Syllabus*, 1920, 89; "Famed Author Geo. Lipscomb Mourned Here," *New York Age,* January 26, 1957; Jillian Duchnowski, "Freeport Black History Month: George Lipscomb Became Professor, Author," RRStar.com, February 18, 2017, https://www.rrstar.com/news/20170218/freeport-black-history-month-george-lipscomb-became-professor-author.

4 *The Report of the President's Commission on Campus Unrest* (Washington, D.C.: Government Printing Office, 1970), 101. Margaret Walker Alexander (1915-1998) earned a BA from Northwestern in 1935. She later recalled that Northwestern was an "extremely racist school." But she fondly remembered some of her writing

teachers, including one professor, Edward Buell Hungerford, who was "one of the finest people" she had ever met, and was also author Saul Bellow's professor at Northwestern. Marcia Greenlee, "Black Women and Oral History: Margaret Walker Alexander," (1977) in *Conversations with Margaret Walker,* Maryemma Graham, ed. (Jackson, MS: University Press of Mississippi, 2002), 37-38. See below for more on Alexander.

Notes to Chapter 1

1 Frederick Douglass, "West India Emancipation," speech at Canandaigua, New York, August 3, 1857.

2 Jack Hinz (Roland J. Hinz), interview with the author, September 19, 2012. This was the first of three interviews that I conducted with Jack Hinz. The second took place on October 3, 2012. A third interview took place on April 4, 2018, when we sat down for an extended discussion during which time he provided comments on a draft of this book. Those details have been incorporated throughout the text.

3 Ogletree, interview with the author, May 25, 2018.

4 Ogletree, interview with the author, 2018.

5 John H. Bracey, Jr., (hereafter referred to as John Bracey) interview with the author, June 21, 2018.

6 John Bracey, phone conversation with the author, August 9, 2018.

7 James Turner, interview with the author, May 25, 2012. While it was a surprise to see her husband on TV, Janice Turner was well aware of what was going on leading up to the takeover and was active in the movement as well.

8 "Negro Sit-In at Northwestern," *Chicago Sun-Times,* May 4, 1968. The building the students occupied was officially known as the University Business Office, but it is commonly referred to as the Bursar's Office.

9 In March 1968, the *Daily Northwestern* revealed that for the first time ever, some Northwestern campus security guards were armed. "3 Campus Cops Carry Guns-Arndt," *Daily Northwestern,* March 29, 1968.

10 Bracey, phone conversation with the author, August 9, 2018.

11 There are slightly different versions concerning how the students were able to get inside the building and the details of the occupation. The account rendered here is drawn from several sources, including my interviews with John Bracey and Kathryn Ogletree; "619 Clark Street; N.U.'s Day of Decision," *Daily Northwestern,* May 4, 1968; Northwestern University's official accounts issued after the takeover which are found in the Northwestern University Archives and online; and Northwestern University's history of the takeover found at: Northwestern University, "They Demanded Courageously: The 1968 Northwestern Bursar's Office Takeover," Northwestern Libraries, https://sites.northwestern.edu/bursars1968/history/. Many of the documents related to the takeover can be found at this site. Another version recounts that a student hiding in the Bursar's Office that morning let the other students inside. In her novel, *Where I Must Go,* Angela Jackson, who entered Northwestern in the fall of 1968, provides an account of a young woman's experience at a fictitious Eden University, including her participation in a takeover in the spring of 1968. Jackson's account, although fiction, is based on her own experiences at Northwestern and the stories she heard about the takeover while a

student there. She writes that one of the students had been hiding in the building since the afternoon of May 2 and let the students inside on May 3. Angela Jackson, *Where I Must Go* (Evanston, IL: Northwestern University Press, 2009), 276. Other sources have suggested this was the case. Another account is contained in the FBI's memorandum on the events of May 3-4, 1968 which states that a "member of the janitorial staff opened the doors prior to the official opening of the building at 8:30 a.m." Federal Bureau of Investigation, "Racial Tensions, Northwestern University Campus, Evanston, Illinois," May 8, 1968, 1. From the FBI file, "Bobby [Robert] Rush," accessed from the Internet Archive, https://archive.org/stream/BobbyRush/Rush%2C%20Bobby_djvu.txt. Additionally, there are slightly different accounts of how many guards were on duty at the Bursar's Office that morning. John Bracey recalls there was just one guard, a point confirmed by the *Daily Northwestern's* reporting on the takeover.

12 Bracey, phone conversation with the author, August 9, 2018; "619 Clark Street; N.U.'s Day of Decision," *Daily Northwestern,* May 4, 1968.

13 Bracey, phone conversation with the author, August 9, 2018.

14 Bracey, phone conversation, August 9, 2018. Bracey recalls that the students left their own phone numbers with staff so that they could let them know if anything needed to be replaced.

15 "619 Clark Street; N.U.'s Day of Decision;" "They Demanded Courageously: The 1968 Northwestern Bursar's Office Takeover."

16 Ogletree, interview with the author, 2018. The term "takeover" has a different meaning than the term "sit-in," which is sometimes used to describe the May 1968 action. Kathryn Ogletree remembers using the term "takeover" at the time to describe the action since it more accurately conveyed their intention. As an act of nonviolent protest, a sit-in had a different intention, since business operations could go on even in the midst of such an action, while a takeover was a nonviolent action which was intended to force the complete shutting down of operations both in (and beyond) the occupied space.

17 "619 Clark Street; N.U.'s Day of Decision."

18 "Negroes Protest at Northwestern," *New York Times,* May 4, 1968; "619 Clark Street; N.U.'s Day of Decision."

19 "619 Clark Street; N.U.'s Day of Decision."

20 Different sources provide slightly different totals for the number of students involved in the takeover, ranging from about ninety-four to 120 students. Northwestern lists the names of 107 students on its website: "They Demanded Courageously, The 1968 Northwestern Bursar's Office Takeover." John Bracey recalls that about thirty students initially showed up in the alley on the morning of May 3, 1968. John Bracey, telephone conversation with the author, August 9, 2019. That number would increase as other students joined the takeover soon after the initial occupation and throughout the day. According to the *Daily Northwestern,* there were ninety-four students occupying the building by early Friday morning. In a detailed article documenting the takeover, the newspaper stated that thirty students entered the building's front entrance on Clark Street, while about fifty students entered through the building's rear door. "619 Clark Street; N.U.'s Day of Decision."

21 "Students Seize N. U. Offices," *Chicago Tribune,* May 4, 1968.

22 According to Northwestern student and takeover participant, Wayne Watson the men who unloaded the truck were part of a group of Evanston residents who helped the students. Jeffrey Sterling, MD, and Lauren Lowery, *Voices and Visions: The Evolution of the Black Experience at Northwestern University* (NP: Sterling Initiatives, 2018) loc. 1969-1972, Kindle. Interview materials quoted and drawn from Jeffrey Sterling, MD and Lauren Lowery, *Voices and Visions: The Evolution of the Black Experience at Northwestern University* are the sole property of that work. Quotes attributed to individuals are drawn from that work. My thanks to Jeffrey Sterling and Lauren Lowery for permission to quote portions of those interviews from their work.

23 "619 Clark Street; N.U.'s Day of Decision."

24 The term "leader" is fraught with complexity. While most people consider Ogletree and Turner to be the primary leaders of the takeover, they both emphasized that the takeover was a team effort. Everyone involved played a critical role and no contribution was more significant than any other, a point that Ogletree and Turner reiterated in my interviews with them.

25 Martha Biondi, *The Black Revolution on Campus* (Berkeley: University of California Press, 2012), 84. Bracey, who already knew Jeff Kamen, called Kamen the night before the takeover, telling him that if he came to Evanston the next morning, he'd have an "exclusive" story. Kamen arrived in Evanston at an agreed upon location and waited for Bracey's call. It was then that Bracey told Kamen where they were and what they were doing. Bracey, phone conversation with the author, August 9, 2018. WCFL radio was created by Chicago's Federation of Labor in 1926 and "designed to serve the labor movement and working-class communities." It ceased operations in 1987. Nathan Godfried, "WCFL," *Encyclopedia of Chicago*, http://www.encyclopedia.chicagohistory.org/pages/1331.html.

26 Turner, interview with the author, 2012.

27 Turner, interview with the author, 2012.

28 Robert Cross, "James Turner: The Face of Black Power at Northwestern," *Chicago Tribune,* July 14, 1968.

29 Turner, interview with the author, 2012.

30 John H. Bracey, Jr., "Living the Legacy-From Protest to Progress," panel discussion about the 1968 takeover, held at Northwestern University, May 3, 2018.

31 Hinz, interview with the author, September 2012. Administrators and faculty members present at the meeting were: Payson S. Wild, William S. Kerr, Franklin M. Kreml, Roland J. Hinz, Arthur T. Schmehling, Controller and Assistant Business Manager, Robert H. Strotz, Dean of the College of Arts and Humanities, William I. Ihlanfeldt, Director of Admissions and Financial Aid, Walter Wallace, Associate Professor of Sociology, Gail M. Inlow, Professor of Education and Chairman of the General Faculty Committee, Joe Park, Professor of Education and Chairman of the Faculty Committee on Educational Policies, and Lucius P. Gregg, Jr., Research Coordinator and Associate Dean of Sciences. J. Roscoe Miller to the board of trustees, "Summary Statement Regarding the Basic Issues Involved in the Negro Student Incident of May 3-4, 1968," Kreml papers, NUA.

32 Biondi, *The Black Revolution on Campus,* 87.

33 Miller, "Summary Statement." Miller's statement was also included in "A

Letter to Northwestern," which was sent out to all students, alumni, faculty, and staff following the takeover.

34 Miller, "Summary Statement."

35 FBI, "Racial Tensions, Northwestern University Campus, Evanston, Illinois," May 8, 1968.

36 FBI, "Racial Tensions."

37 Miller, "Summary Statement."

38 Many of the students who took part in the takeover, as well as several faculty members and administrators, were identified in FBI reports on the takeover. Along with Ogletree, Turner, Bracey, and other students, Jack Hinz, Payson Wild, Gail Inlow, and Robert Strotz were also listed in the report. FBI, "Racial Tensions, Northwestern University Campus, Evanston, Illinois," May 8, 1968.

39 "Students Seize N. U. Offices," *Chicago Tribune,* May 4, 1968.

40 Bracey, phone conversation with the author, August 9, 2018.

41 Lerone Bennett, Jr., "Confrontation on the Campus," *Ebony*, May 1968, 27. The "revolution" would expand and, by 1969, there were a reported total of 232 protests led by Black students on campuses across the country. *The Report of the President's Commission on Campus Unrest,* 109. Lerone Bennett, Jr. (1928-2018) was an influential journalist and scholar. He wrote for *Jet Magazine* and *Ebony*, where he later became executive editor. He was the author of many books, including the seminal, *Before the Mayflower: A History of Black America, 1619-1962* (1963). After the takeover, he would teach courses at Northwestern and eventually serve as the first chair of Northwestern's African American Studies department.

42 Miller, "Summary Statement."

43 "Timeline of Events," "1968: Columbia in Crisis," Columbia University Libraries, https://exhibitions.library.columbia.edu/exhibits/show/1968/timeline; Robert D. McFadden, "Remembering Columbia, 1968," *New York Times,* April 25, 2008. Three months prior to the Northwestern takeover, a disaster befell the college world. On February 8, 1968, during a protest of 200 students on the adjoining campuses of two Historically Black Colleges, South Carolina State College (now University) and Claflin College (now Claflin University), three students were killed and twenty-seven injured when South Carolina Highway Patrol officers opened fire on the students. The "Orangeburg Massacre," as it came to be known, was not extensively covered by the media at the time.

44 "1968: Columbia in Crisis," Columbia University Libraries.

45 Quoted in Wilber W. Caldwell, *1968: Dreams of Revolution* (New York: Algora Publishing, 2009), 60.

46 "Negroes Protest at Northwestern," *New York Times,* May 4, 1968.

47-51 Miller, "Summary Statement."

52 Kathy Kelly, "$52,000: It's For New Campus Cops," *Daily Northwestern,* January 5, 1968. In January 1968, Northwestern's security force consisted of eight patrolmen and two supervisors. Increased funds were then allocated to expand the number of officers.

53 J. Roscoe Miller, minutes, meeting of the board of trustees, May 9, 1968, quoted in Harold F. Williamson and Payson S. Wild, *Northwestern University, A History:1850-1975* (Evanston, IL: Northwestern University, 1976), 334.

54 Payson S. Wild, "Memorandum concerning the black student seizure of the University business office, 619 Clark Street on the morning of May 3, 1968," June 30, 1987, in "University Memos and Reports: Incident May 3-4, 1968," box 2, folder 9, Kreml papers, NUA.

55 Hinz, interviews with the author, 2012, and April 4, 2018.

Notes to Chapter 2

1 As cited above, I use the term "negro" in original context only, i.e. quoting directly from primary sources.

2 Vernon Ford, "The Black Athlete at a White University," *Daily Northwestern,* April 25, 1968. Originally from Chicago and a graduate of John Marshall High School, Ford came to Northwestern on a basketball scholarship, graduating with a BA in 1968. In 1971, he earned an MA in sociology from Northwestern and went on to earn his law degree from the University of California, Berkeley. He later worked as an attorney and as a housing consultant for the city of Chicago. "Attention Sociology Majors," *Daily Northwestern,* April 30, 1986; Vernon Ford, "Black Senior Looks Back," *Daily Northwestern,* April 23, 1968.

3 Editorial, reprinted in "Score Northwestern Officials for Attitude on Race Students," *Pittsburgh Courier,* December 26, 1936.

4 Numbers are drawn from Northwestern's website on the history of the takeover. "Meet the Participants," http://sites.northwestern.edu/bursars1968/participants/.

5 Roger Ward, who participated in the takeover, was a 1964 graduate of Evanston Township High School. He entered Northwestern in 1964. A talented athlete, he played on the football team and was a member of the wrestling squad. "Sophs Boost Grapplers' Hopes," *Daily Northwestern,* February 16, 1966. According to John Bracey, at least one other takeover participant also hailed from Evanston.

6 In 1968, a total of 6,400 undergraduates and 2,500 part-time and graduate students were enrolled at Northwestern. Williamson and Wild, *Northwestern University, A History:1850-1975*, 329; J. Roscoe Miller to the board of trustees, "Summary Statement Regarding the Basic Issues Involved in the Negro Student Incident of May 3-4, 1968;" "Students Seize N. U. Offices," *Chicago Tribune,* May 4, 1968.

7 Hinz, interview with the author, April 4, 2018.

8 [James] Jim P. Pitts, "Growth of Black Consciousness at Northwestern," ND, 2. See also: James P. Pitts, "The Politicalization of Black Students: Northwestern University," *Journal of Black Studies,* vol. 5, no. 3, 1975. Pitts' work is invaluable. He took part in the 1968 takeover. He came to Northwestern on a basketball scholarship as an undergraduate, graduating with a BA in 1966. He went on to do graduate work in sociology at Northwestern, earning an MA and a PhD. He was a graduate student and lecturer in sociology at Northwestern during the period surrounding the takeover. In 1968, Pitts undertook a sociological study of Black students' experiences at Northwestern and conducted research before, during, and after the events described here. He described himself as an "active participant in activities and was a member in both the AASU and FMO." Pitts, "The Politicalization of Black Students," 317. His dissertation, *A Case Study: Analysis of Black High School Students-A Generation of Change* (1971), focused on students at Chicago's Marshall High School, Pitts' alma mater. Pitts later became a tenured professor at Northwestern, where he taught for fourteen years. Later, he served as Academic Dean at Ohio Wesleyan University. In 1996, he went to UNC Asheville, where he became vice chancellor for academic affairs. Moe White, "Jim Pitts," *The Urban News,* June 13, 2013.

9 Hinz, interview with the author, 2012; Human Relations Foundation

of Chicago, "A Study of the Racial and Ethnic Climate for Undergraduates at Northwestern University, 1995-1996," in Northwestern University, "Final Report: The Black Student Experience Task Force," Summer 2016, 93.

10 In 1914, the *Daily Northwestern* reported that one percent of students enrolled in the College of Liberal Arts were Jewish; three percent were Catholic. "Methodists in Lead," *Daily Northwestern,* February 17, 1914.

11 Hinz, interview with the author, 2012. Historically, Black people were not the only people discriminated against at the university. But for purposes of focus, this book does not explore the experiences of other students, such as Latinx, Muslim, Asian-American, and Jewish students. Female students were also subjected to unequal treatment and were completely barred from admission during the school's first fifteen years. Over the years, many non-Protestant and non-white students would find the campus to be a less than welcoming place. One of the more notable stories to illustrate this point took place in the fall of 1956, when Northwestern's chapter of Psi Upsilon fraternity made headlines across the U.S. after an invitation to a first-year student, nineteen-year-old Sherman Wu, was withdrawn upon the objection of some fraternity members. As one fraternity member said: "Having an Oriental in the house would degrade [the fraternity] in the eyes of other fraternities and make it more difficult to get dates from the sororities." Wu, an Evanston resident, wrote in the *Daily Northwestern* that he was told, "I would degrade their house because I am a Chinese." "N.U. Fraternity Outs Wu's Son Because of His Race," *Chicago Tribune,* October 31, 1956. Sherman Hsiu Huang Wu (1937-2010) would join a different fraternity. He earned a BA, MA, and PhD from Northwestern. He went on to work on the Apollo lunar missions and served as a professor of electrical engineering at Marquette University for twenty-seven years. Wu's father, K.C. Wu (1903-1984) was a Nationalist Chinese official and served as the mayor of Shanghai and governor of Taiwan. He earned a PhD from Princeton in 1926. In 1954, he immigrated with his family to the United States after accusing the Chinese government of undemocratic practices. After his father and other family members left China, young Sherman was left behind, having been arrested by government officials. He would later be released and joined his family in their home in Evanston. He chose his American name "Sherman" after Sherman Avenue in Evanston. "Dr. K.C. Wu Is Dead; Kuomintang Leader Left Chiang in 1954," *New York Times,* June 7, 1984; Andrew Meacham, "A Reluctant Civil Rights Icon: After Being Subject of a Pete Seeger Song, He Became a Rocket Scientist," *St. Petersburg Times,* May 2010. Although the story of Wu's rejection by the fraternity prompted outrage and condemnation from various entities, Northwestern officials did nothing to address the issue at the time. "The fraternity is a student organization which has its own rules," said James McLeod after refusing numerous times to make a statement on the matter. "N.U. Students Rip Fraternity on Wu Ouster," *Chicago Tribune,* November 1, 1956. Folk singer Pete Seeger *did* do something: In 1958, he wrote and recorded the song, "The Ballad of Sherman Wu."

12 Jon Marshall, "Keeping the Faith," *Northwestern Magazine,* Summer 2002, https://www.northwestern.edu/magazine/northwestern/summer2002/features/

coverstory/index.htm.

13 The city of Evanston was "dry" for many decades. It wasn't until 1972 that the Evanston City Council voted to allow Evanston's hotels and restaurants to serve alcohol.

14 By 1940, the Black community in Evanston was one of the largest in the Midwest, with 6,026 Black residents out of a total population of 64,000. Andrew Wiese, "Black Housing, White Finance: African American Housing and Home Ownership in Evanston, Illinois, Before 1940," *Journal of Social History* 33, no. 2 (1999), http://www.questia.com/read/1G1-58675453/black-housing-white-finance-african-american-housing.

15 Sherman Beverly, Jr., *Edwin B. Jourdain, Jr.: The Rise of Black Political Power in Evanston, Illinois, 1931-1947* (Np: Shorefront Press: 2017), 10.

16 Andrew Wiese, *Places of Their Own: African American Suburbanization in the Twentieth Century* (Chicago: University of Chicago Press, 2004), 63.

17 Editorial, reprinted in "Score Northwestern Officials for Attitude on Race Students," *Pittsburgh Courier*, December 26, 1936.

18 E[dwin] B. Jourdain, Jr. to W.E.B. Du Bois, February 17, 1939, W. E. B. Du Bois Papers (MS 312) Special Collections and University Archives, University of Massachusetts Amherst Libraries, http://credo.library.umass.edu/view/full/mums312-b088-i365.

19 George W. Williams, *Conversations with Blacks in Evanston: An Evaluation of African-American Progress in this Suburb of Chicago* (Baltimore, MD: American Literary Press, Inc., 1998), 53.

20 Thomas Lord, the country club's president, announced that the dance could not be held at the club if Black students were allowed to attend. "Cancel Evanston H.S. Prom Because of Negro Dispute," *Chicago Tribune*, June 8, 1929.

21 Turner, interview with the author, 2012.

22 Pitts, "Growth of Black Consciousness," 1.

23 There exists a "de jure/de facto distinction" regarding segregation. De jure segregation, or statutory segregation, refers to segregation practices governed by laws and policies. De facto segregation is practiced by "private choice." Erica Frankenberg and Kendra Taylor, "De Facto Segregation: Tracing a Legal Basis for Contemporary Inequality," *Journal of Law and Education* 47, no. 2 (Spring 2018), http://www.questia.com/read/1P4-2041728504/de-facto-segregation-tracing-a-legal-basis-for-contemporary.

24 The small number of Black students at Northwestern reflects the small percentage of Americans who attended college overall at this time, but it also reflects the institutional attitude toward integrated education. At the time, college and university officials varied in the ways they invited, supported, and encouraged the admission of Black students. There were also vast differences among colleges and universities concerning admission policies. Some, such as Oberlin College, for example, were early supporters of integrated education, while others were segregated and/or restrictive. The differences also varied regionally. Some reasons behind the absence or low numbers of Black students in many Northern universities and colleges which did not ban outright Black student enrollment are illustrated in the seminal study of Black students in colleges and universities: W.E.B. Du Bois, ed., *The College-Bred Negro: Report of a Social Study Made Under the Direction of Atlanta University* (Atlanta: Atlanta University Press, 1900).

25 Untitled document, [Students' Final List of Demands], nd [1968], Records of the Bursar's Office Takeover, May 1968, 2, box 1, folder 3, NUA.

Hereafter referred to as Final Demands, 1968.

26 Based on the definition of a segregated school as having at least eighty percent of its students with a "particular racial composition." Jeffrey A. Raffel, *Historical Dictionary of School Segregation and Desegregation: The American Experience* (Westport, CT: Greenwood Press, 1998), 130. Of course, many schools and universities throughout the South were strictly segregated. But it is important to note how many in the North were also segregated according to custom, rather than law. Northwestern can also be defined as a "predominantly white institution," or PWI, identified as an institution in which white students account for at least fifty percent of students. While the term "traditionally white institution" also exists, education Professor Brian Bourke argues that such a term suggests that "the predominance of whiteness is simply a product of a slow, almost accidental progression over time and not a product of favoring and producing whiteness as the norm while further subjugating people of color." Brian Bourke, "Meaning and Implications of Being Labeled a Predominantly White Institution," *College and University* 91, no. 3 (2016). A good example of how colleges and universities discouraged Black students and others from attending is found in Edwin Emery Slosson's *Great American Universities* (New York: The MacMillan Co., 1910). "Nothing is said in the catalogue," Slosson wrote in his evaluation of Princeton University in relation to Black student enrollment, "but I think I am safe in saying that if a Negro . . . should present himself for entrance he would be so strongly advised to go elsewhere that he would go." (Slosson, 104-105). For more on the evolution of restrictive admissions policies see: Marcia Graham Synnott , *A Social History of Admissions Policies at Harvard, Yale, and Princeton, 1900-1930,* Dissertation, University of Massachusetts – Amherst, 1974.

27 In 1918, the *Daily Northwestern* reported that of the 1,366 students enrolled in the College of Liberal Arts, fifty-four were Catholic and six were Jewish (five male students and one female student). "Methodists Have Big Grand Slam," *Daily Northwestern,* March 21, 1918. In 1914, the university registrar's office "made public" the figures on the religions of all students registered in the College of Liberal Arts: A total of forty-one percent of students were Methodist, thirteen percent Presbyterian, nine percent Congregational, seven percent Episcopalian, four percent Baptist, three percent Roman Catholic, three percent Lutheran, two percent Christian Science, one percent Christian, one percent Evangelical, and one percent Jewish. Seven percent reported "no affiliation" and another eight percent were categorized as "scattering." "Methodists in Lead," *Daily Northwestern,* February 17, 1914.

28 Northwestern University, *The Syllabus,* 1933, 391; "History of Hillel," Hillel International, https://www.hillel.org/about/hillel-story; "Sheil to Inaugurate Catholic Student Club," *Daily Northwestern,* September 26, 1939.

29 It should be noted that identifying Black students is complicated since some students "kept their racial identities a secret" and "surreptitiously graduated from all-white segregated schools." Robert Bruce Slater, "The Blacks Who First Entered the World of White Higher Education," *The Journal of Blacks in Higher Education,* No. 4 (Summer, 1994): 47. For example, Anita Florence Hemmings received her diploma from all-white Vassar College in 1897, having concealed her

identity as a Black woman for all four years she was enrolled. It was only after she graduated that her secret was discovered. Vassar was desegregated four decades after Hemmings graduated. Olivia Mancini, "Passing as White: Anita Hemmings, 1897," *Vassar Alumnae/i Quarterly* (Winter 2001), https://vq.vassar.edu/issues/2002/01/features/passing-as-white.html.

30 Taylor's graduating class included fifty men and forty-nine women. "Negro to Receive a Degree," *Chicago Tribune,* June 3, 1903; Northwestern University, *Alumni Record of the College of Liberal Arts, 1903* (Evanston, IL: Northwestern University, 1903), 363; *Bulletin of Northwestern University* (Evanston-Chicago: Northwestern University, 1903), 299. (See below for more on Taylor.) A small number of Black students attended Northwestern prior to 1903. The first Black student to enroll at Northwestern was John Jacob Astor Goode (1861-1901). Goode was from Xenia, Ohio. In 1880, he graduated from Evanston Village High School (which later merged with the Evanston Township High School). He attended Northwestern from 1882 until 1885. He later moved to Washington, D.C. and eventually earned his L.L.B. (Bachelor of Laws) degree from Howard University in 1888. William Grant Webster, ed., *The Evanston Village High School (*Chicago: Press of S.D. Childs and Co., 1907), 60; Alumni File, John Jacob Astor Goode, Northwestern University Archives. It should be noted that Northwestern's Evanston campus is separate from Northwestern's law school, as well as its commerce, dental, and medical schools, which are located in downtown Chicago. In the late nineteenth and early twentieth centuries, there were a handful of Black students who attended those schools. In 1878, noted journalist, lawyer, and activist (as well as the husband of Ida B. Wells) Ferdinand Lee Barnett (1858-1936) earned a law degree at Union College of Law, an institution affiliated with Northwestern and Chicago University. "Barnett, Ferdinand Lee," Blackpast.org. https://blackpast.org/aah/barnett-ferdinand-lee-1864-1932. In 1883, Daniel Hale Williams (1856-1931), who performed one of the world's first successful open-heart surgeries, earned a medical degree at Chicago Medical College, an institution affiliated with Northwestern. "Williams, Daniel Hale," Blackpast.org. https://blackpast.org/aah/williams-daniel-hale-1856-1931. In 1895, Emma Ann Reynolds (1862-1917) became the first Black woman to graduate with an MD degree from Chicago Medical College. "History- Emma Reynolds," The Provident Foundation, http: //provfound.org/index.php/history/history-emma-reynolds. Other prominent law school graduates were Graham T. Perry (1894–1960), a 1923 graduate, who later served as assistant attorney general for Illinois, and noted civil rights lawyer and scholar, James Madison Nabrit, Jr., (1900-1997) who received his law degree in 1927. Nabrit was a graduate of Morehouse College. He went on to teach law at Howard University and later served as president of Howard from 1960 to 1969. Nabrit worked for the NAACP's Legal Defense and Education Fund. He was a lead counsel in the landmark case, *Bolling v. Sharpe.* In 1966, he was appointed a U.S. deputy ambassador to the United Nations. "James Madison Nabrit, Jr.," Howard University School of Law, https://web.archive.org/web/20150905130830/http://www.law.howard.edu/1113; "History," Northwestern University Pritzker School of Law, http://www.law.northwestern.edu/about/history/; Jeffrey A. Raffel, *Historical Dictionary of School Segregation and Desegregation: The American Experience* (Westport, CT: Greenwood Press, 1998), 177-178. Among Northwestern's later law school graduates

were several prominent leaders, including Harold Washington (1922-1987), a 1952 graduate who was later elected Chicago's first Black mayor. As far as the Evanston campus, there may well have been at least one Black student who graduated from Northwestern earlier than 1903. In the seminal study, *The College-Bred Negro*, a single Black graduate (unnamed) was credited to Northwestern during the period of 1885-1890. Du Bois, ed., *The College-Bred Negro*, 38.

31 Naomi Willie Pollard Dobson (1884-?) was one of eight children. Her father, John William Pollard (1846-1932), was born in Culpepper County, Virginia. Her mother, Catherine Amanda Hughes, (1856-1937), was from Kentucky. John Pollard's grandparents and parents were free Black farmers in Virginia. Their enslaved ancestors had been manumitted at the end of the American Revolution. Naomi Pollard was born in Missouri and attended Lincoln High School in East St. Louis. After graduating from Northwestern in 1905, she worked as a public school teacher. She later attended the University of Chicago for a year, took a Library Training Course, and joined the staff at the Chicago Public Library from 1911-1914. Chicago Public Library, "Proceedings of the Board of Directors of the Chicago Public Library, 1914-1916," 213, 226. In 1914, she joined the staff at Wilberforce University, serving as a librarian and as an instructor in library economy. Founded in 1856, Wilberforce was the first private Historically Black University in the United States. *Wilberforce University Catalogue, 1915-1916* (Wilberforce OH: Wilberforce University, 1916), 11, 15. In 1916, she married Richard Dobson, a medical doctor, and the couple moved to Sioux City, Iowa. Illinois, Cook County Marriages, 1871–1920, September 17, 1916, retrieved from Ancestry.com. Her parents were profoundly invested in providing higher education for their children. Her father had dreamed of becoming a lawyer and wished to attend Oberlin College. After serving in the 83rd U.S. Infantry (from Kansas) during the American Civil War, he was intent on attending college but contracted smallpox and was unable to pursue his studies. He eventually set up his own barbershop. In 1886, he moved his family from Missouri to Chicago's Rogers Park neighborhood, becoming the first Black family to live in their neighborhood. Two of Dobson's siblings attended Brown University, another attended Dartmouth, and several became star athletes, including her brother, Frederick Douglass "Fritz" Pollard (1894-1986), who, in 1920, along with Bobby Marshall, became one of the first Black players in the NFL and later the first Black head coach in the NFL, among other accomplishments. "Pollard Ranked as Best Half of the Season," *Xenia Daily Gazette,* November 16, 1915; Afia Ohemena, "The Forgotten Pollards," Rogers Park/West Ridge Historical Society, July 28, 2014, https://rpwrhs.org/2014/07/28/the-forgotten-pollards/; U.S. Census, 1910, Cook, Illinois, retrieved from Ancestry.com; John M. Carroll, *Fritz Pollard: Pioneer in Racial Advancement* (Urbana, IL: University of Illinois Press, 1992), 10.

32 In the 1820s, the first known Black Americans to graduate from college earned their degrees: Lucius Twilight (Middlebury College, 1823), Edward Jones (Amherst College, 1826), and John Russwurm (Bowdoin College, 1826). Prior to the end of the American Civil War, a total of approximately forty Black students graduated from American colleges and universities. Northwestern University was not alone in enrolling a small number of Black students. Until the 1950s and 1960s, many other colleges and universities barred Black students entirely from enrolling at

their institutions. In reaction, Historically Black Colleges and Universities (HBCUs) were founded beginning in 1837 with Cheyney University in Pennsylvania, followed by Wilberforce University in Ohio (1843), and Lincoln University in Pennsylvania (1854). The vast majority of HBCUs were founded between 1865-1899, and ninety percent of the schools were located in the South, where Black people were almost universally barred from white institutions. Cynthia L. Jackson and Eleanor F. Nunn, ed., *Historically Black Colleges and Universities: A Reference Handbook* (Santa Barbara, CA: ABC-CLIO, 2003), 2-3.

33 Pitts, "Growth of Black Consciousness," 2.

34 See Joe R. Feagin, Hernan Vera, and Nikitah Imani, *The Agony of Education: Black Students at White Colleges and Universities* (New York: Routledge, 1996).

35 James R. Mingle, "The Opening of White Colleges and Universities to Black Students," in *Black Students in Higher Education: Conditions and Experiences in the 1970s*, Gail E. Thomas, ed. (Westport, CT: Greenwood Press, 1981), 21. While there was a steady rise in the number of Black students enrolled at Northern institutions, by 1920, a total of just one hundred Black students would graduate from universities and colleges in the North. M.G. Allison, "The Year in Negro Education," *The Crisis,* July 1920, 126.

36 John M. Carroll, *Fritz Pollard*, 1992, 10.

37 "Harris Favors Separate Schools for the Negroes," *Chicago Tribune,* November 11, 1906. Abram Winegardner Harris (1858 –1935) was the university's fourteenth president, a position he held from 1906 to 1916. In the 1900 study, *The College-Bred Negro*, it was noted that even in largely or exclusively white schools, there were rarely written policies barring Black students.

38 "'Y' Campaigns Against Negro Athletic Bans," *Daily Northwestern*, March 10, 1938.

39 "Dawn of an Era: Pursuit of Prejudice," *Daily Northwestern,* December 1, 1937; "State-Wide Battle on Illinois Jim Crow," *The Crisis*, February 1937, 61. Although there had been a small number of Black players on Northwestern sports teams prior to 1900, the university, like all other predominantly white colleges and universities in the U.S., maintained largely all-white sports teams until roughly 1947. A few Black students played on Northwestern's football team in the 1930s, and Northwestern's first Black football player was George Henry Jewett (1870-1908), a student in Northwestern's medical school who transferred from the University of Michigan (where he also played football) in 1893. After earning his medical degree, Jewett practiced medicine in Chicago. Lane Demas, *Integrating the Gridiron: Black Civil Rights and American College Football* (New Brunswick, NJ: Rutgers University Press, 2010), 7.

40 John H. Wigmore, letter to the editor, *Daily Northwestern,* April 3, 1914.

41 "State-Wide Battle on Illinois Jim Crow," *The Crisis*, February 1937, 61.

42 *An Introduction to Northwestern* (Evanston, IL: Northwestern University, 1946), 7.

43 "In Loco Parentis," Legal Dictionary in The Free Dictionary, https://legal-dictionary.thefreedictionary.com/in+loco+parentis.

44 Arthur Herbert Wilde, ed. *Northwestern University: A History, 1855-1905*, Volume 1 (New York: The University Publishing Society, 1905), 165, 201.

45 Northwestern University, *Annual Catalogue, 1891-1892* (Chicago: Thayer

and Jackson, 1892); Northwestern University; *Annual Catalogue, 1903-1905* (Evanston: Northwestern University, 1904), 86.

46 Northwestern University, *Annual Catalogue, 1900-1901* (Evanston: Northwestern University, 1901), 214.

47 Wiese, *Places of Their Own*, 63. Decades later, another Northwestern student, William Yancy Bell, Jr., secured housing in a university dormitory. (See below).

48 "Score Northwestern Officials for Attitude on Race Students," *Pittsburgh Courier*, December 26, 1936.

49 Sterling and Lowery, *Voices and Visions*, loc. 1625-1630, Kindle.

50 P.J. Hauser, letter to the editor, "Information Given," *Daily Northwestern*, April 7, 1938. The Emerson Y opened in 1914 and closed in 1969, a few years after Evanston's other YMCA branch on Grove Street was integrated. The building was demolished in 1980. Until 1963, Evanston's YMCA on Grove Street did not allow Black members. In the 1950s, members of the white YMCA hosted a fundraising event, known as the "Aunt Jemima" breakfast and one of its meeting rooms was decorated with a painting depicting enslaved people working in a field. That room was known as the "plantation room" (which until recently was known as the "plant room.") Dirk Johnson, "Now Recorded on Film, Memories of 'the Black Y' Provoke Smiles and Tears," *New York Times*, July 7, 2010; "We've Come a Mighty Long Way," January 10, 2017, McGaw YMCA, http://www.mcgawymca.org/blog/weve-come-a-mighty-long-way/.

51 "Refuse Consideration of Negro-White Dorm," *Daily Northwestern*, May 2, 1939.

52 "Race Prejudice in Illinois," *Richmond Times-Dispatch*, September 23, 1903.

53 Peter Christian Lutkin (1858-1931) had a long career and major impact on the music school at Northwestern. Aside from serving as dean, he also served as a music professor and director of Northwestern's choirs. "Peter C. Lutkin," Library of Congress, https://www.loc.gov/item/ihas.200185357/.

54 "Bar Colored Co-Eds," *The Inter-Ocean*, September 15, 1902.

55 "Colored Student at Northwestern," *The Inter-Ocean*, October 19, 1901.

56 "Race Line Drawn in Co-Eds' Halls," *The Inter-Ocean*, September 15, 1902.

57 Based on a 1900 U.S. Census listing an Ellis family in San Antonio, Texas, with a daughter, Isabella, born December 1878, and newspaper accounts, her name was in fact, Isabella (known as "Belle.") In 1898, before enrolling at Northwestern, she attended Wiley University (now Wiley College), an HBCU in Marshall, Texas. *Yearbook of Wiley University, 1901-1902* (Marshall, TX: Wiley Print, 1902), 61. The life history of her older brother, William Ellis, who became a wealthy banker and who passed as a Mexican, Cuban, and indigenous Hawaiian, is told in Karl Jacoby's *The Strange Career of William Ellis: The Texas Slave Who Became a Mexican Millionaire* (New York: Norton, 2016).

58 "Negro Coed at Evanston Drops Effort to Return," *Chicago Tribune*, November 4, 1902; "Negro Coeds May Fight," *Chicago Tribune*, September 16, 1902.

59 "Negro Coeds May Fight," *Chicago Tribune*.

60 "Negro Coeds May Fight," *Chicago Tribune*.

61 "Negro Co-Ed is the Cause of Wrangle," *The Inter-Ocean*, September 16, 1902. Edmund Janes James (1855-1925) had only been president of Northwestern for six months when he made this statement. He would serve as president until 1904

when he left to become president of the University of Illinois. "The Presidents of Northwestern: Edmund Janes James," Northwestern University Archives, http://exhibits.library.northwestern.edu/archives/exhibits/presidents/james.html.

62 "Negro Coeds May Fight," *Chicago Tribune.*

63 "Negro Coed at Evanston Drops Effort to Return," *Chicago Tribune,* November 4, 1902.

64 "Colored Co-eds Are Barred Out," *The Leavenworth Times,* September 16, 1902; Quoted in "Touching Varied Topics," *The Inter-Ocean,* September 27, 1902.

65 "Race Line Drawn in Co-Eds' Halls," *The Inter-Ocean,* September 15, 1902.

66 "Bar Colored Co-Eds," *The Inter-Ocean,* September 15, 1902.

67 "Bar Colored Co-Eds," *The Inter-Ocean*; "Race Line Drawn in Co-Eds' Halls," *The Inter-Ocean.*

68 "Two Negro Students Enter Northwestern and There is Consternation," *Decatur Daily Review,* September 27, 1903. John Porcius Faulkner (1880-?) was born in Paducah, KY, moving at some later date to Glencoe, Illinois. He later became professor of mathematics at Walden University in Nashville, TN. "Marriages," *The American Journal of Nursing,* Volume 9, 1909, 377. Later, he returned to Chicago and worked as an inspector for the Board of Health. "John Porcius Faulkner," U.S. Draft Registration Card, 1942, Records of the Selective Service System, World War II Draft Cards (Fourth Registration) for the State of Illinois; U.S. Census, 1930, Chicago, Cook, Illinois, retrieved from Ancestry.com.

69 "Two Negro Students Enter Northwestern and There is Consternation."

70 "Two Negro Students Enter Northwestern and There is Consternation."

71 "Two Negro Students Enter Northwestern and There is Consternation."

72 "Negro Students Cast Out," *Palatine Enterprise,* September 26, 1903.

73 "Students Ignore Color Line," *The Inter-Ocean,* June 16, 1903.

74 "Negro Students Cast Out."

75 "Negro Students Cast Out;" Edward F. Younger, "Mrs. Gordon of Savannah, Chief Guest at Chicago," *Atlanta Constitution,* September 20, 1903.

76 Quoted in Dennis Hevesi, "Kay Davis, Coloratura, Soared in Wordless Songs, Dies at 91," *New York Times,* February 22, 2012.

77 "Negro to Receive a Degree," *Chicago Tribune,* June 3, 1903. Lawyer Taylor (1865-1941) was born in Louisville, KY. Before coming to Evanston, he taught school in Austin, TX. *Austin, Texas Directory, 1887-88* (Austin, TX: Morrison and Fourmy, 1888), np. By 1899, he was living in Evanston and attending Northwestern Academy, the preparatory school for the university. After graduating from Northwestern, Taylor was appointed professor of mathematics and physics at Clark University (now Clark Atlanta University) in Atlanta. "Evanston News and Notes," *The Inter-Ocean,* September 28, 1899; *Clark University Register,* 1909-1910; Robert Bruce Slater, "The Blacks Who First Entered the World of White Higher Education ," *The Journal of Blacks in Higher Education* No. 4 (Summer, 1994): 53. Taylor is buried in Woodard Cemetery in Walker Mill, GA. "Lawyer Taylor," *U.S., Find A Grave Index, https://www.findagrave.com/memorial/110210627/lawyer-taylor.* In 2008, Northwestern University named a professorship in Taylor's honor. Galen V. Bodenhausen, professor of psychology and marketing, was the first Lawyer Taylor professor. Pat Vaughan Tremmel, "Bodenhausen Named Lawyer Taylor Professor at Northwestern," September 9,

2008, Northwestern University, News, https://www.northwestern.edu/newscenter/stories/2008/09/bodenhausen.html.

78 "Negro Graduate Cheered by Northwestern Students," *Chicago Tribune,* June 16, 1903.

79 Wendy Leopold, "Former Evanston Mayor Donates Papers to Northwestern," *Northwestern Now,* June 12, 2014, https://news.northwestern.edu/stories/2014/06/former-evanston-mayor-donates-papers-to-northwestern/.

80 "Refuse Consideration of Negro-White Dorm," *Daily Northwestern,* May 2, 1939.

81 "Negro Orator Wins," *The Inter-Ocean, January* 30, 1904; "Negro Student Wins Honor," *Chicago Tribune,* January 20, 1904.

82 Scholars Michael H. Washington and Cheryl L. Nunez observe: "In light of the dearth of black students on northern campuses, the fraternities, like the institutions that housed them, had little need for explicit policies of exclusion; nevertheless, a survey administered in the mid-1920s by the National Interfraternity Conference found that of fifty fraternities, more than half had membership restrictions that excluded blacks." Michael H. Washington and Cheryl L. Nunez, "Education, Racial Uplift, and the Rise of the Greek-Letter Tradition-The African American Quest for Status in the Early Twentieth Century," in *African American Fraternities and Sororities: The Legacy and the Vision,* Tamara L. Brown, Gregory S. Parks, and Clarenda M. Phillips, ed., 2nd ed. (Lexington, KY: University Press of Kentucky, 2012), 159. See the above book for an excellent exploration of the experiences of Black students in the academy and the rise and development of predominantly Black Greek letter groups as a response to those experiences. The post-World War II history of discrimination in Greek letter groups is well documented in Anthony W. James, "The College Social Fraternity Antidiscrimination Debate, 1945-1949," *The Historian* 62, no. 2 (2000). James documents the fact that many fraternities had no explicit rules barring Black members, but enforced unwritten codes regarding membership restriction and discrimination. By 1962, fraternities at Northwestern had achieved what James Pitts referred to as "token desegregation." Between 1962 and 1966, a total of eight Black students joined three formerly-all white fraternities. Pitts, "Growth of Black Consciousness at Northwestern," 3. In 1967, when integration efforts were underway in the entire university, a small number (about seven) of the all-white fraternities and sororities on campus offered membership to a handful of Black students. Three of the groups were historically Jewish organizations. For example, Herman Cage, who would later co-found FMO and participate in the takeover, was a member of Tau Delta Phi, a historically Jewish fraternity. By 1968, five of the twenty-nine fraternities on campus reported having Black members. "Report of the CUL Subcommittee on Negro Fraternities and Sororities," April 10, 1968, 3, Dean of Students, R. Hinz, 1968-1969, box 49, folder 1, Miller papers, NUA.

83 In 1961 Northwestern's Interfraternitiy Council voted to exclude all member organizations with discriminatory clauses in their charters by 1963. Sigma Chi, Alpha Tau Omega, and Sigma Nu fraternities were each "forced to remove these clauses." "Retrospective: What Difference 10 Years Make," *Daily Northwestern,* December 10, 1969.

84 "Negro Orator Wins."

85 Carolyn J. Brown, *Song of My Life: A Biography of Margaret Walker* (Jackson,

MS: University Press of Mississippi, 2014), 19; *Evanston City Directory*, 1920, 322.

86 Quoted in Carolyn J. Brown, *Song of My Life*, 22; "Margaret Walker," The Poetry Foundation. https://www.poetryfoundation.org/poets/margaret-walker.

87 Carolyn J. Brown, *Song of My Life*; "Margaret Walker Center," http://www.jsums.edu/margaretwalkercenter/; Marcia Greenlee, "Black Women and Oral History: Margaret Walker Alexander," 37.

88 Lillian Bell, "The Quibblers Club," *Purple Parrot*, April 1945, 12.

89 In 1939, the Quibblers Club opened its membership to all interested in joining. "Quibblers Chartered," *Daily Northwestern*, May 3, 1939; "Quibblers Announce Policy, Officers," *Daily Northwestern*, October 18, 1939; Minutes, Board of Supervision of Student Activities, October 13, 1930, 1, Student Activities Collection, NUA.

90 "Quibblers Sponsor Negro Week Exhibit," *Daily Northwestern*, February 13, 1945. The South Side Community Center and the Chicago Public Library loaned the items for the exhibit, including paintings, sculpture, books, and magazines.

91 William C. Pyant (1900-1976) was originally from Georgia. He was a graduate of Ohio State University. While a graduate student at Northwestern, he worked as the Boys' Work Secretary at the Emerson Y. He later worked for the Unemployment Relief Service in Chicago and then as a juvenile probation officer for Cook County. He was active in the civil rights movement and also served as the director of Evanston's NAACP chapter. After graduating from Northwestern, he settled in Evanston with his wife Nettie and daughter. The family lived at 1930 Brown Avenue. "Negro Authors to Lecture Here," *Daily Northwestern*, November 11, 1938; "Alpha Mu Welcomes Several New Brothers," *The Sphinx*, Vol. 17 (February 1930): 27; Alpha Phi Alpha Directory, *The Sphinx*, Vol. 17 (February 1930): np; "The Sphinx Speaks," Vol. 19 (December 1933): 20; "Pyant-Polk" *The Sphinx* Vol. 19 (December 1933): 16; U.S. Census, 1940, Cook, Illinois, retrieved from Ancestry.com; *Evanston City Directory*, 1933, 350, 429.

92 "Discuss Housing Problems on Evanston Forum," *Daily Northwestern*, July 7, 1941.

93 "Five Will Join Interracial Chapter Here," *Daily Northwestern*, October 7, 1949. Kappa Alpha Psi was integrated from its founding at Indiana University in 1911.

94 Quibblers Club members, for example, worked to raise money to help improve the recreational facilities at the Emerson Y. Lillian Bell, "The Quibblers Club," *Purple Parrot*, April 1945, 12.

95 "The Quibblers," Northwestern University, *The Syllabus*, 1947, 103; "Quibblers Announce Policy, Officers," *Daily Northwestern*, October 18, 1939.

96 Lillian Bell, "The Quibblers Club," *Purple Parrot*, April 1945, 12.

97 "Negro Authors to Lecture Here," *Daily Northwestern*, November 11, 1938; Sam Jameson, "King Preached to NU, But Crowds Came Out," *Daily Northwestern*, April 18, 1958; "Boycott Leader Gives Human Relations Talks," *Daily Northwestern*, April 15, 1958. In 1958, Martin Luther King, Jr. delivered two lectures at Northwestern for the university's annual Mars lecture series. King's April 15 speech to an enraptured audience was followed by a standing ovation. Program, "The 1958 Mars Lecture Series," April 1958, Northwestern University Archives. King's lectures were titled, "The Crisis in Human Relations" and "The Christian Answer." The Mars lecture series was funded by a bequest from Gerhard Mars, a Northwestern alumnus and Methodist minister. The series invited speakers to

address the subject of "Progressive Christianity."

98 Jourdain to Dr. Du Bois, no date, W. E. B. Du Bois Papers (MS 312) Special Collections and University Archives, University of Massachusetts Amherst Libraries, http://credo.library.umass.edu/view/full/mums312-b060-i057.

99 "Significant Alpha News," *The Sphinx* Vol. 17 (February 1930): 11. W.E.B. (William Edward Burghart) Du Bois (1868-1963) earned BA degrees at both Fisk University and Harvard University. In 1895, he became the first Black student to earn a PhD at Harvard. He later taught at many universities and published numerous works, including the influential *The Souls of Black Folk* (1903). He was a co-founder of the Niagara Movement, a group dedicated to challenging segregation and discrimination. Du Bois was also a co-founder of the movement's successor, the National Advancement of Colored People (NAACP). From 1909 to 1934, Du Bois was editor of the NAACP's journal, *The Crisis*. In the 1950s, he was investigated by the FBI for his adoption of communist and socialist ideas. In many ways, he became disillusioned with the civil rights movement, and some of its leadership, in particular. In 1961, Du Bois moved to Ghana and gave up his U.S. citizenship. Dwayne Mack, "William Edward Burghardt Du Bois (1868–1963)," *The Black Past,* March 19, 2007, https://www.blackpast.org/african-american-history/dubois-william-edward-burghardt-1868-1963/.

100 Beverly, Jr., *Edwin B. Jourdain, Jr.*, 33, 45; George W. Williams, "Mr. Spencer Jourdain," in *Conversations with Blacks in Evanston, Illinois: An Evaluation of African-American Progress in this Suburb of Chicago* (Baltimore, MD: American Literary Press, Inc., 1998), 241.

101 Jourdain won his seat by 385 votes. The Evanston city council then opened an "inquiry" into the election and alleged that thirty-seven fraudulent votes had been cast in the race. "Professor to Aid Negro Ousted by Council," *Chicago Tribune,* February 4, 1932.

102 Beverly, Jr., *Edwin B. Jourdain, Jr.,* 33; William C. Pyant, "Evanston Reelects Bro. Jourdain," *The Sphinx* (May 1932): 10, 27.

103 Jourdain to Dr. W.E.B. Du Bois, February 17, 1939, W. E. B. Du Bois Papers (MS 312) Special Collections and University Archives, University of Massachusetts Amherst Libraries, http://credo.library.umass.edu/view/full/mums312-b088-i365.

104 Jourdain to Du Bois, Northwestern University student population statistics, ca. June 21, 1932, W. E. B. Du Bois Papers (MS 312) Special Collections and University Archives, University of Massachusetts Amherst Libraries, http://credo.library.umass.edu/view/full/mums312-b191-i225.

105 "Harvard is turning into a Southern institution," wrote Harvard student George McKinnon in 1922. "The colored man is not wanted, and every distinction that can be made to make us drop out is being made." McKinnon was a member of the Nile Club, an organization of Black students at Harvard. He made this statement after three Black students were refused admittance into the dormitories and a growing protest was being mounted against university officials in relation to discriminatory policies on that campus. "Charge Harvard Bars Negro Students from Buildings," *Dallas Express,* July 1, 1922.

106 Rose Jourdain, "Emmaline H. Jourdain: Remembering the Lady," *Shorefront Journal,* October 17, 2006, https://shorefrontjournal.wordpress.com/2016/10/27/

emmaline-h-jourdain-remembering-the-lady/.

107 According to Lynn Weiner, Roosevelt University's historian: "Our first students were black, white, Japanese, World War II veterans, new high school students and refugees. We hired professors who were women, black, Jewish, Latino and Asian, in addition to white men. We had the first integrated Board of Trustees and the first black athletic coach of racially integrated teams." Lynn Weiner, "Celebrating Black History Month: Roosevelt Pioneers," The Social Justice Blog of Roosevelt University, February 11, 2015, https://blogs.roosevelt.edu/socialjustice/2015/02/11/celebrating-black-history-month-roosevelt-pioneers/.

108 Lillian Bell, "The Quibblers Club," *Purple Parrot,* April 1945, 12.

109 By 1924, an interracial discussion group was holding meetings, providing students and faculty with a place to discuss "discriminations concerning inter-racial relations." "Interracial Relations, Discriminations to Be Subject of Discussion," *Daily Northwestern,* January 17, 1924.

110 "Students Will See Negro Life," *Daily Northwestern,* July 10, 1928. Subsequent similar trips were organized.

111 In 1966, the Evanston City Council passed a "voluntary" open housing bill which required realtors to list homes for sale on a "nondiscriminatory basis," unless the homeowner "indicates otherwise." This almost pointless legislation was vetoed by the mayor, John Emery. Lewis Harris, "Reality Firms Approve Skokie Plan," *Chicago Tribune,* July 10, 1966; Charles Mount, " 3 Suburbs Plan Voluntary Open Housing," *Chicago Tribune,* June 27, 1966; Marc Zwelling, "Long, Hot Summer Reaches Evanston," *Daily Northwestern,* September 14, 1967. Prior to that, petitions had been presented at various times over the years and the work to bring such legislation to the city council would be ongoing, led by students, faculty members, and city residents. In June 1958, for example, eighty-five professors signed a petition "affirming open occupancy" in Evanston. Rochelle Stanfield, "Free Housing Backers," *Daily Northwestern,* December 3, 1959. In December 1963, two student committees, the Human Relations Committee and the International Students Committee, collected 1,300 signatures on a petition requesting that the Evanston city council "enact laws forbidding racial discrimination in the rental and sale of housing." "Petitions to Council Carry 1,330 Names," *Chicago Tribune,* December 3, 1963; "NU Students Ask Evanston for Open Occupancy Law," *Daily Northwestern,* November 20, 1963; Virginia Walsh, "HRC Open Occupancy Petition Goes to City Council Monday," *Daily Northwestern,* November 27, 1963. At that time, Obi Wali (1932-1993) a graduate student from Nigeria, and John Attico, a graduate student from Ghana, told the commission "of being refused housing in Evanston because of their race." "NU Students Ask Evanston for Open Occupancy Law," *Daily Northwestern,* November 20, 1963. After making public their stories and recounting the humiliation they experienced in looking for housing in Evanston, Attico and Wali were told by Northwestern officials that they would be given housing in the Northwestern apartments. "Negroes May Live in NU Apartments,' *Daily Northwestern,* October 24, 1963. That same year, Wali took part in a panel organized by the Amistad Society in Chicago on the "Negro Writer in an Era of Struggle." "Chicago," *Negro Digest,* December 1963, 50.

112 For many years, Northwestern officials stated that they favored open oc-

cupancy but could not "take corporate action to implement it." "March is Orderly," *Daily Northwestern*, May 11, 1967; "Inter-racial Housing Up to Students," *Daily Northwestern*, May 16, 1944.

113 "The Revolting Students," *Chicago Defender*, May 6, 1968.

114 "State-Wide Battle on Illinois Jim Crow," *The Crisis*, February 1937, 43.

115 "Dorm Votes Negroes Out," *Daily Northwestern*, December 13, 1935.

116 "Dorm Votes Negroes Out;" "N.U. Officials Drop Pearson Hall Inquiry," *Daily Northwestern*, December 11, 1935.

117 "Dorm Votes Negroes Out."

118 "N.U. Officials Drop Pearson Hall Inquiry."

119 "N.U. Officials Drop Pearson Hall Inquiry."

120 "Discrimination Against Negro Students," *Daily Northwestern*, December 15, 1936.

121 "Negro Discrimination: The Campus Acts," *Daily Northwestern*, December 16, 1936.

122 "Discrimination Against Negro Students."

123 "Alpha Mu Chapter," *The Sphinx Vol. 24* (February 1938): 44; "Clarence David Hinton," The Terrible Theta Nupes of Kappa Alpha Psi Fraternity, Inc. http://terriblethetanupes.blogspot.com/2009/09/celebrating-man-of-achievement.html. Lawrence Bernard Jefferson (1918-1991) graduated from Northwestern in 1939, the same year that his brother, Harold Jefferson, also graduated from Northwestern. In 1942, he enlisted in the U.S. Army Air Corps and flew missions with the 332nd Fighter Group (also known as the Tuskegee Airmen). He was awarded the Distinguished Flying Cross. After the war, Jefferson played for the football team, the Chicago Rockets, and he also organized the Chicago Brown Bombers, a semi-pro football team of Black players. He earned an MA in education from the Chicago Teachers College (now Chicago State University) and worked as a teacher in the Chicago Public Schools for more than thirty-five years. From 1971 to 1980, he was the principal at Cook County Jail School. Jerry Thornton, " 'Bernie' Jefferson, 73, Nu Star, School Principal," *Chicago Tribune*, August 19, 1991; "Then: Breaking Barriers," *Northwestern*, Spring 2016, https://www.northwestern.edu/magazine/spring2016/campuslife/then-breaking-barriers-bernard-jefferson-tuskegee-airman.html. In 1942, Clarence Hinton (1917-2008) earned an MD degree from Howard University. He served in the U.S. Army from 1943-46. He later served as Chairman of the Division of Otolaryngology at Howard University Hospital and served as the first Black Chairman of the Section on Otolaryngology of the D.C. Medical Society. Clarence David Hinton "In Memoriam," *Northwestern Magazine*, Spring 2009, https://www.northwestern.edu/magazine/spring2009/alumninews/inmemoriam.html.

124 Thomas D. Eliot, letter to the editor, *Daily Northwestern*, December 18, 1936. Eliot was a professor of sociology at Northwestern. Biographical information about Bell was drawn from *The Syllabus*, Northwestern University's yearbook; Northwestern University, *Seventy-Eighth Annual Commencement* (Evanston: Northwestern University, 1936); "The Sphinx Speaks," *The Sphinx* (December 1933): 21; and from the research that Carl C. Bell, William Yancey Bell, Jr.'s son, has conducted on his father's biography: Carl C. Bell, "William Yancy Bell, Jr.," ResearchGate.

125 "Wm. Yancy Bell Receives M.A. Degree from Northwestern University," *Chicago Defender*, June 12, 1915. William Yancy Bell, Jr.'s father, Bishop William Yancy Bell (1887-1962) earned his MA at Northwestern, a BD degree at Evanston's Garrett

Biblical Institute, and a PhD at Yale University's School of Divinity. He was the founder of the Colored (Christian) Methodist Episcopal Church in Harlem, New York, and served as a pastor at numerous churches throughout his career. He also taught at Howard University. "Dr. William Yancy Bell," https://www.findagrave.com/memorial/34062899/william-yancy-bell; "Score Northwestern Officials for Attitude on Race Students," *Pittsburgh Courier*, December 26, 1936.

126 "State-Wide Battle on Illinois Jim Crow," *The Crisis*, February 1937, 43.

127 "State-Wide Battle on Illinois Jim Crow."

128 The 1885 Illinois Civil Rights Act provided "that all persons within the jurisdiction of the state, regardless of race, or color, shall be entitled to full and equal enjoyment of public accommodations and facilities, and fixes a minimum fine of $25 and a maximum of $500 for convicted violators." As provided in its charter, Northwestern enjoys tax exempt status. The NAACP objected to Northwestern's defense that as a charitable (eleemosynary) institution it was "exempt from liability or wrongful acts of its employees." The suit on behalf of Bell was part of a larger legal battle waged by the NAACP to "call attention to the jim crow practices" not only at Northwestern, but also the University of Chicago, the University of Illinois, and several railroad companies. Representatives of the NAACP wrote to all Illinois state legislators urging them to "revoke, alter, amend or modify the charter of Northwestern University in view of its discriminatory actions and its claim to immunity from the law." They also asked that the university's tax-exempt status be revoked. "State-Wide Battle on Illinois Jim Crow," *The Crisis*, February 1937, 43; "Northwestern Loses Point in Lawsuit For Discrimination," *Chicago Defender*, December 5, 1936.

129 "Discrimination Against Negro Students;" "Score Northwestern Officials for Attitude on Race Students," *Pittsburgh Courier*, December 26, 1936.

130 "Discrimination Against Negro Students."

131 "Discrimination Against Negro Students."

132 "Tittle Raps N.U. Negro Student Stand; Liberal Groups Gird for Fight Against Racial Discrimination," *Daily Northwestern*, December 16, 1936.

133 After 1917, the Western Conference was known as the Big Ten Conference. "Seven Organizations Agree on Issue Raised by Bell Suit," *Daily Northwestern*, December 16, 1936.

134 "Seven Organizations Agree on Issue Raised by Bell Suit."

135-137 "Seven Organizations Agree on Issue Raised by Bell Suit."

138 "Negro Discrimination: The Campus Acts." *Daily Northwestern*, December 16, 1936.

139 "Kennelly Heads Race Study Group," *Daily Northwestern*, November 7, 1939.

140 The committee was a successor to an informal student-faculty interracial committee formed earlier in the 1930s. "Kennelly Heads Race Study Group," *Daily Northwestern*. In 1939, Virginia Kennelly was elected chair of the Interracial Committee. Members included Catherine Payne, Mynor Payne, Eloise Boone, Charlotte Heitlinger, Allen Howard, Ruth Urice, Helen Chandler, Jean Thomas, Norman Blue, Lois LaCroix, Bob Bellamy, Marianna Schaupp, and Isabelle Heck.

141 "Dawn of an Era: Pursuit of Prejudice," *Daily Northwestern*, December 1, 1937.

142 "Refuse Consideration of Negro-White Dorm," *Daily Northwestern*, May 2, 1939. The Student Governing Board was first formed in 1933. It was replaced by the

Student Senate in 1960. The Student Senate was designed to represent the student body more broadly. By 1969, a new student government structure was formed: the Associated Student Government. Michele Corriston and Patrick Svitek, "In Focus: Can ASG be Changed?" *Daily Northwestern,* April 11, 2012.

143 "Interracial Group to Aid in Better Understanding," *Daily Northwestern,* February 7, 1941.

144 "Cooperation is Negro Week Aim," *Daily Northwestern,* February 2, 1940. The event was held again in 1941, renamed "Better Understanding Week." "Interracial Group to Aid in Better Understanding," *Daily Northwestern,* February 7, 1941.

145 "Information Wanted," letter to the editor, *Daily Northwestern,* April 5, 1938.

146 P.J. Hauser, letter to the editor, "Information Given," *Daily Northwestern,* April 7, 1938. Hauser was a member of APA's Epsilon-Lambda chapter in St. Louis. Member Directory, *The Sphinx* (December 1923): np.

147 "Information Wanted."

148 "NU Student Congress Publishes Letters Closing Housing Incident," *Daily Northwestern,* May 20, 1938.

149 "NU Student Congress Publishes Letters Closing Housing Incident."

150 "NU Student Congress Publishes Letters Closing Housing Incident."

151 "The University's Baby Out on the Doorstep," *Daily Northwestern,* April 7, 1938.

152 "The University's Baby Out on the Doorstep."

153 Joanne McDavid, " Inter-Racial committee 'To Carry On'- Kennelly," *Daily Northwestern,* May 3, 1939. The students who sought the integrated dorm for women were: Virginia Kennelly, Pat Clark, Mary Mosby, Alice Dawson, Kana Cole, Eloise Boone, Norma Blue, Jean Boger, Eleanor Blue, Helen Chandler, Katharine Bowls, Virginia Jackson, Nancy Armstrong, Lois LaCroix, and Sara Grimpas. In 1937, students on the Interracial Committee had secured a pledge from Elias Lyman, chair of the board of personnel administration, that the university would support an integrated dormitory on campus—a "race dorm"— in the coming year, provided that there were "a sufficient number of students to make the experiment in social living" financially sound. "Cooperation Promised in Race Dorm," *Daily Northwestern,* January 14, 1937.

154 For more on McCarn, see Linda Eisenmann, *Higher Education for Women in Postwar America, 1945–1965* (Baltimore: Johns Hopkins University Press, 2006) and Kelly C. Sartorius, *Deans of Women and the Feminist Movement: Emily Taylor's Activism* (New York: Palgrave Macmillan, 2014).

155 "Refuse Consideration of Negro-White Dorm," *Daily Northwestern,* May 2, 1939.

156 "Refuse Consideration of Negro-White Dorm."

157 Williamson and Wild, 238-239.

158 This was the revelation from Mary F. Hutchins, a student at Northwestern, whose father served on the board of trustees. Hutchins reportedly overheard a conversation about McCarn and reported what she had heard. "Student Paper Revives 'Race' Charge at N.U.," *Chicago Tribune,* November 17, 1948. Franklyn Bliss Snyder (1884-1958) served as Northwestern University president from 1939 to 1949.

159 Williamson and Wild, 239.

160 Williamson and Wild, 239.

161 In 1950, McCarn was appointed assistant dean of students at the University

of Chicago, the first woman to hold that position. "Name Ruth McCarn to Post at Chicago U.," *The Times,* July 20, 1950. She was later appointed professor of education at the University of Chicago. She retired in 1961. Obituary, "Mrs. Davis McCarn," *Chicago Tribune,* March 12, 1981.

162 Joanne McDavid, "Inter-racial Committee 'to Carry On'-Kennelly," *Daily Northwestern,* May 3, 1939.

163 Mynor P. Payne, letter to the editor, *Daily Northwestern,* May 16, 1939.

164 Lillian Bell, "The Quibblers Club," *Purple Parrot,* April 1945, 12.

165 "Quibblers Chartered," *Daily Northwestern,* May 3, 1939; "Quibblers Announce Policy, Officers," *Daily Northwestern,* October 18, 1939.

166 Lillian Bell, "The Quibblers Club."

167 "We Want Action! Interracial," *Daily Northwestern,* May 12, 1944.

168 "Negro Sorority Invited to Join Panhellenic," *Daily Northwestern,* January 10, 1941. Ruth McCarn had lobbied unsuccessfully to obtain permission to provide the chapter with housing at 628 University Place. Williamson and Wild, 238.

169 "Admittance of K.A. Psi is to Be Respected," *Daily Northwestern,* March 28, 1941; Tom Davies, "Negro Fraternities Will Bid Today for Return to NU," *Daily Northwestern,* May 2, 1967.

170 Russ Kohr, "Tech Fire Highlights Year's News," *Daily Northwestern,* May 23, 1941.

171 John Aaron Wright, *African Americans in Downtown St. Louis* (Chicago: Arcadia, 2003), 44-45; "Charles A. Turpin," Find a Grave, https://www.findagrave.com/memorial/22603/charles-a.-turpin; U.S. Census, 1930, St. Louis, Missouri, retrieved from Ancestry.com.

172 Rufus Clement (1900-1967) was born in North Carolina. He earned a degree in divinity from Garrett Biblical Institute and an MA in history from Northwestern. He was the longest-serving president of Atlanta University, holding that position from 1936 until his death in 1967. Jack Rummel, *African-American Social Leaders and Activists* (New York: Facts on File, 2003), 35.

173 "Campus Committees Discuss Inter-racial Housing Problem," *Daily Northwestern,* April 14, 1944.

174 "Campus Committees Discuss Inter-racial Housing Problem."

175 "Interracial Dorm- Is It a 'Must'?" *Daily Northwestern,* February 22, 1940.

176 "Northwestern Dorms Bar Negro Students," *Chicago Defender,* August 14, 1943.

177 "Northwestern Dorms Bar Negro Students."

178 "Northwestern Dorms Bar Negro Students."

179 David Beard, "Before Barack Obama: The Young Michelle Obama," *PRI's The World,* March 25, 2015. https://www.pri.org/stories/2015-03-25/barack-obama-young-michelle-obama.

180 "Northwestern Sued For $50,000 in Dorm Ban," *Chicago Defender,* December 11, 1943.

181 "Northwestern Sued For $50,000 in Dorm Ban;" David Beard, "Before Barack Obama." Beard reports that Shields won the case, but I was unable to confirm this. Shields was a choir director at Woodlawn AME church in Chicago. It was nighttime when she arrived at Northwestern to check in at Willard Hall. She had registered for Northwestern's church and choral music institute and pre-paid by mail. Her name was clearly written on a list of registered students, but when Shields arrived, the clerk appeared shocked to see she was Black. The clerk summoned the

dormitory director who told Shields she could not room there because she was Black and Black people were not allowed in the university dorms. She was directed to the North Shore community house, a private, off-campus rooming house for Black women. Harry L. Wells, vice president and business manager for Northwestern University, argued that Shields had "done a great service to Northwestern university, when she was sent away from Willard Hall in the middle of the night to a colored rooming-house, 'for we know that Negroes prefer to live with members of their own race.' " "Northwestern Dorms Bar Negro Students." The story is also told in Peter Slevin, *Michelle Obama: A Life* (New York: Vintage Books, 2015), 44-45.

182 "Meet the Quibblers," *Daily Northwestern,* February 22, 1946; "We Want Action! Interracial," *Daily Northwestern,* May 12, 1944.

183 "Group Seeks to Better Race Relations Here," *Daily Northwestern,* May 5, 1944.

184 Chuck Frankel, "These Days, Northwestern WANTS Blacks," *Honolulu Star Bulletin,* March 15, 1971.

185 "We Want Action! Interracial," *Daily Northwestern,* May 12, 1944.

186 "Do We Support Inter-Racial?" *Daily Northwestern,* May 17, 1944.

187 "Do We Support Inter-Racial?"

188 The meeting was sponsored by the Chicago Council against Racial and Religious Discrimination and included forty other organizations. "Notes for an Editorial on Race Prejudice," *Daily Northwestern,* June 28, 1946.

189 "Notes for an Editorial on Race Prejudice."

190 "Northwestern U. Dean Upholds Segregation of Negro Students," *Chicago Defender,* March 8, 1947.

191 "Daily Forum: Should NU Disregard Race in Housing?" *Daily Northwestern,* January 29, 1947.

192 "Daily Forum: Should NU Disregard Race in Housing?"

193 "N.U. Registration Shows 13% Gain," *Evanston Review,* October 4, 1945, 5.

194 Classifieds, *Evanston Review,* January 24, 1946, 65.

195 R.B. Goldsberry, "Negro Vets Not Wanted in N.U. Dorms," *Chicago Defender,* July 20, 1946.

196 "Evanston Lets N.U. Build More Huts for Ex-GIs," *Chicago Tribune,* February 5, 1946. Later, fifty more huts were authorized for construction with the only restriction that they be removed in five years. "Evanston Lets N.U. Build More Huts for Ex-GIs."

197 "Northwestern Gets Ok on Jim Crow Dorm," *Chicago Defender,* May 11, 1946.

198 "Northwestern Gets OK On Jim Crow Dorm."

199 Quoted in Beverly, Jr., *Edwin B. Jourdain,* 97.

200 R.B. Goldsberry, "Negro Vets Not Wanted in N.U. Dorms," *Chicago Defender,* July 20, 1946.

201 R.B. Goldsberry, "Negro Vets Not Wanted in N.U. Dorms." One university official reportedly responded to the NHA by stating that "Northwestern has no Negro housing problem as we have no Negro veterans," a statement that was pointedly untrue.

202 R.B. Goldsberry, "Negro Vets Not Wanted in N.U. Dorms." One university official reportedly responded to the NHA by stating that "Northwestern has no Negro housing problem as we have no Negro veterans," a statement that

was entirely untrue.

203 "Dean Defends School Policy on Housing," *Daily Northwestern,* February 2, 1947.

204 "Dean Defends School Policy on Housing."

205 "Our Aim: To Correct Negro Housing Evils," *Daily Northwestern,* January 24, 1947.

206 "Our Aim: To Correct Negro Housing Evils."

207 Jim Davis, "NU Housing Poll Draws 'Color-Line,' " *Daily Northwestern,* February 20, 1947.

208 Davis, "NU Housing Poll Draws 'Color-Line.' "

209 Davis, "NU Housing Poll Draws 'Color-Line.' "

210 Davis, "NU Housing Poll Draws 'Color-Line.' " William "Bill" Blackwell Branch (1927-) was born in New Haven, CT, and grew up in Washington, D.C. and Charlotte, NC. A speech major at Northwestern, he graduated in 1949. While at Northwestern, Branch won numerous prizes for oratory in the prestigious Northern Oratorical league and Kirk contests. He was also cast as an understudy in a national production of *Anna Lucasta* in Chicago. In 1951, Branch's first play, *A Medal for Willie,* was produced by the Committee for the Negro and the Arts at the Club Baron in Harlem. The morning after opening night, Branch had to report for induction into the U.S. Army. He served three years in the U.S. Army before attending Columbia University, where he earned an MFA in playwriting. He attended the Yale University School of Drama and went on to a successful career as a playwright, television and film producer, and as a professor at numerous schools including Smith College, Cornell University, and the University of Maryland. He was later awarded a Guggenheim fellowship and also received an Emmy Award nomination. "William Branch" in *From the Ground Up: Grassroots Theater in Historical and Contemporary Perspective* (Norton, VA: Roadside Theater, 1992), 19.

211 "Inter-racial Club," *Daily Northwestern,* September 29, 1949.

212 "The Quibblers," *The Syllabus,* Northwestern University yearbook, 1947, 103.

213 "Students Expect Housing Results," *Daily Northwestern,* February 26, 1947.

214 "N. U. Campus House Doors Swing Open to Negro Males in January," *Chicago Defender,* October 8, 1949.

215 "International House for Men Slated at N.U.," *Chicago Tribune,* October 9, 1949.

216 Cynthia Grant Bowman, *Dawn Clark Netsch: A Political Life (*Evanston: Northwestern University Press, 2010), 19. Dawn Clark Netsch (1926-2013) was one of the editors on the *Daily Northwestern* who took part in the campaign to end campus housing discrimination. She later went on to serve as a state senator from Illinois, Illinois comptroller, and a professor of law at Northwestern. She served on the board of the ACLU of Illinois and was a longtime advocate for advancing civil rights. Liam Ford, " 'Straight Shooter' Dawn Clark Netsch Dies at 86," *Chicago Tribune,* March 5, 2013; "Dawn Clark Netsch," ACLU Illinois, https://www.aclu-il.org/en/news/dawn-clark-netsch, March 5, 2013.

217 Williamson and Wild, 241-242.

218 "International House," *Daily Northwestern,* April 21, 1948.

219 Barbara Stoner, letter to the editor, *Daily Northwestern,* May 14, 1947.

220 Bill Branch, letter to the editor, *Daily Northwestern,* May 9, 1947.

221 W.R. Rosenmeyer, "Bill Branch Tells of Racial Unrest," *Daily Northwestern,* January 5, 1947.

222 Rosenmeyer, "Bill Branch Tells of Racial Unrest." Branch's three brothers were veterans of World War II. One brother, Frederick, was the first Black officer in the U.S. Marine Corps. In 1943 Frederick Clinton Branch (1922-2005) was drafted and entered the U.S. Marine Corps, one of the first Black men to join after it had been desegregated by executive order of President Roosevelt. In November 1945, he was commissioned as a 2nd Lieutenant and later promoted to captain. Kevin L. Bradley, "Captain Frederick C. Branch: The First African American Commissioned Officer in the USMC," Rediscovering Black History, December 16, 2014, https://rediscovering-black-history.blogs.archives.gov/2014/12/16/captain-frederick-c-branch/.

223 Advertisement, *Daily Northwestern,* November 15, 1946.

224 Rosenmeyer, "Bill Branch Tells of Racial Unrest."

225 Paul Doebler, "Activities Soar During Hot Spell," *Daily Northwestern,* September 22, 1949.

226 "J. Roscoe Miller," Northwestern University Archives, http://exhibits.library.northwestern.edu/archives/exhibits/presidents/miller.html.

227 Wally Priest, "Int'l House Gets 1st Priority," *Daily Northwestern,* August 5, 1949.

228 "International House for Men Slated at N.U.," *Chicago Tribune,* October 9, 1949.

229 Jim Shanahan, "Men's Internat'l House to Open," *Daily Northwestern,* September 27, 1949.

230 At the time, there were just twenty Black male students enrolled at Northwestern. "International House for Men Slated at N.U.," *Chicago Tribune,* October 9, 1949; "Northwestern Opens Campus House For Men," *Chicago Defender,* January 14, 1950. The 1889 building was the former Norwegian-Danish Theological Seminary.

231 Jay Pridmore, *Northwestern University: Celebrating 150 Years* (Evanston, IL: Northwestern University Press, 2000), 180.

232 Pridmore, *Northwestern University,* 180.

233 John L. McKnight also served as president of Asbury Hall during his residency there. Today, he is an emeritus professor of education and social policy and co-director of the Asset-Based Community Development Institute at Northwestern. After graduating from Northwestern in 1953, McKnight served in the U.S. Navy during the Korean War. He went on to work for the Chicago Commission for Human Relations. Later he served as the Midwest director of the United States Commission on Civil Rights and director of the ACLU in Illinois. He was recruited to help shape the first federal affirmative action legislation, Executive Order 10925, signed by John F. Kennedy in 1961. In 1969, Northwestern University hired him to launch the Center for Urban Affairs (Today known as the Institute for Policy Research). Bill Healy, "Forgotten History: How Two Words Changed The Job Prospects For Black Americans," Social Justice News Network, May 5, 2016. http://sjnnchicago.medill.northwestern.edu/blog/2016/05/05/forgotten-history-two-words-changed-job-prospects-black-americans-bill-healy/; "Affirmative Action History," University of Rhode Island, https://web.uri.edu/affirmativeaction/affirmative-action-history/; "About John McKnight," Abundant Community, http://www.abundantcommunity.com/home/block_and_mcknight_biographies/about_john_mcknight.htm.

234 "Untrodden Toes," *Daily Northwestern,* January 1, 1953.

235 "Officials Approve MIC Plan," *Daily Northwestern,* February 3, 1953.

236 Pitts, "Growth of Black Consciousness at Northwestern," 4.

237 "Government," *Daily Northwestern,* November 19, 1959.

238 "Government," *Daily Northwestern,* November 19, 1959.

239 "Controversy Over Race and Religion at Northwestern U.," *The Daily Reporter,* November 23, 1950.

240 "Controversy Over Race and Religion at Northwestern U."

241 Pridmore, *Northwestern University,* 196.

242 Pridmore, *Northwestern University,* 196.

243 Initially drafted by Tom Hayden, with later input from a variety of student leaders, the Port Huron Statement served as an inspiration and blueprint for students around the country who took the concept of "participatory democracy" to heart. Tom Hayden, "Crafting the Port Huron Statement: Measuring Its Impact in the 1960s and After," in *Port Huron Statement: Sources and Legacies of the New Left's Founding Manifesto,* Richard Flacks and Nelson Lichtenstein, ed. (Philadelphia: University of Pennsylvania Press, 2015), 19.

244 College enrollment in degree-granting programs rose from 3.6 million in 1960 to 7.9 million in 1970. Louise B. Russell, *The Baby Boom Generation and the Economy* (Washington, DC: Brookings Institution, 1982), 41.

245 Rochelle Stanfield, "Free Housing Backers," *Daily Northwestern,* December 3, 1959.

246 "Policy Statements-Funny Things," *Daily Northwestern,* November 10, 1964; Stanfield, "Free Housing Backers."

247 Pridmore, *Northwestern University,* 196.

248 Mary Bitting, "Prof Asks Picket of Discriminating Houses," *Daily Northwestern,* April 27, 1960.

249 "Interracial Club Plans Crusade," *Daily Northwestern,* January 11, 1950.

250 SNCC was founded at a meeting organized by civil rights leader Ella Baker (1903-1986) at Shaw University in North Carolina in 1960. In the wake of the student sit-ins throughout the Southern states, Baker and others recognized the potential organizing impact a national student-led movement could have on the civil rights movement in general. Baker was executive secretary of the Southern Christian Leadership Conference.

251 "Daily Calendar," *Daily Northwestern,* May 7, 1964; "Curtis Hayes," Civil Rights Digital Library, http://crdl.usg.edu/people/h/hayes_curtis.

252 "King Aides, Selma Participants to Address Rally," *Daily Northwestern,* April 2, 1965.

253 The movement included nonviolent actions such as rallies, boycotts, and protests, all designed to raise issues concerning a variety of areas, including employment and housing discrimination. "Chicago Freedom Movement (1965–1967)," Blackpast.org, https://blackpast.org/aah/chicago-freedom-movement-1965-1967.

254 During a convention held in June 1962, many student activists contributed to the final version of the Port Huron Statement. SDS member Barbara Haber recalled the group who contributed to the final document: "We were a group of perhaps fifty young people (and a few elders), mostly white (a few of our black civil rights comrades attended) mostly from elite schools, more men than women (although the numbers are distorted by sexism; no one kept records, and the women have tended to be forgotten)." Barbara Haber, "A Manifesto of Hope," in *Port Huron Statement:*

Sources and Legacies of the New Left's Founding Manifesto, 141.

255 Sam Frizell, "The Radical Education of Bernie Sanders," *Time*, May 26, 2015, http://time.com/3896500/bernie-sanders-vermont-campaign-radical/.

256 "NU Coed Plans to Establish Evanston Chapter of SDS," *Daily Northwestern*, November 2, 1965. The constitution of the SDS chapter was approved by the Student Senate in December 1965. Jack Fuller, "Dean Gives Plans to Senate," *Daily Northwestern*, December 3, 1965. Northwestern's SDS chapter was the third founded in the Chicago area, along with chapters at the University of Chicago and Roosevelt University. By March 1966, SDS had 5,500 members in 151 chapters across the country. "5500 Members! 151 Chapters!" *New Left Notes*, March 18, 1966, 1.

257 "NU Coed Plans to Establish Evanston Chapter of SDS;" "SDS Will Contact NU Official About Negro Housing in City," *Daily Northwestern*, November 4, 1966.

258 "First SDS Meeting Pulls 100 as 2 Other Groups Lend Help," *Daily Northwestern*, November 18, 1965.

259 Members of Students for Civil Rights worked with a local chapter of F.R.E.E. in Evanston (For Real Estate Equality) on ending housing discrimination in the North Shore. Loren Chudy, "Analysis: Political Action Groups," *Daily Northwestern*, April 22, 1966; "Northwestern News Briefs," *Daily Northwestern*, October 8, 1965.

260 Announcement, *Daily Northwestern*, May 17, 1966. Ochs performed at Cahn Auditorium on May 21, 1966.

261 Panelists included Melvin Tumin, a Princeton sociologist and expert on race relations who had a degree from Northwestern, and University of Mississippi professor, James Silver, whose book *Mississippi: The Closed Society*, analyzed the evils of racism in the state. Wolfgang Saxon, "Melvin M. Tumin, 75, Specialist in Race Relations," *New York Times*, March 5, 1994.

262 "Civil Rights Leader to Participate in 1965 Symposium on 'Rebellion," *Daily Northwestern*, December 4, 1964.

263 Tom Hayden, "Crafting the Port Huron Statement: Measuring Its Impact in the 1960s and After," in *Port Huron Statement: Sources and Legacies of the New Left's Founding Manifesto*, 18. A bit of rebellion took place during a seminar hosted by Moses after the panel: there, thirty-five students drafted a letter to university officials. Why was it, they asked, that the university still had not notified area landlords "that they will be taken off the university's list of approved off-campus housing if they discriminate against students"? Michael Whitney, "NU to Notify Landlords of its Policy," *Daily Northwestern*, February 4, 1965. That policy had been approved the previous fall and still had not been implemented. The students staged a protest and presented a set of demands to officials. After a meeting, officials agreed to act and promptly notified all local landlords. Al From, "Wild to Send Letters by Friday," *Daily Northwestern*, February 9, 1965.

264 Andrew H. Malcolm, "Moses: Equality in a 'New' Society," *Daily Northwestern*, February 9, 1965.

265 Joan Lorenson, " 'Rebellion' Hasn't Spread, Say Campus Administrators," *Arlington Heights Herald*, July 8, 1965.

266 Lorenson, " 'Rebellion' Hasn't Spread, Say Campus Administrators."

Notes to Chapter 3

1 Quoted in Andrew H. Malcolm, "Focus: Out of Focus," *Daily Northwestern,* November 12, 1965. Judy Innes visited Northwestern and provided a less than flattering evaluation of what she observed. "[I]f you want to stop students from being rebellious, opinionated, hot-headed, and idealistic, I've discovered a foolproof recipe—lodge them in luxury and insulate them from the outside world with a thick protective padding of money. This revelation came to me on the campus of Northwestern University." Innes argued that the university was dominated by the Greek system and fueled by wealthy parents, and that the homogenous student body was interested in very little beyond social life. Innes quoted one student, who described the makeup of the student body: "they take ten percent Jewish students, fifteen percent Catholics, a half percent Negroes, and five percent Uglies."

2 Tim Schellhardt, "NU Intensifies Chicago Recruitment," *Daily Northwestern,* October 15, 1965.

3 "HRC Committee May Plan Racial Discrimination Study," *Daily Northwestern,* October 24, 1963.

4 "HRC Committee May Plan Racial Discrimination Study." In the 1950s, the student government established a Human Relations Committee whose purpose was to "serve as a watchdog to fight against discrimination." Terry Turner, "SC and FNV Submit Convention Platforms," *Daily Northwestern,* May 6, 1954. It investigated cases of suspected discrimination in Evanston businesses and residences on the university's approved off-campus housing list. "Croake to Investigate Reports of Bias," *Daily Northwestern,* September 30, 1964.

5 Al From, "Northwestern Statement Denies Bias in Employment, Admissions," *Daily Northwestern,* November 8, 1963; Al From, "Religious Quota Denied by Admissions," *Daily Northwestern,* January 30, 1964.

6 Chuck Remsberg, "Religion Query Elimination Climaxes Long Fight," *Daily Northwestern,* March 8, 1957. Reiley would later defend the practice of requiring applicants to submit their photographs, explaining that they merely helped "personalize" applicants. From, "Religious Quota Denied by Admissions."

7 Remsberg, "Religion Query Elimination Climaxes Long Fight."

8 Dick Longworth, "No Admission Bias Here, McLeod Says," *Daily Northwestern,* February 20, 1957.

9 Longworth, "No Admission Bias Here, McLeod Says;" "No Reason for Religion on Admissions Blank," *Daily Northwestern,* February 22, 1957. Even some critics of the required religion question argued that such information could be collected in another way, after a student enrolls, for example.

10 Longworth, "No Admission Bias Here, McLeod Says."

11 Longworth, "No Admission Bias Here, McLeod Says."

12 Chuck Remsberg, "Religion Information Query Struck from 1958 N.U. Admissions Blank," *Daily Northwestern,* March 5, 1958; "No Reason for Religion on Admissions Blank," *Daily Northwestern,* February 22, 1957.

13-15 Remsberg, "Religion Information Query Struck from 1958 N.U. Admissions Blank."

16 "Religious Advisers to Receive Info," *Daily Northwestern,* April 18, 1957. After campus religious advisors expressed concern that they would be "denied the information" about students' religions, McLeod and others pledged that they would find a new procedure to provide advisors with that information, but only after students had been admitted. Remsberg, "Religion Information Query Struck from 1958 N.U. Admissions Blank;" "Religious Advisers to Receive Info," *Daily Northwestern,* April 18, 1957.

17 "Admissions Pot Boils As Letter, Meeting Set," *Daily Northwestern,* April 23, 1964.

18 Al From, "Religious Quota Denied by Admissions," *Daily Northwestern,* January 30, 1964.

19 From, "Religious Quota Denied by Admissions."

20 "Reiley Attacks Daily, Threatens Reporter," *Daily Northwestern,* February 12, 1964. Al From (1943-) was editor of the *Daily Northwestern* from 1964-1965. He went on to a successful career as a journalist and political strategist, later founding the Democratic Leadership Council (DLC). Mollie Leavitt, "The Northwestern Wing," *North by Northwestern,* November 18, 2015, http://www.northbynorthwestern.com/story/the-northwestern-wing/.

21 Pitts, "The Politicalization of Black Students," 282.

22 Michael Whitney, "Kreml Denies Coding System," *Daily Northwestern,* September 25, 1964; Baran S. Rosen, "Former Admissions Policy Questionable," *Daily Northwestern*, December 3, 1969.

23 Jeff Lyon, "Admissions Conflict Erupts Again," *Daily Northwestern,* March 6, 1964.

24 Al From, "Reiley Named to New Position," *Daily Northwestern,* April 13, 1964.

25 Michael Whitney, "Kreml Denies Coding System."

26 Whitney, "Kreml Denies Coding System."

27 In 1962, the ADL had first charged discrimination in admissions at Northwestern University. At the time, Payson Wild, vice president and dean of faculties, said there were no religious or racial restrictions on applicants. Whitney, "Kreml Denies Coding System."

28 "Top Priority," *Daily Northwestern,* September 29, 1964.

29 "Wild Sets Up Admissions Committee," *Daily Northwestern,* May 27, 1964.

30 Al From, "Reiley Named to New Position," *Daily Northwestern,* April 13, 1964.

31 From, "Reiley Named to New Position."

32 "Follow That Lead," *Daily Northwestern,* April 27, 1965.

33 Pitts, "The Politicalization of Black Students," 280. Prior to the passage of that legislation, U.S. Congress member Adam Clayton Powell, Jr. (1908-1972) had attached anti-segregation riders (which became known as "Powell amendments") to any legislation authorizing funds for schools. In 1961, Powell became chairman of the Education and Labor Committee and continued to lobby for desegregation in education. "The Powell Amendment," *The Harvard Crimson,* March 1, 1956, https://www.thecrimson.com/article/1956/3/1/the-powell-amendment-pwhen-president-eisenhowers/.

34 Northwestern recruitment efforts were also coordinated with the Cooperative Program for Educational Opportunity, the National Scholarship Service Fund for Negro Students, and the National Achievement Scholarship Program. Roland J. Hinz, "Northwestern University Responses to the Black Student Petition Received April 22, 1968," Records of the Bursar's Office Takeover, May 1968, 3, box 1, folder 3, NUA.

Another catalyst for integration was President Lyndon Johnson's Executive Order 11246, signed in September 1965, requiring federal contractors to "take affirmative action to ensure that . . . employees are treated during employment, without regard to their race, creed, color, or national origin." Joy Ann Williamson-Lott, *Black Power on Campus: The University of Illinois, 1965-75* (University of Illinois, 2003), 26. At the same time as Hinz started his job at Northwestern, the city of Evanston also began to grapple with many of its longstanding issues regarding racial discrimination. In the wake of the U.S. Supreme Court's 1954 ruling on *Brown v. Board of Education,* which declared unconstitutional any laws establishing separate public schools on the basis of race, and the passage of the 1964 Civil Rights Act, Evanston was undergoing change, some forced, some willing. Despite these changes, Evanston still showed signs of racial disparity and worse: In June 1966, a three-foot cross was burned on the lawn of the home of Marilyn Alexander, a seventeen-year-old student at Evanston Township High School and president of the Junior NAACP. "Cross Burned on Evanston Front Lawn," *Chicago Tribune,* June 15, 1966.

35 With the backing of the school board, the school superintendent began to implement policies to desegregate Evanston's public elementary schools, an effort that would lead to discord among residents in the coming years. Efforts to desegregate schools began in earnest in 1965. Several schools were targeted for desegregation, including Foster school (which had one hundred percent Black student enrollment) and Dewey school (which had sixty-seven percent Black student enrollment). School superintendent Oscar M. Chute announced the goal of achieving an "even mix in every school" within the district's fifteen schools (which also included several schools in nearby Skokie, IL). "Evanston Plan Given to Integrate Schools," *Chicago Tribune,* May 18, 1965; Casey Banas, "O.K. Evanston School Quota," *Chicago Tribune,* November 22, 1966. Chute retired before the desegregation process was implemented. His successor, Gregory Coffin, (1926-2002) took over in October 1966. Over the next two years, Coffin became the focal point of many angry critics as he sought to carry out desegregation efforts, including busing students and transferring teachers to other schools. Coffin sought to achieve total desegregation, but he also proposed a more holistic and progressive operation. "True integration would come," he observed, "after white teachers had been taught to understand the problems of Black pupils, when the school system became more responsive to the community, and when the 'built-in racism' of the white-authored text books had been eliminated." Residents were divided over his efforts and they packed the school board meetings that became increasingly tense. Two years into his job, Coffin was all but fired by a divided school board. (His contract was not renewed.) Seth S. King, "Affluent Evanston, Ill., Divided Over Move to Drop School Integration Leader," *New York Times,* August 24, 1969. Coffin later joined the faculty at Northwestern and remained active in the civil rights movement.

36 Williamson-Lott, *Black Power on Campus,* 26. According to a 1970 U.S. government study on campus unrest, Black students constituted approximately five percent of the total national college enrollment in 1964. By 1969, the percentage increased to six percent. That same report states that from about "1940 through 1969, the percentage of black men and women in the age group 25-34 with four or more years of college increased less than the percentage of whites of the same age

group. The gap between the level of higher education for Blacks and whites, so wide at the beginning of the thirty-year period, has grown even wider. That fact is more significant than the numerical increase in black college enrollment." In 1970, twenty-two percent of Black Americans "of college age" were enrolled in college, compared with thirty-eight percent of white Americans of the same age. *The Report of the President's Commission on Campus Unrest,* 105-106.

37 "Hinz Takes Over as Dean of Admissions," *Daily Northwestern,* July 23, 1965.

38 Joan Schuman, "New Admissions Director Searches for Future Northwestern Alumni," *Daily Northwestern,* January 12, 1966.

39-41 Schuman, "New Admissions Director Searches for Future Northwestern Alumni."

42 Photographs of students were now only required after they had been admitted. Cathy Newman, "NU Admissions Offices Gets the 'Pics' of the Crop," *Daily Northwestern,* December 3, 1969.

43 Hinz, interview with the author, 2012.

44 Hinz, interview with the author, 2012.

45 "$39.3 Million Received for First Plan of '70s," *Daily Northwestern,* May 26, 1967.

46 By 1970, the university had raised $115 million toward its goal. Ann Beasley, "$1.5 Million Grant Aids Plan for '70s," *Daily Northwestern,* April 1, 1970.

47 McLeod came to Northwestern in 1946 and served as university chaplain. In 1952 he was appointed dean of students. After leaving that role in 1967, he remained at Northwestern as professor of history and literature of religion. "James Mcleod Quits as N.U. Dean," *Chicago Tribune,* October 18, 1966; "James McLeod Will Resign," *The Daily Chronicle,* October 19, 1966.

48 "Trustees OK Hinz as Dean, V-P," *Daily Northwestern,* May 16, 1967.

49 "N.U. Appoints Vice President for Students," *Chicago Tribune,* May 17, 1967.

50 Hinz, interview with the author, April 4, 2018.

51 "Ihlanfeldt Succeeds Hinz as Director of Admission," *Daily Northwestern,* September 14, 1967.

52 Bob Greene, "How Hinz is Trapped by Role," *Daily Northwestern,* November 15, 1968.

53 Greene, "How Hinz is Trapped by Role."

54 Hinz, interview with the author, 2012.

55 Charles Mount, "100 at N. U. Damage R. O. T. C. Classroom," *Chicago Tribune,* January 15, 1970.

56 "N. U.'s Lawyer Raps Student Dope Proposal: Believes 'Non Police' Plan Illegal," *Chicago Tribune,* April 4, 1968.

57 John MacLean, "N. U. Whites Protest Being Forced to Move," *Chicago Tribune,* May 1, 1969.

58 John W. Walter, Jr., "Students Seeking a Place in World," *Chicago Tribune,* June 18, 1968.

59 David Thompson, "Dean Hinz to Quit N. U. Post Aug. 31," *Chicago Tribune,* July 10, 1970.

60 Abigail Foerstner, "Striking Memories: Looking Back 25 Years," *Chicago Tribune,* April 30, 1995.

61 Hinz, interview with the author, 2012.

62 Pitts, "Growth of Black Consciousness at Northwestern," 8. (See note

above for more on James Pitts.)

63 Editorial, "Intensified Recruitment and Methods," *Daily Northwestern,* October 19, 1965; Jim Clare, "Program to Recruit Negroes," *Daily Northwestern,* March 4, 1966; "Northwestern University Responses to the Black Student Petition Received Monday, April 22, 1968," 3. The Lawndale Tutoring Project, a short-lived tutoring program for students in Chicago's Lawndale neighborhood, had been launched by Northwestern students in 1965. "This is Lawndale," *Daily Northwestern,* March 31, 1966. The program did not receive support from the university.

64 "Admissions Director Predicts Heterogeneous Class of 1970," *Daily Northwestern,* April 19, 1966.

65 James Pitts notes that compared to most white students at Northwestern, most Black students were "materially disadvantaged." But compared to a majority of Black people, they would be considered "middle class." Many students depended on financial aid and had to work in order to fulfill the requirements of receiving that aid. This put them in sharp contrast with the wealthier white student body, another source of tension. Pitts, "The Politicalization of Black Students," 292-293, 285.

66 "Parker Student Given Scholarship," *Chicago Tribune,* July 28, 1966. Frances W. Parker High School closed in 1977.

67 Pitts, "The Politicalization of Black Students," 292.

68 "Admissions Director Predicts Heterogeneous Class of 1970," *Daily Northwestern,* April 19, 1966.

69 "Northwestern University Responses to the Black Student Petition Received April 22, 1968," 3.

70 By 1967, Northwestern, along with 2,400 institutions across the country, would be required by the U.S. Office of Education to complete a "Higher Education Compliance Report Form." The questionnaire was designed to investigate and "uncover racial discrimination" within colleges and universities receiving federal funds, with information required from each school concerning its scholarship allocations, recruitment of athletes, admissions policies, and fraternity and sorority "racial policies." Those found to be practicing discrimination would be subject to investigation and faced a potential loss of federal funds. "NU to Receive Civil Rights Forms," *Daily Northwestern,* May 10, 1967.

71 "Admissions Director Predicts Heterogeneous Class of 1970." NUCAP was funded partially by the Wieboldt Foundation of Chicago. "Interracial NUCAP: Emotional, Turbulent," *Daily Northwestern,* September 24, 1968. Project Upward Bound was created in 1965. It was "designed to bridge the gap between the ghetto school and the university campus." Winston Cenac, "Students 'Upward Bound,' " *Daily Northwestern,* July 5, 1968. Lake Forest College and the University of Illinois also participated in the program. The program recruited low-income students to the campuses to take courses in preparation for entering or applying to college. The first students in the program came from Marshall High School in Chicago.

72 Northwestern University, "Why Students Made Demands," https://sites.northwestern.edu/bursars1968/history/why-students-made-demands/.

73 Hinz, interview with the author, 2012.

74 Joan Schuman, "University Officials Say 'Thumbs Up' to Class of ' 70," *Daily Northwestern,* September 15, 1966.

75 "Northwestern University Responses to the Black Student Petition Received April 22, 1968," 2-3. Between 1965 and 1967, the number of first-year Black students at Northwestern University went from five to seventy. The class of 1970 also included a greater percentage of students who received scholarships and financial aid, in part a result of Title V of the Higher Education Act of 1965. Enrollment numbers are drawn from "They Demanded Courageously, The 1968 Northwestern Bursar's Office Takeover;" Williamson and Wild, 329; "N. U. Class is One of Largest," *Chicago Tribune,* September 25, 1966; and "Largest Freshman Class Arrives," *Daily Northwestern,* September 15, 1966. Because the administration was no longer asking applicants to state their religion, other methods of assessing the make-up of the student body were adopted, including conducting student surveys and consulting club and fraternity membership rosters. In January 1967, a survey by the American Council on Education revealed some figures concerning Northwestern students: 44.3 percent of students identified as Protestant, 19.1 percent, Catholic, 17.8 percent Jewish, and 13.8 declared no religious preference. Roy Harris, "Protestants in Minority in Frosh Class," *Daily Northwestern,* January 17, 1967. In the spring of 1967, it was estimated that fifteen percent of male students were Jewish, based on the numbers of those pledging fraternities. Bill Harsh, "Most Jewish Men Pledge 1 of 3 Frats," *Daily Northwestern,* May 12, 1967.

76 James C. McLeod to new students, Summer 1966. Quoted in "One Generation Ago: A Scrapbook, An Observance of an Era," video, Norris University Center, May 18, 1991. Written, produced and directed by Cherilyn Wright and Barbara Perkins. Marjorie I. Mitchell Multimedia Center of Northwestern University Libraries, https://media.northwestern.edu/media_objects/0c483k33v.

77 Sterling and Lowery, *Voices and Visions,* loc. 1178-1181, Kindle. Among the students were Christine Price, John Higginson, Marianne Jackson, Leslie Harris, Arnold Wright, Juaquita Harris, Dorothy Carter, Josephine Bronaugh, Mario McHarris, Herbert Melton, (William) Eric Perkins, Lea Redmond, Charles Shepard, Andre Bell, Michael Smith, Stephen Broussard, Milton Gardner, and Lonnie Ratcliffe.

78 Cross, "James Turner: The Face of Black Power at Northwestern."

79 The groundbreaking program was launched by anthropologist Melville J. Herskovits (1895-1963) in 1948. Herskovits was an influential, if controversial, figure, well known for his 1941 book, *The Myth of the Negro Past.* At Columbia University, Herskovits studied under Franz Boas, and later came to Northwestern University. The African Studies program he created soon became internationally famous and the Melville J. Herskovits Library of African Studies, launched in 1954, remains the largest separate Africana collection in the world. Herskovits also founded the African Studies Association. "Melville J. Herskovits," Wikipedia entry, https://en.wikipedia.org/wiki/Melville_J._Herskovits.

80 Cross, "James Turner: The Face of Black Power at Northwestern."

81 Cross, "James Turner: The Face of Black Power at Northwestern."

82 Bracey, interview with the author, 2018. After Bracey left Howard University he took a year off from school and worked as a GS-2 clerk in the mail room of the U.S. Army Signal Engineering Agency in Arlington Hall near the Pentagon.

83 The Amistad Society was a precursor to the Black Studies Movement.

Russell Burns, "New Negro History Society," *Muhammad Speaks*, nd, 1963; Biondi, *The Black Revolution on Campus*, 98; Photo Caption, *Muhammad Speaks,* October 11, 1963.

84 "Hecklers Cut Daley Talk to NAACP," *Chicago Sun-Times*, July 5, 1963. In July 1963, about 20,000 people took part in a "Freedom March" during the NAACP's national convention held in Chicago. Many hundreds of people, including John Bracey, were there to protest the city's policies of segregation and discrimination. When Chicago Mayor Richard J. Daley took the stage to address the rally, he was booed off the stage by protesters. "Jeer Mayor Daley from Platform at 4th of July Rally," *The Dispatch*, July 5, 1963. The planned and organized public opposition to Daley was just one of the actions Bracey took part in—and became known for—prior to coming to Northwestern.

85 Bracey, interview with the author, 2018.

86 Bracey, interview with the author, 2018.

87-94 Ogletree, interview with the author, 2018.

95 Turner, interview with the author, 2012.

96 Kathy Polhemus, "A Conversation on Racism," *Daily Northwestern*, April 14, 1969.

97 Sterling and Lowery, *Voices and Visions,* loc. 1634-1638, Kindle.

98 Sterling and Lowery, *Voices and Visions,* loc. 1634-1638, Kindle.

99 Jason Mast and Rosalie Chan, " 'It's Like a Legend:' Remembering the 1968 Bursar's Office Sit-In," *North by Northwestern,* February 8, 2017; http://www.northbynorthwestern.com/story/its-like-a-legend-remembering-the-1968-bursars-off/.

100 Kathleen Flaherty, "Alumni Talk of Racism at NU 40 Years Ago," *Daily Northwestern,* November 1, 2008.

101 Ogletree, interview with the author, 2018.

102 Flaherty, "Alumni Talk of Racism at NU 40 Years Ago."

103 Ogletree, interview with the author, 2018.

104 According to James Pitts, some white parents also objected to their children living with Black roommates. "The Politicalization of Black Students," 286.

105 Eva Jefferson Paterson, interview with the author, September 10, 2012.

106 "Few Negative Reactions to Roommate Integration," *Daily Northwestern,* September 23, 1966.

107 Kathryn Ogletree, "Living the Legacy-From Protest to Progress," panel discussion about the 1968 takeover, held at Northwestern University, May 3, 2018. The issue of roommate interactions would soon be explored by a Northwestern graduate student in psychology, O.W. Markley, whose PhD dissertation, "Having a Negro Roommate as an Experience in Intercultural Education," was completed in 1968.

108 Ogletree, email to the author, December 1, 2018.

109 Ogletree, interview with the author, 2018.

110 Ogletree, "Living the Legacy-From Protest to Progress."

111-113 Ogletree, interview with the author, 2018.

114 Turner, interview with the author, 2012.

115 Cross, "James Turner: The Face of Black Power at Northwestern."

116 Pitts, "The Politicalization of Black Students," 290, 280.

117 Bracey, "Living the Legacy-From Protest to Progress;" Sterling and Lowery, *Voices and Visions,* loc. 1634-1638, Kindle.

118 Ogletree, interview with the author, 2018. James Pitts also documented this fact, stating that whenever Black students gathered in a dormitory lounge to talk or to listen to music and dance, white students would become "visibly annoyed." Pitts, "The Politicalization of Black Students," 288-289.

119 Ogletree, interview with the author, 2018.

120 Ogletree, interview with the author, 2018.

121 For a fascinating study of the experiences of Black students at Northwestern, see Sarah Susannah Willie, *Acting Black: College, Identity, and the Performance of Race* (New York: Routledge, 2003).

122 Cross, "James Turner: The Face of Black Power at Northwestern."

123 Bracey, "Living the Legacy-From Protest to Progress."

124 In 1963, the *Daily Northwestern* reported that there were a total of eight Black faculty members on Northwestern's Evanston and downtown campuses. "University Policy," *Daily Northwestern,* November 8, 1963. By 2015, a total of sixty-two Black or African-American tenure-line faculty members were employed at Northwestern, comprising 4.6% of all faculty. Office of Institutional Diversity and Inclusion, "2016 Report on Faculty, Staff, and Student Diversity and Inclusion at Northwestern," Northwestern University, 17. From Institutional Research and Reports on the Status of Northwestern Women, https://www.northwestern.edu/womenscenter/get-info/institutional-research-and-reports-on-the-status-of-northwestern-women.html. By the fall of 2016, "According to the Northwestern Data Book, 3.5 percent of tenure-line and full-time faculty . . . — including those in graduate schools — were black." Troy Closson, "Unmet Demands," *Daily Northwestern,* May 3, 2018.

125 Bracey, "Living the Legacy-From Protest to Progress."

126 Turner, interview with the author, 2012. Sociologist John Gibbs St. Clair Drake (1911-1990) and co-author Horace R. Cayton, Jr. published the groundbreaking *Black Metropolis: A Study of Negro Life in a Northern City* in 1945. Drake taught at Roosevelt University and later founded the university's African and African American Studies programs.

127 Turner, interview with the author, 2012; Bracey, interview with the author, 2018.

128 Both Bracey and Stuckey would later be counted among the founders of Black Studies. Groundbreaking historian Ples Sterling Stuckey, Jr. (1932-2018) was a graduate of Du Sable High School in Chicago and later taught at Wendell Phillips High School in Chicago. He was a co-founder of the Amistad Society. He first enrolled at Northwestern in the 1950s, and would earn BA, MA, and PhD degrees at the university. He briefly took a break from his studies to take on many roles within the civil rights movement, including working as an organizer with the Congress of Racial Equality (CORE) in Chicago. In 1971, he became a professor of history at Northwestern and helped shape the African American Studies Department. He later taught at several other universities, including the University of California, Riverside. He was the author of many influential works, including, *Slave Culture: Nationalist Theory and the Foundations of Black America* (1987). "Sterling Stuckey, Renowned Historian, Dies," *Diverse Issues in Higher Education,* August 17, 2018, http://diverseeducation.com/article/123233/; Sam Roberts, "Sterling Stuckey, 86, Dies; Charted African Culture in Slavery," *New York Times,* August 28, 2018; Biondi, *The Black Revolution on Campus,* 98; Herbert G. Ruffin II, "Ples Sterling Stuckey,

Jr. (1932-2018)," *The Black Past,* December 18, 2018, https://www.blackpast.org/african-american-history/stuckey-ples-sterling-jr-1932-2018/.

129 Bracey and Stuckey also started an off-campus seminar to study the work of European theorists.

130 Turner, interview with the author, 2012.

131 Turner, interview with the author, 2012.

132 Ogletree, email to the author, December 2, 2018.

133 Ogletree, interview with the author, 2018.

134 Polhemus, "A Conversation on Racism."

135 The additional expenses of room and board, along with other fees, put the cost at $3,500 per year. Pitts, "The Politicalization of Black Students," 317; Michael Conway, "NU Officials Study Possible Tuition Hike," *Daily Northwestern,* January 5, 1967.

136 Pitts, "Growth of Black Consciousness at Northwestern," 8.

137 Ogletree, interview with the author, 2018.

138 Ogletree, interview with the author, 2018.

139 Photograph caption, *Daily Northwestern,* April 7, 1967.

140 Turner, interview with the author, 2012.

141 Ogletree, "Living the Legacy-From Protest to Progress."

142 Turner, interview with the author, 2012.

143 Ted Arndt to N. Ekberg, April 14, 1968, "Dean of Students, R. Hinz, 1967-1968," box 49, folder 1, Miller Papers, NUA. In March 1968, the *Daily Northwestern* light-heartedly reported the "first panty raid of the spring quarter" when four hundred male students "stormed" the women's dormitories and threw firecrackers at the windows. Bob Greene, "Spring's First Rites," *Daily Northwestern,* March 29, 1968.

144 Turner, interview with the author, 2012.

145 "My Soul Looks Back in Wonder," staged reading, fiftieth anniversary of the takeover, Northwestern University, May 4, 2018.

146 Ogletree, interview with the author, 2018.

147 Kathleen Flaherty, "Alumni Talk of Racism at NU 40 Years Ago," *Daily Northwestern,* November 1, 2008. A perusal of the portraits of fraternity members published in Northwestern's 1968 yearbook, *The Syllabus,* reveals that the majority of fraternities were (apparently) entirely white in membership. Chapters of the fraternities discussed in this book, Sigma Chi, Phi Gamma Delta ("Fiji,") and Triangle, had no Black members.

148 Pitts, "Growth of Black Consciousness at Northwestern," 20; Steve Sink, "Fiji Called to UDC for Second Hearing," *Daily Northwestern,* May 23, 1967.

149 The incident allegedly took place either on Sheridan Road or near (or in) Allison Hall, a women's campus dormitory. Bill Harsh, "Security Added at Fiji House," *Daily Northwestern,* May 19, 1967. Takeover participant Vernon Ford's recollection of this story is found in Jason Mast and Rosalie Chan, " 'It's Like a Legend.' " Pitts recounts the incident in "Growth of Black Consciousness at Northwestern," 20.

150 Bob Eaton, "Student Judiciary Requires Change in Statutes: McLeod," *Daily Northwestern,* April 14, 1962.

151 "UDC Change Needed," *Daily Northwestern,* April 26, 1962.

152 "UDC to Hear Fiji Case Again Today; Still Withholds Ruling," *Daily Northwestern,* May 24, 1967; "Fiji Case is Closed," *Daily Northwestern,* May 25, 1967.

153 "UDC to Hear Fiji Case Again Today; Still Withholds Ruling;" "Fiji Case is Closed," *Daily Northwestern,* May 25, 1967.

154 "UDC to Hear Fiji Case Again Today; Still Withholds Ruling."

155 Pitts, "Growth of Black Consciousness," 20-21; Bill Harsh, "Security Added at Fiji House," *Daily Northwestern,* May 19, 1967.

156 "Fiji Case is Closed," *Daily Northwestern,* May 25, 1967.

157 Steve Sink, "Fiji Called to UDC for Second Hearing," *Daily Northwestern,* May 23, 1967.

158 Pitts, "Growth of Black Consciousness at Northwestern," 21. With over half the student population belonging to the thirty fraternity and eighteen sorority chapters on campus, Greek life had a significant impact at Northwestern. In 1962, there had been "token desegregation" of Northwestern's fraternities, but over a four-year period only eight Black students were accepted into the fraternities and most of them were star athletes. Pitts, "Growth of Black Consciousness," 3. The majority of fraternities and sororities remained majority white, and national efforts to desegregate Greek organizations were not successful. In 1953, a campaign to abolish "bias clauses" in fraternities was launched by a group of Northwestern students who introduced a referendum to end discrimination in the Greek groups. It was defeated. Pridmore, *Northwestern University,* 196. The issue of discrimination within fraternities would draw national attention in subsequent years. In 1965, the Stanford University chapter of Sigma Chi was suspended by the national fraternity for pledging a Black member. "Frat Pulls for Negro Member," *Chicago Defender,* April 15, 1965. In February 1966, "Greeks Against Discrimination," a campus group was launched "to halt discrimination and prejudice at Northwestern." "New Equality Group to Hold First Meet" *Daily Northwestern,* March 2, 1966. In 1967, the issue of discrimination in Greek letter groups was again the subject of investigation by the Student Senate, led by Roger Friedman, president of the freshman class. Steve Sink, "NU Greek Discrimination Probe Begins," *Daily Northwestern,* April 4, 1967.

159-161 "Fiji Case is Closed," *Daily Northwestern,* May 25, 1967.

162 Roland J. Hinz, "Northwestern University Responses to the Black Student Petition Received April 22, 1968," Records of the Bursar's Office Takeover, May 1968, 3, box 1, folder 3, NUA.

163 "Negro Co-Ed is Homecoming Queen at N.U.," *Chicago Tribune,* October 21, 1967.

164 "Sorority Pledge List," *Daily Northwestern*, September 29, 1967. Judy Klemesrud, "Sororities: The Exuberance is Fading," *New York Times,* October 13, 1968. *Jet* magazine took note of the two pledges in its February 22, 1968 issue. Hinton's father, Clarence Hinton, had graduated from Northwestern in 1938.

165 Vernon Ford, "The Year Just Past: An NU Negro View," *Daily Northwestern,* January 3, 1968.

166 Daphne Maxwell Tubbs, letter to the editor, "Grad 'Thanks' NU," *Daily Northwestern,* July 10, 1970.

167 Daphne Maxwell Reid, panel discussion, fiftieth anniversary of the takeover, Northwestern University, May 4, 2018. Reid noted that members of the Black press arrived at the event in droves to cover the story, but many Northwestern

officials and students were not happy. Her surprise election was not an entirely positive experience for her. Once her name was announced in front of the crowd, "[I]t got real quiet," she recalled in a 2008 article by Nancy Deneen. " 'I smiled, received my flowers and left the stage.' The memory still stings." Nancy Deneen, "Daphne Maxwell Reid '70 Actress, Designer, Film Producer," *Weinberg Magazine,* Spring-Summer 2018, http://www.weinberg.northwestern.edu/after-graduation/weinberg-magazine/crosscurrents-archive/2008-spring-summer/reid.html; Daphne Maxwell Tubbs, "Grad 'Thanks' NU." At the time, there was some degree of outcry against the coverage of the homecoming ceremony. In a *Daily Northwestern* article by editor John Walter, he reported that Maxwell had been left "standing alone and unescorted" after she was elected Homecoming Queen. In a letter to the *Daily Northwestern* FMO officer, Milton Gardner objected to the paper's portrayal of the incident. Not only was it written without having talked directly to Maxwell, Gardner argued, but it also argued incorrectly that she was crestfallen at not being "integrated into the white festivities for homecoming." The story, Gardner argued, was "the creation of a guilt-ridden liberal." "FMO Disagrees on 'Memory,'" *Daily Northwestern,* November 7, 1967.

168 Pitts, "Growth of Black Consciousness at Northwestern," 8, 17.

169 "They Demanded Courageously, The 1968 Northwestern Bursar's Office Takeover." Originally from Kansas City, Cage graduated from Northwestern with a BS degree in 1969 and went on to earn his MBA from Northwestern in 1973. He currently runs his own financial consulting business in Chicago. "Reconciling Works," https://www.reconcilingworks.org/about/board/.

170 Colin Boyle, "For Members Only Panelists Discuss History, Future of Black Community at NU," *Daily Northwestern,* February 21, 2018.

171 Some sources also list Milton Gardner as a co-founder of FMO. See for example, Brett Pulley, "Black Alums Party for Scholarship," *Daily Northwestern,* July 10, 1986.

172 Charles E. Shepard, "For Members Only (F.M.O.): From Moderation to Militancy," c. 1969.

173 Pitts, "The Politicalization of Black Students," 294-295.

174 Ogletree, interview with the author, 2018.

175 "They Demanded Courageously, The 1968 Northwestern Bursar's Office Takeover."

176 Daphne Maxwell Tubbs, "Grad 'Thanks' NU;" Lynn Elber, " 'Fresh Prince' Star Reid Focuses on a Creative Life," *AP,* December 7, 2018; Daphne Maxwell Reid, "Living the Legacy-From Protest to Progress."

177 "They Demanded Courageously, The 1968 Northwestern Bursar's Office Takeover."

178 Ogletree, interview with the author, 2018.

179 Vernon Ford, "The Year Just Past: An NU Negro View," *Daily Northwestern,* January 3, 1968; Vernon Ford, "The Black Athlete at a White University," *Daily Northwestern,* April 25, 1968.

180 Steve Sink, "Pines, Caulfield, Behr to Head Senate," *Daily Northwestern,* April 20, 1967; Barbara Foeller, "Freshman to Vote on Dow, Drug Policy This Weekend," *Daily Northwestern,* January 19, 1968; "Shanahan Voted Senate President," *Daily Northwestern,* April 18, 1968.

181 "Organizational Meeting for Negro History Club Set," *Daily Northwestern,* December 1, 1967.

182 Pitts, "Growth of Black Consciousness at Northwestern," 17; Pitts, "The Politicalization of Black Students," 290.

183 Kathy Polhemus, "A Conversation on Racism," *Daily Northwestern,* April 14, 1969.

184 Pitts, "The Politicalization of Black Students," 295.

185 Ogletree, interview with the author, 2018.

186 Pitts, "Growth of Black Consciousness at Northwestern," 26.

187 Bracey, interview with the author, 2018. Bracey recalled that when he and his friend went to look at the Foster Street apartment that they'd eventually end up subletting from two other students, the landlord suspected that they were investigating housing discrimination. Bracey and his friend ended up moving into the apartment, becoming the first Black residents on the block.

188-192 Bracey, interview with the author, 2018.

193 Vernon Ford, "Black Senior Looks Back," *Daily Northwestern,* April 23, 1968.

194 Ogletree, interview with the author, 2018.

195 Ogletree, interview with the author, 2018. Hinz noted that meetings with Black students to discuss "campus, summer program, and admission problems" took place in the spring of 1967. Later, Hinz stated that the Admissions Office wanted to "formalize such meetings in order to acquire better counsel from the University's black community regarding the recruitment of black students." "Northwestern University Responses to the Black Student Petition Received Monday, April 22, 1968," 3.

196 Ogletree, interview with the author, 2018.

197 Ogletree, interview with the author, 2018.

198 Pitts, "The Politicalization of Black Students," 293.

199 "No Negro Sororities at NU: Thrash," *Daily Northwestern,* April 19, 1967.

200 Nancy Snapp, "Panhel to Host Shepard Meeting," *Daily Northwestern,* May 3, 1967; Cross, "James Turner: The Face of Black Power at Northwestern." In 1969, Alpha Kappa Alpha founded Gamma Chi, a chapter at Northwestern. Alpha Phi Alpha, Kappa Alpha Psi, and Alpha Kappa Alpha currently have chapters at Northwestern University.

201 Tom Davies, "Negro fraternities Will Bid Today for Return to NU," *Daily Northwestern,* May 2, 1967. The initial idea to reactivate the groups had largely sprung from the local Evanston community. As integration efforts were underway at Northwestern, two fraternity alumni who lived in Evanston, John Wallace, a teacher at Evanston Township High School and chairman of Alpha Phi Alpha expansion, and Andrew Rodez, president of Kappa Alpha Psi's alumni chapter, (and an Evanston Police officer) began to gauge potential interest among students for bringing the fraternities back to campus. Although Kappa Alpha Psi's Theta Chapter was deactivated, it remained a "municipal chapter," with its members still part of the group. According to the *Daily Northwestern,* Wallace first approached Hinz about bringing the chapter back to campus. At about the same time, juniors Roger Ward and Vernon Ford also began to consider reactivating the Kappa Alpha Psi chapter on campus and reached out to Samuel Bolden, a local Kappa Alpha Psi member. Tom Davies, "NU Officials Examine Negro Fraternity Reactivation Plans," *Daily Northwestern,* April 19, 1967.

202 Tom Davies, "Fraternity Reactivation Plans," *Daily Northwestern,* April 19, 1967.

203 Editorial, "What's Going On?" *Daily Northwestern,* May 18, 1967.

204 "Frat Denies Northwestern Racist Charge," *Chicago Defender,* October 30, 1967.

205 "Black Fraternity Wins Reinstatement At Northwestern U.," *Chicago Defender,* April 13, 1968.

206 "Frat Denies Northwestern Racist Charge," *Chicago Defender,* October 30, 1967. Albert J. Weiss of the Anti Defamation League of Chicago concurred with the university's position. In a letter to Franklin Kreml, Weiss argued that "predominately negro fraternities and sororities" would only encourage a separation of Black and white students. "ADL Asks Rejection," *Daily Northwestern,* May 26, 1967. Walter Wallace, Lucius Gregg, Jr., and Jack Hinz were among those who initially opposed (but later supported) the predominantly Black groups, all agreeing, as Hinz wrote, that such organizations would "tend to segregate these students from the rest of our student body and would work in opposition to the efforts which we have made in recent years to integrate student life at Northwestern." Jack Hinz to J. Roscoe Miller, June 19, 1967, "Dean of Students, R. Hinz, 1967-1968," box 49, folder 1, Miller Papers, NUA.

207 Tom Stanley, letter to the editor, *Daily Northwestern,* May 18, 1967.

208 "Separate But Equal," *Daily Northwestern,* May 12, 1967.

209 Tom Davies, "Negro fraternities Will Bid Today for Return to NU," *Daily Northwestern,* May 2, 1967.

210 Williamson and Wild, 287. When the CUL was first formed in the 1950s, there were no student representatives on the council. President Miller held veto power over the CUL. John Walter, "Senate Backs Frat, Housing March," *Daily Northwestern,* May 9, 1967.

211 Tom Davies, "Negroes Form Own Groups," *Daily Northwestern,* January 25, 1968; Jack Hinz to J. Roscoe Miller, June 19, 1967, "Dean of Students, R. Hinz, 1967-1968," box 49, folder 1, Miller Papers, NUA.

212 Roland J. Hinz, "An Open Letter to all Northwestern Students," September 1967, "Dean of Students, R. Hinz, 1967-1968," box 49, folder 6, Miller Papers, NUA.

213 Davies, "Negroes Form Own Groups."

214 Among the members and pledges of Kappa Alpha Psi were: Stanley Hill, Roger Ward, Vernon Ford, Dan Davis Clinton Bristow, Gregory Harper, Roland Person, James Hill, Leon Coleman, Fred Heard, John Trimble, William West, Stephen Broussard, Earl (Chico) Freeman, Robert Scott, and Michael Smith. Alpha Phi Alpha members and pledges included: Andre Bell, Lonnie Radcliffe, Nelson Johnson, Dale Kelley, and Arnold Wright. All of the above mentioned would take part in the takeover. By January 1968, seventeen men and six women at Northwestern had joined the Chicago area chapters of the two fraternities, Alpha Phi Alpha and Kappa Alpha Psi, and two sororities, Delta Sigma Theta and Alpha Kappa Alpha. Tom Davies, "Black Frats' Start Poses Questions," *Daily Northwestern,* April 17, 1968; Tom Davies, "Negroes Form Own Groups," *Daily Northwestern,* January 25, 1968.

215 Tom Davies, "Negro Frat, Student Differ on NU Pledge Interest," *Daily Northwestern,* October 17, 1967.

216 Rolf Schulze, "The Student Rebellion in the United States: A Case Study of a Cool Confrontation with Academic Racism," *Sociological Bulletin,* Vol. 19. (March 1970): 14-15.

217 Ogletree, interview with the author, 2018.

218 Kathy Polhemus, "A Conversation on Racism," *Daily Northwestern*, April 14, 1969.

219 Pitts, "The Politicalization of Black Students," 298.

220 This reference was cited in the university's official response to the Black students' demands of April 1968.

221 Cross, "James Turner: The Face of Black Power at Northwestern."

222 Hinz, interview with the author, 2012.

223 Hinz, interview with the author, 2012.

224 Ogletree, interview with the author, 2018.

225 Bracey, interview with the author, 2018.

226 Ogletree, interview with the author, 2018.

227-229 Turner, interview with the author, 2012.

230 Jeffrey A. Raffel, *Historical Dictionary of School Segregation and Desegregation: The American Experience* (Westport, CT: Greenwood Press, 1998), 131.

231-232 Turner, interview with the author, 2012.

233 Ruth Moss, "Lawndale Goes to College," *Chicago Tribune,* October 24, 1965.

234 Moss, "Lawndale Goes to College."

235 Northwestern University, "Confrontation on the Campus," May 6, 1968, box 2, folder 8, Kreml papers, NUA.

236-237 Moss, "Lawndale Goes to College."

238 Bracey, interview with the author, 2018.

239 Jim Clare and Frank Zoretich, " 'Invisibility' is Main Problem Facing Negroes at NU," *Daily Northwestern,* March 2, 1966. The article included sophomore Vernon Ford's observation that "Race is not a problem at Northwestern, because the Negro doesn't exist here." Clearly, Ford's statement was made sarcastically, but reporters extrapolated from it, perhaps relying on a reading of Ralph Ellison's 1952 novel, *Invisible Man.* The caricature of Black students being "invisible" at Northwestern would emerge occasionally in other, later instances, and was often challenged by Black students.

240 "Recruitment Plan Exceeds Hope, Hinz Announces," *Daily Northwestern,* April 1, 1966.

241 "Confrontation on the Campus," May 6, 1968.

242 Victor Goode and Eric Perkins, Report, October 28, 1968, in "Admissions Scholarship Committee, 1956-1968," box 2, folder 6, Miller Papers, NUA.

243 Pitts, "The Politicalization of Black Students," 283.

244 Bracey, "Living the Legacy-From Protest to Progress."

245 Clare and Zoretich, " 'Invisibility' is Main Problem Facing Negroes at NU."

246 "Doc Glass' Home Away from Home for Negroes," *Daily Northwestern,* March 3, 1966.

247 James Pitts, unpublished term paper for Group Leadership B24-O, Northwestern University, Fall 1965, 1-2, NUA.

248 Pitts, unpublished term paper, 1-2.

249 Pitts, unpublished term paper, 4.

250 "Doc Glass' Home Away from Home for Negroes," *Daily Northwestern,* March 3, 1966.

251 "Doc Glass' Home Away from Home for Negroes."

252-254 Ogletree, "Living the Legacy-From Protest to Progress."
255 Turner, interview with the author, 2012.
256 Hinz, interview with the author, 2012.
257 Turner, interview with the author, 2012.
258 Ogletree, interview with the author, 2018.
259 "Black Student Statement and Petition to Northwestern University Administrators," Received Monday, April 22, 1968, 4. Records of the Bursar's Office Takeover, May 1968, 1, box 1, folder 3, NUA.
260 Turner, interview with the author, 2012.
261 Turner, interview with the author, 2012.
262 Bracey, interview with the author, 2018.
263 Jason Mast and Rosalie Chan, " 'It's Like a Legend.' "

Notes to Chapter 4

1 Marla Strassberger, "Pine Leaves Student Senate, NU," *Daily Northwestern,* September 26, 1967.

2 Roger Friedman, email to the author, January 18, 2019.

3 Loren Chudy, "Analysis: Political Action Groups," *Daily Northwestern,* April 22, 1966.

4 "SDS at NU," *Daily Northwestern,* November 16, 1965; Loren Chudy, "Analysis: Political Action Groups."

5 Dan Lovely, "SDS Marches Downtown," *Daily Northwestern,* April 19, 1966.

6 David O'Brien, letter to the editor, "Challenge," *Daily Northwestern,* November 16, 1965.

7 David O'Brien, letter to the editor, "Restraint," *Daily Northwestern,* November 2, 1965.

8 Dan Lovely, "SDS Marches Downtown."

9 Dan Lovely, "SDS Marches Downtown."

10 "SDS Protests U of C's Draft Policy," *Daily Northwestern,* May 17, 1966. Fager was also active in many other ways. In 1966, she confronted university officials and demanded that they reveal Northwestern's policy of releasing lists of student members of SDS and other groups to the FBI, eventually forcing the administration to declare that it would not release any such lists. Officials also pledged that "the FBI is not now on campus, and it has never been in the past." Fager said she had been "pestered" by officials to provide them with the membership list of SDS at Northwestern. She reluctantly complied, offering the names of only five students. Joan Schuman and Loren Chudy, "Decision Pends on NU Policy on Giving Names of Students in Political Groups," *Daily Northwestern,* May 17, 1966; "NU Will Not Release Membership Lists," *Daily Northwestern,* May 20, 1966.

11 Announcement, *Daily Northwestern,* January 27, 1967. Tom Holmes was elected vice president. Steering committee members included George Vickers, Ed Steinhart, and Larry Felt. Steven Lubet is currently a professor of law at the Northwestern University Pritzker School of Law. "Steven Lubet," Northwestern Pritzker School of Law, http://www.law.northwestern.edu/faculty/profiles/stevenlubet/.

12 Eric Miller, *Hope in a Scattering Time: A Life of Christopher Lasch* (Grand Rapids, MI: William B. Eerdmans, 2010), 137. Lasch became a well known critic of the American political and cultural scene. He was an advocate of the New Left and radical reform of U.S. institutions and policies, but he also had a keen critical eye, analyzing the left, progressives, and radicals with the same trenchant analysis he brought to bear on his critique of American society and politics in general. He served as professor at the University of Iowa before accepting an appointment at Northwestern, where he served as professor of history from 1966 to 1970. In 1970, he was hired by the University of Rochester, where he served as professor and chair of the history department. Among his many influential books are, *The Agony of the American Left* (1969), *The Culture of Narcissism* (1979), and *The True and Only Heaven: Progress and Its Critics* (1991). William Grimes, "Christopher Lasch Is Dead at 61," *New York Times,* February 15, 1994.

13 Along with other faculty members, including George Fredrickson, Robert

Wiebe, Michael Marcus, and Marvin Shinbrot, Lasch was a member of the Faculty Committee on Vietnam, a group that held teach-ins and participated in other anti-war activities. Joann Lublin, "Nine Profs Teach-In Tonight on Recruiting," *Daily Northwestern,* February 13, 1969. Raymond Mack, considered an expert on race relations, joined Northwestern's faculty in 1953. He later chaired the sociology department and served as vice president and dean of faculties. Megan Fellman, "Raymond W. Mack, Expert on Race Relations, Dies at 84," Northwestern University, August 29, 2011, https://www.northwestern.edu/newscenter/stories/2011/08/raymond-mack-obituary.html#sthash.I22rKvd2.dpuf. Robert Wiebe, also known for his progressive views and activism, was hired as a faculty member in 1960 and became a renowned historian, whose works include the influential history of the American progressive era, *The Search for Order, 1877-1920* (1967). "Wiebe, Robert H.," Northwestern University, Archival and Manuscript Collections, https://findingaids.library.northwestern.edu/agents/people/1122. After earning a PhD from M.I.T. in 1965, Michael Marcus came to Northwestern. He later taught at Texas A&M University, the City College of New York, and the CUNY Graduate Center. "Professor Michael Marcus, City College of New York," https://www2.isye.gatech.edu/~dai/cap/distinguished-lectures/marcus.html. Marvin Shinbrot (1928-1987) was quite outspoken politically. According to one of his close friends, he "personally handed out flyers protesting the Vietnam war and civil rights violations; he spoke out against the role of the university as a slumlord. This attitude brought him many enemies—he was branded 'the most dangerous man in Northwestern University, possibly the United States,' by a reactionary professor; he was gassed at the police riots associated with the Democratic National Convention of 1968; his family was harassed—they received bomb threats and rocks through their windows." Ultimately, the university would "discontinue his contract" in 1972. He later moved to Canada, where he taught at the University of Victoria. Reinhard Illner "Marvin Shinbrot: 1928-1987," *Transport Theory and Statistical Physics*, February 1989, 2. https://www.northwestern.edu/newscenter/stories/2011/08/raymond-mack-obituary.html.

14 Roger Friedman, email to the author, January 20, 2019.

15 Roger Friedman, email to the author, January 20, 2019.

16 Friedman, email to the author, January 22, 2019.

17 Friedman, email to the author, January 18, 2019; "Friedman Elected Frosh Class President," *Daily Northwestern,* November 23, 1966.

18 Friedman, email to the author, January 18, 2019.

19 Friedman made this statement at a Presidents Round Table meeting, composed of university officials and student government representatives. "Financial Aid Should Not Hinge on Accum: Ihlanfeldt," *Daily Northwestern,* January 12, 1967.

20 Steve Sink, "Senate Backs City Open Housing," *Daily Northwestern,* March 31, 1967.

21 Michael Conway, "Officials' Reaction Mixed on Senate Housing Plea," *Daily Northwestern,* April 4, 1967.

22 Friedman, email to the author, January 20, 2019.

23 Steve Sink, "NU Greek Discrimination Probe Begins," *Daily Northwestern,* April 4, 1967. Just weeks later, the Interfraternity Council passed a resolution to require fraternities to sign a pledge that there were no "official or unofficial chapter policies" which "condone or allow discrimination on the basis of race, religion, or

national origin." Despite the passage of the resolution, however, the Student Senate continued its investigation into discriminatory practices within Greek organizations. Tom Davies, "Bill to Be No Problem-Wray," *Daily Northwestern,* April 21, 1967. An effort to pass legislation barring fraternities and sororities from discriminating against prospective members had been ongoing. In 1954, the Student Governing Board backed a ban on discrimination, which would, by 1960, only allow Greek-letter groups on campus if they were able to prove to a student and faculty panel that they were "fighting discrimination in their national organization." But the Council on Undergraduate Life, in a decision backed by President Miller, voted to reject the ban. "Council's Bias Ban Rejection Strands," *Daily Northwestern,* July 9, 1954; Tom Davies, "Negro Fraternities Will Bid Today for Return to NU," *Daily Northwestern,* May 2, 1967.

24 "Power Backs 'Gentle' Outing," *Daily Northwestern,* April 26, 1967.

25 Announcement, *Daily Northwestern,* May 10, 1967.

26 Friedman, email to the author, January 18, 2019.

27 Ellis Pines, notes to the author, October 12, 2018.

28 Pines, notes to the author, October 12, 2018. The Chicago Business Industrial Project was designed to enlist "corporate executives in understanding and responding to the needs of inner-city neighborhoods." Andrew Scott, "Columcille Founder Remembered," *Pocono Record,* June 21, 2018.

29 John Walter, "Pines Leaves Student Senate, NU," *Daily Northwestern,* September 26, 1967.

30 Pines, notes to the author, October 12, 2018; John Walter, "Fifty Hear Ellis Talk on Himself, Power," *Daily Northwestern,* September 26, 1967.

31 Advertisement, "How Student Power Can Be Used at Northwestern," *Daily Northwestern,* April 18, 1967. Pines also backed an investigation into discrimination among fraternities and sororities. By the spring of 1967, the Student Senate passed a bill prohibiting discrimination in fraternity and sorority rush. Kathy Waters, "Relations Committee Sets Meeting with NU Officials," *Daily Northwestern,* February 12, 1969.

32 Jack Fuller, "Pines: New Force," *Daily Northwestern,* April 25, 1967; "SDS Votes Support for Rader, Pines' Movement," *Daily Northwestern,* April 21, 1967.

33 "Northwestern U. Protest," *Chicago Tribune,* April 19, 1967; "Pick 'Student Power' Leader in N.U. Race," *Chicago Tribune,* April 20, 1967. In May 1967, Pines and others presented a set of demands to the university administration which included calling for the university to take a public stand on the issue of open housing. "Flag Incident at N.U. Brings an Apology," *Chicago Tribune,* May 6, 1967. An increasing move toward what some might term "radicalism" among students was cited in November 1967 with the WBBM airing of a television documentary, "Pot Party at a University," which showed Northwestern students smoking marijuana. It caused considerable concern among university administrators, and eventually led to an investigation by the FCC. Aldo Beckman, "N.U. Student Tells TV Pot Parry Plea," *Chicago Tribune,* May 11, 1968; "Pot Party Induced," *Decatur Daily Review,* May 17, 1969.

34 Jack Fuller, "Pines: New Force," *Daily Northwestern,* April 25, 1967; Steve Sink, " 'Bitch-In' Turns Sit-In at Pearsons," *Daily Northwestern,* April 18, 1967.

35 Interview with Ellis Pines, quoted in Reed Wilson, "Ellis Pines and The Student Power Movement at Northwestern: The Pursuit of Personal Authenticity

and Political Legitimacy in the Face of Existential Angst and Social Alienation, 1966-1968," unpublished paper, June 2010, 12.

36 Donna Rosene, "Pines Contradicts Miller at Conference," *Daily Northwestern,* May 16, 1967.

37 Steve Sink, " 'Bitch-In' Turns Sit-In at Pearsons," *Daily Northwestern,* April 18, 1967.

38 Steven Sink, "Dr. Miller to Meet Pines This Morning," *Daily Northwestern,* April 19, 1967.

39 Photograph caption, *Daily Northwestern,* April 19, 1967.

40 Joan Schuman, "Grievances Presented to Dr. Miller-Invited to Student Forum on May 2," *Daily Northwestern,* April 20, 1967. Russell Barefield, a graduate research assistant, soon resigned from the SPM, allegedly under pressure from university administrators who argued that he could not be kept on the university payroll if he continued to be involved in student activities. "Power Group Says Barefield Quits Under University Pressure," *Daily Northwestern,* May 2, 1967. A protest followed, during which time Pines and others hung an American flag upside down from a second story window in Harris Hall. It was, they said, a symbol of "free speech under distress." Photograph caption, *Daily Northwestern,* May 4, 1967. Students also wore American flag lapel pins upside down. Steve Sink, "Bitch-in Set Today," *Daily Northwestern,* May 3, 1967. Franklin Kreml later affirmed that Barefield had been ordered to cease his involvement in the SPM, but now said that he would be permitted to stay in both his university job and the SPM. John Walter, "Kreml Absolves Administration," *Daily Northwestern,* May 4, 1967. Pines later apologized for the flag incident.

41 "Pines, Caulfield, Behr, Elected," *Daily Northwestern,* April 20, 1967.

42 John Walter, "Student Power Movement Officially Dissolved-Pines," *Daily Northwestern,* May 9, 1967.

43 "Pick 'Student Power' Leader in N.U. Race," *Chicago Tribune,* April 20, 1967; "Daily Picks Top 10 NU Stories," *Daily Northwestern,* May 26, 1967.

44 "Pines, Caulfield, Behr, Elected," *Daily Northwestern,* April 20, 1967.

45 Donna Rosene, "Pines Contradicts Miller at Conference."

46 Steve Sink, "Aldermen, Wild to Debate Open Housing," *Daily Northwestern,* April 21, 1967.

47 "March is Orderly," *Daily Northwestern,* May 11, 1967; Marc Zwelling, "Long, Hot Summer Reaches Evanston," *Daily Northwestern,* September 14, 1967.

48 Steve Sink, "Bitch-In Set Today," *Daily Northwestern,* May 4, 1967; Tom Davies, "Negro fraternities Will Bid Today for Return to NU," *Daily Northwestern,* May 2, 1967.

49 Duane Anderson, "On the Lookout for Rush Bias," *Daily Northwestern,* September 21, 1967. In a report issued later, the committee investigating bias in Greek-letter group rushing practices reported that "no flagrant examples of rush discrimination were observed by freshman rushees last fall, but discrimination may be inherent in the fraternity system at Northwestern." "Rush Week is Clean, Bias Committee Says," *Daily Northwestern,* February 6, 1968.

50 Joan Schuman, "Grievances Presented to Dr. Miller-Invited to Student Forum on May 2," *Daily Northwestern,* April 20, 1967.

51 Roy, Harris, "Miller Tells NU Policies to 1000," *Daily Northwestern,* May 16, 1967; "Dr. Miller Asks Students to Meet Him in Forum," *Daily Northwestern,* April 25, 1967.

52 "Miller Meeting Today Closed to Non-Students," *Daily Northwestern,* May 12, 1967.

53-55 Friedman, email to the author, January 18, 2019.

56 "Men in Blue Uniforms Field Questions on War Morality," *Daily Northwestern,* November 16, 1967.

57 Marla Strassberger, "NU Groups Protest War Effort," *Daily Northwestern,* April 18, 1967.

58 "SDS Raises Rader Bail Money," *Daily Northwestern,* April 21, 1967; "Arrested for Viet Protest," *Chicago Tribune,* April 20, 1967.

59 "Rader to Speak at SDS Tonight," *Daily Northwestern,* May 18, 1967. While at Northwestern, Rader (1944-1973) served as vice president of the Student Senate. A political science major, he was just one course shy of graduating when he refused to take a final required course "in protest," he said, "against 'the system.' " Facing the possibility of being drafted, he considered going to Canada, but instead enlisted in the Special Forces and later joined a reserve unit. He soon became deeply committed to opposing the war. After his arrest, Rader was found guilty and sentenced to four years in jail, a sentence that was later overturned. Rader would continue his activism against the war. He went on to play a prominent role in the anti-war movement. (In 1973, Rader died by suicide.) By the fall of 1967, CADRE members at Northwestern sought to raise the issue of the war and the draft by sponsoring talks, attending rallies, and circulating literature, including a "draft resistance statement." "CADRE to Pass Draft Statement," *Daily Northwestern,* November 14, 1967. CADRE's draft resistance statement was signed by fifteen individuals, including both students and faculty, who stated that they intended to burn their draft cards.

60 CADRE's co-founder was David F. Greenberg. Gary Rader, "Draft Resistance," *New York Review of Books,* September 14, 1967 https://www.nybooks.com/articles/1967/09/14/draft-resistance; "Alum Burns Draft Card," *Daily Northwestern,* April 18, 1967. While at Northwestern, Rader worked with Professor Kenneth Janda to develop a computerized system to notify scholars when new research articles were published in their areas of interest. Kenneth Janda and Gary Rader, "Selective Dissemination of Information: A Progress Report from Northwestern University," *American Behavioral Scientist,* January 1, 1967, https://doi.org/10.1177/000276426701000506.

61 "SDS Votes Support for Rader, Pines' Movement," *Daily Northwestern,* April 21, 1967.

62 Joann Lublin, "SDS Plans Own Newssheet to Voice Views of Minorities," *Daily Northwestern,* September 29, 1967. In a visit to Northwestern, poet Alan Ginsberg told student Kenny Byrne about the "Gentle Thursday" events held in San Francisco, planting the seed for a similar event to be held on Northwestern's campus. Joann Lublin, " 'Gentle Thursday' Planned; Exercise in Love, Kindness," *Daily Northwestern,* April 25, 1967.

63 Judy Kulstad, "Gentle Thursday: Black Friday?" *Daily Northwestern,* April 26, 1967.

64 Photograph caption, *Daily Northwestern,* October 6, 1967.

65 One of the earliest public acts of opposition among faculty occurred in the spring of 1966 when seven Northwestern professors wrote to President Johnson and called upon him to support a cease fire in the conflict. "Northwestern Profs Protest Viet Conflict," *Daily Northwestern,* May 17, 1966.

66 "An Open Letter to President Johnson from Northwestern University Faculty Members, Graduate Students and Undergraduates," *Daily Northwestern,* May 24, 1966.

67 Marla Strassberger, Bill Harsh, and Bill Smith, "2,000 Hear War Protests at Teach-In," *Daily Northwestern,* April 14, 1967; Flyer, "Vietnam Teach-In: A Program of Speakers on the War and American Society," Thursday, April 13, 1967, Student Protests, NUA. The teach-in took place from 3 p.m. to midnight.

68 Marla Strassberger, Bill Harsh, and Bill Smith, "2,000 Hear War Protests at Teach-In."

69 Petition, October 10, 1967, "Dean of Students, R. Hinz, 1967-1968," box 49, folder 1, Miller Papers, NUA. Miller defended the faculty's right to "act individually or collectively to make their views known and to seek support for them." But he also stated that they "should not identify the University with their activities." Miller to Hinz, November 2, 1967, "Dean of Students, R. Hinz, 1967-1968," box 49, folder 1, Miller Papers, NUA.

70 Letter to J. Roscoe Miller, October 7, 1967, "Dean of Students, R. Hinz, 1967-1968," box 49, folder 6, Miller papers, NUA.

71 Kreml, May 5, 1967, box, 2, folder, 7, Kreml papers, NUA.

72 Dale J. Walther, letter to the editor, *Daily Northwestern,* May 10, 1967.

73 Walther, letter to the editor.

74 Marianne Jackson, letter to the editor, *Daily Northwestern,* May 18, 1967.

75 Jackson, letter to the editor.

76 Friedman, email to the author, January 18, 2019.

77 Friedman, email to the author, January 18, 2019.

78 Letter to J. Roscoe Miller, October 11, 1967, "Dean of Students, R. Hinz, 1967-1968," box 49, folder 6, Miller papers, NUA. Northwestern students had proposed parietal hours in 1966. At the time, male students could be penalized if they were caught in the room of a female student and vice versa. Many students found this rule to be entirely antiquated. Once administrators (reluctantly) agreed to look into the issue, an editorial in the *Daily Northwestern* sarcastically wrote: "And so, in 1966, this university takes another great stride into the Thirties." "Stride into the Thirties," *Daily Northwestern,* January 28, 1966.

79 Anonymous to Miller, ND, "Dean of Students, R. Hinz, 1967-1968," box 49, folder 6, Miller papers, NUA.

80 Hinz, "An Open Letter to All Northwestern Students."

81 "Trib Editorial Blasts Bitch-in," *Daily Northwestern,* May 5, 1967.

82 John Walter, "Senate Calls Down Power Movement," *Daily Northwestern,* May 5, 1967.

83 Walter, "Senate Calls Down Power Movement."

84 Ellis Pines, notes to the author, October 12, 2018.

85 Pines and his colleagues dissolved the SPM as an official organization over the weekend of May 6-7, 1967. John Walter, "Student Power Movement Officially Dissolved-Pines," *Daily Northwestern,* May 9, 1967.

86 Walter, "Senate Calls Down Power Movement."

87 Pines argued that he had made up the work from a course in which he had taken an incomplete and thereby brought his grades up to standard. The

university disputed this and held him to the rule that any student with two grades lower than "C" had to resign from all extracurricular activities. Marla Strassberger, "Pine Leaves Student Senate, NU," *Daily Northwestern,* September 26, 1967.

88-90 Strassberger, "Pine Leaves Student Senate, NU."

91 Friedman, email to the author, January 18, 2019.

92 Joann Lublin, "To Voice Views of Minorities," *Daily Northwestern,* September 29, 1967.

93 Friedman, email to the author, January 23, 2019.

94 Announcement, *Daily Northwestern,* January 27, 1967.

95 Friedman, email to the author, January 23, 2019.

96 "Judicial Rights Sought," *Daily Northwestern,* November 16, 1967; Bill Harsh, "Pines, Now SDS Worker, Blasts New Parietal Plan," *Daily Northwestern,* October 13, 1967. Along with Friedman, students George Vickers and Barb Caulfield, who was president of the Student Senate, worked with faculty members Christopher Lasch, Robert Wiebe, and Howard Becker to try to overhaul student judicial proceedings. At the time, students had little autonomy and their rights were often violated in ways that would likely be illegal today. For example, in 1967, campus security deployed detectives within men's dormitories to conduct surveillance and "nab homosexuals in the men's room." In one dorm, detectives reportedly spied "on homosexuals from a room separating two rows of toilet stalls." "Homosexuality on campus is the 'number one' problem for law enforcement officials across the country" chief of campus security, Ted Arndt told the *Daily Northwestern.* "We are going to arrest everyone we catch now," he pledged. "Homosexuality Cited as a Major Campus Problem," *Daily Northwestern,* September 29, 1967.

97 Joann Lublin, "SDS Plans Own Newssheet to Voice Views of Minorities," *Daily Northwestern,* September 29, 1967.

98 Friedman, email to the author, January 18, 2019.

99 Friedman, email to the author, January 23, 2019.

100 Barbara Caulfield (c. 1947-2010) went on to earn a law degree from Northwestern and was later appointed a U.S. District judge in California. She taught law at several universities, including Northwestern, and she also directed a trial advocacy program at Harvard. Bob Egelko, "Barbara Caulfield, Attorney, Federal Judge, Dies," *SF Gate,* November 19, 2010. https://www.sfgate.com/bayarea/article/Barbara-Caulfield-attorney-federal-judge-dies-3165997.php.

101 Charles V. Hamilton and Stokely Carmichael (Kwame Ture), *Black Power: Politics of Liberation in America* (New York, Vintage Books, 1967, 1992), 47.

102 Bracey, "Living the Legacy-From Protest to Progress," panel discussion about the 1968 takeover, held at Northwestern University, May 3, 2018.

103 Bracey, "Living the Legacy-From Protest to Progress."

104 Daphne Maxwell Reid, panel discussion, fiftieth anniversary of the takeover, Northwestern University, May 4, 2018.

105 Ogletree, interview with the author, 2018.

106-109 Ogletree, interview with the author, 2018.

110 Bracey, "Living the Legacy-From Protest to Progress."

111 Turner, interview with the author, 2012.

112 Ogletree, interview with the author, 2018.

113 Ogletree, interview with the author, 2018.

114 Ogletree, email to the author, September 8, 2018.

115 Pitts, "Growth of Black Consciousness at Northwestern," 31.

116 Ogletree, "Living the Legacy-From Protest to Progress." For an informative study of the experiences of Black female students at predominantly white colleges and universities in the 1960s, see Elizabeth Higginbotham, *Too Much to Ask: Black Women in the Era of Integration* (Chapel Hill, NC: University of North Carolina Press, 2001). To be sure, the university exercised more extensive control over the entire female student population than it did over male students; women, for example, were subject to curfews. Barbara Haber provides an interesting observation on the control of female students on university campuses in the 1960s and earlier. "Rules, such as the then common curfews for women, ostensibly aimed at protecting helpless women from uncontrollable men," Haber wrote, "were actually used to rationalize the limitation of women's freedom and autonomy." Haber, "A Manifesto of Hope," in *Port Huron Statement: Sources and Legacies of the New Left's Founding Manifesto*, 145.

117 Ogletree, interview with the author, 2018.

118 Ogletree, interview with the author, 2018.

119 Tom Davies, "Negroes Form Own Groups," *Daily Northwestern*, January 25, 1968.

120 Ogletree, email to the author, December 1, 2018.

121 "Fund Started to Help Students," *Daily Northwestern*, February 28, 1968.

122 Cross, "James Turner: The Face of Black Power at Northwestern."

123 Turner, interview with the author, 2012.

124 Turner, interview with the author, 2012. Turner recalled that the organizing efforts of Black student groups around the country made a significant impact on him and others. In 1966, for example, members of the Black student union at San Francisco State College (now University) demanded the creation of a Black Studies Department; a demand that was met by the university in 1969. Williamson-Lott, *Black Power on Campus*, 29.

125 Perkins and Goode submitted a proposal to William Ihlanfeldt for their planned trip and requested funding. They received travel funds from the Wieboldt Foundation. Victor Goode and Eric Perkins, Report, October 28, 1968, "Admissions Scholarship Committee, 1956-1968," box 2, folder 6, Miller Papers, NUA; Cross, "James Turner: The Face of Black Power at Northwestern;" William Ihlanfeldt to Miller, December 16, 1968, "Admissions Scholarship Committee, 1956-1968," box 2, folder 6, Miller Papers, NUA.

126 Victor Goode and Eric Perkins, Report, October 28, 1968.

127 Victor Goode and Eric Perkins to William Ihlanfeldt, October 28, 1968, box 2, folder 6, Miller Papers, NUA.

128 Ogletree, interview with the author, 2018, and email to the author, September 7, 2018.

129 Tom Davies, "Negroes Form Own Groups," *Daily Northwestern*, January 25, 1968.

130 Davies, "Negroes Form Own Groups."

131 Bosley Crowther, "Students Cheer Talk of Violence," *New York Times*, January 22, 1968. Crowther debated critic Leslie Fieldler in what became a very contentious encounter concerning their disagreement over the portrayal of violence in art, namely in the 1967 film *Bonnie and Clyde*. Crowther thought the film's use of "glamorous violence" was dangerous. "Crowther Versus Fiedler is Failure to

Communicate," *Daily Northwestern,* January 23, 1968.

132 Jack Fuller, "White Power System Must Be Defeated-Panelists," *Daily Northwestern,* January 18, 1968.

133 Carol Oliver, letter to the editor, "Wasted Symposium," *Daily Northwestern,* January 26, 1968.

134 Northwestern student George Vickers (c. 1944-2018) served as co-chair of the symposium. Vickers, who later earned an MA and PhD in sociology from Washington University, went on to become a professor of sociology at the Graduate Center and Brooklyn College of the City University of New York and director of the Institute for Central American Studies in New York. He devoted much of his career to human rights work in the Americas. He also served as executive director of the Washington Office on Latin America. Symposium participant James Lawson was a key figure in the civil rights movement and was an influential teacher of the tactics of nonviolent protest. He trained many who participated in various actions in the South, from the sit-ins at lunch counters to the freedom rides. "James Lawson Biography," Biography, https://www.biography.com/people/james-lawson/. Hamilton was a professor at Roosevelt University and is currently a professor at Columbia University. Ernest Chambers currently serves as a state senator in Omaha. Staughton Lynd (1929-) served as director of Freedom Schools in the Mississippi Summer Project of 1964. In April 1965, he chaired the first march against the Vietnam War in Washington D.C. A visit to Hanoi in protest of the war translated into Lynd's being blackballed by several universities. He was an influential leader and author of the *Intellectual Origins of American Radicalism* (1968). "Staughton Lynd," *Encyclopedia.com,* https://www.encyclopedia.com/history/encyclopedias-almanacs-transcripts-and-maps/staughton-lynd. Eduardo Mondlane (1920-1969) was born in Mozambique. He graduated from Oberlin College and earned a PhD in sociology at Northwestern. He became an assistant professor of anthropology at Syracuse University, where he helped develop the university's East African Studies Program. Later, he moved to Tanzania to become involved in neighboring Mozambique's movement for independence from Portugal. He was elected president of the organization *Frente de Libertação de Moçambique* or FRELIMO. In 1969, Mondlane was assassinated. In 1975, Mozambique was liberated. Kathy Kelly, "Violence Week Opens Tuesday," *Daily Northwestern,* January 12, 1968; "An African Revolutionary to Speak to Symposium," *Daily Northwestern,* January 12, 1968. Stokely Carmichael (later known as Kwame Ture) (1941-1998) is credited with coining the term "Black Power." A graduate of Howard University, he was chair of Student Non-Violent Coordinating Committee (SNCC) and participated in a variety of nonviolent civil rights actions in the South. He later repudiated a nonviolent and integrated approach to issues of racial justice. He joined the Black Panther Party, but later ended his association with the group, moved to Guinea in 1968, and devoted the rest of his life to Pan-Africanism. J.Y. Smith, "Kwame Ture, Civil Rights Activist, Dies At Age 57," *Washington Post,* November 16, 1998.

135 Wright and Perkins, "One Generation Ago: A Scrapbook, An Observance of an Era."

136 Pitts, "Growth of Black Consciousness at Northwestern," 38.

137 John H. Bracey, interview with Daniel Chard, September 10, 2013, UMass Amherst

Oral History Collection, http://credo.library.umass.edu/view/full/murg1_207_2013-i064.

138 Hamilton and Carmichael (Kwame Ture), *Black Power: Politics of Liberation in America*, 44.

139 Williamson-Lott, *Black Power on Campus*, 32-33.

140 Marc Zwelling, "Long, Hot Summer Reaches Evanston," *Daily Northwestern*, September 14, 1967; "Cop Brutality Hearings Open in Evanston," *Chicago Tribune*, August 23, 1967. After an investigation into the incident, the police department and the city's Human Relations Commission decided not to take any further legal action against the officers. "Plan to Aid Police Image in Evanston," *Chicago Tribune*, September 19, 1967.

141 Pitts, "Growth of Black Consciousness at Northwestern," 25.

142 Clovis E. Semmes, letter to the editor, "Black Students," *Daily Northwestern*, January 16, 1968.

143 James Turner, "Black Students and Their Changing Perspectives," *Ebony*, August 1969, 137.

144 "My Soul Looks Back in Wonder."

145 Cross, "James Turner: The Face of Black Power at Northwestern."

146 Pitts, "The Politicalization of Black Students," 296.

147 Vernon Ford, "The Black Athlete at a White University," *Daily Northwestern*, April 25, 1968.

148 University Discipline Committee Statement, April 15, 1968, Records of the Bursar's Office Takeover, May 1968, box 1, folder 3, NUA, 1.

149 Pitts, "Growth of Black Consciousness at Northwestern," 32.

150 University Discipline Committee Statement, April 15, 1968, NUA, 1.

151 University Discipline Committee Statement, April 15, 1968, NUA, 1.

152 "Fight Victim Recovers from Stab Wound in Back," *Daily Northwestern*, January 3, 1968.

153 Pitts, "Growth of Black Consciousness at Northwestern," 32.

154 University Discipline Committee Statement, 2.

155 "Party Crashers Invade Sigma Chi," *Akron Beacon Journal*, December 4, 1967.

156 "424 Profs Commend N. U. Pact," *Chicago Tribune*, May 7, 1968. The *Daily Northwestern* covered the incident, but the *Chicago Tribune* would only report on it after the May 1968 takeover, getting most of the fundamental details wrong.

157 Final Demands, 1968, 1.

158 Pitts, "The Politicalization of Black Students," 296.

159 Jack Hinz is a member of Phi Gamma Delta.

160 Pitts, "The Politicalization of Black Students," 297.

161 Pitts, "The Politicalization of Black Students," 297; Pitts, "Growth of Black Consciousness at Northwestern," 34.

162 Tom Davies, "Negroes Form Own Groups," *Daily Northwestern*, January 25, 1968.

163 Pitts, "Growth of Black Consciousness at Northwestern," 34.

164 Pitts, "Growth of Black Consciousness at Northwestern," 35.

165 Ogletree, interview with the author, 2018.

166 Pitts, "Growth of Black Consciousness at Northwestern," 33, 35.

167 Pitts, "The Politicalization of Black Students," 297-298.

168 Pitts, "The Politicalization of Black Students," 298.

169 Pitts, "The Politicalization of Black Students," 298.

170 Bill Harsh, "UDC Has Role Between Judge, Advisor," *Daily Northwestern,* January 12, 1968.

171 Ogletree, interview with the author, 2018.

172 Pitts, "The Politicalization of Black Students," 298.

173 "Campus News Briefs," *Daily Northwestern,* February 6, 1968.

174 Seward Weber to Chapter President of Sigma Chi Fraternity, April 26, 1968, "Sigma Chi, 1968," box 49, folder 5, Miller papers, NUA.

175 Seward Weber to Chapter President of Sigma Chi Fraternity, April 26, 1968. Miller papers. NUA.

176 Seward Weber to Chapter President of Sigma Chi Fraternity, April 26, 1968. Miller papers. NUA.

177 From drinking to hazing to harassing security officers, some students' behavior was reportedly creating a very difficult and uncomfortable environment on campus. The situation had reportedly become so bad that the local Western Union telegram deliveryman informed Arndt that he would no longer set foot on campus without a security escort. Ted Arndt to N. Ekberg, April 14, 1968, "Dean of Students, R. Hinz, 1967-1968," box 49, folder 1, Miller Papers, NUA. Edward "Ted" Arndt (c. 1931-2005) was born and raised in Evanston. A graduate of Evanston Township High School, he served for eleven years on the Evanston police force before joining Northwestern's security force. He was appointed chief of security in October 1966. He headed a new campus security division which was separated from the university's traffic and parking services in August 1966.

178 "Guns are Dangerous," *Daily Northwestern,* April 3, 1968. In January 1967, students voted against allowing campus security officers to carry guns. But by 1968, the administration decided to authorize their use. "Kerr Postpones Firearm Decision," *Daily Northwestern,* March 1, 1967.

179 Ogletree, interview with the author, 2018.

180-182 Roy Harris, "Memorials Set for Dr. King," *Daily Northwestern,* April 5, 1968.

183 Harris, "Memorials Set for Dr. King." As recently as March 1967, the university had announced that it would "not apply corporate pressure to achieve across the board open housing in Evanston." "NU to Remain Quiet on Housing Debate Says Administrator," *Daily Northwestern,* March 28, 1967.

184 Harris, "Memorials Set for Dr. King."

185 Harris, "Memorials Set for Dr. King."

186 "Northwestern Mourns Dr. King," *Daily Northwestern,* April 9, 1968; Pitts, "The Politicalization of Black Students," 304.

187 "Ease Tension Here; Start to Dig Out," *Chicago Tribune,* April 9, 1968; Mary Mitchell, "In Parts of Chicago, The Aftermath Of King's Assassination Still Reverberates," *Chicago Sun-Times,* April 10, 2018.

188 "Students Collect $1570 for Riot Victims," *Daily Northwestern,* April 10, 1968.

189 "Halt Disorders in Areas Near Jackson Park," *Chicago Tribune,* April 8, 1968; "Students Collect $1570 for Riot Victims." The Evanston branch of Chicago Help Corps, along with the campus coordinator for SCLC were the main organizers of the effort.

190 Upon leaving Evanston, headed to Chicago's west side, they were stopped

by an Evanston police officer who asked what they were doing, driving a truck so heavily loaded with supplies. After Bracey made a quick phone call to Evanston's police captain (who vouched for him), they were given the go-ahead and the police officer even personally escorted Bracey and Watson all the way to the Evanston border. Bracey, interview with the author, 2018.

191 "Northwestern Mourns Dr. King," *Daily Northwestern,* April 9, 1968.

192 The student had been stopped at Wells and North Avenue by a crowd of hundreds of rioters; his car was pelted by rocks, shattering one of his windows and injuring him slightly. Steve Sink, "Riots Miss Campus, Affect Students," *Daily Northwestern,* April 9, 1968.

193 Bob Greene, "Tension, Distrust, Fear," *Daily Northwestern,* April 9, 1968.

194 Ted Arndt to N. Ekberg, April 14, 1968, "Dean of Students, R. Hinz, 1967-1968," box 49, folder 1, Miller Papers, NUA.

195 Bob Greene, "Hinz Recovering from 'Quiet Vacation,' " *Daily Northwestern,* April 10, 1968.

196-197 Greene, "Hinz Recovering from 'Quiet Vacation.' "

198 Bob Greene, "Tension, Distrust, Fear." After Bob Greene graduated from Northwestern in 1969, he worked for the *Chicago Sun-Times* and later for the *Chicago Tribune,* where he became a well known columnist. He wrote numerous books and contributed to a number of publications. In September 2002, Greene was forced to resign after admitting to sexual relationship fourteen years earlier with a high school student. Robert Feder, "Bob Greene, 10 Years Later," *TimeOut Chicago,* September 12, 2012, https://www.timeout.com/chicago/tv/bob-greene-10-years-later-trying-to-do-the-best-job-i-can.

199 Pitts, "The Politicalization of Black Students," 304.

200 Steve Sink, "Riots Miss Campus, Affect Students," *Daily Northwestern,* April 9, 1968.

201 Pitts, "The Politicalization of Black Students," 304.

202 Bob Greene, "Tension, Distrust, Fear," *Daily Northwestern,* April 9, 1968.

203-205 Greene, "Tension, Distrust, Fear."

206 Pitts, "The Politicalization of Black Students," 304.

207-208 Ogletree, interview with the author, 2018.

209 Pitts, "The Politicalization of Black Students," 305.

210 Ibram X. Kendi (formerly Ibram H. Rogers), *The Black Campus Movement: Black Students and the Racial Reconstitution of Higher Education, 1965-1972* (New York: Palgrave Macmillan, 2012), 123.

211 Pitts, "The Politicalization of Black Students," 303-304.

212 Ogletree, interview with the author, 2018.

213 Professor Walter Wallace and Dean Lucius Gregg, Jr. "both changed their views and now favor recognition" of the groups, the CUL's report read. "They remained opposed, in principle, to Greek letter groups, but feel that options to join such groups should be as available to Negro students as to White students so long as such groups dominate student life at the university." "Report of the CUL Subcommittee on Negro Fraternities and Sororities," April 10, 1968, 4; "Hinz Grants Final Approval to Black Frats," *Daily Northwestern,* April 11, 1968.

214 The Council on Undergraduate Life, with final approval from Hinz, granted permission for reinstatement. "Black Fraternity Wins Reinstatement At

Northwestern U.," *Chicago Defender,* April 13, 1968. Among the members and pledges of the fraternities were many who would soon take part in the takeover, including, Alpha Phi Alpha members and pledges, Stanley Hill, Clinton Bristow, and Stephen Broussard.

215 "Report of the CUL Subcommittee on Negro Fraternities and Sororities," April 10, 1968, 4.

216 Tom Davies, "Black Frats' Start Poses Questions," *Daily Northwestern,* April 17, 1968.

217 Flyer, undated, Records of Student Protests and Strikes at Northwestern University, 1965-1979, NUA. Many Evanston government officials had long opposed passing open occupancy legislation. In 1959, Evanston mayor John R. Kimbark argued that there "can be no good purpose served by the enactment of such an ordinance." He also argued that such a law would "label minority groups as 'second class citizens.' " "Mayor Appoints Group to Study Racial Needs," *Evanston Review,* May 19, 1960. In May 1967, Franklin Kreml delivered a statement on open occupancy before the executive committee of the Evanston Housing committee, stating that the university "believes in open occupancy and is commendatory of individuals and groups, in our outside academic community, who are seeking the amelioration and elimination of discriminatory practices." Kreml did not, however, state that the university would take a stand in favor of open occupancy legislation, arguing that such a stand would deny the "freedom of individuals within the university community who do not agree that legislation is the way to achieve open housing." Ed McCahill, "Praise N.U. Administrators," *Chicago Tribune,* May 18, 1967. The *Chicago Defender* called Northwestern's position a "clear abdication of moral leadership." "Northwestern U.," *Chicago Defender,* November 22, 1967. As calls for an open housing law intensified, the university shifted its position. On April 8, 1968, just days after the assassination of Martin Luther King, Jr., William S. Kerr, Northwestern's business manager, made a statement in front of the Human Services Committee of the Evanston city council to "reassert our strong support for a broad and comprehensive open housing law." "Northwestern Meeting Its Responsibility," *Chicago Defender,* June 13, 1970.

218 Flyer, undated, NUA. The two-hour demonstration included an address by President Miller to the protestors, supporting their rally and pledging that the university held firm to a "policy of non-discrimination in admission, housing, and employment." Additionally, William S. Kerr announced that that the university would support a "strong and unequivocal open housing law" in Evanston. Joann Lublin, "NU Firmly Urges Open Housing," *Daily Northwestern,* April 9, 1968.

219 Lublin, "NU Firmly Urges Open Housing;" "N. U.'s President Meets With 500 Demonstrators," *Chicago Tribune,* April 9, 1968.

Notes to Chapter 5

1 "Black Student Statement and Petition to Northwestern University Administrators," 1, April 22, 1968, NUA.

2 Ogletree, interview with the author, 2018.

3 Ogletree, email to the author, September 7, 2018.

4 Ogletree, email to the author, September 7, 2018. By 1969, AASU had ceased to operate, its functions having been absorbed by FMO. "Turner Takes Cornell Post," *Daily Northwestern,* June 27, 1969.

5 Cross, "James Turner: The Face of Black Power at Northwestern."

6-8 Ogletree, interview with the author, 2018.

9 "Black Student Statement and Petition to Northwestern University Administrators," 3.

10 "Black Student Statement and Petition to Northwestern University Administrators," 3.

11 "Black Student Statement and Petition to Northwestern University Administrators," 2.

12 Pitts, "The Politicalization of Black Students," 307.

13 "Black Student Statement and Petition to Northwestern University Administrators," 3.

14 "Black Student Statement and Petition to Northwestern University Administrators," 2.

15 "Northwestern University Responses to the Black Student Petition Received April 22, 1968," 5.

16 "Black Student Statement and Petition to Northwestern University Administrators," 3.

17 "Black Student Statement and Petition to Northwestern University Administrators," 4.

18 Bill Harsh, "NU Black Students Make Demands of University," *Daily Northwestern*, April 26, 1968.

19 J. Roscoe Miller to the board of trustees, "Summary Statement Regarding the Basic Issues Involved in the Negro Student Incident of May 3-4, 1968," Kreml papers, NUA

20 Miller, "Summary Statement."

21 Harsh, "NU Black Students Make Demands of University." An original copy of the petition in the Northwestern University Archives includes a handwritten note that reads: "Response: Meeting this evening (4/24/68) with signers and Victor Good [*sic*] and Eric Perkins." Records of the Bursars Office Takeover, May 1968, box 1, folder 1, NUA.

22 Harsh, "NU Black Students Make Demands of University."

23 John Walter, "Senate Votes Autonomy for Students," *Daily Northwestern,* March 1, 1968. On February 24, 1969, the U.S. Supreme Court ruling in the case *Tinker v. Des Moines* effectively dismantled the concept of *in loco parentis* when it ruled in favor of students who had been suspended for holding a protest against the war in Vietnam and wearing black armbands. The court's ruling held that "Students

don't shed their constitutional rights at the school house gates." "Tinker v. Des Moines," http://www.uscourts.gov/about-federal-courts/educational-resources/supreme-court-landmarks/tinker-v-des-moines-podcast.

24 Kathy Waters, "Two Versions of Rights and a Student's View," *Daily Northwestern,* February 24, 1969; Kathy Waters, "Hinz to Reject Students' Rights Bill," *Daily Northwestern,* January 16, 1969. Students would continue to work with CUL and other officials on revisions of the bill.

25 Before being granted self-rule, each living unit had to submit a constitution to the Student Senate for verification. Steve Sink, "NU Grants Self Rule," *Daily Northwestern,* April 26, 1968.

26 Bob Greene, "Rules Will Be Enforced, Say NU Officials," *Daily Northwestern,* April 19, 1968.

27 "Self-Rule Not Be Dealt-Shanahan," *Daily Northwestern,* April 19, 1968; Bob Greene, "The Bill of Rights: How it Changed on Way to Ballot," *Daily Northwestern,* April 18, 1968. For many years, students had advocated for the official adoption of a student bill of rights. Al From, "CUL to View Rights Again," *Daily Northwestern,* February 26, 1964.

28 Steve Sink, "No Penalty for Walkout," *Daily Northwestern,* April 19, 1968.

29 The four-part plan for the advancement of student rights was written by undergraduate students Roger Friedman, George Vickers, and Allan Foster, along with graduate student Edward Steinhart. Among the rights the plan outlined were: the right for students to make their own rules "concerning their social lives;" the right to "administer their own disciplinary measures;" the right to "a voice in decisions on educational policies directly affecting them;" the right to "refuse to serve on committees powerless to make final decisions;" and the right to have an "outlet for their views which would be more representative than existing campus news media." Marla Strassberger, "Pine Leaves Student Senate, NU," *Daily Northwestern,* September 26, 1967.

30 Strassberger, "Pine Leaves Student Senate, NU."

31 "New Freedoms Get Final O.K. by N.U. Heads," *Chicago Tribune,* April 26, 1968. The self-rule movement was advocated by student groups and presented to the Student Senate before going to the university administration. Initially, the university was not in favor of it. It was focused on granting autonomy to all "living units" on campus, including dormitories and fraternity and sorority residences. With self-rule, students would no longer have to "abide by the university regulations concerning their conduct." "N.U. Students Meet Tonight on 'Self Rule,' " *Chicago Tribune,* April 5, 968.

32 Bob Greene, "A Great Day for Hinz," *Daily Northwestern,* April 26, 1968.

33 Greene, "A Great Day for Hinz."

34 Steve Sink, "NU Grants Self Rule," *Daily Northwestern,* April 26, 1968.

35 John Walter, "Senate Votes Autonomy for Students," *Daily Northwestern,* March 1, 1968. The only time the word race is mentioned in the student bill of rights is in the right to seek admission, which was protected "regardless of race, color, national origin, religious creed, sex, or political belief." "Text of Proposed Student Bill of Rights," *Daily Northwestern,* March 1, 1968. The bill also addressed the right to protest, but as worded, it would not have protected the students in the takeover.

It read: "Students have the right of assembly, to demonstrate, inform, or protest, so long as the normal workings of the university community are not disrupted and no university property is damaged." Over the coming months, each of the twenty-two rights would be considered individually by the Council on Undergraduate Life, with many rights eventually authorized, some with amendments. Steve Sink, "Student Rights Bill Retains UDC," *Daily Northwestern,* May 16, 1968.

36 Pitts, "The Politicalization of Black Students," 299.

37 Kathy Waters, "Drafted Grads Get Readmission Priority: Miller," *Daily Northwestern,* April 3, 1968. Wild projected a loss of $750,00 in revenue from tuition that would not be received as male students were drafted. Additionally, the university faced cutbacks in federal funds as more federal money was being "poured into the war." John Walter, "Viet War Halts Faculty Growth," *Daily Northwestern,* April 2, 1968.

38 "Strike Aimed at Colleges is Not Felt Here," *Chicago Tribune,* April 27, 1968. According to a written statement announcing the strike, April 26 was "designated as the day of the international students strike. Students and faculty on campuses throughout the world will be participating in various ways commemorating those who have suffered and died because of our government's iniquitous policies, devoting their attention to the bitter realities of 1968. Let us at Northwestern join them. Let us divorce ourselves from ' business as usual,' from the indifference which nourishes injustice and oppression. Let us consider on this day in both in class and out of class, those aspects of America which prompted Martin Luther King to identify our country as the greatest purveyor of violence in the world today." Typed statement, ND. "Dean of Students, R. Hinz, 1967-1968," box 49, folder 1, Miller Papers, NUA.

39 Joann Lublin, "Dustin Asks Student Support," *Daily Northwestern,* April 24, 1968.

40 In the June 1968 primary in Illinois, McCarthy won thirty-nine percent of the vote. Hubert Humphrey came in second with seventeen percent of the vote. "1968 Democratic Party presidential primaries," Wikipedia, https://en.wikipedia.org/wiki/1968_Democratic_Party_presidential_primaries. And, in May 1968, for the first time in its sixty years, Northwestern's own political convention would elect a Democratic "president" when McCarthy won the (mock) convention's vote. Wally Judd, "Sit-in, Autonomy Best Stories," *Daily Northwestern,* May 28, 1968; Steve Sink, "NPC picks Sen. McCarthy," *Daily Northwestern,* April 23, 1968.

41 "N. U. Students Cavort Thru Spring Rites," *Chicago Tribune,* April 27, 1968.

42 Joann Lublin, "Students Welcome Spring Gently," *Daily Northwestern,* April 26, 1968. The event had been held the year earlier when it had been known as "Gentle Thursday."

43 Lublin, "Students Welcome Spring Gently."

44 John W. Walter, Jr. (1947-2008) graduated from Northwestern with a degree in journalism in 1969. He went on to work for various newspapers and was the founding editor of *USA Today.* Later, he served as managing editor and then executive editor of the *Atlanta Journal-Constitution.* "In Memoriam," *Northwestern Magazine,* Spring 2009, https://www.northwestern.edu/magazine/spring2009/alumninews/inmemoriam.html.

45 Bill Harsh, "NU Black Students Make Demands of University," *Daily Northwestern,* April 26, 1968; Pitts, "Growth of Black Consciousness at Northwestern," 44-45.

46 Harsh, "NU Black Students Make Demands of University."

47 Editorial, "Confrontation: Again, Time to Think," *Daily Northwestern,* May 2, 1968.

48 "Northwestern University Responses to the Black Student Petition Received Monday, April 22, 1968," 1.

49 "Northwestern University Responses to the Black Student Petition Received Monday, April 22, 1968," 3.

50 John Walter, "Senate Focuses on Self-Rule, NU Blacks," *Daily Northwestern,* April 26, 1968.

51 "Northwestern University Responses to the Black Student Petition Received Monday, April 22, 1968," 7.

52 "N. U. Negro Students to Get Meeting Room," *Chicago Tribune,* April 30, 1968.

53 "Northwestern University Responses to the Black Student Petition Received Monday, April 22, 1968," 4.

54 "Northwestern University Responses to the Black Student Petition Received Monday, April 22, 1968," 4.

55 "Northwestern University Responses to the Black Student Petition Received Monday, April 22, 1968," 5.

56 "Northwestern University Responses to the Black Student Petition Received Monday, April 22, 1968," 7.

57 "Northwestern University Responses to the Black Student Petition Received Monday, April 22, 1968," 6.

58 Final Demands, 1968, 1.

59 "Hinz Urges Black White Dialogue," *Daily Northwestern,* May 2, 1968.

60 "Hinz Urges Black White Dialogue."

61 Ogletree, interview with the author, 2018.

62 "Northwestern University Responses to the Black Student Petition Received Monday, April 22, 1968," 1.

63 Bill Harsh, "Hinz Discloses Reply to Blacks' Grievances," *Daily Northwestern,* April 30, 1968; University Discipline Committee Statement, April 15, 1968, Records of the Bursar's Office Takeover, May 1968, box 1, folder 3, NUA.

64 "Northwestern University Responses to the Black Student Petition Received April 22, 1968," 1.

65 University Discipline Committee Statement, April 15, 1968, 4.

66 University Discipline Committee Statement, April 15, 1968, 4. The statement recommended the following: more Black people should be employed among university administrative staff; changes should be made "in all social groups and other organizations that will end de facto segregation;" facilities for Black student activities should be provided; Black student representatives should be appointed to committees to make sure Black students' views are represented; arrangements should be made for incoming first-year students to meet Black students, faculty, and administrators during New Student Week; and "a series of campus-wide meetings to help Northwestern adjust to the 'new reality of a multi-racial campus' " should be convened. University Discipline Committee Statement, April 15, 1968, 4; Bill Harsh, "Hinz Discloses Reply to Blacks' Grievances," *Daily Northwestern,* April 30, 1968.

67 University Discipline Committee Statement, April 15, 1968, 3. As evidenced by letters found in the Northwestern University Archives (Miller papers), some members of Sigma Chi and their parents were outraged by the UDC's punishments of Sigma Chi members following the December 1967 fight.

68-71 Hinz, Interview with the author, 2012.

72 University Discipline Committee Statement, April 15, 1968, 4.

73 University Discipline Committee Statement, April 15, 1968, 4.

74 Cross, "James Turner: The Face of Black Power at Northwestern."

75 "Hinz Urges Black White Dialogue," *Daily Northwestern,* May 2, 1968.

76 "Administration Accepts Plan for Rights Commission," *Daily Northwestern,* May 2, 1968.

77 Title VIII of the 1968 Civil Rights Act.

78 Kathy Kelly, "Northwesterners Participate in Open Housing March," *Daily Northwestern,* April 12, 1968.

79 "Statement of Intent," Collection 57, Evanston Housing Records, 1900-1995, Evanston History Center Archives, Evanston History Center, Evanston, IL.

80 John Maclean. "O.K. Stiffer Housing Law," *Chicago Tribune,* April 30, 1968.

81 Bill Harsh, "Black Leader Blasts NU Response to Grievances," *Daily Northwestern,* May 1, 1968.

82 Harsh, "Black Leader Blasts NU Response to Grievances."

83 Cross, "James Turner: The Face of Black Power at Northwestern;" Harsh, "Black Leader Blasts NU Response to Grievances."

84 Harsh, "Black Leader Blasts NU Response to Grievances."

85-90 Harsh, "Black Leader Blasts NU Response to Grievances."

91 "Hinz Urges Black White Dialogue," *Daily Northwestern,* May 2, 1968.

92 "Hinz Urges Black White Dialogue."

93 Harsh, "Black Leader Blasts NU Response to Grievances."

94 "Hinz Urges Black White Dialogue."

95 "Hinz Urges Black White Dialogue."

96 Joann Lublin, "NU Whites React to Demands," *Daily Northwestern,* May 3, 1968. Joann S. Lublin graduated with a degree in journalism from Northwestern and went on to earn a master's degree in communications from Stanford University. She is the management news editor for *The Wall Street Journal* and shared a Pulitzer Prize in 2003 for her reporting on corporate scandals. "Earning It: Hard-Won Lessons from Trailblazing Women," Gender and the Economy, https://www.gendereconomy.org/joann-s-lublin-on-earning-it-hard-won-lessons-from-trailblazing-women/.

97-100 Lublin, "NU Whites React to Demands."

101 "Turner Sets Deadline for NU Response," *Daily Northwestern,* May 3, 1968.

102 "Turner Sets Deadline for NU Response."

103 "Turner Sets Deadline for NU Response."

104 "Turner Sets Deadline for NU Response."

105 Miller, "Summary Statement."

106 Miller, "Summary Statement."

107 "Turner Sets Deadline for NU Response."

108-110 Final Demands, 1968, 1.

111 Final Demands, 1968, 2.

112- 117 Final Demands, 1968, 1.

118 Final Demands, 1968, 5.

119 Final Demands, 1968, 5.

120 Italics added. "Turner Sets Deadline for NU Response," *Daily Northwestern,* May 3, 1968.

121 Bob Greene, "Black Press Meeting: Integration Rejection," *Daily Northwestern,* May 3, 1968.

122 Greene, "Black Press Meeting: Integration Rejection."

123 Greene, "Black Press Meeting: Integration Rejection."

124 "Blacks Want Response to Grievances" *Daily Northwestern,* May 3, 1968.

125 "Turner Sets Deadline for NU Response," *Daily Northwestern,* May 3, 1968.

126 Ogletree, interview with the author, 2018.

127 Ogletree, interview with the author, 2018.

128 Ogletree, interview with the author, 2018.

129 Final Demands, 1968, 5.

130 Bracey, "Living the Legacy-From Protest to Progress," panel discussion about the 1968 takeover, held at Northwestern University, May 3, 2018.

131 Bracey, interview with the author, 2018.

132 Bracey, interview with the author, 2018.

133 Sterling and Lowery, *Voices and Visions,* loc. 1562-1566, Kindle.

134 Ogletree, email to the author, September 7, 2018.

135 Bracey, interview with the author, 2018.

136 Sterling and Lowery, *Voices and Visions,* loc. 4140-4143, Kindle.

137 The critically acclaimed and Academy-Award nominated film, *The Battle of Algiers* (*La Battaglia di Algieri*) (1966) recounts events during the Algerian War for Independence from France which had only recently (1962) ended with independence won for Algeria. Banned for five years in France, the film served as a primer for effective protest and was an inspiration for many people fighting unjust power structures. The film was loosely based on Saadi Yacef's book, *Souvenirs de la Bataille d'Alger.* Director Gillo Pontecorvo shot the film in documentary style. Roger Ebert noted that the film, which played for fourteen weeks in Chicago upon its release, was particularly influential during the height of the Vietnam War. Many turned to it for inspiration and insight, including the Black Panther Party. By 2003, officials in the U.S. Pentagon also reportedly made a study of the film after the U.S. invaded Iraq. Roger Ebert, "The Battle of Algiers," October 2004. https://www.rogerebert.com/reviews/great-movie-the-battle-of-algiers-1967; Michael T. Kaufman, "The World: Film Studies; What Does the Pentagon See in 'Battle of Algiers'?" *New York Times,* September 7, 2003.

138 Ogletree, interview with the author, 2018.

139 Wayne Watson, panel discussion, fiftieth anniversary of the takeover, Northwestern University, May 4, 2018.

140 Bracey, interview with the author, 2018.

141 Bracey, interview with the author, 2018; Sterling and Lowery, *Voices and Visions,* loc. 2332, Kindle.

142 Bracey, phone conversation with the author, August 9, 2018.

143 Turner, interview with the author, 2012.

144 Bracey, phone conversation with the author, August 9, 2018.

145 Bracey, phone conversation with the author, August 9, 2018.

146 Bracey, interview with the author, 2018.

147 Bracey, interview with the author, 2018.

148 "They Demanded Courageously, The 1968 Northwestern Bursar's Office Takeover."

149 Bracey, phone conversation with the author, August 9, 2018.

150 "They Demanded Courageously, The 1968 Northwestern Bursar's Office Takeover."

151 Ogletree, interview with the author, 2018.

152 Sterling and Lowery, *Voices and Visions,* loc. 1912-1914, Kindle.

153-155 Turner, Interview with the author, 2012.

156 Advertisement, *Daily Northwestern,* May 2, 1968.

157 The Student Senate resolution was a highly diluted version of the petition's demands. It called for four elements: a course in Black history to be offered in the fall 1968 quarter; continued "dialogue"; a hall set aside for Black students to room together; and fifty percent recruitment of Black students from inner cities. Resolution, May 2, 1968, Records of the Bursar's Office Takeover, May 1968, box 1, folder 3, NUA.

158 Student Senate President Barb Caulfield issued a statement following the meeting: "We must look at this not as a problem of Negroes looking for separation . . . but as a plea by students of our constituency who need help with their problems." Student senators Clyde Jeffers and Frank Morris joined Paterson in proposing their resolution, which asked for "unqualified" support of the Black student demands. Richard Boudreaux, "Senators Support Black Proposals," *Daily Northwestern,* May 3, 1968. Paterson had just won her seat on the senate by a large majority in the election held days earlier. A "radical slate," endorsed by *The Real Press*, had been "wiped out" in the same election. Elliot Brown, "Smith, Morris, Wick Elected in Class Race," *Daily Northwestern,* April 18, 1968.

159 Cross, "James Turner: The Face of Black Power at Northwestern."

160 "Turner Sets Deadline for NU Response," *Daily Northwestern,* May 3, 1968.

161 "Greensboro, NC, Students Sit-in for U.S. Civil Rights, 1960," Global Nonviolent Action Database, Swarthmore College, https://nvdatabase.swarthmore.edu/content/greensboro-nc-students-sit-us-civil-rights-1960.

Notes to Chapter 6

1 "Yesterday's events brought to head the crisis between black and white on campus," the *Daily Northwestern* observed. Editorial, "A Crucial Day," *Daily Northwestern,* May 3, 1968.

2 Theophilus Green, "Black Leader of White Majority," *Jet Magazine,* July 9, 1970, 24.

3 Hinz, interview with the author, 2012.

4 Northwestern University, press release, May 3, 1968, University memos and reports, Incident May 3-4, box 2, folder 9, Kreml papers, NUA.

5 Northwestern University, press release, May 3, 1968.

6 "619 Clark Street; N.U.'s Day of Decision," *Daily Northwestern,* May 4, 1968.

7 Video, interview with takeover participants Debra [Avant] Hill, Adrianne Hayward, and Sandra Hill. Kira Boyd, "How a 1968 Protest at Northwestern University Still Resonates," June 9, 2015, Medill Reports Chicago, http://news.medill.northwestern.edu/chicago/video-how-a-1968-protest-at-northwestern-university-still-resonates/.

8 Ogletree, interview with the author, 2018.

9 Miles Wolff, *Lunch at the 5 & 10* (Chicago: Ivan R. Dee, 1970), 31.

10 Ogletree, interview with the author, 2018.

11 Bracey, phone conversation with the author, August 9, 2018.

12 Ogletree, interview with the author, 2018.

13 Bracey, phone conversation with the author, August 9, 2018.

14 Ogletree, interview with the author, 2018.

15 Turner, interview with the author, 2012. Others also left the building temporarily. Daphne Maxwell Reid left briefly to go to a doctor's appointment. Bracey, "Living the Legacy-From Protest to Progress," panel discussion about the 1968 takeover, held at Northwestern University, May 3, 2018.

16 Turner, interview with the author, 2012.

17 Turner, interview with the author, 2012.

18 Ogletree, interview with the author, 2018.

19 Paterson, interview with the author.

20 "My Soul Looks Back in Wonder."

21 "World of Pictures," *Chicago Defender,* May 4, 1968.

22 Both Adams (1947-2013) and Kelley served as team captain and both were elected the team's most valuable players, along with setting various records during their time playing at Northwestern. *Northwestern Basketball, Media Guide, 2017-2018* (ND, NP): 93. Upon graduation, Kelley was drafted by the New York Nets and Adams by the San Diego Rockets.

23 "NU Athletes Act as Individuals, Not Players," *Daily Northwestern,* May 4, 1968.

24 Vernon Ford, "The Black Athlete at a White University," *Daily Northwestern,* April 25, 1968.

25 "NU Athletes Act as Individuals, Not Players."

26 Biondi, *The Black Revolution on Campus,* 86.

27 Bracey, "Living the Legacy-From Protest to Progress."

28 Bracey, phone conversation with the author, August 9, 2018.

29 Venice Isa Deese, Jr. (1936-2013) was born in Texas and later moved with his family to Evanston. He graduated from Evanston Township High School, where he played on the basketball team and ran track. He attended Kendall College and later worked for Illinois Bell from 1968 until 1994 when he moved to Three Rivers, Michigan. Obituary, "Venice Isa Deese," http://www.efhchapel.com/obituaries/print?o_id=2200429. Eickhoff, Farrand, Halverson Chapel, Inc.

30 Bracey, "Living the Legacy-From Protest to Progress." Deese may have been at the very end of his shift at the Bursar's Office when the takeover occurred roughly twenty minutes before 8 a.m. In April 1968, head of campus security Ted Arndt reported that Deese worked the shift from midnight to 8 a.m. Ted Arndt to N. Ekberg, April 14, 1968, "Dean of Students, R. Hinz, 1967-1968," box 49, folder 1, Miller Papers, NUA. According to the *Daily Northwestern,* Northwestern security guards' shifts were scheduled for 8 a.m. to 4 p.m.; 4 p.m. to midnight; and midnight to 8 a.m. Kathy Kelly, "$52,000: It's For New Campus Cops," *Daily Northwestern,* January 5, 1968.

31 Bracey, "Living the Legacy-From Protest to Progress."

32 Several Northwestern students were quite active at Evanston Township High School (ETHS). They gave lectures on Black history and served as counselors and mentors to students. At this time, there was a strong movement of Black student activism at ETHS. Students in the AASU at Northwestern were working with high school students and parent groups in order to initiate changes at the school, including hiring more Black staff, changing the curriculum to include Black history and culture, and gaining permission to celebrate Martin Luther King, Jr.'s birthday. In February 1968, for example, a group called Federation of Citizens for an Unsegregated Society (FOCUS) picketed the high school accusing the school board of "holding secret meetings" and hiring too few Black teachers. "25 in Rights Group Picket Evanston High," *Chicago Tribune,* February 23, 1968. Later, they would assist in organizing a sit-in and a walk-out at ETHS. In January 1969, students staged a two-hour sit-in in the school superintendent's office, having been coached by Milton Gardner and Wayne Watson on how to approach the action and work for their demands. Bob Greene, "Another Sit-In: The Message is Black," *Daily Northwestern,* January 17, 1969. In February 1969, seventy-five students staged a walk-out and issued various demands after a newly-painted mural depicting both Black and white students on the wall of the high school had been removed, without explanation. A group called Concerned Blacks and Citizens Council submitted a variety of demands following the incident which included the firing of school administrators, including the head of security. Northwestern students took part in the negotiations that followed. Among their demands to administrators were: that the mural be replaced, an apology be issued, and the administrators responsible be "ousted." Charles Mount, "Evanston High Mural Erased; 75 Walk Out," *Chicago Tribune,* February 27, 1969.

33 Turner, interview with the author, 2012.

34 "Students Seize N. U. Offices," *Chicago Tribune,* May 4, 1968.

35 On Friday, May 3, the two men came to the building in support of the action and departed some time in the afternoon. According to an FBI report, Rush and Brown had planned to "remain with the demonstrators," but, owing to an un-

specified "disagreement over the demands," left in the late afternoon. It should be noted that many details within the FBI reports on the takeover are incorrect. FBI, "Racial Tensions, Northwestern University Campus, Evanston, Illinois," May 8, 1968, 2. That fall, Rush (1946-) and others would found a chapter of the Black Panther Party in Illinois. At the time of the takeover, Rush was a student at Roosevelt University and had recently been discharged from the U.S. Army, after serving four years. In 1992, he was elected U.S. Representative for Illinois's First Congressional District; a seat he has held since that time.

36 Biondi, *The Black Revolution on Campus,* 86. Stephen J. Broussard (c. 1948-2009) grew up in Chicago. He graduated with a degree in journalism from Northwestern in 1970 and went on to earn his law degree at Northwestern in 1973. "Stephen Broussard," In Memoriam, *Northwestern Magazine* (Fall 2009), https://www.northwestern.edu/magazine/fall2009/alumninews/inmemoriam.html.

37 "619 Clark Street; N.U.'s Day of Decision," *Daily Northwestern,* May 4, 1968.

38 Schulze, "The Student Rebellion in the United States," 14-15.

39 Schulze, 22.

40 Roger Friedman, email to the author, January 18, 2019.

41 Newsletter #3, ND, Records of the Bursar's Office Takeover, box 1, folder 3, NUA.

42 Turner, interview with the author, 2012.

43 Bracey, interview with the author, 2018. Bracey learned that the students were not all SDS members after reading the account of the action in Linda Gartz's memoir, *Redlined: A Memoir of Race, Change, and Fractured Community in 1960s Chicago* (Berkeley, CA: She Writes Press, 2018).

44 Bracey, interview with the author, 2018.

45 Ogletree, interview with the author, 2018.

46-48 Turner, interview with the author, 2012.

49 "Sit-in, Negotiations Continue, No Accord Reached on Demands," *Daily Northwestern,* May 4, 1968.

50 Hinz, interview with the author, 2012

51 "Sit-in, Negotiations Continue, No Accord Reached on Demands,"

52 Hinz, interview with the author, 2012.

53 "Negroes Protest At Northwestern," *New York Times,* May 4, 1968.

54 Kathy Waters, "Can't Give Up Control: Wild," *Daily Northwestern,* May 4, 1968.

55 "Negroes Protest At Northwestern;" Robert Nolte, "Negroes Get Reply to Demands," *Chicago Tribune,* May 4, 1968. Williamson and Wild argued that one third of the faculty was "sympathetic" to the students, one third was opposed to their tactics, and one third was "ambivalent." Williamson and Wild, 335.

56 Waters, "Can't Give Up Control: Wild."

57 Schulze published his findings in "The Student Rebellion in the United States: A Case Study of a Cool Confrontation with Academic Racism." *Sociological Bulletin,* Vol. 19. (March 1970). After teaching at Northwestern, Schulze joined the faculty of the sociology department of San Diego State University, where he is now an emeritus professor.

58 "Things are 'As Usual' Up North," *Daily Northwestern,* May 4, 1968.

59 Bracey, interview with the author, 2018.

60 "Lt. Col. Lucius P. Gregg," *The History Makers,* http://www.thehistorymakers.org/biography/lt-col-lucius-p-gregg.

61 Bracey, interview with the author, June 21, 2018; Biondi, *The Black Revolution on Campus,* 83; Ariela J. Gross and Leslie M. Harris, "In Memoriam: George M. Fredrickson," *Perspectives on History,* May 2008, American Historical Association, https://www.historians.org/publications-and-directories/perspectives-on-history/may-2008/in-memoriam-george-m-fredrickson.

62 Bracey, interview with the author, 2018.

63 Bracey, phone conversation with the author, August 9, 2018.

64 Bracey, phone conversation with the author, August 9, 2018.

65 Bracey, interview with the author, 2018.

66-68 "Things are 'As Usual' Up North," *Daily Northwestern,* May 4, 1968.

69 Bob Greene, "Our Incredible Friday: Dr. Miller's Long Night," *Daily Northwestern,* May 4, 1968.

70-71 Turner, interview with the author, 2012.

72 "619 Clark Street; N.U.'s Day of Decision."

73 Turner, interview with the author, 2012.

74 Ogletree, interview with the author, 2018.

75 Hinz, interview with the author, 2012.

76 Waters, "Can't Give Up Control: Wild."

77 "Seize N.U. Office," *The Pantagraph,* May 3, 1968; Joann Lublin, "NU Firmly Urges Open Housing," *Daily Northwestern*, April 9, 1968.

78 "30 White Occupy Hinz' Office," *Daily Northwestern,* May 4, 1968.

79 "Students Seize N. U. Offices," *Chicago Tribune,* May 4, 1968.

80 "Negro Sit-In at Northwestern," *Chicago Sun-Times,* May 4, 1968.

81 "30 White Occupy Hinz' Office," *Daily Northwestern,* May 4, 1968.

82 FBI, "Racial Tensions, Northwestern University Campus, Evanston, Illinois," May 8, 1968, 3.

83 "30 White Occupy Hinz' Office," *Daily Northwestern,* May 4, 1968.

84 "30 White Occupy Hinz' Office."

85 "30 White Occupy Hinz' Office." The Sandbox Committee was formed by students following recent protests, including a February 1968 protest against Dow Chemical Company. (See below for more on that protest.) The committee also organized Northwestern's role in Evanston's fair housing march in April 1968. It was named after a "sandbox-like area" in the plaza at the newly-constructed Rebecca Crown Center where protests often took place. "Students Establish Anti-Bias Groups," *Daily Northwestern,* April 10, 1968; Kathy Kelly, "Northwesterners Participate in Open Housing March," *Daily Northwestern,* April 12, 1968.

86 "30 White Occupy Hinz' Office."

87 "619 Clark Street; N.U.'s Day of Decision."

88 Friedman, email to the author, March 8, 2019.

89 Joann Lublin, "Curiosity Draws Bystanders to Bursar's Office," *Daily Northwestern,* May 4, 1968.

90 Greene, "Our Incredible Friday: Dr. Miller's Long Night."

91 Lublin, "NU Firmly Urges Open Housing;" FBI, "Racial Tensions, Northwestern University Campus, Evanston, Illinois," May 8, 1968, 4.

92 Photograph caption, *Chicago Defender,* May 6, 1968.

93 "Reveal Frosh Football Grants," *Daily Northwestern,* April 19, 1966.

94-96 "619 Clark Street; N.U.'s Day of Decision."

97 "Black Power Wins at N.U.," *Chicago Tribune,* May 5, 1968.

98 "Negroes Seize Northwestern U Office," *Arizona Republic,* May 4, 1968. The UPI story read: "Negro students seized the business office of swanky Northwestern University Friday demanding that school officials stamp out alleged 'white racism,' give black separate housing on campus and serve 'chitlins and collard greens' in the cafeteria." "Separate Dorms, 'Chitlins' Are Issues in Campus Row," UPI, May 3, 1968.

99 Thomas Picou, "NU Student Protest Hit Unjustly By White Press," *Chicago Defender,* May 6, 1968.

100 Greene, "Our Incredible Friday: Dr. Miller's Long Night."

101 "Joseph N. Boyce," interview, *The History Makers,* December 12, 2012; http://www.thehistorymakers.org/biography/joseph-n-boyce.

102 Joseph N. Boyce (1937-) worked as a Chicago police officer before being hired by the *Chicago Tribune* in 1961. He would go on to work for *Time* and the *Wall Street Journal* and he would serve as a faculty member at Columbia University's Graduate School of Journalism and Indiana/Purdue University's Indianapolis School of Journalism. "Joseph N. Boyce," *The History Makers,* 2012.

103 Bracey, telephone conversation with the author, August 9, 2018.

104 Bracey, "Living the Legacy-From Protest to Progress."

105 Bracey, telephone conversation with the author, August 9, 2018.

106 Sterling and Lowery, *Voices and Visions,* loc. 2373-2377, Kindle.

107 Ogletree, interview with the author, 2018.

108 "A Letter from Northwestern," May 14, 1968, Records of the Bursar's Office Takeover, May 1968, box 1, folder 3, NUA.

109 "619 Clark Street; N.U.'s Day of Decision."

110 "619 Clark Street; N.U.'s Day of Decision."

111 "Skylight Broken in Besieged Office," *Daily Northwestern,* May 4, 1968.

112 "Sit-in, Negotiations Continue," *Daily Northwestern,* May 4, 1968.

113 Here is the full list of those present at the negotiations: students representing FMO and AASU: John Bracey, Harold Daniels, Amassa Fauntleroy, Vernon Ford, Victor Goode, Kathryn Ogletree, Michael Smith, James Turner, Roger Ward, and Arnold Wright. Representing the administration and faculty: Robert H. Baker, Lucius P. Gregg, Jr., Jack Hinz, William Ihlandfeldt, Gail M. Inlow, Franklin M. Kreml, Joe Park, Robert H. Strotz, Walter L. Wallace, and Payson S. Wild. "Draft agreement between Afro-American Student Union and FMO and a Committee Representing the Northwestern University Administration," May 4, 1968, 9, Records of the Bursar's Office Takeover, May 1968, NUA. The draft of the agreement was signed by all present at the meeting (listed above.) A final version is also found in the Northwestern University Archives. The final version incorporated the addenda from the draft version.

114 "Black Students Win Many Demands After 38-Hour Bursar's Office Sit-in," *Daily Northwestern,* May 6, 1968.

115 Turner, interview with the author, 2012.

116 Hinz, interview with the author, 2012.

117 Letter to Franklin Kreml, May 5, 1968, "Correspondence: Incident May 3-4, 1968," box 3, folder 6, Kreml papers, NUA.

118 FBI, "Racial Tensions, Northwestern University Campus, Evanston, Illinois," May 8, 1968, 10.

119 FBI, "Racial Tensions, Northwestern University Campus, Evanston, Illinois," May 8, 1968, 7.

120 Michael Selinker, "A Turning Point," *Daily Northwestern,* May 3, 1988.

121 Ogletree, interview with the author, 2018.

122 "Former VP Kreml Dies at 91," *Daily Northwestern,* January 30, 1998; Eric Pace, "Franklin M. Kreml Dies at 91," *New York Times,* February 5, 1989.

123 "Repudiate Order," *Daily Northwestern,* April 18, 1968.

124-127 Bracey, interview with the author, 2018.

128-130 Hinz, interview with the author, 2012.

131 "N.U. Students End Seizure of Building," *Chicago Tribune,* May 5, 1968.

132 Bracey, interview with the author, 2018.

133 Turner, interview with the author, 2012.

134 Turner, interview with the author, 2012.

135 Ogletree, "Living the Legacy-From Protest to Progress."

136 Turner, interview with the author, 2012.

137 Bracey, interview with the author, 2018.

138 Bracey, interview with the author, 2018.

139 Walter L. Wallace to Franklin Kreml, May 21, 1968, Kreml papers.

140 Ogletree, interview with the author, 2018.

141 Ogletree, interview with the author, 2018.

142 Hinz, interview with the author, 2012.

143 J. Roscoe Miller to the board of trustees, "Summary Statement Regarding the Basic Issues Involved in the Negro Student Incident of May 3-4, 1968."

144 "Agreement between Afro-American Student Union and FMO and a Committee Representing the Northwestern University Administration," May 4, 1968, 2, Kreml Papers, box 2, folder 8, NUA. (Hereafter cited as Agreement, May 4, 1968.)

145 Agreement, May 4, 1968, 2.

146 Michael Hotchkiss, "Princeton Sociologist Walter Wallace Dies at Age 88," *Princeton News,* December 8, 2015, https://www.princeton.edu/news/2015/12/08/princeton-sociologist-walter-wallace-dies-age-88; "Walter L. Wallace," *The Black Past,* https://blackpast.org/aah/wallace-walter-l-1927; "In Memoriam: Walter Wallace, 1927-2015," *The Journal of Blacks in Higher Education,* December 22, 2015, https://www.jbhe.com/2015/12/in-memoriam-walter-wallace-1927-2015/. In the introduction to her thesis, Robinson (Obama) observed: "My experiences at Princeton have made me far more aware of my 'Blackness' than ever before. I have found that at Princeton no matter how liberal and open-minded some of my White professors and classmates try to be toward me, I sometimes feel like a visitor on campus, as if I really don't belong." Michelle LeVaugh Robinson, "Princeton-Educated Blacks and the Black Community" (senior thesis, Princeton University, 1985): 2.

147 Agreement, May 4, 1968, 1.

148 Agreement, May 4, 1968, 1.

149 Agreement, May 4, 1968, 2.

150 Agreement, May 4, 1968, 2.

151 Final demands, 1968, 6.

152 Agreement, May 4, 1968, 7.

153 Agreement, May 4, 1968, 4.

154 "A Letter from Northwestern," May 14, 1968.

155 John Bracey said that all the demands were met, but he explained that Kreml made a deal with the students during the negotiations: "He also told us straight up," Bracey recalled, "he said, 'I'm under tremendous pressure from white alums who want me to clean that building out and either lock you up or throw you off campus.' And he said 'I don't think that's good for the institution. And so we have to come up with a way that I can satisfy your concerns and satisfy the concerns of people that have supported this institution long before you got here.' That's when he said could he be allowed to say that he had not given us all of our demands and that we were still negotiating some demands." Bracey, interview with the author, 2018. According to Bracey, the students accepted this position, saying they could work with that. " 'You've got to go calm your people down as to why you didn't lock us up,' " Bracey remembered responding. " 'I get that. I get that. So say whatever you have to say.' " Kreml told the students that no matter what statements he made to the press afterward, they should " 'remember what I said in this room because that's what I'm going to stand on. Trust me on that.' And we did. And they did." Bracey, interview with the author, 2018. Kathryn Ogletree does not recall such a deal being made. "The only thing I can say definitively," she wrote to me in an email on October 30, 2018, "is that I did not agree to any kind of punishment or to stating that some of the demands were denied so that the University could save face. I am beginning to believe that there may have been several levels of negotiations, some of which I was not part of. This is not surprising since there was a tendency to not take me seriously on the part of the University (and sometimes on my own team) because I was female and only a freshman." There was at least one demand that was not (explicitly) met: that the "Administration restructure the UDC or create a new judiciary to adequately and justly cope with racial problems and incidents." Final Demands, 1968, 5. But clearly, both administrators and students agreed that ongoing negotiations concerning the implementation of the agreement would be undertaken and discussions in all areas covered by the demands would continue. In a report prepared by university officials for the board of trustees, several demands were listed as being "denied." But they were, in actuality, accepted. For example, the demand that the university would "add studies in Negro history, literature and art" was reported as being denied. But these so-called denials were explained in careful language that nullified the whole concept of a denial: "In the discussion of this denial in the negotiations on Saturday," the report stated, "the reason for the denial was explained, the explanation was accepted, and a counter plea made for consultation and advisory arrangements, which was acceded to because of their consonance with the general workings of the university and the helpfulness of maintaining such intercourse among the administration, faculty, and students in all matters of importance." J. Roscoe Miller to the board of trustees, "Summary Statement Regarding the Basic Issues Involved in the Negro Student Incident of May 3-4, 1968."

156 Agreement, May 4, 1968, 2-3.

157-160 Agreement, May 4, 1968, 3.

161 Turner, interview with the author, 2012.

162 Ogletree, interview with the author, 2018.

163 Turner, interview with the author, 2012.

164 Bob Greene, "Hinz Gets the Final Answer," *Daily Northwestern,* May 6, 1968.

165-168 Greene, "Hinz Gets the Final Answer."

169 Turner, interview with the author, 2012.

170 Greene, "Hinz Gets the Final Answer."

171 Roland J. Hinz, statement, May 4, 1968, NUA, document, accessed from "They Demanded Courageously, The 1968 Northwestern Bursar's Office Takeover."

172 Greene, "Hinz Gets the Final Answer."

173 Bracey, interview with the author, 2018.

174 Ogletree, interview with the author, 2018.

175 Ogletree, interview with the author, 2018.

176 "Black Power Wins at N.U.," *Chicago Tribune,* May 5, 1968.

177 The Northwestern students had learned from the students at Columbia University. Following the eviction of Columbia students by the police, photographs of the interior of the recently occupied buildings, depicting destruction within them, emerged in the media. Later, it was learned that the destruction had been caused by the police, not the students. Leaders of later strikes and occupations urged that all buildings be cleaned and photographed by occupying students as evidence that they had done no harm to their contents or interiors. "1968: Columbia in Crisis," Columbia University Libraries, https://exhibitions.library.columbia.edu/exhibits/show/1968/protests/strike.

178 Bracey, "Living the Legacy-From Protest to Progress."

179 Kathy Waters, "NU Blacks - Here to Stay, - Celebrate Successful Sit-in," *Daily Northwestern,* May 6, 1968.

180 Waters, "NU Blacks - Here to Stay, - Celebrate Successful Sit-in."

181 Michael Selinker, "A Turning Point," *Daily Northwestern,* May 3, 1988.

182 Waters, "NU Blacks - Here to Stay, - Celebrate Successful Sit-in."

183 Waters, "NU Blacks - Here to Stay, - Celebrate Successful Sit-in."

184 "Black Students Win Many Demands After 38-Hour Bursar's Office Sit-in," *Daily Northwestern,* May 6, 1968.

185 "N.U. Students End Seizure of Building," *Chicago Tribune,* May 5, 1968; "Black Students Win Many Demands After 38-Hour Bursar's Office Sit-in."

186 "Black Students Win Many Demands After 38-Hour Bursar's Office Sit-in."

Notes to "Dear Northwestern University"

1 Anonymous to J. Roscoe Miller, July 11, 1968; Letter to J. Roscoe Miller, May 6, 1968; Letter to Roland Hinz, May 5, 1968; David A. Dudley to Roland J. Hinz, May 7, 1968; Message written on envelope of the 1967-1968 alumni annual fund; Michael Votta to Ronald [*sic*] J. Hinz, May 6, 1968; anonymous, postcard, nd; Walter F. Gray to John Searles, May, 8 1968, "Correspondence: Incident May 3-4, 1968," Kreml papers, NUA.

Notes to Chapter 7

1 Agreement, May 4, 1968, 1.

2 "Black Power Wins at N. U.," *Chicago Tribune,* May 5, 1968.

3 "Here is Text of Student and N. U. Pact," *Chicago Tribune,* May 5, 1968. The *Daily Northwestern* published the agreement in full on Monday, May 6, 1968.

4 "N.U. Students End Seizure of Building," *Chicago Tribune,* May 5, 1968. Hinz was later told by a *Chicago Tribune* staff member that on the night the agreement was reached, the *Tribune's* editor, W.D. "Don" Maxwell, dictated the re-write of the article over the phone from a cocktail party he was attending. The staff member also told Hinz that not everyone on the paper's staff shared Maxwell's views. Hinz, interview with the author, April 4, 2018.

5 Boyce later referred to the re-write of his piece as an act of censorship. "Joseph N. Boyce," interview, *The History Makers*, December 12, 2012, http://www.thehistorymakers.org/biography/joseph-n-boyce.

6-8 "A Sad Day for Northwestern," *Chicago Tribune,* May 6, 1968.

9 "Kreml Blasts Tribune's Sit-in Coverage," *Daily Northwestern,* September 30, 1968. A week after the *Chicago Tribune's* story and editorial appeared, a protest letter signed by fifty-nine of Northwestern's seventy journalism graduate students was printed in the paper. In September 1968, during a weekend alumni leaders workshop, Franklin Kreml told an audience of 1,500 that in its coverage of the takeover, the *Chicago Tribune* had "misrepresented the university 'thoughtfully and maliciously.' " "Kreml Blasts Tribune's Sit-in Coverage," *Daily Northwestern*, September 30, 1968. The "city's largest newspaper lied," he asserted, and did "irreparable damage" to the university. Kreml made these comments apparently unaware that any reporters were present. They were, and his sentiments were transmitted far beyond the auditorium walls. Later, the *Daily Northwestern* bestowed upon Kreml one of its annual (tongue in cheek) "Tired Typewriter Awards." Kreml was the recipient of the "Oops! Did I say that?" award. (And to the *Chicago Tribune*, it awarded the "Wild-Eyed Revolutionary Award, to the Dangerous Organization Which Is Most Hell-Bent to Advance its Extremist Viewpoints on an Unsuspecting and Quiet Campus.") "The First Annual Tired Typewriter Awards," *Daily Northwestern,* January 9, 1969.

10 John Walter, "Student Seizure of Building-Never Again?" *Daily Northwestern,* May 6, 1968.

11 Northwestern University, "Confrontation on the Campus," May 6, 1968, box 2, folder 8, Kreml papers, NUA.

12 "No Surrender, N.U. Aid Says," *Chicago Tribune,* May 6, 1968.

13 Copy of "A Sad Day for Northwestern," *Chicago Tribune,* May 6, 1968, "Correspondence: Incident May 3-4, 1968," box 3, folder 5, Kreml papers, NUA.

14 Martin Gansberg, "Ferment on Campuses Challenges Rules," *New York Times,* May 6, 1968. Roger Friedman stated that there were "no repercussions" for the students who occupied Hinz's office because the university had agreed not to " 'discipline' any of the black students for the Bursar's Office Takeover, and that extended to us who had gone into his office." Roger Friedman, email to the author,

January 20, 2019.

15 Letter to J. Roscoe Miller, June 3, 1968, "Correspondence: Incident May 3-4, 1968," box 3, folder 5, Kreml papers, NUA.

16 Anonymous to President Miller, July 11, 1968, "Correspondence: Incident May 3-4, 1968," box 3, folder 7, Kreml papers, NUA; Anonymous to Jack Hinz, ND, "Correspondence: Incident May 3-4, 1968," box 3, folder 7, Kreml papers, NUA.

17 "University Pact Sparks Furor," *Evanston Review*, May 13, 1968.

18 F.P. Shanahan, Statement, Student Senate, May 3, 1968, Records of the Bursar's Office Takeover, May 1968, box 1, folder 3, NUA; Richard Boudreaux, "Shanahan Calls for 'Support NU' Meeting," *Daily Northwestern,* May 7, 1968.

19 Minutes of the Evanston City Council, May 6, 1968, 5.

20 Letter to the editor, *Daily Northwestern,* May 9, 1968.

21 "424 Profs Commend N. U. Pact," *Chicago Tribune,* May 7, 1968.

22 Letter to the editor, *Daily Northwestern,* May 9, 1968.

23 "What Next?" *Daily Northwestern,* May 6, 1968; "Northwestern Students Call Negro Demands 'Segregationist,' " *Chicago Tribune,* May 6, 1968.

24 "Negro Students Jubilant," *Evanston Review,* May 6, 1968.

25 "University Pact Sparks Furor," *Evanston Review,* May 13, 1968.

26 "Alarming Precedent," *Evanston Review,* May 6, 1968.

27 Letter to the editor, "University's Grant of Segregated Housing," *New York Times,* May 11, 1968.

28 "The Revolting Students," *Chicago Defender,* May 6, 1968.

29 "No Surrender, N.U. Aid Says," *Chicago Tribune,* May 6, 1968.

30 "Northwestern Cool After Sit-In," *Chicago Defender,* May 7, 1968; "No Surrender, N. U. Aid Says."

31 Northwestern University, letter announcing thirtieth annual reunion, "University Memos and Reports: Incident May 3-4, 1968," box 2, folder 9, Kreml Papers, NUA.

32 "University Pact Sparks Furor," *Evanston Review,* May 13, 1968.

33 "Alum Leads Crown Protest of Black Sit-in Agreement," *Daily Northwestern,* May 14, 1968.

34 "Alum Leads Crown Protest of Black Sit-in Agreement;" Letter to "Students attending Northwestern University," May 13, 1968, Kreml papers, NUA.

35 Hinz, interview with the author, 2012.

36 Bob Greene, "Return to Equilibrium," *Daily Northwestern,* May 7, 1968.

37 Greene, "Return to Equilibrium."

38 "424 Profs Commend N. U. Pact," *Chicago Tribune,* May 7, 1968.

39 "No Surrender, N.U. Aid Says," *Chicago Tribune,* May 6, 1968.

40 J. Roscoe Miller to the board of trustees, "Summary Statement Regarding the Basic Issues Involved in the Negro Student Incident of May 3-4, 1968."

41 Memorandum, "University Memos and Reports: Incident May 3-4, 1968," box 2, folder 9, Kreml Papers, NUA. The responses were only to be sent in response to people whom Miller did not know personally. Miller wrote more extensive letters to those he knew personally.

42 Letter to J. Roscoe Miller, May 8, 1968, "Correspondence: Incident May

3-4, 1968," box 2, folder 12, Kreml papers, NUA.

43 "Aftermath," *Daily Northwestern,* May 9, 1968.

44 Bill Smith, " 'No Extra Police on Campus,' NU, City Say," *Daily Northwestern,* May 22, 1968.

45 "Water Balloon Thrown at Blacks," *Daily Northwestern,* May 6, 1968.

46 Turner, interview with the author, 2012.

47 Sterling and Lowery, *Voices and Visions,* loc. 1531, Kindle.

48 Bill Harsh, "Turner Warns of 'Hysteria,' " *Daily Northwestern,* May 10, 1968.

49 Bob Greene, "Return to Equilibrium," *Daily Northwestern,* May 7, 1968.

50 "NU to Mail Letter About Black Accord," *Daily Northwestern,* May 28, 1968.

51 "Confrontation on the Campus," May 1968, Kreml papers, NUA.

52 Payson S. Wild, "Memorandum concerning the black student seizure of the University business office, 619 Clark Street on the morning of May 3, 1968," June 30, 1987, "University Memos and Reports: Incident May 3-4, 1968," box 2, folder 9, Kreml papers, NUA.

53 "424 Profs Commend N. U. Pact;" Resolution, Northwestern University Student Senate, NUA; "Senate Says Motives Ok, Not Methods," *Daily Northwestern,* May 4, 1968. A petition in support of the agreement was also signed by a total of 424 faculty members, which inlcuded part-time faculty (out of a total of 995). Faculty petition in "Correspondence: Incident May 3-4, 1968," box 3, folder 7, Kreml papers, NUA; "Confrontation on Campus," Kreml papers, box 3, folder 7, NUA.

54 Petition, "Correspondence: Incident May 3-4, 1968," box 3, folder 7, Kreml papers, NUA.

55 Hinz, interview with the author, April 4, 2018

56 Photograph caption, "Man of the Day," *Daily Northwestern,* May 17, 1968.

57 Sara Jane Goodyear, "N. U. Parents Voice Concern Over Revolt," *Chicago Tribune,* May 19, 1968.

58 Goodyear, "N. U. Parents Voice Concern Over Revolt."

59 Goodyear, "N. U. Parents Voice Concern Over Revolt."

60 Hinz, interview with the author, 2012.

61 Audio recording, James Turner, (speaking about the Bursar's Office Takeover) May 9, 1968, Northwestern University, Library Repository Audio and Video, https://media.northwestern.edu/media_objects/7d278t113.

62 Richard Boudreaux, "Shanahan Calls for 'Support NU' Meeting," *Daily Northwestern,* May 7, 1968.

63 Bob Greene, "Panel Hails Resolution," *Daily Northwestern,* May 10, 1968.

64 "Bi-racial Teach-in," *Daily Northwestern,* May 6, 1968.

65 "Turner to Discuss Black Student Sit-in," *Daily Northwestern,* May 7, 1968; "Biracial Teachin."

66-68 Audio recording, James Turner, May 9, 1968, Northwestern University.

69 Advertisement, *Chicago Tribune,* May 11, 1968.

70 Television listings, *Chicago Tribune,* June 1, 1968. Later, Turner appeared on the Mike Douglas show, along with guests Jesse Jackson and Sammy Davis, Jr. "Turner to Appear on TV," *Daily Northwestern,* February 4, 1969. Turner was also a featured speaker at numerous events, including an off-campus workshop sponsored by People to Overcome White Racism, titled, "America is Revolting." "James Turner

to Speak at 'Revolting' Workshop," *Evanston Review,* September 9, 1968.

71 Turner, interview with the author, 2012.

72 "Anarchists, Rebels and Fakers," *Chicago Tribune,* July 16, 1968.

73 Chesly Manly, "New Left, Black Power Guide Campus Revolts," *Chicago Tribune,* May 19, 1968.

74 "Florida State President Quits," *Decatur Daily Review,* May 15, 1968.

75 Howard H. Rosenheim, press release, May 7, 1968, Records of the Bursar's Office Takeover, May 1968, box 1, folder 3, NUA. Rolf Schulze observed the dramatic contrast between the two schools: "To many outside and casual observers it would have appeared quite unlikely that such a reputedly conservative school as Northwestern university could avoid violence, while seemingly more liberal schools, such as Columbia University, were unable to avoid disruptive violence and destruction." Schulze, "The Student Rebellion in the United States," 12.

76 Howard H. Rosenheim, press release.

77 Howard R. Rosenheim to all alumni, May 16, 1968, Records of the Bursar's Office Takeover, May 1968, box 1, folder 3, NUA.

78 "1968: Columbia in Crisis," Columbia University Libraries; https://exhibitions.library.columbia.edu/exhibits/show/1968/timeline.

79 Glen Elsasser, "Kirk Defends Police Use at Columbia U," *Chicago Tribune,* May 6, 1968.

80 Elsasser, "Kirk Defends Police Use at Columbia U."

81 Karen W. Arenson, "Grayson Kirk, 94, President of Columbia During the 1968 Student Protests, is Dead," *New York Times,* November 22, 1997.

82 Steve Sink, "Trustees to Investigate Accord," *Daily Northwestern,* May 10, 1968.

83 Chairmen of the departments of the College of Arts and Humanities to the board of trustees, May 12, 1968, "Correspondence: Incident May 3-4, 1968," box 3, folder 7, Kreml Papers, NUA.

84 Chairmen of the departments of the College of Arts and Humanities to the board of trustees, May 12, 1968.

85 This sentiment is present throughout the voluminous collection of correspondence received in reaction to the takeover, found in "Correspondence: Incident May 3-4, 1968," box 2-3, Kreml Papers, NUA.

86 Wild, "Memorandum concerning the black student seizure of the University business office."

87 Bob Hunter, "University Trustees Okay Administration Agreement," *Chicago Defender,* May 15, 1968.

88 Hunter, "University Trustees Okay Administration Agreement."

89 Hunter, "University Trustees Okay Administration Agreement."

90 Resolution, Northwestern University Board of Trustees, May 14, 1968, 2, Bursar's Office Takeover, May 1968, box 1, folder 2, NUA.

91 Hunter, "University Trustees Okay Administration Agreement."

92 Resolution, Northwestern University Board of Trustees, May 14, 1968, 2.

93 Resolution, Northwestern University Board of Trustees, May 14, 1968, 3.

94 "Kreml Blasts Tribune's Sit-in Coverage," *Daily Northwestern,* September 30, 1968.

95 Resolution, Northwestern University Board of Trustees, May 14, 1968, 1.

96 "A Letter from Northwestern," May 14, 1968.

97 "A New Day-A New Deal," *Chicago Defender,* May 13, 1968.

98 Roger Williams, Jr., letter to the editor, "Hail Northwestern," *Chicago Defender,* May 25, 1968.

99-105 Ogletree, interview with the author, 2018.

106 Bracey, interview with the author, 2018.

107 Quoted in Biondi, *The Black Revolution on Campus,* 92.

108 "NU Sees the Light," *Chicago Defender,* May 8, 1968.

109 Richard C. Christian, president of the Northwestern University Alumni Association, September 1968, box 2, folder 11, Kreml papers, NUA.

110 Letter to J. Roscoe Miller, May 6, 1968, "Correspondence: Incident May 3-4, 1968," box 2, folder 11, Kreml papers, NUA.

111 Letter to J. Roscoe Miller, May 6, 1968, "Correspondence, Incident May 3-4, 1968," box 3, Kreml Papers, NUA..

112 Doris E. Saunders, "Confetti," *Chicago Defender,* May 8, 1968. After graduating from Northwestern, Doris E. Saunders (1921-2014) served as a librarian at the Chicago Public Library. She later worked for Chicago-based Johnson Publishing Co., publisher of *Ebony* and other publications. During her tenure at Johnson, she launched a reference library, focused on twentieth-century Black history, and also headed up the company's book publishing division, launched in 1962. She was editor of several books including, *The Day They Marched* (1963) and *The Kennedy Years and the Negro* (1964) and author, with Gerri Major, of *Black Society* (1976). She later went on to serve as professor and chair of the Department of Mass Communications at Jackson State University. Aside from writing for the *Chicago Defender,* Saunders also hosted a radio talk show on WBEE in Chicago, "The Doris Saunders Show." *Jet,* May 10, 1962, 28; Doris E. Saunders Papers, Chicago Public Library, https://www.chipublib.org/archival_post/doris-e-saunders-papers/; "Saunders, Doris (1921–)," Encyclopedia.com.,https://www.encyclopedia.com/women/dictionaries-thesauruses-pictures-and-press-releases/saunders-doris-1921.

113 J. Roscoe Miller to Harold Walker, June 18, 1968, "Correspondence: Incident May 3-4, 1968," box 2, folder 11, Kreml papers, NUA.

114 Thomas H. Floyd, Jr. to Howard H. Rosenheim, June 4, 1968, "Correspondence, Incident May 3-4, 1968," box 3, folder 3, Kreml Papers, NUA.

115 Letter to J. Roscoe Miller, May 6, 1968, "Correspondence, Incident May 3-4, 1968," box 2, folder 12, Kreml Papers, NUA.

116 Letter to Howard H. Rosenheim, June 13, 1968, "Correspondence, Incident May 3-4, 1968," box 3, folder 3, Kreml Papers, NUA.

117 Amundsen-Mayfair City College to board of trustees of Northwestern University, telegram, May 14, 1968, box 2, folder 11, Kreml papers, NUA.

118 Leon M. Despres to Northwestern University, May 7, 1968, "Correspondence: Incident May 3-4, 1968," box 2, folder 11, Kreml papers, NUA.

119 "Northwestern Students Call Negro Demands 'Segregationist,'" *Chicago Tribune,* May 6, 1968.

120 "Northwestern Students Call Negro Demands 'Segregationist.'"

121 Letter, May 8, 1968, box 2, folder 11, Kreml papers, NUA.

122 "Negro Housing Plan Approved for N.U.," *Chicago Tribune,* July 25, 1968;

"Black Sit-in Won't Hurt NU: Hinz," *Daily Northwestern,* September 24, 1968.

123 Biondi, *The Black Revolution on Campus,* 93; "$300,000 Gift by M'Cormick Trust to N.U.;" *Chicago Tribune,* July 31, 1968; "Jewel Pledges $75,000 to N.U.'s First Plan for '70s," *Chicago Defender,* May 25, 1968.

124 "Negro Housing Plan Approved for N.U.," *Chicago Tribune,* July 25, 1968.

125 Sheryl Fitzgerald, "NU Confrontation Pact: A Model of Cooperation," *Chicago Defender,* October 10, 1968.

126 Under threat of expulsion, the students withdrew. "U. of Chicago Acts, Puts End to Sit-in," *Chicago Tribune,* May 16, 1968. More protests would take place at the University of Chicago during the next year, 1969.

127 "Demands on De Paul Listed by Negroes," *Chicago Tribune,* May 16, 1968. Another weeklong takeover and hunger strike were also taking place at Roosevelt University in Chicago at this time. Numerous students protested the university's refusal to offer historian Staughton Lynd a teaching contract, among other concerns. Scores of students were arrested, suspended, or expelled as a result of the action. "Police Seize Another 11 at Roosevelt U.," *Chicago Tribune,* May 15, 1968.

128 "De Paul Gives Blacks Reply to 9 Demands," *Chicago Tribune,* May 22, 1968. The impetus toward student activism would continue into the fall of 1968, when a major school boycott was underway in Chicago, with 20,000 Black students, along with 700 teachers, staging a walk-out after submitting a set of demands for more influence on curriculum and school policy. Among the many Chicago schools whose students participated in the walk-out, was Ogletree's alma mater, Harrison High School. The result of the protest at Harrison was not without incident: police were called in and fourteen students were arrested. "Chicago Student Fighting Flares," *Quad City Times,* October 9, 1968. At a rally held in support of the walk-out on what was deemed "Liberation Monday," James Turner was one of the featured speakers. Faith C. Christmas, "700 Teachers Join Boycott," *Chicago Defender,* October 22, 1968. A massive teacher and student strike and boycott had been staged in Chicago in 1963, with an estimated 200,000 to 250,000 students participating in a walk-out to protest segregation and inequality. Mark Walsh, "Documentary Recalls a 1963 Boycott of Segregated Chicago Public Schools," *Education Week,* October 25, 2017, http://blogs.edweek.org/edweek/education_and_the_media/2017/10/documentary_recalls_a_1963_boycott_of_segregated_chicago_public_schools.html.

129 Minutes of the Evanston City Council, May 6, 1968, 5.

130 Frederick A. Luecker, "Comments by Former Chairman," from *Report of the Evanston Human Relations Commission, 1969* (Evanston, IL, 1969), 1.

131 Ben Williams, "Comments by Executive Director," *Report of the Evanston Human Relations Commission, 1969* (Evanston, IL, 1969), 3. The commission heard complaints from citizens, sponsored talks and discussion groups on racism, launched a number of programs and partnerships, and investigated issues in the areas of policing and housing.

132 Photograph, *Evanston Review,* July 25, 1968.

133 "Prejudice Explained," *Evanston Review,* September 16, 1968.

134 "The Changing Mood of Local Blacks," *Evanston Review,* May 12, 1969.

135 Irving Louis Horowitz and William H. Friedland, "Sit-in at Stanford" in *Black Power and Student Rebellion,* James McEvoy and Abraham Miller, ed. (Belmont,

CA: Wadsworth Publishing, 1969), 148.

136 "Black Students Form Political Organization," *Chicago Defender,* May 14, 1968.

137 Turner, interview with the author, 2012.

138 Bob Greene, "Another Sit-In: The Message is Black," *Daily Northwestern,* January 17, 1969.

139 Charles Mount, "Negro School Plan Weighed in Evanston," *Chicago Tribune,* August 4, 1968.

140 John W. Walter, Jr., "N. U. Office Seizure Emphasizes Split," *Chicago Tribune,* June 17, 1968.

141 The *Daily Northwestern's* shift from using "Negro" to Black appears to have started directly after the takeover in the spring of 1968.

142 Bob Greene, "Panel Hails Resolution," *Daily Northwestern,* May 10, 1968.

143 [Faculty members] Arthur J. Freeman, Martin M. Block, Laurie M. Brown, Jules A. Marcus, and Stuart L. Meyer to the editor of the *Chicago Tribune,* May 6, 1969.

144 Letters to the editor, *Daily Northwestern,* May 9, 1968.

145 Bob Greene, "Panel Hails Resolution."

146 Audio recording, James Turner, May 9, 1968, Northwestern University.

147 "Northwestern University Accepts Black Demands," *Chicago Defender,* October 9, 1968.

148-153 Turner, interview with the author, 2012.

154 Cross, "James Turner: The Face of Black Power at Northwestern."

155 Ogletree, interview with the author, 2018.

156 Paterson, interview with the author.

157 Ogletree, interview with the author, 2018.

158 Ogletree, interview with the author, 2018.

159 Hinz, interview with the author. April 4, 2018.

160 "My Soul Looks Back in Wonder."

161 Thomas Powers, "N. U. Grads Told Meaning of Freedom," *Chicago Tribune,* June 16, 1968.

Notes to Chapter 8

1 "Education: "The Cynical Idealists of '68," *Time*, June 7, 1968. The *Time* article, which focused on the class of '68, included a profile of takeover participant Vernon Ford. Ford was described as "one of the key members of the militant Black Power movement on campus" who "has helped make Northwestern aware of the Negro students' determination to carve out their own niche on white campuses."

2 Enrollment numbers are drawn from "They Demanded Courageously, The 1968 Northwestern Bursar's Office Takeover" and "N. U. Official, Black Leader Tell Progress," *Chicago Tribune,* October 9, 1968.

3 "N.U. Students Face Relaxed Campus Rules," *Chicago Tribune,* September 23, 1968.

4 "N. U. Official, Black Leader Tell Progress," *Chicago Tribune,* October 9, 1968.

5 Kathy Waters, "9-Member Relations Group Set," *Daily Northwestern,* October 9, 1968. Northwestern's student government had long had a subcommittee on human relations. This new committee was an "all-university" committee, with members representing faculty, administrators, and students. The new committee had been proposed just before the takeover. "Administration Accepts Plan for Rights Commission," *Daily Northwestern,* May 2, 1968.

6 Roland J. Hinz, "Implementation of Black Student Agreement of May 4, 1968," October 10, 1968, Records of the Bursar's Office Takeover, May 1968, box 1, folder 3, NUA.

7 Waters, "9-Member Relations Group Set." Later, the Black student advisory council would be formed. Professor George Frederickson and Political Science Professor William W. Ellis, one of Northwestern's few Black faculty members, were appointed as faculty members on the committee. "Human Relations Unit Set Up at N.U.-3 Negroes Included," *Chicago Tribune,* August 22, 1968.

8 "Interracial NUCAP: Emotional, Turbulent," *Daily Northwestern,* September 24, 1968.

9 Originally from Trinidad, C.L.R. (Cyril Lionel Robert) James (1901-1989) was a Pan-African and Marxist historian best known for his 1938 history of the Haitian revolution: *The Black Jacobins: The Black Jacobins: Toussaint L'Ouverture and the San Domingo Revolution.*

10 Hinz, "Implementation of Black Student Agreement of May 4, 1968." Jeremiah Congress Mbata (1919-1989), a historian from South Africa, was a prominent anti-apartheid activist, who worked alongside Nelson Mandela. He was later hired by James Turner to teach at Cornell University. Glenn C. Altschuler and Isaac Kramnick, *Cornell: A History, 1940–2015* (Ithaca, NY: Cornell University Press, 2014), 168; Bill Harsh, "NU Officials, Blacks Will Report Progress," *Daily Northwestern,* September 24, 1968.

11 Initially, there was some opposition to the establishment of an African American studies program. The *Daily Northwestern* reported that some people were "intellectually opposed to the concept of Afro-American studies." By March 1969, however, the plan was moving forward. A permanent committee on Afro-American studies had been approved, with the goal of offering a degree program at some

point in the future. As Kathryn Ogletree pointed out, the program, and later the department, would undergo an evolution as a debate took place over what its primary academic focus should be. "Afro-Amer. Plan Gets CAS Okay," *Daily Northwestern*, March 7, 1969; "Department of African American Studies," Northwestern University, https://www.afam.northwestern.edu/about/department-history.html. For more on the establishment of the department see, Martha Biondi, *The Black Revolution on Campus*.

12 Turner, interview with the author, 2012.

13 Bill Harsh, "NU Officials, Blacks Will Report Progress," *Daily Northwestern*, September 24, 1968. The gift was made by Chicago Thoroughbred Enterprises.

14 Hinz, "Implementation of Black Student Agreement of May 4, 1968;" "Northwestern University Accepts Black Demands," *Chicago Defender*, October 9, 1968. Paul Black was appointed in November 1968, replacing Calvin Smith. He had formerly been a teacher at Central YMCA High School in Chicago. "Paul Black Named Black Counselor," *Daily Northwestern*, November 4, 1968. In the fall of 1968, Calvin Smith resigned to focus on his doctoral studies. Harsh, "NU Officials, Blacks Will Report Progress."

15 *Daily Northwestern*, November 1, 1968.

16 "Negro Housing Plan Approved for N.U.," *Chicago Tribune*, July 25, 1968.

17 "Northwestern Meeting Its Responsibility," *Chicago Defender*, June 13, 1970. The North Shore Hotel had long been used by Northwestern for student housing as well as a location to host university social events.

18 Hinz, "Implementation of Black Student Agreement of May 4, 1968."

19 Bill Harsh, "Progress Reported on Black Agreement," *Daily Northwestern*, October 9, 1968.

20 Michael Kilian, "Students' Drive for More Power at N. U. Growing," *Chicago Tribune*, February 2, 1969.

21 Turner, interview with the author, 2012.

22 Bill Harsh, "NU Officials, Blacks Will Report Progress," *Daily Northwestern*, September 24, 1968.

23 Harsh, "NU Officials, Blacks Will Report Progress."

24 "Committee Nominees Expected by Friday," *Daily Northwestern*, May 6, 1968.

25 Ogletree, interview with the author, 2018.

26 Charles E. Shepard, "For Members Only (F.M.O.): From Moderation to Militancy," c. 1969.

27 Michael Smith, Victor Goode, Eric Perkins, and Milton Gardner, respectively. Northwestern University Black Alumni Association, https://nubaa.wordpress.com/tag/northwestern-black-student-experience/.

28 Ogletree, interview with the author, 2018.

29 Ogletree, interview with the author, 2018. In January 1969, one woman was serving in a leadership role in FMO: Christine Henderson, who was corresponding secretary. Photo caption, *Emphasis, Daily Northwestern*, February 2, 1969. Still, the overall absence of female leaders in FMO was largely replicated in other student organizations and government. Barb Caulfield, who served as Northwestern's first female president of the Student Senate, was a rarity. And it was not until the end of the 1960s that the women's liberation movement and women's rights movement began to make more of an impact at the university.

30-32 Ogletree, interview with the author, 2018.

33 John Bracey, email to the author, June 8, 2018.

34 Members of the anti-war groups were predominantly male, although women were also members, including Suzanne Foote (Hanks) who was a member of CADRE and an organizer of at least one anti-war teach-in on campus. Joann Lublin, "Nine Profs Teach-In Tonight on Recruiting," *Daily Northwestern,* February 13, 1969.

35 The boycott was targeted at area liquor stores that sold California wines. "SDS Boycotts Wine Shops," *Daily Northwestern,* February 2, 1967.

36 Nancy Biberman, "Women in the Strike," *At Issue,* May 13, 1968.

37 Mark Rudd, "The Missing History of the Columbia '68 Protests," *New York Times*, April 22, 2018. Rudd, an SDS member and student leader of the Columbia University protests, went on to become a member of the Weatherman Underground. His memoir *Underground: My Life with SDS and the Weathermen* (New York: Harper Collins, 2009) provides a fascinating glimpse into the workings of the student protest movements, including the rampant sexism that existed within many organizations.

38 By 2015, a total of 400 female faculty members held tenure-line positions at Northwestern, comprising 28.7% of all faculty. Northwestern University, Office of Institutional Diversity and Inclusion, "2016 Report on Faculty, Staff, and Student Diversity and Inclusion at Northwestern," 15, https://www.northwestern.edu/diversity/resources/reports/.

39 About a third of the faculty of the schools of Music and Speech were female, while the faculty in the College of Arts and Sciences was less than one percent female. As far as women in the administration went, one administrator offered his view: "At the dean's level pressures of the job make it easier for a man to handle. Besides, a woman might get upset or over-emotional regarding faculty relations." "NU Women: Liberated or Left Out?" *Daily Northwestern,* October 10, 1969. The above article appeared in the *Emphasis* magazine of the *Daily Northwestern.*

40 Ogletree, interview with the author, 2018.

41 Steve Sink, "Trustees to Investigate Accord," *Daily Northwestern,* May 10, 1968.

42 Sink, "Trustees to Investigate Accord."

43 Rumsfeld sent a telegram to Miller just days after the takeover, alerting him to the question of the legality of providing separate housing for Black students. He also expressed his support, writing that he believed university officials had handled the incident with responsibility and thoughtfulness. Donald Rumsfeld to J. Roscoe Miller, telegram, May 10, 1968, "Correspondence: Incident May 3-4, 1968," box 3, folder 1, Kreml papers, NUA.

44 "University Pact Sparks Furor," *Evanston Review,* May 13, 1968. One Northwestern graduate recalled that years ago the university had, without controversy, offered separate housing for Jewish students after their mothers requested that their daughters be allowed to room together in a campus dorm, a request that had been granted. Letter, May 8, 1968. "Correspondence: Incident May 3-4, 1968," box 2, folder 1, Kreml papers, NUA.

45 Title VI-Nondiscrimination in Federally Assisted Programs, Sec. 601., Civil Rights Act of 1964, Pub.L. 88-352, 78 Stat. 241 (1964).

46 "U.S. Hits NU On Black Student Pact," *Chicago Defender,* June 1, 1968. A

handful of other universities, including Rutgers and Cornell, had allowed separate residential facilities for Black students to be established. But most others "refuse[d] to establish separate residence or cafeterias, claiming that the provision of separate services and benefits based on race or ethnicity violated title 6 of the Civil Rights Act of 1964." Williamson-Lott, *Black Power on Campus*, 30.

47 Louise Hutchinson, "Part of N.U. Pact Illegal," *Chicago Tribune,* May 30, 1968; "N.U. Responds to Civil Rights Charge," *Chicago Tribune,* May 30, 1968.

48 "Northwestern Revamps Negro Housing Plan," *Stevens Point Journal,* July 25, 1968.

49 "Northwestern's Accord With Negroes Is Barred," *New York Times,* May 31, 1968.

50 "N. U. Negroes Will 'Clarify' Pact For U. S.," *Chicago Tribune,* May 31, 1968.

51 "N. U. Negroes Will 'Clarify' Pact For U. S."

52 Hinz, interview with the author, April 4, 2018.

53 "Rights Tested at NU," *Evanston Review,* September 26, 1968.

54 "Rights Tested at NU."

55 "Kreml Blasts Tribune's Sit-in Coverage," *Daily Northwestern,* September 30, 1968.

56 The investigators included two from HEW's Washington D.C. office of Civil Rights, two from the Chicago regional HEW office, and one from HEW's Bureau of Higher Education. "U.S. Asks: Does NU Discriminate?" *Daily Northwestern,* October 23, 1968. Northwestern was one of 200 campuses across the country that HEW would investigate that fall to ensure compliance with Title VI of the 1964 Civil Rights Act—"that no institution receiving funds from the government may discriminate in respect to race, creed or color." Tom Davies, "HEW: Many Schools, Little Time," *Daily Northwestern,* October 25, 1968.

57 Davies, "HEW: Many Schools, Little Time."

58 "U.S. Asks: Does NU Discriminate?" *Daily Northwestern,* October 23, 1968.

59 Kathy Waters, "HEW Investigators Not Critical: Hinz," *Daily Northwestern,* October 24, 1968.

60 "Northwestern University Responses to the Black Student Petition Received Monday, April 22, 1968," 4.

61 Kathy Waters, "Veto Black Dorm; Current Set-Up Ok'd," *Daily Northwestern,* February 28, 1969.

62 Waters, "Veto Black Dorm; Current Set-Up Ok'd."

63 Waters, "Veto Black Dorm; Current Set-up Ok'd."

64 "Civil Rights Office Okays NU Reaction to Probe," *Daily Northwestern,* January 10, 1969.

65 "Blacks Say Slow Action on Housing, Other Issues Contribute to Tensions," *Daily Northwestern,* March 19, 1969.

66 "Black Students Air Gripes," *Daily Northwestern,* January 31, 1969.

67 "N.U. Students Face Relaxed Campus Rules," *Chicago Tribune,* September 23, 1968.

68 Ogletree, interview with the author, 2018.

69 Hinz, interview with the author, April 4, 2018.

70 Turner, interview with the author, 2012.

71 Paterson, interview with the author, 2012.

72 Charles E. Shepard, "For Members Only (F.M.O.): From Moderation to Militancy," c. 1969.

73 Carl Shierhorn, "IFC Tables Egg Incident Fine Motion," *Daily Northwestern,*

October 31, 1968.

74 Eva Jefferson Paterson, interview with the author, 2012.

75 "Blacks Set Their Own Homecoming Dance," *Daily Northwestern,* November 1, 1968; "Queen, King Reign," *Daily Northwestern,* November 4, 1968.

76 Elliot Brown, "Separatism Reflects Present Culture: Black," *Daily Northwestern,* December 2, 1968.

77 Michael Kilian, "Students' Drive for More Power at N. U. Growing," *Chicago Tribune,* February 2, 1969.

78 Elliot Brown, "Fountain Square Election Protest Draws 50," *Daily Northwestern,* November 5, 1968.

79 Kilian, "Students' Drive for More Power at N. U. Growing."

80 "N.U. Students Face Relaxed Campus Rules," *Chicago Tribune,* September 23, 1968.

81 "N.U. Students Face Relaxed Campus Rules."

82 "N.U. Students Face Relaxed Campus Rules."

83 Hinz, interview with the author, 2012.

84 Roger Friedman, email to the author, January 20, 2019.

85 Kilian, "Students' Drive for More Power at N. U. Growing."

86 Kilian, "Students' Drive for More Power at N. U. Growing."

87 Wally Judd, "Sit-in, Autonomy Best Stories," *Daily Northwestern,* May 28, 1968.

88 Editorial, "The Agreement," *Daily Northwestern,* May 7, 1968.

89 Roberta Kirsten, "Women Write on Rights," *Daily Northwestern,* May 15, 1969; Mark Winiarski, "Women's Liberation Talk Gets Her Into Trouble-But Marlene Dixon Talks!" *Daily Northwestern,* March 5, 1969; Advertisement, *Daily Northwestern,* May 19, 1969; Baran Rosen, "Coeds Free Image," *Daily Northwestern,* October 10, 1969.

90 "Overhaul Curriculum, Campus Life, Massive Hagstrum Report Urges," *Daily Northwestern,* October 14, 1968. English professor Jean Hagstrum served as chair of the Faculty Planning Committee.

91 "Disenchanted SDS Members Restructure Group, Elect Rice," *Daily Northwestern,* December 2, 1968.

92 Flyer, "Dis-Orientation Week," Student Protests and Strikes at Northwestern University, NUA. This was the second annual dis-orientation week. The first, held in 1967, reportedly suffered from poor publicity and low turn-out. Richard Boudreaux, "Group Plans to 'Tell it Like it Is,' " *Daily Northwestern,* September 24, 1968.

93 "SDS to Protest Election," *Daily Northwestern,* October 24, 1968.

94 Flyer, "Elections?" nd, Student Protests and Strikes at Northwestern University, NUA.

95 Elliot Brown, "Fountain Square Election Protest Draws 50," *Daily Northwestern,* November 5, 1968.

96 Along with Tom Hayden and others, Flacks took part in drafting the Port Huron Statement (1962), the blueprint for SDS and the New Left.

97 Advertisement, *Daily Northwestern,* November 22, 1968.

98 "Nude-In a Big Cover-Up," *Daily Northwestern,* November 25, 1968.

99 Kilian, "Students' Drive for More Power at N. U. Growing."

100 Kilian, "Students' Drive for More Power at N. U. Growing."

101 Kilian, "Students' Drive for More Power at N. U. Growing."

102 "Symposium Gets Gregory," *Daily Northwestern,* November 22, 1968; "Panels Disrupted At Northwestern," *New York Times,* January 12, 1969.

103 Joan Lublin, "Crowds Shake Panel at Cahn," *Daily Northwestern,* January 9, 1969. Thomas Ayers was the father of Bill Ayers, an SDS member at the University of Michigan who would later join the Weatherman Underground.

104 "Of Ways Men Make Change," *Daily Northwestern,* January 6, 1969. Other speakers included author and professor, Michael Harrington, founding member of the Democratic Socialists of America, and Richard Goodwin, adviser to Presidents Kennedy and Johnson. "The Men and Their Issues," *Daily Northwestern,* January 6, 1969.

105 Kilian, "Students' Drive for More Power at N. U. Growing." Rubin (1938-1994) would soon be arraigned on a variety of charges, including "crossing state lines to incite violence" during the Democratic National Convention in Chicago in August 1968. Joann Lublin, "Yippie! It's Rubin!" *Daily Northwestern,* January 8, 1969. Rubin was one of the famous "Chicago 7."

106 "Panel Format Killed?" *Daily Northwestern,* January 10, 1969.

107 "Shaving Cream Hurled on Viet Speaker at N.U.," *Chicago Tribune,* November 15, 1968.

108 Audio recording, James Turner, May 9, 1968, Northwestern University.

109 For more on the ways protest movements intersected (namely within the civil rights and anti-war movements) see Simon Hall, *Peace and Freedom: The Civil Rights and Antiwar Movements of the 1960s* (Philadelphia: University of Pennsylvania Press, 2005).

110 Philip Lentz, "SAS Tactics Like Blacks' of May '68," *Daily Northwestern,* November 25, 1969.

111 Paterson, interview with the author, 2012. Paterson recalled that the 1968 Dow protest significantly contributed to her reassessment of her own beliefs. See text for more on that protest.

112 Kathy Polhemus, "Black Students Seek White Cooperation," *Daily Northwestern,* April 3, 1969.

113 Polhemus, "Black Students Seek White Cooperation."

114 "From the Editor," *Emphasis, Daily Northwestern,* February 14, 1969.

115 *Emphasis, Daily Northwestern,* February 14, 1969.

116 Stephen Plotnick, "What Can We Do?" Emphasis, *Daily Northwestern,* February 14, 1969.

117 Kilian, "Students' Drive for More Power at N. U. Growing."

118 "U.S. Campuses Termed 'Ripe for Revolution,'" *The Argus,* March 7, 1969.

119 Kilian, "Students' Drive for More Power at N. U. Growing."

120 John Walter, "Student Seizure of Building-Never Again?" *Daily Northwestern,* May 6, 1968.

121 "New N.U. Students Warned on Dissent," *Chicago Tribune,* September 23, 1968.

122 Northwestern University, "Procedure for University Administration in the Event of Campus Disorders," October 1968, Records of the Bursar's Office Takeover, May 1968, box 1, folder 3, NUA, 3-4.

123-125 Northwestern University Board of Trustees, Resolution, May 14, 1968, 2, Records of the Bursar's Office Takeover, May 1968, 3, box 1, folder 3, NUA.

126 Williamson-Lott, *Black Power on Campus,* 86.

127 "The Universities Are Asking for It," *Chicago Tribune,* September 11, 1968. The students at the University of Illinois were attempting to have their grievances addressed concerning housing, financial aid, and other issues. They refused to leave the student union after it had closed and instead continued to discuss their demands. When some students began to break furniture and damage other property within the union, university officials called in the local and state police. "300 Negro Students Seized in U. of Illinois Protest," *New York Times,* September 11, 1968. For more, see Williamson-Lott, *Black Power on Campus: The University of Illinois, 1965-75.*

128 Emphasis in the original. Ibram X. Kendi, *The Black Campus Movement,* 123. And, as Kendi notes, in the wake of the widespread student uprising, "Laws of all sorts in all states sought to regulate campus activism, from denying federal aid to 'rioters' to making it illegal to seize property." *The Black Campus Movement,* 141.

129 Resolution, Northwestern University Board of Trustees, May 14, 1968, 3, Bursar's Office Takeover, May 1968, box 1, folder 2, NUA

130 Northwestern University, "Procedure for University Administration in the Event of Campus Disorders," 1.

131 "Ellis Pines Comes Back," *Daily Northwestern,* January 5, 1968.

132 Napalm had been deployed by the U.S. military as early as World War II.

133 "Napalm and the Dow Chemical Company," *Two Days in October,* The American Experience, October 17, 2005. https://www.pbs.org/wgbh/americanexperience/films/two-days-in-october/.

134 "A Turning Point: Six Stories from the Dow Chemical Protests on Campus," University of Wisconsin-Madison, https://1967.wisc.edu/.

135 Student Life and Archival Program of the University of Illinois Archives, "1967 Protest and Sit-In against Dow Chemical," https://archives.library.illinois.edu/slcold/researchguides/coldwar/vietnam/dowprotest.php.

136 Franklin Kreml argued that an "extreme view could be taken of any holdings we have," while officials were firm in their position that Northwestern's choice of stock holdings would not be influenced by any opinions held by students or faculty. John Walter, "NU Owns $811,899 of Dow Stock," *Daily Northwestern,* January 24, 1968.

137 "500 Protesters March on Crown," *Daily Northwestern,* February 15, 1968.

138 "YAF Cuts Ties with National; Sets Dow Plans," *Daily Northwestern,* January 31, 1968.

139 Letter to the editor, "Welcome Dow," *Daily Northwestern,* January 19, 1968.

140 Bill Harsh, "Hinz Warns Protesters About Obstructing Dow," *Daily Northwestern,* January 16, 1968.

141 "Anti-Dow Students Set Rally," *Daily Northwestern,* January 16, 1968.

142 "Ellis Pines Comes Back," *Daily Northwestern,* January 5, 1968. Pines had withdrawn from Northwestern in the fall of 1967.

143 Reed Wilson, "Ellis Pines and The Student Power Movement at Northwestern: The Pursuit of Personal Authenticity and Political Legitimacy in the Face of Existential Angst and Social Alienation, 1966-1968," unpublished paper, June 2010, 24.

144 John Walter, "Pines Says He is Happy as a Student," *Daily Northwestern,* January 9, 1968.

145 Photograph caption, "500 Protesters March on Crown," *Daily Northwestern,*

February 15, 1968.

146 Bob Greene, "How Hinz is Trapped by Role," *Daily Northwestern,* November 15, 1968.

147 Bob Greene, "Everyone is Talking-But to Themselves," *Daily Northwestern,* April 18, 1969.

148 Greene, "How Hinz is Trapped by Role;" "500 Protesters March on Crown," *Daily Northwestern*; "Non-Violence: They Planned it That Way," *Daily Northwestern,* February 15, 1968.

149 "Local Police Should Protect Dow Only if Law is Broken," *Daily Northwestern,* January 30, 1968.

150 "Local Police Should Protect Dow Only if Law is Broken."

151-154 Greene, "How Hinz is Trapped by Role."

155 Hinz, interview with the author, 2012. Hinz was also identified in the FBI reports concerning the takeover. FBI, "Racial Tensions, Northwestern University Campus, Evanston, Illinois," 2.

156 Greene, "How Hinz is Trapped by Role."

157 Greene, "How Hinz is Trapped by Role."

158 "Jaundiced Eyes," *Daily Northwestern,* February 16, 1968. On the day of the scheduled interviews, the students were brought to the interviews in campus security cars. The interview site had been moved to McGaw Hall at 2705 Ashland Ave. Hinz announced the move, stating that the change had been made "to prevent disturbance of others on the main campus." But he pledged that "orderly demonstrations would be permitted." "Dow Chemical To Recruit At N. U. Fieldhouse," *Chicago Tribune,* February 9, 1968; Thomas Powers, "2 N. U. Co-eds Defend the Flag from Anti-War Demonstrators," *Chicago Tribune,* February 15, 1968.

159 "Jaundiced Eyes."

160 Letter to the editor, "Laugh at Protest," *Daily Northwestern,* February 22, 1968.

161 "Evanston All Night Meet-in," *Dixon Evening Telegraph,* February 26, 1969. The demonstration was planned to take place in front of the Job Placement Center office at 1940 Sheridan Road, where the Dow recruiters were slated to interview the student job candidates.

162 Steve Sink, "Dual-Site Dow Protest Planned," *Daily Northwestern,* February 13, 1969. Organizers of the Dow protest initially planned two simultaneous protests from 9 a.m. to 4 p.m. at both the campus job placement center and McGaw Hall. But only one protest took place.

163 "A Little Something For Everyone," *Daily Northwestern,* February 26, 1969.

164 Kathy Waters, "Extra Security is Planned for Dow Visit," *Daily Northwestern,* February 25, 1969.

165 Waters, "Extra Security is Planned for Dow Visit;" Joann Lublin, "Students Unshaken by Threat," *Daily Northwestern,* January 18, 1969.

166 Elliot Brown, "Dow Protest in Turmoil," *Daily Northwestern,* February 26, 1969.

167 Brown, "Dow Protest in Turmoil."

168 William Jones and Charles Mount, "Sit-in Held by Students in N.U. Hall," *Chicago Tribune,* February 26, 1969.

169 Brown, "Dow Protest in Turmoil." In the aftermath of the "bedlam" on campus, the question of just who had called the police was raised. Both university

officials and Evanston police confirmed that no one at Northwestern had called them. An Evanston police captain told the *Daily Northwestern* that he had ordered the riot-equipped officers there himself and that they had already been placed on alert long before the protest began. "A Nice Whodunit: Did NU Call cops?" *Daily Northwestern,* February 26, 1969.

170 Brown, "Dow Protest in Turmoil."

171 William Jones, "Sit-In Held By Students In N. U. Hall," *Chicago Tribune,* February 26, 1969.

172 Hinz, interview with the author, 2012.

173 Photograph caption, *Chicago Tribune,* February 26, 1969.

174 Brown, "Dow Protest in Turmoil."

175 "6 N.U. Students Fined," *Chicago Tribune,* April 19, 1969; Elliot Brown, "Six Students Fined for Dow Protest," *Daily Northwestern,* April 21, 1969. The students' court hearing would later be set for April 1969. Four students would also be disciplined by the UDC. Richard Boudreaux, "UDC Cases Made Biggest Headlines," *Daily Northwestern,* May 26, 1969.

176 Flyer, "Arrested," February 25, 1969, Student Activities Collection, NUA.

177 Brown, "Dow Protest in Turmoil."

178 "Ferment at Northwestern," *New York Times,* February 26, 1969.

179 "A Little Something For Everyone," *Daily Northwestern,* February 26, 1969.

180 "A Little Something For Everyone."

181 Brown, "Dow Protest in Turmoil."

182 Brown, "Dow Protest in Turmoil."

183 William Jones, "Sit-In Held By Students In N. U. Hall," *Chicago Tribune,* February 26, 1969.

184 "Calm at Northwestern," *New York Times,* February 27, 1969.

185 UPI photograph caption, *The Republic,* February 27, 1969.

186 Northwestern University, "Procedure for University Administration in the Event of Campus Disorders," 4.

Notes to Chapter 9

1 The People of the State of Illinois, V. Clinton Bristow Et Al., 1972, Appellate Court of Illinois, 1972.

2 "Report of the Proceedings of the University Discipline Committee Regarding Events of March 3 and 4, 1969, Including Incident at the Willard Hall Dining Room and an Incident at the Triangle Fraternity," March 8, 1969, 2, Records of the Bursar's Office Takeover, May 1968, box 1, folder 3, NUA.

3 John Walter, "Willard Events Recalled at UDC," *Daily Northwestern,* March 10, 1969. Reports of the incident were first made to the head of the Willard food service, then to the housemother of Willard Hall before reaching Thrash. "Busboys Fault 'System' for Slow Solution," *Daily Northwestern,* March 7, 1969.

4 "Report of the Proceedings of the University Discipline Committee Regarding Events of March 3 and 4, 1969," March 8, 1969, 2.

5 "Report of the Proceedings of the University Discipline Committee Regarding Events of March 3 and 4, 1969," March 8, 1969, 2.

6 "3 Are Hurt in Black Raid on N.U. Frat," *Chicago Tribune,* March 5, 1969.

7 Charles Mount, "N.U. Busboys Walk Out to Defend a Pal," *Chicago Tribune,* March 6, 1969.

8 The People of The State of Illinois, v. Clinton Bristow Et Al., 1972, Appellate Court of Illinois, 1972.

9 Accounts of what happened at the Triangle fraternity house vary. Some witnesses reported seeing "a group of blacks running down an alley behind the house with bats and rocks just before the attack." And some reported a "similar, less destructive" disturbance at the house two hours earlier. Following the incident, an unsubstantiated report circulated that a fourth Triangle fraternity member had been beaten by Black students elsewhere on the campus. "3 Are Hurt in Black Raid on N.U. Frat," *Chicago Tribune,* March 5, 1969; Robert Nolte and Charles Mount, "Members of N.U. Fraternity Quit House After Black Attack," *Chicago Tribune,* March 7, 1969; "Four Students Hurt as 20 Blacks Invade, Fight in Triangle," *Daily Northwestern,* March 5, 1969; "Negroes Invade Fraternity at Northwestern," *Mt. Vernon Register,* March 5, 1969.

10 "UDC Opens Fight Hearing to Press," *Daily Northwestern,* March 7, 1969.

11 Hinz, interview with the author, 2012.

12 "Negroes Invade Fraternity at Northwestern."

13 Mount, "N.U. Busboys Walk Out to Defend a Pal."

14 One student was also charged with battery, not a felony charge. "Hinz Takes UDC to Black Meeting," *Daily Northwestern,* March 6, 1969.

15 "Negroes Invade Fraternity at Northwestern."

16 "Dean Urged to Resign," *Decatur Daily Review,* March 7, 1969.

17 Mount, "N.U. Busboys Walk Out to Defend a Pal."

18 "Negroes Invade Fraternity at Northwestern."

19 "Hinz Takes UDC to Black Meeting," *Daily Northwestern,* March 6, 1969.

20 Mount, "N.U. Busboys Walk Out to Defend a Pal;" "Police Hunt Two Students, Have Warrants for Arrests," *Daily Northwestern,* March 6, 1969.

21 "UDC Opens Fight Hearing to Press," *Daily Northwestern,* March 7, 1969.

22 Mount, "N.U. Busboys Walk Out to Defend a Pal."

23 "UDC Opens Fight Hearing to Press."

24 Mount, "N.U. Busboys Walk Out to Defend a Pal." The statement was signed by Michael Smith, FMO governor of campus affairs, Milton Gardner, FMO correlator of communications, and Eric Perkins, FMO director of community affairs. All three had been participants in the May 1968 takeover.

25 Ogletree, interview with the author, 2018.

26 Hinz, interview with the author, 2012.

27 "Hinz Hits N.U.'s Sororities, Fraternities," *Chicago Tribune,* June 16, 1968.

28 John Walter, "Sigma Chi Barred from Rush for Full Year! IFC President Protests," *Daily Northwestern,* July 26, 1968.

29 Walter, "Sigma Chi Barred from Rush for Full Year! IFC President Protests." The fight took place on June 21, 1968.

30 "N.U. Sigma Chi Chapter Put on Probation," *Chicago Tribune,* July 27, 1968.

31 "UDC Meets-No Sigma Chi Change," *Daily Northwestern,* August 9, 1968. In July 1968, HEW officials pledged to investigate Sigma Chi fraternity to find out if it violated federal civil rights laws since the group had no Black members. "Northwestern Faces a Federal Probe of Fraternity Bias," *Des Moines Tribune,* July 31, 1968.

32 Bill Harsh, "UDC to Reconsider Sigma Chi Ban," *Daily Northwestern,* September 24, 1968.

33 The letters urging a reconsideration of the case are found in "Sigma Chi 1968," box 49, folder 5, Miller papers, NUA.

34 "N.U. Will Give Sigma Chi's New Hearing," *Chicago Tribune,* August 3, 1968; Bill Harsh, "UDC to Reconsider Sigma Chi Ban," *Daily Northwestern,* September 24, 1968.

35 Kathy Waters, "UDC Shortens Sigma Chi Rush Ban," *Daily Northwestern,* October 7, 1968.

36 "Negroes Disciplined at Northwestern," *Southern Illinoisan,* April 14, 1969.

37 "Hinz Takes UDC to Black Meeting," *Daily Northwestern,* March 6, 1969.

38 "Hinz Takes UDC to Black Meeting."

39 Hal Hollister, "2 NU Students are Charged," *Evanston Review,* March 10, 1969; "Hinz Takes UDC to Black Meeting."

40 "Police Hunt Two Students, Have Warrants for Arrests," *Daily Northwestern,* March 6, 1969.

41 Photograph caption, "The Meeting is Closed," *Daily Northwestern,* March 6, 1969.

42 "Hinz Takes UDC to Black Meeting."

43 "Hinz Takes UDC to Black Meeting."

44 "Media Erred in Coverage, Blacks Say," *Daily Northwestern,* March 7, 1969.

45 "Media Erred in Coverage, Blacks Say."

46 "Backlash of Reason," *Chicago Tribune,* March 7, 1969. In its scathing editorial, the *Chicago Tribune* lambasted Hinz, quoting the *Daily Northwestern's* editorial at length.

47 "Hinz: An Ultimatum," *Daily Northwestern,* March 6, 1969.

48 "Dean Urged to Resign," *Decatur Daily Review,* March 7, 1969; "Protest N.U. Editorial by Taking Papers," *Chicago Tribune,* March 8, 1969.

49 "Hinz: An Ultimatum."

50 "Protest N.U. Editorial by Taking Papers."

51 "N.U. Won't Comment of Change," *Chicago Tribune,* March 6, 1969.

52 "University Shiftover," *Daily Chronicle,* March 11, 1969. The *Daily Northwestern* later wrote that Miller was "elevated" to this new position. "Retrospective: What Difference 10 Years Make," *Daily Northwestern,* December 10, 1969.

53 "University Shiftover;" "2 Presidents for Northwestern?" *Evanston Review,* March 10, 1969.

54 "University Shiftover."

55 "Top-level Shake-Up! Miller Plans Jobs Split, Eventual Campus Exodus," *Daily Northwestern,* March 5, 1969.

56 "Top-level Shake-Up! Miller Plans Jobs Split, Eventual Campus Exodus."

57 The Student Senate attempted to address the tension on campus by announcing that it would hold a special "rumor-clearing meeting" on Friday, March 7, in order to fill what was seen as an "information void" on campus. Some senate members tabled a motion to urge members of Triangle to drop the felony charges against the two students. Senate member Eva Jefferson Paterson objected to tabling the motion and warned that "all black students might leave the university if the two students now being sought by Evanston Police are expelled." Black students, she argued, believe that the "only way to move toward solving the problem is to have charges dropped and keep the problem inside the university." "Senate Sets Open Talk," *Daily Northwestern,* March 7, 1969.

58 Roland J. Hinz, "Statement to the Student Body," *Daily Northwestern,* March 7, 1969.

59 Robert Nolte and Charles Mount, "Members of N.U. Fraternity Quit House After Black Attack," *Chicago Tribune,* March 7, 1969.

60 Hinz, "Statement to the Student Body."

61 Hinz, "Statement to the Student Body."

62 Bill Harsh, "Continuance Delays Busboys Ruling," *Daily Northwestern,* March 10, 1969.

63 Harsh, "Continuance Delays Busboys Ruling;" Charles Mount, "2 Surrender in Fraternity Fracas at N.U.," *Chicago Tribune,* March 8, 1969.

64 Hal Hollister, "2 NU Students are Charged," *Evanston Review,* March 10, 1969.

65-67 Mount, "2 Surrender in Fraternity Fracas at N.U."

68 Announcement, *Daily Northwestern,* March 7, 1969.

69 John Walter, "Willard Events Recalled at UDC," *Daily Northwestern,* March 10, 1969.

70 "Report of the Proceedings of the University Discipline Committee Regarding Events of March 3 and 4, 1969," March 8, 1969, 2.

71 Walter, "Willard Events Recalled at UDC."

72 Joann Lublin, "3 Mothers Take Sides at Hunger Strike Site," *Daily Northwestern,* April 21, 1969.

73 Walter, "Willard Events Recalled at UDC."

74 "Report of the Proceedings of the University Discipline Committee Regarding Events of March 3 and 4, 1969," March 8, 1969, 1.

75 Italics added. Bill Harsh, "Continuance Delays Busboys Ruling," *Daily Northwestern,* March 10, 1969.

76 "Report of the Proceedings of the University Discipline Committee on Friday, March 14, in McGaw Hall Regarding the Events of March 3 and 4, 1969, at Willard Hall and the Triangle Fraternity," March 14, 1969, 2, Records of the Bursar's Office Takeover, May 1968, box 1, folder 3, NUA; "N.U. Busboy Insists Upon, Gets Hearing," *Chicago Tribune,* March 9, 1969.

77 "Report of the Proceedings of the University Discipline Committee on Friday, March 14, in McGaw Hall Regarding the Events of March 3 and 4, 1969, at Willard Hall the Triangle Fraternity," March 14, 1969, 1.

78 "Report of the Proceedings of the University Discipline Committee Regarding Events of March 3 and 4, 1969," March 8, 1969, 2.

79 Harsh, "Continuance Delays Busboys Ruling."

80 Final Demands, 1968, 2.

81 Harsh, "Continuance Delays Busboys Ruling."

82 "Report of the Proceedings of the University Discipline Committee on Friday, March 14, in McGaw Hall Regarding the Events of March 3 and 4, 1969, at Willard Hall the Triangle Fraternity," March 14, 1969, 1.

83 Hal Hollister, "2 NU Students are Charged," *Evanston Review,* March 10, 1969.

84 Holt argued that a fair proceeding was impossible for the following reasons: "1. The absence of substantive University rules and regulations defining misconduct allegedly committed by the respondents. 2. The absence of procedural rules and regulations governing the conduct and functioning of university disciplinary authorities, including this committee; 3. The absence of specific provisions stating the possible punishment for the alleged misconduct; and 4. With regard to the two respondents presently involved in criminal proceedings, the possibility of self-incrimination resulting from their participation in these hearings." "Report of the Proceedings of the University Discipline Committee on Friday, March 14, in McGaw Hall Regarding Events of March 3 and 4, 1969, at the Willard Hall and the Triangle Fraternity," March 14, 1969, 1, NUA. James G. Carr also served as an attorney for the students. The students charged criminally were represented by Leo E. Holt and Donald Frey.

85 Charles Mount, "Fraternity at N.U. Won't Drop Charges," *Chicago Tribune,* March 15, 1969.

86 "Report of the Proceedings of the University Discipline Committee on Friday, March 14, in McGaw Hall Regarding the Events of March 3 and 4, 1969, at Willard Hall the Triangle Fraternity," March 14, 1969, 1-2.

87 Mount, "Fraternity at N.U. Won't Drop Charges."

88 Mount, "Fraternity at N.U. Won't Drop Charges."

89 Kathy Polhemus, "Blacks Release Letters, Claim Triangle 'Cop Out,' " *Daily Northwestern,* May 22, 1969.

90 Kathy Polhemus, "Black Students Seek White Cooperation," *Daily Northwestern,* April 3, 1969.

91 "Blacks Say Slow Action on Housing, Other Issues Contributes to Tension," *Daily Northwestern,* March 10, 1969.

92 "UDC Opens Fight Hearing to Press," *Daily Northwestern,* March 7, 1969.

93-95 "Blacks Say Slow Action on Housing, Other Issues Contribute to Tensions."

96 "Blacks Ask for Support of Students," *Daily Northwestern,* April 2, 1969;

Kathy Polhemus, "Students Discuss Racial Crises," *Daily Northwestern,* April 4, 1969.

97 Polhemus, "Students Discuss Racial Crises."

98 "Blacks Ask for Support of Students," *Daily Northwestern,* April 2, 1969.

99 "Threaten Black Student Walkout at NU: Meeting Set Today to Plan Protest Move," *Chicago Defender,* March 17, 1969.

100 The FMO also issued a formal statement to this effect. "Threaten Black Student Walkout at NU: Meeting Set Today to Plan Protest Move," *Chicago Defender,* March 17, 1969; "Hayakawa Favors No U.S. Funds for Rioters," *The Independent,* March 17, 1969.

101 Donna Rosene, "Seven More Blacks Charged by UDC for Triangle Incident," *Daily Northwestern,* March 31, 1969.

102 Charles Mount, "Seven Blacks Face Hearing in N.U. Brawl," *Chicago Tribune,* March 21, 1969.

103 Mount, "Seven Blacks Face Hearing in N.U. Brawl."

104 Rosene, "Seven More Blacks Charged by UDC for Triangle Incident."

105 Editorial, "UDC and Closed Doors: Wrong," *Daily Northwestern,* April 15, 1969.

106 Mount, "Seven Blacks Face Hearing in N.U. Brawl."

107 The group was also referred to as "Concerned White Students." "Black Support Rally Today," *Daily Northwestern,* April 11, 1969. After graduating from Northwestern, Richard J. (Dick) Cohen (1949-) earned a law degree from William Mitchell College of Law in Saint Paul, Minnesota. In 1976, he was elected to the Minnesota legislature where he served as a member of the Minnesota House of Representatives and now serves as a member of the state senate. "Senator Richard Cohen," Minnesota Senate DFL Caucus, http://www.senatedflcaucus.com/members/richard-cohen.

108 "Black Support Rally Today," *Daily Northwestern,* April 11, 1969.

109 Phil Lentz, "Weber Supports Blacks," *Daily Northwestern,* April 14, 1969.

110 Lentz, "Weber Supports Blacks."

111-113 "Hinz Pledges Action, Blacks Not Impressed," *Daily Northwestern,* April 11, 1969.

114 Bob Greene, "Blacks End 121-Hour Hunger Strike with Vow to 'Confront University,' " *Daily Northwestern,* April 22, 1969.

115 Bill Harsh, "UDC Suspends 15 Blacks, Puts 6 on Pro After Attorneys Negotiate Triangle Case," *Daily Northwestern,* April 14, 1969.

116 "Report of the Proceedings of the University Discipline Committee on Sunday, April 13, in McGaw Hall Regarding Events of March 4 at the Triangle Fraternity," April 18, 1969, 1, Records of the Bursar's Office Takeover, May 1968, box 1, folder 3, NUA.

117 "Hunger Strike Hits N.U., U. of C.," *Chicago Tribune,* April 17, 1969.

118 "Negroes Disciplined at Northwestern," *Southern Illinoisan,* April 14, 1969.

119 Harsh, "UDC Suspends 15 Blacks, Puts 6 on Pro After Attorneys Negotiate Triangle Case;" "Continue Case in N.U. Raid," *Chicago Tribune,* April 15, 1969. Each of the three students charged criminally had been participants in the takeover. On October 24, 1969, after a ten-day criminal trial in Cook County, overseen by Judge James Mejda, a jury acquitted the students of burglary, but found them

guilty of criminal damage to property. Ultimately, they were sentenced to three years of probation. Triangle fraternity members testified in court and identified the three defendants. After the verdict, the students' lawyer, Leo E. Holt, asked for a mistrial after two jurors said they had changed their minds about the case during deliberation. It was denied. An appeal was later filed in 1972. It was denied. "Trial Begins for 3 Blacks," *Daily Northwestern,* November 14, 1969; "Convict 3 Students of Fraternity Raid," *Chicago Tribune,* October 25, 1969; The People of the State of Illinois, v. Clinton Bristow Et Al., 1972, Appellate Court of Illinois, 1972; "Identify Blacks in Court Case," *Daily Northwestern,* October 21, 1969; "Three Students Found Guilty in Raid," *Daily Northwestern,* October 27, 1969.

120 "Judge Refuses to Drops Counts for Burglary," *Daily Northwestern,* October 22, 1969. Northwestern officials did not make good on their promise, and during the trial, they failed to appear in court "to state that the punishment the students had already received was fair and was enough." Clinton Bristow, letter to the editor, "NU Didn't Talk," *Daily Northwestern,* October 28, 1969; "Three Students Found Guilty in Raid," *Daily Northwestern,* October 27, 1969.

121 Sterling and Lowery, *Voices and Visions,* loc. 1995-2002, Kindle.

122 Sterling and Lowery, *Voices and Visions,* loc. 1995-2002, Kindle.

123 Sterling and Lowery, *Voices and Visions,* loc. 1995-2002, Kindle. A number of the twenty-one students were those who were initially charged by the UDC.

124 Harsh, "UDC Suspends 15 Blacks, Puts 6 on Pro After Attorneys Negotiate Triangle Case."

125 "Report of the Proceedings of the University Discipline Committee on Sunday, April 13, in McGaw Hall Regarding Events of March 4 at the Triangle Fraternity," April 18, 1969, 1, NUA.

126 "Report of the Proceedings of the University Discipline Committee on Sunday, April 13, in McGaw Hall Regarding Events of March 4 at the Triangle Fraternity," April 18, 1969, 2, NUA.

127 "Report of the Proceedings of the University Discipline Committee on Sunday, April 13, in McGaw Hall Regarding Events of March 4 at the Triangle Fraternity," April 18, 1969, 1-2, NUA; Robert Svejcara, "21 Punished in Fraternity Raid at N.U.," *Chicago Tribune,* April 14, 1969; "Negroes Disciplined at Northwestern," *Southern Illinoisan,* April 14, 1969; Editorial, "Law on Campus," *Chicago Tribune,* April 17, 1969; Bill Harsh, "UDC Suspends 15 Blacks, Puts 6 on Pro After Attorneys Negotiate Triangle Case," *Daily Northwestern,* April 14, 1969; "3 Students Found Guilty in Raid," *Daily Northwestern,* October 27, 1969.

128 Editorial, "Law on Campus," *Chicago Tribune,* April 17, 1969.

129 Ogletree, interview with the author, 2018.

130 Ogletree, interview with the author, 2018.

131 "Blacks Charge 'Blackmail' Discipline," *Daily Northwestern,* April 15, 1969.

132 Bill Harsh, "How Incident Became a Crisis," *Daily Northwestern,* April 18, 1969.

133 "Report of the Proceedings of the University Discipline Committee on Sunday, April 13, in McGaw Hall Regarding Events of March 4 at the Triangle Fraternity," April 18, 1969, 1, NUA.

134 Bill Harsh, "NU Attorney Rejects 'Blackmail' Charge," *Daily Northwestern,* April 16, 1969.

135 "Blacks Charge 'Blackmail' Discipline."

136 Quick himself had been present at the special Sunday hearing, where he had made a statement, objecting to the students' request for new charges to be brought against them. Harsh, "UDC Suspends 15 Blacks, Puts 6 on Pro After Attorneys Negotiate Triangle Case;" "Report of the Proceedings of the University Discipline Committee" April 18, 1969, 2.

137 Harsh, "UDC Suspends 15 Blacks, Puts 6 on Pro After Attorneys Negotiate Triangle Case."

138 Donna Rosene, "Triangle Slams Verdict: 'Whitewash,'" *Daily Northwestern,* April 15, 1969.

139 Rosene, "Triangle Slams Verdict: 'Whitewash.'"

140 Rosene, "Triangle Slams Verdict: 'Whitewash.'"

141 Editorial, "Questions," *Daily Northwestern,* April 17, 1969.

142 Photograph caption, *Daily Northwestern*, April 15, 1969.

143 "Blacks Charge 'Blackmail' Discipline."

144 "'People's Court' to Try UDC," *Daily Northwestern,* April 14, 1969.

145 "Hinz is Home," *Daily Northwestern,* April 16, 1969. Only one of the twenty-one students punished by the UDC in the Triangle case was a senior. He was placed on probation for the remainder of the term. All others were first-year students, sophomores, and juniors.

146 "Blacks and Press," *Daily Northwestern,* April 16, 1969.

147 Joseph L. Turner, "Hunger Strike to Back Punished NU Students," *Chicago Defender,* April 16, 1969.

148 Turner, "Hunger Strike to Back Punished NU Students."

149 Turner, "Hunger Strike to Back Punished NU Students."

150 Ogletree, interview with the author, 2018.

151 Kathy Polhemus, "21 Blacks Will Conduct Hunger Strike in Protest," *Daily Northwestern,* April 16, 1969.

152 Polhemus, "21 Blacks Will Conduct Hunger Strike in Protest;" Turner, "Hunger Strike To Back Punished NU Students."

153 All were takeover participants. Bob Greene, "Late at Night, Only the Cold is Left," *Daily Northwestern,* April 21, 1969.

154 Polhemus, "21 Blacks Will Conduct Hunger Strike in Protest."

155 "Four Hospitalized in Hunger Strike," *Daily Northwestern,* April 21, 1969.

156 Elliot Brown, "SDS Sympathy Strike," *Daily Northwestern,* April 16, 1969.

157 Ellis Pines, notes to the author, October 12, 2018. Pines left Northwestern again in the spring of 1968 and lived for a time in Mexico and later in California, where he married and had a son. But he later returned to Northwestern and graduated in 1970 with a degree in communication. Today, he is a vice president at TMP Worldwide, an advertising and communications company. "Ellis Pines," TMP Worldwide, https://dc.tmp.com/our-leadership-ellis-pines/. "Northwestern," Pines reflected, "was my coming of age." Judith Forman, "Ellis Pines," *Daily Character,* 1995. He continues to support Northwestern University. "I genuinely love the Purple," he wrote in an email to me on October 12, 2018.

158 Ellis Pines, notes to the author, October 12, 2018.

159 The University of Chicago strike was held to protest the expulsion and

suspension of eighty-one students who had taken part in a sixteen-day sit-in on campus and a demonstration at the university president's home. "U. of Chicago Students End Hunger Strike," *Mount Vernon Register News*, April 25, 1969.

160 "Hunger Strike Hits N.U., U. of C.," *Chicago Tribune*, April 17, 1969.

161 "Hinz Defends NU's Stand," *Daily Northwestern*, April 17, 1969.

162 "Hinz Defends NU's Stand."

163 "Hunger Strike Hits N.U., U. of C."

164 "Strike at Northwestern," *New York Times*, April 17, 1969; Turner, "Hunger Strike To Back Punished NU Students."

165 "Strike at Northwestern."

166 Kathy Polhemus, "21 Blacks Begin Hunger Strike," *Daily Northwestern*, April 17, 1969.

167 "Hunger Strikers Call for Changes," *Evanston Review*, April 21, 1969; "Four Hospitalized in Hunger Strike," *Daily Northwestern*, April 21, 1969.

168 Ogletree, interview with the author, 2018.

169 Polhemus, "21 Blacks Begin Hunger Strike."

170 Elliot Brown, "SDS Sympathy Strike," *Daily Northwestern*, April 16, 1969; "Hunger Strikers Call for Changes," *Evanston Review*, April 21, 1969.

171 Tom Davies, "Northwestern May Be Biggest Loser," *Daily Northwestern*, April 17, 1969.

172 "4 Are Hospitalized After College Fast," *New York Times*, April 21, 1969.

173 "Black Strike Continues; Mediation Offer Rejected," *Daily Northwestern*, April 18, 1969.

174 Roger Friedman, email to the author, January 20, 2019.

175 Polhemus, "21 Blacks Begin Hunger Strike."

176 "4 Are Hospitalized After College Fast;" "Hunger Strikers Call for Changes," *Evanston Review*, April 21, 1969; Turner, "Hunger Strike to Back Punished NU Students."

177 In December 1969, Hampton (1948-1969) was shot and killed in his residence in Chicago when officers of the State's attorney's office, Chicago Police, and the FBI raided his home.

178 Jerry Carfangno, "Panther Leader Talks Revolution," *Daily Northwestern*, April 17, 1969.

179 The proposal was made by William E. Cross, Jr. of Evanston's West Side Service Center and Ben Williams, executive director of the Evanston's Human Relations Commission. "Black Strike Continues; Mediation Offer Rejected," *Daily Northwestern*, April 18, 1969.

180 Richard Boudreaux, "Place Ticket Elected to Head ASG," *Daily Northwestern*, April 17, 1969.

181 Boudreaux, "Place Ticket Elected to Head ASG."

182 Boudreaux, "Place Ticket Elected to Head ASG."

183 Richard Boudreaux, "No Banquet Talk for ASG Proxy," *Daily Northwestern*, April 18, 1969.

184 "Black Strike Continues; Mediation Offer Rejected," *Daily Northwestern*, April 18, 1969.

185 "Black Strike Continues; Mediation Offer Rejected."

186 During one of the protest marches following a vigil, Richard Cohen accompanied Milton Gardner to a meeting in Parkes Hall where administrators and several students were discussing the housing situation for Black students. "Four Hospitalized in Hunger Strike," *Daily Northwestern,* April 21, 1969.

187 Elliot Brown, "SDS Sympathy Strike," *Daily Northwestern,* April 16, 1969.

188 "Four Hospitalized in Hunger Strike." At the hearing held at the Cook County Circuit Court, each of the six students was fined fifty dollars. They had been charged with state and city disorderly conduct violations, but their attorneys managed to have the state charges dropped. They each pleaded guilty. One of the students, former Northwestern SDS president, Steven Lubet, said it had been "a typical example of the workings of the American Judicial System" where "the price of pleading innocent is greater than the price of pleading guilty." Elliot Brown, "Six Students Fined for Dow Protest," *Daily Northwestern,* April 21, 1969.

189 Editorial, "Talking Time, or Else," *Daily Northwestern,* April 21, 1969.

190 Joann Lublin, "3 Mothers Take Sides at Hunger Strike Site," *Daily Northwestern,* April 21, 1969.

191 Lublin, "3 Mothers Take Sides at Hunger Strike Site."

192 Lublin, "3 Mothers Take Sides at Hunger Strike Site."

193 "4 Are Hospitalized After College Fast," *New York Times,* April 21, 1969.

194 "Stomach Pains Hospitalize 3 N. U. Strikers," *Chicago Tribune,* April 21, 1969. Conflicting reports stated that three or four students were hospitalized. The *Daily Northwestern* reported that three strikers, Winston Cenac, Bill Henderson, and Adrian Williams, were hospitalized for at least twenty-four hours and were later released. Kathy Polhemus, "Hinz Says NY Vice-Presidents Willing to Start Talks With Blacks," *Daily Northwestern,* April 23, 1969.

195 "Down But Not Out," *Daily Northwestern,* April 21, 1969. Cenac was also Freshman class president, elected in November 1968. "Cenac Romps to Presidency," *Daily Northwestern,* November 14, 1968.

196 Phil Lentz, "Blacks Charge Police Stalled," *Daily Northwestern,* April 29, 1969.

197 Bob Greene, "Late at Night, Only the Cold is Left," *Daily Northwestern,* April 21, 1969.

198 "Four Hospitalized in Hunger Strike," *Daily Northwestern,* April 21, 1969. FMO leaders would object to Schwartz's later position that the punishments should be allowed to stand. "Accept UDC Stance," *Daily Northwestern,* April 28, 1969; Kathy Polhemus, "Blacks Blast Schwartz for 'Cop-Out,' " *Daily Northwestern,* April 29, 1969.

199 Bob Greene, "Blacks End 121-Hour Hunger Strike with Vow to 'Confront University,' " *Daily Northwestern,* April 22, 1969.

200 "Four Hospitalized in Hunger Strike," *Daily Northwestern,* April 21, 1969.

201 "Four Hospitalized in Hunger Strike."

202 Greene, "Late at Night, Only the Cold is Left."

203 Greene, "Late at Night, Only the Cold is Left."

204 Greene, "Blacks End 121-Hour Hunger Strike with Vow to 'Confront University.' "

205 Editorial, "Talking Time, or Else," *Daily Northwestern,* April 21, 1969.

206 "Rebel Students in Atlanta Free Trustees," *Los Angeles Times,* April 20, 1969. The university is part of the Atlanta University Center Consortium whose

members include Morehouse College, Morehouse School of Medicine, and Spelman College.

207 Kendi, *The Black Campus Movement,* 127-129.

208 "Cornell Blacks Hold On, Atlanta Trustees Freed," *Wisconsin State Journal,* April 20, 1969.

209 Homer Bigart, "Cornell is Tense as 21 Students Face Arrest in Armed Seizure," *New York Times,* May 14, 1969.

210 Paul B. Hewitt, letter to the editor, "Comments on a Week of Change," *Daily Northwestern,* April 21, 1969.

211 Hewitt, letter to the editor, "Comments on a Week of Change."

212 Greene, "Blacks End 121-Hour Hunger Strike with Vow to 'Confront University.' "

213 Greene, "Blacks End 121-Hour Hunger Strike with Vow to 'Confront University.' "

Notes to Chapter 10

1 Tim Petrusak, "Rights Drive Reflects Ferment," *Daily Northwestern,* February 5, 1965.

2 Ogletree, phone call with the author, October 25, 2018.

3 Sterling and Lowery, *Voices and Visions,* loc. 1812-1815, Kindle.

4 Kathy Polhemus, "Some Blacks Won't Return," *Daily Northwestern,* May 19, 1969. The 1969-1973 commencement records reveal that not all of those students who initially submitted withdrawal applications left the university. The majority of the twenty-one students would eventually graduate from Northwestern. Out of the list of twenty-one students, there were only three students for whom I could find no record of graduation. These students may have been among those who submitted withdrawal applications.

5 Arthur Siddon, "Angry, Impatient, Distrustful, Blacks Battle for Negro History," *Chicago Tribune,* May 31, 1969.

6 "Militant Student Groups Crusade for Special Privileges, Courses," *Asbury Park Press,* January 30, 1969.

7 Peggy Mulville, letter to the editor, "Who Settled What?" *Daily Northwestern,* May 9, 1969.

8 Mulville, letter to the editor, "Who Settled What?"

9 John Walter, "Some Thoughts on Us, and NU," *Daily Northwestern,* April 25, 1969.

10 Editorial, "What a Difference a Year Makes," *Daily Northwestern,* May 26, 1969.

11 Phil Lentz, "NROTC Status at NU Might Be Weakened," *Daily Northwestern,* September 23, 1969; "1500 Students Hurl Insults at N. U. Group," *Chicago Tribune,* May 23, 1969.

12 Robert Nolte, "Students Try to Balk N. U. R.O.T.C. Drill: Guests Kept From Mcgaw Hall," *Chicago Tribune,* May 30, 1969.

13 "UDC to Try 5 Protesters Today," *Daily Northwestern,* May 19, 1969. Brandt was charged with assaulting a campus security officer. The others were charged with physically interfering with a regularly scheduled class. Former Student Senate president Barb Caulfield acted as the students' attorney and represented them at the UDC hearing.

14 Roger Friedman, email to the author, January 20, 2019.

15 Roger Friedman, email to the author, January 20, 2019.

16 "N.U. Suspends 1 for Trying to Disrupt Drill," *Chicago Tribune,* May 21, 1969.

17 By the fall, Brandt was working for the *Chicago Sun-Times* and had not been drafted. "Protester Brandt Still Civilian After Sept. Reclassification," *Daily Northwestern,* September 9, 1969. Northwestern student William Sandberg admitted that he had written a letter to the members of Brandt's draft board to inform them of Brandt's suspension and recommending that "appropriate action be taken." Sandberg said he took this action in opposition to Brandt's and other SDS members' political activity and protests. "Student Admits Telling Draft Board; Blasts Brandt and SDS Activists," *Daily Northwestern,* July 3, 1969.

18 Roger Friedman, emails to the author, January 20, 2019 and February 15, 2019.

19 "War," *Daily Northwestern,* September 23, 1969.

20 *The Report of the President's Commission on Campus Unrest,* 39.

21 John Walter, "Some Thoughts on Us, and NU," *Daily Northwestern,* April 25, 1969.

22 Roger Friedman, email to the author, January 20, 2019. Friedman's book is co-authored with Monte Akers and Nathan Akers, *Tower Sniper: The Terror of America's First Active Shooter On Campus* (Houston, TX: John M. Hardy Publishing Company, 2016).

23 Kathy Polhemus, "Hinz Says NY Vice-Presidents Willing to Start Talks With Blacks," *Daily Northwestern,* April 23, 1969.

24 Polhemus, "Hinz Says NY Vice-Presidents Willing to Start Talks With Blacks."

25 "Hinz Says NU Vice-Presidents Willing to Start Talks With Blacks," *Daily Northwestern,* April 23, 1969; "Housing is Topic for Hinz, Blacks," *Daily Northwestern,* April 29, 1969. Long after the Triangle case concluded, the students still faced its ramifications. By January 1970, some of the students were back in meetings with the university officials to "determine whether the case should be reconvened." Carl Shierhorn, "UHAB Reviews Triangle Incident," *Daily Northwestern,* January 20, 1970. The request to reopen the case came from Triangle members, who argued that they had not yet received restitution for the damage done to the fraternity house. By October 1970, the University Hearing and Appeals Board ordered each of the twenty-one students to pay $35.75 in restitution before graduation. But the students, several of whom had already graduated by then, disputed the reported restitution figure, stating that Triangle members had increased the amount twice since the incident, raising it from $500 to over $1,000, and no documents had been submitted to substantiate the amount. The students also argued that by order of the UDC, they had agreed to settle the amount in negotiation with the university, not with Triangle. A later attempt to reopen the case was opposed by Alban Weber, attorney for Northwestern. Nan Hunter, "Blacks: No Restitution Talks," *Daily Northwestern,* January 21, 1970; Nan Hunter, "NU Lawyer Says Blacks Should Pay," *Daily Northwestern,* January 28, 1970; Thom Stauss, "Triangle Settlement Awaits Judgment in Civil Court Case," *Daily Northwestern,* October 8, 1970.

26 Bob Greene, "Miller Says Sentences Will Stand," *Daily Northwestern,* April 23, 1969. On the strike's sixth day, April 21, Miller met with "a committee of parents of black students," along with an attorney representing the students. One of the parents at that meeting reported that Miller had "received us graciously and unresponsively." Bob Greene, "Blacks End 121-Hour Hunger Strike with Vow to 'Confront University,' " *Daily Northwestern,* April 22, 1969.

27 (Advertisement) "Statement of University Chancellor Dr. J Roscoe Miller Concerning the UDC decision of April 13th," *Daily Northwestern,* April 23, 1969.

28 "Miller Won't Cut Frat Raid Penalties," *Chicago Tribune,* April 23, 1969; Bob Greene, "Miller Says Sentences Will Stand," *Daily Northwestern,* April 23, 1969.

29 (Advertisement) "Statement of University Chancellor Dr. J Roscoe Miller Concerning the UDC decision of April 13th."

30 "Blacks Blast Miller's Stand," *Daily Northwestern,* April 24, 1969.

31 Turner, "Hunger Strike To Back Punished NU Students."

32 "Hunger Strike Hits N.U., U. of C.," *Chicago Tribune,* April 17, 1969.

33 "Hunger Strike Hits N.U., U. of C."

34 Editorial, "What a Difference a Year Makes," *Daily Northwestern,* May 26, 1969.

35 Hinz, interview with the author, April 4, 2018.

36 Hinz, interview with the author, April 4, 2018.

37-40 Hinz, interview with the author, 2012.

41 J. Roscoe Miller to the board of trustees, "Summary Statement Regarding the Basic Issues Involved in the Negro Student Incident of May 3-4, 1968."

42 Miller, "Summary Statement."

43 Miller, "Summary Statement."

44 Editorial, "The Agreement," *Daily Northwestern,* May 7, 1968.

45 On August 24, 1970, a physicist at the University of Wisconsin was killed in an explosion on campus. This event caused widespread alarm, especially among university administrators. James W. Vice, University of Chicago's acting dean of students, stated: "The university is extremely volatile during times of change . . . There is great concern on this campus and throughout the nation about what might happen this fall." Robert Nolte, "Campuses Gird for Season of Guerrilla Violence," *Chicago Tribune,* September 13, 1970.

46 Additionally, twelve states passed criminal statutes to "authorize jail sentences and fines for anyone who willfully denies free use of university property and facilities to members of the university community." Federal legislation was also passed to deny federal financial aid to students who "disrupt campus activities." *The Report of the President's Commission on Campus Unrest,* 40.

47 "Backlash of Reason," *Chicago Tribune,* March 7, 1969.

48 Jack Rosenthal, "President's Panel Warns Split on Youth Perils U.S.; Asks Him To Foster Unity," *New York Times,* September 27, 1970. The President's Commission on Campus Unrest convened in June 1970. (It is popularly known as the Scranton Commission, named after its chairman, William Scranton). Its final report included a separate section devoted to examining the "Black Student Movement." In June 1970, Eva Jefferson Paterson was invited to testify in front of the committee (as was Northwestern graduate, Margaret Walker Alexander). After providing testimony, Paterson's invitation to serve on a White House Conference on Youth was revoked by a White House official. She was reportedly "snubbed" owing to the widespread misconception that she was too "radical" and advocated using violence as a protest method. But she had only been explaining why some activists turned to that tactic. She was an advocate of nonviolence at all times, including on Northwestern's campus. "N.U. Student Snubbed by Nixon Aide," *Chicago Tribune,* August 20, 1970. In September, Paterson appeared as a guest on David Frost's television show, along with other student leaders and U.S. Vice President Spiro Agnew. Her clear, direct, and brilliant debate with the vice president on that show served to make her even more famous and respected than she had been before.

49 Others profiled in the FBI documents were student Steven Lubet and professors Marvin Shinbrot and Michael Marcus. An Evanston police officer, along with other unnamed sources, reportedly supplied the FBI with information concerning the takeover and its participants. FBI, memorandum, "Racial Tensions, Northwestern University Campus, Evanston, Illinois," May 8, 1968, 11-12. In 1971, the FBI's heretofore secret COINTELRO was exposed to the public for the first time. The program had been operating since 1956, authorized by FBI director J. Edgar Hoover. It was designed to disrupt, discredit, and spy on individuals and

groups deemed "subversive," including members of Black student groups, SDS, the Black Panther Party, and others. The U.S. Army also conducted its own domestic surveillance in a program known as "Continental United States Intelligence" (ConusIntel) which ultimately fed the names of 18,000 Americans into its "computers, dossiers and files." Northwestern administrators, faculty, and students were also targeted in this program. In February 1971, it was learned that U.S. Army intelligence officers had conducted "sabotage and espionage investigations" on and around the Northwestern campus, and students and several professors (including Marvin Shinbrot and Michael Marcus) had been the subject of surveillance. Baran Rosen, "Army Agent Gives NU Spy Details," *Daily Northwestern*, February 25, 1971; Richard Halloran, "Army Spied on 18,000 Civilians in 2-Year Program," *New York Times,* January 18, 1971.

50 "Hinz Says NU Vice-Presidents Willing to Start Talks With Blacks," *Daily Northwestern,* April 23, 1969.

51 Photograph Caption, *Daily Northwestern,* May 5, 1969.

52 John MacLean, "N. U. Whites Protest Being Forced to Move," *Chicago Tribune,* May 1, 1969.

53 "N. U. Students Condemn Dorm Racial Plan: Proposal to Seek Injunction Rejected," *Chicago Tribune,* May 2, 1969.

54 Sheila Wolfe, "Students Get Greater Role at N. U., U. C.," *Chicago Tribune,* October 26, 1969.

55 Later known as University Hearings and Appeals System. Jim Dexter, "UHAS: The First Year Was a Trial," *Daily Northwestern,* September 22, 1970.

56 In November 1971, Northwestern University President Robert H. Strotz argued against the University Hearing and Appeals Board (UHAB) hearing a case concerning two white fraternity members who had engaged in a physical altercation. He specifically cited the Triangle incident as the reason why UHAB would not hear the case. The university now wanted the two fraternities to handle the matter "between themselves" or through the Interfraternity Council. Ray Casas, "DU-Delta Conciliation Meeting Today," *Daily Northwestern,* November 2, 1971. By 1970, Greek organizations were in decline. In 1966, sixty percent of first-year students at Northwestern joined a fraternity or sorority. Just five years later, later only thirty-five percent of first-year students joined. John Kifner, "Fraternity at Northwestern U. Evicts Members," *New York Times,* January 16, 1971. Kifner's story recounts the closing of Phi Kappa Sigma at Northwestern. The chapter was suspended by the national fraternity for its involvement in supporting the student strike in the spring of 1970 and for failing to uphold the fraternity's "traditions."

57 Elliot Brown, "UDC, CUL Replaced by Judiciary, Council," September 23, 1969; Elliot Brown, "ASG Picks 13 Students for Judiciaries," October 24, 1969. A general faculty committee had also been appointed. Northwestern alumna Dawn Clark Netsch, now a law professor at Northwestern, had been appointed to serve on the committee.

58 Richard Boudreaux, "Disband CUL Immediately: Senate," *Daily Northwestern,* January 21, 1969. The Student Senate had called for the immediate dissolution of the CUL, arguing that the CUL was "ineffective" in handling Senate legislation, particularly in the case of the student bill of rights. Richard Boudreaux, "Senate

Pushes CUL Demise After Hinz' Slap at Bill of Rights," *Daily Northwestern*, January 17, 1969.

59 Sheila Wolfe, "Students Get Greater Role at N. U., U. C.," *Chicago Tribune*, October 26, 1969; Williamson and Wild, *Northwestern: A History*, 325.

60 Janet Stockard, "NU Equal Opportunities Official Takes Office," *Daily Northwestern*, October 1, 1970. Northwestern's first Equal Opportunity Employment plan was submitted to HEW's regional civil rights office on June 19, 1969. HEW officials rejected the university's first several plans "for want of appropriate analysis of problem areas." Northwestern faced the loss of millions of dollars in federal funding if its plan was not accepted and implemented. Milt Policzer, "NU, HEW Agree After Years of Negotiation," *Daily Northwestern*, June 21, 1971; "Adams Changing NU's Image," *Daily Northwestern*, June 21, 1971.

61 In 1970, Michael Smith would graduate with a BA degree in sociology. He earned a masters degree in sociology from Northwestern in 1972.

62 "Top Level Shake-Up in FMO Structure," *Daily Northwestern*, June 27, 1969. At the time, a rumor was denied that the FMO leaders had been impeached. An FMO member said they had "served us well." But, this member added, "after 9 months at the helm of any organization on this lousy campus, you're crazy to keep at it."

63 "Top Level Shake-Up in FMO Structure."

64 "Blacks Make New Admissions Demands," *Daily Northwestern*, October 7, 1969.

65 Bonnie Solow, "Blacks Recruit in Schools," *Daily Northwestern*, December 3, 1969.

66 "Daily Board Names Five More Editors," *Daily Northwestern*, April 24, 1969; Chris Roush, "Q&A: Lublin Talks About Her WSJ Career," Talking Biz News, https://talkingbiznews.com/2/qa-lublin-talks-about-her-wsj-career/, April 12, 2018. In 1968, Marla Strassberger (Kruglik) had been identified by the administration as one of the "possible members or probable associates" of Northwestern's SDS chapter. Roland Hinz to J. Roscoe Miller, July 2, 1968, Miller papers, NUA.

67 Ogletree, interview with the author, 2018.

68 "UDC Opens Fight Hearing to Press," *Daily Northwestern*, March 7, 1969.

69 Tom Davies, "Northwestern May Be Biggest Loser," *Daily Northwestern*, April 17, 1969.

70 Sue Greenberg, "Dissent Brings Another Look," *Daily Northwestern*, May 1, 1969.

71 At the SDS national convention held in Chicago in the summer of 1969, the organization was highly factionalized. One group, the Revolutionary Youth Movement (later called the Weatherman and then, after its members began committing crimes and evading law enforcement, the Weather Underground), advocated for SDS members to take more aggressive and violent actions in protest of the war and other issues. Leaders included Bernardine Dohrn, Bill Ayers, and Mark Rudd. The group nominally took over SDS by electing their slate of candidates, while a small faction of the traditional SDS remained operative for a while. The SDS members who favored violence (bombings) as a tactic would forever damage the nonviolent student protest movement and the New Left in general. After years of evading law enforcement, some members of the Weather Underground turned themselves in and faced no prosecution. In 1991, Dohrn was appointed adjunct professor of law at Northwestern University. Her husband, Bill Ayers, whose father had been a trustee

at Northwestern and was a participant in the Confronting Change symposium, was hired at the University of Illinois, Chicago. Hinz later said the increasing violence would turn off many activist students who decided "this isn't what I want to be connected with." Hinz, interview with the author, 2018. In 2006, New Students for a Democratic Society was formed, taking its name "from the legacy of the original SDS which created the largest student movement in U.S. history." "History," National Students for a Democratic Society (SDS), http://www.newsds.org/p/history.html.

72 Turner, interview with the author, 2012.

73 Turner, interview with the author, 2012.

74 Ogletree, interview with the author, 2018.

75 Ogletree, interview with the author, 2018.

76 Williamson-Lott, *Black Power on Campus,* 2.

77 Kendi, *The Black Campus Movement,* 4.

78 Ogletree, interview with the author, 2018.

79 Biondi, *The Black Revolution on Campus,* 93.

80 Biondi, *The Black Revolution on Campus,* 3.

81 After graduating from Northwestern with a degree in education in 1971, Dorothy Harrell earned a law degree. She worked for the National Education Association in Washington, D.C. for many years, and enjoyed a long career as a teacher. She currently works with school districts to address the academic achievement gaps between white and Black students. She also serves as president of the Beloit Branch of the NAACP in Wisconsin. Anna Marie Lux, "Fifty Years After MLK, Women Work to Make His Dream Reality," *GazetteXtra,* March 31, 2018. https://www.gazettextra.com/news/education/fifty-years-after-mlk-women-work-to-make-his-dream/article_0ec5280a-9d04-57cb-b54a-a72fcad4fcc6.html.

82 Sterling and Lowery, *Voices and Visions,* loc. 1833-1844, Kindle.

83-85 Turner, interview with the author, 2012.

86 According to a 2016 report issued by Northwestern University, in 2015, a total of 514 Black or African American undergraduate students were enrolled at Northwestern, comprising 6.7% of the total undergraduate population. Other statistics for that year include: Hispanic/Latino students, 987 or 12.8%; Asian American, 1,492 or 19.4%; Pacific Islander 0 or 0%; American Indian, 3 or 0%; Multi-Racial, 393 or 5%. The report noted that owing to a 2010 U.S. Department of Education revision in the methodology used for reporting student ethnic and racial categories, the data on race and ethnicity collected in 2010 and afterward was not consistent with the data for previous years. It also stated that "the 2015 incoming freshman class showed a slight decrease in enrollment of African American and Hispanic/Latino undergraduates in terms of proportion while the total undergraduate minority population was the largest and most diverse in Northwestern's history." "2016 Report on Faculty, Staff, and Student Diversity and Inclusion at Northwestern," 36, 32. Overall college enrollment numbers for all students, including Black students, increased over recent decades, but the percentage of Black students who earned degrees remains disproportionately small. For example, in 2012, Black adults composed fourteen percent of all U.S. college-aged students (ages eighteen to twenty-four), yet just nine percent of bachelor's degrees were earned by Black students that same age. That same year, whites accounted for fifty-eight percent of college-aged students,

but sixty-nine percent of young adults with bachelor's degrees. Krogstad, Jens Manuel and Richard Fry, "More Hispanics, Blacks Enrolling in College, But Lag in Bachelor's Degrees," Pew Research Center, April 24, 2014. http://www.pewresearch.org/fact-tank/2014/04/24/more-hispanics-blacks-enrolling-in-college-but-lag-in-bachelors-degrees/. Other reports point to low enrollment of Black students at so-called "top tier" and ivy league universities. Meanwhile, school segregation in the U.S. in general is reportedly increasing. According to one report, the number of segregated schools in the U.S. approximately doubled between 1996 and 2016. Will Stancil, "School Segregation is Not a Myth," *The Atlantic,* March 14, 2018.

87 Turner, interview with the author, 2012. After the takeover there would be, of course, more students actions, from a 1995 twenty-three-day student hunger strike demanding the creation of an Asian-American Studies major to a 2015 series of protests after the administration announced plans to significantly alter the Black House by moving offices of other university offices within it (see below for more on later protests). Henry Bushnell and Josh Rosenblat, "Student Protesters Interrupt Northwestern Athletic Facility Groundbreaking Ceremony," *Inside NU,* November 13, 2015. https://www.insidenu.com/2015/11/13/9731594/northwestern-athletic-facility-groundbreaking-ceremony-interrupted-by. The fight to protect the Black House continues. "End of AAB Strike Gives New Direction to Protest," *Daily Northwestern,* May 9, 1995.

88 The 1969 hunger strike would be represented in the 1970 yearbook.

89 Northwestern University, *The Syllabus*, 1969, 56-57.

90 *The Syllabus*, 1969, 55.

Epilogue Notes

1 William Sloane Coffin, Jr. (1924-2006) was a hero to Jack Hinz. The Yale University chaplain and pastor at New York's Riverside Church was an outspoken critic of the war in Vietnam and a proponent for human rights. He not only led through his sermons and rhetoric, but was also active in numerous protests and demonstrations. In January 1968, along with others, including Benjamin Spock, he was indicted by a Federal grand jury for "conspiracy to counsel, aid and abet draft resistance." His conviction was appealed and later overturned. Coffin's cousin, Gregory Coffin, served as superintendent of Evanston's District 65 schools and led the work to integrate Evanston's elementary schools. (See above for more about Gregory Coffin.)

2 Anna Marie Lux, "Fifty Years After MLK, Women Work to Make His Dream Reality," *GazetteXtra,* March 31, 2018, https://www.gazettextra.com/news/education/fifty-years-after-mlk-women-work-to-make-his-dream/article_0ec5280a-9d04-57cb-b54a-a72fcad4fcc6.html.

3 Roger Friedman, email to the author, January 20, 2019.

4 "Negroes Seize Northwestern U. Office," *Arizona Republic,* May 4, 1968.

5 "619 Clark Street; N.U.'s Day of Decision," *Daily Northwestern,* May 4, 1968.

6 Cross, "James Turner: The Face of Black Power at Northwestern."

7 Turner, interview with the author, 2012.

8 Hinz, interview with the author, 2012.

9 Ogletree, interview with the author, 2018.

10 Ogletree, interview with the author, 2018.

11 Hinz, interview with the author, 2018.

12 Hinz, interview with the author, 2012.

13 Ogletree, interview with the author, 2018.

14 Homer Bigart, "Cornell is Tense as 21 Students Face Arrest in Armed Seizure," *New York Times,* May 14, 1969.

15 Former Quibblers Club member and Northwestern alumnus, Bill Branch, would later be hired by James Turner to teach at the Africana Studies and Research Center at Cornell University, "William Branch" in *From the Ground Up,* 15.

16 "Roland J. Hinz Resigns Post as N.U. Dean," *Chicago Tribune,* July 12, 1969.

17 David Thompson, "N.U. Picks J.F. Stull as Dean of Students," *Chicago Tribune,* August 22, 1970.

18 Elliot Brown and Carl Schierhorn, "Eva Jefferson Wins ASG Presidency in NU's Largest Election Turnout Ever," *Daily Northwestern,* April 15, 1970.

19 Helen H. King, "Eva Jefferson: Young Voice of Change," *Ebony,* January 1971, 71.

20 James M. Naughton, "Agnew and Student Leaders Hit Impasse in TV Debate," *New York Times,* September 22, 1970.

21 Paterson, interview with the author, 2012.

22 Paterson, interview with the author, 2012.

23 Theophilus Green, "Black Leader of White Majority," *Jet Magazine,* July 9, 1970, 24.

24 Hinz, interview with the author, 2012.

25 Linda Smith, "NU's Administrators Oppose Vietnam War," *Daily Northwestern,* October 14, 1969.

26 Smith, "NU's Administrators Oppose Vietnam War."

27-32 Hinz, interview with the author, 2012.

33 Thompson, "N.U. Picks J.F. Stull as Dean of Students."

34 Hinz, interview with the author, 2012. A couple of weeks after Hinz announced his resignation, Robert Strotz was appointed president of Northwestern. Strotz, who had taken part in the May 4, 1968 negotiations, pledged to "keep N.U. out of politics." "Strotz: I'll Keep N.U. Out of Politics," *Chicago Tribune,* July 23, 1970.

35 David Thompson, "Dean Hinz to Quit N. U. Post Aug. 31," *Chicago Tribune,* July 10, 1970.

36 "Job Vacancy," *Chicago Tribune,* July 11, 1970.

37-41 Hinz, interview with the author, 2012.

42 "Consultant Joins Northern Staff," *Daily Chronicle*, November 10, 1970.

43 Hinz, interview with the author, 2012.

44-53 Ogletree, interview with the author, 2018.

54 Bracey, interview with the author, 2018.

55 Bracey, "Living the Legacy-From Protest to Progress," panel discussion about the 1968 takeover, held at Northwestern University, May 3, 2018.

56 Paterson, interview with the author, 2012.

57 Hinz, interview with the author, 2012.

58 Bracey, "Living the Legacy-From Protest to Progress."

59 Hinz and Turner would be reunited again at the fortieth commemoration of the takeover in 2008. Ashley Lau, "1968 Protest Remembered," *Daily Northwestern,* May 3, 2008.

60 Turner's wife Janice worked in Ithaca College's Educational Opportunity Program and she later served as an associate dean of the College of Arts and Science at Cornell. Kara Cusolito, "Lasting Impact: James and Janice Turner Have Made Their Mark on Ithaca," *Ithaca Times*, October 12, 2011, http://www.ithaca.com/news/lasting-impact-james-and-janice-turner-have-made-their-mark/article_b7f8db52-f45e-11e0-8920-001cc4c002e0.html.

61 Cusolito, "Lasting Impact: James and Janice Turner Have Made Their Mark on Ithaca."

62 Pete Walsh, "Fire Destroys Cornell Africana Center," *Ithaca Journal,* April 1, 1970; George Lowery, "A Campus Takeover That Symbolized an Era of Change," *Cornell Chronicle*, April 16, 2009. http://news.cornell.edu/stories/2009/04/campus-takeover-symbolized-era-change.

63 Patricia Nordheimer, "Many Precious Items . . . Lost," *Ithaca Journal,* April 1, 1970.

64 Turner, interview with the author, 2012.

65 Turner, interview with the author, 2012.

66-69 Ogletree, interview with the author, 2018.

70 Hinz, interview with the author, 2012.

71 Hinz, interview with the author, 2012.

72 Bracey, interview with the author, 2018.

73 Bracey, interview with the author, 2018.

74 Bracey, interview with the author, 2018; John H. Bracey, interview with

Daniel Chard, September 10, 2013, UMass Amherst Oral History Collection, http://credo.library.umass.edu/view/full/murg1_207_2013-i064; Bracey, phone conversation with the author, August 9, 2018.

75 Wayne Watson earned three degrees at Northwestern University: a BA in education in 1968, an MA in education and sociology in 1970, and a PhD in education administration in 1972. He would later serve as president of Chicago State University and chancellor of Chicago City Colleges. "Wayne Watson," *The History Makers,* http://www.thehistorymakers.org/biography/wayne-watson-39.

76 After graduating in 1970, Bell was hired as the assistant to the dean of students in 1971. He later served Director of Admissions and Financial Aid from 1972 to 1987. "Insurance Man New Asst. Dean," *Daily Northwestern,* October 12, 1971; Len Anderson, Jr., "NU to Improve Recruiting," *Daily Northwestern,* September 23, 1980; Neil Milbert, "Northwestern Won't Lower Standards For More Victories," *Chicago Tribune,* April 22, 1990; Antoine Lewis, "A Minority Priority," *Daily Northwestern,* November 6, 1986. In 1971, Semmes earned a BA and later a PhD (1978) from Northwestern. He also earned an MA in sociology from the University of Illinois, Chicago. He later went on to serve as acting director of Black Studies at the University of Illinois and as Professor of African American Studies at Eastern Michigan University. In 2009, he was appointed Director of the Black Studies Program at University of Missouri-Kansas City. "UMKC names Clovis Semmes as Director of Black Studies," *UMKC Today,* May 6, 2009, https://info.umkc.edu/news/umkc-names-clovis-semmes-as-director-of-black-studies/. Daniels later worked as director of admissions at Miami University in Ohio.

77 Zuzanna Wisniewska, "Isola Jones," *The Black Past,* July 29, 2018, https://blackpast.org/aah/jones-isola-1949. Paterson earned her BA degree from Northwestern in 1971 and earned her law degree from UC Berkeley Law School. For twenty-six years, she worked for the Lawyers' Committee for Civil Rights, serving for thirteen years as that organization's executive director. "Roger Ward," Evanston Township High School, July 31, 2015, http://www.eths1964.com/class_profile.cfm?member_id=6130149; Chris Bonjean "Jackson Appointed Cook County Circuit Judge," Illinois State, Bar Association, October 22, 2014, https://www.isba.org/iln/2014/10/22/jackson-appointed-cook-county-circuit-judge; "Daphne Maxwell Reid on Her 'Fresh Prince' Days, Black Activism, Fashion Designs & More," *Lee Bailey's Electronic Urban Report,* February 26, 2018, https://www.eurweb.com/2018/02/daphne-maxwell-reid-opens-black-history-contributions-fresh-prince-eur-exclusive/. Reid, who signed with the prestigious Eileen Ford Agency, worked as a model while she was a student at Northwestern. Ellis Pines, who later entered the advertising profession, recalled hiring Reid for commercials. The two served together on Northwestern's Student Senate. Pines, notes to the author, October 12, 2018.

78 In 1986, after Northwestern alumni organized a Black Student Alumni Association, one of its first projects was to raise funds to establish a scholarship in Milton Gardner's name. The Gardner-Exum Scholarship Fund honored Gardner and professor William Exum, former chairperson of the Department of African American Studies. Deborah D. Douglas, "Black Grads Seek Notice," *Daily Northwestern,* October 13, 1986; Brett Pulley, "Black Alums Party for Scholarship," *Daily Northwestern,* July 10, 1986; "Gardner Exum Scholarship," Northwestern

University, https://www.northwestern.edu/msa/resources/scholarships/index.html.

79 Stephen Broussard, (c. 1948-2009) "In Memoriam," *Northwestern Magazine,* Fall 2009, https://www.northwestern.edu/magazine/fall2009/alumninews/inmemoriam.html.

80 "Cuny School of Law," http://www.law.cuny.edu/faculty/directory/goode.html.

81 Perkins attended graduate school at the University of Rochester and the City University of New York, City College. My thanks to Roger Friedman for providing me with details concerning the biography of his friend, Eric Perkins.

82 Ogletree, interview with the author, 2018.

83 Ogletree, interview with the author, 2018.

84 "My Soul Looks Back in Wonder."

85 Ogletree, interview with the author, 2018.

86 Mark Watanabe, "NU Blacks Ask 13 Concessions," *Daily Northwestern,* May 17, 1972; "FMO Says It Won't Move Into 'Unsafe' Black House," *Daily Northwestern,* October 17, 1972; "Black House Ready by Feb. 5," *Daily Northwestern,* January 30, 1973; "Women at NU Get 619 Emerson St.," *Daily Northwestern,* September 26, 1973. The Women Studies program has evolved over the years and is now part of Gender and Sexuality Studies.

87 "Turner Reflects on Past, Future of Blacks," *Daily Northwestern,* February 14, 1973.

88 "Turner Reflects on Past, Future of Blacks."

89 "Turner Reflects on Past, Future of Blacks." Turner was perhaps paraphrasing noted writer John Oliver Killens (1916-1987). In 1973, Killens reflected on the surge of activism in the 1960s, followed by what he identified as a decline. He wrote: "our struggle for liberation was indeed a long distance race, for we are out for nothing short of winning the entire human race and we were up against a formidable foe, and to win this race would require planning, pacing, discipline and stamina, and a belief in our ability to win the long protracted struggle. Indeed we must construct one hundred year plans. We must construct institutions for generations yet unborn." Killens, "Wanted: Some Black Long Distance Runners," *The Black Scholar,* November 1973, 2.

90 Jason Mast and Rosalie Chan, " 'It's Like a Legend:' Remembering the 1968 Bursar's Office Sit-In," *North by Northwestern,* February 8, 2017, http://www.northbynorthwestern.com/story/its-like-a-legend-remembering-the-1968-bursars-off/. The plaque was dedicated on the fiftieth anniversary of the takeover, May 3, 2018. It was sponsored by Northwestern Alumni and the Northwestern University Black Alumni Association (NUBAA).

91 James P. Pitts and Kathryn Ogletree, "Northwestern University's Recent Alumni: In Black and White," Evanston, IL: Northwestern University, 1978.

92 Nery Ynclan, "Sociology Report Indicates NU Racial Trend Changing," *Daily Northwestern,* October 18, 1978.

93 Kevin Blackistone, Carolyn D. Davis, and Michael Wilbon, untitled document [History of the 1968 Takeover], nd., 4.

94 Nancy Rawles, "Racial Tension at Northwestern . . . Not as Obvious, But It's Still There," *Daily Northwestern,* February 20, 1978.

95 Jason Mast and Rosalie Chan, " 'It's Like a Legend.' "

96 "Living the Legacy-From Protest to Progress." In 2015, Northwestern officials announced plans (later canceled) to move other campus administrative offices into the Black House, an announcement that elicited widespread protest from a broad coalition of students, faculty, and others, including members of FMO. "Black alumni and underclassmen fell to our knees in front of heartless administrators, pleading for the space our predecessors had fought for," wrote a Northwestern undergraduate student about the campaign to save the space that had been won by the students in 1968. Natalie Frazier, "A Black Ass Nightmare: My Four Years at Northwestern," *Blackboard,* Northwestern University's Black Student Magazine, April 2016, http://www.blackboardmag.com/my-black-ass-nightmare-four-years-at-northwestern/. Frazier was one of 300 students, faculty members, and others who joined in a much-publicized protest staged during a groundbreaking ceremony for a new sports complex on campus in November 2015. Mariana Alfaro, "Students Protest Institutional Racism, Interrupt Groundbreaking Ceremony," *Daily Northwestern,* November 13, 2015. The coalition of student groups included FMO, Students for Justice in Palestine, Inspire Media, Alianza, the Asian Pacific American Coalition, MEChA de Northwestern, the African Students Association, and CaribNation. The action was taken in solidarity with students at the University of Missouri, along with students from a variety of other universities, who were "openly expressing their experiences of marginalization, oppression, and trauma within campuses and institutions meant to serve and educate them." The Black Student Experience Task Force, "The African American/Black Student Experience: Final Report," Northwestern University, Summer 2016, 61. Ibram X. Kendi points out that many contemporary struggles on campuses center around defending what already exists, rather than creating new, forward looking systems and structures, arguing that the student activists of the late 1960s were "were institution building, not merely defending what had already been built." Karanja Keita Carroll, "The Black Campus Movement: An Interview with Ibram H. Rogers [Kendi]," *Journal of Pan African Studies* 5, no. 8 (2012), http://www.questia.com/read/1G1-316072931/the-black-campus-movement-an-interview-with-ibram.

97 "The African American/Black Student Experience: Final Report," 3. The highest percentage (8.4%) of students identifying as Black was achieved in 1989, and thereafter that percentage decreased, falling to 5.3% by 2001. Ally Mutnick, "For Class of 2016, Percentage of Black Students Highest in 23 Years," *Daily Northwestern,* October 29, 2012. The percentage has since risen slightly. In the fall of 2017, six percent of all undergraduates at Northwestern identified as Black. Troy Closson, "Unmet Demands," *Daily Northwestern,* May 3, 2018.

98 Preetisha Sen, "Jabbar R. Bennett to Serve as NU's First Associate Provost for Diversity and Inclusion," *North by Northwestern,* July 21, 2015. At Northwestern, Bennett directs the Office of Institutional Diversity and Inclusion and also serves as associate professor of medicine. "Jabbar R. Bennett," Office of the Provost, Northwestern University, https://www.northwestern.edu/provost/about/bios/jabbar-bennett.html.

99 Mariana Alfaro and Peter Kotecki, "University Report: Being a Black Student at Northwestern is 'Exhausting,' " *Daily Northwestern,* September 20, 2016.

100 "The African American/Black Student Experience: Final Report," 30.

From 2011 to 2012, six "bias incidents" were recorded by university officials: harassment of a Latinx student on Sheridan Road, a "Beer Olympics" party hosted by the Northwestern Ski Team in which "racially themed costumes and chants were witnessed," and an egg throwing/racial slur incident on the tennis courts. "The African American/Black Student Experience: Final Report," 24. More recently, swastikas and racist and anti-Semitic graffiti have been found around campus. Tyler Page, "More Swastikas, Racist Graffiti Found in Library," *Daily Northwestern,* April 16, 2015. And, in 2019, printed stickers with statements tied to neo-Nazi and white supremacist groups have been found on campus. "Student Reports Finding Another White Supremicist Sticker on Campus," *Daily Northwestern,* April 21, 2019.

101 Dan Baumann, "Hate Crimes on Campuses Are Rising, New FBI Data Show," *Chronicle of Higher Education,* November 14, 2018, https://www.chronicle.com/article/Hate-Crimes-on-Campuses-Are/245093. According to the *Daily Northwestern,* by 2016, Jewish students accounted for rougly fifteen percent of the student body, a figure that was down from the figure of over seventeen percent that was reported in 1967. Erica Snow, "Northwestern Jewish Community Challenges Study that Calls University an Anti-Semitic 'Hotspot,' " *Daily Northwestern,* November 18, 2016.

102 Northwestern Student Affairs, Campus Inclusion and Community, "A Summary of Recommendations and a Prioritized Action Plan," https://www.northwestern.edu/inclusion/reports-reviews/black-student-satisfaction-report/index.html.

103 Northwestern Student Affairs, Campus Inclusion and Community, "A Summary of Recommendations and a Prioritized Action Plan."

104 This was the phrase spoken several times at the 2018 commemorations. Perhaps it is a play on the famous rallying cry, *a luta continua,* or, the struggle continues. The phrase was first used during Mozambique's war for independence, 1964-1874.

105 Bursar Commemoration Demands, May 1, 2018, https://docs.google.com/document/d/1-GhZsfBg6R_Og6O3YigYOWKfUupzpdtqBH_E2F7fojM/edit; Troy Closson, Rishika Dugyala, and Jonah Dylan, "Students Demand University Action on Black Student Experience, Departmentalization, Dining Transition," *Daily Northwestern,* May 4, 2018.

106 Syd Stone, "At News Conference, Student Activists Discuss Demands Delivered to Administrators," *Daily Northwestern,* May 10, 2018; 2018; Bursar Commemoration Demands, May 1, 2018, 1. Other demands included establishing departments for the Asian American Studies and Latina and Latino Studies programs at Northwestern and supporting campus workers rights, including providing a "living wage and exemplary working conditions" and halting the use of E-Verify. Black Lives Matter NU, email to the author, March 25, 2019; Bursar Commemoration Demands, May 1, 2018, 5.

107 Latinx Asian American Collective, Students Organizing for Labor Rights, Black Lives Matter NU, letter to the editor, *Daily Northwestern,* May 3, 2018. In explaining their 2018 demands, the students also demanded that the university protect students' right to protest. They asserted that there was a "glaring hypocrisy of the university commemorating the Bursar's Office Takeover while simultaneously punishing students who engage in similar actions today." Latinx Asian American Collective, Students Organizing for Labor Rights, Black Lives Matter NU, letter to the editor, *Daily Northwestern,* May 3, 2018.

108 Bursar Commemoration Demands, May 1, 2018, 1.

109 How can the "university engage in its celebration of the Bursar's Office Takeover," the students asked, "— attempting to position itself as sympathetic to the grievances of our community's marginalized members — while its administration continually fails to take action to support them? We are exhausted with the rhetorical flourishes of the university's statements claiming its commitment to the well-being of marginalized people on this campus; instead, we want action." Latinx Asian American Collective, Students Organizing for Labor Rights, Black Lives Matter NU, letter to the editor, *Daily Northwestern,* May 3, 2018.

110 Amina Kilpatrick, "John Bracey Honors Longtime Friend Prof. Emeritus James Turner at Two-Day Symposium," *Cornell Daily Sun,* April 16, 2019, https://cornellsun.com/2019/04/16/john-bracey-honors-longtime-friend-prof-emeritus-james-turner-at-two-day-symposium/.

111 Troy Closson, Rishika Dugyala, and Jonah Dylan, "Students Demand University Action on Black Student Experience, Departmentalization, Dining Transition."

112 Below the text on the banner, a timeline marked the year 1968 with the statement, "We were courageous." At the year 2015, it read: "We were concerned." And at 2018, it read: "We are coming for you."

113 "Living the Legacy-From Protest to Progress," May 3, 2018.

114 Turner, interview with the author, 2012.

115 Turner, interview with the author, 2012.

Illustration Credits:

Cover Photographs:

Front cover photographs (left to right): students outside the Bursar's Office, Northwestern, May 3, 1968; Jack Hinz and James Turner in front of the Bursar's Office, May 3, 1968; Northwestern student at the front of the Bursar's Office, May 3, 1968. All photographs are from the Records of the Bursar's Office Takeover, May 1968, Northwestern University Archives, Northwestern University. Reprinted by permission of the Northwestern University Archives.

Back cover photographs (top to bottom): Hunger strike at Northwestern, April 1969, Northwestern University Archives; International House residents, Northwestern, 1949, Northwestern *Syllabus* Yearbook, 1949; Track Team, Northwestern, 1898, Northwestern *Syllabus* Yearbook, 1900; Northwestern University Office of the Dean of Students' Stamp, May 8, 1968; Page from Northwestern *Syllabus* Yearbook, 1903. Reprinted by permission of the Northwestern *Syllabus* Yearbook and the Northwestern University Archives.

Photographs and Illustrations:

Students on Low Library Ledge, *Columbia University, April 1968*. From University Archives, Columbia University, Office of Public Affairs, Protest & Activism Photograph Collection, Collection number: UA#109. Reprinted by permission of University Archives, Columbia University.

Margaret Walker Alexander. From the George Cleveland Hall Branch Archives, Box 9, Photo 50, Vivian G. Harsh Research Collection, Woodson Regional Library, Chicago Public Library. Reprinted by permission of the Chicago Public Library.

Edwin Bush Jourdain, Jr. From the Evanston History Center Archives. Reprinted by permission of the Evanston History Center.

Quibblers Club Members, 1945. From *Purple Parrot,* April 1945, Northwestern University. Reprinted by permission of Students Publishing Co., Northwestern University.

Sit-in at a Woolworth's lunch counter in Durham, North Carolina, February 10, 1960. From N&O Negative Collection, State Archives of North Carolina, Raleigh, NC.

"I Back Hinz" button, 1968. Courtesy of Jack Hinz.

Roger Friedman, 1966. Courtesy of Roger Friedman.

Herblock cartoon, May 5, 1968. A 1968 Herblock Cartoon, ©The Herb Block Foundation. Reprinted by permission of the Herb Block Foundation.

Photograph of Professor John H. Bracey, Jr. of the W.E.B. Du Bois Department of Afro-American Studies, University of Massachusetts Amherst, c. 1972. Reprinted by permission of the Department of Special Collections and University Archives, W.E.B. Du Bois Library, University of Massachusetts Amherst.

Photographs and illustrations from the *Daily Northwestern*. Reprinted by permission of the *Daily Northwestern*, Students Publishing Co., Northwestern University.

"No Room for Them??" Illustration accompanying the campaign to "To Correct Negro Housing Evils." *Daily Northwestern*, January 24, 1947.

SDS anti-war protest in downtown Evanston. *Daily Northwestern*, April 19, 1966.

Cartoon, "Problems of Democracy." *Daily Northwestern*, October 24, 1967.

Jack Hinz announcing the passage of self-rule, Northwestern University, April 25, 1968. "Nu Grants Self Rule," *Daily Northwestern*, April 26, 1968.

Negotiation Table, 217 Scott Hall, Northwestern University, Saturday, May 4, 1968. *Daily Northwestern*, May 6, 1968.

Kathryn Ogletree and James Turner in front of the Bursar's Office after the agreement had been reached. *Daily Northwestern*, May 6, 1968.

The interior of the Bursar's Office after the takeover ended. *Daily Northwestern*, May 6, 1968.

Cartoon, Joseph A. Mendenhall at Northwestern University, by Bill Reed. *Daily Northwestern*, November 25, 1968.

Roland J. Hinz, Hesitant About Calling Police. *Daily Northwestern*, January 30, 1968.

Roger Friedman addressing an open housing rally in Evanston, April 8, 1968. *Daily Northwestern*, April 9, 1968.

Photographs from Northwestern *Syllabus* Yearbook. Reprinted by permission of the Northwestern *Syllabus* Yearbook, Students Publishing Co., Northwestern University.

Members of the Menorah Society, Northwestern University, 1937. Northwestern *Syllabus* Yearbook, 1937.

Lawyer Taylor. Northwestern *Syllabus* Yearbook, 1903.

Members of Northwestern's Hinman Debating Society, 1905, with John Porcius Faulkner. Northwestern *Syllabus* Yearbook, 1906.

Members of Alpha Mu, Northwestern's chapter of Alpha Phi Alpha, 1930. Northwestern *Syllabus* Yearbook, 1930.

William Yancy Bell, Jr. with other members of Northwestern's YMCA chapter. Northwestern *Syllabus* Yearbook, 1935.

Nanette "Nannie" Turpin Thomas (Hopkins). Northwestern *Syllabus* Yearbook, 1933.

Residents of the International House, Northwestern University. Northwestern *Syllabus* Yearbook, 1948.

Residents of Asbury Hall, 1953. Northwestern *Syllabus* Yearbook, 1953.

Naomi Willie Pollard Dobson. Northwestern *Syllabus* Yearbook, 1905.

Student rally, Northwestern University, 1969. Northwestern Syllabus Yearbook, 1969.

Kathryn Ogletree. Northwestern *Syllabus* Yearbook, 1970.

"King is Dead." Northwestern *Syllabus* Yearbook, 1969, photograph by Gary Price.

Spring comes to Northwestern, Deering Meadow, Northwestern University, 1968-1969. Northwestern *Syllabus* Yearbook, 1969.

Jack Hinz and James Turner in front of the Bursar's Office, Northwestern University, May 1968. Northwestern *Syllabus* Yearbook, 1969, photograph by Gary Price.

Evanston police officer on duty at the Bursar's Office, Northwestern University, May 3, 1968. Northwestern *Syllabus* Yearbook, 1969.

Evanston police officers arrest a student protester, Dow protest (and counter-protest), Northwestern University, February 1969. Northwestern *Syllabus* Yearbook, 1969.

Northwestern Students' Hunger Strike at the Rebecca Crown Center Plaza, Northwestern University, April 1969. Northwestern Syllabus Yearbook, 1970.

The staff of the *Daily Northwestern*. Northwestern *Syllabus* Yearbook, 1969.

Cover, *Syllabus* yearbook, Northwestern University, 1969. Northwestern *Syllabus* Yearbook, 1969.

Demonstration photographs from Northwestern *Syllabus* Yearbook, 1969

Photographs and documents from the Northwestern University Archives. Reprinted by permission of the Northwestern University Archives.

Photograph of the crowd outside the Bursar's Office, 619 Clark Street, Northwestern University, Evanston, IL, May 3, 1968, photograph by James Sweet.

Bursar's Office, 619 Clark Street, Northwestern University, May 3, 1968, photograph by James Sweet.

Football Team, Northwestern University, 1936.

Ruth O'Brien McCarn, Northwestern University.

James Roscoe Miller. University Relations.

Pre-integration Northwestern, early 1960s.

Roland "Jack" Hinz. University Relations.

Daphne Maxwell Reid, c. 1967. University Relations, photograph by Jim Biery.

Student Power Movement flyer, "Bitch-In No. 2," Northwestern University, March 1967. Student Activities Collection.

Christopher Lasch. University Relations.

Ellis Pines, c. 1967.

Alpha Omicron Pi sorority dance, Northwestern University, fall 1967 or winter 1968. Courtesy of Audrey Hinton.

Students gather after the assassination of Martin Luther King, Jr., Northwestern University, April 1968.

Students at an east side window of the Bursar's Office during the takeover, May 3, 1968, photograph by James Sweet.

Northwestern students in front of the Bursar's Office, Friday morning, May 3, 1968, photograph by James Sweet.

Northwestern students block the front entrance to the occupied Bursar's Office, May 3, 1968, photograph by James Sweet.

Jack Hinz leaves the Bursar's Office after a consultation with James Turner, May 3, 1968, photograph by James Sweet.

Lucius Perry Gregg, Jr. University Relations.

George Marsh Frederickson. University Relations.

John Bracey leans out of a window in the Bursar's Office, May 3, 1968, photograph by James Sweet.

James Turner talks with members of the press outside the occupied Bursar's Office, May 3, 1968, photograph by James Sweet.

Members of the press gather around James Turner with Jack Hinz, May 3, 1968, photograph by James Sweet.

James Turner with Venice Deese, Jr., photograph by James Sweet.

James Turner being interviewed outside the Bursar's Office, May 3, 1968, photograph by James Sweet.

Franklin M. Kreml. University Relations.

Walter L. Wallace. University Relations.

Inside the Bursar's Office, May 1968, Michael Smith, Steve Colson, Dan Davis, and Eric Perkins. Courtesy of Steve Colson.

Hunger strike rally, Rebecca Crown Center Plaza, Northwestern University, April 1969.

Crowds and sympathy picket members at the hunger strike, Rebecca Crown Center Plaza, Northwestern University, April 1969.

Reporter interviewing a hunger strike participant, Rebecca Crown Center Plaza, Northwestern University, April 1969.

Hunger strike participants, Rebecca Crown Center Plaza, Northwestern University, April 1969.

Hunger strike participant, Rebecca Crown Center Plaza, Northwestern University, April 1969.

Hunger strike rally, Rebecca Crown Center Plaza, Northwestern University, April 1969.

Eva Jefferson (Paterson), photograph by James S. Roberts.

The second location of the Black House, 1914 Sheridan Road, Evanston.

Documents from the Northwestern University Archives:

List of Demands, April 22, 1968; University Response to the Students' Demands, April 1968; Revised and Final Demands, May 1968; Draft of the May 4 Agreement, 1968. Reprinted by permission of Northwestern University Archives.

Photographs by the Author:

The Bursar's Office, Northwestern University, April 2019.

"#TheTakeoverToday. You Never Completed Our Demands," May 3, 2018.

A Note to the Reader

I have made every effort to confirm the information contained in this history. In some cases, it was difficult to confirm the accuracy of some of the dates cited here since various sources list different dates for some events, all within just a couple days of each other. In other cases, sources had somewhat conflicting accounts of certain details related to specific events. I have tried to make sure to note that some incidents recounted here are alleged and/or reported. I have tried to recount events in the most objective and thorough manner possible. The author and publisher do not assume and hereby disclaim any liability to any party in connection with this publication.

About the Author

Jenny Thompson is Director of Education at the Evanston History Center in Evanston, Illinois. She also works as a public history consultant. A graduate of San Francisco State University, she has an MA in American Studies from the George Washington University and a PhD in American Studies from the University of Maryland. She has taught courses in American history and culture at the University of Maryland and at Roosevelt University in Chicago. Her work focuses on twentieth-century American history and culture, the cultural history of American wars, and the history of images. She is the author of *War Games: Inside the World of 20th-Century War Reenactors* (Smithsonian Books, 2004). Her essays have appeared in various anthologies and publications, including the *New York Times.*